AVIATION AWARDS OF IMPERIAL GERMANY IN WORLD WAR I AND THE MEN WHO EARNED THEM

Also by Neal W. O'Connor

AVIATION AWARDS OF IMPERIAL GERMANY IN WORLD WAR I
Volume I: The Aviation Awards of the Kingdom of Bavaria (1988)

AVIATION AWARDS OF IMPERIAL GERMANY IN WORLD WAR I
Volume II: The Aviation Awards of the Kingdom of Prussia (1990)

AVIATION AWARDS OF IMPERIAL GERMANY IN WORLD WAR I
Volume III: The Aviation Awards of the Kingdom of Saxony (1993)

AVIATION AWARDS OF IMPERIAL GERMANY IN WORLD WAR I
Volume IV: The Aviation Awards of the Kingdom of Württemberg (1995)

AVIATION AWARDS OF IMPERIAL GERMANY IN WORLD WAR I
Volume V: The Aviation Awards of the Eight Thuringian States and the Duchy of Anhalt (1998)

AVIATION AWARDS OF IMPERIAL GERMANY IN WORLD WAR I
Volume VI: The Aviation Awards of the Grand Duchies of Baden and Oldenburg (1999)

AVIATION AWARDS OF IMPERIAL GERMANY IN WORLD WAR I
Volume VII: The Aviation Awards of Eight German States and the Three Free Cities (2002)

AVIATION AWARDS OF IMPERIAL GERMANY IN WORLD WAR I AND THE MEN WHO EARNED THEM

Volume VII: The Aviation Awards of Eight German States and the Three Free Cities

NEAL W. O'CONNOR

Schiffer Military History
Atglen, PA

Front Cover: The painting entitled *Morning Class* depicts a trio of German scout fighter aircraft on an early morning sortie above the Somme campaign in the summer of 1916. The flight leader in his twin-gunned Fokker D-III is the legendary strategist Oswald Boelke who is shown signalling to his wingmen in their Halberstadt D-II fighters. *Artwork by S.W. Ferguson.*

Rear Cover: Five of the awards discussed in this book. At the top, the Brunswick War Merit Cross 1st Class and the Lippe War Honor Cross for Heroic Deed. At the bottom, the Princely Hohenzollern Honor Cross 3rd Class with Swords, the Waldeck Merit Cross 3rd Class with Swords and the Schaumburg-Lippe Cross for Faithful Service.

Front flap: Portrait painting of *Leutnant* Erwin Böhme, recipient of the *Orden Pour le Mérite*, the Knight's Hohenzollern with Swords, both Iron Crosses and the Brunswick War Merit Cross 2nd Class.

Book design by Robert Biondi.

Library of Congress Catalog Number: 2002111329.

Printed in China.
ISBN: 0-7643-1626-5

Published by Schiffer Publishing Ltd.
4880 Lower Valley Road
Atglen, PA 19310
Phone: (610) 593-1777
FAX: (610) 593-2002
E-mail: Schifferbk@aol.com.
Visit our web site at: www.schifferbooks.com
Please write for a free catalog.
This book may be purchased from the publisher.
Please include $3.95 postage.
Try your bookstore first.

In Europe, Schiffer books are distributed by:
Bushwood Books
6 Marksbury Ave.
Kew Gardens
Surrey TW9 4JF
England
Phone: 44 (0)208 392-8585
FAX: 44 (0)208 392-9876
E-mail: Bushwd@aol.com.
Free postage in the UK. Europe: air mail at cost.
Try your bookstore first.

CONTENTS

Appendices

The biographies that appear in this book and the page number where they begin are listed below. Where all award dates are known, the biographies appear chronologically, Where all awards dates are not known, the biographies appear in alphabetical order. The same holds true for the sections with photographs of recipients without biographies.

AUTHOR'S PREFACE AND ACKNOWLEDGEMENTS

Upon accepting the instruments of surrender on the deck of the USS *Missouri* in Tokyo Bay which ended World War II, General of the Army Douglas MacArthur said, "these proceedings are closed." With this volume, the series on the aviation awards of Imperial Germany in World War I is likewise concluded, the seventh and last of them.

For virtually everyone reading these lines, therefore, there is no need so late in the game to once again set the stage for the discussion that follows, to recount how these awards came the way of the young airmen or dwell on the limitations a researcher encounters in a work of this kind. It is enough to say this book proceeds along the same lines as its predecessors. First, there is a bit of background on the origins and military development of each of the entities. This is followed by some detail on the orders and decorations each conferred for military merit and bravery. Finally, the wartime careers of a select number of their aviation recipients appear on both the famous and others whom history, at least in the English language, has largely overlooked. Appendices providing more detail appear last.

In this book we find the remaining German states not covered earlier, eight of them in all, plus the three Free Hanse Cities of Bremen, Hamburg and Lübeck. The eight states appear first in alphabetical order. Thus we find the Duchy of Brunswick leading off the discussion followed by the Grand Duchy of Hesse, the Principality of Hohenzollern, the Principalities of Lippe and Schaumburg-Lippe, the Grand Duchies of Mecklenburg-Schwerin and Mecklenburg-Strelitz and the Principality of Waldeck.

As before, it is important to acknowledge the help received in preparing this volume. Among individuals, the mentoring of the late A. Edward Ferko who contributed so much to the first five books in this series was again sorely missed. In the on-the-ground research carried out at archives in Germany for this book, the author this time had the benefit of the personal assistance of six gentlemen at various times and in various places. From Germany, this was *Professor Dr. Dr.* Holger Steinle from the *Deutsches Technikmuseum Berlin*. From the United States, they were Charles C. Freihofer III, Peter M. Grosz, Peter Kilduff, Eric C. Ludvigsen and George A. Seymour. Dieter H.M. Gröschel, M.D., also in the United States, once again provided much of the military background of the individual states and cities in this volume. He also rendered invaluable service in translating into English some of the often difficult-to-read old handwritten *Schrift* that one finds on documents and service records. Dr. Gröschel also translated certain passages of award foundation statements whose archaic language and meaning can defeat even the best of today's German speakers (but not Dr. Gröschel).

Photographs have always been the most interesting and appreciated feature of the series. As one volume has led to another, it has been the most challenging one too. The challenge is to present the reader with fresh images, more and more difficult when one is constantly dealing with the same circumstances involving the same men (how many really "new" pictures are there of Manfred von Richthofen?). How well that challenge has been met this time must be left to the reader but were it not for the following individuals and institutions, it would not have been met at all.

In Germany, *Dr.* Ernst Aichner, Charlotte von Cossel, *Dr.* Achim Fuchs, *Oberstabsfeldwebel a.D.* Falk Hallensleben, Rainer Haufschild, Margot Hemer, Reinhard Kastner, Ernst Ladek, Jürgen Ladek, Jörg Mückler, *Dr.-Ing.* Niedermeyer, *Dr.* Joachim Niemeyer, *Major Dr.* Harald Potempa, Jörg Schmalfuss, Wilhelm Steifensand, *Professor Dr. Dr.* Holger

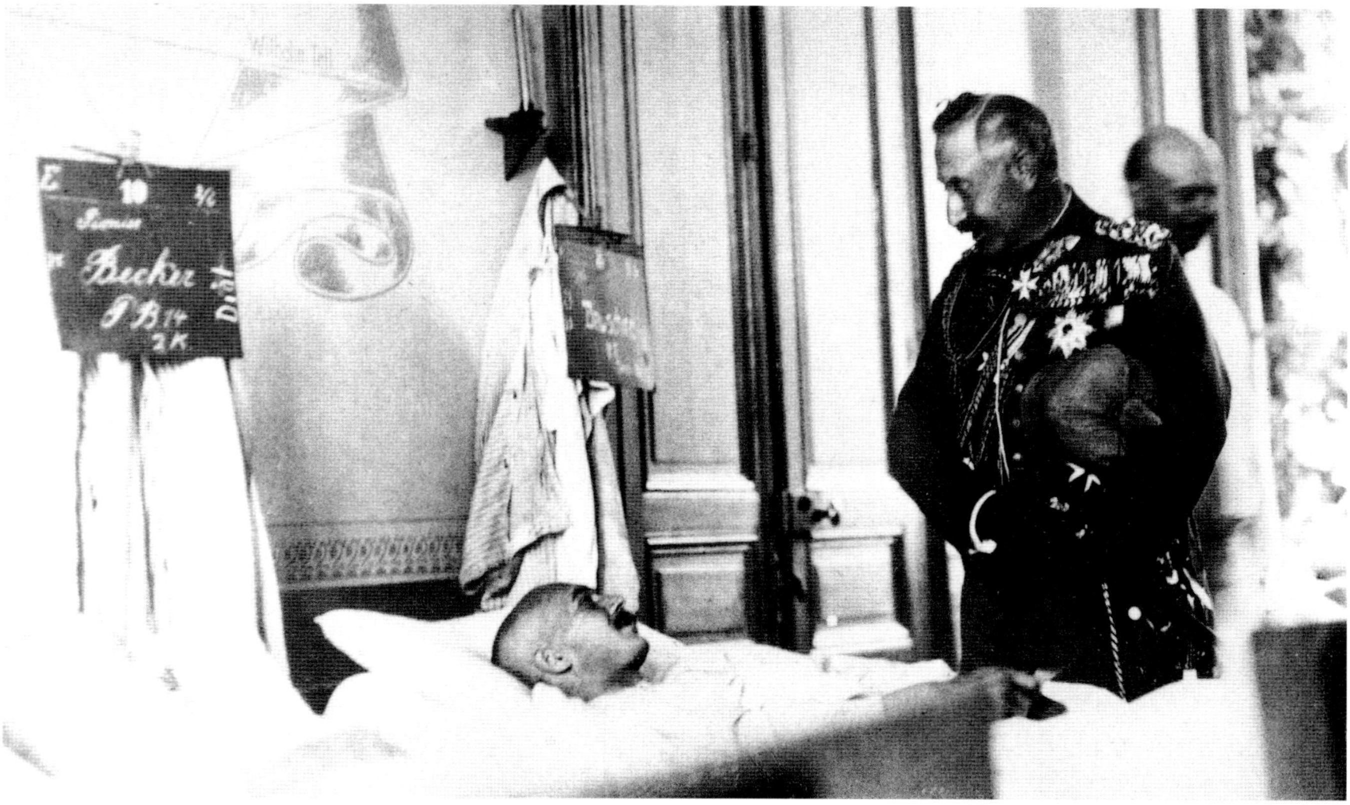

The *Kaiser* in full regalia visits the wounded wearing the *Grossordensschnalle* below that contains the major war orders and decorations of his empire as well as two of his allies. The awards of all but one of the states and cities covered in this book are present on this bar. The 1914 Iron Cross 2nd Class is followed by the Bavarian Military Max-Joseph Order, the Saxon St. Henry Order, the Württemberg Military Merit Order, the Austrian Order of Maria Theresa, the Baden Military Karl Friedrich Order, the Oldenburg Friedrich August Cross, the Saxe-Weimar White Falcon Order, the Hessian General Honor Decoration "for Bravery," the Mecklenburg-Schwerin Military Merit Cross, the Mecklenburg-Strelitz Cross for Distinction in War, the Brunswick War Merit Cross, the Saxe-Meiningen Cross for Merit in War, the Anhalt Friedrich Cross, the Princely Hohenzollern Honor Cross, the Schaumburg-Lippe Cross for Faithful Service, the Lippe War Merit Cross, the Hanseatic Cross from Hamburg, Bremen and Lübeck and the Turkish Imtiaz Medal. Many of these were specially sized to present a neat appearance. But missing is anything from Waldeck or Germany's third ally, Bulgaria. This magnificent bar is now in a private collection.

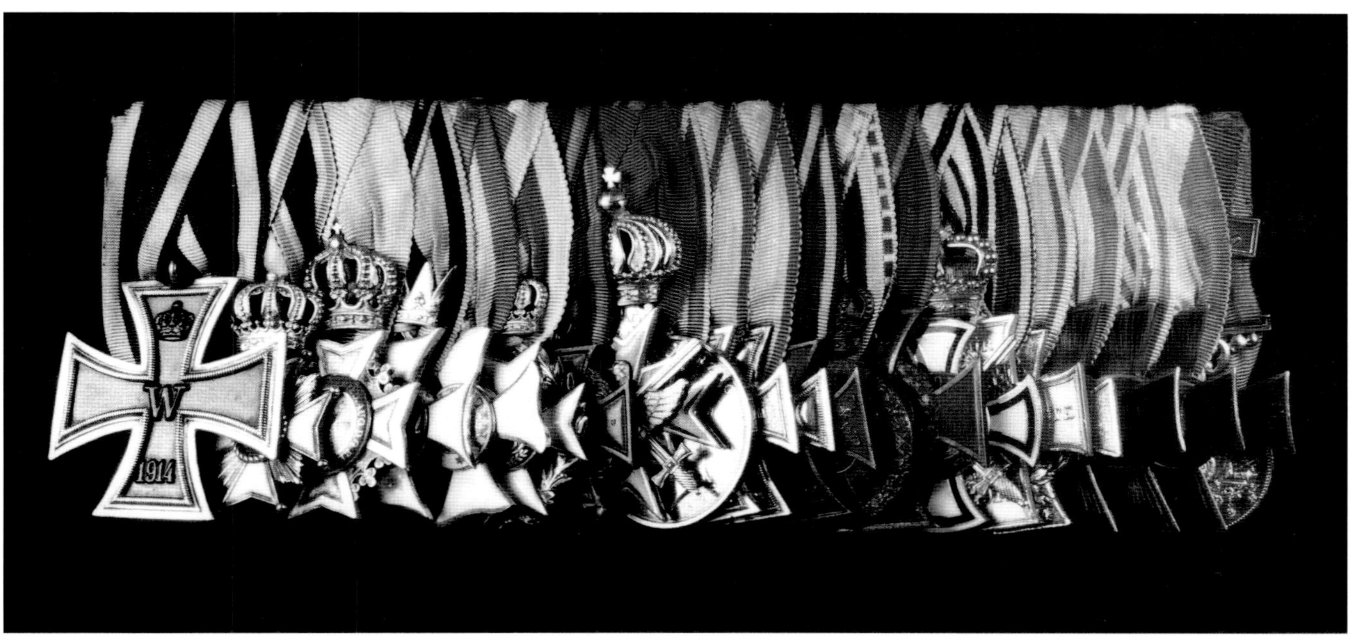

Steinle, Manfred Thiemeyer, *Dipl.-Ing.* Dieter Veltjens and Reinhard Zankl. In Great Britain, Alex Imrie, Ray Rimell and Terry C. Treadwell. In Switzerland, Hans Herbert and Monika Hemer Munte. In the United States, the late A. Edward Ferko, Charles C. Freihofer III, Francis P. Garove, Dieter H.M. Gröschel, M.D., Peter M. Grosz, Peter Kilduff, Eric C. Ludvigsen, Knox Martin, the late William R. Puglisi, George A. Seymour and Greg VanWyngarden.

For the subjects covered in this book, a number of institutions were visited personally, often in company with the six gentlemen mentioned earlier. There, invariably, one was met with the utmost courtesy and cooperation. Taking them according to the subjects appearing in this book, they were: For Brunswick, *Niedersächisches Staatsarchiv in Wolfenbüttel*; For Hesse, *Hessisches Staatsarchiv Darmstadt*; for Hohenzollern, *Staatsarchiv Sigmaringen*; for Lippe, *Nordhein-Westfälisches Staatsarchiv Detmold*; for Schaumburg-Lippe, *Niedersächsisches Staatsarchiv in Bückeburg*; for Mecklenburg-Schwerin and Mecklenburg-Strelitz, *Mecklenburgisches Landeshauptarchiv*; for Waldeck, *Hessisches Staatsarchiv Marburg*; for Bremen, *Staatsarchiv Bremen*; for Hamburg, *Senat der Freien und Hansestadt Hamburg Staatsarchiv*, and for Lübeck, *Hansestadt Lübeck Archiv*. In working on earlier volumes, other institutions have been visited which also provided information for this book. They were: In Berlin, the *Deutsches Technikmuseum Berlin* and the *Luftwaffenmuseum der Bundeswehr;* in Freiburg im Breisgau, the *Bundesarchiv-Militärarchiv*; in Ingolstadt, the *Bayerisches Armeemuseum*; in Karlsruhe, the *Generallandesarchiv Karlsruhe*; in Munich, the *Bayerisches Hauptstaatsarchiv-Kriegsarchiv* and in Rastatt, the *Wehrgeschichtliches Museum Schloss Rastatt*. Dr. Gröschel, Mr. Grosz, Mr. Kilduff, Mr. Seymour and *Professor Dr. Dr.* Steinle also personally assisted in the researches in those institutions.

As the Errata and Addenda chapter attests, mistakes inevitably have occurred in earlier volumes in this series. Corrections by readers have been gratefully received although most have requested anonymity and have asked not to be mentioned by name. The author welcomes similar corrections for anything in this volume for which he, again, must assume sole responsibility.

Neal W. O'Connor
Princeton, New Jersey

"Days and weeks passed. Flying and nothing but flying! Firing and firing! Successes. Failures. Victories. Celebrations. A comrade lost. Another shot down. Anxious hours. Sad hours. But always the war dragged us along. No one belonged to himself. We all belonged to the Fatherland."

Malaula! The Battle Cry of *Jagdstaffel 17*
by the *Pour le Mérite* ace, Julius Buckler

CHAPTER I

NOTES REGARDING FREQUENTLY MENTIONED PRUSSIAN AWARDS

This chapter first appeared in Volume IV as an aid to readers who might want to have more information than otherwise would have been provided on Prussian awards which were bestowed throughout the Empire and which all of the airmen featured in books since then, as well as this one, earned in the course of their wartime careers. By now, however, the following will be old hat to almost every reader. Thus the discussion of each of these awards will be shortened this time to the bare essentials to conserve space and the patience of the reader.

Orden Pour le Mérite: Prussia's highest military honor for distinguished service or personal bravery in the face of the enemy. During World War 1,685 awards were made with 78 going to officers in the *Fliegertruppe* (Aviation Troop or Air Service). A separate and higher grade of the order existed, the *Orden Pour le Mérite mit Eichenlaub* (with Oakleaf). It was meant to recognize the most important of military achievements (the original language of the foundation statement called for it going to an officer who had captured or successfully defended a fortress or who had "won a battle"). This grade of the order was awarded a total of 124 times in World War I. No flier received it although Germany's premier fighter pilot, Manfred *Freiherr* von Richthofen, was proposed for it but unsuccessfully so.

Royal House Order of Hohenzollern: Prussia's intermediate award in World War I for officers between the *Orden Pour le Mérite* and the Iron Cross 1st Class. The best figure for swords awards of the order for World War I comes to 8,291. No breakout of aviation awards of the order has ever been discovered.

Red Eagle and Crown Orders: Two other Prussian orders which could be awarded with Swords to officers for military merit or bravery. Swords awards of these orders virtually disappeared in World War I for junior officers in favor of the Knight's Hohenzollern. One major exception was Manfred von Richthofen who received the Red Eagle Order 3rd Class with Crown and Swords in lieu of his failed nomination for the *Orden Pour le Mérite mit Eichenlaub*. Another exception was the highly unusual award of the Crown Order 4th Class with Swords to a then non-commissioned officer, Rudolf Windisch (see the chapter on the Waldeck Honor Cross with Swords for details). Prewar, junior officers received the Red Eagle and Crown Orders in their lower classes without Swords for exemplary service in peacetime circumstances.

Member's Cross with Swords of the Royal House Order of Hohenzollern: A highly exclusive honor decoration affiliated with the House Order. It was awarded with Swords a total of only 17 times in World War I with 11 of these, an unusually high percentage, going to airmen.[1]

Golden Military Merit Cross: Another bravery decoration open to non-commissioned officers and men. Because of the eventual total of 1,770 awarded for World War I, it came to be considered as the highest bravery award among the troops and was often referred to as the *Pour le Mérite für Unteroffiziere* ("*Unteroffiziere*" literally stands for "Corporals," but here it

[1] For years, the total number of World War I awards of the Member's Cross with Swords was thought to be sixteen according to an official list published in the 1930s with ten of these going to airmen. Now it has been found there was another aviation recipient, Edmund Nathanael, who was omitted from the list because he was a Jew.

was used as a generic term for all enlisted personnel). Men in the various air services received a total of 69 awards of this decoration for World War I.

Iron Cross: Usually classed as a decoration although it was constituted as an order in that there were several grades, namely, the Star to the Grand Cross (awarded only twice, once in 1815 and once in 1918), the Grand Cross (five awarded for World War I), the 1st Class (around 218,000 awarded for World War I) and the 2nd Class (something over 5,210,000 awarded for World War I). As the numbers for World War I indicate, the Iron Cross in the 2nd Class soon lost its original exclusivity. All the airmen featured in this volume held both the 1st and 2nd Class Iron Cross.

The War Ribbon: The term for the ribbon from which Prussian orders and decorations awarded for military merit and bravery in the face of the enemy were worn. For combatants, it was black with two white side stripes, the ribbon for the Iron Cross 2nd Class. For non-combatants, it was just the reverse, white with two black side stripes. The *Orden Pour le Mérite* had a neck cravat that was black with two silvered rather than white side stripes. There were certain high grades of the Red Eagle and Crown Orders where swords awards when worn from a sash used the statutory colors of their respective ribbons rather than the war ribbon. There were also provisions for adding a third white (or silvered) stripe to the war ribbon for subsequent higher awards of a Prussian order under certain circumstances. For a fuller discussion of these refinements, see Volume II on Prussian awards or the expanded version of this chapter in Volumes IV, V and VI.

The *Orden Pour le Mérite*

The Knight's Cross with Swords of the Royal House Order of Hohenzollern

The Red Eagle Order 3rd Class with Crown and Swords

The Prussian Crown Order 4th Class with Swords

The Member's Cross with Swords of the Royal House Order of Hohenzollern

The Golden Military Merit Cross

The Iron Cross 2nd Class and 1st Class

CHAPTER II

THE DUCAL HOUSE OF BRUNSWICK

The Duchy of Brunswick goes back to the ninth century Saxon Duke Bruno, after whom it was named. In 1127, the land was acquired by the Guelphs through the marriage of Henry the Proud, Duke of Saxony and Bavaria, to Gertrude, the daughter of the Holy Roman Emperor Lothair II. The Guelphs were rivals of the House of Hohenstaufen for the imperial title and when Conrad III of Hohenstaufen became German king in 1138, he moved to seize Henry's duchies and war between the two houses erupted. Things were smoothed over, however, when Frederick I of Hohenstaufen became the emperor in 1155. Frederick's mother, Judith, was the sister of Henry the Proud and this family tie resulted in the two houses in Germany becoming united. Henry the Proud's only son was Henry the Lion and he succeeded his father as Duke of Saxony and Bavaria (and it was Henry the Lion after whom the Brunswick house order was named when it was founded in 1834). Typically, this cordial state of affairs did not last long. Friction developed between Frederick and the Lion which resulted in Henry's duchies except for Brunswick and Lüneburg being confiscated. Over the subsequent years, there were many divisions of the remaining lands among the various branches of the family with those of Brunswick-Lüneburg, Lüneburg itself, Celle and Lüneburg-Calenburg becoming the most significant. During the Thirty Years War (1618-1648), the dukes played an important role on the Protestant side. Then in 1692, Duke Ernst August of Calenburg was raised to the dignity of an elector and his domain became the Electorate of Hanover. He married a granddaughter of James I of England which resulted in Ernst August's son, Elector George Louis, becoming King George I of England in 1714. The emergence of "the little Corporal" in the person of a formerly obscure Corsican artillery officer, Napoleon Bonaparte, who had made a name for himself by dispersing a mob of Parisian royalists with "a whiff of grapeshot" in 1795 was to have a profound effect on the fortunes of both Brunswick and Hanover.

Two allied coalitions had already been formed in largely futile efforts to thwart Napoleon's continental ambitions when in 1805, after already proclaiming himself French emperor, he also assumed the title of King of Italy and annexed Genoa to France. Two years before, he had already overrun Hanover thereby firmly putting himself at odds with King George III of England who was also Elector of Hanover (the upshot of this takeover was that most of the Hanoverian army made its way to England to form the King's German Legion and await the day for revenge). Now a Third Coalition against Napoleon was formed comprised of England, Austria, Russia and Sweden with a dithering Prussia signing up late in 1806. Moving with his characteristic speed and with troops from Bavaria, Württemberg and Baden in his vanguard, Napoleon surrounded 20,000 Austrians at Ulm on October 17, 1805 and forced their surrender. He then moved on to achieve his most brilliant victory over a combined army of Austrians and Russians at Austerlitz on December 2 that same year. In the harsh Treaty of Pressburg that followed (December 26, 1805), Austria was forced to concede territory to, among others, Napoleon's then German brothers-in-arms. In the process, Bavaria and Württemberg were elevated to the status of kingdoms and Baden became a grand duchy.

Napoleon also called Prussia to account for what up until this time had been its vacillation and parceled out some of its smaller possessions to his favorite commanders. In compensation, he allowed Prussia to have Hanover. Then in 1806, in an expedient as he tried to work out an arrangement with England concerning their respective sea trade with Europe, he offered Hanover back to George III. The trouble was, he hadn't bothered to inform King Friedrich Wilhelm III of Prussia of his intention. Friedrich Wilhelm was incensed and for once, decided to act. With Saxony and Brunswick at his side, he declared war on France. Brunswick's contribution to his arms consisted of two infantry regiments. This time, Austria and Russia stood by while a polyglot army made up of troops from France, Bavaria, Württemberg, Baden, Hesse-Darmstadt, Würzburg and Frankfurt moved through southern Germany, catching the ill-prepared Prussians, Saxons and Brunswickers and defeating them at the twin battles of Jena and Auerstadt on October 14, 1806.

Duke Karl II of Brunswick, a field marshal in the Prussian army, married to the eldest daughter of the Prince of Wales and a Knight of the Garter, was wounded at Jena and died at Altona on November 10, 1806. Saxony was forced to make a separate peace with France and then moved into the French camp completely. The other German forces fled eastwards where Russia finally came to their aid for another stand against the "Monster" (another of Napoleon's sobriquets). But they, too, were crushed at Friedland on June 14, 1807. In the Treaty of Tilsit that resulted the next month, more of the map of Europe was reworked according to Napoleon's design. Prussia ceded the land that became the Grand Duchy of Warsaw. Saxony got a bit of Prussia too and now as a member of Napoleon's Confederation of the Rhine, became a kingdom. Its new king, Friedrich August, was also given the (empty) title of Grand Duke of Warsaw. It was little Brunswick that paid the most fearful price. It was simply abolished and made part of the Kingdom of Westphalia under the rule of Napoleon's brother, Jerome. Duke Friedrich Wilhelm of Brunswick, the youngest son of the now dead Karl II to whom the throne had descended, was forced to flee to the safety of Austria, there to bide his time and nurture his hatred of the French.

An uneasy peace lasted until 1808. Then war once again broke out but this time far from Austria. Napoleon had attempted to install yet another of his brothers – Joseph Bonaparte – as king of Spain but the Spaniards would have none of that. Austria and an eager Friedrich Wilhelm figured that with French attention and resources now focused on the Iberian Peninsula, the time was right for them to strike back. In early 1809, Friedrich Wilhelm agreed to raise a corps consisting of a regiment of infantry (two battalions with a total of 1,000 men) and a regiment of hussars (eight squadrons each comprised of 125 men) with an attached horse artillery battery of four guns. The usually accepted story is that it was at this time that the Brunswickers were outfitted with the black uniforms adorned with the skull and crossbones insignia as symbols of the dire

The last ruler of the Duchy of Brunswick, Duke Ernst August, with a decorative border containing the legend "The Brunswickers in the World War," a panoply of arms with the rampant horse symbol of the House of Hanover, a 1914 Iron Cross and the Brunswick War Merit Cross which the Duke instituted on October 23, 1914. Here he is wearing the uniform of *Husaren-Regiment von Zieten* (*Brandenburgisches*) *Nr.3.* of which he was a Colonel *à la suite*. The regiment had old ties with the British royal family and prewar, its *Chef* was a *Generallfeld-marschall* in the German Army, Arthur, Prince of Great Britain and Ireland, Duke of Connaught. At the neck, the Duke displays the Grand Cross of the Prussian Red Eagle Order. Over his left shoulder is the sash of the Prussian High Order of the Black Eagle (the badge at his right hip is hidden in this photograph) The upper breast star is that of the Black Eagle and the lower one is the Grand Cross star of the Hanovarian Guelphic Order.

retribution the Duke had vowed to extract from the French and its allies and for which they were to become famous. There is a more benign version which may or may not be apocryphal. This has it that the only cloth available in sufficient quantities to equip the troops was black and it was thus only a matter of expediency and not some sinister intent that the uniforms turned out this way. However they came to be, it resulted in Friedrich Wilhelm being dubbed *Der Schwarzer Herzog* ("The Black Duke") and his men *Der Schwarze Band* ("The Black Band").

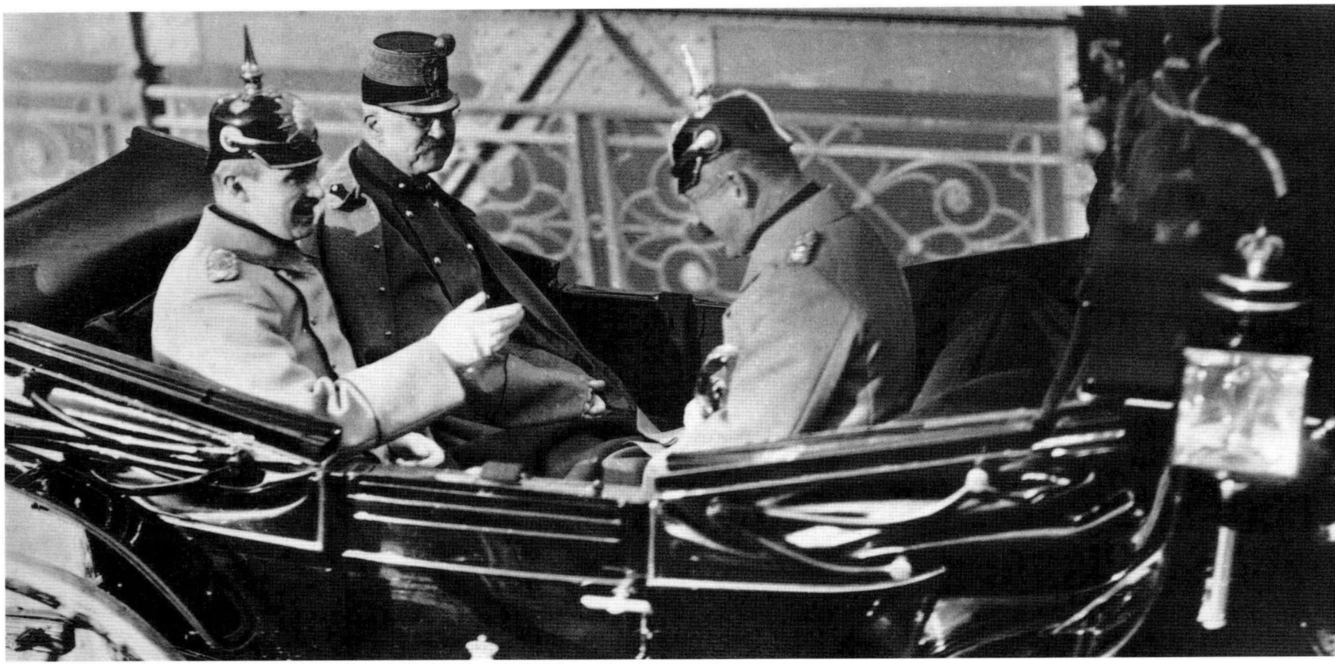

Above: Ernst August's father, also named Ernst August (in shako), Duke of Brunswick and Lüneburg, formerly the Crown Prince of Hanover, was also the Duke of Cumberland. He should have ruled Brunswick after the death of his own father but his house was impeached from the succession in 1884 and he lived a bucolic but unfulfilled life in Austria. The Duke harbored no love for things Prussian but here on some unknown occasion he seems friendly enough with two other German royals, Grand Duke Friedrich Franz IV of Mecklenburg-Schwerin (left) and Prince Max of Baden. Right: In place of the elder Ernst August, Brunswick was at first administered under the regency of Prince Albrecht of Prussia until his death in 1913. Then the regency was turned over to Duke Johann Albrecht of Mecklenburg-Schwerin (with an Iron Cross 2nd Class and Mecklenburg-Schwerin War Merit Cross 2nd Class in his buttonhole in this post card). A love match, described in the text, brought the duchy back to the Ernst August family in 1913.

Hostilities broke out at several points but were short lived. The Brunswickers took on the Saxons in Bohemia in May 1809 and then pushed into Saxony itself the next month. The Saxon king appealed to Jerome for help and a series of inconclusive, hit and run actions ensued until an armistice with the Austrians was signed that July. This was hardly what the Black Duke had in mind and it left him in an impossible situation since he could hardly carry on alone. But he decided on a fighting march to the north German coast where the British, now engaged in Portugal against the French, promised warships to transport his troops to England and an opportunity to come to grips with the real enemy there. Halle was taken before he encountered much resistance but at Halberstadt there was a sharp and costly engagement with the Westphalians. The Black Duke suffered about 400 casualties but this was more than offset by the opposing force's 600 dead and wounded plus some 2,000 captured. Only 100 or so Westphalians escaped and 300 odd of their men, in a move not uncharacteristic of the time, joined up with the Brunswickers. Replenished with captured stores, they now pushed through the old capital of Brunswick on their continued march north. The enemy in pursuit failed to come to grips with them and the Black Band, now numbering 1,600, embarked upon British men-of-war in August bound ultimately for the Isle of Wight. There they regrouped and reembarked, landing at Lisbon on October 8, 1810.

In the Peninsula, the infantry, now known as the Brunswick-Oels *Jägers*, fought in the west with the regiment of hussars assigned to the east. The latter had arrived direct from England in July 1813 and were involved in several operations including a botched (by the British general in command) raid on Terragona which resulted in a forced evacuation. They also participated in the August 1813 battle at Villa Franca, losing nine killed, 26 wounded and 18 missing. In 1814, they were part of the force that invaded Sicily. The *Jägers*, on the other hand, were engaged continuously from the Battle of Fuentes d'Onoro in May 1811 to the Battle of Orthez in February 1814. Its total losses came to 252 of whom 43 were killed, 156 wounded and 53 went missing. On Christmas Day, 1814, the *Jägers* left English service. The hussars remained in England until the middle of 1815.

On March 1, 1815, Napoleon, in exile on Elba after his disastrous Russian campaign and defeat at the Battle of the Nations at Leipzig in October 1813, magically appeared with about 1,000 followers on the French coast near Cannes. In a triumphant march northwards, France once again rallied to him, King Louis XVIII fled to Belgium and Napoleon entered Paris on March 20 to begin his rule of one hundred days. The allies were once again forced into action. A formidable array of armies from Britain, Austria, Prussia, Russia, the Netherlands and other allies including Brunswick was mobilized and began to move against France from different directions. The northernmost force included the Brunswickers along with troops from Britain, Hanover, Nassau and the Netherlands, all under the command of Sir Arthur Wellesley, Duke of Wellington. To the southeast of Wellington was an army of 124,000 Prussians under Field Marshal Gebhard Leberecht von Blücher who had made his reputation at Wahlstatt, Möckern and Leipzig. Both Wellington and Blücher were poised in Belgium by early June 1815 ready to invade France but were under orders to stay put until the other allies advancing from the east could come into play. Napoleon saw another chance to defeat his enemy in detail however, and struck first, hoping to split the two armies and take them on one at a time. He very nearly succeeded (Wellington was quoted after the Battle of Waterloo that it was "a damn near run thing"). On June 15, Napoleon attacked the Prussians and at the Battle of Ligny the next day, the Prussians were defeated and forced back east just as the French emperor had planned. He then turned towards Wellington even while some of his forces were trying to make sure Blücher kept his distance. The French moved to capture the vital crossroad junction at Quatre Bras where the Brunswick brigade with the Black Duke himself in their command were part of the Netherlands Prince of Orange's opposing forces. The fighting at Quatre Bras was desperate as Wellington poured in more reinforcements. The June 16 battle cost the Brunswickers 188 officers and men killed, 396 wounded and an indeterminate number of missing. One of the fatalities was the Black Duke himself. As he tried to reform his men early that evening, a musket ball lodged in his liver and he died almost immediately.

Wellington pulled his troops back from Quatre Bras on the 17th and positioned them on a ridge astride the road to Brussels to await the advance of Marshal Ney. The Black Band, now a Corps consisting of 4,586 infantry, 866 cavalry and 16 guns of artillery with 510 men under the command of an *Oberst* Olfermann (whom Friedrich Wilhelm had called for in his dying words), was in reserve when shortly before noon on June 18, the Battle of Waterloo commenced with an attack on the British center. Brunswick troops did not become engaged until more than three hours later when there was a second French cavalry charge in force. During this and in a second French cavalry attack, the Brunswickers acquitted themselves well and were, in fact, commended for their bravery. Towards the end of that confused day, with the issue still very much in doubt as Napoleon threw in the Imperial Guard in a last ditch gamble to gain victory, Wellington himself rode up to exhort the Brunswickers to stand fast even though they were perilously low in ammunition. It was at this crisis point that Blücher arrived on the scene, having eluded the French force that was supposed to pin him down. The Prussian intervention carried the day and Napoleon fled the field and four days later, signed his final abdication. The men of the Black Band had played their part in ridding Europe of Napoleon forever. Combined losses of their troops at Quatre Bras and at Waterloo were put at 260 dead, 918 wounded and 378 missing out of total of about 23,000 coalition casualties. By the time the campaign was wound up, it was estimated that it had cost them 22% of their total strength.

Friedrich Wilhelm was succeeded by his eldest son who ruled from 1815 as Karl III under the regency of the Prince Regent of Great Britain (later King George IV). Karl III fled the duchy in September 1830 and the government of the duchy was taken over by his only brother, Wilhelm. Wilhelm ruled provisionally until April 1831 when the German Diet, who had declared Karl unfit, confirmed him definitely. Between 1816 and 1831, the Brunswick infantry was reorganized several times and had become an infantry regiment of three battalions plus a *Jäger Leib* battalion by the time Duke Wilhelm took the throne. The hussars became a guard regiment in 1825 and were renamed the Brunswick Hussars in 1830.

In 1848, two infantry battalions and the artillery took part in the Schleswig campaign. The following year, they were joined by the *Jäger* and the hussars. The same infantrists and hussars served in the Prussian 2nd Reserve Corps in the 1866 war against Austria and her allies but saw no action. With Prussian arms in the ascendancy, the Brunswick army consisting of *Herzoglich Braunschweigische Infanterie-Regiment Nr.92.* (with the fusilier battalion serving as *Leib* unit), *Husaren-Regiment Nr.17.* and the sixth (Brunswick) battery of the Prussian *Feldartillerie. Regiment Nr.10.* joined the North German Confederation army.

In the Franco-Prussian War, the 92nd Infantry and the Brunswick artillery formed a part of the 20th Division, 10th Corps (Hanover, Oldenburg and Brunswick under General Voigts-Rhetz) of the Second Army. They crossed the Moselle at Pont-à-Mousson, marched north and fought in the Battle of Mars-la-Tour at Vionville and formed part of the reserves in the Battle of Gravelotte. The artillery was in the front line with the Guard. After the victory, the Brunswickers took part in the siege of Metz. The typhoid epidemic plaguing many German units afflicted 14% of their men. With the Second Army, they saw action again in the Battle of Orleans December 3-4, 1870 and then against General Chanzy's Army of the Loire, on the Loire itself and on the Loir. The infantry lost 156 men at Vendôme, 73 as prisoners. In a renewed attempt to relieve Paris, General Chanzy attacked the Germans in the new year, and the Brunswickers saw action at Poncé, Ruillé, La Chartre and in the Battle of Le Mans on January 11 and 12 where the 10th Corps carried the day by breaking through the French defenses. Until the armistice, the infantry had only a few skirmishes with the French, having only small losses.

The Brunswick hussars belonged to the 13th Brigade of the 5th Cavalry Division, the cavalry reserve of the Second Army. They saw action at Spichern and Pont-à-Mousson in early August 1870 and arrived in time to ride in a regimental attack in the Battle of Mars-la-Tour on August 16, losing eight men killed and 45 wounded. Among the latter was their commanding officer, von Rauch who was wounded again two days later at Gravelotte. Until the end of the war, the hussars rode protective patrols along the northern and western perimeter of besieged Paris.

The 92nd Infantry lost 99 officers and men killed, 224 wounded and 73 taken prisoner during the War of 1870/71. An additional 71 died from illness, making total casualties of 467 or 15% of their total strength. For the 17th Hussars, the comparable figures were 22, 69, 28 and four respectively, a total of 123 or 17% of their strength. In only two days of fighting at Waterloo, the Brunswickers had lost almost three times as many men as they did in the entire 1870/71 campaign.

The hussars received permission to wear the skull and crossbones insignia of the Black Band on their *Pelzmütze* (fur cap) in 1883 and through World War I were known as the "Death's Head Hussars." The Brunswick units lost their ducal status in 1886, becoming Royal Prussian troops with the designation *Braunschweigisch.* The Brunswick artillery battery was transferred to the newly established *Königlich Preussisches Niedersächsisches Feldartillerie-Regiment Nr.46* in 1899 as its second battery.

Duke Wilhelm died in October 1884 and with him, the senior line of the House of Guelph became extinct. He should have been succeeded by Ernst August, the Duke of Cumberland, Duke of Brunswick and Lüneburg, formerly Crown Prince of Hanover. He had been living the life of a country gentleman on an estate in Austria and Bismarck would have none of him. Callously, Bismarck blocked the normal succession and turned the duchy over to a Regent in the person of Duke Albrecht of Prussia in 1885. Albrecht died in 1906 and the Regency continued with the appointment of Duke Johann Albrecht of Mecklenburg-Schwerin. Meantime, the rightful Duke of Brunswick continued in his Austrian retreat, pretty much the forgotten man. There is the story of Edward VII of Great Britain stopping his royal train at Gmunden, a watering spot on Austria's Lake Traunsee, so that Ernst August could pay his respects. The Duke of Cumberland showed up like some ancient

Duke Ernst August took over the rule of the duchy in 1913 after nearly 30 years of it being administered by regents appointed by Prussia. The then 25-year old handsome youth had been deputized by the family to thank the *Kaiser* for the respects shown when his older brother's death in an accident occurred on German soil in 1912. Ernst August discharged his duties so well that the *Kaiser*'s youngest child and only daughter fell in love with him. The feelings were reciprocated, initial opposition from the groom's anti-Prussian parents was overcome and the happy couple were married in Berlin on May 24, 1913. In a burst of generosity, the *Kaiser* restored the throne to Ernst August and the impeachment that had barred the house was formally annulled by the Federal Diet on November 1, 1913. With the collapse of the *2nd Reich* and the *Kaiser*'s abdication, Ernst August was forced to vacate his throne on November 8, 1918

The Duke was Colonel and nominal commander of both the 92nd Brunswick Infantry Regiment and the 17th Hussars whose uniforms he wears above. Both of them bore the sinister skull and crossbones insignia on their service caps with the Hussars also displaying it on their distinctive *Pelzmütze* (fur cap or busby). The device had been adopted by an ancestor, Duke Friedrich Wilhelm, in his early 19th century wars against Napoleon as a symbol of the vengeance he hoped to wreak on the French. The first two Prussian hussar regiments of the line, both known as *Leib*, or Body- or Life Guard regiments, also wore the skull and bones and were commonly referred to as the "Death's Head Hussars" along with the 17th.

apparition wearing a British general's uniform of Crimean War cut decked out with an "antiquated Garter riband." He may have been something of a laughing stock but the enmity that Ernst August and his family held towards Bismarck and anything that smacked of the new German empire was very real. This persisted even after the newly installed impetuous Wilhelm II had sacked Bismarck. So bad was the feeling that when he and his wife traveled across Germany to visit relatives in Denmark (she had been the youngest daughter of King Christian IX), they would not even alight from their train or motor car lest their feet touch German soil.

King Frederick of Denmark, the Duchess' brother, died in 1912. The family deputized their eldest son, Prince Georg, to represent them at Frederick's state funeral. But on his way across Germany by car, the young man crashed and was killed. Because royalty had died on his lands, the *Kaiser* sent two officers plus an honor detachment of his elite Garde du Corps to Georg's services. This show of respect could not be ignored and protocol dictated that the bereaved family render proper thanks to the Berlin court for the *Kaiser's* gesture of respect. The Cumberlands sent their remaining surviving son who also bore the name of Ernst August to render the appropriate niceties which he is said to have carried out in commendable fashion, although a bit stiffly. But not stiffly enough to find himself enraptured by the seventh and last child of Wilhelm and Auguste Viktoria and their only daughter, the 20-year old Viktoria Luise. The feelings were reciprocated but, as might be expected, the Cumberlands initially opposed the union. Love triumphed however, permission was granted and the happy couple were given a gala wedding in Berlin on May 24, 1913. The proud father of the bride in an uncharacteristic show of generosity presented his new son-in-law with the Duchy of Brunswick as a wedding present, the old Duke of Cumberland having renounced any rights he may have had to the duchy in his son's favor.

Because the wedding that took place was one of the last great royal events prior to the start of World War I, a description of it might not be out of place in ending this brief discussion of the ducal house of Brunswick. The gala celebration was capped by the traditional *Fackeltanz* (torch dance) which was only performed at royal weddings and in which no one not holding the title Royal Highness could take part. Pages in medieval livery bearing candle-lit candelabra led off the dancers who paraded around the White Hall at the royal palace in Potsdam for what was probably the last time ever. Six years later, the father and mother of the bride were in exile, another of the dancers, Tsar Nicholas II of Russia, and his family had been murdered, the bridegroom's father had been stripped of his titles of Duke of Cumberland and Prince of Great Britain and Ireland as well as his order of the Garter by the British government and the short-lived Duke of Brunswick, the young Ernst August, was forced to abdicate his throne on November 8, 1918.

When the war started, Brunswick fielded its three contingents as elements of the X Hanovarian Army Corps in its 20th Division, *Braunschweigisches Infanterie-Regiment. Nr.92.* (1809), *Braunschweigisches Husaren-Regiment Nr.17.* (1809) and *Niedersächsisches Feldartillerie-Regiment Nr.46., 2. Batterie* (1809). The 19th Division formed the other element of the X Army Corps. In 1914, the Corps was part of von Bülow's Second German Army in the invasion of Belgium and France and was present at the Battle of the Marne. After service in Champagne, the division embarked on the first of a sea-saw series of shuttles between the Western and Eastern Fronts, going to Galicia at the end of April 1915 where it was attached to the army of *Generalfeldmarschall* August von Mackensen. It was returned to France in September, fighting again in Champagne. From November 1915 until June 1916, it was stationed in the Aisne sector until it was again entrained for the east where it helped stem the Russian advance. The division was brought back to France in November 1916 and participated in the stand against the ill-starred Nivelle Offensive in April and May 1917 incurring such heavy losses that, together with the casualties already suffered, the effectiveness of the two divisions was considerably reduced and it had to be relieved. July 1917 saw the Corps back on the Russian Front for a third time, first in Galicia and then in Kurland. With Russian forces collapsing, the pressures of Third Ypres brought it back to Flanders at the end of September but casualties again required that the division be withdrawn after less than a month. It was next assigned to the relative quiet of Artois, the slaughter in Flanders having finally subsided in December. Ludendorff's big March 1918 offensive saw the division heavily engaged once more. Losing something like 50% of its effectives in the opening weeks of that drive, the division had to be withdrawn in early April for a complete reconstitution. By the end of July, it had been in action around Soissons in the third and last of Ludendorff's abortive drives where it took heavy punishment from the French and the newly arrived Americans. September and October saw it in stubborn retreat from Arras to Cambrai and then spent the remainder of the war east of the Meuse without being heavily engaged.

In an appreciation of the performance of the 20th Division, the histories compiled on the 251 divisions of the German Army in the war rated it a "first-class division" that "had fought well throughout the year (1918) and suffered enormous losses." And among the officers of its three Brunswick contingents, they were enormous indeed. In the 92nd Infantry, 165 Active and Reserve officers and equivalent ranks who were members of the regiment died during the war either with the regiment itself or with units to which they were later seconded (including three men in the *Fliegertruppe*; see Appendix II). Officer casualty figures for the 17th Hussars came to 25 with a much higher percentage of them as airmen, indicative of how many cavalrymen chose aviation as a career when trench warfare rendered their chosen profession virtually useless (in all, nine former 17th Hussars died in the *Fliegertruppe*; see Appendix II). The 46th Field Artillery lost at least 13 officers, four of them in the air service (see Appendix II).

Following the usual format in this series, there now follows a discussion of the military awards of the Duchy of Brunswick in World War I and brief biographies of some of their aviation recipients, some famous but an almost equal number about whom very little, if anything, has ever appeared in the English language.

CHAPTER III

THE MILITARY AWARDS OF THE DUCHY OF BRUNSWICK

THE ORDER OF HENRY THE LION

Among the most elaborate of German orders insignia (in most classes) was the Order of Henry the Lion, founded on April 24, 1834 by Duke Wilhelm of Brunswick and Lüneburg who named what turned out to be the Duchy's only house order after his illustrious 12th century ancestor. It originally came in four classes, Grand Cross, Commander 1st Class, Commander 2nd Class and Knight. As was customary, the Grand Cross consisted of a sash badge and eight-pointed breast star. It also could come with a collar. The two grades of Commander were differentiated by its own distinctive star for the 1st Class while the 2nd Class consisted only of a badge. Unusually, the badges of all three of the higher grades were, apart from minor differences in manufacture over the years, essentially the same size while the Knight's badge was typically smaller, about three-quarters the size of the other grades. There were also affiliated Merit Crosses established at the same time as the foundation of the order.

During its lifetime leading up to World War I, there were enlargements of the order, the most important of which, for us, was the addition of swords to all classes of the order in 1870. The others occurred in these years:

1877 - A Knight 2nd Class was established which could also be awarded with swords.

1879 - Swords (in gold) were added to the Merit Cross 1st Class and (in silver) to the Merit Cross 2nd Class.

1903 - A medal (in silver) called the Honor Decoration was founded as another award affiliated with the order.

1908 - A 1st Class grade of the order was added which ranked between the Grand Cross and the Commander 1st Class.

An Officer's Cross was added which ranked between the Commander 2nd Class and the Knight 1st Class.

A 4th Class grade was added which ranked between the Knight 2nd Class and the Merit Cross 1st Class.

A bronze medal was added which became the Honor Decoration 2nd Class. The silver medal became the Honor Decoration 1st Class.

An award called the Merit Decoration for Arts and Science was instituted in two classes, 1st Class (in silver-gilt) and 2nd Class (in oxidized silver).

1909 - The placement of swords on the order's badges was altered. Since 1870, swords had been placed (awkwardly one might say) under the lower arm of the crosses. Now, more conventionally, they ran through the center of the arms. For Grand Cross, Commander 2nd Class, Officer's Cross and Knight 1st Class badges, the swords were in silver, for the other grades in gold when placed in this position. Swords on the breast stars which always ran through the center of the medallions were in gold for the Grand Cross and 1st Class and in silver for the Commander 1st Class.

Provision was also made for swords to be placed above the top arm of the crosses in the so-called "on-Ring"

Opposite
Top: The Order of Henry the Lion was founded on April 24, 1334 by Duke Wilhelm of Brunswick and was the duchy's only house order. It was named after his illustrious 12th century ancestor. The insignia for most of the grades of the order, including the Knight 1st Class with Swords (top obverse and reverse) and the Knight 2nd Class with Swords (bottom obverse and reverse), was among the most-elaborate of all Imperial German awards. The Knight 1st Class and Knight 2nd Class were the same except for finish, gold for the 1st Class (silver-gilt after 1909) and silver for the 2nd Class. Swords between the limbs of the cross mark these awards as from 1909. Before that, the swords were affixed below the lower arm of the crosses.

Bottom: In addition to different finishes, there were minor variations in style. The 1st Class badge shown here was made by H. Jürgens in Brunswick who took over the contract in 1912. On the Jürgens piece, the horse's tail is up and the crown's arches are upright. On the 2nd Class badge, made by the firm of F. Siebrecht, also in Brunswick, and dated between 1909 and 1912, the tail is down and the crown has been rounded-down.

Below: In 1870, coincident with the war against France, swords were added to all classes of the order to distinguish awards that were made for wartime military merit or for bravery "in the face of the enemy" from those that were made away from the battlefield or, in the case of civilians, for services to the state. As mentioned on the previous page, swords were originally placed in the rather ungainly position under the lower arm of the crosses as shown in the photograph below left. Then in 1909, as also shown on the previous page, they were placed in the more conventional position between the arms of the crosses. Swords could also be placed in the so-called "on-Ring" position as with this Commander's badge shown in the photograph above right. This was to indicate that the recipient had previously earned a lower class of the order "with Swords."

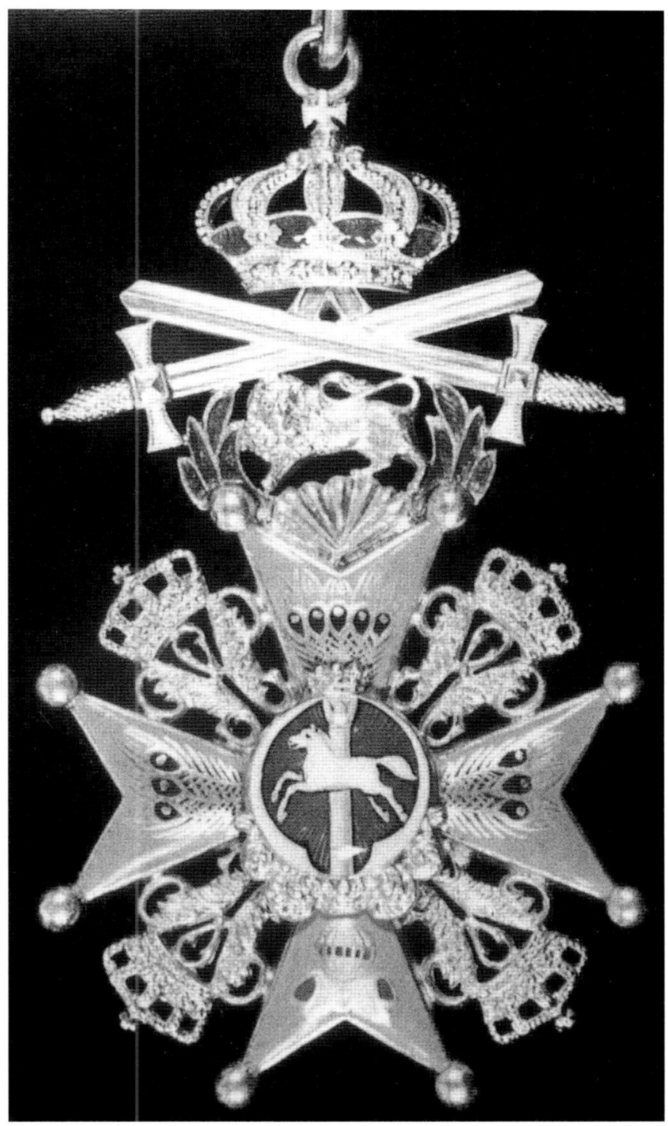

position (although that term was not used in the language of the statute amendment covering this feature). When swords were placed there, it was meant to indicate that a recipient had previously earned a lower grade of the order "with Swords." The swords in these cases were in gold for the Grand Cross, both Commander badges and for the Knight 1st Class. For the other grades, the swords were in silver. There was no provision for the placement of swords in the on-ring position on the Officer's Cross.

The Honor Decoration and the Merit Decoration for Arts and Science were not employed as awards won "in the face of the enemy" and thus will not be considered further here.

The insignia of the order in its original four classes were typical works of the jeweler's art but arguably the most elegant and most intricate of all the 19th century Imperial German orders insignia. The badges of the Grand Cross, Commander and Knight (and later the Knight 2nd Class when that grade was divided in two) were pale blue enameled Maltese crosses edged in gold (silver for the Knight 2nd Class) with ball finials. The red enamel center medallion held a white enamel stallion in full stride behind which was a white enamel column topped by a small gold ducal coronet and gold six-pointed star. The medallion was edged by ragged white enamel "teeth." The upper arm of the crosses had a spray of five green enamel peacock feathers applied over the blue; the two horizontal arms had a spray of three each. The lower arm had a white, gold and red knight's coroneted helmet in enamels. Between all four arms there was an ornate crowned initial "W" (for Wilhelm) in gold (silver, again, for the Knight 2nd Class). As mentioned, swords, if present, were placed under the lower arms of the crosses prior to 1909 and thereafter through the arms for swords awards made in the first instance and in the "on-Ring" position if the recipient had earned an earlier award "with Swords." No "Swords with Swords-on Ring" combination were ever made

Duke Ernst August of Brunswick, here in the dress uniform of his 17th "Death's Head" Hussars, signed this document dated 24 August 1916 awarding the Grand Cross with Swords of the Order of Henry the Lion to *General der Kavallerie Freiherr* von König. It was one of only two such known awards during World War I. The other swords Grand Cross went to *Generalfeldmarschall* Paul von Hindenburg in 1915. Von König was a veteran of the Wars of 1866 and 1870/71 and was called out of retirement to serve again in 1914 and became the Commanding Officer of Divisional Train Echelon No.56. Why he merited such an unusual recognition is yet to be discovered.

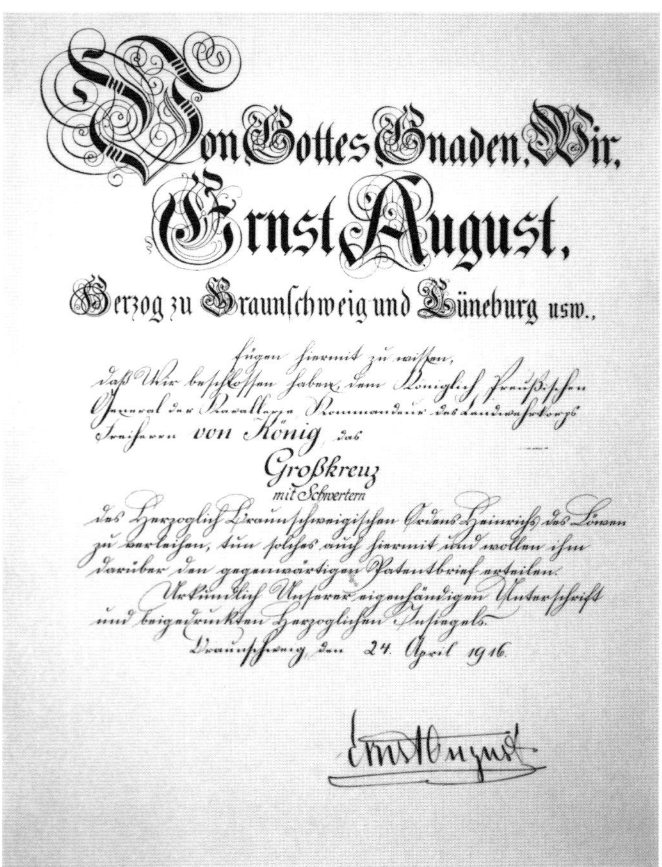
Von Gottes Gnaden, Wir,
Ernst August,
Herzog zu Braunschweig und Lüneburg usw.,

von König
Großkreuz
mit Schwertern

24. April 1916

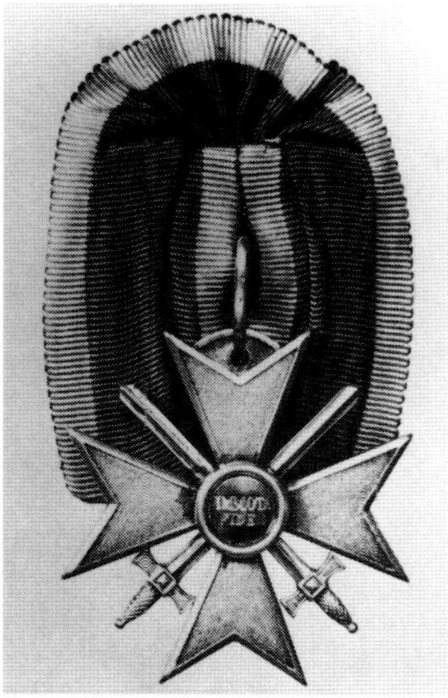

The 4th Class cross of the Order of Henry the Lion with the obverse (left) without Swords and the reverse (right) with Swords and displaying the order's motto *Immota Fides* ("Unshakably Faithful").

The Merit Cross 2nd Class with Swords, a decoration affiliated with the order. Research has failed to discover a single award of the Merit Cross in either 1st or 2nd Class with Swords during World War I.

apparently. Surmounting the upper arm of these crosses was a lion *passant guardant* flanked on each side by sprigs of six green enameled laurels. And above this was a five-arched crown.

On the reverse, these badges had plain blue enamel arms with a red center medallion carrying the order's motto in gold capital letters on two lines, *IMMOTA FIDES* (which can be translated as "Unshakably Faithful" or "Steadfast and Faithful"). This was surrounded by a gold (or silver in the case of a Knight 2nd Class) band on which the foundation date of the order appeared in the Latin numerals MDCCCXXXIV.

Unusually, the Grand Cross badge and Breast Star could be awarded "*mit Brillanten*," set with precious stones, diamonds in most cases, either real or paste Herr Jörg Nimmergut in his work, *Deutsche Orden und Ehrenzeichen Bis 1945*, cites just three such awards, in April 1837 to Prince Wittgenstein, in May 1911 to State Minister Dr. von Otto and in December 1914 to State Minister Hartwieg. Both von Otto and Hartwieg were Chancellors of the Order.

When the 1st Class grade of the order as well as the Officer's Cross and the 4th Class badge were created in 1908, those crosses represented a marked departure from the other insignia of the order. They were plain in the extreme, completely lacking in the embellishments and (to some) the fussy details that had marked the other badges of the order and which continued to be awarded in their original form. The 1st Class badge, which, like the Grand Cross, was also a sash badge, retained the Maltese cross form of pale blue enamel but nothing else. Its arms were plain, there was no crown or lion atop the top arm, no laurel sprigs, no ball finials, no crowned monograms between its limbs, no red enameled center medallion – in short, practically nothing to associate it with the previous badges of the order. There was simply a center medallion on the obverse with a gold crowned "W" set on a background of silver rays surrounded by a gold band and on the reverse the motto of the order set on two lines. This new grade of the order even lacked the sculptured suspension ring of the other higher grades. Instead, it had what has been termed a "pie-slice" suspension on the upper arm of the cross through which a gold wire loop passed as an attachment to the sash. This style suspension was similar to that then being employed on the badges of the Orden *Pour le Mérite* and the Prussian Honor Knight of the *Johanniter Orden*. One can only conclude that it was indeed Prussia that influenced the design of these new badges, or at least a desire for a Prussian "austerity" on the part of Duke Johann Albrecht of Mecklenburg-Schwerin who was ruling the Duchy as Regent in 1908 (and who would continue to do so until 1913 when the young Duke Ernst August assumed the throne as a wedding present from the father of the bride, the *Kaiser*, as described in the previous chapter).

The similarly simplified Officer's Cross, a pin-back badge that was worn without a ribbon on the lower breast, was, like the 1st Class badge, a plain pale blue enameled Maltese cross. It did, however, retain the red enameled center medallion with white crowned post and prancing white horse surrounded by a gold band topped by the small ducal crown that marked the other badges. The back of the Officer's Cross was plain except for jeweler's marks. The 4th Class badge was another Maltese cross but with no enameling on its arms, these being in matte silver. It, too, retained the enameled red center medallions of the other badges on both the obverse and reverse. And, like the 1st Class badge, it employed the "pie-slice" suspension.

Breast stars for the Grand Cross, 1st Class and Commander 1st Class grades were imposing pieces of workmanship in their own right. For the Grand Cross, the body was a silver eight-pointed star on which the ball finialed pale blue enamel Maltese cross with an outsize center medallion was applied. Within a decorative silver outer band the order's motto appeared in gold letters against red enamel. Inside this was another decorative silver band and finally, in the center, there was the gold crowned initial "W." The back of the star, as customary, was plain with just jeweler's marks. The star to the 1st Class grade was also eight-pointed and in silver but did not have the representation of the order's cross applied. Instead, there was just a center medallion with the familiar white post and horse on red enamel. Above the crowned post was another crown from which

The *Kaiser* (left and resplendent here in Turkish uniform) and his brother, *Prinz* Heinrich (right), were both holders prewar of the Grand Cross without Swords of the Order of Henry the Lion. There is no evidence that any of these royals received swords to their orders during the course of the war.

General der Infanterie Otto Emmich was among many of the high ranking officers who held the Grand Cross without Swords prior to the war.

Prinz Oskar of Prussia and his brothers, the Crown Prince, Eitel Friedrich, Adalbert, August Wilhelm and Joachim were also Grand Cross recipients.

Grossadmiral Alfred von Tirpitz was one of the few officers who received the Grand Cross with Swords on some unknown date before World War I.

peacock feathers emanated. Below the post and horse a white enameled helmet was applied. Both the peacock feathers and the helmet rested on a blue enameled band on which *IMMOTA* on the left and *FIDES* on the right appeared in raised gold letters. The back of the star was, like the Grand Cross, plain except for jeweler's marks. The star to the Commander 1st Class was not a "star" at all but rather more like a large pin-back badge. It was an attractive piece in the form of a silver Maltese cross that had raised edges with silver ball finials. On each limb of the cross there were five raised rays of progressive lengths. The now familiar crowned "W" monogram in gold appeared between the four arms of the cross. A red enamel center medallion carried the order's motto in gold block letters on two lines. The medallion was surrounded by a substantial gold wreath of laurel and oak leaves broken at the bottom by a small curved plaque upon which the order's foundation date appeared in raised Latin numerals. The back of the star was also plain, in matte silver with jeweler's marks.

The Merit Crosses took the form of a *cross pattée*, one whose arms curve outwards and in this case, with slightly elongated vertical members. It was of the "Leopold" style where the ends of each arm are slightly concave. The 1st Class was in gold (silver-gilt from 1912) and the 2nd Class in silver. The 1st Class had the additional embellishment of a laurel wreath in green enamel with small red "fruit" between the arms of the cross. The center medallion carried a raised crowned "W" with no enameling. Surrounding the medallion was a braided oval circle. Ball finials were centered under each of the lower three arms of the cross. The order's motto appeared in raised letters in the following sequence: Upper arm: *IM* Left arm: *MO* Right arm: *TA* Lower arm: *FI* on an upper line and *DES* below that on a lower line. The crosses were uniface, that is, entirely plain on the reverse.

The sash, neck and breast ribbons for the order as well as for the affiliated Merit Cross, the Honor Decoration and the Merit Decoration for Arts and Science were the same: a rich, rather darkish red moire with bright yellow edge stripes.

It has already been stated that swords awards of the order were extremely rare, and this was particularly so during the period immediately leading up to the war and the war years themselves. This applied to the Merit Cross as well. Table 3-1 shows the number of such awards from 1908 through 1918 and is based on research carried out by this writer in the Brunswick archives in Wolfenbüttel.

Table 3-1
Swords Awards of the Order of Henry the Lion in the Years 1908-1918

Grade of the Order	1908	1909	1910	1911	1912	1913	1914	1915	1916	1917	1918
Grand Cross with Swords	0	0	0	0	0	0	0	0	1	0	0
1st Class with Swords	0	0	0	0	0	0	0	0	0	1	0
Commander 1st Class with Swords	*	3	0	0	0	1	0	0	0	0	0
Commander 2nd Class with Swords	*	2	1	0	0	2	1	0	0	0	0
Officer's Cross with Swords	2	1	0	1	0	0	0	0	0	0	0
Knight 1st Class with Swords	*	3	0	1	0	0	0	0	0	0	0
Knight 2nd Class with Swords	*	1	0	0	0	1	0	0	0	0	0
4th Class with Swords	1	0	0	0	0	0	0	0	0	0	0
Merit Cross 1st Class with Swords	*	0	0	0	0	2	1	0	0	0	0
Merit Cross 2nd Class with Swords	*	6	0	2	0	2	1	0	0	0	0

* = 1908 entries are omitted on the roll

These data are repeated in Appendix VI but there the non-swords awards during this same period are also shown. This makes the point that while swords awards were few and far between, a relatively liberal use of the order and the Merit Cross (as well as the Honor Decoration) was made to reward, as the statutes of the order put it, "those who have distinguished themselves in our service, military or civil, in war or the arts and sciences" but without the presence of swords.

This writer's research was carried out in 1995. Earlier, in 1987, the team of *Herr* Roger Reckewell and *Herr* Jens Fischer made a much more thorough study of the awards of the order and its affiliated decorations going back, as far as these awards are concerned, to 1834 entitled *Orden, Ehren- und Abzeichen des Herzogtums Braunschweig-Lüneburg von 1809 bis 1908.* They categorized awards in four time periods, April 25, 1834 to October 18, 1884, October 19, 1884 to 1891, 1892 to May 7, 1908 and May 8, 1908 to 1918. Unfortunately, they did not break down the latter period by individual years, including the war years, which were this writer's main interest and the reason for carrying out his own research. Appendix VII compares the Reckewell/Fischer findings with those of this writer. There are a number of small discrepancies, no doubt due to errors in counting by this writer. But there are some interesting findings too, principally that while Reckewell/Fischer show no awards of either Merit Cross with Swords in the years 1908 to 1918, this writer found 14, three in the 1st Class and 11 in the 2nd. Also, this writer could find only one Grand Cross award with Swords while Reckewell/Fischer list two. The one found by this writer went to a *General der Kavallerie Freiherr* von König whose document dated 24 August 1916 is pictured here. No doubt the second Grand Cross with Swords award counted by Reckewell/Fischer was the known one to *Generalfeldmarschall* Paul von Hindenburg in 1915. And yet that is not listed on the roll this writer inspected. How many more swords awards may have been omitted? We know of at least one more Grand Cross with Swords award that went to Czar Ferdinand of Bulgaria because the insignia is in a private collection today. And would there not have been more such "courtesy" Grand Crosses with Swords awards made during the war, first of all to the *Kaiser* and then to other royalty and leading military figures to say nothing of Duke Ernst August himself whose rank was *Oberst*? One would think so yet no evidence of such awards has been found. One would also think that lower classes of the order in reasonable numbers would have gone as swords awards to other officers since all Brunswick had for them during most of the war was a one-class decoration called the War Merit Cross which was introduced on October 23, 1914 and then enlarged with a 1st Class badge in March of 1918 along with a special clasp for holders of the now 2nd Class badge who met certain criteria (this decoration and the clasp will be discussed in the next chapter). For high ranking officers in command positions and for repeated and outstanding acts of courage on the battlefield by junior officers, the War Merit Cross was rather small potatoes. Were there other swords awards of the order to men like these that were never recorded? We will shortly be discussing the very real possibility that one such swords award of the order went to an airman whose name does not appear on the roll. Even if there were a few such unrecorded awards, the fact remains: for some reason, swords awards of the order during the war were deliberately held down.

Further evidence of the truth of the statement just made comes from an examination of a list of officers who served in the Brunswick cavalry regiment during the war, the 17th Hussars. Table 3-2 shows the 25 Regular and Reserve officers who held grades of the order. All but two had been awarded prewar and then only two had come with swords. The lone Officer's Cross with Swords in 1917 went to a 61-year old commander of a replacement depot (rank not given) who had been relieved of that job in August of the previous year. The award of the Knight 1st Class with Swords in 1915 had gone to the regiment's oldest serving officer, a 65-year old Major relegated to running rail transport. He had earned a Knight 2nd Class with Swords back in 1889 so in all likelihood, it actually was a Knight 1st Class with Swords-on-Ring and it was the one that does appear for 1915 on the roll in the Wolfenbüttel archives. Neither award would seem to qualify for being won "in the face of the enemy" in the strict sense of that term and would appear to have been rewards to a couple of elderly retreads for their lengthy service rather than anything to do with actual combat.

Table 3-2
Number of Awards of the Order of Henry the Lion Held by Officers of *Braunschweigisches Husaren-Regiment Nr. 17.* in World War I

Regular Army Officers

Award	Number	Date
Order of Henry the Lion Officer's Cross without Swords:	1	(1917)
Order of Henry the Lion Knight 1st Class with Swords	1	(1915)[1]
Order of Henry the Lion Knight 1st Class without Swords	1	(prewar)
Order of Henry the Lion Knight 2nd Class with Swords:	2	(both prewar)
Order of Henry the Lion Knight 2nd Class without Swords:	12	(all prewar)
Order of Henry the Lion 4th Class without Swords:	6	(all prewar)

Reserve Army Officers

Award	Number	Date
Order of Henry the Lion Knight 1st Class without Swords:	1	(prewar)
Order of Henry the Lion Knight 2nd Class without Swords:	1	(prewar)

Note 1: Believed to have been the Knight 1st Class with Swords-on-Ring (see text).

Source: *Die Braunschweiger Husaren im Weltkriege 1914-1918.*

Prewar, wartime (where they exist) and postwar rank lists have also been consulted to reinforce the point about the scarcity of swords awards of the order. Appendix III shows officers serving in the Prussian Army and the 13th Württemberg Army Corps as of May 6, 1914 who held various grades of the order with swords. There were but 23 men in all, a mere handful, therefore, considering the strength of that formidable body. Appendix IV shows officers serving in the German Navy as of February 14, 1918 who held any grade of the order with or without swords. There were but three men there who held a swords award. This also shows how exclusive the order was overall since only 16 men held the order without swords. Appendix V shows a similar compilation for officers serving in the small postwar *Reichsheer* as of April 1, 1924. By that time, not a single man held the order in any grade with swords and there were only 23 non-swords holders. There is also a naval rank list for officers serving as of November 20, 1926. No appendix for that is needed. By then, there was no one aboard who held any grade of the order, with or without swords.

Just one more set of numbers before moving on. The late orders scholar, *Dr.* Kurt-Gerhard Klietmann, in his *Pour le Mérite und Tapferkeitsmedaille* in 1966 had a tabulation of combined swords and non-swords awards of the order for the years 1913 to 1918 (why that breakdown was not explained nor was the source for his findings cited). Reworking the figures found by this writer in the Brunswick archive to conform to *Dr.* Klietmann's tabulation permits a side-by-side comparison of our respective findings. This is shown in Appendix VIII. His total number of awards during this period came to 701. This writer's total comes to 1,125. In every grade, this writer's findings were substantially higher than those of the doctor's. Apparently, we were each working from different sources.

And with that background to the Order of Henry the Lion, we can now turn to its one possible aviation recipient.

LEUTNANT JOACHIM LAMBERT ROBERT HERMANN VON BERTRAB

The late air historian, A. Edward Ferko, a determined researcher if there ever was one, made it a top priority of his to attempt to contact as many surviving German World War I airmen as he could in the days when many were still living. For those who had died in the war or subsequently, he tried reaching the man's family members, sometimes with considerable success but oftentimes with only frustration for his efforts. Ed was generous in return. He could often tell the family more about their relative than they knew themselves and much was their joy when Ed could provide photographs that had been lost over the years or about which the family was completely unaware. Ed was also generous to this writer. While he never thought the matter of awards was of much importance, he always made it a practice to ask about them on my behalf. Such was the case with the family of *Leutnant der Fliegertruppe* Joachim von Bertrab who had survived the war but who had died in 1922 at the early age of just 27.

After contacting the von Bertrab family, however, Ed received the reply he often did and the one he feared the most. All of the family possessions including the personal effects of the flier had been lost in the maelstrom of World War II. Towards the end of that conflict, the Russians overran the town of Menz, about 55 miles north of Berlin where the family home was then located. The house and everything in it had been totally destroyed by fire. But the uncle who wrote Ed could recall his nephew's awards. The reply mentioned the Iron Cross 1st and 2nd Class but then two additional awards that were totally unexpected and caused great excitement in this camp were also mentioned in the letter Ed received. One was the "*Braunschweiger Orden III. Klasse mit Schwertern*" and the other was a Brunswick "*Ehrenkreuz*" (the "Brunswick Order 3rd Class with Swords" and a Brunswick "Honor Cross"). The uncle's mention of an order in the 3rd Class is exactly in line with the dual nomenclature adopted when the three new grades were added to the order in 1908. The line-up was: Grand Cross, First Class, Second Class (comprising the Commanders 1st and 2nd Class and the Officer), Third Class (comprising the Knights 1st and 2nd Class), Fourth Class and the Merit Cross (1st and 2nd Class). As a *Leutnant*, von Bertrab would have been in line for the Knight 2nd Class. And, of course, the reference to an Honor Cross must have meant Brunswick's only other decoration in wide use for military and homefront merit and bravery in the field, its War Merit Cross (again, this award is the subject of the next chapter).

Above and two opposite: *Leutnant* Joachim von Bertrab of *Jagdstaffel 30* became the subject of three of the patriotic post cards so widely circulated in Germany. His brief 22-week career as a fighter pilot came to an end on August 12, 1917 when he was shot down by the later famous British ace, Edward Mannock, and taken prisoner. But on April 6, 1917, he was indeed "*erfolgreich*" (successful). On that day, he received credit for four British planes, up to that time the most downed by a German airman in one day. It is believed that this native-born Brunswicker who before transferring to the air service served in the Brunswick artillery regiment was the only airman (and possibly the only junior officer) to be decorated with Brunswick's only house order with swords, the Order of Henry the Lion. In the photograph above, the award is represented by the middle ribbon in the buttonhole under that for the Iron Cross 2nd Class and above the ribbon of the Brunswick War Merit Cross. In the other two photographs, the order is again represented by the middle ribbon and in both cases the ribbons carry small crossed swords appurtenances.

What an uncle might say about such an arcane subject 61 years after the event (Ed's correspondence occurred in 1978) could be one thing but there is photographic evidence that seems to support the uncle's statements completely. Von Bertrab was the subject of three of the post cards circulated by the Berlin photographer, W. Sanke, which are pictured here. In one pose, von Bertrab is wearing three ribbons in his buttonhole in addition to his Iron Cross 1st Class and his Imperial Pilot's Badge. In the other two, he is wearing a three-ribbon *Feldschnalle* (field, or small, ribbon bar). In the three-ribbons-in-the-buttonhole photo, below the ribbon of the Iron Cross 2nd Class, the middle ribbon, which has the tonal values of the Order of Henry the Lion's red ribbon with yellow edge stripes, a small pair of crossed swords can clearly be seen. This appurtenance would be appropriate to an order that had both civil and military divisions as the Order of Henry the Lion did indicating that the order had been won "with Swords." The tonal value of the third ribbon in this photograph appears to be the same as the second but in the other two poses, the second and third ribbons are clearly different as would be the case with the Brunswick War Merit Cross with its (for combatants) dark blue ribbon with yellow end stripes. And although it appears a bit blurred in both of the *Feldschnalle* photographs, a small pair of swords can be seen on the middle ribbon in these poses. Thus it can be said with considerable confidence that despite the fact it is not recorded on the roll of the order, von Bertrab did, in fact, receive the Knight 2nd Class with Swords of the Order of Henry the Lion and almost certainly, the only airman so honored during the war.

Joachim von Bertrab was born in the small town of St. Andreasberg/Zellenfeld nestled in the Harz Mountains of northern Germany, some 43 miles from Brunswick, the capital of the duchy. Shortly thereafter, his father, a forester, was transferred to Menz where Joachim grew up. At the tender age

Above: Von Bertrab flew this distinctively marked Albatros D.III believed to be in the 2100/16 to 2149/16 series. Markings specialists are in general agreement that the fuselage and rudder were black although one historian believed the aircraft was overpainted purple. It appears the crosses were also overpainted white which resulted in their appearing pale gray with a white border. The comet or shooting star comes in for different interpretations. One camp believes it was in yellow edged in pale gray. Another opinion has it in red with white or very light yellow shading. Either way, it was a most striking aircraft. Here von Bertrab strikes a rather Napoleonic pose wearing one of the Royal Flying Corps leather flying coats so favored by German airmen. It could well have been liberated from one of the crew of his fifth and last victory on May 15, 1917 when both the pilot and observer of the F.E.2d von Bertrab shot down that day were taken prisoner (the crews of all his earlier four victories scored on a single day, April 6, 1917, were either killed outright or later died of their wounds).

Below: Von Bertrab shows the cockpit details of his aircraft to Duke Ernst II of Saxe-Altenburg on *Jasta 30*'s airfield at Phalempin. Often, a chance meeting with royalty like this could produce a decoration but apparently not this time. Von Bertrab's only awards were from Prussia and his native state of Brunswick.

of 12, however, he was shipped off to far-away Bad Kösen between Leipzig and Erfurt to attend *Gymnasium* (grammar-school) there. But Joachim was intent on a career in the military (or, more likely, it was decided for him) and two years later, he was enrolled in the Cadet School in Naumburg which was practically next door to Bad Kösen and probably the reason he went to grammar-school there in the first place. Just when he was commissioned is not known but his pre-air service unit was the *Niedersächsisches Feldartillerie-Regiment.Nr.46* whose staff and first section was based in Wolfenbüttel, just south of Brunswick, and whose second was in Celle, northeast of Brunswick. So von Bertrab had all the credentials to qualify for Brunswick awards – a native by birth and service in one of its contingents.

Just when von Bertrab made the switch from an artilleryman to a flier and where he trained is equally unknown but like all the pilots coming to the newly formed *Jagdstaffeln* (fighter flights) from their formation in August of 1916 through most of 1917, he had first served in *Feldflieger-Abteilung 71* (Field Aviation Detachment or Unit 71), a two-seater formation. But unlike most of the pilots in such units, von Betrab had also put in time on single-seater aircraft. He had been attached to

The impressive line-up of 14 of *Jasta 30*'s Albatros D.IIIs (foreground) and what must be the first batch of its newly arrived D.Vs (farther down the line), no doubt at the Phalempin airfield and probably sometime between May and August of 1917. Von Bertrab's D.III with its distinctive paint scheme and marking can be seen 6th from the rear. The second-to-last machine, a D.V, has the same overpainted rudder and fuselage but it is not possible here to make out whether it, too, carries the comet/shooting star design of his D.III. If it did, it could indicate that not long before von Bertrab was shot down and taken prisoner in a balloon attack on August 12, 1917, he had one of the new D.Vs similarly painted. The markings specialists will be interested in those that can be seen on the other aircraft in this photograph, especially those which carry initials on the fuselage. The third D.III in line with the "S" is said to have been the mount of *Lt.* Oskar Seitz who scored no victories during his service in *30* from April 16, 1917 to July 20 that year. The second D.III with the "0" could be the then *Vzfw.* Hans Oberländer's. He scored five times in his more than one year tour with *30* (May 15, 1917 to May 23, 1918) to add to his first, a Nieuport downed on October 25, 1916 when he was with *FFl.Abt. 71*. The "Br" D.III (number six in line) might have been flown by *Lt.* Heinrich Brügmann (the only *30* pilot whose last name began with those two letters). Brügmann, also scoreless, was mortally wounded in a combat on August 15, 1917. The D.V with the stylized "E" next in line might be *Lt.* Paul Erbguth's. After his second, and last, confirmed victory on September 21, 1917, he was awarded the Knight's Cross of the Military St. Henry Order on December 2 that year. All this is pure speculation of course. This writer freely admits he is no markings expert and should leave that department to those who are.

Fokkerstaffel Metz, a small grouping of the then new *Eindecker* (monoplane) built by the Fokker factory in Schwerin. Flying out of its airfield at Metz-Frescaty, *FS Metz* was intended to provide protection for the two-seaters but in the hands of aggressive pilots, the little birds with their synchronized forward-firing machine gun soon became a much feared offensive weapon. *Fokkerstaffel Metz* formed the nucleus of *Jasta 17* when it was mobilized on November 11, 1916. Von Betrab, however, was assigned to another of the then-forming fighter flights, *Jasta 30. Jasta 30* became operational at the Phalempin airfield on January 25, 1917, eight pilots in all, including von Bertrab, under the command of *Oberleutnant* Hans Bethge. Bethge was an old hand having served in the first bombardment squadron code-named *Brieftauben-Abteilung-Ostende* (Carrier Pigeon Detachment Ostend) and then having switched over to fighters, with *Kampfeinsitzer-Kommando Bertincourt* (Single-Seater Fighter Command Bertincourt). *KEK B*, in turn, became *Jasta 1* upon the formation of these permanent fighter flights and were at first equipped with the new Fokker D.I and D.II biplanes (soon to be discarded when the better Albatros and Halberstadt D-Types arrived).

In *Jasta 1* under the command of *Hauptmann* Martin Zander, Bethge was credited with three confirmed victories between August 29 and December 26, 1916.[1] Concurrently that December, eight new *Jastas* were formed, numbers *26, 28, 29, 30, 31, 32, 33* and *35*. Experienced leaders for each were needed and with Bethge's seniority and performance in *Jasta 1*, he was a natural to take charge of one of them. His appointment became effective on January 15.

Von Bertrab arrived at *Jasta 30* on March 3, 1917. He was a replacement for the unit's first casualty. *Gefreiter* Heinrich Schneider had been shot down over Ploegsteert in Flanders on February 15 and taken prisoner. His aircraft was identified as Halberstadt D.III 234/16 by German researchers working from existing War Diary records between the two world wars but in the British capture report, the aircraft is listed as Halberstadt D.V 1108/16. One finds such small discrepancies from time to time in the work these pioneer German researchers did and other sources. This is especially true when it comes to identifying the type of enemy aircraft credited to German fighter pilots from what they recorded and more recent studies like Trevor Howard's carefully researched *The Sky Their Battlefield* and the Grub Street series, *Above the Lines, The Jasta Pilots*, etc. (see the Bibliography at the end of this book). Bethge's 4th victory on March 28 was the first recorded by *Jasta 30*. On that morning, leading his flight against five enemy aircraft, he shot down and killed 2nd Lt. H. Welch of No.1 Squadron, RFC in his Nieuport 17 A.6615. That same day, possibly due to battle damage in the fight, Bethge crashed in his Albatros D.III and although the plane was a total write-off, he emerged unhurt. This seemed to break the ice for shortly, *Jasta 30* was to go on something of a scoring spree.

April 1917 ("Bloody April" to the British flying services because of the large number of casualties they suffered at the hands of the disciplined and better equipped German *Jastas*) opened with victories on the 3rd and 5th, another Nieuport 17 and a Sopwith V-2 Strutter both credited to *Leutnant* Gustav Nernst (who would be killed later in the month, on the 21st, in his Albatros D.III 2147/16 in a combat involving Sopwith Triplanes and F.E. 2b "Pushers" over Arras). Then on April 6 came von Bertrab's big day, the biggest, in fact, of his military career. He claimed and was credited with four British aircraft on two morning patrols that day. Table 3-3 gives the details. And there we encounter some of the small discrepancies mentioned in the previous paragraph between the findings of those interwar German researchers and, in this case, Howard's *The Sky Their Battlefield*. Setting those aside, the important thing was that this was a signal event in the annals of the German Army Air Service thus far in the war. Von Bertrab was the first of its men to score four victories in one day. Before the war was over, only three other German fighter pilots would reach that mark and three more would surpass it.[2]

[1] In recognition for his first victory on August 29, Bethge, already possessing the Iron Cross 2nd Class, was awarded the Iron Cross 1st Class on September 9. A first victory at this stage of the war often brought a holder of the 2nd Class the higher grade. Along with his 1st Class cross that day came his *Ehrenbecher dem Sieger im Luftkämpfe* (Honor Goblet to the Victor in Air Battle), an impressive silver (at the time) ball-footed drinking mug depicting two eagles locked in combat which was given to fighter pilots and two-seater crews to mark their initial victories. Bethge went on to a distinguished career, scoring 15 more victories in 1917 and two in 1918, the last, his 20th, on March 10. Already a holder of the Knight's Cross with Swords of the Royal House Order of Hohenzollern (although, curiously, the announcement of the award did not appear in the *Militär-Wochenblatt* (Military Weekly Paper) until August 20, 1918), he was proposed for the *Orden Pour le Mérite* but before it could be approved, Bethge was killed in an air combat over Passchendaele in Flanders on March 17. In keeping with the normal Prussian practice of not making posthumous awards, the matter was then shelved.

[2] The three other German airmen credited with four victories in one day were Hans Müller of *Jasta 18* on September 14, 1918, Manfred von Richthofen of *Jasta 11* on April 29, 1917 and Kurt Wolff of *Jasta 11* on April 13, 1917. The three German airmen who went von Bertrab one better were Otto Bernert of Jasta Boelcke on April 24, 1917, Heinrich Gontermann of *Jasta 15* on August 19, 1917 (including four balloons) and Fritz Röth of *Jasta 16b* on May 29, 1918 (five balloons; Röth had also burned four balloons in *Jasta 23b* on April 1, 1918; his first three victories, all balloons on January 25, 1918, brought him an immediate Knight's Hohenzollern with Swords).

While swords awards of the Order of Henry the Lion were always rare and virtually non-existent in World War I, the order without swords was bestowed quite liberally among the military in peacetime. *Hauptmann* Hans Masius of the Army Airship Service received the Knight 2nd Class without Swords just before the outbreak of the war. In addition to both Iron Crosses, his order bar here "reads" the Prussian Crown Order 4th Class without Swords, the Centenary Medal, the Mecklenburg-Schwerin Military Merit Cross 2nd Class, the Ducal Saxe-Ernestine House Order, Knight 1st Class with Swords, the Bavarian Military Merit Order 4th Class without Swords and his Brunswick House Order. Commanding several army airships, Masius bombed Paris in the LZ.35 in March 1915 and revisited the city on successive nights at the end of January 1916. With these ships as well as the LZ.72 and LZ.107, he also struck at targets along the coasts of Belgium and England before the German Army abandoned its service in June of 1917 as too costly and ineffective. Below Masius is seen with the officers and crew members of his last command, the LZ.107.

Table 3-3

Von Bertrab Victory Number and Date	Interwar German Researcher's Notes	"The Sky Their Battlefield" Entry
1. April 6, 1917	Martinsyde 7765 No. 27 Sq., 7:35 a.m. at Ath, 2/Lt. J.R.S. Proud	Martinsyde G.100 7465 No. 27 Sq., 8:15 a.m. at Ath, 2/Lt. J.R.S. Proud (DOW as POW)
2. April 6, 1917	Sopwith 1 1/2 Strutter 7544 No. 45 Sq., 10:30 a.m. at Obigies, 2/Lt. G.St.G. Campbell and G.E. Blake	Martinsyde G.100 7478 No. 27 Sq., 8:30 a.m. at Ath, Lt. J.H.B. Wedderspoon (KIA)
3. April 6, 1917	Sopwith 1 1/2 Strutter (no number) No. 45 Sq., 10:30 a.m. s.e. of Leuze, 2/Lt. J.A. Marshall and Capt. D.W. Edwards	Sopwith 1 1/2 Strutter A.1093 No. 45 Sq., 10:48 a.m. at Lille, 2/Lt. J.A. Marshall (KIA) and 2/Lt. F.G. Truscott (DOW)
4. April 6, 1917	Sopwith 1 1/2 Strutter 7806 No. 45 Sq., 10:35 a.m. at Pecq, Capt. W.D. Brashay and 2/Lt. S.A. Truscott	Sopwith 1 1/2 Strutter A.2381 No. 45 Sq., 10:50 a.m. at Pecq, 2/Lt. C.St.G. Campbell (KIA) and Capt. D.W. Edwards (KIA)
5. May 15, 1917	F.E.2d A.6446 No. 20 Sq., 8:30 a.m. at Quesnoy, 2/Lt. E.J. Grout and AM/2 A.R. Tyrell	F.E.2d A.6446 No. 20 Sq., 7:20 a.m. n. of Lille, 2/Lt. E.J. Grout (POW) and 2/AM A. Tyrrell (POW)

Notes: Between March 24 and April 14 in 1917, German Time and British Summer Time were the same. Beginning on April 15, 1917, German Summer Time was one hour ahead of British Summer Time. DOW = Died of Wounds KIA = Killed in Action POW = Prisoner of War

If indeed von Bertrab were a recipient of the Order of Henry the Lion with Swords, this had to be the basis for the award. And after such a brilliant start, the rest of his air war was to be marked by only one more victory before it came to an abrupt end. On May 15, he forced a No.20 Squadron F.E.2d to come down in German lines in the early morning hours. For von Bertrab, now, another long dry spell in the victory column ensued while his mates claimed three more in May, eight in June and five in July with Bethge being credited with five of these during that time. On Sunday, August 12, *Vizefeldwebel* Josef Heiligers scored his fourth and last victory in the evening hours of that day (he would be killed in action on November 20, 1917). Earlier, around 4:00 p.m. German Time, von Bertrab had tried his hand at a new target, an observation balloon over Souches. While absorbed in that effort, he had the bad luck to be intercepted by the man whom many believe should have the title of the most successful British fighter pilot of the war, Major Edward Mannock.[3] Mannock shot up von Bertrab's Albatros D.V which came down near Farbus Wood in British lines. The aircraft was pretty much a wreck (only the engine was salved and the number of the plane was never recorded in the capture report) but von Bertrab himself was all right but had to sit out the rest of the war in a prison camp. What an ignominious end to possibly the only German airman of the war, and possibly the only junior officer in all of its armed services, to hold a swords award of Brunswick's exclusive Order of Henry the Lion.

[3] Mannock is generally credited with 61 solo and shared victories and not the 73 sometimes accorded him. Thus the 72 given to William A. Bishop would put Mannock in second place. But most of Bishop's claims have now been discounted since they were never supported by other British pilots, by ground observers or by hard evidence. Also discounted is the raid on an airfield he claimed to have made on June 2, 1917 during which he was credited with three victories and which resulted in the award of the Victoria Cross. It remains the only instance where Britain's highest award for gallantry was based on one man's word alone there being no other officer (whether friendly or enemy) present to corroborate the circumstances.

CHAPTER IV

THE MILITARY AWARDS OF THE DUCHY OF BRUNSWICK

THE MILITARY MERIT CROSS AND THE WAR MERIT CROSS

These two decorations for bravery are being covered together since the Military Merit Cross was so seldom bestowed in World War I (if at all) that the subject is all but academic while the War Merit Cross was in wide use during the war with many of the men in whom we are interested receiving that award.

The Military Merit Cross was established by Duke Wilhelm of Brunswick on December 11, 1879 for "heightened, repeated and especially brave deeds" by men holding the rank of *Feldwebel* and below. It was a plain, straight-armed St. George's cross struck in gold and except for one element, it was a dead ringer for the Prussian Golden Military Merit Cross which King Wilhelm I of Prussia had founded on February 27, 1864 for men of the same ranks who displayed bravery in the face of the enemy. Both the Prussian and Brunswick pieces displayed the words *KRIEGS VERDIENST* ("War Merit") in block letters on two lines on the obverse under which there was a small branch of oak. The difference was on the reverse. The Prussian cross had the crowned initials "*WR*" (for Wilhelm *Rex*). The Brunswick cross had the crowned initial "*W*" (for Wilhelm). Duke Ernst August of Brunswick renewed the award on August 18, 1914 and in the *Dr.* Klietmann work, *Pour le Mérite und Tapferkeitsmedaille*, he suggests that there were no bestowals between the time of its founding and the time of its renewal. On the renewed Brunswick cross, the initial "*W*" on the reverse was replaced by the "*EA*" monogram, also crowned. But more than that, someone must have decided that it would not be prudent to continue to ape the Prussian award and the entire form was changed to a rather "fat" Maltese cross. Klietmann further suggests that after its renewal, it was bestowed in "only a few cases." On the other hand, *Herr* Nimmergut in his *Deutsche Orden und Ehrenzeichen bis 1945* casts doubt on whether any were ever awarded at all. He says that up to October 1914, only 25 crosses had been struck and after that, no further statements were made concerning it. From this he infers that none was ever awarded and points to an exchange of correspondence between the orders chancelleries of Brunswick and Prussia up to the end of 1915 concerning the eligibility of Brunswick troops for Prussia's highest bravery award to non-commissioned officers, its Golden Military Merit Cross. In the event, the first award of the Golden Military Merit Cross in the war did not occur until October 1916 and of men in Brunswick contingents, only five received it, all in 1918. Three were members of the 92nd Infantry and two were from the 46th Artillery Regiment.

Meantime, the new War Merit Cross had been instituted on October 23, 1914, originally in just one class. Whether it had already been decided that this would replace the Brunswick Military Merit Cross henceforth or whether there was still some thought that it would be awarded and this was a move to protect its exclusivity is not known. In any event, the War Merit Cross came to be widely awarded both for front line military merit and bravery as well as for meritorious service to the war effort on the home front. The badge was a dark bronze *cross pattée* in the form of a Templar's Cross with sides curving outwards with straight ends, much like the Prussian Iron Cross on which it was undoubtedly modeled although much smaller, unusually so in fact being about 30 mm vs. the 42-44mm. of the 1914 Iron Cross 2nd Class. On the obverse, the upper arm had a raised crown, in the center the monogram "*EA*" appeared with two sprays of oak leaves on each of the middle arms and on the lower arm there was the year date "*1914*" in raised letters. The reverse also carried raised lettering, the word *Für* ("For") on the upper arm, *Verdienst im* ("Merit in") across the middle arm

The Brunswick Military Merit Cross was established by Duke Wilhelm on December 11, 1879 as a reward for "heightened, repeated and especially brave deeds" by senior non-commissioned officers and lower ranks. Its obverse was identical to the Prussian Golden Military Merit Cross which had been created in 1864. Only the monogram on the reverse differed. It appears, however, that it was never actually awarded. Duke Ernst August of Brunswick renewed the decoration on August 18, 1914 and probably so as not to continue to ape the Prussian decoration, its design was changed to the Maltese cross shown below and Ernst August's monogram replaced that of Wilhelm's. It, too, was a scarce award, said to have been given in only "a few cases."

and *Kriege* ("War") on the lower arm. The ribbon, also narrower than usual, was dark blue with smaller yellow stripes towards each end for military merit and bravery. For home front service, the badge was the same but the ribbon was just the reverse, yellow with dark blue stripes towards each end. Both officers and men in the ranks as well as civilians were eligible for the cross.

An interesting document was found in the Munich War Archive dated 1 April 1915 concerning the award of the War Merit Cross to citizens of Brunswick serving in the Royal Bavarian Army. It read:

> Only those members of the field army and navy who are citizens of Brunswick and possess the Iron Cross may be recommended for an award of the Ducal War Merit Cross of Brunswick. Brunswickers who serve in Bavarian troop contingents may still be recommended if they are decorated with a Bavarian war decoration and not the Iron Cross. Recommendation lists are to be sent by the troop contingents to the ducal state ministry in Brunswick-Lüneburg.

Brunswick citizenship may have been a requirement initially for others to receive the War Merit Cross but that was certainly no longer the case as the war went on. We shall see many awards to fliers who were non-Brunswickers or who had never served in a Brunswick formation.

On March 20, 1918, Duke Ernst August added a 1st Class grade of the War Merit Cross. It was a pin-back decoration, again in dark bronze, but larger, almost the size of the 1914 Iron Cross 1st Class (41mm vs. 41.5mm - 44mm). The original breast badge was then called the War Merit Cross 2nd Class. At the same time, a device termed the *Bewährungs-Abzeichen* was created for certain holders of the 2nd Class badge. The requirements to earn it were quite stringent. First, a recipient had to be a Brunswick native as of August 1, 1914 or if a non-Brunswicker, an officer in one of its formations. Second, he had to have had two years of "unbroken" service in the field. That was caveatted to permit up to two months of hospital and/or home leave time during the period of qualification. Third, the recipient had to have a record of good conduct (usually, that applied only to men in the ranks, being presumed for officers). All requirements were waived in the case of death so, apparently, posthumous awards were contemplated from the beginning. Nothing was said about prisoner-of-war status so the man we met in the previous chapter who suffered that fate, Joachim von Bertrab, may or may not have compiled sufficient time to have earned the clasp to his 2nd Class cross.

There is no single word in English which easily conveys the meaning of "*Bewährungs.*" The verb from which the noun derives has the general meaning of "prove" or "certify." One English-speaking German has translated the word as "test of character" which certainly conveys the meaning very well but is not succinct enough in describing a device like this. So this writer, quite arbitrarily, has chosen to adopt merely the word "proved." And for the word "*Abzeichen*" which usually translates to "badge," the term "clasp" has been chosen since the *Bewährungs-Abzeichen* was a device affixed to the ribbon and not something worn separately. Perhaps some reader will come up with a better interpretation than the term "Proved Clasp."

Except for size and it being slightly concave, the obverse of the 1st Class cross was the same as that of the 2nd Class cross. The reverse of the 1st Class cross was blank. The "Proved" clasp was a small (22mm wide by 30mm high) silvered bronze device which had the Brunswick prancing horse surrounded by a crowned wreath of oak leaves under which was a pair of crossed Roman-style swords. Knowledgeable medals specialists are of the belief that original clasps had loops on the reverse of the device for sewing them on the ribbon while later manufactured examples, considered copies, had two prongs as the means of attachment.

No roll of the War Merit Cross could be located in the archive in Wolfenbuttel and both Klietmann and Nimmergut are silent on the number bestowed. Possibly, therefore, no roll has survived. This is a pity because, without doubt, we would find there many more airmen who received the award than have been discovered from other sources. Some idea of how liberally the decoration was bestowed, however, can be had by examining the same rank lists that were referenced in determining the distribution of the Order of Henry the Lion in the previous chapter.

The Navy rank list of serving officers as of February 14, 1918 (and therefore just before there was a 1st Class cross and the "Proved" clasp) contains the names of 113 recipients of the then one-class War Merit Cross. Appendix IX breaks these down by rank categories. The Army list for officers in the much smaller *Reichsheer* as of April 1, 1924, now showing awards of the 1st Class, 2nd Class with "Proved" clasp and plain 2nd Class, contains 207 such recipients, a rather surprisingly large number. But of these 207, only 33 men (about 16%) held the "Proved" clasp, a measure of its exclusivity (see Appendix X for the complete breakdown). The Navy list as of November 20, 1926 shows how the officer force had shrunk in the intervening years and hence how few War Merit Cross recipients remained (only 13 of them and none with the "Proved" clasp; see Appendix XI).

For military achievements and bravery in the field in World War I as well as for home front merit, Brunswick relied almost solely on its War Merit Cross, a breast badge founded on October 23, 1914. Then on March 20, 1918, a 1st Class pin-back decoration (right) was added. At the same time, the *Bewährungs-Abzeichen* was created for the now 2nd Class badge. The device signified two years of "unbroken" service at the front (see the text for full requirements). "*Bewährungs*" does not translate easily into English but its general meaning is "to prove" or "to certify." Thus here it has been arbitrarily called the "Proved" clasp. Original pieces are thought to have had loops for sewing it on the ribbon. A clasp with prongs would be indicative of a later manufactured piece.

Perhaps the best indication of how widely the War Merit Cross was awarded, at least within a Brunswick contingent, comes from the book that traces the history of the 17th Hussars in World War I. Table 4-1 lists War Merit Cross data given there for its 146 Regular and Reserve officers (there were four officers for whom awards information was omitted). It is of interest to note that of the 146, 15 (or nearly 10%) held both the 1st Class and the 2nd Class with "Proved" clasp. Another 45 officers (or 30%) held both the 1st Class and the plain 2nd Class. Just two (under 2%) had the 2nd Class only with "Proved" clasp and 65 more (or 45%) had the 2nd Class without clasp. Thus the 19 officers (or 13%) who failed to earn a class of the award were in the definite minority.

Table 4-1
Number of Awards of the War Merit Crosses Held by Officers of *Braunschweigisches Husaren-Regiment Nr.17.* in World War I

Regular Army Officers

War Merit Cross 1st and 2nd Class with "Proved" Clasp:	9
War Merit Cross 1st and 2nd Class:	23
War Merit Cross 2nd Class with "Proved" Clasp:	0
War Merit Cross 2nd Class:	26
Officers Not Holding Either Class of the War Merit Cross:	11
Officers Whose Awards Are Not Listed:	4

Reserve Army Officers

War Merit Cross 1st and 2nd Class with "Proved" Clasp:	6
War Merit Cross 1st and 2nd Class:	22
War Merit Cross 2nd Class with "Proved" Clasp:	2
War Merit Cross 2nd Class:	39
Officers Not Holding Either Class of the War Merit Cross:	8
Officers Whose Awards Are Not Listed:	0

Source: *Die Braunschweiger Husaren im Weltkriege 1914-1918.*

From that book and other sources, including the archive of the late A. Edward Ferko which is now in the Special Collections Library of the University of Texas at Dallas in Richardson, Texas, 45 airmen have been found who earned the War Merit Cross in the war (two more were found in the 1924 Army Rank List but since nothing is known of the aviation units in which they served, their rank at the time or even their first names, they have been omitted). These 45 recipients can be found in Appendix XII. Surely, a mere 45 considering the numbers found elsewhere must understate by a wide margin the true number of airmen who were entitled to the award. But among the 45, we have the famous, including eight *Pour le Mérite* recipients, and the not-so-famous for whom, in most cases, very little is known about their careers in the air. And since again in most cases, the dates of the awards are not known, the stories of those men who have been selected for discussion will be told in alphabetical order rather than the order in which they received their awards. There will be one exception to that and it involves the simultaneous awards of the cross to three airmen in late 1915. And it is with that story we begin.

THREE AWARDS IN ONE DAY (OR BEING IN THE RIGHT PLACE AT THE RIGHT TIME)

On October 23, 1915, a group of dignitaries and high ranking officers including Duke Ernst August of Brunswick and Prince August Wilhelm of Prussia visited the airfield of *Feldflieger-Abteilung 23* near the town of St. Quentin, 45 miles east of the British held city of Amiens. That afternoon, *Oberleutnant* Ernst

Freiherr von Althaus and *Leutnant* Hans-Joachim Buddecke, fighter pilots attached to the two-seater formation, were to demonstrate their new Fokker *Eindeckers* for the benefit of their august guests. They did better than that. In the middle of the proceedings, an alarm was raised. British planes were on their way and von Althaus and Buddecke rose to challenge them.

It was Buddecke who drew blood, being credited with downing B.E.2c 2017 of No.13 Squadron, RFC, the unit's first combat loss in an engagement south of St. Quentin. The crew of Captain C.H. Marks and 2nd Lt. W.G. Lawrence, brother of the later famous T.E. Lawrence ("Lawrence of Arabia"), were both killed. It was Buddecke's second confirmed victory, another poor old B.E.2c, that being 2008 of No. 8 Squadron, which he had gotten on September 19. In Buddecke's own book, *El Schahin* (*Der Jagdfalke*) ("The Hunting Falcon"), he mentions that another later *Pour le Mérite* ace, also a *Leutnant* at this time and a member of *Feldflieger-Abteilung 23*, Rudolf Berthold, returned from a flight that afternoon but like von Althaus, he had yet to score a victory in the air (Berthold's first came on February 2, 1916 while von Althaus' had occurred earlier, on December 5, 1915 [and not on December 3 as has been reported sometimes]). Buddecke himself says that when the guests were leaving the airfield, Ernst August handed out "three of his crosses on its pretty blue-gold ribbon." Buddecke, of course, received one (supposedly protecting a high personage from an enemy bombing attack was the reason behind Manfred von Richthofen's and Hans Imelmann's awards of the Saxe-Coburg and Gotha Duke Carl Eduard Medal 2nd Class with Swords and Date on November 9, 1916 when both were blossoming fighter pilots with *Jasta 2*, given on the personal orders of Duke Carl Eduard himself for the two men having shot down a B.E.2c apiece which were on a bombing sortie in the vicinity of the Duke's headquarters – see pages 179-185 in Volume V of this series). The second cross went to von Althaus whose original awards, including the Brunswick War Merit Cross (2nd Class), are in the possession of the *Luftwaffen-museum* at Gatow airfield near Berlin. But who got the third? Buddecke does not say. But there are two possibilities.

A cross to Rudolf Berthold can be ruled out however. His original awards were for many years part of the Foundation for Aviation World War I's collection and are now with the Deutsches Technikmuseum Berlin. A Brunswick War Merit Cross is not among them. This leaves a fourth Eindecker pilot who had scored his first victory on October 11, 1915, *Leutnant* Otto Parschau, and *23's Abteilungsführer, Hauptmann* Karl Seber. Although a well-known photograph of Parschau in dress uniform wearing a *Grossordensschnalle* (large orders bar)

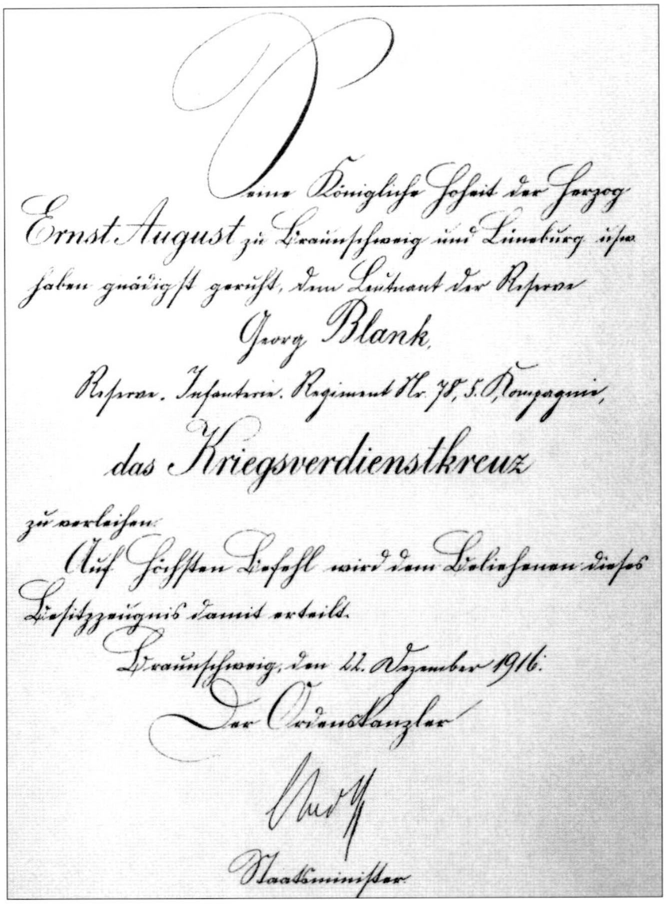

Seine Königliche Hoheit der Herzog Ernst August zu Braunschweig und Lüneburg haben gnädigst geruht, dem Leutnant der Reserve Georg Blank, Reserve-Infanterie-Regiment Nr. 78, 5. Kompagnie, das Kriegsverdienstkreuz zu verleihen.

Auf Höchsten Befehl wird dem Beliehenen dieses Besitzzeugnis damit erteilt.

Braunschweig, den 22. Dezember 1916.

Der Ordenskanzler

Staatsminister

Two examples of the bestowal documents to the War Merit Cross, the original cross (above) dated 22 December 1916 and (below) the newly instituted 1st Class cross dated 28 May 1918. Contrast these with the simple typewritten *Vorläufiges-Besitzzeugnis* ("Preliminary Certificate of Possession").

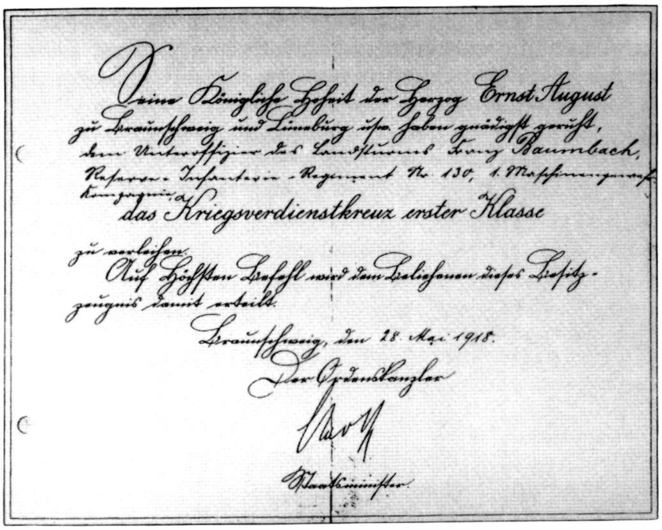

Seine Königliche Hoheit der Herzog Ernst August zu Braunschweig und Lüneburg haben gnädigst geruht, dem Unteroffizier [illegible] Baumbach, Reserve-Infanterie-Regiment Nr. 130, 1. Maschinengewehr-Kompagnie das Kriegsverdienstkreuz erster Klasse zu verleihen.

Auf Höchsten Befehl wird dem Beliehenen dieses Besitzzeugnis damit erteilt.

Braunschweig, den 28. Mai 1918.

Der Ordenskanzler

Staatsminister

clearly shows the presence of the Brunswick War Merit Cross, Parschau was assigned to the fighter detachment of *Kampfgeschwader 1* at the time and Buddecke does not mention his presence during the October 23 proceedings. If this writer were asked to guess, he would say protocol would require the Duke to recognize *23's* leader in handing out his cross on this occasion and possibly Parschau received his in a similar visit to *KG 1* by the Duke. Thus the more likely beneficiary of the third cross was Seber.

Von Althaus, Buddecke and Parschau have all figured to one degree or another in all volumes in this series except for the first one (Bavaria). Seber appeared in Volume III (Saxony) and received just one passing reference in Volume IV (Württemberg). Finding new things to say about these men is not easy but worth a try since it also provides the opportunity to use photographs that have not been seen before in this series.

OBERLEUTNANT ERNST *FREIHERR* VON ALTHAUS

The leader of *Jasta 10, Leutnant* Albert Dossenbach and Baden's most highly decorated airman (thus rating a full biography in Volume VI in this series), was killed in combat on July 3, 1917. *Rittmeister* Manfred *Freiherr* von Richthofen, now commanding the four flights of *Jagdgeschwader Nr. 1* of which *Jasta 10* was one, tapped *Oberleutnant* Ernst *Freiherr* von Althaus to be Dossenbach's replacement. Von Althaus had been flying as just a regular member of *Jasta 14* and had nothing to show for his efforts since running up a string of eight victories between December 15, 1915 and July 1916 in *Kampfeinsitzer-Kommandos-Sivry* and *-Vaux* which had earned him the *Orden Pour le Mérite* on July 21, the eighth fighter pilot of the war so far to have earned the high award. The appointment would seem to have indicated a change in his fortunes when promptly, on July 24, he scored his ninth victory over a formidable opponent, a Sopwith Camel (B.3825) of No.70 Squadron, RFC. That notwithstanding, a week later von Althaus was relieved of his command and taken off combat. What happened? Why was a such a highly decorated old-timer so abruptly dismissed (among other honors, von Althaus also held Saxony's highest bravery recognition for officers, its Military St. Henry Order, which he had earned as a dismounted cavalryman in January 1915 for an earlier daring patrol action on the Western Front)? The question has been answered in various ways.

Perhaps the most frequently mentioned reason for von Althaus' untimely dumping was that his eyesight was failing and, indeed, he did go blind in the interwar years. Others have speculated that it was more due to his independent ways and his inability or unwillingness to conform to the tactics insisted upon by his new boss, the demanding von Richthofen. Still one more view is that von Althaus was a worn out man, even deeply depressed at this stage (although the Camel victory would seem to belie that) and he simply wasn't up to command responsibility. It has also been suggested that it was a combination of these factors that prompted von Richthofen to act just as it appeared von Althaus was getting started again. To them, possibly another theory should be added to the pot. Allusions to von Althaus' playboy ways have also existed over the years but never has anything specific surfaced until now. Although von Richthofen was by no means the prig that we now know Max Immelmann was, von Richthofen was nonetheless a strict conformist, temperate in drink and smoking and maybe with women, even celibate. While tolerant of his men (as long as they performed in the air), his exuberant younger brother, Lothar for example, his standards were high. On July 6, Manfred had been wounded in an air battle and was lucky to escape with his life. But even as he lay in hospital, he was getting daily reports of the goings-on at his *Geschwader*. Could something of von Althaus' behavior have gotten back to him which became the deciding factor as much as anything else? Thanks now to a discovery made by Dr. Dieter H.M. Gröschel of Charlottesville, Virginia, we can see that von Althaus' ways had become a problem before.

In the military archives in Freiburg, Dr. Gröschel found the memoirs of the German officer who was the *de facto* head of the Turkish Army Air Service from 1915 to 1918, *Major* (in the Turkish Army, a *Hauptmann* in the German Army) Erich Serno. Twice in 1916, Serno journeyed back to air headquarters in Charleville, France to discuss his requirements with the later *Oberst* Hermann von der Lieth Thomsen who was *Feldflugchef* (Chief of Field Aviation) up until the reorganization of the German Army Air Service in October 1916 whereupon Thomsen became Chief-of-Staff to the Commanding General of the (Army) Air Force (*Kogenluft*). Serno wrote that he always had Thomsen's full support and understanding except that on one occasion they did get into an argument. Thomsen wanted to transfer von Althaus to the Turkish Air Service and Serno had no difficulty in understanding why because even from distant Istanbul, von Althaus' habits were well known. Serno described them and the consequences he feared in these words:

> I had an idea why he wanted to get rid of him. Von Althaus was famous among aviators for gambling, love of women and even worse habits. I rejected his transfer to Turkey vehemently despite all arguments from Colonel

On October 23, 1915, a group of dignitaries including Duke Ernst August of Brunswick, hamming it up for the camera at lower left, visited the airfield of *FFl.Abt. 23* to observe a demonstration of its new Fokker *Eindeckers*. During the show, enemy planes were reported in the vicinity. Hans-Joachim Buddecke and Ernst *Freiherr* von Althaus rose to protect their guests and in the engagement, Buddecke shot a British B.E.2c down. Upon departing, the Duke presented his War Merit Cross to both Buddecke and von Althaus. A third cross was also handed out, this probably going to *23*'s leader, *Hauptmann* Karl Seber, and not to another *Eindecker* pilot who was there, Rudolf Berthold, who did not fly that day. In the photograph at the lower right, the tall man at the extreme left is Seber followed by Prince August Wilhelm of Prussia and Berthold.

This seldom seen profile view of Ernst *Freiherr* von Althaus in the uniform of his pre-air service Saxon *1. Husaren-Regiment König Albert Nr.18.* shows off his splendid proboscis to good (?) advantage.

Von Althaus with a Fokker E.IV at *Kampfeinsitzer-Sivry* in 1916. He was at the height of his career at this time, scoring seven of his eventual nine victories that year.

> Thomsen. What kind of damage to Germany, to the German Army and to aviation could develop! Finally, Colonel Thomsen saw my point of view and agreed with me although he rarely changed one of his decisions.

Von Althaus' "even worse habits" will be left to the mind of the reader but strange it is that a year later, Thomsen would have approved the transfer requested by von Richthofen that would place a man with that reputation as the head of one of the elite fighting units of the German Army Air Service. Had von Althaus changed in the interim? Not likely, one would think. In any event, the War Diary of *Jagdgeschwader Nr.1* which appeared in a 1935 book by the squadron's Adjutant, *Oberleutnant a.D.* Karl Bodenschatz under the title *Jagd in Flanders Himmel* ("Hunting in Flander's Skies" and expertly translated into English in 1996 by Janice L. Hayzlett under the title "Hunting with Richthofen"), offers no help on von Althaus' departure from the command of *Jasta 10*. It merely notes that on July 30, in accordance with *Kogenluft* (order) 64550, the leader of *Jasta 10* is transferred to *Jastaschule II* (Fighter School 2) and *Leutnant der Reserve* (Werner) Voss, *Jasta 14*, is transferred to *Jagdgeschwader Nr.I* in conformity with *Kogenluft* (order) 64549 and is appointed leader of *Jasta 10*. The War Diary doesn't even mention von Althaus' victory on July 24, a more than curious omission in view of the fact one of the main purposes of the diary was to note such daily activity. Von Althaus must already have been in the dog house when von Richthofen returned from hospital on the following day to resume command to ax him a week later. In the narrative that Bodenschatz wrote that fleshes out the terse entries of the War Diary, von Althaus is again "sent to Coventry" in terms of his ninth victory and his dismissal. Of the latter, all that is said is:

> The thirtieth of July is a good day for the squadron. Lieutenant Voss arrives as the new detachment leader of Flight 10 and, with him, an "ace" has once again arrived:

An enemy plane shot down behind one's lines always attracted a crowd. Here German troops surround what was left of the Farman that became von Althaus' eighth victory on July 21, 1916. That earned him the much coveted *Orden Pour le Mérite* on the very same day.

very young, wiry, thirty-four victories behind him, and the order *Pour le Mérite*.

All in all, it would appear to be rather shabby treatment. Let us hope it was not deserved.

OBERLEUTNANT HANS-JOACHIM BUDDECKE

Although *Feldflieger-Abteilung 23* was a Prussian formation, it had an uncommonly large number of its airmen who were decorated with Saxony's premier bravery order, the Military St. Henry Order. There were seven of its members who earned the high award for service with the unit, all in 1915 and 1916. Only *Feldflieger-Abteilung 24*, which was Saxon, had more awards to their men and then only by a margin of one, a late 1917 Knight's Cross when the unit had been redesignated *Flieger-Abteilung (A)264*. Two of the 1915 awards in *23* went to men who were involved in the October 23, 1915 incident just described wherein Duke Ernst August of Brunswick handed out three of his War Merit Crosses. They were *23's* Commanding Officer at the time, *Hauptmann* Karl Seber, soon to be heard from, and the then *Leutnant* Hans-Joachim Buddecke.

As also mentioned in the von Althaus biography, Buddecke had scored his first victory on September 19, 1915 when he was credited with a B.E.2c near St. Quentin. The B.E. was part of No.8 Squadron, RFC flight that had as its target the bombing of the city of Cambrai some 24 miles north of St. Quentin, Already the crew of the British aircraft, 2nd Lt. W.H. Nixon and Captain J.N.S. Stott, had forced another plane from *23* down after a short fight. Buddecke closed to the near collision distance of 10 meters, if the account of the action is to be believed, and before the B.E. went down had fired nearly 700 rounds, the extremely high number of 109 of which went home. Nixon, the pilot, was killed and Stott taken prisoner. On October 16, thus with still only the one victory under his belt, Buddecke was presented with his Knight's Cross of the Military St. Henry. The September 19 action formed the entire rationale for the

Above: The wreckage of B.E.2c 2017 shot down by Hans-Joachim Buddecke on October 23, 1915 during the visit by Duke Ernst August of Brunswick to *Feldflieger-Abteilung 23*. Its crew did not survive.

At the left, Buddecke in the uniform of a Turkish *Hauptmann* with his *Pour le Mérite* and the Turkish Liakat Medal in Gold with Sabers. He also earned its higher Imtiaz Medal in Gold with Sabers. The aircraft is an Albatros C.I. Above, Buddecke as the *Staffelführer* of *Jasta 4* in the fall of 1916 in a Halberstadt D.II said to be a delight to fly after wrestling with difficult-to-control *Eindeckers*.

award. And it is likely that the event was also marked by Buddecke receiving the Iron Cross 1st Class for a first victory just as Max Immelmann had been awarded one right after his first victory on August 1 that year (another B.E.2c!). Before an important event occurred in Buddecke's career, he scored a third victory on November 11 (need we say it?) over a B.E.2c of No.8 Squadron, RFC, one of two it lost that day. Each had only a single occupant, the observers having been left behind so that a heavier bomb load could be carried. High winds and cloud caused several of the B.E.s to become separated from their escorts and undefended as they were from the rear, became easy prey for the then potent Fokker *Eindecker*.

In December 1915, Buddecke was transferred to Turkey where he immediately took effect and earned fame. His record there leading up to the award of his *Orden Pour le Mérite* on April 14, 1916, only the third airman so honored thus far in the war, has always intrigued this writer because most sources give him only seven confirmed victories by that date with as many as seven unconfirmed. As most readers well know, the first two air recipients of the award, Oswald Boelcke and Max Immelmann, had had eight confirmed victories at the time they received it and eight became the standard for earning it throughout 1916 (at least for the old-timers anyway; new men like Manfred von Richthofen and Hans von Keudell failed to get the order when their scores reached eight). If Buddecke did, in fact, have only seven confirms at the time of his award, this writer has always rationalized that by observing that victories in the Dardanelles were much harder to come by and besides, perhaps "the rule of eight" had not been made such a hard and fast one as it would later become that year (the fourth through ninth air awards of the order all came in July 1916 with four of the recipients having just scored their eighth confirmed victory and the other having added one more before the award caught up with him).

Now, from the memoirs of the aforementioned *Major* Serno, we have his calculation of Buddecke's number of victories at the time of his award. Serno says Buddecke's first success in the theater came on January 6, 1916 and all sources agree on that. Then he says by April 14, Buddecke had four *more* confirmed victories and six, not seven, unconfirmed, giving him the required eight after all. Of interest, too, is the fact that Serno had his problems with Buddecke as well as with von Althaus. If Serno is to be believed, and there is no reason not to, Buddecke was hardly the "paragon of virtue" that Inmelmann, for example, was said to be. It seems Buddecke was addicted to gambling which was endemic in Turkey. A local railroad official in Smyrna had lost large sums to Buddecke which he was not able to pay. Instead, he gave Buddecke a freight car, a scarce commodity there, presumably so Buddecke could ship private goods in some kind of illicit trade and make up the debt that way. Buddecke turned around and sold the use of the car to a Jewish merchant for a lot of money (was the reference to a "Jewish" merchant a bit of antisemitism here?). When word of this reached the Turkish authorities, Serno says he was forced to act although he claims it was Buddecke who asked for the transfer. At any rate, it was back to Germany, the Western Front and an appointment with death for the unfortunate man.

Buddecke had returned to the Western Front from Turkey once before but hardly in disgrace. On August 25, 1916, he took over as the first Commanding Officer of the newly formed *Jagdstaffel 4* with two such stalwarts as his old comrade from *Feldflieger-Abteilung 23*, Rudolf Berthold (then with six victories and a *Pour le Mérite* to come on October 12 after two more) and Wilhelm Frankl (with eight victories and the *Pour le Mérite* already dangling from his neck) plus a comer with but one victory at the time, Otto Bernert (who would score six more times under Buddecke before the year was out and would go on to his own *Pour le Mérite* in April 1917). Buddecke himself got three more confirms as *Jasta 4*'s leader and then with winter reducing aerial activity on the Western Front, it was back to Turkey again for Buddecke. There he would score only twice more, a "double" on March 30, 1917. Serno reports that Buddecke left Turkey the second time on February 15, 1918 but considering the length of the journey and time for reassignment at the front, that could not be. It had to be earlier for on February 19, flying now as just a regular pilot with *Jasta 30*, Buddecke received credit for his 13th and as it turned out, last victory. Excerpts taken from the unit's war diary by one of the interwar German researchers identifies it as a Sopwith Camel of No.80 Squadron, RFC whose pilot, Lt. S.H.L. Potter was wounded at 2:00 p.m. (German Time) in a combat over La Bassée but who got back across his lines all right. *The Sky Their Battlefield* raises other possibilities however. While confirming that Lt. S.L.H. (note the different arrangement of the initials) Potter of the squadron was wounded and returned safely, it credits two other No.80 Camels to Buddecke and to the leader of *Jasta 30, Oberleutnant* Hans Bethge, both in the same combat in which Potter was wounded and with both British pilots killed. For Bethge, it was his penultimate victory out of a total of 20 before he himself was killed in an air battle on March 17.

This writer had always assumed that Buddecke's return to the Western Front was probably occasioned by the need for pilots for the up-coming, long planned for German last gasp offensive of the war which was to kick off in March of 1918.

As described in the text, Buddecke was returned from Turkey to the Western Front in early 1918, booted out, apparently, by the chief of the German Air Service mission there, *Hauptmann* (*Major* in the Turkish Army) Erich Serno, for alleged profiteering in connection with a gambling debt. This charge may explain why Buddecke was not only reassigned but why he was sent to a *Jasta* as just a regular pilot and not as a Commanding Officer despite his rank and the *Pour le Mérite*. Then on March 8, his old comrade, Rudolf Berthold, his arm still in a sling from a wounding five months before, got Buddecke to come over from *Jasta 30* to his *Jasta 18* to help him run it in the air. Two days later, Buddecke fell in an air combat. Here we see the large assemblage accompanying his coffin to its final resting place in the Invaliden cemetery in Berlin where he was born. It is worth comparing Buddecke's *Ordenskissen* in this photograph with the one carried at his services in the field, two views of which have appeared in earlier volumes in this series (see page 208 in Volume II and page 80 in Volume III). In both of those, all of his 15 orders, decorations, medals and badges were not present. But here, on a more elaborate cushion fully twice the size of the one used in the field, all his honors seem to have been mounted. At observances like this, at least one brother flier was usually deputized to represent the air service but if any were present, they are too far back in the procession to be identified in this photograph.

And the fact that a man of his rank wearing Prussia's highest military tribute was not given a command but merely assigned as a regular pilot was due to the need for Buddecke to have some time to acclimate himself to the combat conditions in the air war of 1918 which had changed greatly since Buddecke had last flown there over a year ago. But now with Serno's report, one has to wonder whether Buddecke was having to do a bit of penance before being reinstated to a job commensurate with his record in the air. At any rate, once again his friend, Berthold, came through. Berthold had been severely wounded by a bullet in his right arm in combat on October 10, 1917 as the leader of *Jasta 18* and it was slow to heal. His arm was still in a sling when he asked for Buddecke to come over on March 8, 1918 to assist him in running *Jasta 18*, probably as its leader in the air while Berthold retained command on the ground. It was a fateful move. Two days later, Buddecke fell in a combat with Camels of No.3 (Naval) Squadron. Credit is generally given to Captain Arthur T. Whealy whose 10th claim it would have been (out of an eventual total of 27). It has also been reported that Berthold was wounded in the same fight. From photographs of Berthold's condition at the time (see those on Page 69, Volume I and Page 78, Volume III in this series taken when Buddecke arrived at *Jasta 18*), it is hard to believe he could have been up in the air that day. Some even say Buddecke lost his life in going to the aid of Berthold. If so, the gambler from Smyrna went out with honor.

HAUPTMANN KARL SEBER

Even if the leader *of Feldflieger-Abteilung 23, Hauptmann* Karl Seber, were not the third recipient of the Brunswick War Merit Crosses handed out by Duke Ernst August on the occasion of his October 23, 1915 visit to *23*'s airfield Seber would still be an interesting figure. But like so many of the early two-seater men who, by 1917, had put their days of hard combat flying behind them and took on staff or training duties, not much is known of Seber's later service in the war.

Like Buddecke, Seber was a recipient of the Knight's Cross of the Saxon Military St. Henry Order in *FFl.Abt.23*, one of the seven that have already been mentioned.[1] Seber's cross was approved on July 4, 1915 along with three others in the unit that day. As was frequently the case with the air awards of this order, a single event was emphasized in the citation although, in reality, it was a fine overall record as much as anything else that counted towards the award. And so it was with Seber. While it was said that he had "performed heroically as an observer on many occasions," it was for his performance and that of his pilot on November 18, 1914 that drew special praise.

[1] At least 20 of the pilots and observers in *FFl.Abt.23*, but not Seber, received the Albert Order, Saxony's lesser of its three bravery orders (1918 data are largely missing from the roll so there could have been more). So far as we know, no man in *23* received Saxon's intermediate bravery order, its Merit Order, which was almost exclusively reserved for native Saxons. Once again, the Saxon *FFl.Abt.24* and its successor unit, *Flieger-Abteilung (A)264*, topped *FFl.Abt.23* and its successor unit, *Fl.Abt.23*, in these departments. There were at least 27 awards of the Albert Order and six awards of the Merit Order in *24/(A)264* during the war. Still, for what was technically a non-Saxon formation, the men of *FFl.Abt. 23/Fl.Abt.23* seem to have been unduly honored by that kingdom. See Volume III in this series for more discussion of this.

Karl Seber (standing) and an unknown pilot with an Aviatik B-Type. The absence of visible national markings and with no Iron Cross ribbon present on Seber's tunic suggest that this was a prewar scene. It has to be dated after January 27, 1914 however, the *Kaiser*'s birthday on which that year he authorized a badge for military observers, one of which Seber wears. This photograph came from A. Edward Ferko years ago. Ed, a serious researcher, had a sense of humor too. He wrote on the back, "Dig that quilted coat lining!"

Seber's three-ribbon bar has his Iron Cross 2nd Class and Knight's St. Henry in positions one and two. The third could well be the Brunswick War Merit Cross.

Seber flanked by two of his men, *Rittmeister* Max Schueler von Krieken (left) and the then *Leutnant* Hans-Joachim von Seydlitz-Gerstenberg. The puppies look like a matched pair.

Seber was just a regular crew member of *23* at that time; he would not assume the leadership of the unit until the following month. On the day in question, he was paired with the then *Oberleutnant* Gottfried Glaeser (promoted *Hauptmann* on August 20, 1915). Their objective which was attacked in "squadron" strength was the rail yards at the critical supply and communications center of Amiens. In the typical overstatement when it came to assessing damage to the enemy, they were said to have been totally destroyed by the raid. On their return to base, Seber and Glaeser were attacked by a "technically far superior" French plane, meaning that it was equipped with a machine gun. Also typical of that time, all Seber had with which to protect themselves was a pistol but he banged away with that in the unequal combat. Their aircraft was said to have been hit many times with several striking vital spots including the gas tank. Nonetheless, the enemy plane was forced down, or so it was stated. Whether downed or just breaking off combat, the crew received no official credit for a victory. Had they, it would have been just the second recorded instance of an aerial victory by the German Army Air Service. The first had come just a few days earlier, on November 5, when the later *Hauptmann* Richard Flashar and his observer downed a French Parasol Type (Flashar is another man about whom we will hear more before this chapter concludes). When Seber's St. Henry came, there was also one for Glaeser. While we know that Seber soldiered on until the end of the war, November 18, 1914 must have been a high point, if not *the* high point, of his wartime career.

LEUTNANT OTTO PARSCHAU

The well-known photograph of *Leutnant* Otto Parschau referred to earlier was used on the ubiquitous post card number 380 from the Sanke studio in Berlin. It shows a smartly turned out Parschau with an immaculate bemedalled tunic, dress belt and gleaming boots posing in front of a railway sleeping car, part of *Kampfgeschwader 1*'s mobile living quarters, wearing his brand new *Orden Pour le Mérite* (the card has appeared in so many other books on World War I aviation that it is not reproduced here in favor of some which have had less exposure). The photograph also shows the presence of the Brunswick War Merit Cross on his order bar. The question has already been asked: was his one of the three handed out by Duke Ernst August on his visit to *Feldflieger-Abteilung 23* on October 23, 1915? We have guessed not because there is no evidence he was on *23's* field that day. Besides, Parschau was involved in a number of other demonstrations of the new Fokker *Eindecker* before other admiring audiences which included royalty like Duke Ernst August. For example, air historian Peter Kilduff has unearthed a letter written by the then neophyte Max Immelmann from the field of *Feldflieger-Abteilung 62* at Douai dated June 25, 1915 which read:

> Recently, we received two small combat monoplanes from the Fokker factory. Primarily to see these fighting machines, yesterday the Crown Prince of Bavaria visited the field and inspected us and *Abteilung 20*. Director Fokker, the builder of combat aircraft, was presented to him. He, as well as a Lieutenant Parschau, flew the aircraft and fired from the air to the ground. Fokker especially amazed us with his skill.

Much has been written elsewhere about Parschau's brief, but spectacular for its day, career as a fighter pilot, particularly his victories which resulted in his becoming the sixth German airman of the war to earn the *Orden Pour le Mérite*. So here we will try to add some other things about the man that have not generally been brought up before.

Parschau was an old hand, relatively speaking, of the early unarmed Fokker monoplanes used as scouts and an even older one as a military aviator having earned his pilot's license on July 4, 1913. And unlike the other fighter pilots of the day who had to cut their teeth in two-seaters before taking over one of the new single-seater fighting planes, Parschau flew solo from the start. At the outset of the war, he was assigned Fokker A.II (M 5L) which had been the personal property of an *Oberleutnant* von Buttlar (it would be interesting to know whether von Buttlar was compensated for his aircraft or whether it was confiscated and even more interesting to know why von Buttlar was not permitted to fly it himself instead of having to give it up to someone else). Parschau picked up what he dubbed his "green machine" in Belgium and flew it for nearly a year. With *Feldflieger-Abteilung 22, Brieftauben-Abteilung-Ostende* and *Feldflieger-Abteilung 42*, he was on roving commissions throughout that time, first in Champagne from September 28 to November 30, 1914, then over in Flanders from December 1 to February 2 in the new year, next back to Alsace Lorraine until February 20 and then on two stints on the Eastern Front, from March 6 until April 20, 1915 in East Prussia and finally from April 24 for a short time in West Galicia. In a letter to Anthony Fokker from there, Parschau complained about his by-now worn out old bird. He quoted a fellow officer, *Hauptmann* Jasper von Oertzen, as saying, "it should go to a museum" to which Parschau added, "and he's right!"

By July 1915, Parschau was back in the west with *Feldflieger-Abteilung 62* and in the company of the likes of Oswald Boelcke and Max Immelmann. He also had a new machine, Fokker A.III with the serial number A.226/14 and armed with a fixed forward-firing synchronized machine gun. He would soon trade this in for a production E-Type which were coming on stream now. One would have thought that first scoring honors with Fokker's new creation would have gone to Parschau but those went to another *Eindecker* pilot in *Feldflieger-Abteilung 48, Leutnant* Kurt Wintgens, on July 15. Actually, Wintgens had claimed Morane Parasols on July 1 and July 4 flying his E but these were not confirmed. By the time Parschau left *62* to return to *BAO* on the day after Wintgens' first confirmed victory, no one else in *62* had scored in *Eindeckers* either since the senior pilot of the unit, Boelcke, was still familiarizing himself with the one that had arrived there on June 24 and was still using a two-seater operationally. And it was in the first armed one of those delivered to the unit, LVG C.I 162/15, that Boelcke and his observer, *Leutnant* Heinz Helmut von Wühlisch (who will come up in a later chapter in this book), achieved their first victory on July 4. Thereafter, Boelcke used an *Eindecker* exclusively and when a second one arrived, he took over the new ship and Immelmann got the older one.

Parschau's turn to score did not come until October 11, 1915 when, at last, he was credited with a Farman over the Argonne. By that time, Boelcke had brought his total to four with three kills in his *E*, Immelmann likewise had reached four the day before, all in *Eindeckers*, and Wintgens' tally stood at three. *BAO* was back in Flanders when Parschau got his second, B.E.2c 2074 of No.12 Squadron, RFC, on December 19 in a

"The Happy Warrior," a smiling *Leutnant* Otto Parschau with his armed E-Type Fokker *Eindecker* (above) probably upon his return from a sortie as it was generally considered bad luck by the airmen, a superstitious lot, to be photographed before taking off on patrol. In the other pose, the absence of a *Pour le Mérite* and swords affixed to the ribbon of his Iron Cross 2nd Class (indicative of the Hohenzollern House Order) on his *Litewka* (double-breasted tunic) dates this scene prior to July 1916 when he received both awards in rapid succession. His Hohenzollern came immediately after his sixth victory and the *Pour le Mérite* the day after his eighth and final success in the air. The *Wagen* was part of the mobile living quarters of *Kampfgeschwader 1*.

Above: Parschau, as yet without a victory but wearing the Iron Cross 1st Class, and his unarmed Fokker A.II (M 5L) scout. Stenciled on the fuselage are the location and dates of where and when he flew this machine in 1914 and 1915 on both the Western and Eastern Fronts. Despite the poor quality of the photograph, these can be made out fortunately (see text for details).

Below: Fokker A.III A.226/14, Work Number 216, on the Douai airfield of *Feldflieger-Abteilung 62*, probably early July 1915, now armed with a synchronized Spandau with unusual gun butt. Parschau has boldly lettered his name on the fuselage for all the world to see but the cropping of the original photograph prevents us from seeing all of the personal markings.

combat over Bruges. The next day, *BAO*, whose cover name was no longer necessary, adopted a new designation more appropriate to its duties, *Kampfgeschwader der Obersten Heeresleitung 1* (*Kagohl 1* – "Fighting Squadron of the Army High Command 1"). The remaining six victories that Parschau scored, all in 1916, have been well documented over the years but a transcript recently found dated 25 March 1918 signed by the Commanding Officer of *Bombengeschwader 1* (the successor designation for *Kagohl 1* and commanded at the time by the *Pour le Mérite* bomber "ace," *Hauptmann* Alfred Keller) is curiously at odds with what are the generally accepted facts of several of them. Table 4-2 shows the four discrepancies. The transcript dates Parschau's third victory as February 6, 1916 while *Above the Lines* quotes the date most often found, March 12. The two lists differ on the type of aircraft constituting Parschau's fifth victory on June 29, a more understandable variance since there was considerable confusion on that subject. There is a difference of one day between the dates cited for his sixth victory, also more understandable than the one month disparity for number three. What really surprises is what the transcript puts down as his seventh victory, a Caudron, and what *Above the Lines* shows, an observation balloon. Very curious indeed.

Before coming to Parschau's final and fatal combat, something should be said about Parschau's other awards. By the time he picked up an Austrian Military Merit Cross 3rd Class with War Decoration and the Austro-Hungarian Field Pilot's Badge for his efforts on the Eastern Front, brief as they were, he already held the Iron Cross 1st and 2nd Class. Thus, unlike Immelmann and so many other German airmen, Parschau did not receive the Iron Cross 1st Class for a first victory. It would be of interest (at least to this writer anyway) to know the date of Parschau's award and compare that as well as the date of his 2nd Class award with those of the earliest known fighter pilot recipient of both of those Prussian decorations. That man was the later *Hauptmann* and *Pour le Mérite* fighter ace, Rudolf Berthold. Berthold started off as an observer in *Feldflieger-Abteilung 23* attached to the German 2nd Army and its drive through Belgium and into France in the opening weeks of the war. For the reconnaissance that discovered the gap that had been allowed to grow between the German 2nd Army and the German 1st Army on its right flank through which the enemy was pouring troops and which caused the 1st Army's Commander-in-Chief, *Generaloberst* Karl von Bülow, to order a retreat from the Marne on September 9, Berthold was given the Iron Cross 2nd Class four days later. Then for continued good work and valuable reports, Berthold received his 1st Class award on October 4, 1914. In both cases, Berthold was the first man after von Bülow himself to wear the two decorations in the German 2nd Army.

Table 4-2

(Day, Month and Year)

Victory Number	**Bogohl 1 Transcript** Date	Aircraft Type	**"Above the Lines"** Date	Aircraft Type
1.	11.10.15	Farman	11.10.15	Farman
2.	19.12.15	B.E.	19.12.15	B.E.2c
3.	6.2.16	Farman	12.3.16	French a/c
4.	21.3.16	Voissin (sic)	21.3.16	Voisin
5.	29.6.16	English Fighter	29.6.16	Voisin
6.	1.7.16	Caudron	2.7.16	Two-seater
7.	3.7.16	Caudron	3.7.16	Balloon
8.	9.7.16	Observation Balloon	9.7.16	Balloon

Above: Parschau doesn't appear to be too happy as he is congratulated on the site of his second victory by an officer with the unusual shoulder holster. The locale was Oostkampe near Bruges. The date was December 19, 1915. Both Parschau and *Leutnant* Martin Gerlich, 2nd from Parschau's right, wear identical woolly turtle-necks. Gerlich later became the Adjutant in *Kampfgeschwader 3*. The officer at the extreme right is *Hauptmann* von Gersdorff, an early (Spring 1916) air recipient of the Hohenzollern House Order with Swords as Parschau's Commanding Officer in *Kampfgeschwader 1*.

Below: Parschau wiped out both a hangar and his *Eindecker* in this undated photograph. To what extent he might have been injured in this crash is not known. There was something of a scoring hiatus between his 2nd and 3rd victories (12 weeks) and his 4th and 5th (11 weeks) so, while it's only speculation, it's possible this put him out of action for a time in the first half of 1916.

Returning now to Parschau's awards, the sixth victories of both Boelcke and Immelmann had earned them the then rarely bestowed Knight's Cross with Swords of the Royal House Order of Hohenzollern and as is well known, the *Orden Pour le Mérite* after their eighth victories, the first air recipients of both of these awards. These levels then became the standard for other fliers to receive those two orders throughout 1916 until November that year when word was put out that henceforth the *Pour le Mérite* would be given to airmen only for "extraordinary achievements" (this was meant for fast-rising stars like Manfred von Richthofen who was made to wait until his victory score was exactly twice the old mark; it was not applied to an "old-timer" like *Oberleutnant* Hans Berr who got his *Pour le Mérite* on December 4, 1916, a little more than five weeks after his eighth victory by which time his score stood at 10). Accordingly, Parschau got his Hohenzollern on July 3, the day he added one more to his score. His *Pour le Mérite* came on the 10th, just a day after his eighth and final victory. That day of his eighth success in the air also saw Parschau transferred from *Kagohl 1* to an all-fighter detachment, *Abwehrkommando-Nord* (Defense Command North). Within the week, he was named its leader and the unit, which had been assigned to *Feldflieger-Abteilung 32*, was given independent status with the new designation, *Kampfeinsitzer-Staffel B* ("B" for Bertincourt, *AKN*'s airfield). With the *Pour le Mérite*, Parschau's awards ended as did his life before the momentous month of July was over.

There is even confusion on the matter of his death, however. All agree that it was in a combat on July 21 that he was struck by a glancing shot to the head and mortally wounded by a bullet in his stomach. Apparently, the exact time of the action was never recorded anywhere in records that have survived so it is not clear who his victor might have been or even which enemy, England or France, he was fighting. Most sources have concluded it was the Royal Flying Corps who were responsible, focusing in on the D.H.2s of No.24 Squadron and the F.E.2bs of No.22 Squadron that had fights with large formations of German aircraft that morning and later the same evening. Indeed, the later Major John O. Andrews of 24 Squadron claimed a Fokker over Allaines, just north of Peronne on the

Below: Parschau in the cockpit of one of the best German fighting machines of its day, the Halberstad D.II. All the pilots praised its handling over the *Eindeckers* which had to be constantly manhandled while the D.II was said to fly by itself when hands were taken off its controls. This photograph could have been taken on one of the last days of his life when he was the leader of an independent all-fighter detachment called *Abwehrkomando-Nord/Kampfeinsitzer-Staffel B*. It could also be the aircraft in which he lost his life in an air battle on July 21, 1916.

Abschrift.

Abschüsse des Leutnant P a r s c h a u bei der Brieftauben-abteilung „O" bezw. beim Kampfgeschwader 1 O.H.L. St.1.

Am 11.10.15	1 Farman mit Cold M.G.
„ 19.12.15	1 engl. B.E.D.D.
„ 6.2.16	1 Farman
„ 21.3.16	1 Voissin D.D.
„ 29.6.16	1 einsitz. engl. Jagdflugzeug
„ 1.7.16	1 Caudron D.D.
„ 3.7.16	1 Caudron doppelmotorig
„ 9.7.16	1 Fesselballon

Für die Richtigkeit:

Stempel:

Königl.Pr.Bombengeschw.1
O.H.L.

B.U., den 25. März 1918
gez. Unterschrift.
Hauptmann und Kommandeur.

Above: An interesting transcript dated 25 March 1918 and the accuracy of which was attested to by the *Pour le Mérite* leader of *Bombengeschwader 1*, *Hauptmann* Alfred Keller, listing Parschau's victories by date and type of aircraft. Four of the entries differ from what has usually been accepted as fact (see text for details). Why this was prepared at such a late date is not known.

road to Bapaume at 8:00 a.m., his first of an eventual 12 solo and shared victories credited to him. But there were other Fokker claims made by British pilots too. In all, the Germans lost three of their fighter pilots that day. In addition to Parschau, there was *Vizefeldwebel* Wolfgang Heinemann of an unknown detachment who was killed near Douai and *Leutnant* Werner Schramm, one of Parschau's *AKN* men who had come over from *Kagohl 1* with him. Schramm was killed over Combles, about four miles northwest of Allaines, in the action which took place with 24 and 22 Squadrons that evening.

But the French have their own view as to Parschau's victor. They credit the later 45-victory ace, Lt. Charles Nungesser, with bringing down an Aviatik at an unspecified time or location that day for his 10th victory. Parschau is thought to have been flying a new Halberstadt D.II, not yet familiar to allied pilots, so the misidentification would be understandable. At any rate, they recorded Parschau's name, rank, some of the units in which he served and even his birth date and place (November 11, 1890 in Allenstein in East Prussia) correctly in assigning the credit to one of their own.

Whoever was responsible, Parschau was beyond help. Although he had managed to get himself and his plane down somehow and was rushed to a field hospital, it was too late. As the story goes, he died that evening on the operating table. Parschau and his comrade in death, Schramm, were given a funeral worthy of a "reigning prince" (as Manfred von Richthofen described the ceremonies for Boelcke 14 weeks and a day later) and were buried side-by-side in the military cemetery just outside the town of St. Quentin.

And with that, we end the story of the three awards of the Brunswick War Merit Cross in one day and the two men who are known to have been involved and the two who may have been. We now tell the remaining mini-biographies of recipients of the decoration in alphabetical order.

Parschau and one of his Bertincourt-based men, *Leutnant* Werner Schramm, were both killed in action on July 21, 1916 and joint funeral ceremonies were held for them. Above, the military escort and band form up while an officer is ready to march off holding Parschau's *Ordenskissen* topped by his *Pour le Mérite*.

As the solemn procession wends its way through the streets of St. Quentin, another officer (above right) walks in front of Schramm's hearse bearing his pillow with two Iron Crosses and a Pilot's Badge. To the right, a military chaplain and high ranking officers trail behind one of the hearses. Below, the impressive entourage on its final route to the cemetery outside of town while French civilians, including several children watch the proceedings from a respectful distance The Germans exhibited a real flair for this kind of pomp and circumstance.

LEUTNANT ERWIN BÖHME

Erwin Böhme has the unfortunate distinction as being remembered today mostly as the man whose aircraft undercarriage brushed the upper left wing of the Albatros D.II of the leader of *Jagdstaffel 2*, the legendary *Hauptmann* Oswald Boelcke. It occurred on the afternoon of Saturday, October 28, 1916 in a hot fight with D.H.2 fighters of the Royal Flying Corps. The damage to Boelcke's plane appeared slight at first as he descended, seemingly under control. But parts of the wing gave way, the glide steepened into a dive and Boelcke died from the impact as the Albatros slammed into the ground. Böhme's undercarriage was damaged in the collision but not critically. He was able to control his ship and break off combat only to watch in horror as his *Staffelführer*'s aircraft went into its death plunge. No blame for the mid-air accident fell on Böhme but that day remained etched in his mind until his own death a little more than a year later (and so upset was he at the time that he did not even recall that upon landing back at his own field, the weakened undercarriage gave way and he nosed over).

It has only been in recent years that Böhme's own considerable accomplishments in the war have been given the attention they deserve, thanks in large measure to research carried out and articles written by *Dr.-Ing.* Niedermeyer of Dietzenbach, Germany and Mr. Douglas V. Fant of Dallas, Texas which have appeared in the quarterly World War I aviation journal *Over the Front*. Their work has included an extensive examination of letters written by Böhme to his family and to his young fiancée. Yet in none of that has any mention been found of Böhme's award of the Brunswick War Merit Cross. In fact, Böhme was unduly modest about his accomplishments and the rewards they brought as we shall see.

The outbreak of war found Böhme just returned to his home in Holzminden from six years of working in German East Africa as an engineer for a German firm developing the colony. He was planning on pursuing one of his passions, mountain climbing, in the Swiss Alps when the call to the colors came. He immediately reported to the unit in which he had performed his compulsory military service but this man who had reached the ripe old (for an airman) age of 35, plagued as he was with recurrent bouts of the malaria he had contacted in Africa and which would continue to come and go until the very end, had other things in mind than being an anonymous ground pounder. Somehow, despite the fact that he had no previous flying experience, Böhme managed to be accepted into the then small German Army Air Service. On August 30, 1914, the war less than a month old, he was ordered to report to *Flieger-Ersatz-Abteilung 1* at Döberitz. Two weeks later, he was transferred to the school at Leipzig-Lindenthal to begin his formal pilot training and by the following month, was promoted *Unteroffizier*. So adept a pupil did he prove to be that by early December, he had already passed two of the three required examinations to earn the Pilot's Badge. Front flying was the quicker way to completing the third course and Böhme yearned for that opportunity. But two, possibly three, things held him back for more than a year. First, the malaria continued to weaken him from time to time and, besides, pilot training was an urgent need in an expanding air force and Böhme was a good instructor as it turned out. The third factor might have been his age and the maturity that went with it which helped in dealing with the young tyros turning up at the flight schools. During this period in his aviation life, by June 1915, he had further been promoted to *Vizefeldwebel*.

Towards the end of November 1915, Böhme got some home leave on his way, at last, to a front line assignment. That December, he joined *Kampfstaffel 10* of *Kampfgeschwader 2*, the second of the early bombardment squadrons which was just at this time adopting its new designation from its original one, *Brieftauben-Abteilung-Metz*. Böhme caught up with *Kasta 10* in the Saarbrücken area, some 40 miles from Metz. His flight was still forming and being equipped with the armed Albatros C.I. Before he made his own first front line flight, a Christmas Eve present arrived for Böhme. He was made *Offizier-Stellvertreter* with the prospects of a commission in sight. The squadron moved in its long trains of captured French passenger cars to a position at Mörchingen, arriving there on December 30. Böhme's air war had begun and despite poor weather conditions, regular patrols were carried out without, as Böhme put it, "the fortune to meet a Frenchman" (*Kasta 10*'s task was to protect the German artillery positions from attack by French airmen). With the German drive on Verdun kicking off on February 21, 1916, *Kagohl 2* was moved to Metz-Frescaty and went on the offensive too, bombing rail junctions at the enemy-held cities of Bar-le-Duc and Ligny and hitting the fortress of Verdun itself. Then as the battle for Verdun see-sawed back and forth and the French brought in more air reinforcements,

Opposite: Of the older fighter pilots in the Imperial German Army Air Service, *Leutnant* Erwin Böhme, here at age 37 or 38 in the well-known Sanke post card produced after his receipt of the Hohenzollern House Order, was the most successful with 24 confirmed victories. Here he wears the ribbon of that award with a small crown and crossed swords device in the first position followed by the ribbon indicating his Iron Cross 2nd Class whereas the order of precedence called for it to be just the other way around. These ribbons are followed by those of his Brunswick War Merit Cross and the Austrian Military Merit Cross 3rd Class with War Decoration, the latter having the small wreath indicative of that distinction.

C.766

the two *Kagohls* operating there were switched over to the much maligned *Sperrefliegen* ("Barrier Flights"), the practice of patrolling up and down the front line to deny the enemy planes from entering German air space.

Böhme's Commanding Officer at *Kasta 10* was Wilhelm Bölcke, the older brother of the already famous Oswald (fresh from his ninth victory on the Somme and now assigned to the Verdun sector; the "ö" with the umlaut rather than the "oe" was favored by everyone in the family but Oswald). On March 5, Oswald visited his brother, flying in with his "much perforated" Fokker *Eindecker*. This is the first recorded meeting between Erwin and Oswald that was to have such a profound effect on the lives of both men, first at their next meeting on August 14, 1916 at Kovel in Russia and then on that 28th of October in the skies over Bapaume. Certainly, the idea of Böhme becoming a fighter pilot himself must have been planted by Boelcke's visit to *Kasta 10* if it had not already come to mind. Apparently, Böhme's family were expecting that he would be receiving the Iron Cross 2nd Class around this time for in a letter to one of his brothers, Gerhard, who was also in service, dated two days after Boelcke's visit, Erwin wrote, "Your dream of my decoration was too soon." He further went on to say such things did not happen as quickly as with what he called "the rising generation" (meaning the relative newcomers like himself) which he felt was only right. Laurels had to be earned, including his still-to-be-acted-upon promotion to officer. But then, curiously, in a continuation of the letter dated March 8, he writes that he was wrong in saying he had not as yet received the Iron Cross. Did it come that very day? But, of course, receive it he did with much more to follow and just when it was awarded is of little consequence in the final analysis.

In the earlier section of the letter we are discussing, Böhme also said that his "bird" had not been hit despite heavy French anti-aircraft fire. In the later section, he had to retract that statement too. As he and his 47-year old observer, a *Dr*. Sanders, were fruitlessly pursuing a Farman over Verdun on the morning of March 8 due to Sanders' jammed gun and his frozen fingers, a second Farman dove on them and then a Nieuport Scout attacked from underneath, hitting the fuselage and wings of their aircraft. Böhme courageously dove on the Nieuport even though not having a forward-firing gun, he could do little to harm it. That did the trick, however, and the Frenchman quickly took himself out of the fight. Böhme repeated the ruse with the same effect when shortly thereafter, he chased another Farman away from the tail of another machine of his flight. The very next day, Böhme installed a machine gun for his own use on a new Rumpler he had picked up at the *Armee-Flug-Park* at Metz-Frescaty the afternoon of his combats the previous morning, turning in an Albatros, perhaps the one he and Sanders had been flying, in an exchange. In May, Böhme got a two week leave part of which he spent at Döberitz where he flew to a wedding anniversary celebration in a Gotha G.1 with another brother, Martin, a *Riesenflugzeug-Abteilung* (Giant Aircraft Detachment or Unit) observer. His leave coincided with the long-awaited promotion to *Leutnant* that had come through on May 3. In late May, he was back at Verdun and even though that struggle continued in all its fury (on May 22, Fort Douaumont, which had been easily overrun by Brandenburgers of the 24th Regiment four days after the initial German attack, was retaken by the French 5th Division at terrible cost only to be lost again on the 24th) and would continue until the final French counter offensive from October 24 to December 18, 1916 regained all the lost ground (and Fort Douaumont again), a change of venue was in the cards for Böhme and the men of *Kagohl 2*.

On June 4, 1916, the Commanding General of the Russian Southwest Army Group, Aleksei Brusilov, opened a massive offensive named after him which turned out to be the only successful action of the war for that ally in the Triple Entente. It smashed the Austrian defenses on a two-hundred-mile front, causing the Austrian Fourth and Seventh Armies to collapse. The grave situation alarmed Hindenburg and Ludendorff and their appeals were answered by the transfer to the Eastern Front of men and resources sorely needed in the west (one must wonder what the outcome of the war might have been had not Germany been repeatedly called upon to shore up its shaky partner both in the east and on the Italian Front). *Kagohl 2* was one of the units pulled out and sent east, in its case to Kovel in the Ukraine. One of the other pilots moving along with Böhme was the then pretty much unheralded *Leutnant* Manfred *Freiherr* von Richthofen who had returned to *Kagohl 2* in March 1916 after formal training at Döberitz. According to Böhme, his unit, equipped with six Albatros C.III machines, went into action for the first time in their new surroundings on July 5. With virtually no enemy air opposition, the men of *Kagohl 2* had a field day bombing and strafing the unprotected Russian

Opposite: Böhme's first front line posting after passing out of flight school was to the newly designated *Kampfgeschwader 2* which he joined in December 1915 as a pilot in its *Kampfstaffel 10*. In late June 1916, the entire unit was shipped to Kowel in the Ukraine as part of the German reinforcements rushed there to counter the Brusilov Offensive, named after the Russian general commanding the attack. These two photographs were taken there that summer. In the better-known view above, he and his observer, a *Leutnant* Lademacher (in leather flying togs), stand in front of their Albatros C.III 766/16. In the less often scene below, Böhme and Lademacher are now on board and we get a better look at the arresting crocodile marking running along the fuselage.

Above: Five of the six brand new Albatros D.Is that were delivered to *Jasta 2*'s Bertincourt field on September 16, 1916 with which the men of Boelcke's Staffel went out in force for the first time the following day. The pilots admiring their new steeds are, from left to right, *Lt.* Erwin Böhme, *Lt.* Wolfgang Günther, *Oblt.* Stefan Kirmaier and the then *Offz.-Stv.* Max Müller.

Below: A crowd of Boelcke's fledgling pilots greet their revered leader at Lagnicourt aerodrome in October 1916 to learn whether "he had another Englishman for breakfast." Boelcke prepares to step down from Albatros D.II 386/16, the aircraft in which he was killed on October 28. It is now thought that Böhme is at far left and next to him is Kirmaier followed by Manfred von Richthofen (in other identifications of this photograph, Böhme's and von Richthofen's positions have been reversed). Fourth from the left is Wortmann (with glasses), then Günther (in front of Wortmann), König, Müller and Höhne. Only Günther and Höhne were not killed in the war.

troops. Their only real risk was being forced down in enemy lines by a stray shot or mechanical failure where they could expect no mercy from the soldiers they were harassing so effectively. Considering that enemy planes were seldom encountered in the air during this time, Böhme did remarkably well. On August 2, he was given official credit for shooting down a Russian Nieuport in the Rodzyse area, not far from where Brusilov's headquarters were located at the time. Earlier, on July 11 and 13, he and his unknown observer had claimed two "large battle planes" but these went unconfirmed. Still, these feats, really quite remarkable given the situation on that front, brought no Iron Cross 1st Class for Böhme but could we not theorize that possibly it was at this time he was awarded his Brunswick War Merit Cross (for his service in the east, the grateful Austrians did award him their War Merit Cross 3rd Class with War Decoration as they did to von Richthofen as well)?

But meantime, things had happened in the west that would again change the fortunes of several of the men of *Kagohl 2*. The great Max Immelmann had been killed in his *Eindecker* on June 18, 1916. Germany could not afford to lose its other great air hero, Boelcke, still back at Verdun, and by Imperial Decree he was ordered off active combat status (but not before he shot down a Nieuport on June 27 over Douaumont for his 19th confirmed victory, "illegally" Böhme characterized it). Boelcke was given several options during his enforced rest one of which was a tour of operations in the east including Turkey. And this he chose. Then on July 1 on the Somme, a combined Anglo-French offensive opened which turned into a blood bath to equal Verdun and put further strain on Germany's fast dwindling manpower (estimates vary but German casualties in the half-year battle at Verdun were on the order of 400,000 killed, wounded, missing and prisoners while the French lost perhaps a half million; before the Somme battles ground to a halt on November 20, Britain had suffered some 420,000 casualties in their head-on assaults, including 60,000 on the first day alone, but Germany had incurred even more, 450,000, in their misguided attempts to recover every bit of ground the moment it was lost). The British attempt on the Somme was only in part to relieve the pressure on Verdun. Field Marshal Sir Douglas Haig had been planning his offensive for some time although he had wanted to strike in Flanders further to the north but acquiesced to French pleas that it be closer to Verdun. Besides all that, the Brusilov Offensive, which sputtered to a temporary halt in late June, got going again in August and continued to advance in September. It had, however, outrun its supply lines and by October, it was all over. Although the Russians captured 400,000 prisoners, it had lost the cream of its army, some one million men. The key objectives of Lublin and Lemberg south of Warsaw were never taken. It was the last gasp for the Russians in the east. German eyes could now turn west where the Allies had wrested supremacy of the air away from the Germans. The "Fokker Scourge" was over as the *Eindecker* found itself facing superior numbers of much better fighting machines.

Returning now to mid-August, Boelcke had left Constantinople and was making his way back to the Western Front where the new *Jagdstaffeln* were being formed. Boelcke had been an advocate for all-fighter formations and he was naturally slated to take one over. By the 14th of the month, Boelcke was at *Kagohl 2* in Kovel visiting his brother Wilhelm, still Böhme's Commanding Officer in *Kasta 10*. It was there and on that date, according to *Dr*. Niedermeyer's research, that Boelcke received his orders to take over *Jasta 2* and where he personally selected according to Böhme, not only himself, but von Richthofen and three others who were not identified by Böhme.[1] Böhme, as did von Richthofen and the others, jumped at the chance to serve under a demigod like Boelcke flying the new biplane fighters that were to replace the now worthless-for-combat *Eindeckers* (but which, according to air historian Alex Imrie, still made up the backbone of the German fighter aircraft at the front at this time; at the end of August, there were still 145 E-Types and only single examples of the Albatros D.I and D.II and 25 Halberstadt and 35 Fokker biplane fighters at the front according to him). Böhme had long dreamed of becoming a fighter pilot. As early as March 26, 1916, he was fully expecting that "before long" he would be assigned an *Eindecker* to use in addition to his regular duties as a two-seater pilot. He was looking forward "mightily" to the new plane. Although the dates are not recorded, Böhme apparently did get some time in on the new little birds but as he said, "only now and then." He was thrilled by the prospects of "daring anything with these aircraft that respond so lithely" and with which "one can properly hunt the enemy" (Böhme would later write that he thought the designation "*Jagdstaffel*" (literally, "Hunting Section or Flight") was well chosen).

---

[1] According to *Dr*. Niedermeyer, the three were the *Leutnante* Hans Imelmann, Herwarth Philipps and Christian von Scheele. From the meager records available to this writer, only von Scheele can be identified as being in *Kagohl 2* at this time. He had served as an observer in *Feldflieger-Abteilung 32* where on July 21, 1915, he and his pilot, *Oberleutnant* Wolfgang Weese, forced a Voisin down in German lines near Bapaume. This resulted in Weese receiving the first air award of Baden's Military Karl Friedrich Order (see Volume VI). Von Scheele then became a pilot with *BAM/Kagohl 2*. Imelmann, Philipps and von Scheele all became early casualties in *Jasta 2*. Another early *Jasta 2* casualty, *Leutnant* Hans Reimann, was with *Kasta 8* of *Kagohl 2* prior to joining *Jasta 2* so he may well have been one of the other three whom Boelcke selected.

MEN OF *JASTA 2/BOELCKE* WITH WHOM BÖHME SERVED IN 1916 AND EARLY 1917 SHOWN IN CONTEMPORARY POST CARDS OF THE DAY

(Victories in That Time Shown in Brackets)

Hptm. Oswald Boelcke (21). The caption says this was the last photograph taken of him in his fighter plane but that was hardly the case. Here he is in the prototype Fokker D.III (350/16, Work Number 700) at the Fokker factory in Schwerin in March 1916. Boelcke was killed in Albatros D.II 386/16.

Lt. Dieter Collin (2)

Lt. Otto Höhne (6)

Oblt. Stefan Kirmaier (8)

Offz.-Stv. Max Müller (5)

Offz.-Stv. Leopold Reimann (4)

Lt. Manfred von Richthofen (16)

Lt. Werner Voss (28)

After traveling back to Germany and a spot of leave, Böhme reported to his new boss at *Jasta 2* on September 8. The unit was awaiting its first batch of the new twin-gunned Albatros D.I and in the meantime, Böhme was assigned what he termed a "refurbished" Halberstadt D.II ("refurbished" seems a strange word for an aircraft then new to the front; perhaps his had suffered some earlier damage). Boelcke himself flew lone patrols in Fokker D.III 352/16 and in it scored victory numbers 20 through 26 between September 2 and 15. Six of the Albatros arrived on September 16 to an excited group of Boelcke's pups. Six were enough to convince the leader that on the morrow, he would put them and their mounts to the test. It was a glorious beginning. Böhme, von Richthofen and *Leutnant* Hans Reimann all drew blood and, for good measure, Boelcke notched his 27th. A little commented upon fact, however is that these four victories did not all come in the same engagement. Böhme's victim, Sopwith 1 1/2 Strutter A.1913 from No.70 Squadron, RFC went down on the unit's first patrol of that day. None of the others scored on that sortie. The other three victories came on a second patrol later that morning, all F.E.2bs from No.11 Squadron (with the new (August 12) *Pour le Mérite* ace, *Leutnant* Wilhelm Frankl, getting a fourth from that same unfortunate unit in the same fight). Four victories on the first day of combined action was cause enough for a celebration that evening but it was further marked by the award of the Iron Cross 1st Class to Böhme. A recommendation for the award had apparently been made while he was still at Kovel and it had just now been approved. Böhme reports that Boelcke personally pinned the badge on Böhme's tunic and it would be nice to think that with his own badge yet to reach him at *Jasta 2*, Boelcke took off his and gave it to Böhme. A little over a year later, another badge would arrive at the now redesignated *Jasta Boelcke* for Böhme but it would be one he would never be destined to wear.

By the time the fateful day of October 28 arrived, Boelcke's *Staffel* and its *Führer* had posted a remarkable record. Boelcke himself had brought his total score up to 40 and eight of his men had either begun their victory strings or had added to what they had rung up before. Böhme had scored three more times for a total of five confirmed victories. *Oberleutnant* Stefan Kirmaier had gained four within a ten day period in October to tack on to the three he had been credited with as an *Einaecker* pilot attached to *Kampfeinsitzer-Kommando-Jametz*, the fighter detachment cooperating with *Artillerie-Flieger-Abteilung 203*. Von Richthofen was already showing his stuff, leading the pack after Boelcke with six of his own. *Offizier-Stellvertreter* Leopold Reimann, over from *Jasta 1* with a victory there, had gotten four under Boelcke plus two unconfirms. Hans Reimann had added two more for a grand total of four but he was gone, killed in action on September 23. *Offizier-Stellvertreter* Max Müller, already thrice decorated by his native Bavaria including both its Gold and Silver Bravery Medals for his two-seater work, the only airman to ever hold both, and later Max *Ritter* von Müller with a posthumous Military Max-Joseph Order, scoreless in September had gotten two in October, his first of an eventual 36. The boyish Hans Imelmann was one up on Müller with three. And finally, *Leutnant* Otto Höhne, the only one of this group to survive the war, also had three (another fact that has drawn little comment over the years is that Höhne's first victory was scored on the evening of September 16, thus before *Jasta 2* went out in force the next day. It was another F.E.2b from No.11 Squadron whose mates suffered those four losses the next day. Was Höhne out on a solo hop familiarizing himself with his new D.I when the action occurred?). If all of that sounds like a numbers game, that's really not far from what it was, with recognition in official dispatches, promotion and medals closely linked to the number of one's victories.

Böhme carried out lengthy correspondence with his brothers, his parents and especially a young woman in Hamburg to whom he would become engaged. She must have chided Böhme for talking "numbers" when tallying his victims for just 10 days before Boelcke's death, he replied to what he detected as a "mild reproach" for his apparent callowness. Part of what he said was:

> With us, every fight is a personal fight, man against man, with the same weapons and the same chances ... With us, each dogfight is like a joust, a knightly, or to put it in more modern terms, a sporting duel. I have nothing against the single man with whom I fight. I only want to put him and his aircraft out of commission so that he will harm us no more ... I respect him, but nonetheless he will be recorded as a number ... Because each dogfight is personal, one also scribes his success personally, and if the victories pile up on you, one must count them.

And for Böhme, the numbers did indeed start to pile up. These have been recorded and documented so thoroughly elsewhere that they need not be recounted one by one as has been done so far. It should suffice to just touch on some of the other highlights of the 11 months Böhme had left on earth, many of which are due to the diligent work of others not the least of whom is *Dr.* Niedermeyer.

Boelcke's successor was Kirmaier and fittingly so since he was the most senior in rank and experience with single-seaters. But he didn't last a month, shot down and killed on

November 22 after being caught unawares from the rear (an account of the action by Kirmaier's victor himself, the later Air Vice Marshal John O. Andrews, appears on Page 168 in Volume VI in this series). Another Bavarian, but this time an outsider, was put in charge of the *Staffel*. He was the soon-to-be 31 year-old *Oberleutnant* Franz Josef Walz (and soon-to-be promoted *Hauptmann* as well, on January 20 of the following year). One must wonder whether there wasn't some resentment that one of their own wasn't chosen. Yet Böhme, in correspondence says that Walz was chosen by the men of *Jasta 2* (highly unlikely, as *Kogenluft* did not consult fliers on who their Commanding Officers would be; perhaps the one exception to that was the handwritten "will" of Manfred von Richthofen that, "should I not return," appointed *Hauptmann* Wilhelm Reinhard as his successor; so great was von Richthofen's prestige that such a directive could not be ignored). Whether Walz was seen as a popular choice or not, *Jasta 2* was seemingly getting just the right man if aggressiveness in the air counted for anything. As the leader of *Kasta 2* of *Kagohl 1*, he had been credited with six confirmed victories between April and late July of 1916, good enough for a fighter pilot to receive an immediate Hohenzollern at the time. But things didn't work that fast for the men in the two-seaters, or at least not for Walz because it was not until more than a month later when his Hohenzollern caught up with him on September 5 while on a temporary assignment at *Flieger-Ersatz-Abteilung 1* at Schleissheim following a hospital stay due to a wound suffered in combat on July 30. Walz returned to *Kagohl 1* on October 11 and was put in charge of *Kasta 1* but the need to staff the new *Jagdstaffel* leaderships with experienced hands saw him take over *Jasta 19* just three weeks later, on November 3. And then with Kirmaier's death, the call had come to move over to *Jasta 2* on November 28. Of the men already on board *Jasta 2* whom *Kogenluft* might have chosen, von Richthofen would have been the leading candidate if scoring and other honors were the main criteria. He had just scored his ninth and 10th victories two days before Kirmaier was picked off, had already received his Hohenzollern on the 11th of the month and was wondering where his *Pour le Mérite* was. And like Walz, von Richthofen was a Regular Army Officer which always was a factor in command decisions of this kind in 1916. But, as most readers need not be told, von Richthofen would have to wait until the following January before getting his "Blue Max" and his own *Jasta* to lead.

Walz turned out to be less than an inspiring leader, a fact that has been reported before in this series (see pages 54 and 55 in Volume IV for example). Under him, *Jasta Boelcke* (*Jasta 2* was so renamed on December 10, 1916 in honor of its fallen first leader) went into a long decline. At first, things went well but then casualties and transfers of some of its best men took their toll. By the spring of 1917, just two men, Otto Bernert and Werner Voss, were its only stalwarts. Walz himself had failed to score. Then Bernert left to take the command of *Jasta 6* on May 1 and Voss had had enough. He did the unthinkable. He went over Walz's head and lobbied for his removal. Voss could have been court-martialled but his record of 24 victories and the *Pour le Mérite* apparently saved him. The upshot had all the appearance of a face-saving whitewash. Voss got a command, *Jasta 5*, and Walz, who had at last scored a seventh victory on May 14 (albeit over a then-obsolescent D.H.2), was temporarily left in charge of *Jasta "B." Kogenluft* waited until the following month and then transferred Walz to the Bavarian *Jasta 34* on June 9, bringing back Bernert to take over *Jasta "B."* No doubt the brass congratulated itself on handling a delicate situation skillfully and with minimal fuss.

Böhme himself had had little opportunity to gain an opinion of Walz's leadership. After scoring two more times under Walz to bring his total number of confirmed victories to nine, Böhme went on three weeks leave on January 9, 1917. He returned on February 3 and immediately showed that the time off had not dulled either his flying skills or his appetite for air fighting. The next day, he received credit for a B.E.2c and a D.H.2 although the latter may actually have been able to get back to its lines with its pilot wounded, Then six days after this "double," the only one of his career, he added number 12, another D.H.2. These were important victory numbers because they brought him into "Hohenzollern territory," whereby a fighter pilot having reached the 10 or-more level at this stage of the war on the Western Front might expect that recognition anytime thereafter. The next day, February 11, his chance to extend that string was cut short by what appears to have been an act of mercy on Böhme's part. He had latched on to a Sopwith 1 1/2 Strutter and had shot it up sufficiently that he thought it was going to be forced to land within German lines. Unlike many another fighter pilot on both sides wanting to make sure of a kill even though his quarry was not going to make it home, Böhme refrained from delivering a *coup de grâce* (for an example of the ruthlessness often displayed in situations of this kind, see the descriptions of Manfred von Richthofen's 49th victory on April 29, 1917 that appear in many books on him). In following his quarry down, Böhme, for his charity, received a burst from the observer's gun which lodged a bullet in his left arm and what would have been his 13th victory escaped.

After getting patched up, it was decided that Böhme could be put to better use for the time being as an instructor at

The late air historian, A. Edward Ferko, provided the identifications of these aircraft, attributing both to Erwin Böhme. Albatros D.III 2119/16 with a dark "B" against a white (?) band is parked on the field of *Jastaschule 1* at Valenciennes during the time Böhme was an instructor there after his wounding on February 11, 1917. And, below, Albatros D.V 4578/17 whose view is thoughtlessly blocked by a captured Sopwith Triplane with now a light "B" against a dark band is parked at *Jasta Boelcke* sometime after Böhme took over its command on August 18, 1917. It is not known if this were the aircraft he was flying when shot down in flames and killed on November 29 that year. He fell in British lines in Flanders but the capture report failed to list a number for the craft. Perhaps the fire destroyed the evidence.

Jastaschule 1 at Valenciennes. Some consolation for this enforced vacation from the front came in the form of the Knight's Cross with Swords of the Royal House Order of Hohenzollern which was approved on March 12 and duly made the list of awards published in the *Militär-Wochenblatt* of March 24. There was some talk about his being named to lead *Jagdstaffel 11* when Manfred von Richthofen went on leave at the beginning of May but this came to naught, the temporary command devolving on Manfred's younger brother, Lothar. On June 24, the first of the permanent *Jagdgeschwadern* was ordered to be formed within the German 4th Army comprising *Jagdstaffeln 4, 6, 10* and *11* and the next day, *Rittmeister* Manfred *Freiherr* von Richthofen was named its commander. A new Commanding Officer for his old *Jasta 11* was wanted and a former member, the then *Leutnant* Kurt Wolff who had won the *Pour le Mérite* there and had been in charge of *Jasta 29* since May 6, was brought back and given the job. The opening at *29* was the break Böhme was hoping for. When he heard the news that he was to be its new leader, his joy was "colossal." He had worried that he might have been considered too old, and now about to turn 38 at the end of the month, well he might have. Böhme was to score only once in his new capacity, on July 14 although that same day he knew he had "winged" two other enemy planes but feared that they might have been out of the sight of ground observers, too far on the other side of the lines to be confirmed. And he was right; no credit for them was granted. On August 1, *Jasta 29* was moved up to Flanders and there on the 10th, Böhme was wounded a second time, this being a bullet that grazed the back of his right hand which would continue to hamper him for some time and cut down on his flying time. He had been attacking a two-seater out on an artillery shoot when an enemy fighter caught him from below.

It was on August 18 that Böhme got a telephone call ordering him to return to his beloved *Jasta Boelcke* and take charge. He was well aware of the hard times that had beset it in recent months and it was no longer the proud outfit that it once was. By this time, Walz had been long gone, first to *Jasta 34* on June 9 and then from the following month a complete change of scenery – to *Flieger-Abteilung 304b* in Palestine as its Commanding Officer. There Walz would redeem his reputation, winning the *Pour le Mérite* for his leadership and the respect of his British opponents (the Royal Air Force that is, not the authorities; Walz was taken prisoner on September 30, 1918, the day after General Edmund Allenby had launched a hugely successful attack on a 16-mile front against two Turkish armies; the authorities did not release him until November 30, 1919). The then *Leutnant* Otto Bernert, who had posted a spectacular record in *Jasta Boelcke* between March 19 and April 24, 1917 (14 aircraft and three balloons shot down including five planes on the 24th), was brought back from *Jasta 6* which he had been leading since departing *Jasta B* as Walz's replacement. He really should not have been given the tough job of restoring some luster to his old unit. He probably shouldn't even have been flying at all. He was worn out and under him, there was only one victory recorded and this by a man who had been aboard since February and whose first victory this was. Then Bernert badly injured himself in a crash while over-shooting a landing and Böhme got the call. Böhme turned *Jasta 29* over to another veteran, *Oberleutnant* Otto Schmidt, who had scored two victories in two-seaters and up to this time, four more as a fighter pilot (and who would end the war with a total of 19 and a failed nomination for the *Orden Pour le Mérite*).

In the short time Böhme had to shape up *Jasta Boelcke*, he did what all *Jasta* commanders were supposed to do, he led by example, scoring 11 times himself. Others under his wing did well too, most notably the later *Leutnant* Paul Bäumer who topped Böhme's tally by one on his way to his eventual 43 confirmed victories and a Golden Military Merit Cross and after being commissioned, a *Pour le Mérite* before the war's end. Table 4-3 shows the traceable victories scored by Böhme and his men between August 18, 1917 through November 29, 1917. The 34 victories in a 15-week period shown there was certainly a creditable performance and is evidence enough that Böhme was beginning to bring the unit back into a semblance of its old form. And exactly half of the 34 were scored during November when the weather was generally atrocious and in the words of the Royal Flying Corps communiqué for November 6-12, 1917, "the weather has been persistently bad for aerial work," and "during the period under review (13th to 19th inclusive) the weather has been unfavorable for aerial work" and, finally, "during the period under review (20th to 26th November inclusive) the weather has been very bad for flying." Seventeen confirmed victories in one month under such conditions shows that Böhme had indeed turned things around and were headed in the right direction. Of course, commendable as that performance was, it was nothing like a similar 15-week period from September 2, 1916 when Boelcke scored the unit's first victory, to December 13 by which time 82 victories had been achieved (21 by Boelcke himself before he was killed, 14 by Manfred von Richthofen, 46 by other members of the *Staffel* including Böhme's six plus one on September 27 that could not be individually assigned and was counted as a squadron victory). But the 34 victories in the August-November 1917 period compare quite favorably with the results realized by *Jasta Boelcke* in the 15 weeks between March 4 and June 16,

1917 which included the killing time of "Bloody April." Then, 42 victories had been confirmed but it needs to be noted that the majority of those, 34 of them, had been accounted for by the remarkable runs of just two men, Bernert and Voss, who got 17 apiece. Only four other pilots of the unit shared in the remaining eight victories. The picture is further distorted by the fact that all of the 34 downed by Bernert and Voss were scored in the first two months of the period. Bernert's last came on April 24 (his 5-in-1 day). Voss' last came on May 9. After they had left and until Böhme took over to resuscitate the once proud outfit, there was the long dry spell during which a scant three victories were all that could be shown for another near 15 weeks of flying.

Table 4-3
Victories Confirmed in *Jagdstaffel Boelcke*
Between August 18, 1917 through November 29, 1917

Name of Pilot and Highest Rank Held	Victories in the Period	Victories In the War
Lt. Paul Bäumer	12	43
Lt. Gerhard Bassenge	2	7
Lt. Erwin Böhme*	11	24
Lt. Carl Gallwitz	3	10
Lt. Fritz Kempf	1	4
Lt. Walter Lange	1	1
Lt. Max *Ritter* von Müller	3	36
Lt. Wilhelm Papenmeyer	1	4

* = Killed in Action During this Period

When Böhme reached the 20-victory level on October 16 and then added ones on October 31 and November 6, he would have been less than human if his thoughts were not on a *Pour le Mérite*. From Flanders on November 9, he wrote to his now fiancée about that in such a modest manner that it undoubtedly understated his true feelings about the award. The relative paragraph reads:

> You appear to be concerned that for your sake, ambition has seized me and I am chasing the Order of Merit. I have already amply earned the decoration in that I have conquered my Annamarie. Moreover, the award is now no longer so freely awarded as in the initial stages of the fighter detachments; Immelmann and Boelcke received it after their eighth victories and Richthofen after his sixteenth. Besides, all decorations possess for me only value in that they are an assessment of what I have done. So, for me it is actually immaterial whether I receive another medal or not. However, I would be happy to receive the Order of Merit because the award would constitute recognition of the valiant fighter detachment that I command.

Spoken like a true Commanding Officer in that, if the award came, it would honor not just himself but all the men of *Jasta Boelcke*. But Böhme could count. He would have known that the last air *Pour le Mérite* prior to his letter had gone to *Leutnant* Walter von Bülow-Bothkamp over in *Jasta 36* on October 8 when his score stood at 21. In fact, the matter was coming to a head on November 20 when he dispatched his 23rd and penultimate victim. Having worked its way through channels to *Kogenluft* and with their endorsement to the General Commission Dealing with Royal Prussian Orders, the proposal that Böhme receive the high award got the latter's endorsement around this time and a document would have been drawn up with his name, rank and unit entered in graceful script. All that was needed was the signature of Böhme's All-Highest War Lord, the *Kaiser*, to give him legal entitlement to the order. That came on November 24 and in situations of this kind when an immediate investiture was not possible, a telegram signed by *Kogenluft* himself, *Generalleutnant* Ernst von Hoeppner, would have been immediately dispatched to Böhme in the field with the badge following by post.

We have no record of Böhme's reaction to the award or even what kind of celebration ensued about it within the *Staffel*. But there must have been great joy by all, not the least the recipient himself who could take great pride in the fact that he was only the fourth airmen to actually earn the award in *Jasta Boelcke* after the three greats, Manfred von Richthofen, Werner Voss and Otto Bernert. But then, how do we account for the fact that in a flurry of correspondence dated on the evening of November 24 itself and again on the 26th, 27th and 28th all written to his intended, there is apparently no reference to the award at all? His last letter to his beloved Annamarie is the shortest of all and the most poignant:

> 29 November 1917
> My love! Now just a quick affectionate morning greeting! The detachment is already waiting for me. This evening I will write a proper letter to you.
>
> Your Erwin

One must also wonder if Böhme was delaying telling his Annamarie about his *Pour le Mérite* until the badge was actually in his hands which, as we will shortly see, would have been that very evening. But for Erwin Böhme, that evening would never come.

On his second patrol of the day on the 29th, over the devastated and sodden Flanders plain, near the ruins of what once was the village of Zonnebeke north of the now virtually treeless Polygon Wood, Böhme was credited with his 24th and final victory. It was a Sopwith Camel, just before 2:00 p.m. German Time (it should be noted, however, that the British showed no Camel losses at all that day). Böhme and two of his men were still milling about the area looking for more game when they came upon a lumbering Armstrong Whitworth F.K.8 two-seater taking photographs. In the lead, he dropped down on this inviting target. Royal Flying Corps Communiqué No. 116 gives the essential details of what followed:

> Enemy Aircraft - 2nd Lts J Pattern & P Leycester, 10 Squadron, were taking photographs when they were attacked by three Albatros scouts. The pilot opened fire with his forward gun, then manoeuvred in order to give his Observer a free field of fire, and after a short burst the leading EA burst into flames and crashed.

A fuller account of the action was given by John Pattern himself to a British author in an interview when Pattern was in his nineties shortly before his death. According to Pattern:

> About a quarter of a mile on the enemy side of the lines, I turned southeast and Leycester started to work his camera. The anti-aircraft fire, which had been intense, had stopped, but I didn't take much notice. I should have known better; it was a sure sign that enemy fighters were in the vicinity. Suddenly, I heard the clatter of Leycester's machine gun above the roar of the engine. I looked round to see what he was shooting at, and nearly had a heart attack. Slanting down from above, getting nicely into position 30 yards behind my tail, was an Albatros.
>
> I immediately heaved the old A.W. round in a split-arse turn, tighter I think than I had ever turned before. I felt a flash of panic as I lost sight of the Hun, but Leycester must have been able to see him all right as he kept on firing. My sudden turn had done the trick. The Albatros overshot and suddenly appeared right in front of me. Because of the relative motion of our two aircraft, he seemed to hang motionless, suspended in mid-air. I could see the pilot's face as he looked back at me.
>
> I sent a two-second burst of Vickers fire into him. His aircraft seemed to flutter, then slid out of sight below my starboard wing. I was pretty certain that I had hit his petrol tank. Behind me, Leycester was still blazing away. He was using tracer, and it may have been one of his bullets that ignited the petrol pouring from the Hun's ruptured tank. When I caught sight of the Albatros again, it was burning like a torch and side-slipping towards the ground, trailing a streamer of smoke. For an instant I saw the German pilot, looking down over the side of the cockpit. Then the smoke and flames enveloped him.

"Then the smoke and flames enveloped him." The death most feared by airmen. Böhme's Albatros D.Va fell in British lines. Before burial, his body was searched. A document clearly in reference to a German award was among the things found. It was of little consequence to those handling it but they could make out that it had something to do with an award by the *Kaiser* a few days before. It could well have been a copy of the telegram Böhme had received informing him of his award of the *Orden Pour le Mérite*, or even the actual telegram itself. The language of these announcements was pretty standard and Böhme's would probably have read something like this: "*Seine Majestät der Kaiser und König haben in Anerkennung Ihrer glänzenden Erfolge als Jagdflieger und Ihrer vorzüglichen Staffelführung Ihnen den Orden 'Pour le Mérite' zu verleihen geruht*" ("His Majesty The Emperor and King has in recognition of your outstanding successes as a fighter pilot and your excellent squadron leadership been pleased to bestow upon you the Order 'for Merit.'").

The wreckage of Böhme's aircraft became number G.92 on the British capture list but nothing was salved so complete was its destruction. Tributes to the fallen hero immediately flowed in. These have been quoted in the work done by *Dr.* Niedermeyer and Mr. Fant but because they say so much about the man (to say nothing of the flowery language of the day), and for those readers who may not have seen their excellent studies, they are not out of place here too.

From *Hauptmann* Helmuth Wilberg, *Kofl* of the German 4th Army:

> Army High Command, 4th Army
> Commander of Aviation
>
> At Headquarters, 30 November 1917
>
> Yesterday, at the head of the Boelcke Fighter Detachment, which was commanded by him, and after achieving his 24th victory, Lieutenant Böhme fell in an air combat on the other side of the front.
>
> Educated by his friend and leader, Boelcke, in the art of superior offensive skills, this magnificent, hard and battle-tested man, with singular energy and dogged effort, and unflustered by the heaviest losses in the Battle of Flanders, had the intelligence and judgement and fought to achieve new brilliance and laurels for the old crown of glory of the proud detachment.
>
> Inextricably bound with the history of the Boelcke Detachment, the name of Lieutenant Böhme, as well as

Right: Böhme came down in flames near the village of Zonnebeke on November 29, 1917. Zonnebeke is about five miles northeast of Ieper (in Flemish; to the British it was Ypres but it was always "Wipers" to the Tommies). Ypres was one of the most powerful towns in Flanders during the Middle Ages with a flourishing cloth industry. It was held by the British throughout the war.

Below: Not much to salve here. What is left of Sopwith Pup B.1800 attracts the usual onlookers. The 54 Squadron plane was shot down by Böhme on the morning of October 13, 1917 for his 18th confirmed victory. The officer in greatcoat is not identified but could it be Böhme himself? No.54 Squadron lost three other Pups that day to German pilots of other *Jagdstaffeln*.

every flier with the 4th Army, will remain as shining and never to be forgotten examples of manly virtue.

Wilberg
Commander of Aviation, 4th Army

And from *Generalleutnant* Ernst von Hoeppner:

Commanding Officer of the Imperial Air Force 30 November 1917

I extend my heartfelt sympathies to the Detachment over the death of their valiant leader. In spite of his advanced age, just like the youngest pilot, he wrested victory after victory from the enemy as the head of his trustworthy group of pilots.

By the highest decree of the Supreme Command, which itself did not reach our fallen soldier, he and his Detachment's service in the Battle of Flanders was honored through the bestowal of the Order for Merit upon Lieutenant Böhme.

He was the last of Boelcke's intimate circle of friends in the Detachment. His death renews our duty to preserve Boelcke's spirit.

The Commanding General of the Imperial Air Force v. Hoppner

And this to Böhme's brother, Gerhard, who was serving as a veterinarian officer in an artillery regiment from a man who already had known the loss of more than his share of old comrades:

Said to be the funeral ceremonies in the field of Erwin Böhme with the dramatic backdrop of the dismantled wings of an early Aviatik B.I or C.I. No *Ordenskissen* which might confirm that these rites were for the respected leader of *Jasta Boelcke* can be seen although the heavy overcoats on the two guards of honor fit in with a late November day. Some kind of decorative motif appears on the face of the coffin but what it might have been or if there were an inscription that might provide additional clues cannot be made out in the photograph. Böhme fell in British lines and his remains were buried there. So if these services were for him, the casket was just an empty symbol.

When Böhme's body was searched, the British troops on the scene found a communication addressed to him which they found largely unintelligible but they could make out that it had something to do with an award bestowed by the *Kaiser*. It could well have been the telegram from *Kogenluft* informing Böhme that his *Pour le Mérite* had been approved on November 24, 1917. The package with the badge itself had arrived in the squadron mail at *Jasta* "*B*" on the 29th, apparently just after he left on his last patrol. That afternoon, Böhme was credited with a Sopwith Camel for his 24th confirmed victory. But then he himself was brought down in flames when attacking an Armstrong Whitworth F.K.8 from No.10 Squadron, RFC. Among the many tributes flowing in was one from Manfred von Richthofen, his old comrade from *Kagohl 2* days who like Böhme, had been hand-picked by the famed Boelcke to become a fighter pilot. Von Richthofen, in writing one of Böhme's brothers, observed that now both "your splendid brother and the great master" were united in Valhalla, the great hall in Norse mythology where Odin receives and feasts the souls of heroes slain in battle.

In the Field, 1 December 1917
To Gerhard Böhme

I just received the painful news of the death of your brother. In war, one becomes hard and cold. However, his death has touched me very deeply – you yourself know how close a friend your brother was to me.

On the last afternoon before his death, he was here visiting me at Avesnes-le-Sec, my new airfield – full of joy over the development of our dear old Boelcke Detachment, which he had led solely and single-handedly to its old heights.

Leutnant Martin Böhme was a younger brother of Erwin and followed him into aviation, serving as an observer in the Giant aircraft of *Riesenflugzeugabteilung 501* which together with its sister *Rfa 500* cooperated in raids on England with the Gothas of *Kampfgeschwader/ Bombengeschwader 3*. Martin lost his life in the crash of Staaken R.VI (Aviatik) 34/16 in Flanders on April 21, 1918 after returning from an attack on St. Omer, 33 miles west of Ypres in Flanders. This portrait of Martin was painted by Professor Hans Kohlschein, the brother-in-law of a third Böhme son. The professor also did a rendering of Erwin in March 1917 when he was recuperating from the first of the two wounds he suffered in air combat.

Below: This is the Giant R.34 in which Martin Böhme crashed and three of the men who died with him. It came down at Westroosbeke in Flanders on April 21, 1918. Left to right, *Oblt.* Hans Strum, *Oblt.* Johannes Leistner and *Flieger* Peter Antoni. Along with them, three others also perished, all enlisted men. It has never been established whether the R.34 crashed due to battle damage or whether it was one of the landing accidents that plagued these huge ships. Martin baled out just before the crash and although his 'chute deployed, he was apparently too close to the ground to have it break his fall. When help reached him, he had already expired. Leistner, the R.34 commander, had received two Saxon awards for his earlier service in *Feldflieger-Abteilung* 59, its Albert Order Knight 2nd Class with Swords on September 15, 1915 and then its premier bravery order, the Military St. Henry Order in the Knight's Class on January 12, 1916.

Now they are both united in Valhalla: your splendid brother and his great master, who of us all was closest to him.

Please call on me soon dear Mr. Böhme, so that we may jointly remember and honor the deceased brother and friend.

With sincere condolences, your
Manfred Baron von Richthofen

When the disconsolate men of *Jasta Boelcke* returned to their field that Thursday afternoon following Böhme's fall, there was a final irony. In the unopened mail awaiting the Commanding Officer's attention, there was a package containing the *Pour le Mérite* he would never wear.

OBERLEUTNANT RICHARD FLASHAR

If Erwin Böhme, the subject of the previous biography, is largely remembered today as the man who collided in mid-air with Oswald Boelcke causing the latter to crash to his death, we can say that *Oberleutnant* Richard Flashar is a forgotten man. Forgotten because almost no one remembers that, along with his observer, he was given credit for the first officially confirmed German aerial victory of the war. Many World War I aviation books and articles still state that the first success of the Imperial German Army Air Service was scored by the crew of *Hauptmann* Hugo Geyer, pilot, and *Oberleutnant* Egburt Kühn, observer, of *Feldflieger-Abteilung 48*. On April 28, 1915 aboard their Aviatik B.192a/13, they shot down a French Voisin over Altkirch, 12 miles south of Mulhouse in Alsace. But there is an Army Order of the Day stating that Flashar and his observer, an *Oberleutnant* Demuth, had been victorious on November 5, 1914 and then later, the men received gold watches from the Inspectorate of Aviation commemorating the occasion. Even better, we have Flashar's account of the action which was published in his memoirs.

By November 1914, the Western Front had become nearly stabilized along a 400-mile trench line that ran from the North Sea to Switzerland although in what came to be called the First Battle of Ypres, the Germans were still trying to punch through the British Expeditionary Force and the tiny Belgian Army to capture the ports of Dunkirk and Calais. Farther south, on the morning of the 5th, the then *Leutnant* Flashar and Demuth were detailed to make a long range reconnaissance around Maux. It was a clear and warm day and when they reached their assigned altitude of 2,000 meters, about the maximum height for aircraft

Above: Looking more like a slightly overfed school master with his pince-nez rather than the respected *Jastaführer* that he was, *Oberleutnant* Richard Flashar wears a cluster of three awards in an unconventional but attractive arrangement, looping their ribbons through a buttonhole on the front of his tunic. Under his Knight's Hohenzollern and Iron Cross 2nd Class, his Brunswick War Merit Cross can be seen. The Hohenzollern dates the scene as sometime after February 1918

Below: No question about it. On the ground, the fliers often lived in comfort. Here is the manor house requisitioned for *Jasta 5* in Boistrancourt, some six miles to the east of Cambrai. Its field nearby was to be the *Staffel*'s home from March 11, 1917 to March 21, 1918.

Party time at *Jasta 5*. The men seem to be on their best behavior as they entertain three nursing sisters. Standing left to right: *Vzfw*. Dilcher, *Lt*. Strobel, *Offz.-Stv*. Löwensen, *Lt*. Schumann, and *Oblt*. Flashar. Seated left to right: an unknown visitor, possibly a doctor/chaperon from the hospital, *Lt*. Vorländer and *Lt*. Schulte. Sitting on the floor left to right: Lt. Büssing and *Offz.-Stv*. Sturm. Sprawled on the floor left to right: *Vzfw*. Könnecke and *Offz.-Stv*. Mai. The time is June 1917, right after Flashar was appointed *Jasta 5*'s Commanding Officer on June 10.

of that time, they could clearly observe the enemy road and rail traffic. They spent an undisturbed three hours in the air and mission accomplished, they turned towards their own lines, headed for the airfield of their *Feldflieger-Abteilung 33* at Loire Farm near Coney-le-Chateau. Above the roar of his engine, the crew suddenly heard a knocking sound. It stopped, then repeated itself, stopped again and then was heard once more. Naturally disturbed, the men looked over the entire plane but everything seemed to be in order with the engine still running at full power with a steady throb. Flashar then turned around to see if something might have been wrong with the rudder (as the pilot of a two-seater, he at this time was seated in the rear cockpit with his observer in front of him). Much to his surprise and shock, he found a French Parasol-Type not two plane lengths away with its cockades looming large. They were under attack and the knocking sounds had been bullets from a carbine which the enemy observer was manning as they had slapped into the Aviatik.

Flashar, like all the pilots that early on, had no experience in air-to-air fighting but he instinctively banked to get out of the line of fire and this alerted Demuth to the situation. When Flashar straightened out, he found the Frenchman still glued to their tail. Demuth then came to life and got off a string of shots with the rifle he had (wisely) carried aloft. At that, the enemy plane disappeared and they found nothing but empty sky. There was nothing to do now but land. Upon touching down, they were met with a huge welcome. The action had taken place near their airfield and it had been followed through binoculars by their anxious comrades who had figured they were goners. Demuth's shots had somehow taken effect and the French aircraft had crashed in a field about three kilometers away, its engine buried deeply into the ground. The German 1st Army Order of the day said in part:

> On 5 November 1914, Senior Lieutenant Demuth, in an aircraft piloted by Lieutenant Flashar, shot down a French

Now the field hospital of the German 2nd Army returns the favor and entertains men of *Jasta 5* and others on July 10, 1917. Flashar is 5th from the left. The officer standing to his lower left, probably another doctor, wears two pin-back awards below his Iron Cross 1st Class which appear to be the Mecklenburg-Schwerin Military Merit Cross 1st Class (above) and the Oldenburg Friedrich August Cross 1st Class.

> aircraft on our side of the lines. For their victorious air battle, I express my recognition to both men.
>
> (Signed) von Kluck

There were no *Ehrenbechers* at that stage of the war (they would come in around Christmas of 1915 when Flashar, and presumably Demuth as well, received one of the first of these victory goblets) and unless the crew received the Iron Cross 2nd Class of which there is no mention, *Generaloberst* Alexander von Kluck's praise and official recognition by the air service for their victory was all that they received at the time. Then, according to Flashar, later in 1916, a wealthy Cologne citizen, inspired by the many air victories of Boelcke and Immelmann, made a proposal to the High Command that he would donate a certain sum of money to any flier upon the occasion of downing his first enemy plane. This idea was rejected politely on the basis that a stipend to the military for doing their job was out of the question but suggested that the money go to needy dependents of fliers who had fallen. As further balm for any wounded feelings the would-be donor might have had, he was told that the two officers who had scored the first German aerial victory would be given "an honorary gift" by the Inspectorate of Aviation. And so it was that on Christmas 1916, Flashar received a gold watch suitably inscribed to him as the pilot of the first victorious German aircraft followed by the date of the action. It was his second *Ehrenbecher* one might say.

Flashar was a Regular in the German Army having been commissioned in June of 1911 in *4. Hannoversches Infanterie-Regiment Nr.164* whose 3rd Battalion was quartered in Erwin Böhme's home town of Holzminden and whose staff and its other two battalions were located in Hameln, 30 miles away. At some undetermined date before the war, he completed his pilot training and flew with *Feldflieger-Abteilung 33* from the opening days of the war (perhaps he was lucky in that; 12 of his old regiment's prewar officers were killed in action in the first two months of the war). The photograph here clearly shows his Brunswick War Merit Cross, a product, no doubt, of his old affiliation and although the date of its award is not known, it was clearly an air award. By 1916, during the summer of which he was promoted *Oberleutnant*, Flashar was in command of

Above: *Jasta 5* at full strength with 16 of their gaily decorated machines at Boistrancourt in July 1917. The Albatros 5th from the left carries a stylized dragon in red on its fuselage. This was Albatros D.V 2065/17 which was used at first by Flashar when he assumed command of the unit.

Below: *Offz.-Stv.* Karl Bey, the stout fellow between the two captured RFC airmen, achieved his first and only air victory on October 17, 1917 when he brought down Bristol F2b A.7231 of No.11 Squadron and then entertained his "guests" at the Boistrancourt field. Flashar is to the right of the captured British pilot. Bey would be killed in action on November 23, 1917. Another "stout fellow" is in this picture, *Vzfw.* Fritz Rumey, at the extreme right, had been wounded in the thigh in a combat on September 24 but, obviously, was back in action by now. The Bristol was used as a squadron hack and probably was the one that with the addition of German national markings, had the words *Nicht Schiessen Gute Leute* ("Don't Shoot Good People") lettered prominently on its upper wing.

Above: Flashar was visited by Manfred von Richthofen on at least two occasions in March 1918 probably, as air historian Alex Imrie points out, to discuss the operational deployment of fighters in the German offensive about to start. Here at Boistrancourt on March 13, Richthofen, with a slight bow, exchanges salutes and makes eye contact with one of Flashar's men (possibly Fritz Rumey). Flashar, with glasses, is just behind the Baron. The officer 2nd from the right is *Lt.* Wilhelm Lehmann who took over *Jasta 5* when Flashar was given the command of *Jagdgruppe 2* and who was killed on June 26. The Albatros D.V behind the men was an ex-*Jasta 4* machine and does not have the unit's distinctive red outline on its rudder although it could be overpainted green. The rudder of the aircraft next in line which can just be seen appears to have the green and red combination which made the "Green-Tails" of *Jasta 5* so famous on the Western Front.

Opposite
Top: *Lt.* Hans Joachim von Hippel inherited Flashar's Albatros D.V 2065/17, the "Dragon Machine," and on February 18, 1918, while in combat with elements of No.56 Squadron, RFC, lost his lower right wing at 13,500 feet. By some miracle, he was able to bring it down to a landing at Folie Farm where it ground looped as seen here. Von Hippel emerged unscathed. The *Jasta 5* War Diary reports that Manfred von Richthofen shepherded von Hippel down, protecting him from further attack. A pensive Flashar, in light tunic, poses with his old bird while von Hippel looks on.

Bottom: Flashar's later mount, an Albatros D.V, with a mailed fist personal marking and the straight, or Balkan, crosses, making this sometime after March 1918. The *Jasta 5* War Diary makes no reference to a crash by Flashar but perhaps the slight nosing over was not worthy of mention. It does seem rather late, however, for a *Staffelführer* to be saddled with an old D.V.

Kampfstaffel 8 of *Kampfgeschwader 2* so he shared in the Russian adventure described in the previous biography on Erwin Böhme. Just when Flashar made his conversion to a fighter pilot is just another of many things we do not know about the man but he shows up in the War Diary of *Jagdstaffel 5* as coming into that unit as its *Staffelführer* on June 10, 1917.

Those who have been reading this book sequentially will recall that the hot shot Werner Voss with 28 victories and a *Pour le Mérite* had been practically a one man show in *Jasta Boelcke* along with Otto Bernert in the first half of 1917. Fed up with what he perceived as the lackluster performance of his Commanding Officer, Franz Walz, he took his case to the higher-ups, angling for the job himself. He had a co-conspirator in the attempted coup, a young nobleman, *Leutnant* Rolf *Freiherr* von Lersner. This circumvention of military protocol could not go unpunished but what to do? Obviously, von Lersner's case was simple. He was transferred out and made to suffer the indignity of being returned to a two-seater unit from whence he came (and where, in *Kagohl 3* on August 25, 1917, he was killed). But one could hardly treat a *Pour le Mérite* man with a record like Voss' that way. There was an opening in *Jasta 5* that needed filling. The 38-year old leader there, *Hauptmann* Hans von Hünerbein had been killed on May 4 in the fiery crash of an aircraft he was testing. So Voss was sent there, ironically getting a command after all.

In *Jasta 5*, Voss continued his torrid pace, adding six more victories in rapid succession which brought his score to 34 by June 6. Then, abruptly and surprisingly, the rug was pulled out from underneath him. The order cut on June 10 appointing Flashar as *Jasta 5*'s new boss also transferred Voss to *Jasta 14* but only as Acting Leader. Another put-down was the fact that of all the 24 *Jagdstaffeln* that had been mobilized in 1916, *Jasta 14* at this time had the poorest scoring record of them all (and would retain that dubious distinction until the end of the war). As is well known, however, Voss' stay in this sort of purgatory was to be very brief. On July 30, he got back a top command when he took over Manfred von Richthofen's *Jasta 10* from the aforementioned Ernst *Freiherr* von Althaus. There Voss would go on to score 14 more victories himself and pass into legend when he died in a one-sided combat with crack pilots of No.56 Squadron, RFC on September 23, 1917.

As the leader of *Jasta 5* for the nearly one year that he was to hold that post, Flashar proved to be no better in the scoring department than Walz had been in *Jasta Boelcke*. He, too, would add only one victory as a fighter pilot. This came on September 19 when he and a young charge, *Leutnant* Rudolf Matthaei (about whom we will hear more in the next biography), each downed Moranes from No. 3 Squadron, RFC said to be out on training flights in the Cambrai area. For Flashar, it was a BB-Type biplane. For Matthaei, it was a P-Type single-wing Parasol. The difference between Flashar and Walz must have been in leadership. Under Flashar's tutelage, three of the greatest German fighter pilots of the war saw their careers begin and then flourish. There would have been a fourth, too, had the man not been transferred out of *Jasta 5* just as he got started. The three were Fritz Rumey, Otto Könnecke and Josef Mai. The fourth was Paul Bäumer. All four were decorated with Prussia's Golden Military Merit Cross as non-commissioned officers and after being commissioned, three received the *Orden Pour le Mérite* and the fourth would have had the war lasted just a bit longer. Table 4-4 tabulates this picture when *Jasta 5* was under the direct command of Flashar from June 10, 1917 to May 12, 1918, the day, incidentally, when the Golden Military Merit Crosses to Rumey and Könnecke were approved.

Proof, if proof were needed, that Flashar was highly regarded despite a meager victory record came in the form of a Knight's Cross with Swords to the Royal House Order of Hohenzollern that was announced in the *Militär-Wochenblatt* of February 19, 1918. Ordinarily, a fighter pilot, even a *Staffelführer*, had to have a more respectable score to earn the award this late in the war. Recognition via greater command responsibilities also came Flashar's way when on that May 12, he was named the head of *Jagdgruppe 2*, a temporary tactical grouping of *Jagdstaffeln* that comprised *Jastas 5, 34, 37* and *42*. And with this bigger job and even though *Jasta 5* still reported to him, Flashar's name disappears from its War Diary and we lose track of him for the rest of the war.

Table 4-4
Victories Under the Direct Command of *Oblt.* Richard Flashar in *Jagdstaffel 5* During the Period June 10, 1917 and May 12, 1918
(Total Victories in the War Shown in Brackets)

Pilot	Victories	Golden Military Merit Cross	Orden Pour le Mérite
Vzfw./Lt. Fritz Rumey	17 (45)	May 12, 1918	July 10, 1918
Vzfw./Lt. Otto Könnecke	14 (35)	May 12, 1918	September 26, 1918
Offz.-Stv./Lt. Josef Mai	11 (30)	June 24, 1918	Proposed Too Late
Vzfw./Lt. Paul Bäumer	3 (43)	February 12, 1918	November 2, 1918

Above: Von Richthofen is back again at *Jasta 5* on March 17 flying in with Fokker Dr.1 525/17, a *Jasta 6* machine. He is talking directly to *Lt.* Hans Joachim von Hippel and Flashar is 2nd from the right. The mechanic seems pleased to be privy to the conversation. Von Richthofen scored no victories in 525/17.

Below: After a year stationed at Boistrancourt near Cambrai, *Jasta 5* moved to the airfield near Cappy on the Somme and began operations there in late April 1918. The men are, left to right: Oppenhost, Könnecke, Lehmann, Trieber, Zettelmayer (*Jagdgruppe* 2 Adjutant), Flashar, Schaumberg (*Jasta 5* Adjutant), Rath, Schlömer, Mai, von Hippel, Rumey and Voigt. No more manor house like at Boistrancourt though. Cappy, a dreary place, was an advance field made necessary by the German offensive along the Somme that had kicked off on March 21. It was from Cappy that Manfred von Richthofen took off on his last flight exactly a month later. Here the men lived in Quonset huts.

Above: *Jasta 5* got its first triplanes on May 9, 1918. They were machines from *Jagdgeschwader Nr.1* which was being re-equipped with the new Fokker D.VII. *Jasta 5* had to make do with these leftovers, until they got their own D.VIIs and by August, according to Alex Imrie, few, if any, triplanes were on strength at *Jasta 5*. Flashar is in the light tunic in this earlier scene at Boistrancourt.

RITTMEISTER HANS-ACHIM VON GRONE

As a son of a retired *Generalmajor*, Hans-Achim von Grone's profession seems to have been decided for him when, at age 17, he was inducted into *Braunschweigisches Husaren-Regiment Nr.17*. as a *Fahnenjunker* at the end of March 1908. There he gained his Lieutenancy in January 1910 and it was with them that he rode off to war in 1914. The stalemated Western Front by the end of that year had little use for mounted horsemen and von Grone found more interesting employment as an infantry officer, first with the 73rd Infantry Regiment in October and then with Oldenburg's 91st Infantry Regiment in January and February of 1915. That latter connection resulted in the award of Oldenburg's Friedrich August Cross 2nd Class in February as well as an Iron Cross 2nd Class, evidence that his performance must have been exemplary. But almost immediately after that recognition, a change from the ground war occurred.

At the beginning of March that year, von Grone was assigned to *Feldflieger-Abteilung 21* in some kind of non-flying capacity. It was enough, however, to whet his appetite for more than just a ground job in the *Fliegertruppe*. He reported first to *Flieger-Ersatz-Abteilung 4* at Posen in mid-June and then was at *FEA 5* at Hanover by late July, training to become an observer. In those early years, the course was a short one and he was off to a front line posting by August by way of the *Armee-Flug-Park* for the German South Army at Lemburg, the chief city of West Ukraine in the northern foothills of the Carpathian Mountains (today the city's name is Lvov). On August 16, he joined *Feldflieger-Abteilung 24* and two days later got the good news that he had been promoted *Oberleutnant*, not bad for a youth who would celebrate his 25th birthday the next day. Von Grone was to have a fairly long stint with *54* in East Galicia which lasted until the end of November 1916. During his tour there, he, like many of the German airmen on the Eastern Front, received the Field Pilot's Badge from his Austrian allies, his coming on December 16, 1915 (despite its official name, the badge went equally to pilots and observers; it was not until later in the war under Emperor Karl that Austria created a separate badge for observers). Before von Grone left the front and returned to Germany for home leave and reassignment, another award came his way, the Friedrich Cross from Anhalt. One might ask: Why would a son of Brunswick one of whose pre-air service regimental patrons was the Grand Duke of Oldenburg also be decorated by Anhalt? The answer may be geography. Von Grone was born in the village of Ballenstedt which was Brunswick territory. But literally next door lay land belonging to the Duchy of Anhalt. So it may well have been a case of Anhalt merely recognizing a "good neighbor."

Von Grone's leave was up on New Year's Day 1917 and for four months, he put in a stint at *Idflieg* in Berlin. There, on February 28, two years to the month after his service in the 91st Infantry had earned him the Oldenburg Friedrich August Cross 2nd Class, he added the 1st Class of the decoration to his

A veteran of more than 14 months of flying as an observer with *Feldflieger-Abteilung 54* in East Galicia from mid-summer 1915 to the end of November 1916, *Rittmeister* Hans-Achim von Grone makes a dashing figure in his 17th Brunswick "Death's Head" Hussar uniform with its frogged tunic, yellow striped breeches and gleaming boots. His Iron Cross 1st Class dates the photograph sometime after July 1916 when he received it. Yet to come, however, is his Brunswick War Merit Cross awarded in 1917. See text for details on the other awards that are present here. He was captured in Turkey in July 1917 and interned for the rest of the war. Below, men of *FFl.Abt. 54* are joined by Austrian comrades for a pleasant social. On the floor, 4th from the right, is *Leutnant* Leopold Anslinger who scored eight of his 10 confirmed victories in *54* and its successor unit, *Flieger-Abteilung 24*, in 1916 and 1917. Von Grone, with eyes closed and smiling demurely, is seated at far left.

chest. He was soon slated to go back on active duty however, this time seconded to Germany's other ally, Turkey. On the eve of his departure for that assignment, his own people finally got around to recognizing him with the Brunswick War Merit Cross on April 25. His appointment in the Turkish Army moved him up to *Hauptmann* in their service, effective on May 5, and within the week he was off on the long overland journey to Constantinople. Von Grone joined Turkish *Flieger-Abteilung 2* which was serving with the 6th Turkish Army in the Tigris and Euphrates plain. Regular missions began with nothing much of consequence to report until July 10, 1917. A routine flight by two German aircraft turned out to be anything but that unfortunately.

Von Grone was in one of the planes along with his pilot, Arnold Hopff (a *Vizefeldwebel* according to von Grone but listed as just a *Flieger* (Private in the aviation troop) in German records). The other was manned by *Leutnant* Walter Teich and his pilot, an *Unteroffizier* Dürre. They had taken off from Ramadi, a position on the Euphrates occupied by the Turks, and were to reconnoiter the desert between the Euphrates and the Tigris before completing their flight at Tikrit. Their route was northeast of Ramadi and after passing over Lake Tharthar, a water line on Teich's plane burst and they had to make a hurried landing in the wasteland. Bravely, von Grone ordered Hopff to land alongside. Repairs were effected and both aircraft took off again, only to have Teich's machine seize up again moments into the flight and into a second forced landing with the faithful von Grone and Hopff following them down a second time. Nothing could be done with the other plane now and rather than leave it for possible salvage by the enemy, it was burned. Teich and Dürre lashed themselves to the lower wing of von Grone's aircraft and with the extra weight, Hopff was only able to reach an altitude of 150 meters before his aircraft developed engine trouble too and they were forced down. Now they were somewhere southwest of the ancient town of Samarra. It was impossible to get the plane off the ground again and the foursome faced a dreadful prospect. It was still only 9:00 in the morning and the fierce heat of the day was coming on.

What they had already experienced left the men in a state of exhaustion and there was little choice but to attempt to find some shade under the wings of their plane, rest up and wait until the sun was lower before pushing on. By 4:00 in the afternoon, their canteens had been drained and what warm water that remained in the engine had been consumed. The sun set three hours later and after setting their plane on fire too, the wretched men set off in an attempt to reach some form of civilization. After an hour's march, Teich and Hopff were in a state of collapse and could go no further. Von Grone and Dürre had no choice but to leave their two comrades with the promise that if they made it, they would send help. The two set off again around 8:00 p.m., making only slow progress. They would walk for 20 minutes, then rest for another 20 before struggling on. Daybreak found them near Samarra where they were picked up, weak and about ready to collapse totally, by a British patrol. A rescue party was sent out to look for Teich and Hopff but to no avail. Later, they were declared legally dead (although German casualty lists carry their demise as July 9, 1917, it obviously had to be two, probably three, days after that).

From Samarra, von Grone and Dürre were taken to Baghdad and from there, they were transported by boat down the Tigris to the port city of Basra. There they were turned over to the Arabs and interned for two weeks in a prisoner-of-war pen. An Arabian prisoner-transport steamer then took them through the Persian Gulf to Bombay where they were interned for the rest of the war in a German camp at Magar near Poona (Pune) in west central India. Von Grone, in his account of their last flight and capture, makes no mention of the rigors of his captivity but the sea journey from Mesopotamia (today, modern Iraq) to India at the height of summer in the hold of an Arab ship must have been a special kind of hell. With the Treaty of Versailles signed at the end of June 1919, German prisoners began to be repatriated. For von Grone and Dürre, this meant another long journey, from Bombay by ship to Port Said in Egypt and thence from there to Rotterdam where they walked across the German border at Wesel and home at last. They had, at least, survived and while von Grone was not given the consolation of receiving the Brunswick War Merit Cross in the 1st Class, he did, at least, have the satisfaction of knowing his countrymen had not completely forgotten him. While in captivity, in September 1918, he was promoted *Rittmeister* in the German Army.

LEUTNANT GEORG VON HANTELMANN

When people talk about the young German fighter pilot aces of the First World War, the name that first comes to the minds of most is Werner Voss, Manfred von Richthofen's nearest scoring rival, who was killed in a spectacular air battle on September 23, 1917, just five months past his 20th birthday. Others might remember the *Pour le Mérite* 40-victory heavy hitter, Franz Büchner, or the cocky and none-too-popular-with-his-men Kurt Wüsthoff with his 27 victories. Büchner was 20 when the war ended and Wüsthoff, then in a French prisoner of war camp, 21. Some might come up with the name of Oliver *Freiherr* von Beaulieu-Marconnay known for the deathbed

The skull and crossbones between the imperial German and Prussian cockades on the service cap of *Leutnant* Georg von Hantelmann mark him as a former member of one of the "Death's Head" hussar regiments, in his case, the 17th Brunswick Hussars. Von Hantelmann emerged from flying school in February 1918 to go directly into fighters, joining *Jasta 18*. When the *Pour le Mérite* ace, Rudolf Berthold, was appointed the leader of *Jagdgeschwader 2* in March 1918, Berthold demanded that the entire band of *Jasta 18* pilots be transferred to *Jasta 15*, one of the four elements of *JG 2*. Von Hantelmann was one of them and with *Jasta 15*, scored 25 victories before war's end.

Below: Men of *Jasta 18* just before the transfer are shown below. Von Hantelmann is standing at the extreme left in the top row. The date is between March 8 and March 10, 1918 due to the presence of Hans-Joachim Buddecke, third from the right in the first row. Berthold, with arm in sling from his October 1917 wounding, brought Buddecke over from *Jasta 30* to assist him in running *Jasta 18* in the air. Buddecke lost his life in an air combat on March 10.

Pour le Mérite he received on express orders of the *Kaiser*. He had celebrated his own 20th birthday the month before when he was seriously wounded by errant shots from a Fokker D.VII of *Jasta 74* in a combat on October 18, 1918 while he was after a Spad for what would have been his 26th victory. He died on October 28 (so rapid had been his scoring, 15 enemy planes credited to him between August 11 and October 10, that when he got his *Pour le Mérite*, he did not have the customary intermediate Hohenzollern House Order, one of only a handful of German pilots who did not when the higher award came). Another nemesis to the American aero squadrons in the closing weeks of the war was the *Jasta 6* commander, Ulrich Neckel. He, too, was only 20 when he closed out his victory string of 30 on November 6, 1918 and two days later, received the second to last air award of the *Pour le Mérite* (the last air award of the order and the last award of the order in its military form for all time went to another 30 victory man the next day, Carl Degelow). But chances are pretty good that almost no one would come up with the name of Georg von Hantelmann, the youngest of all these men. His victories, 25 in all with another five unconfirmed, puts him in their league but the fact that the proposal for his *Pour le Mérite* came too late for it to be acted upon before the *Kaiser*'s abdication lost him his place on that list and the fame that went with it.

Like the man in the preceding biography, von Hantelmann joined the 17th Brunswick Hussars as a cadet or officer aspirant in February of 1916 serving with them until September 4, 1917 when he secured a transfer to the air service. During that time, on June 15, 1917 and not yet 19, he was commissioned *Leutnant*. After pilot training and unlike the situation prevailing before, he did not put in any front line duty in a two-seater formation but, instead, went directly into fighters, joining *Jasta 18* on February 6, 1918. *Jasta 18* was under the command of *Oberleutnant* Ernst Turck who had taken over after the 1916 *Pour le Mérite* ace, the then *Oberleutnant* Rudolf Berthold had taken a bullet in his upper right arm on October 10, 1917 and had been out of things ever since. But this was about to change. On March 15, 1918, the first leader of the second *Jagdgeschwader, Hauptmann* Adolf *Ritter* von Tutschek, was killed. Even though his arm was still in a sling and he was not fit for combat flying, Berthold, now a *Hauptmann* himself, was fit to command. *Jagdgeschwader Nr.2* was comprised of *Jastas 12, 13, 15* and *19*. Berthold was not about to leave the men of his old *Jasta 18* however. And such was his standing with *Kogenluft* that he got his way. In a move unheard of before and never repeated, a wholesale transfer took place. The men of *Jasta 15* under a just-appointed *Leutnant* August Raben went to *Jasta 18* and the men of *Jasta 18*, von Hantelmann included, under Turck became the. new *Jasta 15*.

For his service in the 17th Hussars, von Hantelmann had picked up an Iron Cross 2nd Class in April 1917 and in September that year, as he was making the transition from trooper to flier, he was decorated by Brunswick with its War Merit Cross. Then, with the requisite number of front line flights in his log, he was able to pin on his Pilot's Badge in April 1918. That was all well and good but breaking into the victory column would prove that he had really earned it. And he thought he had done just that, finally, on May 29 when he put in for a Spad but the claim was not allowed. June was a totally different story. He ended the month with the impressive figure of five confirmed victories to his name. His third, scored on June 12, however, apparently escaped to fight another day. He and a wingmate, von Beaulieu-Marconnay, both were credited with a Camel apiece in the Compiegne area that day. No.43 Squadron, RAF had two of their Camels engaged in combat with German fighters in the area on the 12th but were only shot up and they returned all right with unwounded pilots.

July, on the other hand, turned out to be a disappointing month with nothing to show for his endeavors and August was only slightly better with a sixth victory on the 17th (if, in fact, von Hantelmann was at the front all this time and not away on leave during part of the time; he was not recuperating from injuries either so far as we know; he was to be very slightly wounded on September 18 but so slightly that it hardly affected his performance that month). September was to be von Hantelmann's finest month with 12 planes downed, nine of them Spads. Sleuthing by Norman Franks and his crew, first with their *Above the Lines* and then in subsequent efforts like *Who Downed the Aces in WWI?*, point to von Hantelmann accounting for some well known figures in his bag that month. On September 12, he killed the U.S. 139th Aero Squadron's David Putnam. Putnam, 13 victories, had been flying with the French since December 1917 before transferring to the U.S. Air Service. With *MS 156* and *Spa 38*, he had been credited

Opposite
Top: Von Hantelmann (with cane) in *Jasta 15* sometime after June 1918 when he earned the Iron Cross 1st Class. The others, from left to right with total victories in brackets, are: Unknown, *Lt.* Oliver *Freiherr* von Beaulieu-Marconnay (25), von Hantelmann, *Lt.* Hugo Schäfer (11) and *Vzfw.* Hermann Margot (0). Schäfer, too, was from the hussars but his regiment has not been determined.

Bottom: Von Hantelmann regularly flew this Fokker D.VII 2469/18 with its *Jasta 15* Prussian blue fuselage and red nose on which he symbolically placed the skull and crossbones. But on June 17, 1918, the *Pour le Mérite* ace, *Lt.* Kurt Wüsthoff having just taken command of the unit the day before, borrowed (expropriated?) von Hantelmann's ship and was shot down wounded and taken prisoner.

Above: *Lt.* Josef Veltjens, just over Berthold's right shoulder, celebrates his 20th victory on June 11, 1918, here seated under the nose of his Fokker D.VII that carried his famous winged arrow personal marking. Veltjens would get his *Pour le Mérite* on August 16, the day of his 29th and 30th victories. Von Hantelmenn, seated at Veltjens' right, directs a smirk at the admiring crowd behind the photographer.

Below: Now it is von Hantelmann's turn. His 20th came on October 9, 1918. Apparently, the ground crew prepared a different wreath for each man since the lettering "20" here is just a bit different than Veltjens'. The locale is *Jasta 15*'s field at Charmois near Stenay where the unit took a fierce toll of the Americans. Left to right, *Vzfw*. Klaudat, *Lt*. Glöcklen, *Lt*. von Ziegasar, *Lt*. Veltjens (with *Pour le Mérite*), von Hantelmann, *Lt*. Schäfer (who scored his 11th this day) and *Vzfw*. Weischer. Von Hantelmann was proposed for the *Pour le Mérite* too late for it to be approved.

officially with nine victories but may have had as many as 15 unconfirmed claims including an incredible four unconfirms on June 5 (plus one confirmed) and three on June 14 (none confirmed). Then four days later, on September 16, the fifth ranking French ace with 35 victories, Maurice Boyau who moments before had burned his 20th observation balloon, went down under von Hantelmann's guns. On the 18th, it was the close friend (and perhaps the only friend) of the top American balloon buster, Frank Luke. He was Joseph Wehner, another 139th pilot, who was something of a balloon specialist too (five of his six victories were enemy gas bags). As is well known, Luke, in reprisal for Wehner's loss, went on a real tear. After sharing two balloons on the 18th with Wehner before he was killed that day, Luke destroyed three more of these heavily defended targets, followed up with two more on the 28th and three the following day before being brought down in German lines by ground fire and where he died either from his wounds or, as most people believe, by German soldiers when he refused to surrender to them and opened fire with his .45.

On the day that von Hantelmann scored his 21st victory, October 18, he was notified that he had been awarded the Knight's Cross with Swords of the Royal House Order of Hohenzollern. After adding two more victories within the following week, his name was put forward for the *Orden Pour le Mérite* on October 31. The month also saw his getting the Brunswick War Merit Cross 1st Class. While his *Pour le Mérite* proposal was just beginning to work its way through official channels, von Hantelmann scored his 25th and last victory of the war on November 4. Time was running out for the Germans and for his chance at the glittering blue and gold badge so sought after by every German fighter pilot. The *Kaiser* abdicated on November 9, finally faced with the fact that he no longer had the support of the army he thought would never desert their All-Highest War Lord. On the 10th having been granted refuge by a fellow Knight of the *Johanniter Orden*, his train crossed the border into Holland. Von Hantelmann's proposal for the award and for all those like his that had been languishing on the desks of the bureaucrats at the Royal Prussian General Orders Commission in Berlin came to naught without the *Kaiser* to give his blessing. In the immediate postwar atmosphere, the new German government was not about to sanction the further awarding of Prussian orders (but retrospective awards of the Iron Cross continued until 1924) so if von Hantelmann petitioned for the approval of his award as so many of these men did, it fell on deaf ears.

LEUTNANTE GÜNTHER AND JÜRGEN LÜDEKE

In the section that covers recipients of the Brunswick War Merit Cross without full biographies, we will meet the three flying von Bülow-Bothkamp brothers, Conrad, Harry and Walter. Other brothers served in the *Fliegertruppe* together, sometimes in the same units as Harry and Walter von Bülow did and as did the Baden-born twins, Anton and Johann Dierle, dual winners on the same date of the Grand Duchy's Silver Karl Friedrich Military Merit Medal, its highest bravery tribute to non-commissioned officers (see Volume VI in this series for their stories). Of course, the most famous example of siblings flying together in the war were the two von Richthofens, Manfred and Lothar. Here are two more, Günther and Jürgen Lüdecke, born two years apart in the small village of Hornburg in the District of Wolfenbüttel south of the capital city of Brunswick. Jürgen was the elder, 19 years of age when the war broke out and both did their pre-air service duty in the 17th Brunswick Hussars, Jürgen entering the regiment in October 1913 with the usual starting rank of *Fahnenjunker* (for a man slated for a commission if he proved out) and Günther following on August 2, 1914, the day Germany demanded the right from Belgium to cross their land in executing the von Schlieffen Plan and both Germany and Russia invaded each other's borders in the east. Günther was just 17. Although there are a number of parallels in their wartime careers, what we know about that will be told separately, beginning with Jurgen.

Jürgen Lüdeke secured his transfer to the air service in December 1916 and reported to an *Armee-Flug-Park* near Cambrai already the recipient of three decorations, the Iron Cross 2nd Class (August 28, 1914), the Brunswick War Merit Cross (November 3, 1914) and the Austrian Military Merit Cross 3rd Class with War Decoration (July 14, 1915). He had been promoted *Leutnant* by the middle of February 1915 so having earned an early Iron Cross and the comparable award from his home state as a mere *Fähnrich* was testimony enough of his early promise. From Cambrai Lüdeke was sent to the observer's school that operated in conjunction with the fighter school at Valenciennes and passed that with flying colors (to use an expression) so that by February 1917, he was ready for the front. He drew *Flieger-Abteilung (A)254*, one of two Prussian, one Saxon and one Württembergian two-seater units that had been mobilized the previous December. These were in addition to the six similar Prussian and one Saxon formations that had come on stream just the month before in the reorganization and expansion of the *Luftstreikräfte* that had begun in October 1916 under the new team of *Generalleutnant*

Ernst von Hoeppner and his Chief-of-Staff, the then *Oberstleutnant* Hermann von der Lieth-Thomsen. Lüdeke came to *(A)254* at a propitious time as these units now became the main aviation element for infantry and artillery cooperation. With the Allied spring offensives at Arras, along the Chemin des Dames and in Champagne where *(A)254* was operating in the offing, plenty of action could be expected.

According to the précis of Jürgen Lüdeke's wartime service that appears in the regimental history of the 17th Hussars, he was credited with three aerial victories and it is also stated that he was forced down in German lines three times, once with his aircraft on fire and once with a severely wounded pilot. On none of these occasions was he himself injured however. Of the three victories, only one can be traced. This occurred on August 20, 1917. Up to that time, again as far as it is able to ascertain, there had been two previous victories by *(A)254* crews. The first came on June 27, 1917 when a *Leutnant* Laurisch and a *Leutnant* Thiele were credited with a Spad at Berry au Bac, between Reims and Laon, for their first victories. The other was on the 12th of August when a *Leutnant* Henninger and his pilot, a *Gefreiter* Schuk, got another Spad near Bethelainville. Then came Lüdeke's one traceable victory on the 20th, still another Spad, this one in the vicinity of Chattancourt for which he and a *Flieger* Mertinascht, his pilot, received official credit. The team of Laurisch and Thiele were also successful again that day. A pair of victories within the same two-seater unit in a single day was hardly a common event.[2] In fact, August 20 was quite a day for the entire Imperial German Air Service. On the Western Front, mostly in the area around besieged Verdun where the French launched a massive counterattack that very day which penetrated German defenses to a depth of 2,000 yards, German fighter pilots were credited with 21 confirmed kills. Other two-seater crews had unusual success too. Single victories went to men in *(A)296, Schusta 8* and *Schusta 14*. And a pilot and his gunner in *Schusta 18* scored a double.

According to Lüdeke himself, his victory on the 20th brought him the Iron Cross 1st Class, presented to him personally by *General der Infanterie* Hermann von Francois, commanding the VII German Army Corps at Verdun (where for his leadership there he had just been awarded the Oakleaf on July 27 to his previously awarded (May 14, 1915) *Orden Pour le Mérite*). Not that it makes a great deal of difference, but, curiously, the history of the 17th Hussars dates Lüdeke's 1st Class Iron Cross as July 12, 1917, not sometime shortly after August 20. Some awards, notably the Bavarian Military Max-Joseph Order, were given retroactive dates but not Prussian ones in wartime (postwar awards of the Iron Cross which were approved as late as 1924 were obviously made on a retrospective basis but even here no evidence has been found that the official bestowal date was made retroactive to wartime). Even more strange is the date in the unit's history for Lüdeke's Brunswick War Merit Cross 1st Class. This is listed as coming in September 1917, thus fully six months before it even existed.

So whether the unit history was right in saying Lüdeke had three victories or whether, perhaps, they were referring to three claims only one of which was upheld officially, is something we will probably never know. Whatever his actual score, he not only had a distinguished record in *(A)254* where it was reported that he had made 75 long-range reconnaissance flights but he went on to bigger things in the final year of the war. The *Schutzstaffel* had been redesignated *Schlachtstaffel* in preparation for their role in the coming German spring offensives (from protection flights to battle flights). Lüdeke was appointed the leader of one of them, *Schlasta 6*. It was one of five such flights in *Schlachtgeschwader 3* which had a total complement of 40 aircraft of the fast, light CL-Type Hannoveraner and Halberstadt machines which did such yeoman service throughout 1918 in supporting the infantry in the offensive and defensive battles of that cataclysmic year. The date is not recorded but it could have been coincident with the assumption of his new command that Lüdeke's promotion to *Oberleutnant* came through. He continued to lead *Schlasta 6* until the armistice but not before two other events took place. First, on July 5, he received a well merited Knight's Cross with Swords of the Royal House Order of Hohenzollern. And then, in September, he was joined by his younger brother, Günther. And with that, we pick up his story.

Following in the footsteps of his older brother, Günther joined the 17th Hussars on August 2, 1914, the day before Germany's formal declaration of war against France and just nine days after his 17th birthday. He was commissioned in the regiment on June 18, 1915, not yet 18 therefore, and further emulated his brother by winning the Iron Cross 2nd Class two

[2] A study of the *Nachrichtenblatt* from January 1, 1917 through March 31, 1918, after which the units of victorious German airmen were no longer identified, shows that during this period, two-seater units had crews with multiple victories on a single day on only nine other occasions. After March 1918 and until the end of August 1918 when comprehensive victory lists ceased to be reported, it shows that the same two-seater crew scored multiple victories on the same day only four times. This included a five-victory claim and a four-victory confirmation on May 23, 1918 by the *(A)263* crew of *Vizefeldwebel* Georg Gund, pilot, and *Leutnant* Karl Eisenmenger, observer. They were attacked by fighters, identified as British Sopwith single-seaters. Just to show that overclaiming wasn't limited to the allied side (particularly the British and later, the Americans), the British actually lost only two fighters that day, both Sopwith Camels and each from a different squadron).

Above: *Lt.* Jürgen Lüdeke, 2nd from the right, was one of two brothers from the 17th Brunswick Hussars who transferred to the *Fliegertruppe*. A recipient of both classes of the War Merit Cross, he served as an observer in *Fl.Abt. (A)254* and later assumed the command of *Schlasta 6*. Ludeke was credited with three victories during the course of his service although only one can be traced. Here in *(A)254*, an *Oblt.* Averdam (rear) "blesses" the head of a *Lt.* Thiele who had just been awarded the Iron Cross 1st Class, probably for a victory he and his pilot scored on June 27, 1917. From left to right: *Lt.* Helbig, *Lt.* Mueller, *Lt.* Hoffmann, Averdam, Thiele, Lüdeke and *Lt.* Fremy. According to the caption on the original photograph, the dog's name was "Tell," possibly a contraction of the German *Teller* ("plate" or "dish," i.e. a hungry hound).

Below: The other Lüdeke brother was Günther who earned the Brunswick War Merit Cross (2nd Class) in the 17th Hussars before joining *Jasta 36* directly from flight school at the end of September 1917. No photographs of him have been found during his brief stay there (he was seriously injured in a crash on November 18, 1917). This line-up of *Jasta 36* Albatros D.IIIs pre-dates Lüdeke's arrival (it is April 1917) but the photograph should appeal to markings specialists.

Above: Men of *Fl.Abt. (A)254* on the Konsset airfield in November-December 1917. A shooting star adorns the fuselage of one of the unit's Rumpler C.IV machines. From left to right: Jürgen Lüdeke, *Lt. Graf* von und zu Hoensbroech, *Unteroffz.* Horths, *Lt.* Hoffmann, *Lt.* Mueller, *Vzfw.* Philipps, *Lt.* von Winterfeld and *Lt.* Helbig. It would appear that "Tell" made this photograph too.

Below: There must have been some special reason for the photographer to set up his bellows camera to record the return of three air crews of *Fl.Abt. (A)254* still in their heavy winter flight gear. From left to right: *Vzfw.* Philipps, *Lt.* von Winterfeld, *Lt.* Helbig, *Vzfw.* Franke, *Werkmeister* Reich, *Unteroffz.* Thiele, Lüdeke, *Lt.* Runge and *Gefr.* Strecker. The scene is again *(A)254*'s Konsset field and the same Rumpler C.IV "shooting star" in the photograph above is at the right.

days later and the Brunswick War Merit Cross the following month, on July 15. And like his brother, he effected a transfer to aviation and began pilot training at *Flieger-Ersatz-Abteilung 4* at Posen (now Poznan in Poland) in March 1917. He finished up at the *Geschwaderschule* in Paderborn towards the end of September. By this time and unlike the usual procedure earlier, Günther was not assigned two-seater duties since fighter pilots were needed now, seasoned or not. Accordingly, after some brushing up at *Jastaschule I*, he went directly to *Jagdstaffel 36* in Flanders, reporting in on October 29 just as its Commanding Officer, *Leutnant* Walter von Bülow-Bothkamp, was about to go on a week's leave sporting the new *Pour le Mérite* that he had received on October 8 following his 21st confirmed victory the previous month. Von Bülow was an ex-17th Hussar himself and it is therefore not too much of a stretch of the imagination to assume that these old regimental ties had something to do with Günther's assignment.

Günther Lüdeke's career in *Jasta 36* lasted less than a month. During his brief time with the unit, the weather was unsuitable for flying on more days than not. Several of them were complete wash-outs. But when the skies cleared, as they did, for example, on October 31, there was plenty of action. The notes one of the interwar German researchers made from, presumably, *Jasta 36*'s War Diary show only major events like victories and losses so we do not know whether the untried Lüdeke was allowed up that day. At any rate, nine of *Jasta 36*'s machines were out on a morning patrol. The seasoned *Leutnant* Heinrich Bongartz (with 17 victories already) was credited with an RFC Spad and an R.E.8 only 20 minutes apart. Walter von Bülow's younger brother, Harry, also a member of *36*, got another No.23 Squadron, RFC Spad minutes after Bongartz's R.E.8 for his own second confirmed victory. After midday, 10 aircraft went up for an afternoon sortie (could Lüdeke have been the extra man?). Bongartz scored again, putting him into the 20-victory column and what has been called "*Pour le Mérite*" territory (and which honor he did receive at a *Kaiser* review on December 23 when his score stood at 27). That same afternoon, *Leutnant* Hans Hoyer, a decorated ex-artilleryman, who had been appointed Acting Leader while the senior von Bülow was away, put in for a "Sopwith."[3] The claim was eventually upheld giving Hoyer his seventh overall but it is entirely possible the "Sopwith" credited to him was actually an S.E.5a that made it back all right.

Mostly because of the bad weather, no further successes could be reported by the men of *36* until the 8th of November, a day of considerable aerial activity on both sides. Walter von Bülow, just back from his short leave (where he reported flying a Fokker Triplane at a field near Berlin, presumably for the first time), got his 25th. Also drawing blood on the 8th were Bongartz (his 21st), Hoyer (his eighth) and two *Leutnante*, Hans Gottfried von Haebler (his fourth) and Theodor Quandt (his eighth too).[4] In between more spells of weather unsuitable for much flying, Bongartz was credited with another R.E.8 on the 12th although it was probably the aircraft from No.55 Squadron, RFC which he had driven down almost into the ground when he broke off the action, allowing the enemy plane to return safely albeit with both pilot and observer wounded. The weather broke again on the 15th and the *Staffelführer* and his best man, Bongartz, both put in for kills. Bongartz's was confirmed (although listed in the *Nachrichtenblatt* as an Albatros D.III of all things) but von Bülow's was not.

At the same time von Bülow was going after what was said to be a Spad that went down within its own lines, Hoyer, too, was engaged in a hot combat. He received a stomach wound and came down in a forced landing within German lines but which was right along the front and was under shell fire. With difficulty the wreckage of his Albatros was reached but Hoyer, never regaining consciousness, died of his injuries. He may well have been a victim of the No. 1 Squadron, RFC Nieuport flown by the formidable Captain P.F. Fullard who claimed two Albatros D.Vs in rapid succession just before noon (British Time) that day for his 39th and 40th victories (which were also his last; two days later, he broke a leg playing soccer and was never able to return to the front). Günther Lüdeke was to be the next loss that *Jasta 36* suffered but, fortunately, not as a fatality. On November 18, he took one of the unit's D.Vs up for a test flight when suddenly the engine seized and the plane sideslipped into the ground, just a "heap of ruins" as *36*'s War Diary described it. Lüdeke came away with a broken thigh, serious enough to put him out of action for nearly a year. It was not until September 1918 that Günther got back to a front line posting. It was undoubtedly no coincidence that his new outfit was *Schlasta 6* where Jürgen was still in command. And it was in *Schlasta 6* that the two brothers saw the war out.

---

[3] As a battery commander in the Saxon *1. Feldartillerie-Regiment Nr.32*, Hoyer had distinguished himself in the battles in the Champagne between the end of September and early November 1915, ending up with a head wound. He was decorated with the Knight's Cross of the Saxon Military St. Henry Order on November 30, 1915. After his recuperation, he gained a transfer to the air service in April 1916, evidence once again that a wounding in the ground troops and a stay in hospital often provided the opportunity for a man to get out of the trenches and into the air when fit again.

[4] It is interesting to note that not only Hoyer but Walter von Bülow and von Haebler, too, were Knights of the Military St. Henry Order. Von Bülow's came on October 7, 1917 while leading *Jasta 36*. Von Haebler's was awarded just five days earlier right after he joined *36* but it came in recognition of his earlier service in *Flieger-Abteilung (A)273* (see pages 120-127 in Volume III in this series for their citations and further details of both men's careers).

There is a small postscript to Günther's story. Even though he was never to become one of the big "*Kanonen*" of the Imperial German Air Service, his long service and dedication to duty were not forgotten. On April 9, 1919, he was promoted to the rank of *Oberleutnant* and that September, given the Iron Cross 1st Class, thus once again pulling even with his big brother.

LEUTNANT RUDOLF MATTHAEI

Over 30 years ago, the late A. Edward Ferko authored a biography on a then virtually unknown young German airman named Rudolf Matthaei that appeared in the Spring 1970 issue of the pioneer but now defunct World War I aviation society's publication, *Cross & Cockade Journal*. This publication, the first of its kind, provided a vehicle for early researchers like Ferko to share what was then their near unique knowledge with a small but growing group of people interested in the history of the first full-scale air war. There were others, too, to whom we who came later owe a great debt, men like the late William R. Puglisi and Peter M. Grosz in the United States, the late Heinz J. Nowarra in Germany and Alex Imrie in England. What they did in their day was truly remarkable (and, happily, Messrs. Grosz and Imrie are still at it). Ed Ferko's tribute to Matthaei was a fine example of the diligent research that marked those early efforts. As a salute to Ed Ferko's memory, it seems quite appropriate to run the story of the young Rudolf Matthaei just as Ed wrote it (including his punctuation and abbreviations).

Since that article appeared, great advances in our knowledge of World War I aviation have, of course, been made. Much new information, not available to Ferko and others, has been found and published not the least of which are works like Trevor Henshaw's *The Sky Their Battlefield* and the Grubb Street series under the direction of Norman Franks. Thus here, where appropriate, material like that will be added by this writer in the form of footnotes. Most of the photographs originated with Ferko but the captions are, again, this writer's. So here is what Ed himself wrote those many years ago.

Rudolf Matthaei was born on 10 November 1895 in Hildesheim, the son of Counsel Godwin Matthaei and his wife (nee) Suchier. With his parents and five brothers and sisters, Rudolf spent a happy, carefree childhood in their native city where he later attended the Gymnasium Andreanun. Probably the only shadow that crossed his young life was the unexpected death of one of his older brothers, the barrister Hugo Matthaei, shortly before taking his workers examination at the beginning of February 1914.

With war imminent, Rudolf's desire to become an artillery officer was realized when on 13 February 1914, the 19-year old youth joined the *Niedersächsischen Feldartillerie-Regiment Nr.46* in Wolfenbüttel as a *Fahnenjunker*.

On 7 August 1914, just six days after the declaration of war, *Fahnenjunker* Matthaei was in the field with his unit where they participated in the crossing of the river Marne and battles near Guise, Congy and the Petit Morin. When orders to pull back suddenly arrived on 9 September, the great German advance had ended and *FAR 46* began its life of trench warfare in the vicinity of Reims where the battles of Conde, Sapigneul, Bourgogne and Brimont came into special prominence. On 23 April 1915, Rudolf Matthaei was promoted *Leutnant* in *FAR 46*.

After seven months on the line in the west, *FAR 46* received orders and was transferred immediately to duty on the Eastern Front. In Galicia, he took part in the breakthrough at Tarnow-Gorlice followed by the great advance which took them through the Dukla Pass, across the Wisloka and San rivers and finally over the Russian border on 28 June 1915. Here in front of Pilazkowice and Zygmuntow, *FAR 46* once again settled down for warfare in the trenches.

As a result of a shortage of officers in *Infanterie-Regiment Nr.79, Leut.* Matthaei was temporarily attached to and took command of a platoon in the 10th Company fighting in the battles near Leczna on the Wicperz. *IR 79* remained in the forefront during the successful attack on the heavily defended Russian positions at Walka-Wizanka south of Ostrow and then advanced through Cholm to Brest-Litowsk.

Trouble, never far away, was mounting on the Western Front. Thus it was that *IR 79* was pulled from the line, entrained and returned to France on 18 September 1915 for service with the *3. Armee* in the Champagne. Still only temporarily commanding the 10th Company of *IR 79*, *Leut.* Matthaei nevertheless continued to lead his men with great valor in the grim battles at Roubroy and Ripont. On 23 October, he was returned to *FAR 46* and assigned to its 4th Battery in the firing line on the heights above the Chemin des Dames south of Courtecou. With the onset of winter, operations at the front abated and after a Christmas leave spent at his parents' home in Hildesheim, Rudolf took a Company Commander's course at Leuilly and then returned once again to the front at Colligis.

Weary of ground action, Matthaei at his own request was transferred to the *Fliegertruppe* and ordered to *Fliegerschule* Halberstadt for pilot training. On I June 1916 with his *Feldpilotenprüfung* completed, the youthful veteran received a short leave which was spent in Bavaria, then continued his training at *FEA 5* Hanover and at *FEA Cöln*. At last all

The epaulets and a pristine fresh-from-the-tailor double-breasted *Litewka* mark the newly commissioned *Leutnant* of artillery Rudolf Matthaei, still six months shy of his 20th birthday. Was the wisp of a mustache an effort to appear older than his years? After hard campaigning on both the Western and Eastern Fronts in 1914 and 1915, during which he earned the Iron Cross 2nd Class and the Brunswick War Merit Cross, Matthaei got a transfer to the *Fliegertruppe* in early 1916 and by that October reached the front again with a two-seater unit. Below, Matthaei, with mustache now gone, stands arm-in-arm with his older brother (who still affects one) on the field of the flying school at Halberstadt where he took his initial pilot courses. He is wearing the ribbons of his two awards but the Iron Cross 1st Class would not come until June 1917 after more than seven months as a fighter pilot. The aircraft is a Halberstadt B.I now relegated to training duties.

Above: Change of command at *Jasta 21*, late May 1917. The then *Oblt*. Eduard Schleich, far left, takes over from the unit's first leader, *Hptm*. Richard Schlieben, 5th from left. Matthaei is next to Schleich, then *Oblt*. Nischke, *Unteroffz*. Wagner, Schlieben, *Lt*. Thomas, *Lt*. Stege, *Lt*. Paulus, unknown, *Lt*. Raspe and *Lt*. Thuy. Seated, left to right, *Vzfw*. Thom, unknown and *Vzfw*. Zachmann. On May 25, Schleich scored his first victory and Matthaei his second (some lists say it was his third). Schleich, Emil Thuy and Karl Thom went on to earn the *Orden Pour le Mérite* with Schleich becoming *Ritter* von Schleich with the award of the Military Max-Joseph Order and Thom becoming the first (of 69) aviation recipients of Prussia's Golden Military Merit Cross and the tenth (of 11) aviation recipient of its Member's Cross with Swords of the Royal House Order of Hohenzollern, the only airman to hold all three of these top bravery awards.

Below: Poor quality mars this photograph of Matthaei's Albatros D.V 2167/17 "8" with its *Jasta 21* black and white band. In the rear, Thom's D.V "5" with its stylized "T" can barely be made out.

prescribed instruction was completed and he was assigned on 12 October to *Kasta 9* of *Kagohl 2* based at that time at Leffincourt in the Champagne.

The *Leutnant*'s affiliation with *KG 2* was only a fleeting one for when the newly authorized *Jasta 21* was formed on 25 October 1916 at Le Chatelet by *Hauptmann* Schlieben, young Rudolf, having become acquainted with the *Hauptmann*, requested that he be attached to the *Staffel* as one of its pilots. The request was acceded to and after a number of patrols in January and February 1917, Matthaei was ordered to *Jastaschule* Valenciennes for a four week course of *Jagdflieger* training under the careful tutelage of some of Germany's most experienced fighters. The weeks hurtled by and upon completing the program, he returned to *Jasta 21* in the Champagne where after several difficult but unsuccessful aerial combats, he finally achieved his first victory, a balloon, on 23 March.[5] Before his second victim fell some three weeks later, the long awaited great Spring Offensive by General Nivelle commenced on 16 April in the Aisne-Champagne sector and *Jasta 21* along with fourteen other *Jastas* soon found themselves involved in continual combat with some of France's most skillful and dangerous fighter pilots.

Matthaei's second victory was a single seat Spad which he cut out of a French patrol and forced down inside German lines to be captured.[6] As a result of these and other activities, Matthaei, now a *Kette* leader in *Jasta 21*, was mentioned in Army dispatches along with five other successful pilots and received notification that he had been awarded the silver *Ehrenbecher* for his recent triumphs. The training at *Jastaschule* Valenciennes had paid off.

Following a fourteen day leave, *Leutnant* Matthaei returned to the front to again join battle with the enemy. One further victory fell to his guns while a member of *Obltn.* Eduard Schleich's *Jasta 21* before he petitioned for yet another transfer.[7] This wish was similarly honored and Rudolf soon found himself a member of *Jasta 5*, the famous "Green Tails," then stationed at Boistrancourt southeast of Cambrai. Here in the Cambrai

[5] The official *Nachrichtenblatt* lists only two enemy balloons destroyed on 23 March on the Eastern Front, one by the crew of *Leutnant* Funcke and *Unteroffizier* Metzner of *Flieger-Abteilung 4* and one by anti-aircraft fire and none destroyed on the Western Front. *Above the Lines* dates Matthaei's first victory, a balloon, as 24 March but the *Nachrichtenblatt* makes no mention of it. Extracts taken from *Jasta 21*'s War Diary by an interwar German researcher shows no Matthaei victory on either 23 or 24 March and states that the unit's first confirmed victory did not occur until 12 April 1917 when *Unteroffizier* Eduard Horn brought a Nieuport two-seater down in flames south of Nauroy.

[6] In a separate table in the Ferko article listing Matthaei's victories, the downing of the Spad is dated 16 April 1917. *Above the Lines* puts the date as 15 April with the notation that it was not confirmed. The *Nachrichtenblatt* does not credit Matthaei with a victory on either date (a Spad was credited to a *Jasta 21* man, *Unteroffizier* Max Zachmann, on 15 April listed in its War Diary as the unit's second confirmed victory).

[7] In the Ferko table, this victory is dated 25 May, a Nieuport as number three. *Above the Lines* concurs on the date, type and victory number. The *Nachrichtenblatt* likewise agrees but lists the Nieuport as Matthaei's second confirmed victory. The War Diary's entry is the same as the *Nachrichtenblatt's*. *Above the Lines* credits Matthaei with another balloon victory on 30 April as number four. The War Diary makes no mention of any *Jasta 21* balloon victory on that date and the *Nachrichtenblatt* for some reason has no balloon victory list for the month of April 1917.

As well as its comfortable manor house, the men of *Jasta 5* seem to have requisitioned the owner's long-stemmed wine goblets too. From left to right, the Adjutant, *Lt.* Schaumberg, *Oblt.* Nebel, *Lt.* Strobel, *Lt.* Schuhmann, Matthaei, their leader, *Oblt.* Flashar and *Lt.* Neisen.

The three nurses seen in a previous photograph are entertained again at *Jasta 5*. Standing, left to right, *Lt.* Strobel, *Lt.* Nebel, *Lt.* Schaumberg, Matthaei, unknown, *Offz.-Stv.* Löwensen and *Offz.-Stv.* Mai. Seated at left, *Oblt.* Flashar. In front, left to right, *Vzfw.* Rumey, *Unteroffz.* Bäumer and *Vzfw.* Könnecke. Mai, Rumey, Bäumer and Könnecke later earned the Golden Military Merit Cross, Rumey, Bäumer and Könnecke the *Pour le Mérite*, Mai was proposed for it but too late and of the four, only Könnecke received the Hohenzollern Knight's Cross after being commissioned.

area, the "*Englischmänner*" were plentiful and young Rudolf was seldom at a loss to find opponents on which to test his mettle. In August of that year, while *Obltn.* Flashaar, commander of *Jasta 5*, was on leave, *Leut.* Matthaei assumed temporary command of the "*Kanonen Staffel*"[8] and led it to nine new victories. On one particular occasion, he was cited by the Chief of Staff of *A.O.K.* for attacking a formation of seven British two-seaters, bringing one down and routing the others. The taste of victory was sweet indeed.

Following this short spell of command, Matthaei took yet another brief leave which he was able to spend with his parents in Wiesbaden. It was during this time that he received two additional awards, the Iron Cross, First Class and the *Flieger Abzeichen*.[9] Previously, in the early part of 1915, he had won the *E.K. II* and the *Braunschweigische Verdienstkreuz II*.[10]

On 19 September 1917, *Leut.* Matthaei brought his score to seven with the forcing down of a British two-seater inside German lines where the aircraft and unwounded crew were captured intact. Two additional victories fell to the Green Tailed Albatros expert of *Jasta 5* before he was commissioned to organize and lead one of the newly authorized *Jagdstaffeln* dictated by the "*Amerika Programm*." Enroute to this latest most challenging assignment at Graudenz, the handsome, serious young airman stopped off in Hildesheim to personally inform his parents of his good fortune and future plans. Unknown to the proud couple, this "delay en route" meeting would be the last time they would see their son alive.

Time was at a premium. The great German Spring Offensive was already well along into the detailed planning

[8] Richard Flashar's last name is spelled differently in various records. Ferko chose "Flashaar." The *Jasta 5* War Diary spells it "Flasshaar." "Flashar" seems to be the most common spelling and since it is the one used in the *Nachrichtenblatt*, it was also used in the previous biography on the man. In terms of Matthaei's further victories, all sources agree on the dates and which numbers they represent but there are several instances where they do not agree on the type of aircraft brought down.

[9] The *Jasta 5* War Diary dates Matthaei's Iron Cross 1st Class on 7 June 1917 and his Pilot's Badge on 8 June 1917.

[10] The decoration's legal name was *Kriegsverdienstkreuz* and at this time, there was only the one class.

Lt. Rudolf Matthaei at the peak of his career. He now wears the Iron Cross 1st Class and his Pilot's Badge, the former awarded on June 7, 1917 and the latter on the following day. This studio pose was probably taken in his home town of Hildesheim on his last leave before taking over the command of *Jasta 46* on Christmas Day 1917. His gentle countenance conceals the heart of a warrior who at this time had nine confirmed victories to his name.

Below, Matthaei's 10th and last victim, Sopwith Camel B.5552 of No.4 Squadron, Australian Flying Corps, brought down intact on February 21, 1918. Its pilot, 2nd Lt. A. Couston, was made a prisoner-of-war.

stage and while many commanders were less than satisfied with the competence (or lack of it) displayed by their charges, operational timetables not unlike the Ten Commandments must be obeyed or the consequences suffered. Thus at the beginning of January 1918, Matthaei returned once again to the battlefield. This time, however, he was leading his very own unit, *Jagdstaffel 46*.

Ascq, east of Lille, became their first operational station at the front. But in any case, they did not remain here for long. Poor weather, the desperate need for additional training which could easily be translated into that priceless element, *time*, and the increasing demands of his command conspired to keep the *Staffelführer* from adding to his game bag. After all, the *Staffel* came first! But finally, on 21 February, a careless Australian Camel pilot crossed his sights and in doing so, became the *Leutnant*'s tenth and last victory.[11]

Slightly less than a month later, *Jasta 46*, led by its intrepid commander, participated in the classic "air battle of Le Cateau." This great aerial melee on 18 March saw over 100 British and German aircraft locked in combat as each side attempted to determine who would rule the heavens. During this hectic period in the Spring of 1918, Matthaei was in frequent personal contact with *Rittmeister* von Richthofen since *Jasta 46* was subordinate to, not only in the air but also on the ground, the famous *Jagdgeschwader 1*. On 16 April 1918, *Leutnant* Rudolf Matthaei wrote his parents for the last time. The end was now near.

About 1700 on 17 April, two German fighter aircraft roared across *Jasta 46*'s field at Lieramont and took off into the late afternoon sun. Since the enemy had not shown any great desire for battle that day, the *Staffelführer* decided to join one of his pilots for a short exercise in combat tactics over their field. Matthaei was as usual flying his Pfalz D.III while his "opponent" was piloting an Albatros D.Va. As fate would have it, instead of the special unburnable asbestos-lined trousers which would normally be used during combat operations, *Leutnant* Matthaei wore just an ordinary pair of light service trousers for this practice flight. It was a spur of the moment decision which was to have a fatal outcome.

A mechanic who had stopped to watch the hastily planned duel noted that as Matthaei attained an altitude of about 300 meters, he commenced a left hand turn whereupon the aircraft dropped its nose and began to spin. Apparently the spark was not turned off and as the machine spun down, benzol spilled over, caught fire and the Pfalz hit the ground in flames.

Still living as he was pulled from the burning wreckage, the badly injured pilot was transported under the watchful eyes of a doctor to a nearby hospital. Although Rudolf Matthaei was horribly burnt and both legs were broken, his lips gave no suggestion of the agony and pain he felt. In fact, the courageous young *Staffelführer* joked with his comrades and instructed his personal mechanic to inform his parents of the accident and

On April 17, 1918, Matthaei was about to put one of his men through a mock combat when at only 300 meters, his aircraft was seen to drop into a spin and with its engine still on, fuel spilled on the hot metal which ignited just before the crash.

As the wreckage continues to burn on *Jasta 46*'s airfield at Lieramont, men of the unit have extricated the badly injured pilot and are tending to him before he was rushed off to hospital. Matthaei was alive and even joked about his misfortune.

But it was too late. Towards midnight on the 17th, Matthaei expired, age just 22. Here, grim comrades survey the now burned out remains with only the rudder of his Pfalz D.IIIa untouched by the flames and recognizable for what it was.

[11] Sopwith Camel B.5552, No.4 Squadron, AFC, 2/Lt. A. Couston, POW, shot down near Haubourdin at 10:50 a.m. (British Time) in combat with five Albatros scouts.

convey best regards. At the same time, perhaps sensing the gravity of his condition, he requested that his brother, who was then at St. Mihiel, be notified at once of the events. But even as these final wishes were being carried out, a fatal embolism developed and despite desperate efforts to stave off the inevitable, as midnight approached, death came to gently close forever the eyes of Rudolf Matthaei.

Official reports from both his *Staffel* comrades and higher authority indicated that the tragic crash could only have resulted from an indiscernible weakness or defect in the machine. Subsequently, it was admitted that the Pfalz D.III and D.IIIa were both machines of general unreliability although it would appear that towards the end of Matthaei's service, he favored this type above others.

Ironically enough, just one day prior to his fatal accident, his immediate superior, the Commander of *Jagdgruppe* 2, had submitted to their King and *Kaiser* a recommendation for the award of the *Ritterkreuz des Kgl. Hausordens von Hohenzollern*. But with the death of Matthaei, the award did not materialize.

Leutnant Rudolf Matthaei was first laid to rest in enemy soil but on 12 May 1918, his faithful servant accompanied the body back to the city of his youth and there he found his eternal bed in the family vault in the Centralfriedhof of Hildesheim.

So, because of a tragedy never really explained, a young life ended which could have been of so much service to his country. His death was easier for his parents to bear because he had had a lifetime of complete happiness and to the very last breath, he faithfully believed that his country would in the end be the victor.[12]

[12] Table 4-5 lists Matthaei's victories according not only to Ferko's tabulation but also according to the other sources we have referred to.

Table 4-5
The Victories of *Leutnant* Rudolf Matthaei (Day, Month and Year)

No.	A. Edward Ferko	*Above the Lines*	*Nachrichtenblatt*	*Jasta 21* War Diary	*Jasta 5* War Diary	*Jasta 46* War Diary
1.	23.3.17. Balloon	24.3.17. Balloon	Not Listed	30.4.17. Balloon	—	—
2.	16.4.17. Spad	30.4.17. Balloon	25.5.17. Nieuport	25.5.17. Nieuport	—	—
3.	25.5.17. Nieuport	25.5.17. Nieuport	3rd Not Listed	—	18.8.17. Bristol	—
4.	18.8.17. Bristol	18.8.17. Bristol	4th Not Listed	—	20.8.17. Bristol	—
5.	20.8.17. Bristol[1]	20.8.17. D.H.4[1]	18.8.17. Bristol[1]	—	20.8.17. Bristol[1]	—
6.	4.9.17. Martinsyde [2]	4.9.17. Bristol	4.9.17. Martinsyde[2]	—	4.9.17. Martinsyde[2]	—
7.	19.9.17. Morane	19.9.17. Morane	19.9.17. Morane	—	19.9.17. Morane	—
8.	25.9.17. Sopwith[3]	25.9.17. D.H.5[3]	25.9.17. Sopwith[1]	—	25.9.17. Camel	—
9.	22.11.17. Sopwith	22.11.17. Camel	22.22.17. Sopwith[1]	—	22.11.17. Camel	—
10.	21.2.18. Camel	21.2.18. Camel	21.2.18. Camel	—	—	21.2.18. Camel

Notes:

1. *The Sky Their Battlefield* shows no Bristol F2b loss and only one D.H.4 loss on 20 August 1917.

2. The *Sky Their Battlefield* identifies Matthaei's victory on 4 September 1917 as a Bristol F2b.

3. The *Sky Their Battlefield* shows the loss of only one Camel on 25 September 1917 and this in the sea after a combat with a Friedrichshafen seaplane. It shows no D.H.5 loss that day.

RITTMEISTER MANFRED *FREIHERR* VON RICHTHOFEN

Beginning with Floyd Gibbons' lurid *The Red Knight of Germany* in 1927 (and its syndication in *Liberty* magazine) and ending, for the moment anyhow, with such works as A.E. Ferko's *Richthofen*, Peter Kilduff's *Beyond the Legend* and *The Illustrated Red Baron* and the Grub Street *Under the Guns of the Red Baron*, literally millions of words have been written about the life and times of World War I's premier fighter ace, Manfred *Freiherr* von Richthofen. His victories, his character and most of all the mystery surrounding his death have been examined and re-examined some would say, *ad nauseum*, but the man never fails to fascinate. Because he was Germany's most highly decorated flier of the war, he has appeared in every volume in this series and this last one is no exception. But of all that has been said there and much more elsewhere, what can this writer add that will reward the reader of this volume?

Not much, actually. But there was an incident in connection with von Richthofen's Brunswick War Merit Cross that raises some points of interest (at least of interest to the medals specialist) which is worth relating. Also, in terms of the man's character and demeanor, a posthumous appreciation of von Richthofen by the Commanding Officer of the 92nd Brunswick Infantry Regiment was found while researching Brunswick awards in the archive in Wolfenbüttel. This should please the legion of von Richthofen devotees. But, first, about his Brunswick War Merit Cross.

In a flurry of several awards that came von Richthofen's way in the fall of 1917 as his score passed the 60-mark, and among them was the War Merit Cross from Brunswick. It was approved on September 24 and recorded in the War Diary of *Jagdgeschwader Nr.1* on October 2 along with one of his Hanseatic Crosses. We now skip ahead to 1918 where in late March and early April, the four elements of the squadron, *Jastas 4, 6, 10* and *11* occupied the airfield near the town of Lechelle along the Somme as the first of the three great Ludendorff Offensives drove on Amiens. Their *Offizier zur besonderen Verwendung* (Officer Assigned for Special Duties, or Adjutant), *Oberleutnant* Karl Bodenschatz, had this to say, among many other things, about their beloved leader in the book *Jagd in Flanderns Himmel* published in 1935:

> His clothing was as simple as possible. Around us, most of the time he ran around in just a knitted sweater and his deerskin trousers, the *Pour le Mérite* at his throat. If it was cold, then over these he'd have a leather jacket. You saw him in uniform only on festive occasions, or when guests were there. During the early days (at Lechelle – N.W.O'C), he suddenly came rushing in to the Adjutant to borrow gloves and a belt, because he had to quickly report to "the gentleman from Brunswick" (Duke Ernst August – N.W.O'C). He then came back grinning. He had gotten the inevitable house order, for the second time. "But I can't very well tell the man that!"

Although it was misidentified by Bodenschatz as a house order, it was, in fact, the Brunswick War Merit Cross. This raises some interesting questions. The Duke would have known that the award, then in its only class, had been awarded to von Richthofen the previous September. Considering the importance of the recipient, a proper *Urkunde* (bestowal document) would probably have been prepared which the Duke would have signed. In the Imperial German Order's scheme of things, multiple awards of an order or decoration in the same class were never made.

So how come a second decoration to von Richthofen? The only explanation seems to be that the Duke wanted the honor of presenting his cross to the Great One personally. But hold on. As mentioned earlier, just days before the Duke, on March 20, 1918, had created a 1st Class to his War Merit Cross and added the "Proved" clasp to the now 2nd Class (the first elements of *Jagdgeschwader 1* had reached Lechelle on March 26). If he were going to reward von Richthofen personally, why wouldn't he use the occasion to give him something above and beyond that which he had already received? With a victory score moving into the seventies, von Richthofen certainly merited the 1st Class and probably qualified for the two years of "unbroken front line service" to have the "Proved" clasp as well. But, then, wouldn't have von Richthofen, medal conscious as he was, realized he was getting a new award, making it unnecessary for him to comment the way he did to Bodenschatz? And besides, on the *Ordenskissen* prepared for von Richthofen's reinternment ceremonies in Berlin in 1925 that was later displayed at the home in Schweidnitz, only the 2nd Class cross was in evidence and that without the "Proved" clasp. But there have been other instances where all of a man's awards were not present at ceremonies of this kind, most notably on Boelcke's *Ordenskissen* where three of his awards were not there (the Knight 1st Class with Swords of the Ducal Saxe-Ernestine House Order, the Mecklenburg-Strelitz Cross for Distinction in War 2nd Class and the Austrian Order of the Iron Crown 3rd Class with War Decoration).

For all but the medals specialist, this is probably of little or no consequence. For those more interested in Manfred von Richthofen's character and the regard in which he was held,

In late March, early April of 1918, *Jagdgeschwader Nr.1* was located at Lechelle on the Some before moving on to Cappy. At Lechelle, Manfred von Richthofen was ordered to present himself to Duke Ernst August of Brunswick and received what may have been a second of his War Merit Crosses, the first having been approved on September 24, 1917. If so, it was contrary to regulations since none of the Imperial German States made multiple awards of the same grade or class of their orders and decorations. The text discusses other possibilities. Below, von Richthofen confers with *Oblt*. Richard Flashar on one of his March 1918 visits to *Jasta 5* at Bertincourt.

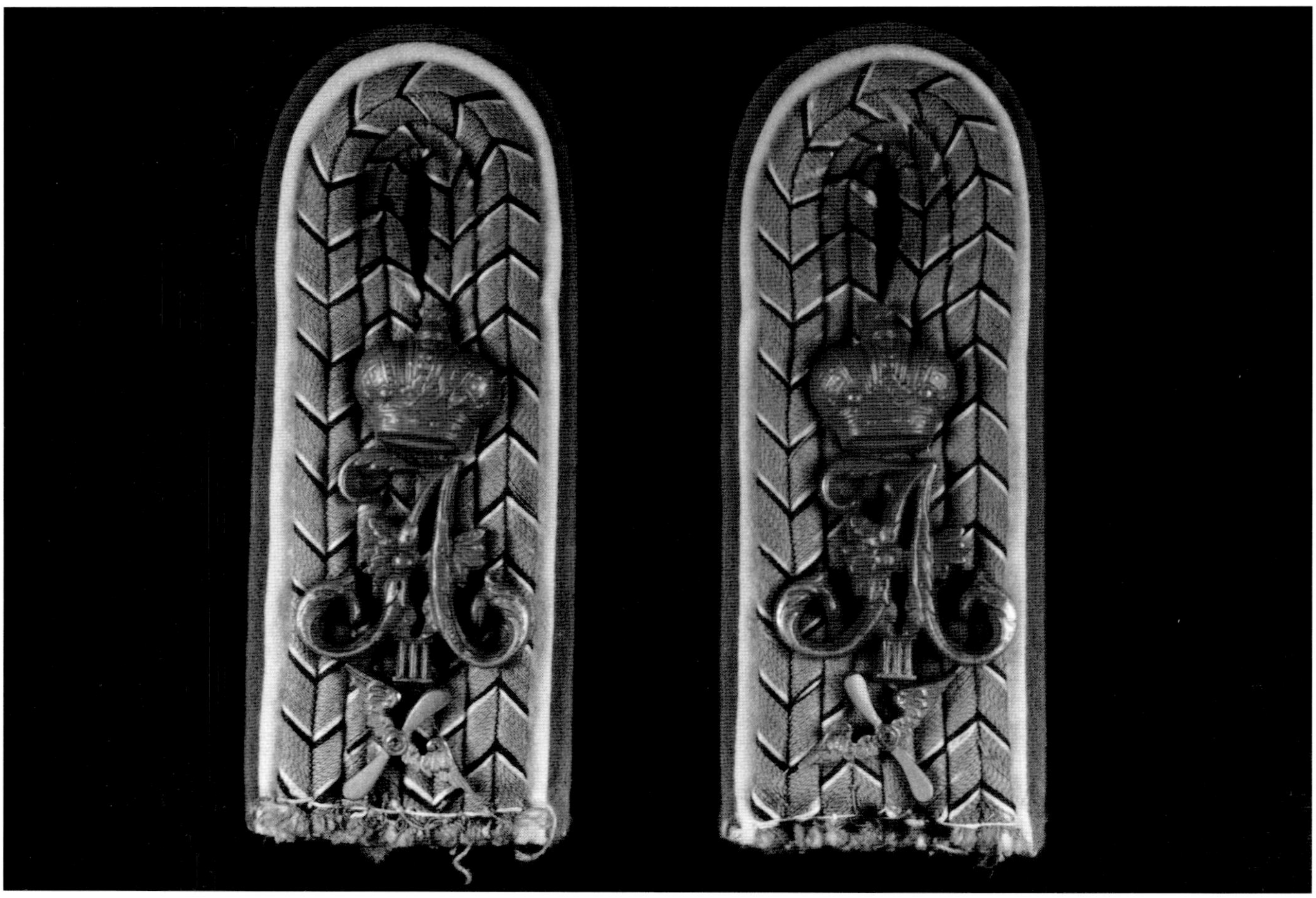

the letter written from the field on June 7, 1918 by the 92nd Regiment's Commanding Officer will make up for the digression into medals small talk. While Bodenschatz's account of von Richthofen needing belt and gloves to present himself properly to "the gentleman from Brunswick" does not mention the Duke by name nor does he specifically say that the meeting occurred at Lechelle, the letter, printed in its entirety here, leaves no doubt about who the "gentleman" was or where the affair took place. It read:

> During this reception, the flying hero, Captain of Cavalry Baron von Richthofen, who, along with his squadron, was nearby in the vicinity of Lechelle, reported to His Royal Highness and received the Brunswick War Merit Gross from the Duke's own hand – an event which will remain a nice memory for those who witnessed it. Our Duke's basic nature, so adverse to any posturing, to any trite display, is so fitting, especially in this solemn war environment which cannot tolerate any appearance of hypocrisy. And the modest young airman's appearance only reinforced the impression of plain simplicity. A marvelous visage, so open, almost childlike! All of the obituaries which were dedicated to this unforgettable man placed much too much emphasis on the masculinity, the sharpness of his appearance. At this moment, with his face animated by a slight embarrassment, a trace of an almost girlish softness became particularly evident in him. I have never seen cleaner, less dissipated features on a man of his age – Manfred von Richthofen, you will remain for all time a model of true, noblest heroism to our valiant, precious German youth! One word of request, of consent, and you could have rested on your laurels in honorable safety, away from danger, after your fortieth, your fiftieth air victory. But as you soared time and time again – to cleaner heights, for you had no equal – like the heavenly heroes of old, as you *outwardly* elevated yourself above the mixture of bravery and despair, of devotion to duty and baseness far below you – at the same time, you also showed us how the strong are *inwardly* above Life and Death in times of great death. To those who feel him ever near him, Death becomes the trusted "good comrade." With a smile, you overcame him, never feared him, the eternal exterminator of all pleasure and all pain! But at home and at the front, after each new aerial victory you achieved, there were hundreds of thousands who, in anxious foreboding, feared that all too soon he would wind the bloody laurels around your temple too. Immelmann, Boelcke, Richthofen! Is it the glory or the curse of this, the youngest and finest of all the armed forces, that its heroic fighters must descend so quickly from the radiant heights of their victorious careers?

Today, some might turn a cynical ear to the florid language of our regimental commander but for the day, it captured the feelings of a nation in mourning.

Opposite: The dress shoulder boards (above) and the service epaulets (below) of a *Leutnant* in Manfred von Richthofen's pre-air service unit, *Ulanen-Regiment Kaiser Alexander III. von Russland (Westpreussisches) Nr.1*. Both carry the oversize cipher of the regiment while the epaulets also have an undersized winged prop device of the *Fliegertruppe*. The underlying color on the boards is white with brass fittings. The epaulets are of grey cloth, flecked with black and white with white and red edges. These were in the collection of the Foundation for Aviation World War I and (what else?) when acquired were said to have belonged to von Richthofen. Their actual provenance was never proved although they were clearly original items from the period. They are now in the possession of the *Deutsches Technikmuseum Berlin* in Berlin.

RECIPIENTS OF THE BRUNSWICK WAR MERIT CROSS WITHOUT BIOGRAPHIES

Oberleutnant Walter Aschoff, an observer with *Kampfgeschwader/ Bombengeschwader 3*, was a recipient of the Brunswick War Merit Cross in both 1st and 2nd Class. Although in the thick of things from 1916 onwards including the early daylight raids on England, he survived the war.

Below, Gothas of *Bogohl 3* on their base at Gontrode in Belgium. The light colored G.IV was Aschoff's aircraft. Against a pale grey (at this time) fuselage, a green snake ran its entire length. It was thus referred to as the "Serpent Machine."

Above: Officers and men of *Kampfstaffel 15* of *Kagohl 3* in December 1916. Aschoff with hair parted in the middle, is on the first step, 2nd from the left. On his left also on the first step is *Kasta 15*'s CO, *Hptm.* Otto Hartmann. On December 15, Hartmann was awarded the Knight's Cross of the Württemberg Military Merit Order (in the ground troops in 1914, he had earned its Gold Military Merit Medal). Hartmann converted to fighters and served in *Jastas 18* and *28*, in the latter as its leader. He scored five victories there to add to the two he was credited with in *Kagohl 3* (where he may also have had two unconfirmed claims). Hartmann fell in flames on September 3, 1917. The only other personnel who can be identified here are a *Vzfw*. Richter, far left in back row, and a *Lt. Graf* von Soden, 2nd from right in back row.

Below: On an original print of the group photograph seen on this page, Hartmann wrote on the back, "To Lt. Aschoff, in remembrance of his departure from Fighting Section 15" and signed his name. Aschoff later commanded *Kasta/Bosta 17* of *Kagohl/Bogohl 3*, the "*Englandgeschwader*."

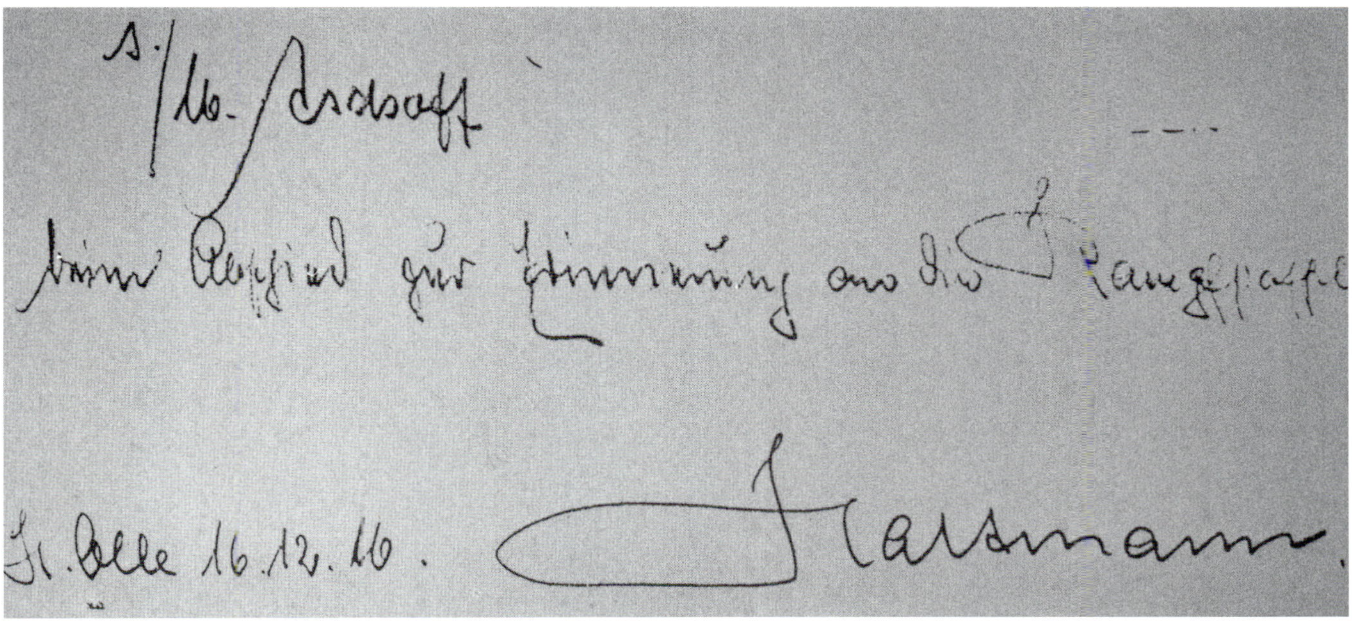

One of Aschoff's original tunics but not of the same style seen in the other photographs. The awards are his original ones which were in the collection of the Foundation for Aviation World War I, These, too, are now in Germany with the *Deutsches Technikmuseum Berlin* along with much else from its former collection. The Wound Badge in Black indicates that Aschoff suffered one or two woundings or injuries during the war. His Knight's Hohenzollern with Swords was awarded on December 4, 1917 and announced in the *Militär-Wochenblatt* on December 28.

Above: *Lt.* Paul Achilles of *Marine Jasta 5* (in helmet and goggles) and *Lt.z.See* Eberhard Cranz of *Marine Jasta 4* (on his left) survey Achilles' nosed-in Fokker D.VII somewhere in Flanders in the closing months of the war. Achilles, with eight victories, held the Brunswick War Merit Cross 2nd Class. The checkerboard marking inconveniently obscures the serial number of this plane.

The *Pour le Mérite* fighter pilot, *Oblt.* Hans Berr was killed in a Boelcke-like mid-air collision with one of his men on April 6, 1917. Born in Brunswick, Berr received the Duchy's War Merit Cross. His pre-air service connection with a fusilier regiment whose *Chef* was the Prince of Reuss resulted in Berr's getting two high Reuss awards and a full biography in Volume V in this series. For another view of the fatal crash scene shown here, see Page 25 of Volume V.

With his comrades in *Jasta 24* in the closing months of the war stands *Lt.* Otto Brandes, 5th from the left. Brandes had received the War Merit Cross 1st Class on May 30, 1918 (when he had been given the 2nd Class has not been found). Brandes joined *24* from *Jasta 15* on February 12 that year and scored his two officially confirmed victories there in August. Seated on the steps, bareheaded and playing with the pooch is the *Staffelführer*, *Oblt.* Hasso von Wedel. He took over the unit one week after its then commander, the *Pour le Mérite Oblt.* Heinrich Kroll, was seriously wounded in action on August 14 ending his combat career.

The men standing, left to right with their number of confirmed victories in the war in brackets, are: *Offz.-Stv.* Friedrich Altemeier (20/21 – Golden Military Merit Cross), *Lt.* Schicke (0 – *O.z.b.V.*), *Lt.* Fischer (0), *Lt.* Leppin (1), Brandes, *Lt.* Rudolf Hepp (1), *Lt.* Stickforth (2), *Unteroffz.* Schmid (0), *Vzfw.* Kurt Ungewitter (7) and *Vzfw.* Tschierschke (0 – also seen spelled Tschiwske). Seated on the steps, left to right, *Oblt.* Hasso von Wedel (5) and *Lt.* Friedrich Wendland (4). *Jasta 24* had been designated a Saxon contingent as from November 24, 1917 and as a consequence, Kroll received its Knight 2nd Class with Swords of the Albert Order and Altemeier its Silver Friedrich August Medal in 1918. The rolls of these awards stop at the end of March 1918 so it is not possible to say if von Wedel or any of the others here were similarly honored after that.

Above: The three flying von Bülow-Bothkamp brothers, Conrad, Walter (with the *Pour le Mérite*) and Harry. Conrad and Walter served in the 17th Brunswick Hussars and Harry in a Saxon Hussar regiment. Conrad and Harry both were awarded the Brunswick War Merit Cross but, strangely, not Walter despite his later prominence as a fighter pilot (28 victories and commands of *Jastas 36* and *Boelcke* and where Harry served under him). Walter was killed in an air battle on January 6, 1918 and Conrad, removed from the Western Front after Walter's death by order of the *Kaiser*, was sent to Finland as a flight instructor. There, on August 11, 1918, on takeoff in a seaplane, there was an engine problem and he crashed to his death.

Right: Harry von Bülow-Bothkamp started off as a pilot in *Feldflieger-Abteilung 53/Flieger-Abteilung (A)272* in late 1916 and recorded six victories as a fighter pilot. After Conrad's death, he, too, was taken off combat duties. Here his unknown observer's hand can be seen through the one of the port windows of this Roland C.II.

The then *Lt.* Hermann Fricke (right) links arms with his "Emil" (pilot), a *Lt.* von Schütze, in *Feldflieger-Abteilung 11* in the late fall of 1915. Their Aviatik C.I has a placard commemorating the unit's 1,000th flight against the enemy. Below, its men celebrate Christmas 1915. A close inspection of the photograph shows Fricke, a native of Wolfenbüttel, wearing the Brunswick War Merit Cross he received there on February 28, 1915 looped through a buttonhole of his tunic. Seated on the floor, center, is the CO, Hilmar von Bülow and on his left, the future fighter ace Josef Jacobs. Both Fricke and Jacobs were later to become Knights of the *Orden Pour-le Mérite*.

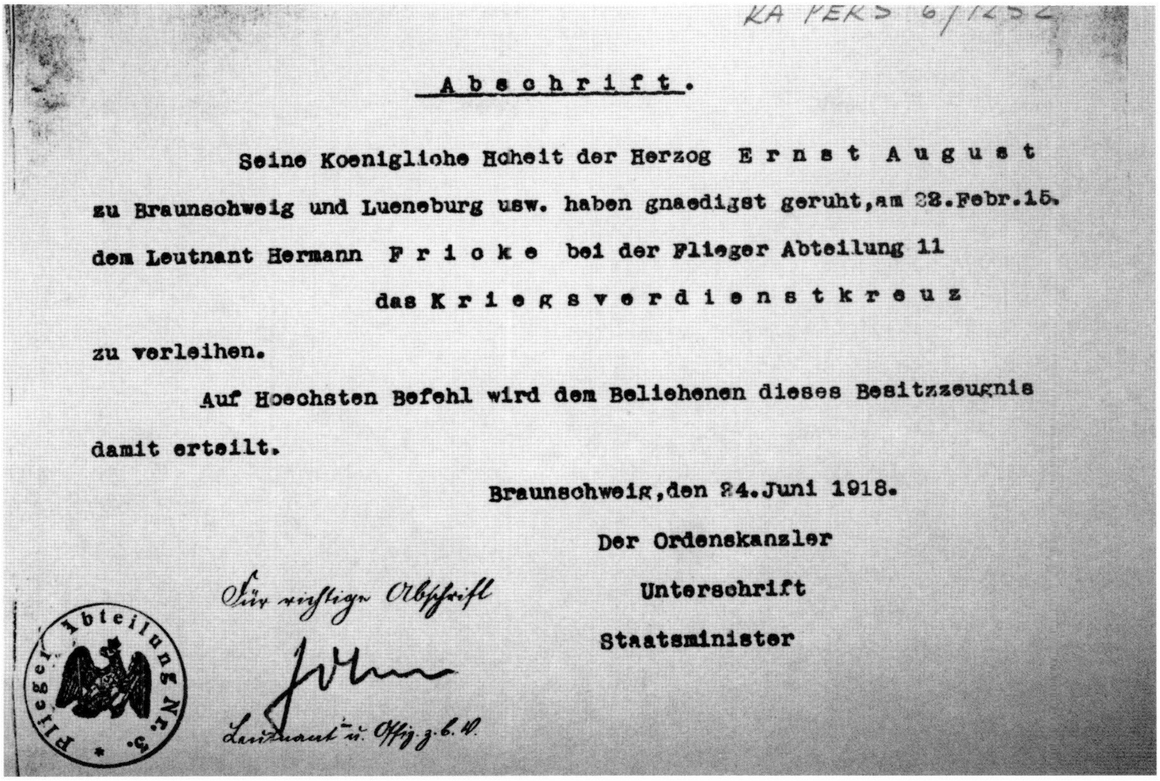

Abschrift.

Seine Koenigliche Hoheit der Herzog E r n s t A u g u s t zu Braunschweig und Lueneburg usw. haben gnaedigst geruht, am 28.Febr.15. dem Leutnant Hermann F r i c k e bei der Flieger Abteilung 11

das K r i e g s v e r d i e n s t k r e u z

zu verleihen.

Auf Hoechsten Befehl wird dem Beliehenen dieses Besitzzeugnis damit erteilt.

Braunschweig, den 24.Juni 1918.

Der Ordenskanzler

Unterschrift

Staatsminister

Transcripts dated 24 June 1918 confirming that Fricke had been awarded the Brunswick War Merit Cross (2nd Class) on 28 February 1915 while with *Feldflieger-Abteilung 11* and the newly instituted 1st Class cross as the leader of *Flieger-Abteilung 3*, apparently on that 24th of June. Fricke was a serial camera expert and was to go on to command *Reihenbildzug-Abteilung 2* with some 15 aircraft especially equipped with these cameras which were a big improvement over the hand-held types.

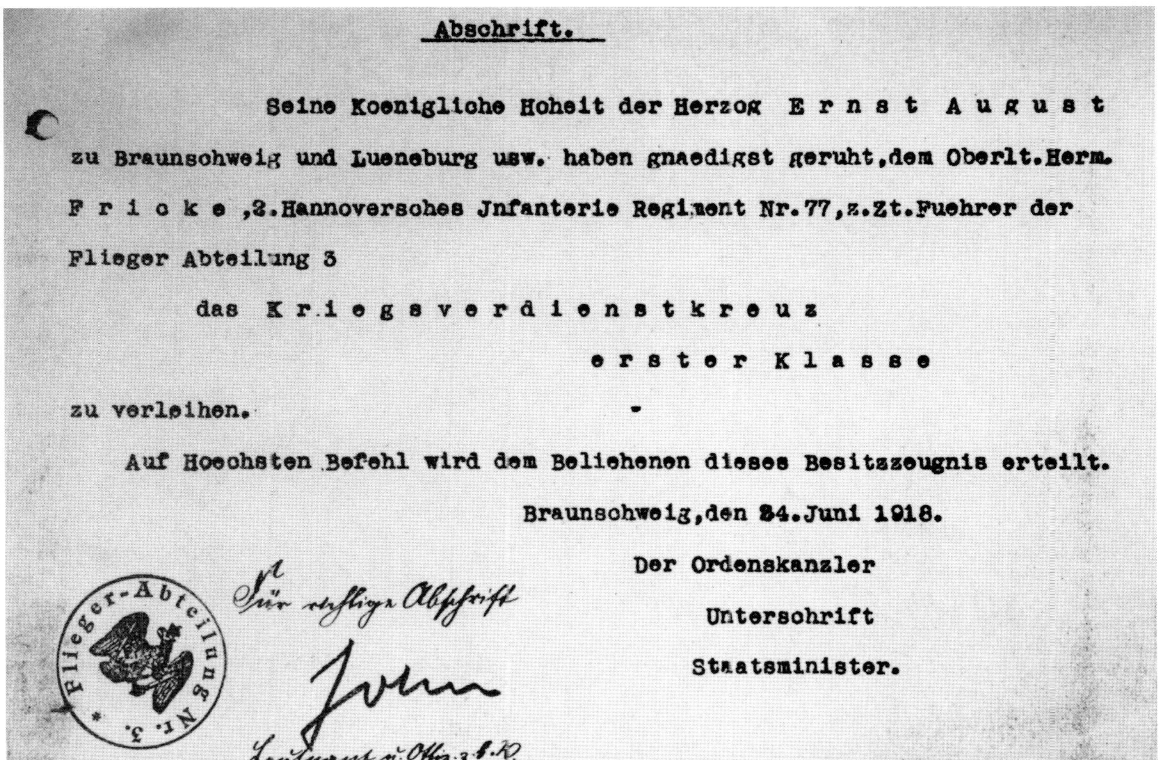

Abschrift.

Seine Koenigliche Hoheit der Herzog E r n s t A u g u s t zu Braunschweig und Lueneburg usw. haben gnaedigst geruht, dem Oberlt.Herm. F r i c k e ,2.Hannoversches Jnfanterie Regiment Nr.77, z.Zt.Fuehrer der Flieger Abteilung 3

das K r i e g s v e r d i e n s t k r e u z

e r s t e r K l a s s e

zu verleihen.

Auf Hoechsten Befehl wird dem Beliehenen dieses Besitzzeugnis erteilt.

Braunschweig, den 24.Juni 1918.

Der Ordenskanzler

Unterschrift

Staatsminister.

The originals of these two photographs were part of the effects of *Lt.* Ernst Hamster of *Jasta 37* that were once in the collection of the Foundation for Aviation World War I. In the view above, the striped tailplane of his Albatros, a *Jasta 37* marking, can be seen and whoever chose the angle for this shot certainly had a flair for the dramatic. It could be a poster for any 1930 Hollywood production. Hamster later changed his name to Hamscher ("Hamster" means the same in both German and English). He scored three times in *Jasta 37* in the fall of 1917 and then is said to have been in *Jasta 65* in 1918 without further success. Unfortunately, his surviving papers told little about his full wartime service. Whatever that was, he was highly decorated as the opposite photo shows. Among his awards were the Brunswick War Merit Cross 1st and 2nd Class with the latter having the *Bewährungs-Abzeichen* or for lack of a better English translation, the "Proved" clasp (see text for other interpretations of the German word).

The original *Grossordenschnalle* and *Feldschnalle* of *Lt.* Ernst Hamster. His full order bar display all his breast badge awards except his Knight's Cross with Swords of the Royal House Order of Hohenzollern which, for some reason, he never had mounted but retained it in its presentation case (see next page). The full bar "reads," Iron Cross 2nd Class, The Hesse General Honor Decoration "for Bravery," the Brunswick War Merit Cross 2nd Class with "Proved" clasp, the Honor Cross for the 1914-18 World War for Combatants, the Baltic Cross breast badge, the Austrian Silver Bravery Medal 2nd Class, the Bulgarian Silver Merit Medal with Crown on its "War Ribbon" and the Hungarian Commemorative War Medal for Combatants. The Baltic Cross indicates Hamster saw service in that area in 1918/1919 and his Austrian, Bulgarian and Hungarian awards in all likelihood mean that he saw service on the Eastern Front as a non-commissioned officer before promoted *Leutnant*. Hamster's *Feldschnalle* is interesting in that here the Knight's Hohenzollern appears in its proper position immediately after his Iron Cross 2nd Class ribbon. Also, now, the ribbon for his Brunswick War Merit Cross with "Proved" clasp takes the next pride of place. Curiously, next in line is his Bulgarian award followed by the Hessen Bravery Medal ribbon and finally, the ribbons for the Hungarian and German World War I Commemorative Medals. A strange arrangement indeed. The military tailor who made up this bar also folded the ribbons in the Austrian style whereas the ribbons on his *Grossordenschnalle* are draped in the Prussian style.

Right: Hamster's Iron Cross 1st Class has been reversed to show the engraving which reads, "In Constant Remembrance of Your Life War Year 1917." Such dedications were often made on the plain back of the cross, this one, no doubt, from his family.

Below: Hamster's other awards including his cased Knight's Hohenzollern with Swords complete with the extra piece of "War Ribbon" that came with it. Upper left, the Commemorative Flier's Badge (for three years' service in the *Fliegertruppe*, probably received postwar in 1920). Upper right, the rarely bestowed on German airmen Bulgarian Pilot's Badge. Lower left, the Brunswick War Merit Cross 1st Class. Lower right, the pin-back version of the Baltic Cross (there was only one class).

Left, *Lt.* Georg Heine, standing, and his observer, *Lt.* Alfons von Zeddelmann, of *Kagohl 1*. Heine was another 17th Brunswick Hussar and with them earned the War Merit Cross on January 27, 1915. The two were the first of *KG I* to fall at Verdun when their LVG C.II was shot down on February 26, 1916. Above, on the Ghistelles field, von Zeddelmann "goes through the ropes" as Heine pretends to catch him. The other man at the right is a *Lt.* Joschkowitz and at the left is *Lt.* Ernst Veiel who received the Württemberg Knight's Military Merit Order in *FFl.Abt. 25* on November 6, 1915, the 24th airman of the war to do so.

Former Marine Infantry *Lt.* Georg Hauptvogel also held the War Merit Cross. In *SeeFlieger-Abteilung I*, he and his pilot, *Flugzeugobermaat* Hermann Behrendt, went down in flames over Thorntonbank on April 1, 1918, credited to a Camel from No.215 Squadron, RAF.

Sous-Lt. Jean Navarre killed Heine and von Zeddelmann and forced down another *KG I* "Avion" on February 26, 1916 for the first French "double" of the war, his fourth and fifth victories from a final total of 12.

This page and opposite
Hermann Heise as a *Hauptmann* in the post-war *Reichswehr* uniform that was much ridiculed for its cord epaulets and (to some) ostentatious sleeve stripes. Not only can the *Bewärhungs-Abzeichen* ("Proved" clasp) be clearly seen on the ribbon of his 2nd Class Brunswick War Merit Cross on his order bar, but for good measure, he has a second one on the ribbon looped through a buttonhole on the front of his tunic. Opposite top we see him in his early flying days with either a 3-Bay Albatros B.1 or a 2-Bay Albatros B.II and below that a Fokker E.I or II and Gotha G.I 10/15 in *Sonderstaffel S.1* which he commanded and which was a special unit that also included three Albatros C.Is to protect the Krupp Works in Essen.

Oblt. Martin Körner in the full regalia of a Turkish *Hauptmann* wearing the Silver Imtiaz and Liakat Medals with Sabers, the War Medal and its joint Pilot's and Observer's Badge was also an early recipient of the Brunswick War Merit Cross. In the war, Körner first gained fame as one of the "*Tannenbergflieger*" whose reports materially contributed to the destruction of the Russian Second Army in August 1914. His valuable photo-reconnaissance work in the Dardanelles in 1915 brought further praise but his career there was cut short when he ran afoul of the head of the German Military Mission to Turkey, *General der Kavallerie* Otto Liman von Sanders. In a telephone call to von Sanders, Körner thought he was talking to an underling and used crude language. Von Sanders ordered him out of the theater in January 1916, refusing an apology. Körner returned to the Western Front where, as the leader of *Fl.Abt. (A)269*, he was killed in action a year later, on January 23, 1917.

Below: Another War Merit Cross holder with but days to live, *Oblt*. Werner Jahns, seated at far left with men of his new command, *Jasta 28w*. He led the unit for all of two weeks before falling on September 24, 1917. Here at Schloss Varsenaere are, left to right: Jahns, *Lt*. Otto Koch, *Lt*. Alfred Welss, *Lt*. Erwin Wenig, *Vzfw*. Paul Wagner (behind Wenig), *Lt*. August Hanko, *Lt*. Waldemar Janssen, *Lt*. Franz Ray and *Lt*. Ernst Hess. Their service in Württemberg *Jasta 28* earned Koch, Welss, Janssen, Ray and Hess its Friedrich Order Knight 2nd Class with Swords and Hanko its Gold Military Merit Medal.

Two Brunswick War Merit Cross recipients, both fatalities. Above, at left in his 17th Hussar tunic, *Lt.* Eduard von Marcard killed in *Fl.Abt.12* on March 17, 1917 after one victory in *KG 4* on May 20, 1916. He and his pilot were Guynemer's 35th victim. Right, *Rittm.* Deodat *Graf* von Oriola in this faded photograph. He fell on the Eastern Front on July 27, 1915. An artist has drawn in his Iron Cross 1st Class as well as the Oldenburg Friedrich August Cross which he earned in both classes.

A solitary guard keeps watch over what was left of Albatros B.II 798/14 at *FEA 3* Gotha on February 2, 1916. Killed in the accident were *Oblt.* Max Kleiser von Kleisheim, observer, and *Lt.* Walter von Rieck-Eggebert, pilot. Von Rieck-Eggebert was another former 17th Hussar who held the Brunswick War Merit Cross. Prewar, his meritorious service gained him the Brunswick Honor Decoration in Silver and the Prussian Red Eagle Order 4th Class.

The then *Lt.* Friedrich Starke, 2nd from right, and other officers of *FFl-Abt. 21* on their field near Reims with one of their LVG B.Is in the spring of 1915. As the provisional certificate of possession attests, Starke received the Brunswick War Merit Cross on January 11, 1915. His other decorations included the Anhalt Friedrich Cross (April 27, 1915), the Iron Cross 2nd Class (January 27, 1916) and the Iron Cross 1st Class (March 24, 1916). Others are, left to right, two unknowns, Alfred Behm, Erich Suchsland, Franz Geertz, two more unknowns, Deodat *Graf* von Oriola (see previous page), unknown, Starke and Eugen von Loessel.

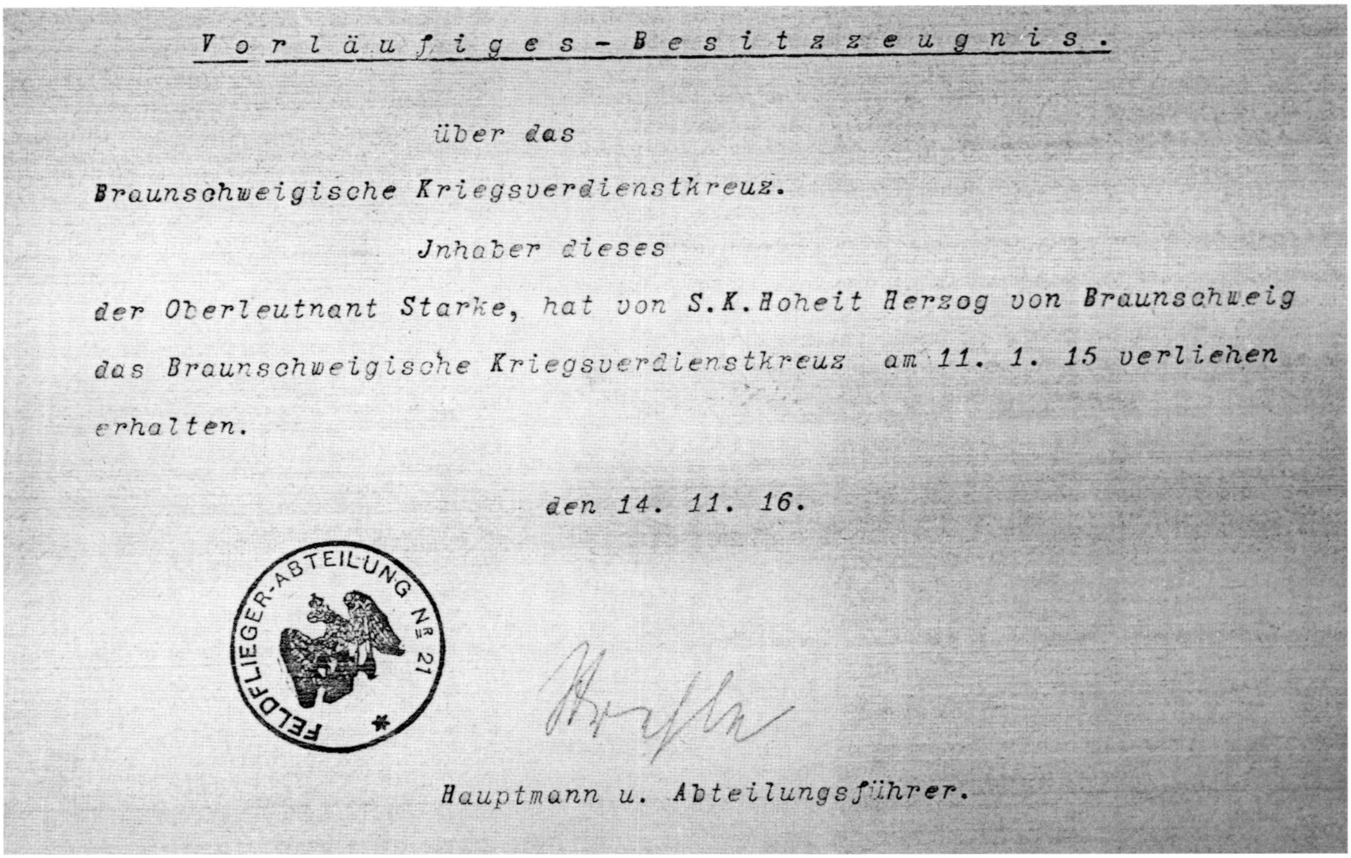

V o r l ä u f i g e s - B e s i t z z e u g n i s .

über das

Braunschweigische Kriegsverdienstkreuz.

Jnhaber dieses

der Oberleutnant Starke, hat von S.K.Hoheit Herzog von Braunschweig das Braunschweigische Kriegsverdienstkreuz am 11. 1. 15 verliehen erhalten.

den 14. 11. 16.

FELDFLIEGER-ABTEILUNG Nº 21

Hauptmann u. Abteilungsführer.

Despite fighter pilot service going back to the fall of 1916 in *Jasta 4*, *Lt.* Burkart Strauch, another Brunswick War Merit Cross recipient, was unable to score a victory although he survived the war. Above, he stands between two nursing sister visitors while the chef pronounces the "benediction." With their *Pour le Mérites*, from the left, Hans-Joachim Buddecke, Ernst *Freiherr* von Althaus and Walter Höhndorf. Still to earn his is Otto Bernert at far right. Below, Strauch as a member of *Jasta 41* with *Lt.* Hans Weiss (Knight's Hohenzollern in *Jasta 11* on April 21, 1918) on his right and at far left, *Vzfw*. Hermann Juhnke (Golden Military Merit Cross on July 16, 1918 for his earlier service in *Fl.Abt. (A)238)*.

Oberstlt. Hermann von der Lieth-Thomsen was appointed Chief of Field Aviation on March 27, 1915 and in that capacity was awarded the Brunswick War Merit Cross on May 3, 1916. Despite his expanded responsibilities as *Kogenluft*'s Chief of Staff later that year, he never received it in the 1st Class.

Right: An unidentified recipient of the Brunswick War Merit Cross, said to have been a pilot in *Jasta 9*. His rank is *Offz.-Stv.* and he must have been an old-timer, having earned the Prussian Crown Order Medal prewar in addition to his wartime awards of both the Oldenburg Friedrich August Crosses.

Another well-known prewar flier was the then *Leutnant*, later *Rittmeister*, Luitpold *Graf* von Wolffskeel here giving a royal visitor in the person of *Prinz* Leopold of Bavaria a ride in Otto No. 81 in 1912. Von Wolffskeel was decorated with the Knight 2nd Class of the Brunswick Order of Henry the Lion (without Swords) on May 9, 1914 and then on March 25, 1915, its War Merit Cross. He was the first leader of Bavarian *FFl.Abt. 2*, the later *Fl.Abt. 45b*.

MORE "*TOTENKOPF HUSAREN*" AND POSSIBLE RECIPIENTS OF THE BRUNSWICK WAR MERIT CROSS

Above: This fine view of Albatros C.III 731/16 at *Feldflieger-Abteilung 1* on its field at Mouzry in August 1916 is worthy of inclusion even if its ex-hussar officer observer, a *Lt.* Metzel, may not have been a recipient of the Brunswick War Merit Cross. All we know about his pilot is that his name was Mader. By August 1916, there were some 354 Albatros C.IIIs at the front and until replaced by more powerful C-types in April 1917, including the Albatros C.VII, was a real workhorse of the *Luftstreitkräfte*. It remained in production until war's end as a trainer. Right: With scarf and goggles around his neck and arms akimbo, this former hussar strikes a jaunty pose at a *Flieger-Ersatz-Abteilung* where he was no doubt in training for his new profession. He, too, may have been a War Merit Cross recipient although the ribbon he is wearing is not that. Nor is it the Iron Cross 2nd Class which was an almost necessary prerequisite before receiving bravery awards from other states. Its light background with two dark side stripes suggests a Württemberg Military Merit Order or Merit Medal however.

Opposite
Top: German officers at the Army aviation supply depot at Cambrai in 1916 entertain four of their British "guests." The glum looking hussar seated in the center is *Lt.* Hans-Joachim Rogalla von Bieberstein. His Iron Cross 2nd Class is represented by ribbons forming a bow which was typically done on the hussar's frogged tunics. Von Bieberstein had two unconfirmed victories in *Jasta 3* before being killed on May 6, 1918 in an Albatros D.Va in an accident over his Rumbeke airfield

Bottom: The photographer was not very careful with his flood lamps when he copied this view of the men of *Jasta 15* and their leader, the 39-victory *Pour le Mérite* ace, *Lt.* Heinrich Gontermann. The "Death's Head" hussar, 4th from the right, is not identified but other familiar faces are *Offz.Stv.* Richard Schleichardt, 3rd from left, *Lt.* Kurt Monnington, 4th from left, *Lt.* Hans Hermann von Budde, 8th from left in white cap, *Lt.* Heinrich Arntzen, 5th from right, and *Lt.* Otto Ludwig Förster, 2nd from right. The date is October 1917 so Gontermann would not see the month out, dying on October 30 from a crash on the 29th while test flying a new Fokker triplane Dr.1 115/17.

CHAPTER V

THE GRAND DUCAL HOUSE OF HESSE

The origins of the House of Hesse (the name itself derives from a Frankish tribe called the Hessi which inhabited the area in the early centuries A.D.) and the House of Brabant can be traced back to the 9th century. In the next six or seven hundred years, between wars, marriages and inheritance, the usual gains, losses and divisions of lands ensued, too complex a matter to worry about here. Perhaps an appropriate place to start would be with Landgrave Philipp who was born in 1504 and who came to be called "the Magnanimous" (and whose name was given to one of Hesse's house orders when it was founded). He was an early champion of Luther and the Reformation for which we was to pay dearly. At age 20, he joined in the brutal suppression of what was known as the Peasant's War. Since the 1400s, the peasants and poorer townspeople had been engaging in periodic protests and disturbances having to do with their grievances, mostly economic and political. But when Martin Luther attacked the church and preached what to them was heresy, religious zeal took over and formed the base for a full scale revolt. The peasants believed that God would be on their side (the *Gott mit Uns* of an earlier day) and that with His intercession, they would prevail. Instead, an army of the Swabian League crushed them in 1525. An estimated 100,000 peasants were slaughtered. Luther himself condemned the revolt and was a contributing factor in its defeat.

Philipp continued to support the cause of Protestantism any way he could. He was instrumental in helping form the Schmalkaldic League along with John Friedrich of Saxony and others to stand against the Holy Roman Empire. Philipp further incurred Emperor Charles' wrath by aiding Protestant Duke Ulrich of Württemberg to regain his throne after he had been deposed. But then a scandal enveloped Philipp in 1540 when he was caught in a bigamous marriage. He was forced to make peace with Charles and beg forgiveness. Then Charles adroitly wooed Maurice of Saxony away from Philipp's camp and war broke out again. At the Battle of Mühlberg in 1547, the Schmalkaldic League suffered a heavy defeat. Philipp surrendered in the belief his station would be respected. Instead, he was thrown into prison and when he emerged in 1552, he was a broken man. Philipp died in 1567 and his holdings were divided among his sons. The eldest, Landgrave Wilhelm IV "the Wise," inherited about half of Hesse and established his capital in Cassel. His line later became known as the Electoral House of Hesse. Philipp's youngest son, Georg I, received lands called the Upper County of Katzzenelbogen and established Darmstadt as its capital. A descendant of his, Ludewig X, joined Napoleon's Confederation of the Rhine and in return, Hesse-Darmstadt was elevated to the status of a Grand Duchy in 1806. He then became Grand Duke Ludewig I and in 1816, adopted the further title of Grand Duke of Hesse and by Rhine by which the house thereafter was formally called. Back in Hesse-Cassel, one of the later heirs of those estates, a man named Karl, found a novel way to improve the finances of his little country. He began the practice of hiring out his soldiery to anyone who met his price. Thus was created the famous (some would say infamous) band of mercenaries known generically as "Hessians." We will now take a slight departure in narrating the development of the Grand Ducal House of Hesse to comment on how these soldiers for hire figured in the American Revolution.

At the time the American colonies proclaimed their independence from Great Britain, Landgrave Friedrich II was on the throne in Cassel. He had married the fourth daughter of King George III of England so when he called for outside help to put the rebels down, Friedrich had an additional reason beyond money to respond (while Catherine the Great of Russia refused to sell England the 20,000 troops requested of her as did Frederick the Great of Prussia). From the opening Battle of Long Island in 1776 right up to the siege of Yorktown in 1781, Hessian mercenaries were in action, often extremely savage on both sides, against the colonials. It is said that Friedrich was paid between four and five shillings per grenadier with a further bounty of the same amount if the man were killed and for every three wounded, a like amount. These Hessians must have been a fearful sight to the often rag-tag American army what with their dark-blue uniforms, colored facings and bristling mustaches fixed firmly in place by liberal applications of boot blacking, all topped by a dome-shaped highly ornamental silver grenadier's cap. Their love of the bayonet at close-in quarters was renowned. Perhaps the Hessians best known action in the war was not one of their finest. As every American schoolboy knows, Washington crossed the Delaware on Christmas night 1776 and went on to become first in the hearts of his countrymen. And it was the Hessians he was after. Washington, and indeed the whole colonial cause, badly needed a victory somewhere. Support for the revolution was fast ebbing and the many Loyalists in the colonies were clamoring for a return to the mother country.

On that Christmas night, Washington had assembled about 2,400 men on the south bank of the Delaware about nine miles upstream from the Hessian garrison in the town of Trenton, New Jersey. Downstream from the town, another 1,800 Pennsylvania militia and between 600 and 800 Regulars were positioned to cross at the same time and block any attempt by the Hessians to retreat in their direction. Some skirmishing around Hessian outposts had alerted the Hessian commander, Colonel Johann Gottlieb Rall, that something was up but he was contemptuous of the American troops anyhow and promised if those "clodhoppers" dared to attack, his men would rout them. Rall was dining and gambling late that night at the home of a wealthy Trenton Tory when another loyalist wanted to interrupt with an important bit of intelligence. Washington was on the move. But the man was turned away, Rall's host, one Mr. Hunt, not wanting to disturb his guest. But the man was allowed to scribble the warning down and the note was sent in to Rall who merely stuffed it into his waistcoat.

The battle was joined just before 8:00 a.m. on December 26, Boxing Day to the British. Unprepared and perhaps the worse for wear due to holiday partying, the Hessians were quickly overwhelmed. It was all over in 90 minutes. A few of Rall's command escaped but most were forced to surrender. Twenty three officers and men were killed with Rall himself one of the fatalities. He had been mortally wounded and as his uniform was stripped away to dress his injuries, that warning note was discovered. When it was shown to him, he is supposed to have said (he spoke no English), "*Hätte ich dies zu Herrn Hunt gelesen, so wäre ich jetz nicht hier.*" ("Had I read this at Mr. Hunt's, I would not be here"). Rall lingered on in terrible pain for more than a day before expiring. Cornwallis was already moving down the Princeton Pike to attack Washington but by an adroit move, his army slipped around and moved on Princeton itself. There it engaged British Regulars and Highlanders and won another victory before successfully escaping into winter quarters. The colonial cause had also won a crucial reprieve and while hard times were still to come before, with the aid of France, the British finally marched out of besieged Yorktown with drums and fifes playing "The World Turned Upside Down" and capitulated, the events in Trenton and Princeton were a major turning point in the American Revolution. Had Rall not been so self-assured and foolhardy and had his troops been on the alert and in position, and had they been able to hold out until reinforced, this writer might be penning these lines in Princeton, Colony of New Jersey in the Loyal Commonwealth of the Americas. But now, to go back to developments in the Hesses.

Hessian contingents would ultimately comprise four regiments of infantry, two of mounted dragoons, two of field artillery and a service detachment. By tracing their histories up to and then through the First World War, we can also work in the history of Hesse-Cassel and Hesse-Darmstadt and the other minor branches of the line.[1] The first Hessian regiment of the line was *Leibgarde-Infanterie-Regiment (1. Grossherzoglich Hessisches) Nr.115*. (Life (or Body) Guard Infantry Regiment (1st Grand Ducal Hessian) No.115). It's origins went back to 1621 when Company Dressler was formed and became the Princely *Leib* company in 1630. In 1697, a district regiment was raised on the Upper Rhine known as Regiment Prince Carl Wilhelm and renamed *Regiment Landgraf* in 1777. It was the antecedent of the infantry *Leibregiment Grossherzogin Nr.117*. The 118th regiment had its roots in county battalions of 1699 that became the garrison regiment *Erbprinz* in 1791 and was enlarged by a field battalion in 1794. The 116th regiment came from district and town regiments in the landgrave's territory

[1] The Houses of Hesse-Marburg and Hesse-Rheinfels had become extinct in 1583 and 1604 respectively and the Hesse-Homburg line likewise in 1866 whereupon the land passed to Grand Duke Ludwig III of Hesse who in the same year was forced to cede that new territory to Prussia. The lines Hesse-Philippsthal and Hesse-Philippsthal-Barchfeld survived into the 20th century but others had fallen by the wayside too (Hesse-Wenfried in 1755 and Hesse-Rheinfels-Rotenburg in 1834).

established between 1741 and 1790 and was incorporated in the *Leibgarde*. This became a regiment and fought from 1792 to 1799 against the revolutionary French army along the Franco-German border together with the 1st company of the new Landgrave Hessian Field Artillery Corps. The other artillery company was attached to the *Landgraf* regiment.

A cheveauleger (dragoon) regiment was newly established in 1790 and was called the Guard Chevaulegers Regiment in 1806, consisting of three squadrons. It saw action in the campaign on the Rhine and then was sold to Britain together with the fusilier battalion and *Regiment Landgraf*. They formed the 2nd Hessian Brigade under Major General von Düring, serving in Holland between 1793 and 1795. The *Landgraf* regiment was also in Austrian service until 1799.

Both Hesse-Cassel and Hesse-Darmstadt had been fighting France, Cassel as a result of subsidies provided by England for its troops and Darmstadt in its own right as part of the Holy Roman Empire. In 1795, Cassel signed a peace with France at Basle and Darmstadt did likewise at Luneville in 1801. The *Leib* regiment was expanded to a brigade in 1803 that incorporated parts of the later 116th and *Landgraf* regiments. The rest of *Landgraf* and regiment *Erbprinz* were also expanded to brigades, the latter as a field brigade, and included the dragoons. Hesse-Darmstadt was to prosper under the patronage of Napoleon but it was a different story with Hesse-Cassel. The Corsican corporal gave Darmstadt the remaining Imperial lands within her borders upon *Landgraf* Ludwig's joining the *Rheinbund* (Confederation of the Rhine) in 1806 and raised Darmstadt to the dignity of a grand duchy that year as already related. Cassel at first got off to a similarly good start under Napoleon and in 1803, having swapped some territories with France, *Landgraf* Wilhelm was elevated to the then-coveted title *Kürfurst* (Elector) of the Holy Roman Empire. The now *Kurfürst* Wilhelm I managed to incur Napoleon's wrath, however, when he partially mobilized his forces when France launched an attack on Prussia in 1806. Napoleon simply dissolved Hesse-Cassel and handed it over to his brother Jerome's new Kingdom of Westphalia. In November 1813, the kingdom having collapsed, Wilhelm was restored to his former position although by now, the title of Prince Elector was an empty one.

Meantime, the now Grand Ducal brigades fought with the French army against Prussia and took part in the Battle of Jena (1806). Brigade *Gross-& Erbprinz* (as it was now called) including a half company of artillery went with the French army's 4th Corps Lefevre to Spain as the *Regiment de Hesse* to fight in the Peninsular War from 1808 to 1812. There they served with great distinction although their contribution was glossed over by the French. The Hessian force was virtually wiped out and only a few survivors eventually struggled back from British prisons. During the Peninsular War, the Hessians were also active elsewhere against the enemies of France. In 1809, the other Hessian brigades, the artillery and the dragoons fought with French Corps Massena against Austria at the battles of Agram and Wagram, losing somewhere between 25-40% of their strength. A provisionary light infantry regiment was created from the guard fusilier and the *Leib* fusilier battalions in 1812, the year Napoleon's *Grand Armée*, 500,000 strong including troops from vassal and allied states like Hesse, embarked on the invasion of Russia.

The Hessian contribution to this force amounted to some 5,000 officers and men, 80-95% of whom never returned. By March 1813, one could count only two officers, seven NCOs and 12 men answering the roll call of the *Leib* brigade. The dragoons had five officers and 42 troopers left. Somehow, the Hessian contingents were reconstituted. The *Leib* guard regiment and the *Leib* regiment (formerly *Landgraf*) were brought up to full strength, a total of 1,300-1,500 officers and men. The guard fusilier regiment (later *Nr.116.*) was brought up to battalion strength. The few returnees from Russia were parceled out to these units and together, along with the artillery corps, formed a part of Marshal Ney's corps. The dragoons, too, were resuscitated with two squadrons of 338 riders in April 1813 and the same number again in July joining the French VI Corps and later its XIIth. They fought the Prussians at Lützen and Gross-Görschen in May and took part in the Battle of Leipzig October 16-19 that year – the so called Battle of the Nations where the combined forces of Austria, Prussia and Russia decisively defeated Napoleon while another French force at nearby Möckern was trounced by the Prussians under Blücher on the first day at Leipzig. The Hessians had again lost more than half their troops with the dragoons casualties amounting to 85% of their strength. Licking their wounds, the remnants fled with the main French body beginning its retreat across Germany and over the Rhine. With that, the Confederation of the Rhine was disbanded and Grand Duke Ludewig I joined the other German states in the allied liberation army. The process of replenishing the Hessian contingents began once again so that by the time Napoleon reappeared in 1815 for the second and last time, his troops were in action again but now facing their former ally.

Ludewig died in 1830 and was succeeded by his eldest son Ludwig. The new Grand Duke Ludwig II renamed all the regiments. The guards became the 1st Infantry Guard Regiment (*Leib* Guard), the guard fusiliers the 2nd Infantry Regiment (*Grossherzog*), the *Leib* the 3rd Infantry Regiment (*Leib-*

regiment) and the *Gross-& Erbprinz* the 4th Infantry Regiment (*Grossherzogin*). During the 1830 and 1848/49 revolutions, the Hessian regiments fought the insurgents, first at home and then in Frankfurt and Baden. The artillery were in Schleswig but saw no action there. A new cavalry regiment was created in 1860 from the guard chevaulegers, the *2. Reiter-Regiment* (*Leib-Chevaulegers-Regiment*) and the guards were renamed *1. Reiter-Regiment* (*Garde-Chevaulegers-Regiment*).

The two Hesses made the understandable mistake of siding with Austria in the war with Prussia in 1866, understandable because of the powerful alliance that was formed against the upstart Prussians under Bismarck. Only a couple of the lesser Thuringian duchies stood by Prussia. Such powerful states as Bavaria, Saxony, Württemberg, Baden, Hanover and Nassau in addition to Hesse-Darmstadt and Hesse-Cassel were sure to crush Prussia, or so everyone was quick to conclude. The result was just the opposite as readers of this series, where the story has been told before in discussing those states, are well aware. Austria and its allies went down to a humiliating defeat as they were beaten in detail in a matter of just seven weeks. In its aftermath, Prussia annexed Hesse-Cassel, Hesse-Homburg, Hanover, Nassau and the Free City of Frankfurt. Hesse-Darmstadt got off relatively easy, having to pay reparations like most of the others but losing only a small portion of its possessions and retaining its privileges. The new (1848) Grand Duke Ludwig III now found himself excluded from the North German Confederation formed by Bismarck in 1867 though. He and his south German neighbors, Baden, Bavaria and Württemberg were left in a sort of limbo now that Austria was no longer a factor in German affairs and with the one-time ally turned enemy, France, just across the Rhine. Militarily, Hesse had not come through the war too badly on the other hand. It had lost only about 15% of its forces, mostly from the third and fourth regiments at a single engagement at Frohnhofen. But Bismarck wasn't through with Hesse completely. On April 7, 1867, by way of a military convention, Hesse was forced to see its entire division transferred to the Prussian army.

In the Franco-Prussian War of 1870, the Hessians were once again heavily engaged. The Hessian 25th Division of the 9th Corps was part of the Second Army. The Guard regiment had the guard *Jäger* battalion attached with the second *Jäger* assigned to the 4th Regiment. The dragoons were combined in the 25th Cavalry Brigade. In the opening days of the campaign, 9th Corps moved from south of Metz to Mars-la-Tour hoping to outflank the French army. In the Battle of Gravelotte on August 18, 1870, 25th Division, along with 18th Division, was moving to try to outflank the enemy again but ran straight into the French center. Severe *chassepot* and *mitrailleuse* (breech-loading needle gun and multi-barrel gun) fire forced them along with the division's advanced artillery corps to retreat into the laps of their own advancing infantry. Losses were over 60%. The 25th and the 18th came under attack by two French corps but despite more heavy casualties, their lines held. The Hessians even advanced to Champenois to more favorable positions. In this engagement, the 25th Division lost about 14% of its strength, almost a third of which were men killed. The 1st Regiment's losses amounted to 10% but the guard *Jäger* battalion's were 28%. The commanding officers of the 3rd and 4th Regiments and of the guard *Jäger* were killed along with a high proportion of other officers. No wonder. They were expected to be in the forefront of their men in any attack and they did what was expected of them.

The division's next major action involved the encirclement of the Metz fortress. Here the typhoid epidemic that had afflicted the Mecklenburgers spread to the Hessians. They developed 499 cases between August 19 and October 29. Nonetheless, Metz fell after a two month siege and 179,000 French soldiers capitulated. The 2nd Army was then ordered to Fountainbleau to join in blocking any attempt by the now republican French Army of National Defense to relieve the siege of Paris from the south. We will now capsulize the rest of the campaign as far as the Hessians were concerned. They pushed the advancing French Army of the Loire back to Orleans and occupied the city on December 3. On the 7th, they were part of the forces moving south into the Sologne toward Salbris. The 1st, 3rd and 4th Hessian regiments and the dragoons moved to the left bank of the Loire with the 1st Regiment taking the famous Chateau of Chambord where they caught 12 ammunition trains and took 200 prisoners. Then they and the 4th Regiment together with cavalry and the divisional artillery took Vienne on the other side of Blois and followed the right wing of the Second Army toward Vendôme. After a false report had them charging off to meet French troops under General Bourbaki which were supposedly bent on another try to relieve Paris, the rest of the 9th Corps turned around and pursued Chancy's army to Le Mans leaving the Hessians to protect their rear. The rest of the war was spent mainly in some minor skirmishing in the sector with action winding down in the northwest. On January 28, 1871, the day Paris fell, an armistice was signed. The Hessian losses during the war were not insignificant.

Table 5-1
The Approximate Losses of the Hessen-Darmstadt Division in the 1870/1871 War

Unit	Strength at Mobilization	Total Losses	Killed	Wounded	Prisoners	Died of Illness (mostly typhoid)
1st Inf. Rgt.	2,121	521 (25%)	130	303		88
2nd Inf. Rgt.	2,120	503 (24%)	125	316		62
3rd Inf. Rgt.	2,122	356 (17%)	86	270		
4th Inf. Rgt.	2,084	210 (10%)	35	110		65
1st Jäger	1,062	295+ (28%)[1]	75	220		
2nd Jäger	1,055	267 (25%)	40	143	50	34
1st Dragoons	670	81 (12%)	13	27	4	37
2nd Dragoons	667	97 (15%)	15	19	36	27
Artillery Corps	170	202 (118%)	34	122		46
Total	12,071	2,532+ (21%+)	553+	1,530+	90+	359+

Note:
1. Only losses at the Battle of Gravelotte. Total losses of the 1st Jägers would have been higher.

After the creation of the German Empire following the successful conclusion of the Franco-Prussian War, the Military Convention of 1867 between Hesse and Prussia was renewed on June 13, 1871 and with effect from January 1, 1872, the Hesse-Darmstadt contingents were assigned Prussian numbers. The merry-go-round of name changes finally ended between 1891 and 1906 and the final designations of the five Hessian infantry regiments, the two dragoon regiments, the two field artillery regiments and the train detachment that fought in World War I can be found in the list of fatalities of prewar officers in these units who were later seconded to the *Fliegertruppe* as shown in Appendix II.

At the start of World War I, these units made up the 25th Division which was also known as the Hessian Grand Ducal Division. Together with the 21st Division whose four infantry regiments were drawn from the nearby Frankfurt, Bad Homburg, Mainz and Hanau areas, they comprised the 18th Amy Corps that entered Luxembourg, Belgian Luxembourg and France in August 1914. The losses in the German Army that month as they marched in open field array were far beyond what the High Command had expected. The 25th Division, for example, saw its 116th Infantry Regiment down to a bare four companies by August 31 after sharp engagements in the Ardennes. Nonetheless, the entire division took part in the Battle of the Marne in the next weeks. After the retreat, it settled into fixed positions on the extreme right flank of the German line around Peronne and spent most of 1915 resting in quiet zones, refitting and being reinforced for the next blood bath soon to come. It was during this time, in March 1915, that the 118th Infantry was detached and assigned to the 56th Division, a newly formed outfit.

The Hessian units minus the 118th were in the spearhead of the massive attack on Verdun which kicked off on February 21, 1916. After some initial success, they were stopped cold and by mid-March, had to be relieved and sent to the rear to be reorganized once again. Back in the line in early April, the 25th Division incurred very heavy losses in attacks in the Caillette Wood area where the French had just counterattacked a few days before. Before the month was out, it again had to be relieved. Their Hessian comrades in the 118th were thrown into the cauldron of Verdun at the aptly named Mort Homme on the left bank of the Meuse in late May where on the 31st it suffered heavily as the French continued their attempts to regain all lost ground regardless of cost. They were engaged there until the middle of July and after a rest found themselves on the Somme in late August, early September where Haig's folly known as the Battle of the Somme had begun on July 1. The 25th Division, too, was there, beginning on September 15

Left: Grand Duke Ernst Ludwig, the ruler of Hesse during the period of World War I. At the neck he wears the Grand Cross with Swords of the Merit Order of Philipp the Magnanimous and below that we see the badge of the Hessian Order of the Golden Lion suspended from its collar. The breast star is the Grand Cross of the Ludewig (or Ludwig) Order. Below left: Prince Heinrich of Hesse-Darmstadt wearing the military orders of the *Pour le Mérite* and the Royal House Order of Hohenzollern and collar and badge of the Prussian High Order of the Black Eagle. The breast star below his order bar is that of the Golden Lion. Below: Prince Joachim of Prussia was a member of *Husaren-Regiment Landgraf Friedrich II. von Hessen-Homburg (2. Kurhessisches) Nr.14.* and has his Grand Cross of the Ludwig Order pinned above his 1st Class Iron Cross.

having been pulled out of Verdun to meet the new threat. In two weeks, the Division was reduced to the point where it had to be withdrawn and was not back on the Somme until the end of November where things were finally winding down.

Although it was in and out of the lines on the Western Front throughout 1917, ending up around Passchendaele in Flanders in the middle of November, the 25th Division was not involved in any really important actions after the beating it took on the Somme the year before. But the desperate last-chance Ludendorff drives of 1918 saw it still once again heavily involved in the fighting. Its gallant conduct at St. Quentin and before Amiens and the good account it gave of itself rated a personal inspection by the *Kaiser* himself on April 20 who, just three days before, had approved the award of the *Orden Pour le Mérite* to a battalion commander of the 117th Infantry, *Hauptmann* Achim von Arnim for his actions to date in the spring offensive, particularly his breakthrough enemy positions on the opening day, March 21 (he came from a distinguished line of soldiers with his *Pour le Mérite* being the 11th that had been awarded to his family). The 25th Division was in action until the very end suffering what was called exceedingly heavy losses, especially in officers. Its former 118th Infantry Regiment, too, was fully involved in the Battle of France in 1918 and in a communiqué on October 26, was singled out for special praise.

With that background, we can now go on and discuss the military awards of the Grand Duchy at the time of World War I and some of their aviation recipients. First, however, this treatise would not be complete without some mention, brief as it will be, about Hesse's rich tradition of high orders that were far beyond the reach of the young airmen.

Two of these went back to the late 1700s and early 1800s. They were, respectively, the Order of the Golden Lion and the Order of Ludewig (more commonly called the Order of Ludwig). Both survived up to the end of World War I. The Order of the Golden Lion came in one class and was given to princes of the Grand Ducal and allied Houses. The Order of Ludwig was a multi-class affair but its Grand Cross ranked equally with the Golden Lion. The Golden Lion was founded on August 14, 1770 by *Landgraf* Friedrich II of Hesse-Cassel. The Ludwig Order's founder was Grand Duke Ludewig I of Hesse-Darmstadt who instituted it on August 25, 1807. Also in Hesse-Darmstadt, but generations later and just prior to the war on June 14, 1914, Grand Duke Ernst Ludwig created a new order which could be awarded to both men and (in some grades) to women for services to the state and his house called the Order of the Star of Brabant (named after a former duchy that had been divided between Belgium and the Netherlands originally and from which Ernst Ludwig could claim antecedents). The badges and stars of the Golden Lion and Order of Ludwig were classic in design but those of the Star of Brabant, particularly the badges, were something else again. With their surreal design, they appeared to be the work of early 20th century Paris cubists and typical of what would be called art deco in the 1920s and 1930s (the Grand Cross badge and the badge and star of the Grand Commander 1st Class were even embellished with, of all things, small turquoise balls). The Star of Brabant has to be the least conventional of all Imperial German orders insignia.

Hesse-Cassel was also the founding house of two one-class strictly military orders and another which was a multi-class affair given for both civil and military merit. The earlier of the military orders was the *Orden pour la vertu militaire* (Order for Military Virtue) created on February 25, 1769 by *Landgraf* Friedrich II. It was a handsome gold-crowned badge (there was no star) very similar in design to the *Pour le Mérite* except that there were lions between the arms instead of eagles and the enamel was in arresting (but highly unmilitary) pink rather than blue. The other military order was established on March 18, 1814 at the time of the Napoleonic Wars. Its founder was *Kurfürst* Wilhelm I. There were two models but both bore the same name, the Order of the Iron Helmet. One version had the sculptured head and shoulders of an armored knight with visor down applied to a cross of Brabant (a Trefoil cross, one with three cups in a circle at each end). The other version had the figure applied to a "German" cross, a *cross pattee* like the Iron Cross only with elongated upper and lower arms. The order was modeled after the then newly (1813) instituted Iron Cross but like the Order for Military Virtue, it was a neck badge. The Order for Military Virtue disappeared in the early 1800s and the Iron Helmets were awarded only in 1814 (for the first form with the Brabant cross) and in 1815 (for the German cross form). The third order was the Wilhelms Order, a creation of *Kurfürst* Friedrich Wilhelm. Its foundation date was August 20, 1851 but it was abolished in 1866 when Prussian annexed Hesse-Cassel.

The war against France in 1814 and 1815 also produced a military decoration from Hesse-Homburg. There, on May 22, 1819, *Landgraf* Friedrich V. Ludwig issued what was called the Swords Cross for services rendered in the war by his landsmen. There was a version of this neck badge in silver gilt and another in just silver. A special cross nearly twice the size of the regular cross and in a slightly different design was given in silver gilt to Grand Duke Ludwig I of Hesse-Darmstadt.

CHAPTER VI

THE MILITARY AWARDS OF THE GRAND DUCHY OF HESSE

THE MERIT ORDER OF PHILIPP THE MAGNANIMOUS

On the birth date of his illustrious ancestor, *Landgraf* Philipp, May 1 in the year 1840, Grand Duke Ludwig II of Hesse-Darmstadt founded the Merit Order of Philipp the Magnanimous. It then became the third ranking order of the Grand Ducal House after the Order of the Golden Lion and the Ludwig Order which were mentioned briefly in the preceding chapter. Originally, it came in four classes, Grand Cross, Commander 1st Class, Commander 2nd Class and Knight. Over the lifetime of the order, which continued until Hesse became a Free State following the 1918 armistice, there were the customary enlargements and qualifications. These should be mentioned.

1849: A Silver Cross was added as a fifth class of the order. Also introduced this year were gold swords for the four higher grades and silver swords for the cross. A change also occurred in the design and shape of the badges and breast stars as described below. The Grand Cross was to rank equally with the Ludwig Grand Cross.

1859: The Knight's Class was divided into a Knight 1st Class and a Knight 2nd Class. Silver swords were designated for the Knight 2nd Class although the guards were to remain in gold.

1881: Crowns were added to all insignia and when applied, it was a mark of extra distinction within a particular grade of the order. These appeared on the breast stars as well as atop the badges.

1893: Henceforth, swords on insignia were meant to signify outstanding achievements in time of war. It was possible for civil personnel under these conditions to be awarded swords insignia in addition to military personnel.

1900: A new grade called the Honor Cross was instituted. It ranked between the Commander 2nd Class and the Knight 1st Class.

1911: Gold rays between the arms of the breast star of the Commander 1st Class were an added feature.

The badge was a white enameled gold-edged *cross pattée* with ends that curved in slightly. At its foundation, the center medallions of the badge and breast stars showed a representation of the full standing figure of Philipp. In 1849, this was replaced by the gold bust of Philipp on a blue enamel background. At the same time, the arms of the badge became a bit less elongated and the medallion changed from oval in shape to round. The obverse medallion was surrounded by the gold letters of the order's motto set on white enamel - *SI DEUS NOBISCUM QUIS CONTRA NOS* ("If God Is With Us, Who Is Against Us"). The reverse medallion on the badge displayed the arms of Hesse, a red-and-white horizontally striped rampant lion on a blue enamel background. The legend surrounding this, also in gold and white and again in Latin, attributed the founding of the order to Grand Duke Ludwig II with the words *LUDOVICUS II MAGN. DUX HASSIAE INSTIT.*

The Grand Cross breast star was the usual 8-pointed kind in silver with the obverse of the medallion applied. The breast star of the Commander 1st Class (which distinguished the Commander 1st Class from the Commander 2nd Class) took several forms. At first, it was just a plain silver cross with the center medallion sometimes enameled and sometimes not. In

Above: The arms of the Grand Duchy of Hesse, a red-and-white horizontally striped rampant lion against a blue field, red and blue being the heraldic colors of Hesse and the ones used for the ribbon of the Merit Order of Philipp the Magnanimous. These arms were also featured on the reverse medallion of the order's badges while the obverse showed the bust of the old *Landgraf* from whom all branches of the House descended.

Below: The obverse (left) and reverse (right) of the Knight's Cross with Swords of the Merit Order of Philipp the Magnanimous. There were two divisions, Knight 1st Class and Knight 2nd Class, identical except for finish (gold and silver respectively). Awards made with swords were a rarity for this order in World War I.

1881, this star became a more conventional one in silver with 4-points with the gold and white enameled badge of the order applied on the plaque. The Honor Cross was a pin-back piece and except for the fact the medallion ring carrying the order's motto was in gold and not enameled, it was identical to the other badges. When gold rays were added to the Commander's star in 1911, it, too, took the form of just a cross without the plaque behind it. The backs of the breast stars and the Honor Cross were plain. Swords, when present, were placed between the arms of the cross and through the center medallion of the breast stars. There was no provision for the Swords-on-Ring feature to indicate a holder of a higher grade of the order without Swords had previously won a lower grade with Swords. The ribbon for all grades, whether awarded with Swords or without, was red with narrow pale blue edge stripes.

Before the war, liberal use of the order without Swords was made within the military to recognize meritorious service not involving the enemy. Swords awards on the other hand were far less frequent as might be expected due to the limited opportunities to earn them (for officers in service at the outbreak of war this meant only the War of 1870 and the colonial campaigns in China and Africa). As of May 6, 1914, there were nearly 500 officers in the Prussian Army and 13th Württemberg Army Corps who held a grade of the Philipps Order without Swords and only 40 who held it with Swords. That picture, by grade of the order and ranks of its recipients, is shown in Appendix XIII. No rank lists for the army were published during the war which showed awards and the Honor Rank List of 1926 omitted them altogether. The navy did publish rank lists in 1916 (as of August 1) and 1918 (as of February 14). Both showed awards. In the 1918 list, only three naval officers held the order with Swords. Two of them were admirals and the grades they had received (a Commander 2nd Class and a Knight 1st Class) indicate they had been awarded earlier on when the men were of lower rank (perhaps in the Boxer Uprising of 1898-1900 in the first case and the War of 1870 in the second).The other award was a Knight 1st Class with Swords to an *Oberleutnant* in the Marine infantry. His was a World War I period award.[1]

How many swords awards of the order were made to men in the army during World War I will probably never be known. Officials in the state archive in Darmstadt have confirmed something that the late German medals authority, *Dr.* Kurt-Gerhard Klietmann, always maintained. All military records dating to the First World War and earlier were destroyed in Allied air attacks during World War II. Presumably, data on Hessian awards up through 1918 were also lost as well. But if the one wartime award of the Philipps Order with Swords within the navy is any indication, it can be said with some assurance that if there were any swords awards to army personnel between 1914 and 1918, there could only have been a handful.

Further evidence that swords awards of the order during the war were a rarity comes from an examination of two postwar rank lists where awards were shown. One was the first published for the tiny *Reichsheer* in 1924 (these continued until 1932) and the other for the navy in 1926. For the army as of April 1, 1924, there were only two officers holding the order with Swords, one a Colonel and the other a Major.[2] Both had the Knight 2nd Class of the order with Swords. For the navy as of November 20, 1926, not a single officer then serving held the order with Swords. Appendix XV and Appendix XVI show this information in more detail (as well as officers in both services then holding Hesse's two wartime bravery decorations, the Warrior's Honor Decoration in Iron and the General Honor Decoration "for Bravery," upon which it primarily relied in World War I). In all of the research into the orders and decorations of the German airmen in the war, none has been found to have been awarded the Philipps Order with Swords. Even the famous Manfred von Richthofen received only the

[1] The recipient was a Heinrich Betz. His Philipps Order does not appear in the 1916 naval rank list, only in the 1918 list. On neither list, however, is he shown possessing an Iron Cross, most unusual in view of the Philipps swords award and the other decorations that appear on both lists. They were the prestigious Prussian Red Eagle Order 4th Class with Swords and the 2nd Class, 3rd Grade of the Chinese Order of the Double Dragon. Swords awards of the Red Eagle to junior officers during World War I were practically non-existent, the major exception being the Red Eagle 3rd Class with Crown and Swords to Manfred von Richthofen in April 1918 shortly before his death. That and the Chinese order suggest they were both earned for actions in China before the war. The absence of an Iron Cross by as late as February 1918 further suggests that Betz might have been a member of the German garrison at the concession port of Tsingtao in East China. Refusing to capitulate, the small German force was attacked by the Japanese on September 2, 1914. It was forced to surrender on November 9 that year after an heroic defense. The garrison went into captivity for the rest of the war, only the pilot of the one serviceable aircraft at Tsingtao, a *Taube*, escaped having been ordered to fly out at the last moment (he was the then *Oberleutnant zur See* Günther Plüschow whose story was told in Volume VI in this series). If Betz had become a prisoner of war this early in the conflict, that could account for his not having an Iron Cross. But what about his Philipps swords award, then, coming sometime between August 1916 and February 1918? It makes for interesting speculation. Perhaps Betz was able to escape later and somehow make his way back to Germany (as Plüschow did after many adventures) and was rewarded by Hesse in what for the navy in World War I was a unique award to a junior officer. Such a feat would certainly have merited an Iron Cross as well. The answer to that might be that it came after the 1918 Rank List had been published. Obviously, Betz's full story and how he came by his Philipps Order with Swords needs further investigation.

[2] The Colonel was Karl von Rettberg who won the *Orden Pour le Mérite* as a Major commanding *Leibgarde-Infanterie-Regiment (I. Grossherzoglich Hessisches) Nr.115.* on November 24, 1917. Prewar, he was a Captain in one of the *Seebataillonen* of the *Marine-Infanterie* and held the Knight 2nd Class without Swords of the Philipp Order. So, obviously, he added swords to his award at some point in World War I. The Major was a man named Jaeschle (first name unknown). He, too was a Captain in another battalion of the Marine Infantry at the start of the war. But as of May 6, 1914 he had already earned his Knight 2nd Class with Swords.

General Honor Decoration "for Bravery" and Hesse's most famous native-born *Pour le Mérite* airman, Julius Buckler, was passed over for the order, receiving instead both the Warrior's Decoration and the General Honor Decoration. One flier (and two airship commanders) held the order without Swords before the war and another, the commander of a *Flieger-Bataillon* in 1914, received it around the time hostilities broke out but whether it was a swords award or not is not clear. Brief biographies of both men now follow, starting with a recipient of the Knight 2nd Class and a man who immediately became famous for a feat he pulled off before the war was even one month old.

OBERLEUTNANT FERDINAND VON HIDDESSEN

Oberleutnant Ferdinand von Hiddessen was one of the first cavalrymen to hang up his spurs and look to the emerging air arm as an exciting new way to carry out the traditional scouting and reconnaissance mission for which they had been trained. As a *Leutnant* in 1914 and shortly to be promoted, he had transferred out of his *Leib-Dragoner-Regiment* (*2.Grossherzoglich Hessisches*) *Nr.24.* in Darmstadt in which he had earned both the Philipps Order 2nd Class and the Prussian Crown Order 4th Class, both without Swords, in recognition of his exemplary work and reported to *Flieger-Bataillon Nr.1.* under the command of a decorated veteran of the colonial campaigns, *Major* Ernst Gundel (the Prussian Orders of the Red Eagle Order with Crown and the Crown Order, both in the 4th Class but in his case, both with Swords). The men in these aviation battalions were immediately parceled out to the aviation units in the field at the outbreak of the war, von Hiddessen going to *Feldflieger-Abteilung 11* on the Western Front. In his nearly four month stay there, he added the Iron Cross 1st and 2nd Class and the Mecklenburg-Schwerin Military Merit Cross 2nd Class to his chest, coming in some part, no doubt, for an audacious flight made over France's capital as German troops were knocking on its door.

On Sunday, August 30, 1914, at around 11:30 in the morning, a lone German *Eindecker* appeared over Paris to the amazement of the populace. It was von Hiddessen. He threw

Below: *Oblt.* Ferdinand von Hiddessen qualified as a pilot prewar and as a former member of the 24th Hessian Dragoons held the Order of Philipp the Magnanimous Knight 2nd Class without Swords. He won a reliability flight competition in 1913, possibly in this DFW "Mars" *Eindecker*. He served in *FFl.Abt. 11* from August 2 until November 26, 1914 and there won both Iron Crosses and the Mecklenburg-Schwerin Military Merit Cross 2nd Class. On Sunday, August 30, he brazenly flew over Paris dropping four small bombs and a 2 1/2 meter long streamer in German national colors with a note saying the German army was at the gates of the city and that there was no recourse but to surrender. Serving with *BAO*, he and his observer were shot down over Verdun on February 4, 1915. Von Hiddessen was wounded in the arm and spent the remainder of the war as a French prisoner.

"Aviation Prosecution at Paris 1914." A fanciful post card depiction of a German crew bombing the capital and fending off attackers. Right, the front page of the Stuttgart South German Newspaper carrying a dispatch dated 3 September 1914 reporting a further attack on Paris by two German *Taube* that dropped 11 bombs. Blasé Parisians shrugged off these early assaults as more of a novelty than anything else. Damage was negligible.

Süddeutsche Zeitung

Morgenblatt für nationale Politik und Volkswirtschaft

Nr. 2 – Preis 5 Pfennig — Sonder=Ausgabe — Stuttgart, 4. September 1914

Frhr. Theodor v. Watter — Kommandeur des 14. Armeekorps

WTB **Karlsruhe,** 4. Sept. (Drahtb.)

Der Kaiser hat den Kommandierenden General des 14. Armeekorps, Frhr. v. Huene, unter wärmster Anerkennung der geleisteten Dienste und herbeigeführten Erfolge in Führung des Armeekorps vor dem Feind und unter Auszeichnung desselben mit dem Eisernen Kreuz 1. Klasse zu anderer Verwendung bestimmt und den Generalleutnant Frhr. v. Watter, Kommandeur der 39. Division, mit der Führung des Armeekorps beauftragt.

Ernst Theodor Frhr. v. Watter ist am 5. Oktober 1856 in Gmünd als Sohn eines Oberstleutnants im Ehreninvalidenkorps geboren, besuchte das Realgymnasium in Stuttgart und die Kriegsschule in Ludwigsburg, wurde 1874 charakterisierter Fähnrich im Infanterie-Regiment 125, 1890 Hauptmann im Infanterie-Regiment 126 (Straßburg), 1896 Bataillonskommandeur im Grenadier-Regt. 123 (Ulm), 1905 Oberst u. Kommandeur des 6. bad. Infant.-Regts. 114 (Konstanz), 1907 des Grenadier-Regiments Königin Olga Nr. 119, 1909 Generalmajor und Kommandeur der 56. Infanterie-Brigade (Rastatt), und am 22. April 1912 Generalleutnant und Kommandeur der 39. Division in Colmar.

Die deutschen Flieger über Paris

GKG **Turin,** 3. Sept. (Drahtb.)

Der Pariser Sonderberichterstatter des „Standard" und der „Gazetta del Popolo" telegraphierte in der Nacht zum Mittwoch

Auch heute haben wieder, wie vor zwei Tagen, und genau zur gleichen Stunde, um 7 Uhr abends, wo die großen Boulevards am belebtesten sind, zwei deutsche Flieger Paris überflogen. Die deutsche Taube flog, wahrscheinlich um den von den Außenforts gegen sie gerichteten Geschützen zu entgehen, zuerst in einer Höhe von 1500 Meter und ging erst über der Stadt auf ungefähr 500 Meter herab. Die Flieger warfen, soweit bis jetzt bekannt wurde, im ganzen 11 Bomben ab, die aber, abgesehen von einem Brand, nicht von bedeutender Wirkung waren. Ein Flieger warf einen Sandsack mit einer angehängten deutschen Fahne herab mit der Aufschrift: Die Wälder von Compiegne stehen in Flammen. Auf Wiedersehen übermorgen in Paris, ergebt Euch". (??) Zwei französische Doppeldecker nahmen sofort die Verfolgung des deutschen Flugzeuges auf. Es wird augenblicklich eine größere Fliegerabteilung mit gepanzerten und mit Maschinengewehren ausgerüsteten Flugzeugen bereit gemacht, die Jagd auf die deutschen Flugzeuge machen sollen.

WTB **Berlin,** 4. Sept. (Drahtb.)

Die „Voss. Ztg." schreibt: Die österreichischen Motorbatterien, die sich so gut bewährten, sind 30,5 Zentimeter-Batterien. Jede Batterie besteht aus zwei Geschützen und wird durch Kraftwagen befördert.

(Nicht amtlich.)

Die Preisgabe von Paris

GKC **Berlin,** 4. Sept. (Drahtb.)

Die Londoner „Evening News" vom 29. August bringen eine Depesche, die vom offiziellen Zensurbureau zugelassen worden ist, des Inhalts, daß Boulogne von den verbündeten Truppen geräumt wurde.

„Die Mitglieder der Regierung der Republik haben Paris verlassen, um der nationalen Verteidigung einen neuen Antrieb zu geben. Ich habe den Auftrag erhalten, Paris gegen den Eindringling zu verteidigen. Diesen Auftrag werde ich bis zum Ende erfüllen!"

(Nicht amtlich. „Agence Havas".)

WTB **Mailand,** 4. Sept. (Drahtb.)

Dem „Corriere della Sera" zufolge geben die Franzosen Paris frei. Das Defensivzentrum liege im Gebiete von Morvant zwischen Dijon und Nevers. Das Oisetal sei jetzt offen. Die Presse ist einstimmig der Ansicht, daß das verschanzte Lager von Paris lange widerstehen werde.

WTB **Zürich,** 4. Sept. (Drahtb.)

Ein Pariser Brief der „Neuen Züricher Zeitung" spricht von zahlreichen Truppennachschüben, besonders von Artillerie nach Norden. Die Bevölkerung aus den Gegenden von Valenciennes und Maubeuge sei kopflos und habe selbst ankommende Engländer für Preußen gehalten. Auch Zeitungsberichte vermöchten sie nicht zu beruhigen. Die Marschgeschwindigkeit der Deutschen jage Schrecken ein. Der Feldpostverkehr sei säumig, die Zensur streng. Die Soldaten erzählten, im Oberelsaß seien Territorialtruppen zurückgelassen worden, die Befehl hätten, beim Vorgehen der Deutschen das Gebiet zu räumen. Je weiter die Reisenden sich von Paris entfernten, umso fühlbarer würde die Entspannung der Nerven, aber auch um so ohnmächtiger die Resignation, mit der sie ihrem künftigen Geschick entgegensehen. Die ihnen begegnenden Verwundetentransporte stimmten sie traurig. Die Soldaten seien vor Uebermüdung ausgemergelt, die heitere Note fehle ganz. Die Soldaten sprechen mit dem größten Respekt von den Deutschen, die ihren Offizieren bewunderungswürdig folgten. Die Maschinengewehre der Deutschen wirkten verheerend. Das Feldgrau sei vorzüglich. Der Gegner sei wie 1870 überlegen. Die französische Artillerie sei erfolgreich. Der Erfinder der Melinit-Patrone, Ingenieur Turpin, soll dem Kriegsminister einen neuen Explosivstoff übergeben haben, dessen furchtbare Wirkung alles bisher Dagewesene übertreffen soll. Im Volksmund spiele diese Bombe Turpins eine große Rolle und werde als der künftige Deus ex machina angesehen. Der deutsche Ausstellungspavillon in Lyon stehe unberührt da unter französischer Flagge.

Ein Seegefecht in Ostasien?

GKG **Berlin,** 4. Sept. (Drahtb.)

Nach einer Kabelmeldung aus Schanghai vom 14. August liefen zwei Kriegsschiffe, jedes mit vier Schornsteinen, arg beschädigt und mit vielen Verwundeten an Bord im Hafen von Hongkong ein. Ueber die Identität der beiden Kriegsschiffe verlautet in Schanghai nichts Offizielles, doch glaubt man, daß es zwei englische armierte Kreuzer gewesen sind, sie wollen einen Zusammenstoß mit deutschen Kreuzern gehabt haben

WTB **London,** 4. Sept. (Drahtb.)

„Daily Telegraph" zufolge bereiten sich die Japaner auf eine längere Kriegsdauer in Kiautschou vor. Sie wollen langsam und methodisch vorgehen und das Menschenmaterial möglichst schonen. Das Parlament werde Kredite bewilligen, um das Heer bis zum nächsten Jahr in Schantung zu unterhalten.

Japanische Blätter bringen Alarmnachrichten aus China. Im Jangtsetal stehe eine Revolution bevor, die mit

four small bombs over the side which were reported to have killed one woman and injured several other people. The crowning insult to the undefended capital, however, was the 2 1/2 meter long streamer in the German national colors of red, white and black that he also loosed. It was reputed to have read, "The German army is at the gates of Paris. There is nothing you can do but surrender." Similar raids continued by German aircraft in the late afternoons of the next three days but whether von Hiddessen also took part in these is not known. The citizens of Paris were fascinated as well as outraged by this violation of a civilian target and were said to pour into the streets looking for the "six o'clock *Taube*."

In November 1914, the first German strategic bombardment unit came into existence, being led by a man about whom we hear next and whose brainchild it was. The unit was given the code name *Brieftauben-Abteilung-Ostende* (Carrier Pidgeon Detachment Ostend), *BAO* for short, and its commander was the then *Major* Wilhelm Siegert. He was able to recruit the most experienced pilots and observers of the day and von Hiddessen was one of them, joining *BAO* on November 26. Unfortunately, von Hiddessen's war and the chance for further honors ended abruptly in February of the following year. By that time, *BAO* had been moved from Belgium to the Verdun Front. On the 4th, von Hiddessen and his observer, *Leutnant* Fritz Mueller, were part of a four plane formation that was returning from a bombing attack when they were engaged by four French aircraft from *Groupe de Bombardement 1*. A 20 minute air battle took place but it was French antiaircraft fire that crippled von Hiddessen's and Mueller's ship. They were forced down in French lines with the carburetor of their machine on fire and crash landed. In the chivalry that opposing airmen displayed *after* the battle in those early years (and which largely carried over to the rest of the war), French fliers personally transported the two injured men to hospital in Verdun. Von Hiddessen had been hit in the arm but Mueller's condition was much more serious. He died six days later while von Hiddessen was forced to sit out the rest of the war in a prison camp.

OBERSTLEUTNANT WILHELM SIEGERT

The September 30, 1914 issue of *Flugsport*, a German flight enthusiasts' magazine, carried the one-line announcement that the then *Major* Wilhelm Siegert had been awarded the Knight 1st Class of the "House Order" of Philipp the Magnanimous. There was no mention of whether it was a swords award or not. These announcements usually lagged the event itself by several weeks at least so it is not possible to know whether it came for some early wartime event or whether it came without Swords and was recognition for some of his peacetime activities as the Commanding Officer of *Flieger-Bataillon Nr.4*. To

Siegert it probably mattered very little in any event. In private, he was quite contemptuous of the whole business of orders and decorations, especially those that went to high ranking officers who were far removed from any personal danger. One of his favorite jokes went this way:

> Question: "What does an aerial bomb and a decoration have in common?" Answer: "Generally, it is dropped far behind the front and hits the not guilty."

Siegert came to aviation in its early years. By 1907, already age 35, he had transferred to the balloon troops. In 1912, after taking flying lessons more or less on the sly, he got his pilot's ticket and later qualified as a full-fledged observer. At the start of the war, he was in command of *Flieger-Bataillon Nr.4.* His peacetime service had earned him the Prussian Red Eagle Order 4th Class with Crown, perhaps not unexpected for a proficient officer of his rank. But he also wore another decoration seldom seen on prewar Army rank lists, the Prussian Life Saving Medal. And it was one of the few awards of his of which he was genuinely proud. On the day after Christmas 1911, he received it for his taking charge of a dangerous situation at a flying exhibition the previous summer. An errant pilotless aircraft somehow got loose and was careening toward a group of spectators. Siegert steered it away from the crowd and was severely injured by the machine's propeller in the process. He would later write in his day book (private diary) in which he would confide his innermost thoughts, "They (the Life Saving Medal and the Flying Badges) are now the only decorations that require the owner to have played blindman's bluff with Death." Siegert did not shirk from danger either once the war got underway. He personally participated in a two-plane bombing attack on Belfort in Alsace on August 29, 1914 for which he received the then precious Iron Cross 2nd Class, Siegert himself saying he was the first of all the officers in *Armeeabteilung Oberrhein* (Army Detachment Upper Rhine) to receive it when it was awarded on September 6. Even Siegert was impressed (for once). He called it the "most beautiful of all orders" but also made sure that all the officers in his small

Right: *Major*, later *Oberstleutnant*, Wilhelm Siegert was the organizational genius at *Idflieg* in Berlin but in the beginning, no desk-bound officer was he personally leading bombing flights against such wide flung targets as Belfort and Dunkirk. Here he is readied for a flight but the exact circumstances are unknown. Siegert received the Knight 1st Class, possibly with Swords, of the Merit Order of Philipp the Magnanimous at the start of the war. The lozenge patterned camouflage on the rudder in the photograph at top with what appears to be the beginning of an Iron Cross national marking in white is an interesting departure from norm.

command also received it in due course. When Siegert was in charge of *BAO*, he likewise flew combat missions and described one at the end of January 1915 at some length. A mixed bag of Albatros B.Is and Aviatiks, with Siegert in one of the latter, "the not completely-fingered chief" as he referred to himself and the injury received with the propeller. Dunkirk was the objective, conveniently pointed out by a ring of "useless" searchlights surrounding it. Siegert claimed 123 of their bombs were unloaded on the port from the 14 aircraft that were involved (the unit's paper strength of 36 planes was never achieved). For this, Siegert was awarded the Iron Cross 1st Class on February 11.

Siegert was taken off active operations in March 1915 to begin a distinguished career as one of the two real brains behind the wartime development of German aviation (the other was the then *Oberstleutnant*, later *Oberst*, Hermann von der Lieth-Thomsen). In Berlin, Siegert became the deputy to the *Feldflugchef* (Chief of Field Aviation) Thomsen, being responsible for all aspects of equipping and deploying the German Army Air Service. When the office of *Kommandierenden General der Luftstreitkräfte* (*Kogenluft* – Commanding General of the Air Force) was established in October 1916, Siegert continued to head up the *Inspektion der Fliegertruppe* (*Idflieg* - Inspectorate of Aviation), a job he had held since August 1916. But even before that, his contributions had resulted in one of the early aviation awards of the then highly exclusive Knight's Cross with Swords of the Royal House Order of Hohenzollern. He had received it on May 22, 1916 (Thomsen had gotten it earlier, on January 27 that year). Even the cynic Siegert said that it was a pleasant surprise" and wrote down the message informing him of it in his day book. The telegram from the Chief of the General Staff had read:

> HM the *Kaiser* has bestowed upon you for your excellent services in organizing aviation and also for promoting the true German offensive spirit of the young air arm weapon the Knight's Cross with Swords of the Royal House Order of Hohenzollern. I congratulate you on this high distinction.
>
> (signed) v. Falkenhayn, General of Infantry

Below: Two officers commanding airships, the Army *Hauptmann* Wilhelm von Quast, fifth from the left above, and the Naval *Kapitänleutnant* Franz Stabbert, below, received the Philipps Order Knight 2nd Class without Swords prewar. Here he poses with his crew of the Z.IV with their newly awarded 2nd Class Iron Crosses. Von Quast died of natural causes on October 26, 1915 in Hamburg.

That same evening over dinner, Siegert's immediate superior, von der Lieth-Thomsen, delivered a flowery speech in praise of Siegert's accomplishments and his new honor. Siegert duly entered Thomsen's remarks in his diary but not before commenting upon them in his usual wry, self-deprecating way. He wrote:

> The Chief of Field Aviation made a speech which could easily have resulted in an acute attack of megalomania. I intend to be unassuming and will attempt to realize only 10% of the qualities ascribed to me. That would be enough. Now, hear:
>
> "My dear Major Siegert!
>
> His Majesty, the Emperor and King, has awarded you for your merits one of the highest and most beautiful war orders. Your merits cannot be summarized more succinctly and to the point in the congratulatory telegram that the Chief of the General Staff of the Field Army sent to you today.
>
> These honoring words will find a happy echo in the entire aviation corps. It knows how to be grateful for your

Stabbert's Philipps Order appears as the last award on his bar. His Zeppelin L.20 (below) was forced to land in Norway on May 3, 1916. Stabbert was one of six of the crew to be repatriated only to be killed on October 20, 1917 when his L.44 was shot down by ground fire above St. Clement in France. None of the crew of 18 survived.

work and knowledge. In memory of this day of honor, I want to present you with a gift and remembrance in the form of a memorial coin. Not of gold or silver but a memorial coin struck with words. These read on one side: 'Work - Will - Perseverance'. And on the other: 'Wisdom - Courage - Strength'. And in the margin I have engraved 'He was given to us at the right hour by a benevolent God!'

Not visibly, dear Siegert, can you wear this memorial coin. That is not necessary. Because everyone who gets to know you will soon feel and experience that from you emanate - work - will - perseverance - wisdom - courage - strength.

It is the grateful wish of all of us that you may apply your eminent qualities, which are only rarely combined in one man, for a long time and for the benefit of the young aviation force!"

What Siegert would say in his diary was one thing. What he was obligated to say in public was another of course. No better example of that occurred on the occasion of his receiving the Commander 2nd Class with Swords of the Saxe-Ernestine House Order from the Duke of Saxe-Altenburg on April 7, 1917. The Duke himself took an active interest in aviation activities at the nearby *Flieger-Ersatz-Abteilung 1* located at the Leina airfield within the Duke's domain. Siegert wrote a fulsome letter of thanks to his "Most Illustrious Duke" and "Most Gracious Duke and Lord" for the "undeserved grace and kindness" shown him for the "high decoration" and expressed the hope for continued Ducal favor in the cause of aviation at Leina. But, privately, Siegert derided the "gigantic Olympic neck decoration" and making a play on words about how such things were earned, including, as Woody Allen would say, just showing up, he vowed never to wear the "magnificent piece" (a full transcript of Siegert's effusive letter to the Duke and the entry in his day book about it appeared in Volume V in this series - see pages 102-106). It's also possible that Siegert was miffed about something that happened to his two bosses that same day, April 7, 1917. On that day, both Thomsen and *Generalleutnant* Ernst von Hoeppner, the Commanding General of the Air Force, were awarded the *Orden Pour le Mérite* for their leadership in the development, planning and operations of the air services since their jobs had been created on October 8, 1916. Perhaps Siegert felt himself equally deserving and what was a decoration from a minor prince compared to a *Pour le Mérite* from his All-Highest War Lord, the Emperor?

The humiliation of Germany's defeat and the privations in postwar Germany only served to sharpen Siegert's tongue against the practice of awarding orders and decorations to those he felt undeserving and in the debate that was then going on about whether the new government should restore the bestowal of the old imperial awards, he came up with a novel solution which once again showed both wit and contempt. The following was part of a statement Siegert made that so incensed the establishment that he was subsequently drummed out of several veterans' societies:

> They (orders and decorations) are probably worn by people who in four and one-half years of war never heard a bang other than noises of a purely personal nature. This tendency to wear decorations should not be overlooked. Perhaps it can be turned into cash of a magnitude that cannot be properly imagined at the present time.
>
> In this context, I visualize a government orders lottery with several drawings. For example: Black Eagle Order – 100,000 tickets at 50,000 Marks each-one winner. Or the *Pour le Mérite* – 500,000 tickets at 100,000 Marks each – five winners. And so on. Red Eagle, Green Eagle, White Eagle, House Order of Ludwig the Irritable, Emil the Bad-Tempered, Star of the Golden Goose with Knife and Fork, ring and ribbon, etc. In this manner the current devaluation of orders and decorations could either be stopped or promoted.
>
> Even the Union of Nations would not refuse to agree and might even propagate the idea on an international scale. At the least, the reparations could be paid off in the shortest possible time with the aid of the lottery proposed by myself, without recourse to other, harder to bear, taxes.

Indeed, Wilhelm Siegert was a remarkable man and one would be hard put to come up with his counterpart in the air services of the other nations involved in the war.

CHAPTER VII

THE MILITARY AWARDS OF THE GRAND DUCHY OF HESSE

THE WARRIOR'S HONOR DECORATION IN IRON

In the first three years of the war, several of the smaller German states brought out new decorations as additional means to recognize bravery and military merit. Often, these constituted a higher class of existing war decorations, were given for repeated acts of bravery or superior service and were more exclusive. The Principality of Lippe, as we shall see, was the first to do this with the introduction of its War Honor Cross for Heroic Deed (December 8, 1914). Then in 1915 (May 23), the Principality of Reuss followed suit with its War Merit Cross as did the Grand Duchy of Saxe-Weimar with its Wilhelm Ernst War Cross (June 10). The next year saw the Duchy of Saxe-Coburg and Gotha establish its Carl Eduard War Cross (July 19). All of these were one-class pin-back decorations. The number of awards were relatively small, often restricted pretty much to people from that state. The next to adopt the idea was the Grand Duchy of Hesse.

March 13, 1917 was the 25th anniversary of the death of Grand Duke Ludwig IV and the succession to the throne of his only surviving son, His Royal Highness, Grand Duke Ernst Ludwig of Hesse and by Rhine. On that date, Ernst Ludwig founded the Warriors' Honor Decoration in Iron, similar to those mentioned above in that it was a one-class pin-back badge worn without a ribbon on the lower left breast and could be awarded to men regardless of rank. The new decoration was meant to honor the glorious achievements of Hesse in this "iron" time of war and to recognize the performance of its own soldiers, sailors and airmen who were in the very forefront of battle over an extended period of time. Four conditions were laid down for eligibility, strict enough to assure that the Warriors' Honor Decoration would never be awarded in large numbers since no proposal for the award would be accepted through official channels unless there was proof supplied that all four conditions had been met. These were:

1. A recipient had to have held Hessian citizenship since at least August 1, 1914.
2. A recipient had to have served more than two years in units active in an area under enemy fire with the exception of temporary stationing in rest or reserve positions. During the two year period, beginning with the day of deployment, any time in hospital or at home lasting more than two months did not count.
3. A recipient had to have been wounded at least once.
4. A recipient had to have displayed bravery and good conduct.

The regulations went on to remind those affected that if there were only partial compliance with these conditions, the proposal would not be considered. The proof mentioned consisted of an excerpt from the War Muster Roll supplemented with evidence of these conditions as well as a supporting statement from the unit in the field or a higher authority. In addition, official proof of citizenship was required. Only with all of this in hand would a proposal be considered satisfactory. And finally, it was stated that as with other Hessian war decorations, the insignia did not have to be returned upon the death of a recipient but could be retained as "mementos" by his heirs.

The badge itself was a black lacquered wreath of laurels on which the silver crowned initials *E L* were superimposed. At the foot of the *L* there was a small silver plaque with the numeral "*25*." The back of the badge was plain. The fact that no Hessian military records apparently survived World War II, once again hampers our ability to give all the aviation recipients their due. The numbers in any case would be few because of the stringent requirements just discussed. The few airmen's names that have been found therefore have come from other sources (see Appendix XVII). But even if a full roll were

Following the lead of several of the smaller German states in the early years of the war, Grand Duke Ernst Ludwig of Hesse founded a distinctive one-class pin-back decoration on the 25th anniversary of his reign, March 13, 1917, naming it the Warriors' Honor Decoration in Iron. It was open to both officers and men subject to strict conditions. In addition to Hessian citizenship, a recipient had to have been under fire for more than two years and wounded at least once as well as displaying outstanding acts of bravery. Below is an example of the formal bestowal document, this to an *Unteroffizier* in a machine gun company.

Ernſt Ludwig
von Gottes Gnaden
Großherzog von Heſſen und bei Rhein.

Wir haben

dem Unteroffizier Wilh. Dewald
3. Masch.Gew.Komp. R.J.R. 80.

unſer

Kriegerehrenzeichen in Eiſen

verliehen und erteilen hierüber gegenwärtige Urkunde.

Darmſtadt, den 14. Februar 1918.

Ernst Ludwig

available, it is doubtful that there would be a more illustrious aviation recipient than the Mainz-born son of a master carpenter who came into the world on March 28, 1894. It is his story that occupies the rest of this chapter.

LEUTNANT JULIUS BUCKLER

Julius Buckler was only one of five German airmen, fighter pilots all, who won Prussia's highest bravery decoration for non-commissioned officers, the Golden Military Merit Cross, and then upon being promoted *Leutnant*, went on to receive the *Orden Pour le Mérite*. And Buckler was the first of them to receive this dual distinction. For Buckler, as was the case with all the others but one, he was skipped over for the usual intermediate award for officers between an Iron Cross 1st Class and the *Pour le Mérite*, the Knight's Cross with Swords of the Royal House Order of Hohenzollern. In Buckler's circumstance, missing out on the Hohenzollern was understandable. His other two awards came practically back-to-back. Table 7-1 presents this information for him and the other four men.

Table 7-1
Aviation Recipients of both the Golden Military Merit Cross and *Orden Pour le Mérite*

Recipient	Golden Military Merit Cross	Member's Cross with Swords Royal Hohenzollern House Order	Knight's Cross with Swords Royal Hohenzollern House Order	Orden Pour le Mérite
Karl Thom	Oct. 11, 1917	Aug. 7, 1918	—	Nov. 1, 1918
Julius Buckler	Nov. 12, 1917	—	—	Dec. 4, 1917
Paul Bäumer	Feb. 12, 1918	—	—	Nov. 2, 1918
Otto Könnecke	May 12, 1918	—	July 20, 1918	Sept. 26, 1918
Fritz Rumey	May 12, 1918	—	—	July10, 1918

Buckler held another distinction among all the *Pour le Mérite* airmen, but certainly not one as eagerly sought as "The Blue Max." He was the only one of them to have the Wound Badge in Gold which signified five or more woundings in the course of the war. In German soldiers' parlance, he was a real *Kugelfanger*, or "bullet-catcher." The first of his wounds came on the Marne in September 1914 when he was serving as an *Infanterist* (Private in the infantry) in the Hessian Grand Ducal Division's *Infanterie-Leibregiment Grossherzogin (3. Ilessisches) Nr.117*. At age 18, he had enlisted in the unit on October 15, 1912. Now, two years later, on October 6, he was promoted *Unteroffizier* as he lay recuperating in his home town of Mainz. Aviation had fascinated him from youth and he took the occasion of his being sidelined to apply for a transfer to aviation. It was readily approved and wearing the Iron Cross 2nd Class that he had earned on the Western Front, Buckler reported to *Flieger-Ersatz-Abteilung 6* in Grossenhain that November. There, if we can believe the account of his career in the book *Pour le Mérite-Flieger* by Walter Zuerl (not to be completely trusted by any means), he found himself to be the only Hessian in the midst of "dyed-in-the-wool Saxons" (Grossenhain was 23 miles northwest of Dresden in Saxony).

Buckler himself wrote or dictated an account of his war years in a book published in 1939, *Malaula! Der kampfpruf meiner Staffel* ("*Malaula*! The Battle-Cry of My Flight"). As a story, it makes for exciting reading. As history, it is to be taken with the proverbial grain of salt. Air historian Greg Van-Wyngarden has a cogent observation on the book. He says, "I think *Malaula*! is largely oral history, a collection of an old pilot's yarns loosely dictated with little reference to official records." How true. In it, Buckler seldom mentions dates and when he does, they are in conflict with other known dates. Even his own victories are not recorded in proper sequence. He mentions situations and encounters with others that simply don't gee with the facts. He confides to the reader his supposed innermost thoughts on various matters, not the least of which is the business of killing. Were they what he truly thought at the time or were they expressed from the distance of over 20 years when the passions of the war and the exuberance of youth had cooled? Despite all that, it is nonetheless worthwhile repeating much of what Buckler has to say and then, where necessary, pointing out where that differs from what we know from more reliable sources.

Three views of the now-promoted *Leutnant* Julius Buckler wearing the *Orden Pour le Mérite* and showing off his Warriors' Honor Decoration in Iron to good advantage. The ribbon bar in the photograph above has his other Hessian award, the General Honor Decoration "for Bravery," unconventionally placed between the ribbons of the Iron Cross 2nd Class and the Prussian Golden Military Merit Cross. Only in the photograph at right is there even the slightest evidence of the strain of more than three years of war, at least 35 successful aerial combats and what would be five woundings showing in his otherwise youthful even, one might say, cherubic countenance.

D.2033
Mops

Mops
5

Opposite and this page: Buckler dubbed his favorite aircraft *Mops* (or "Pug"). On Albatros D.III 2033/16, above and right, it was in dark lettering. On the D.V shown in the other two photographs, it was lettered light (white?). The man with arm in sling is *Vzfw*. Rieger who was injured in a crash following a combat on April 16, 1917. Buckler also had a second plane marked "Lily" but a photograph of it has yet to be found.

Buckler passed his courses at Grossenhain in record time (Zuerl says it took him only four weeks and he completed the work with such distinction that he was granted an extra four weeks leave). The part about his leaving the school with high marks rings true since he was sent on to the field at Leipzig-Lindenthal there to be an instructor rather than going immediately to the front. That posting did not come until the summer of 1915 when he joined *Artillerie-Flieger-Abteilung 209* in the Verdun sector. There, for over a year, his main work was artillery shoots, often with an observer with whom he became close, *Leutnant* Kurt von Rudno-Rudzinski. Then the expansion of the *Jagdstaffeln* provided the chance for Buckler to switch over to fighters and leave the often tedious but always dangerous work of the two-seaters behind. A telegram arrived at *(A)209* asking him if he would like to join the newly forming *Jasta 17*. Buckler does not identify the source but undoubtedly, it came from the man who had just been designated *Jasta 17*'s leader, *Rittmeister* Anton von Brederlow. *Jasta 17* was being formed out of men from *Fokkerstaffel Metz* which had included such stalwarts-to-be as Hermann Göring, Stephan Kirmaier and the two Loerzer brothers, Bruno and Fritz. Its first leader was slated to be *Hauptmann* Kurt Schmikaly but he was wounded in combat on October 22 and died on October 23, 1916 before the appointment could be actioned. Von Brederlow took over on November 11 and Buckler arrived the same day. Before leaving *(A)209*, it had been necessary for Buckler to obtain the permission of his Commanding Officer, *Hauptmann* Werner Funck, for the transfer. Buckler also requested that von Rudno-Rudzinski be permitted to undergo pilot training with the hope that they might be reunited (as they would when von Rudno joined *Jasta 17* in October 1917). Funck gave his permission for the transfer of both men but with "a heavy heart" as Buckler wrote.

The first order of business for the new men of *Jasta 17* was to familiarize themselves with what were called the "old" Fokkers which were the only aircraft then assigned to it (presumably, these were the Fokker D-Types which were actually relatively new but which had turned out to be such disappointments that most of them at this time had already been relegated to trainers). Three and four pilots had to share a single machine and bad weather further cut down on the time each individual could be in the air. But life was good in the meantime. Before, Buckler had lived in Nissen huts ("cold and wet with mice and rats"). Now he had a "splendid" room with central heating and hot and cold running water. Buckler had been further promoted *Vizefeldwebel* back in *(A)209* on June 10. Encouraged by von Brederlow, Buckler also undertook intensive studies to pass the examination to obtain a commission. At first, he claims to have approached the work with considerable enthusiasm. But then something happened to change his mind. He told von Brederlow that he would wait until he could be promoted *Leutnant* based on his merits in the field, not on his success with a text book. From then on, he says, his only thoughts were on flying. Each day, he hoped for good weather, the chance to engage the enemy and a start on his way to earning his officer's epaulets. That day came soon enough.

By mid-December 1916, *Jasta 17* had yet to score a confirmed victory. December 17, a Sunday, found him up alone and cruising over the scarred Verdun battlefield where still another German counterattack was underway that day. Some 200 meters below him, he spied a German two-seater circling over the ruins of Fort Douaumont which the French had finally managed to retake almost two months before. He wondered if it might be a plane from his old *Abteilung*. Then to his shock, he realized it was being stalked by a pusher. The enemy! Buckler pushed the nose of his ship down hard and made a firing pass at what he thought was a Farman. He overshot his target in his rashness and inexperience. The Caudron (for that is what it was) turned on him and the "dance of death," as Buckler describes it, began. Each fired at the other when the opportunity presented itself. Finally, some of Buckler's shots went home. The observer could no longer be seen and the Frenchman began to spin down with Buckler fastened on his tail. At a scant 60 meters, Buckler pulled up as the enemy plane slammed into the earth in a cloud of dust and debris. He escaped in a hail of enemy small arms fire and reported his success to von Brederlow. The Caudron was confirmed as *Jasta 17*'s first official victory, thanks in part, no doubt, to an aerial photograph of the wreck that was considerately arranged for by his former commander at *(A)209* (so perhaps the German two-seater Buckler saved was, in fact, from Funck's unit and this was one way of showing his appreciation). A first victory like this for both *Jasta 17* and a pilot would call for much celebrating and yet, Buckler professes to have had little joy in the event. All he could think of (he says) was the dead crew and somewhere in France, a family mourning the loss of a husband, or a son or a brother. One wonders if those were actually his true feelings at the time. If so, he would have been an exceptionally sensitive young man. Few airmen on either side felt such compassion.

Buckler claims he was still moody about his first kill as Christmas approached and the men of *Jasta 17* received gifts from the German aircraft manufacturers and other patrons of the air service. He should have been feeling very good about himself as two special presents arrived for him. One was a new puppy named *Schnurps* ("Little Brat" or "Little Wise Guy") courtesy of *Hauptmann* Funck (more appreciation for Buckler's victory?). The other was his *Ehrenbecher*, the silver mug marking a man's first victory. On Christmas Eve itself, there was something else to celebrate too. *Vizefeldwebel* Georg Strasser, who had become one of Buckler's closest friend in the *Staffel*, had shot down another Caudron earlier in the day northwest of Fort Douaumont for his own first and the unit's second victory. Much *Sekt* (German sparkling wine) was consumed in the mess that evening.

But Buckler writes that he was still inwardly depressed even as he put on a happy face (and, indeed, in the photographs of him that we have, all we see is a smiling, relaxed and seemingly carefree youth unburdened by such thoughts). Whatever his true feelings, duty called, even on the very next day, Christmas morning.

It seems that Buckler had seen a French observation balloon floating over Pont-a-Mousson for several weeks and vowed to get it. He had already obtained incendiary ammunition and the necessary paper saying that he was specifically on a balloon hunt (the popular notion at the time was that a flier captured with such ammunition aboard without such a permit would be shot). He chose Christmas Day to make his attack, perhaps thinking the French would have their guard down on *Noel*. He was in the first of his Albatros D.IIs marked *Mops* ("Pug"). He climbed to a height of 4,500 meters in the icy blue sky (his description) and headed for the target, a distant 25 kilometers away. From time to time, he lost sight of it but continued en route until there it was, looming in front of him "as big as a house." He opened up with burst after burst until he very nearly rammed the thing. Still, it did not burn and he had to leap-frog over it. Any thoughts of a second pass were quickly erased as he immediately came under attack by three French aircraft. In a long running fight back to his own lines, Buckler had almost made it when one of the enemy's shots struck his engine which promptly quit with a bang. Nothing to do now but glide down, hope his pursuers didn't follow and try to find a suitable landing spot on ground that was everywhere covered in a deep blanket of snow. The Frenchmen had gone but he still had to endure both small caliber and light anti-aircraft fire on his way down. The landing occurred without any injury to himself but as he made for the safety of the village of Mailly which he had identified from the air as being in German hands, machine gun bullets nipped at his heels. Once there, a regimental *Major* provided a late Christmas breakfast complete with hot mulled wine before Buckler got passage back to *Jasta 17*s field at Frascaty near Metz. Buckler feared that he was in for a reprimand for the loss of a plane (whether this *Mops* was a total write-off or could be salved, he does not say). But von Bredelow said nothing about that. He was just glad to get Buckler back all right.

January of 1917 was a quiet time for Buckler and it was not until the next month, on February 11, that he could put in for another claim. But to no avail. Whatever it was (and Buckler does not say), the action was too far behind enemy lines to hope for any confirmation. There would be better luck on St. Valentine's Day. Official records credit him with a Caudron that day over Dacq Wald. But here, in Buckler's chronology of his victories, we encounter one of the mix-ups in events and dates that plague his book. According to him, his second confirmed victory occurred right after an episode that could only have come on April 30, 1917. He himself was considering a balloon attack when he saw five of the distant seven French

Above: Buckler's 4th confirmed victory, a Spad shot down on April 15, 1917. The pilot was a *Sergeant* Papeil of *Escadrille Spa 3* who was entertained by the men of *Jasta 17*. In his writings, Buckler identifies this Frenchman as the one who, upon seeing the wreckage of his aircraft, threw up his hands and uttered "*ma Lola*!" which got converted into *Jasta 17*'s battle cry "*Malaula*!" But it actually was the French pilot he shot down the following month whose Nieuport 17 overturned upon touching down who despaired of his poor bird's fate. Here Papeil with bandaged right eye is flanked by Georg Strasser, Wilhelm Gros, Alfred Träger and Buckler.

Two at right: This is "*ma Lola*," the Nieuport 17 flown by *Adjutant* Alain Joussaud of *Escadrille N.75*, Buckler's 7th victory on May 12, 1917. To the men of *Jasta 17*, "*Malaula*!" meant "up and at 'em" and was said to be their inspiration ever after. In the upper photo, mounted military police keep the inevitable crowd of curious onlookers at bay until the victor could arrive to be photographed after the spectators had been shooed away. Buckler says it was not until sometime in August 1917 before he received the Iron Cross 1st Class but the badge is clearly evident here.

Top: One of *Jasta 17*'s first Albatros D.IIIs flanked on each side by two Albatros D.IIs, probably lined up on the airfield at Metz-Frascaty in early 1917. Chocks are in place and tarps cover the engine housings. The step-ladders provide easy access for mechanics.

Right: *Jasta 17* moved to the field at St. Quentin-le-Petit in March 1917 and here now equipped entirely with D.IIIs are, left to right, Buckler, *Lt.* Heinz Sachsenberg, *Lt.* Wilhelm Gros and *Vzfw.* Georg Strasser. The variety of heavy flight clothing on the first three men is typical. The D.III in the background being checked by ground crew is numbered D.2177.

Right: Now on the airfield at Wasquehal later in 1917, Buckler sports a für-collared, full-length greatcoat to ward off the cold of high altitude flying. No *Mops* can be seen on this D.V so perhaps it is his "Lily," a second machine he had at his disposal.

THE MEN OF *JASTA 17* IN REPOSE

Above: Dressed in their Sunday best in front of their requisitioned quarters near the Ghistelles field at Ostend in July 1917. On the left, bottom to top: Fitzner, Strasser, Wendler (CO), Wolff, Brackwitz and Ehlers. In the center: Schniedewind (left), Schuster (right) and Werner (behind). On the right: Buckler, Traeger, Becker and Zschunke. Schniedewind won the Golden Military Merit Cross in Palestine in 1918. Buckler, often shown as a *Vizefeldwebel* at this time, clearly wears the epaulets of an *Offizier-Stellvertreter* here.

Above: An early 1918 spring day finds the men of *Jasta 17* taking coffee on the terrace. Standing, left to right: Becker and Traeger. Seated, left to right: Spindler, Fleischer, Strasser, Buckler, Werner, Brendel, Schumann and von Esebeck. The day was warm enough for someone to doff his coat and hat and park them on the ancient brick wall.

Below: Sometime over the fall/winter of 1917 with the much respected *Hptm.* Rudolf von Esebeck (standing third from left) in command. Buckler, looking like a younger version of tennis great Andre Agassi, is flanked on his right by *Lt.* Walter Brackwitz and on his left by his former two-seater observer now fighter pilot, *Oblt.* Kurt von Rudno-Rudzinski. *Vzfw.* Gustav Schniedewind, soon to be transferred, is prone on the ground at the right.

Sopwith Camel B.6314 of No.28 Squadron, RFC which was shot down by Buckler on the afternoon of October 11, 1917 for his 17th confirmed victory. The pilot, 2/Lt. William H. Winter was taken prisoner. It was the first combat loss of No.28 Squadron. Earlier that day, Buckler downed an R.E.8 for his first, but not last, "double" of the war. He pulled off that feat two more times in October and on November 18, scored his only "hat trick" of his career.

Buckler wearing his favorite stocking cap with his good friend, *Vzfw.* Georg Strasser.

Buckler displays his usually sunny disposition as he hams it up for the camera.

balloon line go up in flames one after the other. Buckler claims he later found out these were burned by men of *Jasta 19* under the leadership of *Oberleutnant* Erich Hahn. And indeed that was the case, but on April 30, not February 14. The next day, May 1, Hahn received an immediate Knight's Hohenzollern with Swords for the feat, he having accounted for two of the monsters himself.[1] To add to the confusion, at the time Buckler observed *Jasta 19*'s handiwork, he already had six confirmed victories. Not only that but on April 30, Buckler claimed a Nieuport over Dacq Wald which was never confirmed. Buckler's memory must have played him tricks and the description of what he called his second victory on April 30 was actually his second on February 14. For that reason, his account of the action is worth repeating here since it was a rousing fight (if his description of it can be believed that is).

Buckler was alone again (he writes that he couldn't convince any of his comrades to join him that day). He was being buffeted around by some well directed flak and was unaware that a Caudron had sneaked up behind him. It was only when bullets smacked into his right wing that he realized he was under attack. He flung his machine around and the dog fight commenced. The two planes worked themselves down from 1,500 meters to only 150, all the while drifting further into German-held territory. Finally, they were just about over *Jasta 17*'s airfield (if the date were, in fact, February 14, 1917, this would still have been the Frascaty 'drome; *Jasta 17* would move from there to one at St. Quentin-le-Petit on March 1). At that point, the enemy plane went into a long glide emitting smoke. Buckler was sure it was doomed and hoped that the crew could bring it down before it was totally enveloped in flames (a compassionate Buckler once more?). But the glide and the smoke were deceiving. The Caudron was not in trouble at all. As Buckler once again overshot an enemy, the French pilot opened up full throttle and his observer was presented with a "beautiful" target. But he missed and Buckler wheeled around again and was on the Caudron's tail at only 10 meters distance. A short burst of his guns "like on a target range" and it smashed into the ground.

Buckler also relates an action that he dates later in the day that he saw *Jasta 19* shoot up the French balloon line which only adds to the difficulties in squaring what he says with what we know. That same afternoon, we are told, a new balloon line was back up and as darkness gathered, Buckler decided to go after one of them. On his first pass, he held his fire until only 100 meters away and the observer took to his 'chute. But the balloon remained intact and a second strike was necessary. This time, he was successful and the huge bag went up in flames. Buckler calls it his third victory. The facts are that his third victory came on February 15, 1917, the day following his second, and it was another Caudron over Pont-a-Mousson, not a balloon. His first balloon victory of the war did not come until the following April 26 and that occurred in the early morning hours of that day. To make matters worse, Buckler has it that upon returning to his field after the balloon victory, he learned that Strasser had just scored his own first victory. Strasser, as we know, first scored on December 24, 1916 and did not himself score on any of the dates of Buckler's total of six balloon victories of 1917 (Strasser left *Jasta 17* in December and was not around for Buckler's one balloon victory of 1918). And there's more. Buckler describes the celebration in the mess that evening for his and Strasser's victories with "the *Hauptmann*" (meaning *Jasta 17*'s Commanding Officer) presiding. This could only refer to the *Hauptmann* Eberhard von Seel who took over from von Brederlow on May 10, 1917 and was the only man of that rank to command the unit subsequently. Von Bredelow, of course, was a *Rittmeister* and although those ranks were equal, one just didn't confuse one for the other in the German military. So the party Buckler describes, whatever the occasion, had to take place between May 10 and June 12, 1917 when von Seel fell in combat over Montigny.

It is again impossible from Buckler's writings to pin down the exact date of the event which gave *Jasta 17* its famous battle cry "*Malaula*!" If we can believe Buckler's chronology (and we shouldn't), it happened the day after the celebration with "the *Hauptmann*" just mentioned in attendance. At that affair, Buckler and Strasser allegedly agreed that henceforth they would hunt together. And not only that, they would share victories equally regardless of who actually was the one responsible for a successful combat. Strasser was to get the next one so that he "could catch up a bit" (there is no evidence this ever happened subsequently). At dawn the next day, Buckler, Strasser and two others took off but quickly became dispersed, Buckler claiming they still hadn't learned the knack of formation flying (and this after months of frontline patrols?). Somehow, Buckler and Strasser hooked up again and then Buckler realized a Nieuport had fastened itself just behind and below Strasser's Albatros and was in position for a sure kill with Strasser unaware of the danger. But before the Frenchman

[1] Hahn was already a highly decorated officer, In addition to both Iron Crosses, at the time of the balloon action he held the so-called "trio" of Saxon bravery orders, the Knight 2nd Class with Swords of its Albert Order (on April 25, 1915 for service in *Feldflieger-Abteilung 23*), the Knight 2nd Class with Swords of its Merit Order (on October 4, 1916 in *Jasta 19*) and the Knight's Cross of its premier bravery award, the Military St. Henry Order (on December 27, 1916, also in *Jasta 19*). A biography on Hahn appeared in Volume III in this series.

could deliver the *coup de grâce*, Buckler was on him. After just a few rounds, however, Buckler's guns jammed. By now, Strasser was fully alerted and also engaged the enemy. The Nieuport pilot turned the tables on Strasser and in a brilliant maneuver, was on his tail again. Buckler, still with jammed guns nonetheless went straight after the opponent. Buckler claims he could see the consternation on the pilot's face as the distance closed on what could have been a collision course. At that point, the man gave up and spiraled down to a landing, Buckler figuring that the fellow felt he had no chance to escape anyhow.

When touching down, the Nieuport flipped over on its back but the pilot was not seriously hurt. Buckler and Strasser landed nearby and upon reaching the site, found the Frenchman was already in the hands of German troops. They immediately exercised their right to entertain their guest for 24 hours before having to turn him over to the military police. While waiting for a car to transport them to *Jasta 17*'s field, the three men looked over the wreck. At this point, as legend has it, the Nieuport pilot threw up his hands upon seeing the condition of his beloved bird and uttered the cry, "*ma Lola*!" The amused German airmen heard this as "*Malaula*!" and so wrote it down. It instantly became *Jasta 17*'s call to action. Buckler writes that, to them, it meant "up and at 'em," saying that it had a "magic influence" on the men of the unit.

Typically, Buckler does not date this incident but records the French pilot's name as one "Papaine." On April 15, 1917, Buckler was credited with bringing down a *Sergeant* Papeil of *Escadrille Spa 3* for his fourth confirmed victory. The pilot was indeed entertained by *Jasta 17* that evening and it is understandable that Buckler could have misspelled the man's name. But Papeil was flying a Spad VII, not a Nieuport. What may have happened is this. On May 12, 1917, Buckler scored his seventh victory, Nieuport 17 numbered 3674 with a prominent "9" lettered on its fuselage. The aircraft was flown by *Adjutant* Alain Joussaud of *Escadrille N.75*. As the photograph reproduced here shows, it turned over after being forced down. Buckler must have again confused these two incidents in his mind and it may well have been Joussaud who uttered the cry "*ma Lola*" and not "Papaine."

There is a gap in Buckler's 1917 victory string of two months, between the Nieuport on May 12 and his next victory, his eighth over a Sopwith Triplane southeast of Zillebeke in Flanders (*Jasta 17* had been moved from its airfield at St. Quentin-le-Petit to Ghistelles on June 24 where it now faced mainly the British Royal Flying Corps and the Royal Naval Air Service). The victory is dated July 12 in *Jasta 17*'s record book and July 11 in the *Nachrichtenblatt*.[2] Buckler offers a possible explanation for this time interval between victories except for one important thing which will be commented upon shortly. Sometime not long after the May 12 event (according to Buckler's chronology anyway), he was ordered to a *Jastaschule* for a month-long brush-up course. Why, he complained, would the top scorer of *Jasta 17* (no one else was even close) have to go back to school? But orders are orders and he made preparations for the long flight. The school was 280 kilometers to the north (possibly it was *Jastaschule I* at Valenciennes). The first leg of the flight went well but then he encountered heavy cloud cover which forced his "Fokker" down to 50 meters (was it really an obsolescent Fokker in the D.I-D.V series and not his regular Albatros?). After two hours in the air, he finally broke into bright sunshine (two hours of flight at even only, say, 80 miles per hour would have already had him at his objective). At that point, he saw some "specks" rising to meet him. The specks turned out to be three French planes which overtook him (maybe he was flying an old, slow machine after all). What happened next, he says, was largely blocked out of his memory. All he remembers is a blow to the head and a realization that his engine had caught fire.

When Buckler came to, he was lying on the ground next to the wreckage of his "Fokker." Before drifting back into unconsciousness, he heard a feminine voice speaking to him in German. The next he knew he awoke in a hospital bed with two women and a German officer by his side. The women, who were French but spoke German, had seen him fall. Considering everything, Buckler's injuries were not that bad. A split upper lip required 14 stitches and a cut above his left eye, 24. After seven days in hospital, he returned to *Jasta 17* by train for a few more days of rest before he proceeded north again, this time by automobile, to attend his courses. The problem here, however, is that Buckler's first wounding as a flier did not occur until July 17, 1917 by which time *Jasta 17* had moved to Flanders which would have been much closer to Valenciennes and the direction would have been south, not north.

Buckler's recollection of what happened after his return to *Jasta 17* following his time at school again leaves us confused. He says the *Staffel* was now under the command of

[2] The *Jasta 17* record book marked the victory down as Sopwith Triplane N.5384 of 10 (Naval) Squadron flown by Sub/Lt. J.A. Allen who was wounded and came down in British lines. On July 12, Flight Sub/Lt. Allen was forced to land in his own lines wounded, according to *The Sky Their Battlefield*, by a splinter from anti-aircraft fire. His triplane is identified there as No. 5364 from Naval 10 but there is a question mark placed after that number. Whichever is correct, it would appear that in this case the official *Nachrichtenblatt* got the date wrong.

Hauptmann Rudolf *Freiherr* von Esebeck. Von Esebeck did not take over until October 4, 1917 following the wounding of *Jasta 17*'s third leader, *Leutnant* Ernst Wendler on October 1. Wendler, in turn, had replaced *Hauptmann* Eberhard von Seel who had been killed on June 12. Buckler makes no mention of the loss of either von Seel or Wendler which is curious since he scored one victory under von Seel (May 12) and eight under Wendler (four in July, two in August and two in September). There are several other discrepancies in Buckler's account of things around this time but we will only comment upon two.

Buckler suffered a wound in combat on August 12, 1917, serious enough to send him to hospital. With no dates given in Buckler's writings, it is difficult to be sure that his description of an injury he received in an air battle was, in fact, the one he incurred on August 12. He claims he was up alone when he came across two Sopwith Camels which he promptly attacked. He dove on one that "fell like a torch." Buckler and the other Camel pilot warily circled each other, looking for an opportunity to strike. They were around 1,500 meters apart when Buckler received a blow to the cheek. He figured his opponent had fired at that extreme range, speculating that he must have had a telescopic sight. Buckler dove under full power to get away but the enemy plane followed him down, also going flat out. He now realized he had also been hit in the left arm which was dripping blood and virtually useless. Fighting off the unconsciousness that overcame him from moment to moment, Buckler made it safely back to his own field. It took him five weeks to recover before returning to *Jasta 17*. If he did indeed "flame" a Camel just before being wounded, it could not have been on the 12th. He received no credit for a victory of any kind on that date and the British lost no Camels on August 12. Buckler's only Camel victories in 1917 came on August 9 and October 11. He quite obviously has once again recalled things which actually occurred on separate occasions as though they had come on the same day.

Much to the disappointment of this writer, Buckler completely overlooks mention of his awards from his native Hesse but he does give us a good account of his investiture with the *Orden Pour le Mérite* as we shall see. On the other hand, he virtually passes over his Golden Military Merit Cross and completely misstates the date of his Iron Cross 1st Class. He says the latter came around the time of his August 12, 1917 wounding. He actually had it in his possession for some time before that. For example, a photograph of him dated April 15, 1917, reproduced here, clearly shows him wearing the badge. What Buckler also ignores is his promotion to *Offizier-Stellvertreter*. According to an entry in the *Krankenbuchlager* (Hospital Records Depository) in Berlin, the date was also August 12, 1917 and it places him in the *Marine-Kriegs-Lazarett Brügge* (Naval Military Hospital Bruges).

The other account of Buckler's that can't be reconciled with facts is an alleged meeting with the later *Pour le Mérite* ace, Ernst Udet, after each had scored a victory moments apart. Buckler's, according to him, was an R.E.8 whose wings he shot off. Just before that, a then unknown-to-Buckler German pilot had flamed another enemy plane. The two then teamed up and flew back together to Buckler's field. There they introduced themselves to each other. The trouble here is that at no time in 1917 did Udet score a victory on the same date of any of Buckler's seven R.E.8 victories between August 11 and November 18.

As already mentioned, no roll of recipients of the Warrior's Honor Decoration in Iron seems to have survived. But one related document in Buckler's case has. From it, we learn that on October 11, 1917, a proposal was made to Darmstadt that he be awarded the decoration. On November 5, in a letter of transmittal to a headquarters command in Buckler's area, the badge itself and the certificate of possession were forwarded for presentation. Also returned was proof of Buckler's Hessian citizenship, one of the requirements for earning the award. Exactly one week later, on November 12, Buckler's Golden Military Merit Cross was approved in Berlin. He was only the fourth aviation recipient in the war so far to be given what was also commonly referred to as the "Order for Merit for the Little Man" ("Little" here meaning not an officer but a man in the ranks). Concerning it, Buckler merely wrote, "In the meantime, I had also received the Military Merit Cross" (here, Buckler is being quite correct; "Military Merit Cross" was the full legal name of the decoration but the word "Golden" or "in Gold" came to be attached to it in almost every instance to distinguish it from the Military Honor Decoration 1st Class which was an identical badge but in silver, also awarded in World War I). Buckler's use of the word "also" here is interesting. It would seem to refer to his just-awarded Warrior's Honor Decoration in Iron which he otherwise ignores in his writings but which he proudly wore thereafter as the several photographs here show.

There was one notable occasion where Buckler uses a date. It certainly should have been etched in his mind since it was the only time in the war that he pulled off the "hat trick," scoring three victories in one day. Although we can doubt all the details he provides, his account, for once, is essentially correct. In his own words:

> On November 18, 1917, there was a thick mist over the whole Flanders Front. As always, I was first at breakfast.

Großherzogliche
General-Adjutantur
J.-No. [illegible]

Darmstadt, den 5. November 1917.

Dem General - Kommando II. Bayr. Armee - Korps

gemäß Vorschlag v. 11.X.17. II c /4410

1 + 1/. <u>1 K r i e g e r e h r e n z e i c h e n i n E i s e n</u>

mit Besitzzeugnisformular

für Vizefeldwebel Julius B u c k l e r, Jagdstaffel 17 zur weiteren Veranlassung und Ausfüllung des Besitzzeugnisformulares übersandt.

./. 1 Staatsangehörigkeitsausweis zurück.

Buckler was proposed for the Warrior's Honor Decoration in Iron on October 11, 1917. This is the communication from the Darmstadt Adjutant General's Office to headquarters of the 2nd Bavarian Army Corps transmitting the badge for Buckler together with the certificate of possession. Returned along with them is the proof of Buckler's Hessian citizenship, one of the requirements for possession. At right, Buckler with Albatros D.V "*Mops*" around the time of his award in November 1917.

> Three days earlier, I had shot down my 26th enemy. From a gray blanket of cloud, enemy fliers attacked our airfield by day. I had jumped into my "Mops," the engine of which happened to be running already, and caught one who had carelessly come out of the clouds again and I literally chased him into the ground without firing. The machine disintegrated, the pilot remained uninjured and was immediately brought to the *Staffel* (here Buckler is again a bit confused; both the pilot and observer of R.E.8 A.4652 from No.21 Squadron, RFC that Buckler shot down on November 15 subsequently died of their injuries – N.W. O'C).

After making some comments on other matters, including why, after 26 victories, he still hadn't been promoted *Leutnant*, Buckler went on:

> In order to clear my thoughts, I went to the airfield. All the tents were closed. Only mine was open. The engine of my machine was newly overhauled and got a test-run. It ran so extremely well that I felt a great lust to give it a try. Within a few minutes I was in the air and flew an extensive circle of the airfield. I could not fly above 100 meters. At this height, however, visibility was still reasonably good. Why not a short trip to the front? The coward in me asked, "Why? It's useless!" A reason the more to go! And when I am about five kilometers from the front, I observe an enemy over Zillebeke Lake near Ypres. I thought of number 27. The balloon was about 10 kilometers away.
>
> With a speed of 160 kilometers per hour, I thus needed barely six minutes to reach him. I tried out my MGs. They were all right. Then I dived into the mist. The six minutes of blind flying seemed so long to me at the time that four times I came down again from the murk in order to breathe freely again. When the six minutes had passed, the balloon was still a long way behind the enemy lines. I had underestimated the distance. If I entered the mist again, it might well be that I would pass over it or would lose it. So I raced directly towards it at about 50 meters altitude. They pulled it down.
>
> I fired and it was on fire. At the same moment, three enemy aeroplanes took care of me. In addition, everything on the ground with a gun began to fire at me. Then the murk saved me. In it I disappeared. But being in the gray, I had no notion of my position anymore. When I dared to emerge, I saw below shell holes, shot-up landscape, ruined villages. Without compass and sun, I had no indication which way to fly. So I trusted my lucky star and flew in a certain direction and noticed an airfield below me, throttled down and began to glide. But what is that? Enemy aeroplanes next to me in the air! Full power! Control stick into my belly! And again I disappeared into the murk. When I emerged again in a few minutes, I saw before me – unbelievably – an enemy kite balloon!
>
> Hurriedly, I took in the situation. Below me Dickebusch. Over there was my territory. And this gas bag had for the longest time been an enemy observation post for directing their fire on our trenches. At full speed I flung myself at the balloon which already descended speedily. After a few rounds, he was ablaze. Already its observer descended peacefully. This was an unexpected victory! The 28th! I did not wait for attention from below but quickly disappeared into the murk.

Buckler landed at *Jasta 5*'s field for badly needed fuel. There he had a late breakfast (the balloons had gone down between 9:10 a.m. and 9:25 a.m. German Time – N.W.O'C). and before he left for home, he got the good word that German forward observation posts had confirmed that the fighter plane "Mops" had burned two enemy balloons.

The men of *Jasta 17* were up in strength that same afternoon but found the front quiet. Buckler gave the wash-out signal which meant everyone was on his own (if true, Buckler was acting as the leader in the air). For himself, he chose to roam around alone and at 2:15 p.m., shot down an R.E.8 in a low altitude engagement (the plane, A.3669 of No.9 Squadron, RFC actually returned safely with the crew unwounded after apparently being attacked by Buckler over Bixschoote). Not surprisingly, Buckler found himself exhausted from the day's labors and took to his bed. His old observer from his two-seater days, von Rudno-Rudzinski who had joined *Jasta 17* on October 5, himself now a fighter pilot too, locked the door to Buckler's room to insure no interruptions and pocketed the key. Late that afternoon, Buckler was wanted on the telephone. *Kogenluft*, His Excellency General von Hoeppner was calling. There was some confusion until von Rudno was found to unlock the door. On the other end of the line Buckler heard the Commanding General say, "In the name of His Majesty, I congratulate you on your promotion to Active Army *Leutnant* in *Flieger-Bataillon Nr.1*." (another misquote; all records show Buckler was promoted *Leutnant der Reserve*, not an officer in the Regular Army). After hanging up, Buckler was naturally besieged with questions. What did the General say? Buckler merely said it was congratulations on his three victories and repaired to his room. There he sewed on officer epaulets (although this whole sequence of events could be another product of Buckler's imagination, it would not be unreasonable for a man expecting promotion momentarily to have the proper insignia stashed away waiting for the day itself). A celebration was planned anyway for Buckler's triple of the day but when he reported to von Esebeck wearing his new rank, the party turned boisterous and continued on well after Buckler blissfully called it quits before midnight.

The promotion, however, brought no respite from the daily grind. He was up the next day, November 19, and was forced to land after a combat. The circumstances are unknown and Buckler does not comment on them. By the end of the month, *Jasta 17* found itself one of the aviation elements that had been moved down to the Cambrai area to contain a British threat there. On November 20, an attack supported by tanks and without the advance warning of the usual days-long bombardment caught the Germans by complete surprise. In six hours, German lines were penetrated to a depth of 10,000 yards, more ground in one day than the campaign known as Third Ypres in Flanders had just taken after four grueling and costly months. But the British brass had no plans to exploit the unexpected success and by the 30th, determined German counterattacks had reclaimed all the lost ground. The day before, Buckler was up as usual despite poor weather. Late that morning, he had a brief and apparently inconclusive brush with an R.E.8. Pressing on, he spied another balloon and shot it down over Bapaume five minutes after noon. That night, a restless Buckler claims that he had a premonition that on the morrow he would "catch something."

And catch it he did. On November 29, he was flying lone protection for a German two-seater when two Camels below him made to cut it off. Buckler determined to turn the tables on them but before he began his dive, he took the precaution of checking his rear to be sure all was clear. Too late. Ten meters away, another "Lord" (as the Germans were wont to refer to British airmen) was about to take him in flank at what was near impossible-to-miss range. Buckler's body was hit in the back and arms. To break off, he had to use his right foot to control the stick. What he terms a near suicidal dive ended with his piling up in the middle of No-Man's Land. The German counterattack of November 30 saved him. After lying beneath the wreckage of his plane in terrible pain for how long he could not recall, German medics found him. He was taken to a field hospital for initial treatment. The *Staffel* was notified and, according to Buckler, von Esebeck, von Rudno and another arrived with a staff car to carry Buckler on a stretcher to Le Cateau near Cambrai where an operation could be performed.

The concern was that Buckler might lose one or both of his arms. The issue was still in doubt when on December 3, a nurse fussed over him to make sure he was presentable enough to receive important visitors.[3] A *Hauptmann* entered first and in a "low and careful" voice prepared Buckler for what was next to come. Then through the door came "an old gentleman smiling kindly." The old gentleman turned out to be *General der Kavallerie* Georg von der Marwitz, *Oberbefehlschaber* (Commander-in-Chief) of the German 2nd Army and himself a holder of the *Orden Pour le Mérite mit Eichenlaub*. The General seated himself next to Buckler's bed and in a fatherly manner, told what must have been a stunned young man all about his own life, how he was a soldier, had always been a soldier and how he had accepted his own *Pour le Mérite* "not for me, but for my troops." He went on, "How wonderful it must be for the young ones to receive it for a real deed." And with that, the general opened the case he had in his hand, took out the blue and gold cross and draped its long black and silvered ribbon over Buckler's neck. Buckler was still heavily sedated and with the General holding the fingers of one of his hands protruding from the plaster cast, Buckler drifted off. When he awoke three hours later, Buckler had to check to see if the badge were actually there and it all hadn't been a dream. It's a charming story. Let's hope it was true.[4]

Buckler was sent home on December 23 for recuperation in Mainz. There he had a relapse and lived on morphia for several days. He was still in bad shape. It was not until eight weeks after his operation that the cast on his right arm was removed. But the left arm in which an artery had been severed still gave trouble and another operation had to be performed. Two weeks after that, he was allowed up for the first time. If Buckler remembered the date correctly, he did not get back to *Jasta 17* until March 8, 1918 and made his first frontline flight four days later. That day, a Breguet was credited to *Leutnant* Otto Fitzner. Buckler's writings suggest that he had had to step in when it appeared the two-seater was about to escape despite pass after pass of the others in his flight and he was in the lead when it finally fell. Whether giving Fitzner the victory was, as Buckler also implies, a chance for someone else to rack up a score rather than himself is something we will never know.

In April 1918, Buckler opened up his own scoring again with his 31st victory on the 16th and his 32nd on the 21st, both Breguet XIVs. His next was a balloon on May 3. In relating

---

[3] The official date of Buckler's *Pour le Mérite* is December 4, 1917.

[4] General von der Marwitz had a good reason to adopt a fatherly attitude to Buckler. A son of his, Hans-George von der Marwitz, was a *Leutnant* in *Jasta 30* at the time. He had already scored two victories and would go on to command the *Staffel*, be promoted *Oberleutnant* and end the war with a total of 15 confirmed victories.

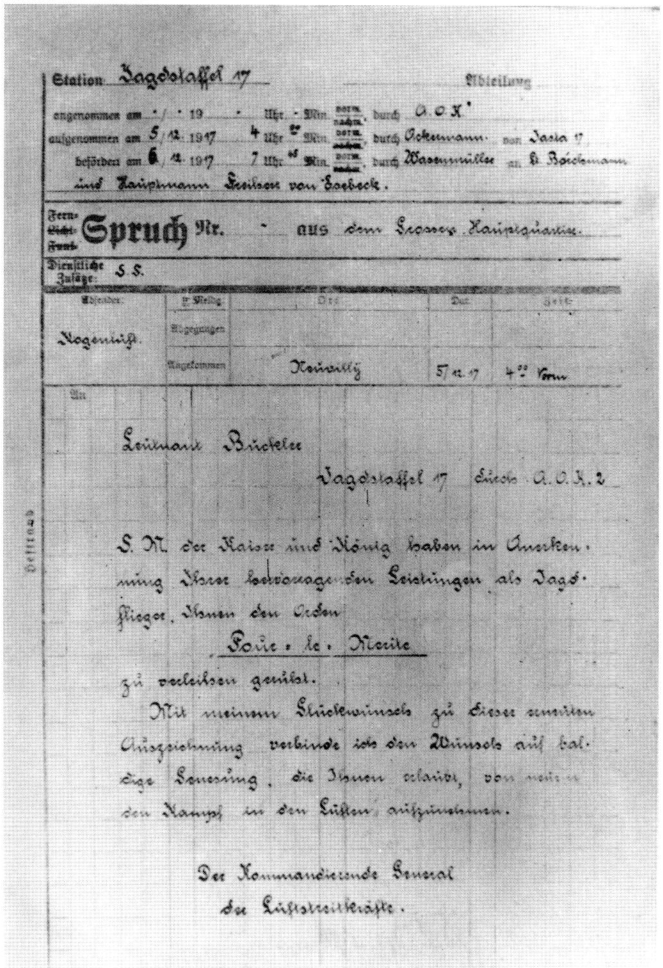

Station Jagdstaffel 17 Abteilung

angenommen am . / . 19 . Uhr . Min. durch A.O.K.

aufgenommen am 5/12. 1917 4 Uhr Min. durch Ockermann von Jasta 17

befördert am 6. 12. 1917 7 Uhr Min. durch Wassermüller an Lt. Bockelmann

und Hauptmann Freiherr von Esebeck.

Fern-Spruch Nr. - aus dem Grossen Hauptquartier.

Dienstliche Zusätze: S.S.

Absender: Kogenluft. Angekommen 5/12.17 4⁰⁰ Vorm.

An:

Leutnant Buckler

Jagdstaffel 17 durch A.O.K. 2

S.M. der Kaiser und König haben in Anerkennung Ihrer hervorragenden Leistungen als Jagdflieger, Ihnen den Orden

Pour le Mérite

zu verleihen geruht.

Mit meinem Glückwunsch zu dieser erneuten Auszeichnung verbinde ich den Wunsch auf baldige Genesung, die Ihnen erlaubt, von neuem den Kampf in den Lüften aufzunehmen.

Der Kommandierende General der Luftstreitkräfte.

Buckler was commissioned *Leutnant* on November 18, 1917 and on December 4, with his score at a round 30 victories, his *Orden Pour le Mérite* was approved. The telegram from *Kogenluft*, *Generalleutnant* von Hoeppner, congratulating him reached *Jasta 17* on December 6. The badge, however, had already been presented to Buckler in hospital where he lay as a result of a serious wounding on November 29 (see text for details). The other photographs show the wagons of *Jasta 17* which Buckler claims to have found abandoned and which he converted into mobile shelters for the men of *Jasta 17* whose aerodromes were prime targets for enemy night bombing attacks. When Buckler returned to *Jasta 17* in August or September 1918, he found the wagons painted *Zirkus Buckler* (Circus Buckler) in expectation that he would now become its Commanding Officer. Whether he actually received this appointment officially or he just led *Jasta 17* in the air during the last months of the war is discussed in the text.

the circumstances of that victory, Buckler again displays his faulty memory. He had made his early morning attack under heavy flak and machine gun ground fire and as he made his escape zig-zagging at low level, he describes being hit in his left foot. In excruciating pain and with the aid of a strap to the rudder bar he had rigged up himself to cope with emergencies of just this kind, he managed to steer with his good right foot and made it back to his field. There, it was found the bullet was still lodged in his foot. No clean wound. Another operation was needed. More hospital time. And this, as Buckler puts it, "at a time when every single German pilot counted." Buckler's May 3 balloon victory is without dispute. What is is that he writes the victory came on May 6, the day on which he did, in fact, suffer his fifth wounding of the war. Strange that a man writing about such things even long afterwards would become so confused.

This time, Buckler recuperated at what he calls a luxurious hospital in Lindau on the shores of Lake Constance. It was there that he received the news that "the good" *Freiherr* von Esebeck had fallen in flames on May 27 in an air battle with a Breguet over Noyon about 18 miles east of Montdidier. Again in what we certainly have good reason to suspect was still another flight of fancy, Buckler says he dreamed of von Esebeck's death two nights before and awoke drenched with sweat and surrounded by worried nurses. Buckler professed great admiration for his fallen *Staffelführer*, "a real leader of

Like many of the more famous German World War I airmen, Buckler was lured back into the new *Luftwaffe* in the mid-1930s and along with his fellow *Pour le Mérite* fighter ace, Josef Jacobs, was commissioned a *Major*. Buckler himself says nothing about his awards other than those from Prussia in his book, "*Malaula*!" But in the photograph at the right we see him with a five-ribbon *Feldschnalle*. The first three ribbons represent his Iron Cross, 2nd Class, the Golden Military Merit Cross and Hesse's General Honor Decoration "for Bravery." The last ribbon on the bar is probably his Hamburg Hanseatic Cross and the one before that could be either the Gold or the Silver Military Merit Medal from Württemberg. A postwar account of *Jasta 17*'s record included a list of the decorations earned by men while serving with the unit but, unfortunately, with none of the recipients identified by name. During the time Buckler served with it, *Jasta 17*'s personnel were awarded one Gold and two Silver Württemberg Military Merit Medals.

men" and one whom given the choice of a *Pour le Mérite* for himself or a decoration or promotion for one of his men, would have always chosen the latter.

When Buckler returned to *Jasta 17* is unclear. He says it was in August. It may have been sometime later. Whenever he did get back, *Jasta 17* was leaderless. *Leutnant* Günther Schuster, a 1917 member of the unit, had been brought over from *Jasta 29* in June to take von Esebeck's place. Then Schuster was wounded in a combat near Soissons on August I and had to be hospitalized. Certainly, Buckler as by far the leading scorer and now with a *Pour le Mérite* was the man for the job. But was he? The between-the-wars German researchers suggest that Schuster came back and was *Jasta 17*'s commander at the time of the armistice. Buckler may never have received official appointment although many other records have placed him as the *Staffelführer* for the last months of 1918. His own writings suggest that he was. There is little doubt, however, that Buckler was the leader in the air when the end came

Buckler's last victories came in October, his 34th, 35th and 36th. He claimed another on November 8 but even Buckler was resigned to the fact that it could not be confirmed. At both the front and at home, conditions were chaotic. The army was being pounded by the combined might of the British, French and Americans. The navy had mutinied at Kiel on November 4 following Admiral Scheer's insane order for a last ditch suicide sortie of the High Seas Fleet. In Berlin, the Socialists were demanding the abdication of the *Kaiser* and a new government. The Communists were inciting outright revolution. At Spa, von Hindenburg was forced to tell his All-Highest War Lord that his beloved army no longer was behind him. At the front and on the masts of ships of the Imperial German Navy, red flags were hoisted. Soldiers' and Sailors' Councils sprang up. Huge numbers of the armed forces had had enough.

It was in that climate that Buckler, he says, was ordered to *Kofl* headquarters at Charleroi to be apprised of the situation and receive orders (suggesting that he was in command of *Jasta 17*). Along the way, he was stopped four times by German soldiers wearing red arm bands. Officers were being assaulted and stripped of rank by often drunken rabble. Though delayed, Buckler's *Pour le Mérite* saw him through. The mobs were still impressed when they saw that (or so Buckler tells us). At Charleroi, he was told just how desperate things were but ordered to go back to *Jasta 17* and await developments. Three days later, it was all over. It had been exactly two years since Buckler had reported to *Jasta 17* and now it had made its last war flight. Buckler gathered the men together, they spoke of their triumphs and mourned their losses. They sang some of the old songs. Originally, they had been planning a festive bash to celebrate the *Staffel*'s second anniversary. But the mood was, according to one of Buckler's last notes in his "*Malaula*," more like that of a funeral.

WARRIORS' HONOR DECORATION IN IRON RECIPIENTS WITHOUT BIOGRAPHIES

Jasta 26 at Erchin in March 1918 with Warriors' Honor Decoration in Iron recipient, *Vzfw*. Fritz Beckhardt, diminutive even by the standards of the day, at the extreme right. In the windows, left to right: *Unteroffz*. Fritz Zogmann, *Lt*. Weiss (*O.z.b.V.*), *Lt*. Werner Dahm and *Offz.-Stv*. Fritz Kublum. Standing left to right: *Vzfw*. Erich Buder (Golden Military Merit Cross), *Vzfw*. Fritz Classen, *Lt*. Claus Reimer, *Lt*. Fritz Loerzer (CO), the then *Oblt*. Bruno Loerzer (*Pour le Mérite* – CO JG III), *Vzfw*. Otto Marquardt, *Offz.-Stv*. Otto Esswein (Golden Military Merit Cross), *Vzfw*. Otto Frühner (Golden Military Merit Cross) and Beckhardt. Beckhardt scored his only confirmed victory in *Jasta 26* on April 11, 1918 and then was sent to *Kest 2* for the remainder of the war.

Right: *Lt*. Walter Graf, an observer with *I. Marine Feldflieger-Abteilung*, Hessian General Honor Decoration "for Bravery" on August 31, 1916 and Warriors' Honor Decoration in Iron on September 4, 1917. Captured sometime in 1918. Above: Another Warriors' Honor Decoration in Iron naval recipient, *Vzflgmstr*. Mayer of *Mar.Feldjastas I, II* and *III* with Albatros D.V "Eva." He was credited with four confirmed victories.

Warriors' Honor Decoration in Iron recipient *Lt.* Oscar Rousselle lost his left eye in an air combat on August 10, 1917 as a member of *Jasta 4*. Nonetheless, he shows us his left profile and new glass eye in the later 1918 photograph at the right, perhaps the better to show his decorations. He had returned to *Jasta 4* after hospitalization and tried to return to frontline combat flying but to no avail. He had to settle for the job of Adjutant for the remainder of the war. In the photograph above taken at an *Armee-Flug-Park*, probably in late 1915 or January 1916, Rousselle can be seen in the background second from the right. He would go on from here to become a pilot briefly with *FFl.Abt. 32* and then went to *FFl.Abt. 23* in February 1916. Rousselle joined *Jasta 4* at the end of June 1917. Second from the left is *Hptm.* Werner Funck, decorated with the Knight 1st Class with Swords of the Saxe-Ernestine House Order on March 8, 1916 in *Art.Fl.Abt. 209*, Buckler's old outfit. Fourth from the left is *Oblt.* Willy Meyer who had won the Knight's Cross of the Saxon Military St. Henry Order on July 4, 1915 in *FFl.Abt. 23*, one of four such awards in the unit on that day.

Below: The officers and men of *Fl.Abt. 7* on an unknown date in 1917 or 1918. The tall mustached officer under the propeller blade, also unknown, is wearing the Warriors' Honor Decoration in Iron.

CHAPTER VIII

THE MILITARY AWARDS OF THE GRAND DUCHY OF HESSE

THE GENERAL HONOR DECORATION "FOR BRAVERY"

A civil award called the General Honor Decoration was founded on September 25, 1843 by Grand Duke Ludwig II who ruled from 1830 until his death on June 16, 1848. Awards then lapsed for more than a year when, on November 14, 1849, his successor, Grand Duke Ludwig III, renewed the decoration and greatly expanded the bases upon which it could be awarded. There were inscriptions on the reverse of the medals that specifically described the reason for its bestowal. The one we will mainly be concerned with here bore the inscription *FÜR TAPFERKEIT* ("for Bravery"). But there were a whole string of others including individual medals for meritorious service, for faithful service, for many years of faithful service, for long years of faithful service, for 50 years of faithful service and two for life saving, one bearing the inscription "for saving human life" and the other "for saving life at the risk of one's own." These inscriptions were encircled by a wreath of laurel on the left and an oak branch on the right. The obverse displayed the bust of the Grand Duke in profile. All the medals used the same ribbon, light blue with narrow red side stripes. The authoritative reference work by *Dr.* Waldemar Hesse Edler von Hessenthal and Georg Schreiber, *Die tragbaren Ehrenzeichen des Deutsches Reich* (The Wearable Decoration of Germany), states that in the wars of 1866 and 1870/71, only 49 awards of the General Honor Decoration "for Bravery" were made.

Ludwig III ruled for 29 years being succeeded by a nephew on June 13, 1877 who took the title Grand Duke Ludwig IV. It was not until June 8, 1889, however, that new coinages were struck that showed the bust of the then reigning monarch. These, in turn, were superseded by a final coinage in 1894. Ludwig IV died on March 13, 1892 and his eldest and then only surviving son, Ernst Ludwig, ascended the throne in that year. His bust then appeared on the new medals. Originally, all of these were struck in silver but in 1917, the precious metals shortage caused the by-then more frequently awarded medal bearing the *FÜR TAPFERKEIT* inscription to be debased and the medal was struck in silvered white metal. Also introduced at this time was an additional General Honor Decoration with the inscription *FÜR KREIGSVERDIENSTE* ("for War Merits") which likewise was struck in silvered white metal. In announcing the creation of the Warriors' Honor Decoration in Iron on March 13, 1917, the regulations regarding Hessian war decorations were supplemented with the following stipulations applying to the award for the medal for bravery and the new one for war merits. The exact wording, somewhat clumsy when translated into English, read as follows:

The General Honor Decoration

a. "For Bravery" (the Bravery Medal), on the war ribbon, as a decoration for participation in actual combat activity with the fighting troops and under enemy fire.

b. "For War Merits," with the war ribbon; not for actual participation in combat activities but for merits in an area under enemy fire, and on rare occasions, in the communication zone, in occupied territory and with the occupation troops, under the following circumstances:

1. Decorated in the War of 1870/71.
2. Possession of the Iron Cross 1st Class.
3. Leader of a Hessian Replacement Battalion or Detachment.
4. Commanders of a Hessian District Command, if

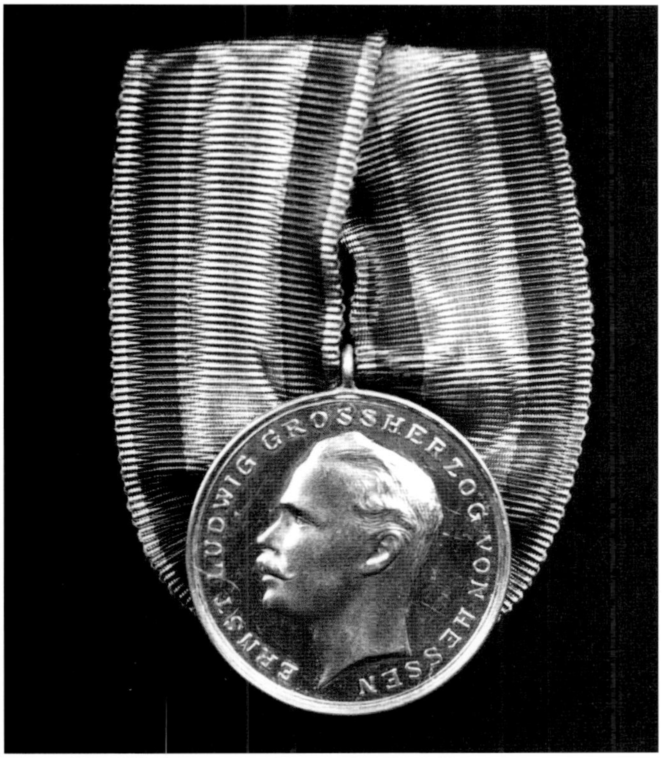

The General Honor Decoration was founded in 1843 originally as a civil decoration. In 1849, it was expanded into an award that was given for a variety of reasons including such things as long and faithful service, meritorious service, life saving and also as a bravery award among the military. The coinage above was the last, struck in 1889 which carried the bust of Grand Duke Ernst Ludwig on its obverse. The inscription on the reverse surrounded by a wreath of laurel on the left and an oak branch on the right indicates that this was the military award *FÜR TAPFERKEIT* ("for Bravery").

Right: Grand Duke Ernst Ludwig of Hesse and by Rhine decorates soldiers in the field. Hessian bravery awards were almost always restricted to Hessian citizens or those serving in Hessian contingents.

> they are either citizens of Hesse or had served for a long time in the face of the enemy.
> 5. Personages close to His Royal Highness the Grand Duke based on their previous merits.

> Personages who possess or receive the Iron Cross with the white-black ribbon would be considered for the General Honor Decoration "for War Merits" with the statutory ribbon (the white-black ribbon with the Iron Cross went to non-combatants including medical and veterinarian personnel – N.W.O'C).

Further stipulations were made concerning the regulations that would be applied to the awarding of the General Honor Decoration "for Bravery" and "for War Merits" (these also applied to two other Hessian war decorations with which we are not concerned here but which might be of interest to those readers whose main concern is not aviation but, rather, orders and decorations; these were the Military Medical Cross and War Honor Decoration, the latter being an award for troops in the communications zone, in occupied areas and for occupation troops themselves). These read:

> The listed war decorations may be awarded if the proposed person has shown himself deserving of a decoration under the conditions that he be a citizen of Hesse, serves in a Hessian unit or did so previously.
>
> Possessing the Iron Cross is not a prerequisite; after having been awarded the Iron Cross or another war decoration (however), additional merits must have occurred, with a severe wounding being excepted.
>
> Proposals have to be submitted and supported through official channels to the Grand Ducal General Adjutant's Office by those authorities or units that are capable to judge the achievement to be rewarded.
>
> Proposals based on former membership in Hessian units during wartime must be supported by those units or one similar.
>
> If all conditions have been met, a proposal to exchange one war decoration for another is permitted.
>
> Any references to conditions met for earlier awards cannot be accepted.
>
> Hessian war decorations are only exceptionally awarded in conjunction with those of other federal states and then preferably to Hessian citizens for distinction in the front line.
>
> One person can be awarded only one of the war decorations listed under I, II and III (i.e., the General Honor Decorations "for Bravery" and "for War Merits," the Military Medical Cross and the War Honor Decoration – N.W.O'C).
>
> Commanding Hessian troops or units is not reason enough for a proposal to higher authorities.

There followed then an example of the proposal form that was to be submitted with the usual particulars of the man's rank and unit, name, date and place of birth, occupation or trade, last address, citizenship (obviously, very important here) and whether the man in question held the Iron Cross 1st and/or 2nd Class, any other war decorations and if so, when. The last space on the form was for the grounds, or support, for the recommendation that was being made. With all these restrictions and the paperwork involved, it is a wonder any awards at all made their way through to a successful conclusion in the middle of an all-consuming war.

There is just one final thing to be said about the General Honor Decoration "for Bravery" before turning to the story of one of its most distinguished aviation recipients. January 23, 1916 was the 125th anniversary of the formation of *Infanterie-Regiment Prinz Carl (4. Grossherzoglich Hessisches) Nr.118.* in Worms in 1791. Grand Duke Ernst Ludwig authorized a special silver clasp with the numerals "23.1.1916." to mark the occasion and pay tribute to the officers and men of the regiment for the hard times they had just been through. The clasp was to be worn on the ribbon of the medal. Twenty nine awards of the clasp were made within the regiment and six were affixed to the flags of its battalions. The Grand Duke must have felt a particular debt to the 118th. No such recognition was given to any of the other Hessian contingents during the war and this included the only three in which Ernst Ludwig was their *Inhaber* (or Member), the 115th Infantry, the 23rd Dragoons and the 25th Field Artillery.

LEUTNANT FRANZ HEMER

It is a loss to history that one of the least known and certainly least written about high scoring German aces of the First World War never recorded his wartime flying experiences for posterity. He was the 18-victory pilot, Franz Hemer, who as a youth prewar was an accomplished cellist who had performed with orchestras and given recitals and who would have had a promising career in front of him had not the war called him to the colors. Perhaps his inherent modesty was the reason he

FRANZ HEMER THE CONCERT CELLIST/FRANZ HEMER THE FIGHTER PILOT

Young Franz Hemer's promising career as a concert cellist was cut short by the outbreak of World War I. After service in the ground troops and a transfer to the *Fliegertruppe*, he had a brief tour as a two-seater pilot before joining *Jasta 6*, one of the four elements of *Jagdgeschwader 1*, on September 10, 1917. By the end of the year, he had been credited with two victories. He picked up his string again in March 1918 and thereafter was a steady scorer, getting victories in every month through early August. On August 9, he was lightly wounded in an air combat, the day after his 18th confirmed victory. He returned to *Jasta 6* on September 25 but never saw action again. A holder of both Iron Crosses and the Hessian General Honor Decoration "for Bravery," he was promoted *Leutnant* during his convalescence and just three days before the armistice, his Knight's Cross with Swords of the Royal House Order of Hohenzollern was approved. The photograph at the right was taken on a *Jasta 6* airfield during Hemer's active flying days as a *Vizefeldwebel* and after the unit had been equipped with Fokker Triplanes in early 1918. In the background is one of them with the unit's black and white striped tailplane markings clearly showing.

never wrote down his memoirs. His family has said that he never talked much about what he did in the war except to say that his small stature probably saved his life after he had become a fighter pilot. Because he weighed less than most young men of his generation, he got a bit more speed out of his aircraft (he was referring to the Fokker Triplane at the time) and he also could fly a bit higher than the others and could attack from above. In fact, his wife, his daughter and son-in-law said they learned more about *Herr* Hemer's life as a World War I flier than they had ever known before as a consequence of a visit this writer was privileged to make to the Hemer home in Frankfurt in 1982 when they were also in attendance. *Herr* Hemer was then approaching his 88th year and had not been well (he had been invited as an honored guest to a 1981 reunion of all surviving World War I aces held in Paris over Armistice Week but had had to decline due to his health). But, as was learned afterwards, "*Poppi*," as his daughter affectionately called him, had become quite excited when he learned that an "*Amerikaner*" who had been involved with that reunion was coming to see him and pay his respects.

Herr Hemer greeted his visitor immaculately dressed and appearing very chipper. He was as much "up" for the occasion

Hemer took his pilot training early in 1917. Here he and "Max," a DFW B.I, have obviously had a slight but embarrassing mishap judging from the wry look on his face and the two amused ground crew facing the camera. The in-flight photograph below was probably taken by his instructor/observer in the front seat while Hemer was in training (see post card explanation on the next page).

as was his guest. Over the customary excellent afternoon coffee and cake, the group all looked over his shoulder as he produced a cherished photo album containing pictures of himself, his comrades and his aircraft during his time with the *Fliegertruppe*. This being a first meeting and with family members present, it was not appropriate to get into the details of when and where he flew and especially any of the circumstances surrounding his many aerial victories. Even the question, "tell me about Richthofen" would have to await another time. But knowing of his visitor's interest in medals, *Herr* Hemer very considerately produced the document to his Knight's Hohenzollern and his "*Tapferkeitsmedaille*," his word for his General Honor Decoration "for Bravery." We never did get around to the "whys" and "whens" of the latter award, unfortunately. His eyes twinkled, however, when his visitor pointed out the late date of his Hohenzollern (November 8, 1918) and how it came just under the wire. But then it was time to go. Surely, there would be another occasion when some of the unanswered questions could be posed. Sadly, that was not to be. *Herr* Hemer died on October 8 that same year. The photographs that appear here and which add so much to his story come through the kindness of his widow, her daughter and her husband for which they have the author's deep appreciation.

Like virtually all the German fighter pilots of 1917, Hemer started in two-seaters. We first pick up his wartime trail at *Armee-Flug-Park 14* on April 20, 1917 as an *Unteroffizier* presumably now trained as a pilot and awaiting assignment. He then went to *Flieger-Abteilung (A)283* where his work must have been commendable since in very short order he was selected to become a fighter pilot, a sure sign that his superiors thought well of him both in terms of his flying skills as well as a spirited, aggressive nature. He went through the course at

Below: Hemer wrote this post card from *Armee-Flug-Park 14* on May 20, 1917 to a *Fräulein* Hilde Steindorff in the Leipzig suburb of Gohlis enclosing with it the in-flight picture shown on the previous photo page. Addressing her as L.H. (standing for *Liebe* (dear) Hilde, it read:

> My new photo taken at 3000 meters altitude. I am not sleeping, but due to the stiff propeller wash I can't look up without (wearing) goggles. Once again, please be content with (just) a card greeting. I am going to the theater tonight, a visiting company, "The Seventh Day." Tomorrow more details.
>
> Always yours,
> F. (Franz)

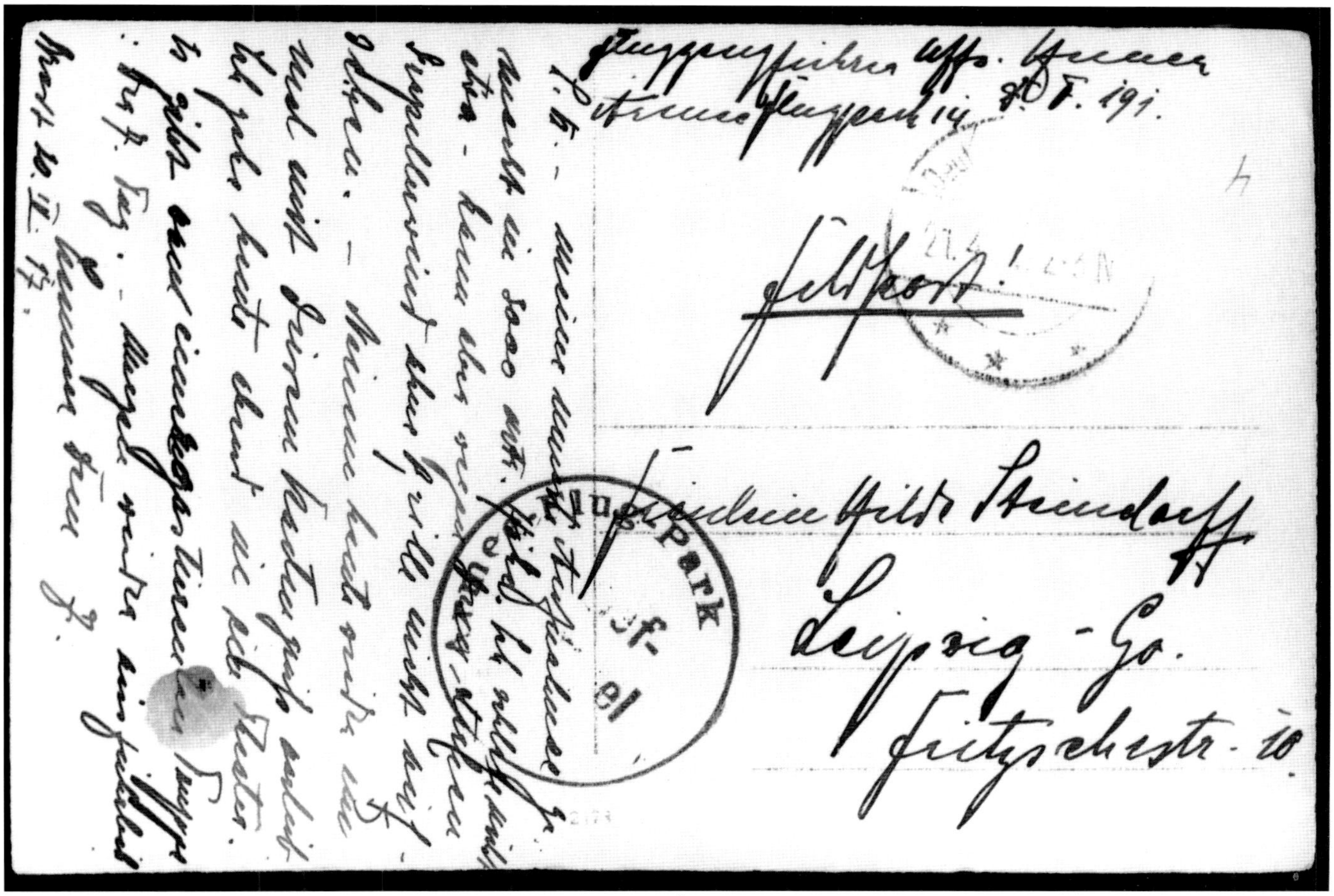

Hemer's first frontline posting was to *Flieger-Abteilung (A)283*. With one of its Rumpler C.Is as a backdrop, the unit is visited by a Bulgarian General, his aide and two other Austrian officers as well as some *Kofl* brass. Hemer, befitting his rank, stays off to the side at the extreme right. 4th from the left is *Hptm.* Lölhöffel von Löwensprung. 7th from the left is *Hptm.* Bruno Hüttig who can be seen wearing the Saxe-Weimar Wilhelm Ernst War Cross earned in 1916 for his pre-air service with an engineer battalion. Below, the then *Unteroffizier* Hemer shares a smoke and a bit of the grape with fellow *Unteroffizier* Futterer, left, and *Feldwebel* Teller in *(A)283*.

Jastaschule I for what must have been a quick one since on September 10, 1917, he was posted to *Jasta 6*, one of the four elements of *Rittmeister* Manfred *Freiherr* von Richthofen's already famous *Jagdgeschwader Nr.1*, the "Flying Circus." *Jasta 6* had just undergone a necessary change of command. A Bavarian, *Leutnant* Hans Adam, had taken over on August 22. His predecessor, *Oberleutnant* Eduard Dostler, also Bavarian, had been killed the day before when his Albatros exploded in flames after being hit by the return fire of an RFC R.E.8 (both men would become *Ritter vons* upon being awarded posthumous Knight's Crosses of the Military Max-Joseph Order, Adam subsequently falling, too, on November 15, 1917). The entire *Geschwader* at this time was grouped together on a field at Marckebeke in Flanders where the bloody battle that came to be called Third Ypres was in full swing. The new arrival there, Hemer, found himself in some heady company not the least of whom was Manfred von Richthofen's then nearest scoring rival, the 20-year old ex-Hussar, *Leutnant* Werner Voss. That very afternoon of September 10, within the space of just 25 minutes, Voss had downed two Sopwith Camels and a Spad for his 43rd, 44th and 45th victories. With the Ringmaster off as of September 6 for four weeks convalescent leave with a score standing at 61, at the rate Voss was going, he might become Germany's premier fighter pilot by the time von Richthofen got back in action (Voss further narrowed the gap when on the very next day after his "hat trick," he got victories number 46 and 47).

Hemer himself did not score until October 27. And while he waited for that first taste of victory, the previous weeks had not been kind to the *Geschwader*. Even though victories far outpaced losses, two further changes in command within the squadron had become necessary due to deaths in action. On September 13, the leader of *Jasta 11*, the 33-victory ace, *Oberleutnant* Kurt Wolff, just promoted the day before, had been shot down in one of the two new Fokker Triplanes which had reached *JG 1* in August, his being FI 102/17, the personal mount of the Baron on loan while von Richthofen was on leave. Then on September 23, Voss, having scored his 48th earlier that day, had been lost in the epic air battle with members of No.56 Squadron, RFC flying the other triplane, FI 103/17 and thus ending, for 1917 anyway, any serious threat to Manfred von Richthofen's title. Although Hemer was given official recognition for victory number one on October 27, available evidence suggests his intended victim may have gotten back all right even though the aircraft was said to have come down "on our side of the lines," that is, in German-held territory. What seems to have happened is this Hemer, with two or three others, attacked an R.E.8 of No.52 Squadron, RFC that afternoon over Gheluvelt, hitting the pilot, Captain G.C. Rogers. Hemer and his comrades must have felt it was a goner and claimed it. This was the only R.E.8 action that day that fit the time and location of the combat. We know the crew of this plane got back all right though Rogers was wounded.

Hemer had another elusive encounter with an R.E.8 on November 12 yet it was enough to produce his second confirmed victory. The combat was northeast of Ypres but again the plane escaped with one of its crew from No.6 Squadron, RFC, Corporal W.A. Elliot wounded. Now there was a long hiatus in Hemer's scoring due in large part to the lessening of aerial action after Third Ypres wound down and the Battle of Cambrai was contained in late November in which the squadron participated. All through December, January and February, the War Diary of *JG 1* noted "no special occurrences" day after day followed by such explanations as "enemy air activity very low," "no enemy air activity," "rain, heavily overcast, heavy ground haze," "heavy fog" and "almost no enemy air activity." Combats were few and far between. The first week of March 1918 was likewise slow. No victories were claimed although one pilot of the *Geschwader* was shot down and killed and two were wounded in their Fokker Triplanes. Things picked up the second week and Hemer was among the first to score. And this time, there was no doubt about the outcome. On March 10, as the men of *JG 1* were getting their orders for deployment in the long anticipated up-coming big spring offensive code-named *Operation Michael* (also called "The Great Battle of France" by the Germans), Hemer had a high altitude (14,000 feet) combat with a Sopwith Camel from No.80 Squadron, RFC over Montbrehain northeast of St. Quentin. The plane was forced to land in German held territory where the unwounded pilot, 2/Lt. C.H Flere, was taken prisoner. Hemer's next victory, his fourth, came only three days later. The *JG 1* War Diary is clear about it, an S.E.5a shot down in flames south of Cambrai at 10:40 (German Time) that morning. The Royal Flying Corps lost only one S.E.5 that day. Also putting in for an S.E.5 on March 13 was *Lt.* Franz Piechuluk of *Jasta 56*. His victim went down at 10:30 a.m. over the village of Gonnelieu, losing a wing although nothing was said about flames. Gonnelieu is less than 10 miles south and a bit to the west of Cambrai. So the two locations fit almost exactly, the time differences are negligible and with only one S.E.5 lost, it would appear both Hemer and Piechuluk were engaged with the same enemy plane and each thought he was responsible for its loss and the death of its pilot, 2/Lt. E.A. Whitehead of No.24 Squadron. And that is the way the *Nachrichtenblatt* saw it too. Each man was accorded an official victory.

Historian Alex Imrie in his book *The Fokker Triplanes* believes this photograph of *Jasta 6* triplanes was taken on the airfield at Lechelle a few days after the unit occupied it on March 26, 1918. The aircraft are in the process of having the national markings changed from the Iron Cross to the straight *Balken* cross. The first machine appears to be Hemer's Dr.1 595/17 with its wavy line personal marking. Some believe the line was yellow, because Hemer had curly blond hair. Others claim it was white. Another marking Hemer used on his aircraft was a rendering of a *brennschere* (curling iron), one more allusion to his wavy hair.

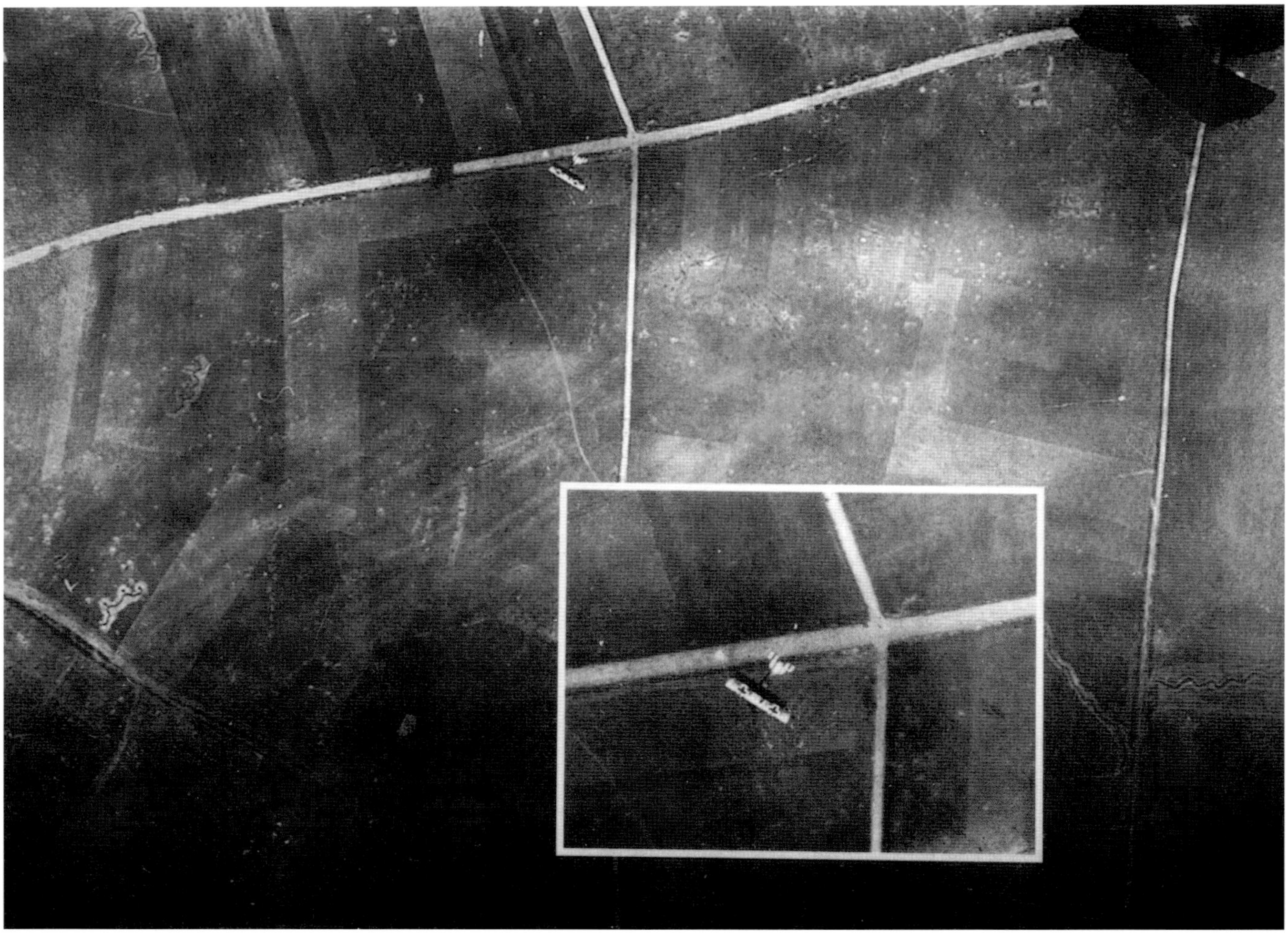

A *Flieger-Abteilung 17* crew were photographing enemy positions near Vaux-sur-Somme on April 21, 1918 when they happened to catch a Fokker triplane from *Jasta 6* searching the area for the missing Ringmaster, Manfred von Richthofen, barely two hours after he had been seen to land in enemy lines. *Jasta 6*'s black and white tailplane markings can be seen in the close-up insert.

As another example of the difficulties one encounters in sorting out the facts in the reference sources at hand, a set of handwritten notes on *Jasta 6*'s day-by-day activities for the year 1918 has survived. These were originally prepared by *Jasta 6*'s last Commanding Officer, *Lt.* Ulrich Neckel (of whom we'll hear more in a subsequent chapter). In those, Neckel dates Hemer's third victory as March 6, not March 10, and says it was an S.E.5 and not a Camel. And in recording Hemer's fourth victory which in this case he does properly, what Neckel fails to note was that this March 13 was another unlucky "13" for the younger von Richthofen brother, the then *Leutnant* and *Staffelführer* of Manfred's old *Jasta 11*, Lothar. His triplane was so badly shot up in a combat that it crashed near Awoingt just east of Cambrai. He was so seriously injured that he was out of action for four months.

By the time of Hemer's next victory, on March 27, the first of Ludendorff's 1918 spring offensives was in full swing. It had kicked off along a 50-mile front on the morning of March 21 after a sudden massive five-hour bombardment which had begun at 4:45 a.m. Some 62 German divisions, many released from the now dormant Eastern Front, using new storm troop tactics smashed into fewer than 30 understrength British divisions of their Third and Fifth Armies. Fog which persisted until the afternoon and shell smoke helped the attackers on the ground but hampered aerial operations on both sides. When the fog lifted, from then until darkness there was intense fighting in the air. This persisted for several days. And on the ground, things were going well for the Germans. So well, in fact, that a euphoric *Kaiser*, feeling the flush of a decisive victory, outdid himself and presented the nominal Commander-in-Chief and his purported subordinate rewards usually given after a battle had been won and not while the outcome, however favorable it looked at this point, was still in the balance. For *Generalfeldmarschall* Paul von Hindenburg it was the Iron Cross with Golden Rays, a breast star (he had worn the Grand Cross of the Iron Cross since December 9, 1916 and the Golden Rays is sometimes referred to as the Breast Star to the Grand Cross). For *General der Infanterie* Erich Ludendorff it was his Grand Cross of the Iron Cross. Both awards came on March 24. Hindenburg's award was unique to World War I. There had been only one such award in the then, as of 1918, 105 year-old history of the Iron Cross. That was in 1815 when it went to *Generalfeldmarschall* Gebhardt von Blücher for his victory at La Belle Alliance in the Napoleonic Wars (both awards were so unique that the first has come to be called the "Blücher Star" and the other the "Hindenburg Star").

After a pause in the air fighting by the stretched German fighter formations on March 26 to permit supplies to reach them and replacements for casualties, aerial action on the next day resumed at fever pitch. In the fierce fighting, the men of the *Jastas* were credited with 25 enemy planes brought down. The British admitted to the loss of 21 of their aircraft with something

The notation on the back of this photograph in the Hemer album dates this March 1918 at the Lieu-St. Armand airfield but *Jasta 6* was there for only a few days in November 1917. More likely, it is sometime in the spring of 1918, possibly at Lechelle (the camp chairs and long-range binoculars seen in the triplane line-up on the preceding page appear to be the same). The men lounging until a call to action are, left to right: *Vzfw.* Franz Hemer, *Lt.* Robert Tüxen, *Lt.* Moritz Bretschneider-Bodemer (KIA July 18, 1918), *Lt.* Martin Skowronski, *Lt.* Hans Kirchstein (KIC July 16, 1918), *Lt.* Johann Janzen (POW June 9, 1918) and *Lt.* Otto Förster.

A fine view of Hemer, his three mechanics and his triplane with the Axial company logo showing up nicely on the propeller. The photograph is dated March 8, 1918 thus just before the start of the German spring and summer offensives and Hemer's 1918 16-victory skein.

like 35 others that got back with battle damage in about half of which there was a wounded pilot or observer. Hemer's contribution this day was Sopwith Dolphin C.3798 from No.79 Squadron which he forced down southeast of Albert just before 8:00 a.m. Albert itself would be taken on the 27th by German troops but the spot where the Dolphin landed was still in British hands. The plane was a total wreck and had to be abandoned but the pilot, 2/Lt. D.W. Lees, was uninjured and lived to fight another day. Both the *JG 1* War Diary and Neckel's notes called Hemer's fifth victory a Bristol Fighter. The Dolphin was a relatively new type to the German airmen and this was just one of a number of misidentifications between the two.

April 1, 1918 saw the birth of the Royal Air Force creating the Third Service by absorbing the Royal Flying Corps and the Royal Naval Air Service into a unified branch. At the front, it would have made little difference to the weary airmen on both sides as the action in the air continued intense. Hemer was up again early that day and again at 8:00 in the morning, he scored shooting down D.H.4 A.7872 of No.57 Squadron. It fell in flames at Achiet-le-Petit near Bapaume killing its crew of 2/Lt. E. Whitfield and Lt. W.C.F. Nicol-Hart. And once again, there was confusion on the type of aircraft. All the German records listed it as a Bristol Fighter. There was similar confusion when Hemer notched his next victory on April 6. In reality, it was another Dolphin, this one being C.3939 from No. 79 Squadron again. The pilot, an American named H.G. Dugan, was able to effect a smooth landing on Hill 102 south of Demuin where he was taken prisoner. But the War Diary (and Neckel) put it down as a Sopwith Camel and somehow the *Nachrichtenblatt* got it recorded as an S.E.5. That was the end of Hemer's scoring for the month of April but the month did not pass without great moment for the men of *JG 1*. As almost everyone reading these lines know, on April 21 the squadron, and indeed all of Germany, suffered a tremendous blow when the *Geschwaderführer, Rittmeister* Manfred *Freiherr* von Richthofen, was shot down over Australian positions as he rashly pursued a novice who was his intended 81st victim at low level along the Somme. These details and the argument over who should receive the credit for ending his string have been thrashed over time and again and need no further elaboration (or speculation) here. Hopes that he had survived were dashed when the British confirmed his death, the news reaching his men on April 23. Von Richthofen's loss was on the front page of every German newspaper the next day.

For Hemer and the rest of the squadron, the air war continued unabated. His next successes came on consecutive days the following month. On May 9, along with three other *Jasta 6* men, all in triplanes, he intercepted a No.3 Squadron, Australian Flying Corps R.E.8 out on a photo op. Hemer shot it up, wounding both pilot and observer and forcing it to land east of Cachy. Generally poor weather prevailed for a second day but, still, the men of *JG 1* had one of their better days on May 10. Of the 14 enemy planes confirmed in the *Nachrichtenblatt* that day, 11 went to men in each of the four *Jastas* of the unit. Seven of the claims were for Camels entirely from one squadron, No.80. Four were, in fact, shot down outright and three others limped back with battle damage. Two of these had to make forced landings. All of these combats took place in the early evening with Hemer's Camel one of those falling in German lines near Cherisy with its pilot killed.

By Allied standards, Hemer had become an ace when he scored his fifth official victory on March 27. The way the Germans looked at it, he became one on May 19 when he was credited with his 10th victory. Ten victories were their measurement for this elite status but the term they used was not "ace." instead, it was "*Kanone*," meaning literally a "cannon" but in today's parlance, "top gun" would be the better translation.

Jasta 6 had been operating from a field at Lomme near Lille since moving from Cappy on April 13 (Cappy was the same field from which von Richthofen took off on his last flight on April 21). Here they were beginning to encounter elements of the French *Armee de l'Air* and so it was that Hemer's 10th victory on May 19 was a Spad which he dispatched just before 8:00 p.m. that evening. The following day, a telegram from *Kogenluft, Generalleutnant* Ernst von Hoppner, was received. By Imperial Decree, henceforth *Jagdgeschwader 1* would become *Jagdgeschwader Freiherr von Richthofen Nr.1*. This came at a time when the squadron was living up to its name, the Flying Circus. All of its elements now began the process of packing up and relocating to fields in the Guise/Laon area to respond to the shifting battle fronts. The third phase of the German offensive, called the Battle of the Aisne, would be launched on May 27. The first drive had finally been stopped in front of its primary objective, Amiens, on April 4. Ludendorff then launched the second phase, the Battle of the Lys, on April 9 and it spread into Flanders. On the 11th, Field Marshal Sir Douglas Haig was forced to issue his famous "with our backs to the wall..." order, so desperate did the situation appear at the moment. But the British put up a magnificent stand (Winston Churchill called it the decisive struggle on the Western Front and, thus, the war). Just as *Operation Michael* had to be called off on April 4, *Operation Georgette* collapsed on April 29. The Allies now girded for the next assault which was to fall between Soissons and Reims along the ridge feature called the Chemin-des-Dames.

The relocation of the *Geschwader* after May 20 and the remarkably light amount of enemy aerial activity in this new sector meant that the men of *JG 1* saw little action for the rest of May. Only on the 31st was there finally much to show when five enemy planes were claimed. June was to be different. The opposition now were the French and the Americans were coming too. Yet it was not until June 28 that Hemer scored again. For the others, it had been a busy time. Although there were some days that due to weather or just a general lack of enemy aerial activity saw no successful actions, the squadron put in claims for 59 aircraft and 14 balloons through the 27th at a cost of only one man killed, three taken prisoner and one wounded. Also during this time, the German streamroller aimed at Chateau-Thierry and an open gate to Paris had been slowed and the newly arrived U.S. 2nd Division's Marine Brigade had slugged its way through Belleau Wood at great cost and to its everlasting glory. The tide of Ludendorff's latest (and last) throw of the dice was beginning to turn against the Germans. Its troops were reaching the limits to which discipline and training could take them. But in the air, the German fliers were showing no signs of weakening despite the numbers being thrown up against them. On the morning of the 28th, in combats that stretched over an hour and a half, six pilots of *JG 1* accounted for seven Spad scouts. Hemer's turn came shortly after noon when he and the soon-to-be-promoted *Leutnant* Erich Löwenhardt, leader of *Jasta 10* and also filling the role of Acting Commander of the *Geschwader* at the time with 30 victories (the last as a result of the morning's work) and a *Pour le Mérite* (as from May 31), each downed Spad two-seaters concurrently. That same day, the squadron could boast of another *Pour le Mérite* member. Word was received that the high award had just been conferred on Hemer's leader since June 10, *Leutnant* Hans Kirschstein. Kirschstein had been fattening his score in the month of June on an almost exclusive diet of Spads and Breguet XIV two-seaters. He had begun that month with a score of 16 victories, reaching the 20-mark on June 3 (after which his proposal for the *Pour le Mérite* could go forward) and by the 24th, he had gotten his 27th confirmed victim. Any celebration

Above: Hemer scored his fourth victory on March 13, 1918 and exactly one week later, posed for this photograph. He had yet to earn his Iron Cross 1st Class. Left: Hemer still in flight clothes points with some amusement to battle damage on the leading edge of the center wing of his Dr.1 while a mechanic looks over the underside of its fuselage. Below: The conversion to the new national markings is now complete on this triplane with Hemer in the cockpit. This is obviously a second and perhaps later ship since his personal "*Locken*" (curl) is lacking here.

of the award and the day's bag of nine must surely have been tempered, however, by the solemn rites paid to one of their own that afternoon when they buried *Leutnant* Werner Steinhäuser of *Jasta 11* who had been killed on June 26 in quest of his 11th victory.

Sober, too, must have been the mood in the squadron on July 3, the day Hemer racked up his 12th victory. He had gotten a Spad at 8:00 a.m. that morning but later in the day, the news was relayed that their leader, *Hauptmann* Wilhelm Reinhard, who in Manfred von Richthofen's written "will" had been recommended to succeed him "should I not return," had crashed while away at Berlin-Adlershof testing new aircraft and had been killed. As if in mourning, practically nothing happened for almost the next two weeks. But, of course, there was nothing like that as the reason. The men of *JG 1* were out daily, sometimes on more than 40 combat sorties in a day, but suddenly the skies seemed to be empty of enemy airmen. Only two victories could be claimed in all this time, one on July 8 and the other on the 14th. July 14 was also the day that *JG 1*'s new commander formally assumed the job. The dispassionate entry in its War Diary merely noted that *Oberleutnant* (Hermann) Göring took over. The men had known of his appointment since July 6 and there must have been deep disappointment, if not some resentment, that an outsider was to be brought in. Was there no one with the necessary record from within the *Geschwader* to take over? There certainly was. Consider the possibilities. In *Jasta 4* there was Ernst Udet, albeit still only a *Leutnant* at the time. On the day Reinhard died, Udet scored his 40th victory. In Hemer's own *Jasta 6* the leader, Kirschstein's score was still 27 but he certainly could have been a candidate (had he received the appointment, however, it would have been short lived; Kirschstein would die as a result of a crash of a Hannover in which he was riding with a novice pilot on July 16). Then in *Jasta 10* there was Löwenhardt with his score, as of July 3, of 34. He was to be promoted *Oberleutnant* on August 9 and this certainly could have been speeded up a bit to give him further qualifications for the post. Finally, there was Lothar von Richthofen. He was about to rejoin *Jasta 11* later in July and resume command following his recovery from his injuries on March 13 and that, too, could have been moved up to allow him to take over following Reinhard's death. Lothar's score was a more than respectable 29. Although still only a *Leutnant* then, what a public relations coup that would have been! The younger brother of the great *Rittmeister* filling the dead hero's shoes. One would have thought that someone at *Idflieg* or even up to the *Kaiser* himself would have capitalized on the shot-in-the-arm potential of such a move. But, no, the *Geschwader* was to get the leader of another *Staffel* (*Jasta 27*) with "only" 21 victories. But Göring had two, perhaps, three things in his favor. First, he was a Regular Army officer. Second, he had the rank and longevity in it. He had been promoted *Oberleutnant* almost a year earlier, in August 1917. The third item is speculation but it would appear that Göring had what is called "friends in high places." Unaccountably, he had received the *Orden Pour le Mérite* on June 2, 1918 when his score was just 18, well under the 20-and-more requirement for a German fighter pilot at this time of the war, and had been stuck there for nearly two months. There was a further ironic note to his appointment. At Adlershof on July 3, it was Göring who first took up the Dornier Zeppelin-Lindau D.I to put it through its paces. Then he turned it over to Reinhard and with him at the controls, there was strut and wing failure and the resultant fatal crash. This, too, could not have been lost on the men of *JG 1* as the Adjutant, *Oberleutnant* Karl Bodenschatz, presented the *Geschwaderstock*, the sturdy walking stick that was the symbol of command, to their new boss.

On July 14, in Champagne, French guns preempted a planned German bombardment by an hour and completely tore apart German positions and formations that had been ready to launch another drive in the first minutes of July 15. East of Chateau-Thierry, the Germans began crossing the Marne at the same time but by nightfall, this attack, too, was in shambles, thanks in large part to American troops. It was here that the U.S. 3rd Division earned its name, "Rock of the Marne." Back in the air, there were more surprises for the Germans. British squadrons had arrived and joined in with the French and the Americans. Although outnumbered, the men of *JG 1* now held the upper hand in equipment. Their Fokker Triplanes had been replaced with the superior Fokker D.VII. The process had begun when D.VIIs first arrived at Cappy in May for *Jastas 6* and *11*. By mid-June, sufficient quantities of the new machine had been delivered to re-equip *Jasta 4*, the last of the four units to give up its triplanes. And with the Fokker D.VII, Hemer had his most successful day of the war on July 16, the day that Kirschstein, his commander, died in that accident that was called "stupid." Hemer accounted for two Sopwith Camels within five minutes of each other around 5:30 p.m. that afternoon. The Royal Air Force's No. 54 Squadron lost two of its Camel pilots killed that day and one who returned wounded but none can be conclusively tied to Hemer. Things on the ground, however, had gone from bad to worse for the Germans. On the 18th, General Ferdinand Foch launched a massive assault against the now-stalled Germans. In the coming weeks, with much territory regained, the elements of *JG 1* would be forced to abandon one airfield after another as the lines pulled back. Paris had been saved and the Allies would never lose the initiative for the rest of the war. But, again, these events hardly affected the combat effectiveness of the *Geschwader*. For the loss of two of its pilots, it chalked up a total of 13 victories over enemy planes. One of these was a Breguet XIV brought down by Hemer for his 15th of the war. Another victorious pilot was the top man himself, Göring, who was credited with a Spad, his 22nd and final one of the war. Thereafter, while others in his command piled up victory after victory, his guns remained silent. It has been said that he believed he was of more value leading his men from behind a desk rather than in the cockpit of an airplane and although a man like Manfred von Richthofen would scarcely have agreed with that point of view, many British squadron commanders, for example, followed the same practice.

The next day, July 19, *Leutnant* Paul Wenzel took over the acting leadership of *Jasta 6* until a permanent appointment could be made. Wenzel had eight victories to his name at that point. If longevity in the unit and the number of victories were the choice between the two, the job would have gone to Hemer but his non-commissioned status precluded any chance for him to have taken over an entire *Staffel*. On the other hand, might not some other form of recognition, promotion or an award, be appropriate now that his score had climbed to the round number of 15? One would think so. So far as promotion went, he still could have been advanced to *Offizier-Stellvertreter* without making the jump all the way to *Leutnant*. In terms of an award, possessing as he did both the Iron Cross 1st and 2nd Class and having served in the Prussian Army before transferring to the *Fliegertruppe* and now with a Prussian flying formation, a record like his could well have merited Hemer the Golden Military Merit Cross. There was enough precedence by this date for a fighter pilot of his standing to be so recognized. Thus far in the war, 11 men with victory scores ranging from a low of nine to a high of 25 had been honored with what was commonly known as the enlisted man's *Pour le Mérite*. Averaging the scores of these 11 holders of the decoration, the number, interestingly enough, comes out to just under 15. Hemer, in other words, was eminently qualified for the award. Here is the picture that existed as of July 18, 1918, the day of Hemer's 15th confirmed victory (only pilots serving on the Western Front appear in this tabulation since other factors than just victories would be taken into account for men serving on other fronts; naval fighter pilots have been excluded too since that service used its own criteria as well).

Table 8-1
Fighter Pilot Recipients of the Golden Military Merit Cross Serving on the Western Front as of July 18, 1918

Rank and Name of Recipient	Victories at Time of Award	Unit in Which the Award was Earned	Date of Award
Vzfw. Karl Thom	12	*Jasta 21*	October 11, 1917
Vzfw. Julius Buckler	25	*Jasta 17*	November 12, 1917
Vzfw. Paul Bäumer	18	*Jasta Boelcke*	February 12, 1918
Offz.-Stv. Friedrich Altemeier	14	*Jasta 24*	April 11, 1918
Vzfw. Otto Könnecke	18	*Jasta 5*	May 12, 1918
Vzfw. Fritz Rumey	17	*Jasta 5*	May 12, 1918
Vzfw. Rudolf Francke	10	*Jasta 8*	May 16, 1918
Offz.Stv. Otto Esswein	11	*Jasta 26*	June 3, 1918
Vzfw. Otto Fruhner	9	*Jasta 26*	June 3, 1918
Offz.-Stv. Josef Mai	14	*Jasta 5*	June 24, 1918
Offz.-Stv. Robert Heibert	9	*Jasta 46*	July 5, 1918

Above: Hemer (far left) now wears the Iron Cross 1st Class in this undated photograph. 3rd from the left is *Leutnant* Paul Wenzel who after Kirschstein's death became the Acting Leader of *Jasta 6* on July 19, 1918. He was slightly wounded on August 1 and then seriously so on August 11.

Below: Wenzel's second wounding sent him to hospital and he was permanently stricken off *JG I*'s roster on August 30. So this photograph must have been taken right after his August 1 "light" wounding (how he continued to fly with an arm in a sling and managed to score his 10th and last victory on the 9th is a good question). From the left, a *Lt.* Matzdorff, *Unteroffz.* Hans Reimers (wounded on September 4 and died the next day), Wenzel, *Lt.* Emil Rolff (killed on August 19 when the new Fokker E.V monoplane he was testing broke up in the air) and Hemer (wounded on August 9). After Rolff's death, *Idflieg* grounded the E.Vs and there is no concrete evidence that the redesignated Fokker D VIII with new wing and strengthened spars ever saw combat again in the last few weeks of the war.

Whatever the reasons might have been, Hemer received neither promotion nor a decoration at this particular time (both would come in due course, however, as we shall see). Recognition in either form would have required the backing of Hemer's overall commander, Göring. But he was not even one week into his new job and it would be understandable if he wanted time to size up his men for himself before going out on a limb for any one of them. Hemer scored again on July 22, one of four enemy planes accounted for by the squadron that day. July 22 also marked a turning point in the fortunes of the German Army in *JG 1*'s sector. That evening, great fires could be seen lighting the skies opposite the Allied lines to the south and east. A general German retreat had been ordered and stores that could not be carried away, many of them captured in the early stages of their offensive, were being burned. The *JG 1* War Diary summed up the situation in these words, "the offensive took its bitter course." At this crucial stage, Göring inexplicably went on leave on July 26 for nearly a month. During his absence, Lothar von Richthofen, just arrived back on July 19 to take up the leadership of *Jasta 11* again, assumed the acting command of the *Geschwader*. This must have pleased the men of *JG 1* (to say nothing of the propagandists in Berlin). However temporary, a von Richthofen was back in charge.

Hemer next figured in on a clean sweep of a Nieuport squadron on August 1. In the space of just 30 minutes, right after 9:00 a.m. that morning, six of them went down to men of *Jastas 4* and *6*. Hemer more than just figured in, he claimed two while four other pilots, including the newly returned *Pour le Mérite Jasta 4* leader, Ernst Udet, got one apiece (he would also down a Breguet at midday and a Spad that evening). The Nieuports apparently were the six that the U.S. 27th Aero Squadron lost on August 1. Three of the pilots were killed and three taken prisoner when they came down in German lines. In the event, Hemer received official confirmation for just one, his 17th of the war, thus denying him the chance for his second "double of the war." August 1 was quite a day for *JG 1*. In addition to the Nieuports and Udet's other two kills (his first "hat trick" of the war but a feat he would repeat exactly one week later), others were in good form as well. Lothar von Richthofen got a Spad an hour after Udet's Breguet and then added another Spad in the evening, again about an hour after Udet's. Udet's score now stood at 43, the younger von Richthofen's at 32. Only the leader of *Jasta 10*, Erich Löwenhardt with his then 48 victories, was ahead of them for top scoring honors of surviving German fighter pilots.

Following August 1, once again there was a week of "no special occurrences" due to poor weather and generally low enemy aerial activity. Only two squadron victories could be claimed. But on the 8th, *JG 1*, true to its tactical mobile mission, was moved to the German 2nd Army's sector in front of Amiens, there to meet its old enemy, the British Royal Air Force. At 4:20 a.m. that morning, with French support on its right, the British 4th Army under General Sir Henry Rawlinson was poised to attack behind a barrage from some 2,000 guns. Preparations for the assault had been masked by 800 odd RAF aircraft (including the 17th and 148th U.S. Aero Squadrons under British control) and 1,100 French machines which had swept the skies of German reconnaissance intruders. The Germans were taken totally by surprise and Ludendorff would later characterize August 8 as the "Black Day" of the German Army. But for the men of the Flying Circus, August 8 and the day following rivaled the famous Marianas "turkey shoot" of a later war.

With the exception of a Camel claimed by Löwenhardt shortly before 1:00 p.m., all of the action for *JG 1*'s pilots on August 8 came in the late afternoon and early evening. Twelve claims were made including what the War Diary listed and the *Nachrichtenblatt* confirmed as a D.H.12 for Hemer, obviously an incorrect entry. Undoubtedly, it was a D.H.4 or D.H.9 type of which 10 were shot down with crews either killed or taken prisoner and a further nine that were in combats but returned in some cases with casualties, The British Camels and S.E.5as suffered even greater losses. It may have been a black day for the German Army but it was no picnic for the RAF either. As Trevor Henshaw says in his masterpiece, *The Sky Their Battlefield*, "there is no other day on which casualties remotely approach those sustained this day." And *JG 1* accomplished their share of this carnage without losing a man either killed, wounded or otherwise injured.

August 9 was virtually a repeat of the day before. In action from morning to night, another 11 of the enemy were claimed by men of all four *Jastas*. Six of these were from a formation of D.H.9s escorted by Camels that were out in the early morning hours to bomb bridges on the Somme. The bag was evenly split between the two-seaters and the fighters. This time, Hemer was not on the claim list. He was struck by a glancing blow to the head and had to retire from the fight. The War Diary in noting this said he remained with the *Geschwader*. But that might be a reference to the fact that his injury was not serious enough to have him struck off charge. Neckel's notes say "to hospital!" which is much more likely the case. At any rate, Hemer's string of 18 victories and his splendid war record was at an end. It was, of course, a coincidence but the day Neckel wrote of Hemer's wounding, he also added the line, "the decline of the German fighter pilot begins!" Or was it a coincidence? The *Luftstreitkräfte* was hard put to lose a man like Hemer.

And lose him the German Air Force did. Although Neckel has it that Hemer returned to *Jasta 6* from convalescent leave on September 25, Hemer apparently never flew in combat again. Hemer, in the meantime, had been promoted *Leutnant* on September 20 so at least his long service and accomplishments in the air had earned him something. Two of the photographs included here picturing him with other comrades were clearly taken after his promotion (his tunic is that of an officer devoid of the "lace" and collar buttons of a *Vizefelfwebel* and with officer's epaulets) and in view of the company he is keeping in them, undoubtedly were taken on a *Jasta 6* airfield. In fact, it would appear that *Jasta 6* was something of a repository for at least one other airman who had had an outstanding record in the air but who then had been wounded and after recovery was assigned to *Jasta 6* late in the war, never to score again either. He was *Leutnant* Julius Schmidt who appears in both the above-mentioned photographs with Hemer. Schmidt had scored all but one of his 15 confirmed victories in *Jasta 3* in 1917 but then was severely wounded in a combat with S.E.5as on September 24 that year. After a year of convalescence, he was sent to *Jasta 6* on September 9, 1918. The *JG 1* War Diary makes no mention of it but according to the notes from one of those interwar German researchers, he took over the duties of the *Offizier zur besonderen Verwendung* (Officer Assigned for Special Duties, or Adjutant). So, like Hemer, he must not have been considered fit for combat operations any longer. Schmidt was a highly decorated officer. A native of Saxony, he received their trio of bravery awards, the Knight's Cross of the Military St. Henry Order and the Knight's Cross 2nd Class with Swords of both the Merit and Albert Orders. In addition to both Iron Crosses, he had also been awarded the Knight's Hohenzollern with Swords (see Volume III in this series for his biography).

Much had happened within the *Geschwader* in the seven weeks that Hemer was away. Two grievous blows were suffered during this time. On the day after Hemer was wounded, Germany's then leading fighter pilot, Erich Löwenhardt, newly promoted *Oberleutnant* on August 7, was killed moments after shooting down an S.E.5a from the famed No.56 Squadron, RAF shortly after noon for his 54th victory of the war. In the same action, he went after another Englishman without realizing that it was under close attack by a *Jasta 11* man, *Leutnant* Alfred Wentz. Löwenhardt came in above and to the right of Wentz with his downward view obscured. A startled Wentz looked up to see the *Jasta 10* leader's yellow Fokker D.VII "close enough to touch." The landing gear of Löwenhardt's aircraft struck Wentz's upper right wing. A large piece of fabric was torn away and immediately Wentz lost all control. His plane went into a steep nose dive and Wentz jumped out of the stricken craft and popped his parachute, landing safely in frontline German positions where an infantryman guided him to shelter. Löwenhardt was not as fortunate. He bailed out too but his 'chute failed to deploy properly and he plunged to his death. Udet, who scored his 50th and 51st victories that same day, took over as Germany's most successful living fighter pilot, never to relinquish that top spot.

Three days later, on August 13, the *Geschwader* lost its next leading contender for the title when Lothar von Richthofen was wounded in the thigh in an air battle. It was another of his unlucky "13s." He had registered his 39th and 40th victories just the day before but there would be no more. He was never able to return to the front by the time of the armistice. The attrition of men and machines had been so severe that on this day and on other occasions in the coming weeks, *JG 1* was down to a single *Staffel* in terms of its effective strength. That, weather, moves to new fields as the enemy advanced and the loss of superstars like Löwenhardt and von Richthofen would all have their effect on its final fortunes.

But there was still Udet and he showed the way in the following week. Of the 16 victories claimed during that period, seven of them were accounted for by him. Then on the 22nd, Göring returned to resume command and Udet was granted his four weeks' leave. He would be missed but still, Göring chose to be the administrator, not the flier. By the time Hemer returned on September 25, 21 victory claims had been submitted, certainly a respectable number for a five week period but hardly up to the heady month of June 1918 with its 85 claims or even the sometimes weather bedeviled July with its 65. And no sooner had Udet returned, than he was gone too. In scoring his 61st and 62nd victories on September 26, he was wounded and that was the end of the war for him. *JG 1* had been relocated to the Metz area at this time where they would take on more of the eager but inexperienced Americans. Despite poor weather for most of October, the German airmen did what they could when they could. An old hand (in experience, not in years) was now leading Hemer's *Jasta 6*. He was *Leutnant* Ulrich Neckel whose name has come up before and will again in a later chapter in this book. Neckel had come in from *Jasta 12* on September 1 to take command with 24 victories to his credit. He would add six more with *Jasta 6* and earn the second-to-last-ever award of the *Orden Pour le Mérite* given to an airmen when he received it on November 7. There was a new star on the horizon too. *Leutnant* Friedrich Noltenius had scored 12 victories in *Jasta 27* in just two months in August and September when he was transferred to *Jasta 6* on September 21. With *6* and later *Jasta 11*, he would bring his number of confirmed victories up to 21 and a nomination for a *Pour le Mérite* (which due to the

Right: Hemer (2nd from the left) back at *Jasta 6* after his promotion to *Leutnant* on September 20, 1918. On his right, *Lt.* Werner Nöldeke, one victory, slightly injured in an accident on July 3, 1918. On Hemer's left, *Lt.* Matzdorff, two victories, transferred to *Jastaschule II* on September 19 (and perhaps therefore back with *Jasta 6* at this time) and *Lt.* Julius Schmidt, an ex-*Jasta 3* man who joined *Jasta 6* on September 9, 1918 after a long recuperation from wounds. Schmidt, like Hemer, never flew in combat again and is believed to have been *Jasta 6*'s Adjutant.

Right: Hemer again at *Jasta 6* after being commissioned. In the center, Schmidt again. First victory with *Kagohl 4* then 14 more in *Jasta 3* before wounding on September 24, 1917. Decorated with all three Saxon bravery honors, Military St. Henry Order and Merit and Albert Orders. On the left. *Lt.* Friedrich Noltenius. Twelve victories in *Jasta 27*, to *Jasta 6* on September 21, 1918. Three victories there and then to *Jasta 11* where he scored his final six victories. His Knight's Hohenzollern was approved on the same day as Hemer's but his *Pour le Mérite* nomination failed to be approved in time for it to be officially sanctioned.

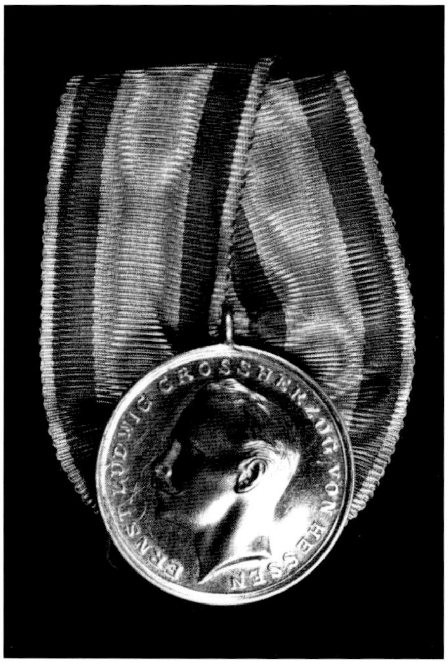

Left, another photograph of Hesse's General Honor Decoration "for Bravery" that Hemer received.

Right, the document to Hemer's Knight's Hohenzollern dated 8 November 1918.

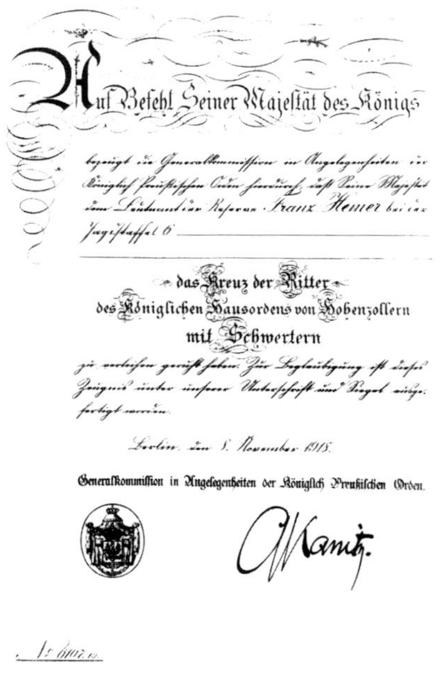

Auf Befehl Seiner Majestät des Königs

das Kreuz der Ritter
des Königlichen Hausordens von Hohenzollern
mit Schwertern

Berlin, den 8. November 1918.

Generalkommission in Angelegenheiten der Königlich Preußischen Orden.

Kaiser's abdication and the later refusal of the postwar government to retroactively approve the award of Prussian orders, never received official approval).

It need not be said here but, of course, it was to no avail. The men of *Jagdgeschwader Freiherr von Richthofen Nr. 1* flew their last sortie on November 6 and scored their last three victories of the grand total of 644 that were attributed to the squadron since its formation. On November 7, in driving rain, *JG 1* moved to its final airfield at Tellancourt and there got the news of the deteriorating situation in Germany that would lead to the armistice. What must have been the mens' thoughts to have to face this after all they and their comrades on the ground had been through? This writer wishes now he had been able to ask *Herr* Hemer about that as well.

In the middle of all the chaos that attended these final weeks of the war, it was fortunate that the bureaucracy of the General Commission on Prussian Orders in Berlin still functioned (as witnessed by Neckel's *Pour le Mérite* and Noltenius' nomination for it). On November 8, the document awarding Hemer the Knight's Cross with Swords of the Royal House Order of Hohenzollern was signed, surely one of the last air awards of the war. It was fitting recognition for a man who was one of the *Luftstreitkräfte*'s elite fighter pilots and yet one who, otherwise, has been so often overlooked when its history is being reviewed.

OTHER RECIPIENTS OF THE GENERAL HONOR DECORATION "FOR BRAVERY"

To conserve space, no other biographies of recipients of the General Honor Decoration "for Bravery" will be developed in the detail that the preceding one on Franz Hemer was. Rather, captions under photographs of some of these men that follow will have to suffice. Six recipients, however, have received fuller attention in earlier volumes in this series and readers may wish to refer to them if these books are in their possession. Several of them, notably Manfred von Richthofen, have appeared in more than just one volume (Richthofen has been in all of them) but these are the ones in which they were featured:

Oblt. Ernst *Freiherr* von Althaus	Volume III
Hptm. Job-Heinrich von Dewall	Volume V
Lt. Albert Dietlen	Volume IV
Hptm. Alfred Keller	Volume II
Rittm. Manfred *Freiherr* von Richthofen	Volume II
Hptm. Eduard Wolfgang Zorer	Volume IV

GENERAL HONOR DECORATION "FOR BRAVERY" RECIPIENTS WITHOUT BIOGRAPHIES

Right: General Honor Decoration "for Bravery" recipient, *Oblt.* Ernst *Freiherr* von Althaus, in his early flight training days and before his *Pour le Mérite* fighter pilot fame. The propeller has the Reschke logo.

Below: *Jasta 40* CO *Lt.* Carl Degelow's own handwriting at the bottom of this photograph places it at the Lome airfield in the fall of 1918 which the unit actually occupied from June 6 through August 24, 1918. *Lt.* Adolf Auer, 2nd from the left, received the Hessian bravery medal on November 17, 1915 as an *Unteroffizier* in a machine gun section on the Eastern Front. Commissioned, he began pilot training in December 1917 and joined *Jasta 40* on the following August 14, scoring just one confirmed victory before being shot down wounded and taken prisoner on October 28. The others are, left to right *Vzfw.* Anton Raab, Auer, *Lt.* Hermann Gilly, Degelow, *Lt.* Hans Jeschonnek, *Lt.* Willy Rosenstein and *Unteroffz.* Hertel. Degelow was the last military recipient of the *Orden Pour le Mérite* when its award came on November 9, 1918.

The first CO of *Jasta 17, Rittm.* Anton von Brederlow, salutes goodbye as he departs on May 10, 1917. Next to him is his brother, Hans. A prewar pilot, Anton won the General Honor Decoration on September 20, 1914. Before taking over *Jasta 17*, he served in two *Feldflieger-Abteilungen* and a *Kasta*. His final commands were in two *Flieger-Abteilungen* in 1917 and 1918 and lastly, *Jagdgruppe 11*. His Knight's Hohenzollern was announced in the *Militär-Wochenblatt* April 30, 1918.

Below: Hessian born *Lt.* Karl Christ, standing 4th from the left with men from *Jagdgruppe 7* was another recipient of the General Honor Decoration. He scored five confirmed victories in *Jasta 28* in 1918. Standing left to right: *Lt.* Sagebuhl, *Lt.* Emil Thuy (wearing the *Pour le Mérite* that he was awarded on June 30, 1918), *Lt.* Otto Koch, Christ, *Lt.* Basse, *Lt.* Braatsch (behind Basse), *Lt.* Kühn and *Lt.* Ruckle. Seated is *Lt.* Hames. Kühn and Ruckle were from *Jasta 33*. The others were all serving in *Jasta 28* at this time. *Jastas 57* and *58* were also part of *Jagdgruppe 7*.

Right: *Lt.* Albert Dietlen qualified for the Observer's Badge on April 10, 1916 and in two-seaters in *Feldflieger-Abteilung 60* scored his first victory on June 20 that year. Rewards were immediately forthcoming for this native Württemberger. He received the kingdom's Gold Military Merit Medal on June 29, the Iron Cross 1st Class on June 30 and the Knight's Cross of Württemberg's Military Merit Order on August 22. Before the year was out, on November 25, he was awarded Hesse's General Honor Decoration "for Bravery." Converting to fighters, Dietlen got his Pilot's Badge on August 10, 1917 and served in *Jastas 23, 41* and *58*. In scoring his ninth victory in *Jasta 58* on April 12, 1918, he was killed some say by a Camel pilot while the interwar German researchers say he collided with the Bristol F2b he was attacking.

Below: Like Albert Dietlen, *Lt.* Ludwig Fritz Dornheim served first as an observer in *FFl.Abt. 60* in 1915 and then joined newly formed *Jasta 7* in August 1916 as a pilot. Transferred to *Jasta 5* in September, he scored his first victory on October 16 and received the General Honor Decoration two months later. Here he suits up in *Jasta 5* while *Vzfw.* Paul Hoppe looks on. It was Hoppe who collided with the *Pour le Mérite* leader of *Jasta 5, Oblt.* Hans Berr, on April 6, 1917 killing both men. Dornheim also received the War Honor Decoration for Heroic Deed.

It could have been some pulp fiction writer in the 1930s who first came up with the idea that the average life of a fighter pilot on the Western Front in the First World War was just three weeks. True or not, *Leutnant* Friedrich Hofmann, seen above apparently readying himself for a flight while mechanics stand by, barely beat that statistic, lasting only four weeks. He joined *Jasta 11* on May 30, 1918 and went down in flames over Passy on June 30 without scoring a victory. He was a month shy of his 22nd birthday. A General Honor Decoration recipient from the Hessian 116th Infantry, Hofmann was shot down by the 41-victory French ace, *Capitaine* Georges Madon (right). Hofmann was Madon's 35th of the war. Below his *Chevalier de la Legion d'Honneur, Medaille Militaire et Croix de Guerre*, Madon wears the Italian Silver Medal for Military Valor and the Romanian Medal for Military Virtue 5th Class, awards that no doubt were sent to the French *en bloc*, leaving it up to them to decide who among their own men were the most deserving of them. Madon's entire war was on the Western Front. Shortly after the armistice, he was made an *Officier* of the Legion of Honor.

TWO PREWAR PILOTS WHO EARNED THE GENERAL HONOR DECORATION "FOR BRAVERY" IN THE WAR

Right: Then civilian and later *Oblt.* Ernst Hamster (later changed to Hamscher) with an Etrich Taube in 1912 or 1913. Hamster received his Hessian award on May 7, 1917. Among his other awards was the Brunswick War Merit Cross in both 1st and 2nd Class.

Below: The then *Oblt.* Alfred Keller at the AEG flying school in 1913 in the pilot's seat of AEG Z.3. His instructor up front apparently is not as assured of Keller's skills as the later *Pour le Mérite* bomber squadron commander is. He prefers a crash helmet to Keller's soft service cap.

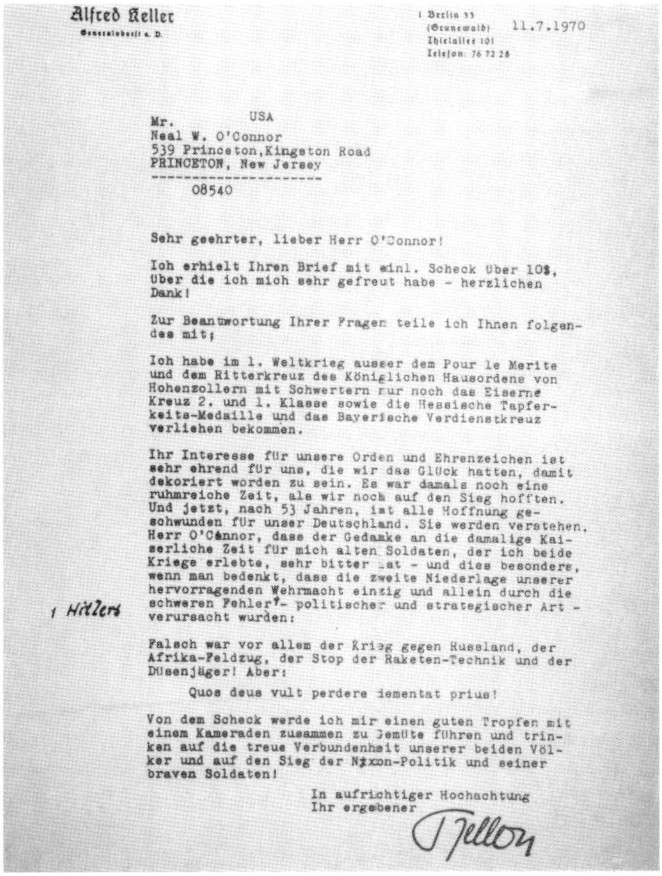

Alfred Keller
Generaloberst a. D.

1 Berlin 33
(Grunewald) 11.7.1970
Thielallee 101
Telefon: 76 72 28

Mr. USA
Neal W. O'Connor
539 Princeton,Kingston Road
PRINCETON, New Jersey

08540

Sehr geehrter, lieber Herr O'Connor!

Ich erhielt Ihren Brief mit einl. Scheck über 10$, über die ich mich sehr gefreut habe - herzlichen Dank!

Zur Beantwortung Ihrer Fragen teile ich Ihnen folgendes mit;

Ich habe im 1. Weltkrieg ausser dem Pour le Merite und dem Ritterkreuz des Königlichen Hausordens von Hohenzollern mit Schwertern nur noch das Eiserne Kreuz 2. und 1. Klasse sowie die Hessische Tapferkeits-Medaille und das Bayerische Verdienstkreuz verliehen bekommen.

Ihr Interesse für unsere Orden und Ehrenzeichen ist sehr ehrend für uns, die wir das Glück hatten, damit dekoriert worden zu sein. Es war damals noch eine ruhmreiche Zeit, als wir noch auf den Sieg hofften. Und jetzt, nach 53 Jahren, ist alle Hoffnung geschwunden für unser Deutschland. Sie werden verstehen, Herr O'Cânnor, dass der Gedanke an die damalige Kaiserliche Zeit für mich alten Soldaten, der ich beide Kriege erlebte, sehr bitter ist - und dies besonders, wenn man bedenkt, dass die zweite Niederlage unserer hervorragenden Wehrmacht einzig und allein durch die schweren Fehler'- politischer und strategischer Art - verursacht wurden:

Falsch war vor allem der Krieg gegen Russland, der Afrika-Feldzug, der Stop der Raketen-Technik und der Düsenjäger! Aber:

Quos deus vult perdere dementat prius!

Von dem Scheck werde ich mir einen guten Tropfen mit einem Kameraden zusammen zu Gemüte führen und trinken auf die treue Verbundenheit unserer beiden Völker und auf den Sieg der Nixon-Politik und seiner braven Soldaten!

In aufrichtiger Hochachtung
Ihr ergebener

Above: A 1970 letter from *Generaloberst a.D.* Alfred Keller in which he provides his World War I awards and then goes on to comment on the state of affairs in his country after two wars. He is highly critical of Hitler, blaming him for mistakes made in the war in Russia, the campaign in Africa, in rocket technology and with the jet fighter (by that he meant Hitler's insistence that the Me 262 be developed as a fighter bomber and not as a pure fighter). He sums up his contempt by quoting the phrase (in Latin), "He whom the gods wish to destroy, first drive mad " In closing he says he will drink a toast to the strong bonds between our two people (Germany and the United States) and, ironically now, for the victory of Nixon politics and his brave soldiers (in Vietnam). Below: In happier times, Keller is flanked by two captured British fliers as he plays host. Keller was probably CO of *FFl.Abt. 40* or *Kagohl 1* at the time although the presence of Lothar von Richthofen (marked "2") suggests that *Kagohl 4*, in which he served, was also involved here.

Left: An ex-8th Hussar holder of the General Honor Decoration, *Lt.* Rolf *Freiherr* von Lersner, with his Albatros D.III during his short career as a fighter pilot with *Jasta Boelcke* in 1917. Von Lersner made the mistake of joining with the *Pour le Mérite* hotshot, Werner Voss, in going over the head of their *Staffelführer*, *Hptm.* Franz Walz, to lobby for Walz's removal due to his lackluster leadership and poor victory record as CO of *Jasta Boelcke* in the spring of 1917 (presumably with Voss getting the job). Such a breech of discipline could not be tolerated. Voss was packed off to *Jasta 5* on May 20 (albeit as its CO) while von Lersner was returned to two-seater duties and relegated to *Kagohl 3*. There he was killed on August 25, 1917. Ironically, the co-conspirators got what they wanted after all. On June 9, Walz was transferred to *Jasta 34* as its leader after which, however, he had a distinguished record with *Fl.Abt. 304b* in Palestine in 1918, winning the *Pour le Mérite* himself on August 9.

Opposite: *Hptm.* Erich Quade's pre-air service unit was the 168th Grand Ducal Hessian Infantry Regiment which accounted for his General Honor Decoration. The arm patch here is that of *Fl.Abt. (A)260* which Quade commanded from October 1917 to April 1918. Below: Earlier, Quade first served with and then was CO of *FFl.Abt. 54* on the Eastern Front from December 1915 to October 1917. He appears in the third row between two Austrian officers in front of the bald NCO with glass in hand. In the last row, 3rd from left and looking much the worse for wear, is the later *Hptm.* Eduard Wolfgang Zorer who was also a recipient of the General Honor Decoration.

Above: Richthofen's "Circle." The War Diary of *JG 1* makes no mention of the *Rittmeister*'s General Honor Decoration but it was clearly one of his numerous awards (displayed on his *Ordenskissen*). Over his right shoulder stands *Lt.* Werner Steinhäuser who also received the decoration. The men are, left to right: *Lt.* Siegfried Gussmann, *Feldwbl.-Lt.* Fritz Schubert (Saxon Silver St. Henry Medal and Merit and Albert Crosses with Swords), *Lt.* Hans-Georg von der Osten, Steinhäuser, von Richthofen, *Lt.* Karl Esser, *Lt.* Fritz Lübbert, *Oblt.*-Hans-Helmuth von Boddien (Mecklenburg-Schwerin Military Merit Cross 1st and 2nd Class), *Lt.* Hans-Karl von Linsingen, *Lt.* Eberhardt Mohnike and *Vzfw.* Edgar Scholz. Schubert's trio of Saxon decorations were unique to an airman.

Right: *Hptm.* Heinrich Scanzoni von Lichtenfel's bar "reads" Iron Cross 2nd Class, Hessian General Honor Decoration and Württemberg Friedrich Order Knight 2nd Class with Swords. He was killed near Adlershof on October 28, 1916 in an accident while test flying an aircraft.

Below: *Oblt.* Hans Schüz received the General Honor Decoration on January 18, 1915. Here he is seen in Turkish service with his Albatros D.III that likewise bears Turkish markings.

Above: *Oblt.* Heinrich Schwandner (4th from the left) and other men said to be on their way to Schleisshein in 1916 (some with send-off nosegays!). Schwandner took command of Bavarian *Kasta 36* of *Kagohl 6* on May 15, 1916 after service from the start of the war with *FFl.Abt. 2b*. In *Kasta 36*, he scored victories on October 23 (a Caudron) and December 27 (a Farman) over Verdun. On the 28th, he was awarded the Bavarian Military Merit Order 4th Class with Crown and Swords, continuing in command when *Kasta 36* became *Schusta 27b* at the turn of the year. He then became the first CO of *Jasta 32* on February 22, 1917. Without a further score, he went down in flames on March 16 that year. The credit is often assigned to *Capitaine* Albert Deullin, CO of *Spa 73*, as his 12th victory. Schwandner received the General Honor Decoration on April 28, 1915. At the far right is *Lt.* Heinrich Geigl, later 13-victory ace and CO of *Jasta 16b*, killed in a collision with a Camel on April 4, 1918.

Below: Promoted *Leutnant* in the Hessian 61st Field Artillery Regiment on January 27, 1915, General Honor Decoration recipient (July 15, 1915) Werner Steinhäuser transferred to aviation in November 1916. After 10 victories, he was killed in combat as a member of *Jasta 11* on June 26, 1918. Marking specialists will enjoy his triplane's band around the fuselage (red?) with crossed "Xs" (yellow?).

Ulanen-Regiment Kaiser Alexander III. von Russland (Westpreussisches) Nr.1. had at least four of its prewar officers seconded to the *Fliegertruppe* in the course of the war. Best known, of course, is Manfred von Richthofen but there also was *Oblt.* Alfred Gerstenberg who served in his *Jasta 11* for seven weeks until severely wounded by a lung shot on October 20, 1917. The others were *Lt.* Erwin Kollberg of *Bogohl 3* who was killed in a Gotha crash on September 3, 1918 and *Oblt.* Erich Rudiger von Wedel (shown at right). Von Wedel arrived at *Jasta 11* on April 23, 1918 just two days after his old cavalry comrade had been lost. He took command of *Jasta 11* on May 2. After scoring his first 12 victories there, he was awarded the Knight's Hohenzollern with Swords on September 29 and finished out the war with a total score of 13. Von Wedel had received the General Honor Decoration on September 28, 1915.

Below: While the attention of others is fixed on something going on in the skies above, the last leader of *JG 1*, *Oblt.* Hermann Göring, seems to scowl his displeasure (was someone showing off?). He prefers a conventional cane here rather than the unit's *Geschwaderstock*. Von Wedel is the tall officer on the right. *Lt.* Wolfram von Richthofen is 3rd from the left, *Lt.* Siegfried Gussmann 5th from the left and *Lt.* Erich Just is 7th from the left. The others cannot be identified.

CHAPTER IX

THE PRINCELY HOUSE OF HOHENZOLLERN

Hohenzollern-Hechingen

Hohenzollern-Sigmaringen

The Princely House of Hohenzollern's beginnings are a bit murky but around 1192, Friedrich III, Count of Zollern, acquired the Burggraviate of Nuremburg through his marriage to Sophie, Countess of Raabs. Their sons, Konrad and Friedrich IV, divided the possessions. Konrad took the Burggraviate and the counties of Raabs and Aberndsberg. His descendants went on to found the Prussian dynasty whose wealth, power and prestige would far eclipse anything the other branch of the family would ever achieve. Friedrich IV's share was only the county of Zollern but over the years, other properties were acquired by Friedrich's successors, the most important of which were the counties of Sigmaringen and Veringen which were ceded to Count Karl I in December 1535. In turn, his sons went on to found the three lines of Hohenzollern-Haigerloch, Hohenzollern-Hechingen and Hohenzollern-Sigmaringen. At Regensburg in March 1623, Johann Georg of Hechingen and Johann of Sigmaringen were elevated to counts of the Holy Roman Empire. The Hechingen line, in further recognition, was admitted to the College of Princes of the empire. Meantime, the Haigerloch line had become extinct in March 1634 and its properties were absorbed into Hohenzollern-Sigmaringen. A mutual succession pact was concluded with Brandenburg (later Prussia) in November 1695 that was renewed in 1707. Both Hechingen and Sigmaringen joined Napoleon's Confederation of the Rhine in 1806 and after his defeat, the German Confederation on June 7, 1815.

Hohenzollern-Hechingen and Hohenzollern-Sigmaringen handed over their sovereign rights to Prussia on December 7, 1849. Among those which were retained, however, was the right to continue to bestow a house order which had been founded in 1841 (see next chapter). Further bestowals were to be subject to Prussian approval although by the time of World War I, it appears that this had become a mere formality at best and little control over the principality's awards was exercised by Berlin as a matter of regular routine. On March 20, 1850, perhaps as balm to any wounded feelings on the part of Prussia's cousins in the principality, the heads of both houses were granted the qualification of "Highness" in a Supreme Cabinet Order issued from the Charlottenburg Palace. Prince Karl Anton of the Sigmaringen branch was further dignified with the title "Royal Highness" by a decree signed by Wilhelm I of Prussia on October 18, 1861. Upon the death of Prince Friedrich Wilhelm of Hohenzollern-Hechingen on September 3, 1869, Karl Anton assumed the title of Prince of Hohenzollern.

As part of their obligation upon joining the German Confederation after Napoleon's fall, the Principalities of Hohenzollern-Hechingen and Hohenzollern-Sigmaringen contributed some 500 infantrists to its army. They were part of the 11th Battalion of the Reserve Regiment. Then in 1820, Infantry Regiment No.40 was formed from the fusiliers of Prussian Infantry Regiment No.36 as an element of the 8th Corps. The 8th Corps was stationed in Luxembourg and was comprised of troops from Baden, Hesse and Arttemberg as well. It saw action in the uprisings of 1830-1832. The next year it was moved into the Rhineland. The regiment went into action again in the revolutionary year of 1848. During this time and up to 1895, it occupied five different garrisons in the Rhineland until it moved to Rastatt in Baden. It was stationed there at the start of World War I. The 40th had been named the Hohenzollern Regiment in 1860 and in 1866, Prince Karl Anton had been attached to it *á la suite*. In 1877, he became the *Chef* of the regiment.

The Hohenzollern Regiment was part of the Prussian Army of the Elbe in the 1866 war with Austria and its allies. The regiment was present at the decisive (for the Prussians) Battle of Königgrätz (Sadowa). Its losses there were small, less than

2% of its force becoming fatalities. In contrast, in the Franco-Prussian War of 1870 where it participated in most of the early battles with the Prussian 1st Army, 9% of its effectives were killed including the regimental commander. Prince Karl Anton died on June 2, 1885 and four years later, the regiment received its final designation, *Füsilier-Regiment Fürst Karl Anton von Hohenzollern (Hohenzollernsches) Nr.40*. Karl Anton's successor, his oldest son Leopold, ruled until his own death in 1905 whereupon he was succeeded in turn by his oldest son, Wilhelm. Wilhelm ruled throughout the war and in addition to being *Chef* of the regiment like his grandfather and father, held the rank of *General der Infanterie* in the Royal Prussian Army.

In World War I, the Hohenzollern Regiment along with three crack regiments from Baden formed the 28th Division of the XIV Army Corps (the Baden units were *1. Badisches Leib-Grenadier-Regiment Nr.109., 2. Badisches Grenadier-Regiment Kaiser Wilhelm I. Nr.110.* and *Infanterie-Regiment Markgraf Ludwig Wilhelm (3. Badisches) Nr.111.*). The principality's other unit, *Hohenzollernsches Fussartillerie-Regiment Nr.13.*, was assigned to the 27th Division as one of its two artillery contingents. The 40th Fusiliers were engaged in the initial collision of the opposing armies as the French thrust into Alsace in what was called the Battle of the Frontiers and in which in foolish headlong charges they were to lose 300,000 men. After punishing the French in September in actions west of Pont a Mousson between Mete and Nancy, the regiment was moved to northeastern France above Arras in October. From then until May 1915, the four regiments were thrown into battles along a plateau known as Notre Dame de Lorette that exhausted them one after the other (the 110th Grenadiers alone reported the loss of 58 officers and 3,814 men between the start of the war and November 30).

During the winter of 1914 and the spring of 1915, the division continued to sustain heavy losses. The regiments most affected were the 110th again, its sister the 111th and the Hohenzollern fusiliers (no casualty numbers for the 40th are known but as an example of the scale of the losses, the 111th Infantry's 1st Battalion was down to only three officers and 272 men as of May 10, 1915 and the regiment was characterized as "completely destroyed"). On May 15, the division was relieved and reorganized but was back in the line after only 10 days to continue in the fighting that came to be known the Battle of Artois. The heavy losses continued to such an extent that the division had to be pulled out of the line again in the middle of June. It was then transferred to Champagne and for the rest of 1915, there were only a few local actions on a quiet front and losses were relatively small.

The first half of 1916 was mostly spent in intensive training. The second half was a different story. The division participated in the Battle of the Somme which had opened on July 1. It suffered heavily in this campaign too and was relieved at the beginning of October and returned to the Champagne sector. At the end of January 1917, the division moved to Verdun and took part in the German attack there on March 4. Throughout that spring and summer and into the first part of September, it was attack and counterattack. Then relief only after the division's effectiveness was so reduced that it could no longer go on without a rest, reorganization and replacements. This came in its old stamping ground in Alsace but was short lived. It went back into the line there on October 20 and then was hastily moved back up northwest again to help counter a British threat that had suddenly materialized at Cambrai on November 20. An attack there supported by tanks had broken through the German lines to a depth of four to five miles on a 10-mile front, huge gains by the standards of Western Front trench warfare. The extent of the success caught the British flatfooted. They had no plan to exploit the breakthrough and hastily assembled German reinforcements, the 28th Division among them, quickly stabilized the situation. In short order, all the lost ground was recaptured. Lost also was one of the few chances to break into open country, sweep up the channel ports and perhaps end the war. From December until the first of the great 1918 spring and summer German offensives, the Western Front went quiet and the 28th Division went into winter quarters in the Ardennes.

The 28th Division was not to be involved in either the opening offensive, *Operation Michael*, the drive on Amiens from March 21 to April 5, or its follow-up drive, *Operation Georgette* on the Lys from April 9 to April 29 between La Bassee and Armentieres. It had been in a holding position in the Butte de Mesnil sector along the Aisne until May 13. After a 10-day rest to be refitted for bigger things, the division was moved to Laon. On the 31st, it joined Ludendorff's third and final 1918 assault that had been launched against the French along a ridge line called the Chemin des Dames on May 27. The Germans were held up at Chateau-Thierry on June 1 and turned towards Vaux and Belleau Wood. The fresh U.S. 2nd Division was instrumental in checking them there. The 40th Fuseliers were given another short rest between June 8 and 13 and then rejoined the Second Battle of the Marne as it came to be called. Badly mauled again, the entire division was pulled out on July 1 and this time it would take more than three weeks before they could be whipped into a semblance of a fighting force. The Germans were now in a bad way. On July 16, Ludendorff had had to issue orders to abandon the offensive. The French with American support opened their own counterattack on the 18th. By August 6, the German threat was over. What had been a large bulge into Allied lines had been erased and the front ran

At the neck, Prince Wilhelm of Hohenzollern, who ascended the throne in 1905 and ruled throughout World War I, wears the Grand Cross of the Red Eagle Order and from the sash, the badge of the High Order of the Black Eagle. The Grand Commander of the Royal House Order of Hohenzollern is suspended from its chain and on collars below that, the Spanish Order of the Golden Fleece and the Spanish Order of Charles III. The top left breast star is that of the Black Eagle and next to it, the Grand Cross star of the Order of Charles III. The lower breast star is that of the Grand Cross of the Spanish Order of Military Merit. Below it is the Princely Hohenzollern Honor Cross 1st Class and in the lead-off position on his bar, the small cross for princely members of the Princely House. The Spanish orders undoubtedly came as a result of his first marriage in 1889 to Maria Theresa Magdalena, daughter of Prince Lodovico of Bourbon, Two Sicilies.

At the neck, Wilhelm in *Feldgrau* has the Grand Cross badge with Swords of the Bavarian Military Merit Order (awarded on October 27, 1914) and aside his Iron Cross 2nd Class the badge of a Commander of Baden's Military Karl Friedrich Merit Order (awarded with Star on December 28, 1914). The upper breast star is to the Bavarian Military Merit Order Grand Cross and the lower is that of the Karl Friedrich Grand Cross to which he was entitled to wear as a Commander of the order with General officer rank. Wilhelm's second marriage in 1915 was to Adelgunde, daughter of King Ludwig III of Bavaria. In addition, Wilhelm was the *Inhaber* (Member) of Bavaria's 22nd Infantry Regiment Prince Wilhelm of Hohenzollern and *Chef* (Chief) of the 28th Division which was comprised of three Baden infantry regiments and his own 40th Hohenzollern fusiliers, all based in Rastatt in Baden at the start of World War I.

in a straight line from Reims west to Soissons. The men of the Hohenzollern Regiment held positions along the Vesle until August 26 when relief was necessary still one more time. The battalions of the regiment were down to a strength of just three companies or less. It was never again to be a first class unit but like the rest of the German army, fought in near continuous rear-guard actions, in and out of the lines from Verdun up to Flanders. Rather ironically, the end found the regiment engaged around Mons on the Belgian border, the scene of the first small (but costly) success of the British Expeditionary Forces' "contemptible little army" in 1914.

CHAPTER X

THE MILITARY AWARDS OF THE PRINCIPALITY OF HOHENZOLLERN

THE PRINCELY HOHENZOLLERN HONOR CROSS

Prince Friedrich Wilhelm of Hohenzollern-Hechingen and Prince Carl of Hohenzollern-Sigmaringen jointly founded the Princely Hohenzollern Honor Cross on December 5, 1841. It was, in effect, the Principality's House Order and was officially designated as such in April 1842. From the beginning, it also had affiliated decorations attached to it. They were, initially, the Honor Cross 1st Class (with Crown), the Honor Cross 2nd Class (without Crown), the Gold Honor Medal (with Crown) and the Silver Merit Medal (without Crown). Then on January 16, 1851, the Princes' Protestant cousin (the Hohenzollerns of the Principality were Catholic), King Friedrich Wilhelm IV of Prussia more or less coopted the idea when he founded the Royal House Order of Hohenzollern, even adopting a similar design for the badges of his new order. Its statutes, signed on August 23 that year, recognized the existence of the Princely House Order which had been taken into the Prussian series of orders by a state treaty concluded on December 7, 1849. It was within that document that the right, and in fact the duty, of the King of Prussia to approve awards of the Princely House Order was sealed. But, as already mentioned, in practice, King Friedrich Wilhelm IV and his successors, Emperors Wilhelm I, Friedrich III and Wilhelm II, probably did not do so as a matter of regular routine.

Typical of an Imperial German order, there were a number of amendments and enlargements to the order over the years leading up to World War I. These were:

- an Honor Cross 3rd Class was added in 1844.
- the first award of the Honor Cross 1st Class with Brilliants was made in 1851.
- revised and final statutes were promulgated in 1852.
- coincident with the war with Austria in 1866, swords were authorized for all insignia to indicate an award made for military merit and bravery in the face of the enemy.
- an additional grade of the order called the Honor Commander Cross was established in 1891 to rank between the Honor Cross 1st Class and the Honor Cross 2nd Class.
- another new grade was added in 1910. This was the Honor Cross 3rd Class with Crown to rank between the Honor Cross 2nd Class and the Honor Cross 3rd Class. Also that year, two additional affiliated decorations came into being, the Gold Merit Cross and the Silver Merit Cross.

The badges of the Princely Hohenzollern Honor Cross were in the form of a *cross pattée*, also called in this case a Rupert's Cross (after the old Order of St. Rupert of the Archbishophric of Würzburg) because the arms of the cross were slightly curved at its ends. In the three higher classes, the arms were enameled white with a black enamel in-line and were edged in gold. In this respect, they were exactly like the badges of the later Royal House Order of Hohenzollern although none of the badges of the three higher classes of the Princely House Order was surmounted by a crown up to the time of World War I (an Honor Commander Cross with Crown was created in 1941 although its issuance is uncertain). On the two 3rd Class badges, however, their arms were not filled in with white enamel although the enameled black in-line was retained. The 3rd Class badges' arms were in silver as was the five-arched crown on the higher 3rd Class grade. The lack of the white enameling on the arms and the overall silver finish was aped, too, by Prussia when it established the honor decoration affiliated with the Royal House Order of Hohenzollern in 1861, the *Kreuz der Inhaber* (Member's Cross).

On December 5, 1841, almost ten years before King Friedrich Wilhelm IV of Prussia established the Royal House Order of Hohenzollern, his Catholic cousins in the far-off Principality of Hohenzollern, Prince Friedrich Wilhelm of Hohenzollern-Hechingen and Prince Carl of Hohenzollern-Sigmaringen, had jointly founded the Princely Hohenzollern Honor Cross. Originally, it consisted of just two classes plus an affiliated Gold Honor Medal and a Silver Merit Medal. A 3rd Class (above) was added in 1844 and in the 1866 war with Austria, swords were added to all insignia to indicate an award for bravery or military merit. The Honor Cross functioned as the principality's house order. Its ribbon, white with three black stripes, was adopted as the statute ribbon for the Royal House Order of Hohenzollern. Twenty men who served in the *Fliegertruppe* are known to have received the Princely Hohenzollern Honor Cross 3rd Class with Swords during the war.

The obverse enameled center medallion of the 3rd Class badge (left) displayed the quartered shield of Hohenzollern surmounted by a crown. A blue enameled riband carried the order's motto, "For Fidelity and Merit." The arms of the crosses in the higher grades were enameled white with a black in-line. On the 3rd Class, the white enamel was omitted. Between the arms of the crosses there was a green enameled wreath of laurels (on the left) and oak (on the right). The overall finish on the 3rd Class badge was silver whereas the higher grades were in gold. The swords on all grades were in gold. The center medallion on the reverse (right) carried the crowned initials *F* and *C*, those of the two founders. The foundation date of the 3rd Class grade, 8 April 1844, appeared on the riband.

The center medallion of all grades of the house order was enameled on the obverse. Against white enamel, the gold edged black and white quartered shield of Hohenzollern appeared below a small gold crown. All the badges except the Honor Cross 1st Class carried a similarly enameled medallion on the reverse (the Honor Cross 1st Class was a pin-back badge and as such, its reverse was plain). On those grades of the order other than the Honor Cross 1st Class, the reverse medallion displayed the gold entwined initials *F C* (for the founding Princes, Friedrich and Carl) beneath another crown. On both sides of these badges the center medallion was surrounded by a riband of blue enamel. On the obverse in gold capital letters the order's motto *FÜR TREUE UND VERDIENST* ("For Fidelity and Merit") appeared. On the reverse, the riband on the Honor Commander Cross and the Honor Cross 2nd Class carried the foundation date of the order in similar gold letters

DEN 5. DEZEMBER 1841. The 3rd Class badges carried its foundation date *DEN 8. APRIL 1844*. A note should be made that originally, from 1844 to 1850, the 3rd Class badge was in plain silver with no enameling whatsoever.

All the badges of the order had a green enameled wreath between the arms of the cross and standing clear of the center medallion (on some early badges there was no space between the center medallion and the wreath). This was another design feature adopted for the Royal House Order of Hohenzollern. On the left (as one faces the badge), the wreath was of laurel and on the right, of oak. The swords, when present, were in gold in all cases and placed conventionally between the arms of the cross. There was no provision for the Swords-on-Ring feature (although one such badge, an Honor Commander Cross with Swords-on-Ring was given once in 1928 to a retired Prussian Major Hermann von Detten who had won the Honor Cross 3rd Class with Swords on September 24, 1914 as a *Hauptmann* and Personal Adjutant to Prince Wilhelm of Hohenzollern).

The 1st Class Honor Cross was unusual in that it was a pin-back piece worn without a ribbon on the lower left breast whereas the highest grades of the house orders of other German

Prince Karl of Hohenzollern was the third son of Prince Leopold who ruled the Principality from 1885 until his death in 1905 whereupon his eldest son, Wilhelm, succeeded him and ruled throughout World War I. The first badge on Karl's order bar is the special badge of the Honor Cross called the Small Cross for Princes of the Princely House, his coming with Swords. Karl was a *Generalleutnant* in the Prussian Army and wears the chain and badge of a Grand Commander of the Royal House Order of Hohenzollern with Swords. The breast star is the Grand Cross of the Prussian Red Eagle Order with Swords. Below that, nearly hidden, is his 1st Class Princely Hohenzollern Honor Cross with Swords. The other neck badge is the Grand Cross of the Order of St. John of Jerusalem in Rome.

The Princely Hohenzollern Honor Cross 1st Class with Swords shows more clearly in the postcard of Prince Franz Josef and his wife Princess Maria Alix, Duchess of Saxony. Franz Josef was Wilhelm's second son and served aboard the commerce raider, Emden, as an *Oberleutnant zur See*. When she was finally caught by HMS Sydney near the Coco Islands, he went into captivity with the rest of her crew. Upon repatriation in 1920, Franz Josef was awarded his 1st Class Honor Cross with Swords and given the title Prince of Hohenzollern-Emden. Maria Alix was a daughter of Friedrich August III, King of Saxony, and thus Franz Josef wears the breast star of the Saxon House Order of the Rue Crown, its highest order of knighthood and chivalry.

states were sash/neck badges. The Honor Commander Cross was a neck badge while the 2nd Class and 3rd Class insignia were breast badges. In 1852, a special grade was established called the Small Cross for Princes of the Princely House. It was approximately the same size as the 2nd Class neck badge and otherwise was the same except that it was surmounted by a gold three-arched crown within which there was a red enameled liner. It was meant to be worn on the order bar however like the 3rd Class and not at the neck. From 1866, it, too, could be awarded with Swords. The ribbon for the neck and breast badges was white with a narrow black center stripe and a slightly broader black stripe towards each edge. This also became the statute ribbon for the Royal House Order of Hohenzollern. In Prussia, however, swords awards of its house order did not use the statute ribbon but rather the "war ribbon," the one employed on the Iron Cross. In Hohenzollern on the other hand, the statute ribbon was employed on both swords and non-swords awards alike.

Prewar, wartime and postwar rank lists have also been consulted here to determine the frequency of swords awards of the Princely Hohenzollern Honor Cross. Appendix XIX shows the picture among serving officers in the Royal Prussian Army and in the 13th Royal Württemberg Army Corps on the eve of the war in May 1914. Just three swords awards show up there, all by men of General rank. The army produced no wartime rank lists showing awards but the Navy one as of February 1918 presents a similarly bleak picture (see Appendix XX). The first postwar rank list for the *Reichsheer* was for 1924 and in it we see a more generous picture, especially with swords awards of the 3rd Class with Crown and 3rd Class only (see Appendix XXI). Also showing up here were three awards of the Merit Cross with Swords (one Gold and two Silver) apparently to men who after receiving their awards during the war were later promoted (these affiliated decorations will be discussed in the next chapter). Unlike previous tabulations, there is no Appendix showing holders of Princely Hohenzollern swords awards for serving officers in the new German Navy as of November 20, 1926. And that is simply because there were none at all, perhaps not too surprising in view of the picture seen in 1918.

Fortunately for a study like this, the roll of swords awards of the Princely Hohenzollern Honor Cross and its affiliated decorations during the war and in the two immediate years following was found in the archive in Sigmaringen during a personal visit in 2000. Thanks to the friendly cooperation of the archive director and his staff, it has been possible to study that and extract overall figures as well as the names of aviation recipients and in a few cases, men who could be identified as recipients prior to their joining the *Fliegertruppe*. Only because of the sheer total number and that common enemy, time, was it not possible to tabulate all the aviation recipients of the lowest of the decorations, the Silver Merit Medal with Swords. For such a small state, the rather large number of swords awards of the various grades of the Honor Cross, 1,280 in all, was unexpected. But as we shall see shortly, the requirements for eligibility of a Princely Hohenzollern award were not quite as stringent as some that we have encountered. The table on page 210 presents the total picture.

On October 30, 1916, Prince Wilhelm approved of regulations governing the award of the Honor Cross with Swords and its affiliated decorations with Swords in the following decree:

> In response to the presentation made to me, I approve - without prejudice to any acts of grace made by My own free will - the following regulations for the award of My House Order for the duration of the war:
>
> I. The classes of the order apply to the following military ranks:
>
>> The Honor Cross 1st Class for Lieutenant Generals, Generals of Infantry, Colonel Generals and Field Marshals.
>
> II. The Honor Commander Cross for Colonels already possessing a Prussian order in the 2nd Class and Major Generals.
>
> III. The Honor Cross 2nd Class for Lieutenant Colonels and Colonels, the latter if not yet in possession of the class of a Prussian order mentioned under II.
>
> IV. The Honor Cross 3rd Class with Crown for Majors.
>
> V. The Honor Cross 3rd Class for Lieutenants, Senior Lieutenants, Captains and Senior Paymasters.
>
> VI. The Merit Cross in Gold will not be affected by this more detailed regulation.
>
> VII. The Merit Cross in Silver for Ensigns with Sword Knot, Warrant Officers and Paymasters.
>
> VIII. The Honor Medal in Gold for the remaining Sword Knot wearers including Acting Officers.

IX. The Merit Medal in Silver for non-commissioned officers without Sword Knot and men in the ranks.

Medical and Veterinary officers, although not mentioned, come under the corresponding class of rank as do Senior and Junior Military Officials.

The order can only be given once during the same campaign and only in one class. An additional award of a higher class of the order after a promotion is not possible.

The order is only awarded for merit in the face of the enemy (bravery, outstanding leadership).

Any acts of grace for war merit in general I shall reserve for Myself until the end of the campaign.

In general, only requests for military orders have to be presented to me for approval; on principle, personal ones are not to be considered.

Considered for the decoration are:

A. The officers, officials and servants in My service and their sons.

B. The officers, non-commissioned officers and men in the ranks of:

My Fusilier Regiment Prince Carl Anton of Hohenzollern No. 40,
My Royal Bavarian 22nd Infantry Regiment Prince Wilhelm of Hohenzollern,
also the 2nd Foot Guard Regiment, the 1st Foot Guard Regiment and
Hohenzollern citizens in the Hohenzollern Foot Artillery Regiment No. 13.

C. The replacement, reserve and militia formations of the military units mentioned under B, as far as active service officers or long service non-commissioned officers serving there who wear the uniform of said regiments with the exception of the Foot Artillery Regiment No. 13.

D. Senior staffs of said regiments with the exception of the Foot Artillery Regiment No. 13.

E. Citizens of Hohenzollern who as such possess Prussian citizenship; also, as an exception from this, members of old Hohenzollern families having kept strong ties with the native country.

F. Outstanding and long serving Prussian officials in the province of Hohenzollern.

Text resumes on page 215

Table 10-1
Awards of the Principality of Hohenzollern, 1914-1920
(excluding an example of each award sent to the Hindenburg Museum in Posen in 1917)

	1914	1915	1916	1917	1918	1919	1920	Total
Honor Cross 1st Class with Swords	13	19	33	22	13	0	1	101
Honor Commander Cross with Swords	5	5	11	6	7	0	1	35
Honor Cross 2nd Class with Swords	5	16	25	10	10	0	0	66
Honor Cross 3rd Class with Crown and Swords	17	20	37	48	20	1	1	144
Honor Cross 3rd Class with Swords	54	122	175	258	303	10	12	934
Total	**94**	**182**	**281**	**344**	**353**	**11**	**15**	**1,280**
Gold Merit Cross with Swords(one awarded with no date)								1
Silver Merit Cross with Swords	5	9	11	35	20	0	0	80
Total								**81**
Gold Honor Medal with Swords	22	90	107	199	209	0	13	640

Silver Merit Medal with Swords (5,875 awarded 1905-1927 according to Link-Gauggel)

Source: *Staatsarchiv*, Sigmaringen

Upon their repatriation along with Prince Franz Josef, other members of the Emden (above) were likewise decorated with the grade of the Princely Hohenzollern Honor Cross appropriate to their rank. Her captain (left) *Kapitän zur See* Karl von Müller, received the Honor Commander Cross with Swords, *Korvettenkapitän* Helmut von Mücke (below left as a *Kapitänleutnant* on his wedding day and not yet wearing his order) was awarded the Honor Cross 3rd Class with Crown and Swords, 13 petty officers the Gold Honor Medal with Swords and an unknown number of other ratings the Silver Merit Medal with Swords. All were approved on January 26, 1920 with a retroactive wartime date of May 19, 1918. At the same time, *Vizeadmiral* Maximilian *Graf* von Spee (below right), Chief of the East Asian Cruiser Squadron who went down with his ship off the Falkland Islands in December 1914, was given a posthumous Honor Cross 1st Class with Swords

"Our *Kaiser* and His Six Sons." By right of birth, all held the Princely Hohenzollern Honor Cross 1st Class prewar. Left to right, Crown Prince Wilhelm, Eitel Friedrich, Adalbert, August Wilhelm, Oskar and Joachim. Eitel Friedrich and Adalbert received swords to the insignia on April 13, 1915, Oskar on July 25, 1916 and the Crown Prince on November 30, 1917. Right, the two "flying princess" of Prussia, Friedrich Sigismund and Friedrich Karl. Friedrich Sigismund was granted swords to his 1st Class Honor Cross on June 25, 1916 but Friedrich Karl never was. He died in British captivity on April 6, 1917 after being forced down on March 21 and wounded in an attempt to reach his lines.

SOME MILITARY LEADERS WHO RECEIVED THE PRINCELY HOHENZOLLERN HONOR CROSS 1st CLASS WITH SWORDS

Kaiser Wilhelm II
December 22, 1914

Paul von Hindenburg
November 8, 1916

Erich Ludendorff
November 8, 1916

Generalstabschef v. Falkenhayn

Erich von Falkenhayn
November 9, 1916

Generalfeldmarschall v. Mackensen.

August von Mackensen
November 22, 1916

Crown Prince Wilhelm
November 30, 1917

MORE MILITARY LEADERS WHO RECEIVED THE PRINCELY HOHENZOLLERN HONOR CROSS 1st CLASS WITH SWORDS

Hermann von Stein
November 4, 1914

Karl von Einem
November 26, 1915

Hans von Beseler
June 22, 1916

Georg von Müller
November 14, 1916

Remus von Woyrsch
April 15, 1917

Bernhard von Kessel
March 17, 1917

G. The military administration and replacement authorities responsible for the province of Hohenzollern (Deputy 14th Army Corps, District Command Stockach).

General Principles:

The award of the Hohenzollern House Order with Swords requires proof of independent merit that had not been rewarded with, or has been applied for, another decoration.

Sword Knot wearers should be in possession of the Iron Cross before being considered for the award.

For non-commissioned officers without the Sword Knot and men in the ranks, allowance must be made to consider those with greater years of service and older age who had not yet obtained any other decoration.

Outstanding military deeds will not be affected by these principles.

Given in Sigmaringen on 30 October 1916

Wilhelm

To English speakers, the sentence structure in these regulations may seem a bit stilted but such was the language of the day. The references to "Ensigns with Sword Knot" and "remaining Sword Knot wearers" should be explained in more detail because they are ranks that have not come up in this treatise so far. In German, the former is *Portepee-Fähnriche* referring to aspirant officers wearing the officer sword knot on the scabbard. The latter term *Portepeeträger* refers to senior non-commissioned officers also wearing the officer sword knot.

Before going on with a few biographies of aviation recipients of the Hohenzollern Honor Cross with Swords, one final regulation concerning the issuance of certificates of possession may be of interest. It was prepared in January 1917 and published in the *Armee-Verordnungsblatt* (Army Official Gazette) on February 5, 1917. It read:

His Royal Highness, the Prince of Hohenzollern, has determined that certificates of possession of Princely Hohenzollern war decorations already awarded or are to

Below: While two of his staff confer with the pilots of *Jagdstaffel 18*, the *Kommandierenden General der Luftstreitkräfte* (Commanding General of the Air Force), *Generalleutnant* Ernst von Hoeppner, inspects the ground crew personnel of the unit, he being the tall gentleman at the far right in a greatcoat. Von Hoeppner received the Princely Hohenzollern Honor Cross 1st Class with Swords (right) on June 14, 1916 when he was the Commanding Officer of the 75th Reserve Infantry Division and just before his appointment to command the Army air services on October 8 that year in its reorganization and expansion. No doubt next to the General and helping with introductions is *Jasta 18's Staffelführer, Leutnant* August Raben. The unit marking was a raven, *Rabe* being the German word for raven. The unit's Fokker D.VIIs were striking with their vermilion noses and white fuselages. Between the two groups of men an Allied machine can be seen, possibly D.H.4 A.7708 from No.55 Squadron, RAF that Raben himself brought down on August 30, 1918 for his fourth and last victory of the war (see page 154 in Volume V).

> be awarded will not be issued by the Orders Chancery. Instead, proof of the award shall be its entry into military papers - war rank lists, war strength lists, transfer papers, military passports. In addition, it is desired that the higher command will give the grantee proof of the legitimacy of possession when handing out the Princely Hohenzollern war decoration and also, as far as possible, hand out such proof for past awards.

In other words, the Orders Chancery in Sigmaringen was not to be bothered with (or go to the expense of) issuing the handsome diplomas that many of the other Imperial German states gave to recipients of their awards. It was left to a recipient's command to enter the proof of possession in the various documents mentioned, a wartime necessity, perhaps, but it still sounds rather tightfisted. And now to a few of those recipients.

HAUPTMANN ERNST DRECHSEL

What started out as a voluntary two-year hitch to satisfy the compulsory military obligations facing most German youths turned into a 20-year career for Ernst Drechsel. Just turned 18, he joined *Grenadier-Regiment König Karl Nr.123.*, the fifth of Württemberg's 10 infantry regiments of the line, in July 1900. Just five months later, something of a record, the young man was promoted *Unteroffizier*. Drechsel must have liked what he saw and they certainly liked him. A promotion to *Fähnrich* came early in 1901 and that April he was sent off to Enger where he studied for eight months at the war school there. Right after his return to his regiment, his Lieutenancy came through in January 1901 and his career path was set. In the prewar years through 1913, he went through a series of assignments grooming him for bigger things to come. There were nearly three years spent at the Württemberg War Ministry, a further three years at the Prussian War Academy and then a real plum, an appointment to the Great German General Staff. Meantime, while at the War Academy, he was upped again to *Oberleutnant* on March 23, 1910. No sooner had the General Staff assignment been made in April 1912 than Drechsel got his first taste of aviation when for two months in the summer of 1913 he attended a course for observers at the air station at Döberitz. That apparently made a deep impression on the now seasoned 31-year old officer. When Drechsel's time was up at the General Staff post on the last day of 1913, he had orders in his pocket to report to *Flieger-Bataillon Nr.1*.

No sooner had Drechsel begun his new work when there was a several month interruption. Coincident with his promotion to *Hauptmann* on February 25, 1914, he took up the temporary job of Company Commander in the 3rd Railway Regiment in Hanau near Frankfurt. But by the end of May, he was back in aviation again, this time with *Flieger-Bataillon Nr.2*. On the 1st of August as the war crisis reached its peak and the old aviation battalions were dissolved and readied to go into the field as flying units, Drechsel was assigned to *Flieger-Ersatz-Abteilung 4*, the aviation replacement center at Posen. By this time, he already wore an award that was not uncommon among his brother officers who had discharged their peacetime duties in commendable fashion. It was the Prussian Crown Order 4th Class (without swords of course). After only two weeks at Posen, this much traveled man was posted to another *FEA*, the one at Hanover, but now as its Commanding Officer. Given his age and seniority, this could have been his home for a considerable period of time but, no, only a little over a month later, he had a frontline command and took over *Feldflieger-Abteilung 31* on the Western Front on September 24. *FFl.Abt.31* was operating as the eyes of the German Third Army whose command had just been assumed by *Generaloberst* von Einem on the 12th, the day the Germans who were occupying positions along the Aisne were forced to evacuate Reims as the French prepared to counterattack the next day (von Einem, still in charge of the 3rd Army, would received the Princely Hohenzollern Honor Cross 1st Class with Swords on November 26, 1915). Before the first war year of 1914 had run its course, Drechsel could pin on two awards, He, along with several of his men in *31*, received the Iron Cross 2nd Class, still a prestigious decoration at the time and worn proudly as the photograph of Drechsel and others at this time attest. Then on December 21, his old connection in the service of the Kingdom of Württemberg was recognized. He and a pilot in *FFl.Abt.28* were given the Knight's Cross of its highest bravery award, the Military Merit Order. Theirs were only the sixth and seventh aviation awards of the Knight's Cross thus far in the war.

Drechsel remained in charge of *31* until the end of April 1915. Then his combat days were over but not his value to the *Fliegertruppe*. From that point on and throughout the rest of the war, he occupied a series of increasingly important staff jobs. After leaving *31*, he was appointed the aviation officer attached to the staff of *Armee-Abteilung Woyrsch* of the 3rd German Army (the then *Generaloberst* Remus von Woyrsch would himself receive the Honor Cross 1st Class with Swords on April 15, 1917). In October 1915, Drechsel took charge of all aviation units assigned to the 3rd Army. The next month, on November 30, he was awarded the Princely Hohenzollern

Above: Men of *Feldflieger-Abteilung 31* in 1914, seven of whom proudly display their newly won Iron Cross 2nd Class including the CO, *Hauptmann* Ernst Dreschel, the portly bare-headed figure in the first row. He was awarded the Princely Hohenzollern Honor Cross 3rd Class with Swords on November 30, 1915 for his leadership of the unit. From left to right, *Lt.* von Hesler (Saxon St. Henry, Merit and Albert Orders), *Oblt.* Meyer (St. Henry, Albert and Zähringen Lion Orders), *Lt.* Gandert, *Unteroffz.* Hucke, Dreschel, ?, *Oblt.* Forster, ?, *Hptm.* Blumenberg, *Unteroffz.* Kulich, *Unteroffz.* Baehtge, *Lt.* Rau and another *Unteroffz.* Baehtge (the pair were brothers).

Below: The date is June 7, 1916, the locale for these men of *Feldflieger-Abteilung 42* is the casino of the 138th Infantry Regiment. The man in the doorway with arm raised is *Lt.* Günther Schroth who received the Honor Cross 3rd Class with Swords on December 1, 1916 while still with the unit. Others who can be identified are at far left with arms folded, *Offz.-Stv.* Edmund Nathanael (Member's Cross with Swords Royal Hohenzollern House Order, Saxe-Weimar Wilhelm Ernst War Cross and its General Honor Decoration in Gold with Swords), holding what may be a map board, *Lt.* Julius Meyer (Württemberg Military Merit and Friedrich Orders and its Gold Military Merit Medal) and seated with left hand on hip, *Lt.* Friedrich Günther (Saxon Merit and Albert Orders). The officer is admonishing a bulldog that bears a striking resemblance to his master.

Honor Cross 3rd Class with Swords, only the fourth such award within the *Fliegertruppe* thus far in the war. Drechsel remained *Kofl 3* for two solid years until October 1917 when he was assigned to *Idflieg* to head up its photographic command. There, on November 11, he received the Saxon Albert Order Knight 1st Class with Swords. On New Year's Day 1918, Drechsel received his final appointment of the war when he was made Inspector of the entire German Army Air Service's photographic service. His value in these important staff positions was rewarded in 1918 (exact date not known) with the Knight's Cross with Swords of Prussia's Royal House Order of Hohenzollern.

LEUTNANT GÜNTHER SCHROTH

In discussing the wartime exploits of recipients of Imperial German orders and decorations, particularly a man who received an award from one of the smaller German states of which he himself was not a citizen, a reason for it is always sought. Fame had a lot to do with it of course. Witness Manfred *Freiherr* von Richthofen's 12 Imperial German orders and decorations from states and cities other than his own native Prussia. But other things accounted for it too. As in the case of the relatively unknown recipient of the Princely Hohenzollern Honor Cross just discussed, frequently there was a regimental connection from his pre-air service days. Similarly, an airman might be honored if that earlier service had been with a unit whose patron, the *Chef* or *Inhaber*, were a royal from one of these lesser states. Simply being in the right place at the right time played its part as well. Probably no better example of this exists than the awards of the Saxe-Coburg and Gotha Duke Carl Eduard Medal 2nd Class with Swords and Date (Bar) which were given to the budding fighter pilots, the same Manfred von Richthofen and a wingmate, Hans Imelmann. The two set off on a quest for souvenirs from the British B.E.2cs each had shot down on the morning of November 9, 1916. On the site of von Richthofen's victim's crash they came upon a party of senior German officers inspecting the remains of the enemy bomber and introductions were made. Von Richthofen professed not to have known at the time but among the group was Duke Carl Eduard himself. That evening, the two airmen were notified by the Duke's Adjutant of their awards, made, presumably, for protecting the Duke's headquarters and the Duke himself from harm. Visits by minor royalty to aerodromes were other occasions for the distribution of awards they controlled. We have seen this in an earlier chapter when the Duke of Brunswick handed out three of his War Merit Crosses on the field of *Feldflieger-Abteilung 23* and later, when he personally decorated (or redecorated?) von Richthofen in 1918. No such reasons have been found, however, concerning the award to the next Hohenzollern Honor Cross recipient whom we discuss, Silesian-born Günther Schroth.

Schroth originally had his sights set on a naval career and one week before he was to turn 19, he joined the Imperial German Navy on April 1, 1913 as a cadet. Five months later, he was out, discharged as unfit due to a problem with his eyesight. The army overlooked the condition and at the end of November that year, he was accepted into the *Colbergsches Grenadier-Regiment Graf Gneisenau (2. Pommersches) Nr.9.* (nor would the air service be as particular as the navy later on). Before his hitch was up, Schroth also served for four months in *Infanterie-Regiment Prinz Moritz von Anhalt-Dessau (5. Pommersches) Nr.42.*, another Pomeranian contingent. He reverted to reserve status at the end of June 1914 as a newly promoted *Unteroffizier*. The mobilization in August called him back to the 9th Grenadiers where he was immediately given the rank of *Offizier-Stellvertreter*. His unit was one of the four infantry regiments that comprised the German Third Division of the German First Army under *Generaloberst* Alexander von Kluck. The First Army made up the right flank of the invasion of Belgium and France in the opening weeks of the war. It entered Belgium on August 13 and had crossed into France on the 24th. Two days later, it took Cambrai and reached the Somme on the 28th. After the Battle of the Marne in which the 9th Grenadiers participated, Schroth's regiment made its retreat north of Soissons and moved on to Roye in early October where it was engaged in the fighting south of there. On October 19, Schroth was wounded, badly enough to spend Christmas and New Year's in hospital. While recuperating, he made a successful application for a transfer to the air service, still another instance of one who did so while laid up with injuries suffered in the ground fighting. He began pilot training on January 21, 1915 at the military flying school at Köslin.

Schroth completed his ground courses and required flights in just four months and at the end of May was posted to *Feldflieger-Abteilung 42* on the Western Front. There, on September 9, he was promoted *Leutnant*. For a 21-year old non-commissioned officer in a two-seater formation that early in the war, this was a considerable achievement. And on December 1, came his otherwise unexplained Princely Honor Cross 3rd Class with Swords. Further evidence of the regard in which he was held came in late March of the new year of 1916 when he was sent to the single-seater school at Mannheim for a couple of weeks in order to familiarize himself with the *Eindecker*. Whether upon his return to *42* he actually flew one of them as protection for its two-seaters is not known but he was well positioned later in the year when the permanent fighter formations, the *Jagdstaffeln*, were formed. On November 24, Schroth was transferred to the newly formed *Jasta 19* under the command of the Bavarian then-*Oberleutnant* Franz Walz. Although Schroth remained with the unit for just a few weeks shy of one full year, he was unable to get credit for a confirmed victory. Perhaps because of that, he was packed off to Palestine, assigned to *Flieger-Abteilung 303* in November 1917.

A few days after New Year 1918, Schroth was transferred as a single-seater pilot again to *Jagstaffel II* of *Heeresgruppe F* one of two German fighter flights supporting its Turkish ally. Still without a success, he became the German officer in charge of the aviation depot in Damascus in June. By September, things were in a bad way in that theater. On the 19th, General (later Field Marshal) Edmund Allenby launched what was possibly the last great cavalry campaign of modern warfare. It quickly broke through the Turkish lines and with Royal Air Force aircraft bombing and strafing the retreating columns, there was a terrible slaughter. On the 22nd, Allenby could report that the 7th and 8th Turkish Armies had virtually ceased to exist. Damascus itself fell on the 30th. Exactly one month later, Turkish emissaries signed an armistice aboard a British battleship at Mudros. All Schroth was able to show for his service on behalf of the Ottoman Empire was its quite commonly awarded War Medal (called the *Eiserner Halbmond* (Iron Crescent) by the Germans because of its design and the Gallipoli Star by the British because it was instituted by Turkey in March 1915 at the start of that campaign in the Dardanelles).

Schroth was fortunate in that he became a prisoner-of-war of the Turks and not the British. They shipped out the Germans they held in captivity almost immediately while the British waited until after the Treaty of Versailles had been signed by the Germans in June of 1919. Schroth arrived back on German soil on December 1, 1918 along with other airmen like the six-victory ace of *Flieger-Abteilung 6* in Turkey, *Offizier-Stellvertreter* Emil Meinecke (as a recipient of Baden's highest bravery award for non-commissioned officers in World War I, the Silver Karl Friedrich Military Merit Medal, a biography on Meinecke appeared in Volume VI in this series). Schroth's former Commanding Officer in *Jasta 19*, the now *Hauptmann* Franz Walz, was not so lucky. Walz's leadership of *Flieger-Abteilung 304b "Pascha"* had earned him the *Pour le Mérite* on August 9, 1918 and the respect of his British opponents. Nonetheless, he did not make it back to German soil until November 30, 1919, a full year after his old pupil Schroth.

LEUTNANT CARL-AUGUST VON SCHOENEBECK

Carl-August von Schoenebeck was another Silesian born recipient of the Princely Hohenzollern Honor Cross 3rd Class with Swords but unlike the award to Günther Schroth, the man just discussed, we have the reason for it from *Generalmajor a. D.* von Schoenebeck himself.

At the Paris reunion of World War I aces over Armistice Week in 1981 that was mentioned in the biography of the Hessian General Honor Decoration "for Bravery" holder, Franz Hemer, one of the German former fighter pilots who were able to accept the invitation was General von Schoenebeck (the other two were Alois Heldmann and Hans-Georg von der Osten and it is of interest to observe that all three had been members of *Jagdgeschwader Freiherr von Richthofen Nr.1*). At the farewell banquet in the Grand Hotel, some of the aces, notably the British and the Canadians, wore their orders, decorations and service medals. General von Schoenebeck was the only German ex-flier to do so and his were represented by miniatures on a chain, the accepted manner of wearing such things in Germany when in civilian dress. When it was appropriate, his seldom awarded Hohenzollern Honor Cross was singled out and, fortunately this time, it was possible to ask the question, "why?" The General's face broke out in smiles. He said that while on a cross-country flight in his training days, he was forced to land near Sigmaringen, the capital of the Principality. It was the first airplane to have landed within its borders (and no wonder; Sigmaringen is located in the mountainous region of the Swabian Jura). As a consequence of that, the Prince awarded him his house order in the fall of 1917 after his career as a fighter pilot had gotten off to a promising start.

Of all the aces at the Paris reunion, General von Schoenebeck was the youngest, being a vigorous 82 at the time. On May Day 1915, only several months after his 17th birthday, von Schoenebeck enlisted as a *Fahnenjunker* (officer cadet or ensign) in a replacement battalion of Baden's premier infantry regiment, *1. Badisches Leib-Grenadier-Regiment Nr.109*. For two months that summer, he was tapped to attend the course for *Fähnrich* aspirants in Döberitz (the rank is very similar to *Fahnenjunker* but indicates more than just an officer cadet but an officer candidate as well). Returning to his battalion that August, von Schoenebeck was appointed a *Fähnrich* on October 14 and in mid-December took over as a platoon leader in the 109th. Not bad for a young man who would not turn 18 until the following month. In this capacity he put in a full year of action in Champagne but fortunately missed the bloody battles on the Somme in the summer and fall of 1916 that caused such

Right: *Leutnant* Carl-August von Schoenebeck held the distinction of being the only German fighter pilot of the war to receive both the Royal House Order of Hohenzollern from Prussia and the Princely Honor Cross from Hohenzollern-Sigmaringen. His ribbon bar is yet to display the Royal Hohenzollern award in this photograph. First in line is the Iron Cross 2nd Class, next the ribbon for Baden's Order of the Zähringen Lion which came in the form of the Knight 2nd Class with Swords on November 27, 1917 in recognition for his pre-air service assignment with its 109th Grenadier Regiment and finally we see the ribbon for his Princely Hohenzollern Honor Cross 3rd Class with Swords which was awarded on October 12, 1917. Von Schoenebeck first served in *Flieger-Abteilung (A)203*, then in *Jastas 11* and *59* and ended the war as the *Staffelführer* of *Jasta 33*, commanding it from July 11, 1918 until the end of the war. Von Schoenebeck was credited with a total of eight confirmed victories.

Below: Almost all fighter pilot-aspirants had spent time in two-seater formations in 1917 before making the transition but von Schoenebeck's stay in *(A)203* was remarkably short, just one month in June 1917. Even though it was summer when this photograph was taken there, it was still cold upstairs and he is dressed accordingly. An altimeter can be seen strapped between the upper struts below the top wing on this DFW-built DFW C.V and a dynamo is fitted to the right landing gear strut. The dark blob under the top left wing is apparently a blemish on the original print of this photo.

heavy casualties in the 109th's sister regiments in the 28th Division including the 40th Hohenzollern Fuseliers. Earlier that year, on March 9, he was further promoted *Leutnant*.

Von Schoenebeck's transfer to aviation became effective in mid-December 1916 and for the next five months, he undertook his pilot training at *Flieger-Ersatz-Abteilung 3* located in the Thuringian town of Gotha, home of the Gothaer Waggonfabrik AG and the Duke Carl Eduard Military Flying School (and today, according to one authority on the subject, the best place in Germany for sausage). On June 1, 1917, he "graduated" and after passing through *Armee-Flug-Park 1*, von Schoenebeck found himself assigned as a pilot to *Flieger-Abteilung (A)203* within the week. Remarkably, that remained his post for only a month. On the surface, one would suspect something had gone wrong, perhaps he had been found lacking in some respect or had had a falling out with his Commanding Officer. Nothing could be further from the truth. He was selected to join the new *Jagdgeschwader Nr.1* whose four flights, *Jastas 4, 6, 10* and *11*, had just been put under the command of *Rittmeister* Manfred *Freiherr* von Richthofen on June 25. Quite an honor for a pilot of a two-seater with only 30 days of frontline experience. Von Schoenebeck drew *Jasta 11* as his berth, the proud unit that von Richthofen himself had led until *JG 1* was formed, another honor since the *Rittmeister* continued to fly with it. The Adjutant of the *Geschwader*, *Oberleutnant* Karl Bodenschatz, would come to call von Schoenebeck the "technical genius" of his *Staffel* so perhaps a reputation for mechanical aptitude had preceded him and had had something to do with his selection to such an elite unit. The date of his arrival at *Jasta 11* is usually set as July 7 and if so, he must have found his new comrades profoundly shaken. Just the day before, von Richthofen had had a near death experience and was already at the St. Nicholas Field Hospital No.76 in Courtrai. He had been in the lead of nine of his men late that morning when they came upon a pack of British F.E.2d "pushers." He swung his flight around so as to attack from their vulnerable rear. Just as smartly, the "Fees" turned to face them so that the observers would have a full forward field of fire. Still at such long range as the two formations closed that von Richthofen had not yet cleared his guns, he suddenly felt a hammer blow in the side of his head and lost his vision immediately. With every bit of willpower, he retained his senses and his vision returned just in time as he spun down so that he was able to make an amazingly good landing under the circumstances.[1]

If July 7 were the arrival date of von Schoenebeck at *Jasta 11*'s field at Marckebeke near Courtrai in Flanders, his first duty after reporting to the Adjutant would have been a courtesy call on his Commanding Officer, the then *Leutnant* Kurt Wolff, a May 1917 recipient of the *Orden Pour le Mérite* thanks to a 21-victory skein in the previous month, "Bloody April." Wolff had inherited von Richthofen's mantle on June 28, the day after the first *Jasta 11* leader after von Richthofen, *Leutnant* Karl Allmenröder, had been killed the day before by ground fire as he was crossing the lines at low level. Allmenröder had held the job all of two days and Wolff, an original *Jasta 11* member under von Richthofen, was brought over from *Jasta 29* where he had been commanding after Hessian General Honor Decoration "for Bravery" and Lippe War Honor Cross for Heroic Deed recipient, Ludwig Dornheim, had been killed on April 29, 1917 (see those awards chapters). Probably, von Schoenebeck had to wait until the afternoon to meet his new Commanding Officer. Wolff had been busy that morning. Precisely at 11:00 a.m. (German Time), Wolff brought down Sopwith Triplane N.6309 of No.1 (Naval) Squadron, RNAS killing its pilot, Flight Sub Lieutenant K.H. Millward, for his 33rd confirmed victory. His slight build and shy manner belied his prowess in the air, a man who was affectionately referred to as "delicate little flower" within the *Geschwader*. Von Schoenebeck was certainly in good hands but not for long. Wolff was out hunting on July 11 after several days of rain and low clouds curtailed operations. In attacking a formation of 15 British aircraft he took a clean shot through the left hand but was able to break off and return safely. He ended up in a bed next to von Richthofen in the hospital in Courtrai.[2]

The air offensive for the second phase of the bloody battle known as Third Ypres had begun earlier in July although the British infantry attack that was designed to sweep up the coast and overrun the German submarine bases and airfields and airship installation across from England was not scheduled until the 25th (and did not actually take place until July 31 after a two week intense artillery bombardment in which over three million shells were spent; when it did, it took place in appalling weather with torrents of rain that turned the Flanders plain into

---

[1] The late A. Edward Ferko in his work, *Richthofen*, theorizes that the shot that creased von Richthofen's skull could not have come from a gun of one of the British observers (as the British would claim) because the range was too great (Ferko put it at some 300 meters). Since there was no anti-aircraft fire in the vicinity, shrapnel from a burst of flak is also discounted. Ferko believed it was almost certain that the shot had to come from the rear, from one of von Richthofen's own men accidentally or carelessly clearing his guns. Ferko quotes the *Rittmeister* as later recalling he had heard firing from the guns of the *Jasta 11* leader, Kurt Wolff. This is but one of the provocative conclusions reached in this highly recommended book.

[2] Wolff returned to his command on September 11, was promoted *Oberleutnant* on the 12th and killed on the 15th flying von Richthofen's triplane F.102/17 without ever adding to his score of 33 (von Richthofen was home on leave at the time). Wolff went down north of Wervicq in a combat with triplanes of No. 10 (Naval) Squadron, RNAS.

Above: Von Schoenebeck, a member of *Jasta 11* since early July 1917, was given the honor of carrying the *Ordenskissen* of his fallen leader, *Oberleutnant* Kurt Wolff. Wolff was killed in action on September 15, 1917. The funeral services for the "delicate little flower" as Wolff was called took place in St. Joseph's Church in Courtrai. Here the procession makes its way to the train station in Courtrai where Wolff's coffin would be shipped to his home in Memel for burial. Wolff had received the *Orden Pour le Mérite* on May 4, 1917 while a member of *Jasta 11*. He then was given the command of *Jasta 29* two days later but recalled to the leadership of *Jasta 11* on July 2 after the *Pour le Mérite* ace, *Leutnant* Karl Allmenröder, was shot down by ground fire as he crossed the lines at low level and killed on June 27.

Right: Prince Wilhelm of Hohenzollern reserved for himself the right to award his Honor Cross with Swords as "an act of grace made by My own free will." And that is just what he did not only in von Schoenebeck's case (see text for details) but also for the then *Oberleutnant zur See* Horst *Freiherr* Treusch von Buttlar-Brandenfels (seated with his Executive Officer, *Leutnant zur See* von Schiller). Von Buttlar had given Wilhelm's son, Crown Prince Friedrich, a joy ride in his airship, the LZ 25, and in appreciation, Wilhelm presented von Buttlar with the order in the 3rd Class with Swords on March 17, 1917. Von Schiller was given a framed portrait of the Prince which miffed him because he, too, would much rather have had a wearable award!

a quagmire which immediately stalled the drive). The aerial fighting had been violent on most days of the month with heavy losses on both sides. On the evening of July 27, one of the most unusual air battles of the war took place. During the course of it, von Schoenebeck was credited with his first victory and could take a measure of revenge for his victim was a Sopwith Triplane from No.10 (Naval) Squadron, RNAS, one of whose pilots had put Wolff out of action on the 11th. It was all part of an ingenious plan to lure the German fighters in the area into a gigantic trap. What happened was this.

Eight No.20 Squadron, RFC F.E.2d two-seaters set off for Menin to act as bait. When spotted by the Germans, they turned tail and made a fighting retreat back to Polygon Wood where 59 RFC and RNAS scouts were up high waiting to pounce on the 20 or so Albatros that had been lured on. As the melee began, other aircraft became involved including some French. The engagement lasted nearly an hour, from 8:45 p.m. to 9:40 p.m. German Time when the *Jasta* pilots broke off and headed home. Claims on both sides were exaggerated perhaps not surprisingly so in such a large and confused combat. Five crews of the No.20 Squadron F.E.s claimed two enemy in flames, four otherwise destroyed and three driven down out of control (No. 20 Squadron F.E. and later Bristol Fighter crews were regarded as quite notorious over-claimers). British naval triplane pilots put in for two destroyed, one shot down and two more out of controls. The S.E.5as of the famous No. 56 Squadron, RFC, who were also involved, claimed two destroyed and two others down out of control. The traceable German air losses in the area that day were actually much lighter. Three of their pilots were killed and two wounded but both of the wounded men got back all right. Another came down in flames in his own lines but, miraculously, escaped uninjured (he was the newly appointed and then six-victory leader of *Jasta 24* and later *Pour le Mérite* recipient, *Leutnant* Heinrich Kroll). Undoubtedly, many of these claims were overlapping as the pilots and gunners in the British formations fired on the same aircraft and genuinely believed that they were responsible for those that were seen to fall. The German claims were a bit more modest but equally flawed. They put in for 12 of which eight received official confirmation. Actually, the British lost only two aircraft in the evening battle, quite remarkable considering the scale of the action. One was an S.E.5a from 56 Squadron and the other Sopwith Triplane N.5492 that von Schoenebeck got. Its pilot, Flight Sub Lieutenant G. Roach who was killed, had just received the machine from No. 10 Squadron's leader, the then Flight Commander Raymond Collishaw. In N.5492, Collishaw had been credited with 18 enemy planes destroyed or shot down out of control. Collishaw himself was in N.533 that evening and put in for an Albatros D.V destroyed and a second one down out of control. These were chalked up as his 37th and 38th victories (out of an eventual total of 60).

The renewed British offensive in Flanders opened on July 31 in terrible weather. What air activity that could take place was marked on the German side mainly by small flights going out during the day searching under low cloud cover for enemy planes. Around 1:00 p.m. that afternoon, von Schoenebeck shot up an R.E.8 from No.9 Squadron, RFC over Frezenberg so badly that it had to make a forced landing within its own lines, both crew members escaping injury. That was good enough for *Idflieg* and von Schoenebeck had his second victory of the war. Other *Geschwader* pilots were credited with four more downed on the day including another R.E.8 by *Jasta 11* member *Leutnant* Karl Meyer just minutes before von Schoenebeck had latched on to his. Meyer's was A.4724 from No. 4 Squadron, RFC whose crew were not as fortunate. Both men were killed, caught while on a protection flight for their own infantry. All in all, it had been a day of relatively light aerial activity but von Richthofen's men had once again showed the way. The total score for the German Army Air Service on July 31 was just seven enemy planes, all in Flanders, and *JG 1* had accounted for five of them. For the next three days everything was grounded by rain and stormy weather. The same conditions persisted more or less into the following week and it was not until August 14 that *JG 1* could accomplish a great deal. On that day, its men got seven confirmed and one that went down in its own lines and was not confirmed. On the 16th, the Flanders offensive was renewed by the British with a second assault. By the end of the month it should have been clear that the original objectives would never be attained and the slaughter stopped. But Third Ypres dragged on until November 20 (the battle is also referred to as Passchendaele after the 150-foot German held ridge which was a dominating feature on the battlefield and which the Canadians finally took on November 6). The breakthrough to the Channel was never achieved and all Field Marshal Sir Douglas Haig had to show for his quarter million British and Dominion dead, wounded and missing was an advance of 9,000 yards into a wasteland.

Poor weather continued to hold things down until September 3 when *JG 1* had another of its big days. Men from all four *Jastas* as well as the Ringmaster himself chalked up 10 victories. One of these was given to von Schoenebeck. It was another triplane, this one from Naval 1. The combat took place at 10:00 a.m. with the Sopwith going down on the other side of the lines east of Hollebeke. A second triplane was credited to *Leutnant* Eberhard Stapenhorst, also of *Jasta 11*, this one at

Opposite
Two Views of Men of *Jagdgruppe 7* under the Command of *Leutnant* Emil Thuy *Orden Pour le Mérite*

Above: Left to right: *Lt.* Koch *Jasta 28*, *Lt.* Schroder *Jasta 28*, *Lt.* von Schoenebeck *Jasta 33*, *Lt.* Basse Unit? (with cigar), *Lt.* Thuy *Jasta 28*, *Lt.* Kühn *Jasta 33*, *Lt.* Ruckle *Jasta 33*, *Lt.* Sagebuhl *Jasta 28* and Hessian General Honor Decoration "for Bravery" recipient *Lt.* Christ *Jasta 28*.

Below: Left to right: *Lt.* Sagebuhl, *Lt.* Koch, *Lt.* von Schoenebeck, *Lt.* Braatsch *Jasta 28*, *Lt.* Thuy, *Lt.* Christ, *Lt.* Schroder, *Lt.* Kühn, *Lt.* Basse and *Lt.* Ruckle. Seated on the steps is *Lt.* Hames.

Jasta 28 was a Württemberg contingent with many of its members decorated by that kingdom. Thuy received its Military Merit and Friedrich Orders. Koch, the Adjutant of *Jasta 28*, also was awarded the Friedrich Order. Ruckle before being commissioned was given the Württemberg Silver Military Merit Medal as a pilot in *Jasta 33*.

Right and below: Leading *Jasta 33*, von Schoenebeck scored his fifth and sixth victories in late August 1918, being credited with Sopwith Camels on both occasions. His seventh came on September 2 but the type of aircraft he claimed has not been recorded. His eighth and last victory was scored in October but neither the date nor what the enemy plane might have been have been found. One of those was obviously this DeHavilland in front of which he is posing for posterity. He wears a "liberated" RFC/RAF belted and lined leather flying coat which was much favored by the German airmen whose own leather jackets and coats, judging from the wide variety seen in photographs, must have been privately purchased.

10:18 a.m. over Wytschaete, thus in the same area. In fact, it seems to be a case of both von Schoenebeck and Stapenhorst being involved with the same plane and apparently not realizing it. The Royal Naval Air Service lost only one triplane that day, N.5381 whose pilot was killed. No other triplane was shot up and forced to land which might have accounted for a second claim. And it is highly unlikely that two experienced pilots like von Schoenebeck and Stapenhorst would have confused, say, a Sopwith Pup or Camel for a *Dreidecker* with which they were by now quite familiar (Stapenhorst had joined *Jasta 11* on June 30, 1917 and already had one confirmed victory prior to September 3). It therefore appears that both men claimed and were credited with the same aircraft. Overclaiming has become a much debated topic in recent years with many brickbats being thrown back and forth as to whom were the worst offenders. That onus often falls on the British and the Americans more than the other participants but the problem, as this example would seem to indicate, existed on both sides. Air historian Alex Revell has an explanation. He argues that the condition came about simply because the pilots in many cases didn't know what the true facts of a combat were. In these instances, they were not able to evaluate their claims correctly. He goes on, "if an RFC/RAF pilot claimed an out of control and it was erroneously allowed, this was not because he was a liar, or indicative of some dastardly plot by higher authority, but because of lack of information."

And with that, his third victory, von Schoenebeck's scoring was over for 1917 and his name virtually disappears from the War Diary of *JG 1*. But not so when it came to other recognition for what he had already accomplished as a fighter pilot. In addition to his now holding both Iron Crosses, his Princely Hohenzollern Honor Cross 3rd Class with Swords was approved on October 12. This was followed by an award from Baden for this former member of its 109th Grenadiers. On November 27, von Schoenebeck was given the Knight 2nd Class with Swords of the Zähringen Lion Order. In other respects, the remainder of 1917 was uneventful and it was not until January of the following year that something of note can be recorded.

On January 25, 1918, von Schoenebeck found himself posted out of *Jasta 11* and headed for a new start-up fighter unit, *Jasta 59*. With him from *Jasta 11* went *Oberleutnant* Hans-Helmut von Boddien who was to assume command. Von Boddien had been with *JG 1* since its inception, partly as a pilot and partly as an administrative officer. He came to his new job with no victories but seniority and a steady hand counted heavily in making such appointments. Nonetheless, it must have been hard for both men to leave an elite unit like *JG 1* led by the charismatic von Richthofen with its battle tested veterans for a group of novice pilots and a *Staffel* that had yet to see combat. Von Boddien, of course, had the comfort of knowing he was going on to larger responsibilities (where he would do well, scoring five victories until September 27 when he was wounded in action and had to be relieved). For von Schoenebeck, his only consolation was that he had fell victim to the well established practice of salting new *Jastas* with experienced men so at least he was being looked upon as an old hand. In his nearly six months with *Jasta 59*, von Schoenebeck, however, was able to add only one more victory, a Camel credited to him on May 9. That notwithstanding, when it came time to find a replacement for a *Staffelführer* whose time was up, von Schoenebeck was tapped for the job.

Oberleutnant Heinrich Lorenz had been commanding *Jasta 33* since its inception in March 1917 and there in the first few months had been credited with four British planes downed to add to one victory scored in June 1916 as a pilot in *Kagohl 1*. On June 15, 1917, he was wounded and out of action for a month. It had been a full year since his return during which time he was unable to score again. The overriding factor, though, was that he was due, perhaps overdue, for a rest. Von Schoenebeck took over on July 11 and proved to be a competent enough leader. He doubled his personal score to eight and the other men under his command, as best as can be reconstructed from available records, got an additional 21 victories in those four remaining months, possibly one or two more. And this came at a cost of only two men killed and one wounded. It must be borne in mind, too, that as one of the "lesser" *Jastas, 33* in the last few months of the war was probably hampered by the shortages of fuel and other materiel that either totally grounded such units from time to time or restricted the number of hours they could be in the air in order that precious supplies could be allotted to the flights of the more elite *Jagdgeschwadern*. And yet, there was one star in *Jasta 33* at this time who certainly wasn't affected by these restrictions and had it not been for this one individual, *Jasta 33*'s record would have been much the poorer. He was *Vizefeldwebel* Emil Schäpe.

Schäpe alone scored 14 of *Jasta 33*'s overall total of 25 victories under von Schoenebeck leadership (which gave him a total of 18 for the war). Had it not been that all but one of these 14 came in October making it too late, perhaps, for the approval of an awards recommendation to make it through channels, Schäpe could well have been one of the last air awards recipients of the Golden Military Merit Cross. At least one award did not elude von Schoenebeck. He was recognized with the Knight's Cross with Swords of the Royal House Order of Hohenzollern although the exact date has not been found (it was not recorded in the *Militär-Wochenblatt* so it probably was a very late 1918 awards which in the breakdown of record keeping in the war's final weeks, failed to be published). That made him not only the one known fighter pilot recipient of the Princely Hohenzollern Honor Cross but also the only known fighter pilot of the war to hold both the Princely and the Royal House Orders. And had it not been that bit of mechanical trouble while flying over the principality, he would never have been able to claim that distinction.

OBERLEUTNANT HEINZ-HELLMUTH VON WÜHLISCH

The von Wühlisch family was well represented in *Husaren-Regiment Fürst Blucher von Wahlstat (Pommersches) Nr.5.* when Germany declared war on Russia on August 1, 1914. Georg and Bruno were *Oberleutnante* and Heinz-Hellmuth was a *Leutnant* having been commissioned in the regiment in August of 1913. Later, August, four and one-half years younger than his brother, Heinz-Hellmuth, would join the 5th Hussars too. All four would survive the war but August, nominally assigned to *Idflieg* after service in the *Fliegertruppe*, would die of natural causes on November 24, 1918. Heinz-Hellmuth would also become an airman but at the outbreak of war, that lay in the future. First there was a ground war to fight.

Russian troops crossed the border into East Prussia on August 2 having mobilized much faster than the Great German General Staff had anticipated and the threat had to be met. The 5th Hussars were the cavalry support for the 36th Division which together with its sister division, the 35th, formed the 17th Army Corps (Danzig). Immediately, they were deployed in East Prussia and there, on August 12, Heinz-Hellmuth was wounded. He celebrated his 22nd birthday in hospital and when released on October 15, he was assigned to the staff of his old regiment. And there, on October 30, he had his first war decoration, the Iron Cross 2nd Class. He continued staff duties with the 36th Division until March 19, 1915 when he effected a transfer to aviation and the next day began observer courses first at *Flieger-Ersatz-Abteilung 4* at Posen and then at *FEA 1* then at Adlershof near Berlin. On May 8, 1915, von Wühlisch was assigned to *Feldflieger-Abteilung 62* on the Western Front. It had just been formed on April 23 and was under the command of *Hauptmann* Hermann Kastner. Among the other comrades he met there were two pilots, one already well seasoned and the other just getting started. Both were destined for great fame. They were Oswald Boelcke and Max Immelmann.

Both Boelcke and Immelmann had arrived at *62* the month before von Wühlisch and were taking up their observers in unarmed LVGs facing French aircraft that did carry machine guns. The day of the German C-Type two-seaters with factory installed armament was just over the horizon at this time. So innovation was the order of the day. The unit's fastest LVG was rigged with an appropriated French machine gun and Boelcke, as *62*'s senior pilot with more than seven months of frontline experience behind him, took it over. Similarly, when the first armed C-Type did arrive at *62*, it went to Boelcke and Immelmann got Boelcke's old ship. Boelcke and von Wühlisch made their first flight in the new machine on June 15. In it, they had an inconclusive brush with an enemy plane that day. The following day, the pair had no less than three engagements with French aircraft. In each of these, their adversary broke off and spiraled down, whether critically hurt or not could not be ascertained. No claims were put in. Immelmann, too, was now regularly engaging the enemy in air combats and the question was, who would score first? In the middle of this, the Dutch aircraft designer in German employ, Anthony Fokker, a crack pilot himself, arrived on *62*'s field to demonstrate his new *Eindecker* with its synchronized forward-firing machine gun. The prospects of real air fighting with the little bird caused great excitement among the pilots. One was assigned to *62* and once again, Boelcke's seniority gave him the edge over the others. He took it up for the first time on June 24. Meantime, however, he was still expected to go on operational missions piloting a two-seater.

Boelcke was up on just such a flight on July 4 with von Wühlisch in the back seat of LVG C.I 162/15. As they cruised along, a French Parasol two-seater flew over them. Boelcke followed in pursuit and caught up with it. The combat lasted some 20 or 25 minutes with Boelcke adroitly maneuvering to allow von Wühlisch to bring his gun into play. In all, von Wühlisch got off 83 rounds, the last of which at last took effect. The Parasol first went into a glide, then nosed over into a steep dive and crashed in a wood in German held territory. Not chancing that something might rob them of a precious first victory, Boelcke landed their plane in a nearby meadow and the two men walked to the crash site. A large crowd had already gathered. Both the French occupants were dead and their corpses showed signs of multiple bullet wounds. That very same day, von Wühlisch's deadly marksmanship was rewarded with an Iron Cross 1st Class. Boelcke had to settle for a mere commendation and his comrades' congratulations since he had possessed his 1st Class Cross before coming to *62*. After this episode, Boelcke took to flying the *Eindecker* exclusively as did Immelmann when a second ship arrived. Boelcke (and von

Oberleutnant Heinz-Hellmuth von Wühlisch was awarded the Princely Hohenzollern Honor Cross 3rd Class with Swords on April 16, 1918 long after his flying days were over and because he was then on the staff of the XIV Army Corps. One of its components was the Hohenzollern Regiment, the 40th Fusiliers and this connection made him eligible for the Principality's house order.

Above: Von Wühlisch's first frontline aviation assignment was to *Feldflieger-Abteilung 62* which he joined on May 8, 1915. Already there were two soon-to-be-famous pilots, Oswald Boelcke and Max Immelmann. Taking a bead during machine gun practice at *62* is *Hauptmann* Ritter. Waiting their turn, left to right, are von Wühlisch, Boelcke, Porr, von Teubern and Immelmann, all *Leutnante* at the time. The other man has not been identified.

Left: Von Wühlisch was Boelcke's observer when they scored their first victory on July 4, 1915. He was then wounded on August 31 and never returned to *62*. But in this 1916 photograph, monocle in eye, he is reunited with his former pilot and Boelcke can be seen wearing the *Pour le Mérite* that he received along with Immelmann on January 12, 1916, the first such air awards.

Wühlisch) had the honor of scoring *62s* first unit victory but Immelmann beat Boelcke in being the first man in the *Abteilung* to score with the Fokker fighter. He shot down a British B.E.2c on August 1 and this, his first victory, also earned him the Iron Cross 1st Class. Boelcke did not bring down an enemy plane with his Fokker until August 19 and thereafter, a scoring contest between the two ensued with first one man going ahead and then the other pulling even and going ahead in his turn (this race, which culminated with Boelcke and Immelmann receiving the Knight's Hohenzollern with Swords in November and the *Orden Pour le Mérite* the following January, is described in Volume III in this series). For years, it was assumed this scoring contest between the two men was conducted on friendly grounds but recent correspondence by Boelcke which has surfaced shows clearly that quite the opposite was true. Boelcke had little regard for Immelmann as a person or for that matter, for his flying abilities (some traits of Immelmann's character as described by a comrade of his in *62* appeared in the Errata and Addenda chapter of Volume VI in this series). Von Wühlisch himself wasn't around to view much of this rivalry. On August 31, he was wounded in the left thigh during an aerial combat and had to be.

Von Wühlisch was released from hospital on September 26, 1915 but was not returned to his old outfit. Instead, he spent a long 13 months at *Flieger-Ersatz-Abteilung 5* in Hanover qualifying as a pilot and in view of his length of time there and subsequent assignment, one would suspect that he also was held there as an instructor. As his work there was nearing its end, von Wühlisch was promoted *Oberleutnant* on October 5, 1916. At the end of that month, he was transferred to *Versuchs- und Übungsflugpark Ost* (Testing and Training Aviation Depot East) where he spent another stretch of eight months. It was, therefore, not until the 1st of July 1917 that he found himself back at the front, now with *Flieger-Abteilung 32*, the former *Feldflieger-Abteilung 64*. Despite his rank, he flew as just a regular pilot with the unit but bigger things were about to come. On December 10, he was named the leader of *Schutzstaffel 10*. On the surface, it looked as though his timing could not have been better. The *Schustas* were in the process of being relieved of their protection duties for two-seaters on reconnaissance and artillery cooperation work and were being converted into ground attack infantry cooperation formations equipped with fast light CL-Type Halberstadt and Hannover aircraft which were to play an important role in the coming German 1918 offensives. Even their name was to change so as to better describe the job they were expected to perform. They would become *Schlachtstaffeln* – Attack Sections or Flights. And then, abruptly, von Wühlisch was relieved of his command on January 23 of the new year and ordered to *Armee-Flug-Park 2* and an organization called *Generalkommando Busigny*. To be removed from a frontline unit after only six weeks in charge and on the eve of a battle that might win the war has to have a better explanation than we are able to offer here but there may be a clue.

On March 12, 1918 and while still with the Busigny Army Corps Headquarters, von Wühlisch received the Prussian Life Saving Medal, a relatively rare award during the war (the *Militär-Wochenblatt* records 747 of them between 1914 and 1918). Its actual approval date would have been something on the order of six to 12 weeks after the event itself. Thus whatever von Wühlisch did to earn the decoration could well have come while he was the head of *Schusta/Schlasta 10*. And if he himself had somehow been injured in a rescue attempt, that might account for his otherwise sudden departure from its command and transfer to staff duties. Whatever the explanation, it was staff work for him for the rest of the war. On April 1, he joined the staff of the XIV Army Corps. Readers may recall that the Hohenzollern regiment, the 40th Fuseliers, was one of the four regiments comprising the 28th Division of that corps. That final assignment of his apparently was deemed sufficient to qualify under the requirements and, accordingly, von Wühlisch was awarded the Princely Hohenzollern Honor Cross 3rd Class with Swords on April 16.

PRINCELY HOHENZOLLERN HONOR CROSS RECIPIENTS WITHOUT BIOGRAPHIES

Above: Inspection time at *Feldflieger-Abteilung 20* early in the war. The second known aviation recipient of the Princely Hohenzollern Honor Cross 3rd Class with Swords was *Hptm.* Erwin Barends who earned it on April 16, 1915 for service with the unit. The stout officer in the greatcoat may be *Generallt.* Walter von Eberhardt, first Inspector of the German Army Air Service. Wooden steps await their viewing of this Aviatik B-Type with its early national markings on the wings.

Below: The second aviation recipient of the Princely Honor Cross was *Oblt.* Heinz von Pflugk-Hartung (sometimes spelled Pflugh-Hartung), 2nd from the left, here shown in *Kasta 39* of *Kagohl 7* with Albatros C.III 761/16. His came on June 30, 1915 for service in *Feldflieger-Abteilung 12*. On his right is *Lt.* Gerhard Bassenge, the later seven victory ace of *Jasta Boelcke*. On his left in flight togs are *Lt.* Rossteucher and *Gefr.* Beese at the ready on the Artemps airfield in 1916.

Patriotic post cards of the day again provide photographs of two of the aviation recipients of the Princely Hohenzollern Honor Cross 3rd Class with Swords, *Oblt*. Lothar Baas (July 1, 1916 in *FEA 2*) and *Lt*. Gustav Salffner (August 25, 1917 in *Fl.Abt. (A)223*). Above: Six men proudly display their new Iron Crosses 2nd Class in *FFl.Abt. 26*. Left to right, *Oblt*. Saenger, Baas, *Oblt*. Hahn, *Oblt*. Ingold, *Lt*. Hug, *Oblt*. Bremer (who already wears the ribbon to his Iron Cross 2nd Class in the buttonhole) and *Vzfw*. Reichert. Baas also won Baden's Zähringen Lion Order in *FFl.Abt. 26* as did Wolfgang Saenger. And what is Reichert doing with a Luger? Below: Salffner (extreme left in first row) is in distinguished company when he was with *FFl.Abt. 62* in 1916. On his left, Meding, Osterreicher, Boelcke, Hermann Kastner CO, Immelmann, von Krause and Hess. Back row left to right, von Mulzer, Fromme, von Cossel (see Waldeck Merit Cross chapter for his biography), Schilling and von Gusnar. As well as Boelcke and Immelmann, Hess and von Mulzer went on to become highly decorated fighter pilots (see Volumes IV and I in this series).

Above: *Hptm.* Leo Leonhardy, leader of *Bogohl 6* in the light *Litewka* with glasses and a garland of flowers on his balding head, visits officers of his *Bosta 9* at Ourq in 1918. He would be the last of the five bomber squadron commanders to be awarded a *Pour le Mérite* when he received it on October 2 that year. Surely, Hohenzollern Honor Cross winner *Lt.* Otto Keller (on May 22, 1918 in *Bosta 9*) is present here, possibly the man on the floor second from the right clasping his knees.

Right: *Oblt.* (Herbert?) von Prittwitz und Graffron, marked '1', got his Honor Cross on August 21, 1918 as a staff officer with Army Group Eichorn-Kiev. Earlier service in *FFl.Abt. 42* had earned him the Saxon Albert Order Knight 2nd Class with Swords in 1915. Far right: Splendidly turned out in his Saxon Guard Heavy Cavalry Regimental tunic, *Lt.* Joachim Albrecht *Graf* von Rothenburg was the last known aviation recipient of the Honor Cross, awarded in 1919 but made retroactive to October 29, 1918. He wears his cross in the buttonhole. He, too, was a holder of the Albert Order Knight 2nd with Swords.

CHAPTER XI

THE MILITARY AWARDS OF THE PRINCIPALITY OF HOHENZOLLERN

THE PRINCELY HOHENZOLLERN MERIT CROSSES, GOLD HONOR MEDAL AND SILVER MERIT MEDAL

As previously mentioned, when the Princely Hohenzollern Honor Cross was founded on December 5, 1841, a Gold Honor Medal (with Crown) and a Silver Merit Medal (without Crown) were also created as decorations associated with the house order. Then in 1842, the coinage was changed slightly and the crown was removed from the Gold Honor Medal. Another affiliated decoration was established in 1910 with the introduction of a Merit Cross which could be awarded in Gold and in Silver. The Merit Cross ranked between the Honor Cross 3rd Class and the Gold Honor Medal. With the addition of swords to insignia, these were placed in the so-called "on-Ring" position for the Gold Honor Medal and the Silver Merit Medal and in the conventional position between the arms of the badges of the two Merit Crosses.

At the time of World War I, the Gold Honor Medal and Silver Merit Medal had the crowned Hohenzollern shield in the center of the obverse medallion surrounded by the house order's motto which in turn was encircled by a wreath of laurel and oak. The reverse carried the crowned monogram *W* (for Wilhelm) with the dated inscription *DEN 1T Januar 1842* in place of the motto. These elements were again surrounded by the wreaths. The Merit Crosses were virtually identical to the Honor Cross 3rd Class except that there was no enameling on the center medallion and the ring surrounding it. Also, on the reverse, the crowned monogram was, again, *W* and the dated inscription was *DEN 1 TEN JANUAR 1910*. The ribbons for all these decorations, both swords and non-swords awards, were the same as the one for the house order.

Table 10-1 on page 210 gave the numbers of awards for the Gold Merit Cross with Swords (1), the Silver Merit Cross with Swords (80) and the Gold Honor Medal with Swords (640 during the years 1914 through 1920). Time did not permit a similar tabulation for wartime awards of the Silver Merit Medal with Swords but the Link-Gauggel study showed a total of 5,875 awarded during the reign of Prince Wilhelm, that is in the years 1905 through 1927. The one Gold Merit Cross with Swords went to a Nikolaus Rank who was Privy Chancellery Secretary at the Adjutancy of his Majesty the King of Bavaria. Another such award was entered for a Senior Paymaster Heinrich Hohl of the 40th Fuseliers dated January 26, 1918 and then the entry was deleted for reasons unknown (the cross to Rank carried no date).

As with all the Hohenzollern insignia, an example of the Gold Merit Cross with Swords was sent to the Hindenburg Museum in Posen presumably for a display. There were no aviation recipients of the Silver Merit Cross with Swords and the roll shows only seven awards of the Gold Honor Medal with Swords to men who served in the *Fliegertruppe*, one of these to an infantryman who later transferred to the air service. Of the remaining six, three of the recipients were anything but fliers. Two held the rank of *Schirrmeister* (Head Ostler or Stableman) and the other was an acting paymaster (see Appendix XXIII).

Only 16 aviation recipients of the Silver Merit Medal with Swords have been identified. Had it been possible to study the roll, we would certainly have many more (see Appendix XXIV). The only name on these lists that the reader schooled in World War I aviation is likely to recognize is that of *Vizefeldwebel* Fritz Beckhardt who in addition to the Princely Hohenzollern Silver Merit Medal with Swords and both Iron Crosses held the Hessian Warriors', Honor Decoration in Iron and its General Honor Decoration "for Bravery." He has achieved a measure of notice primarily because in a home defense unit he flew a fighter with a swastika on each side of its fuselage and he himself was a Jew. It was then, of course, an ancient symbol of good luck and appeared in its original form and not the "flopped" style adopted by the Nazi party and then used during the 3rd *Reich* as Germany's national symbol. In Beckhardt's days, it had none of the sinister connotations it would later acquire.

Gold and Silver Princely Hohenzollern Merit Crosses were established in 1910 (obverse left, reverse right). For World War I, only one Gold with Swords and 80 Silver with Swords were awarded with none going to a man serving in the *Fliegertruppe*.

The Gold Honor Medal and Silver Merit Medal date back to the house order's founding on December 5, 1841. With Swords, the Gold was awarded 640 times for World War I and the figure for the Silver with Swords was well over 5,000. Only seven Gold to men who served in the *Fliegertruppe* are known and only 16 Silver recipients have been found. Again, obverse left, reverse right.

Right: Hohenzollern born *Vzfw*. Karl Kaeppeler received the Gold Honor Medal with Swords on August 8, 1917 for his service in Württemberg *Fl.Abt. (A)252*. Six days earlier, the kingdom had decorated him with its Gold Military Merit Medal. Transferred to *Fl.Abt. 300 "Pascha"* in Palestine, he was killed at Djenin near Jerusalem in unknown circumstances on May 8, 1918.

Below: *Vzfw*. Andreas Emele was a Silver Merit Medal with Swords recipient. He joined *Jasta 80b* on August 23, 1918 fresh out of flight school and got his Pilot's Badge on September 20. With no victories to his credit, Emele was killed in an air battle on October 28.

Below right: *Gefr*. Johann Kohle also earned the Silver Merit Medal with Swords and was obviously suited up as a flier at some point. He was killed in France on April 21, 1917 but his name does not appear on any *Fliegertruppe* casualty list nor has anything been discovered about his service in it.

Right: *Offz.-Stv.* Willy Westphal was a flight leader in *Schlasta 20* when he was decorated with the Golden Military Merit Cross on August 7, 1918. He joined the *Fliegertruppe* from the infantry in August 1916 and a man with the same rank, first and last names received the Gold Honor Medal with Swords in a *Jäger* battalion on December 4, 1916 for previous service there. It is possible that they were one and the same. The Westphal in *Schlasta 20* was credited with four victories during the war. Above, the men of the unit with Westphal in the center displaying their lethal "wares." In the background is one of their Hannover CL.IIs or IIIs and typical of one of these attack flights, all the pilots and gunners were enlisted personnel.

Opposite
Top: Poor quality mars this photograph of *Vzfw.* Fritz Beckhardt in his SSW D.III towards the end of his service in *Kest 2* in 1918. Beckhardt, a Jew, chose the swastika as his personal marking. It was an old good luck symbol and only later was it corrupted by the *Nazis*. For a man with only one confirmed victory, he was highly decorated. In addition to his Silver Hohenzollern Merit Medal with Swords and both Iron Crosses, he earned two awards from Hesse, its exclusive Warrior's Honor Decoration in Iron and General Honor Decoration "for Bravery." It has been reported that he downed two Breguet bombers in September 1918 while flying with *Kest 5* but the source of this information and whether the victories can be substantiated are not known.

Below: Beckhardt, second from the left in the back row and newly arrived at *Jasta 26* from *Schusta 11*, joins others in celebrating Bruno Loerzer's *Pour le Mérite* awarded on February 12, 1918. Loerzer was about to take command of the just-formed *Jagdgeschwader III*. In the front row, left to right: Karl Bolle (*Pour le Mérite* to come), unknown, Loerzer, "Papa" von Richthofen, Heinrich Bongartz, Hellmuth Wilberg and Otto Fruhner (Golden Military Merit Cross to come). Second row: Fritz Loerzer (4th from the left), Helmuth Dilthey (5th from the left) and at the extreme right, Otto Esswein (Golden Military Merit Cross to come).

CHAPTER XII

THE PRINCELY HOUSE OF LIPPE

The Principality of Lippe derived its name from a castle near Lippstadt, a town about 40 miles east of present day Dortmund, where the founder of the family named Bernhard was Lord of the manor in the early 12th century. After his death but within the same century, a descendant of his acquired Detmold and others who followed added the lands of Schwalenburg, Biesterfeld, Weissenfeld and Sternberg in the 14th and early 15th centuries. In 1528, the then-ruler, Simon V, assumed the title of Count and this was confirmed by the Empire the following year. His successor, Count Simon VI, died in 1613 and his territories were divided among his four sons. The eldest, who became Simon VII (the principle of primogeniture was established in 1368), took Detmold, Otto received Brake, Hermann was given Schwalenberg and the youngest, Philipp, inherited Alverdissen, Lipperode and Uhlenburg. Philipp would become the ancestor of the line that took the name Schaumburg-Lippe (see the chapter on that Princely House). Upon the death of Simon VII, still another division of the properties took place between his two sons with Hermann Adolf continuing the line of Detmold and Idocus Hermann taking over Biesterfeld and Weissenfeld where he became the ancestor of those lines. In Detmold, Count Friedrich Adolf was raised to the dignity of Prince of the Empire in October 1720 and through his descendants we come to Prince Leopold III of Lippe who ruled from 1851 to 1875. Leopold was married the year after he ascended the throne to the only daughter of Prince Albert of Schwarzburg-Rudolstadt but the union was childless. As a result, Leopold was succeeded by his brother, Woldemar. When it became obvious that Woldemar, too, would die childless even though married, this created a huge succession problem and for the following chronology of events that would even have an effect on the house order of Schaumburg-Lippe, we are indebted to the scholarly research of Eric C. Ludvigsen of Arnold, Maryland.

Next in line for the throne upon Woldemar's passing would be Prince Alexander who was the younger brother of both Leopold and Woldemar. The problem was that it was evident that Alexander would never produce children either. In polite circles, he was described as *Geisterkrank* ("of unsound mind"). The truth was that he was homosexual. Should the line die out, as it clearly would under Alexander, the strongest claim to the succession appeared to belong to the ruling family of Schaumburg-Lippe. There was a potential bid by the cadet line of the Counts of Lippe-Biesterfeld but they had not ruled anywhere since 1762 when they sold their postage-stamp patrimony to the other branches of the house. The government in Lippe doubted the validity of the Biesterfeld claim but did not speak against it publicly. Instead, in 1890, the government proposed a new regency law to the *Landtag* (Provincial Assembly). The house law of 1667 provided for regencies only for a minor prince and the proposal was drafted in such a way that it would almost surely result in the appointment of a regent from the Schaumburg-Lippe family. The legislature rejected that narrow option so that the matter was still unresolved when Woldemar died on March 20, 1895. Alexander was now nominally reigning Prince but needed a regent. It was now discovered that on October 15, 1890 following the failure of the legislative proposal, Woldemar had decreed that the regent should be Prince Adolph of Schaumburg-Lippe, youngest brother of the reigning Prince Georg II.

Adolph assumed the regency on March 20, 1895 but the *Landtag* and the Biesterfelds vigorously disputed the right of the late Woldemar to have made the choice without reference to the legislature. The problem with Adolph was that he was

Prince Woldemar of Lippe-Detmold ruled from 1875 until his death in 1895. When it became clear that he would die without issue, a huge succession problem developed with the houses of Lippe-Biesterfeld and Schaumburg-Lippe vying for the right of ultimate succession (see the text as to why this came about and its outcome). Here Woldemar wears the Lippe Honor Cross 1st Class with Swords at the neck and the Breast Star that was at the time reserved only for the reigning princes of both houses. The term "Grand Cross" did not come into use until 1911.

The succession was ultimately decided in favor of the Biesterfeld line and the Count of Biesterfeld assumed the throne in 1905 and ruled through World War I as Leopold IV. He wears the Honor Cross Grand Cross badge from the sash and its Breast Star is the uppermost of the three. He also wears the Grand Cross badge at the neck which was a prerogative of the princes of the house. The collar and badge is that of the Lippe Order of Leopold which he founded in 1906 as a merit award in commemoration of the first year of his reign as Prince of Lippe.

the *Kaiser*'s brother-in-law having married Wilhelm's sister, Viktoria. The *Landtag* did not wish to see all the strings being pulled from Berlin as had happened with the Prussian-dominated regencies in Brunswick. The *Landtag*'s majority opposition put them squarely behind the Biesterfeld claim. In a series of agreements that involved the *Bundesrat* (Federal Council), Adolph agreed to vacate the regency in favor of the Biesterfeld branch against a promise that the matter would ultimately be decided by the *Reichsgericht* (Federal Supreme Court). Count Ernst, the senior member of the Biesterfeld family formally entered Detmold on July 10, 1897. He had the ill-grace to mark the occasion by issuing a commemorative medal which didn't endear himself or his regency to the Schaumburg-Lippe people.

Ernst died on September 26, 1904 and was succeeded as regent by his son, Prince Leopold. Prince Alexander of Lippe died on October 25, 1905 and coincident with that and after legal proceedings that went on for years, the Supreme Court legitimized the Biesterfeld claim to the throne and Leopold became Sovereign Ruling Prince of Lippe in his own right, adopting the title Leopold IV and ruled until his abdication on November 12, 1918. So in Bückeburg, the capital city of

Schaumburg-Lippe, what had looked like a sure thing that would have led to the unification of the two principalities under Schaumburg-Lippe dominance had turned to ashes in a startling reversal. Adolf II, the last reigning prince of Schaumburg-Lippe (1911-1918), was a teenager while the squabble was going on (he was born on February 23, 1883) and as an impressionable young man, would probably have felt the loss more keenly than anyone and perhaps took on an obligation to perpetuate a blood feud. Whatever the case, he couldn't abide his cousin in Detmold and one manifestation of that occurred in 1911, the year he ascended the throne. Although there had been a division of the house order between the two principalities in 1890 with a minor alteration in the insignia to differentiate one from the other, this was done by mutual agreement and before the difficulties described above had arisen. Now Adolf went one step further. The center medallion of both house orders displayed the red rose of Lippe on a white enamel background. To show his independence or spite, or both, Adolf changed the white enamel background on the medallion to red for his insignia. That may sound trivial to us but such things were considered significant in those days.

In World War I, the principalities fielded two units, an infantry regiment based in Lippe and a fusilier, or rifle, battalion based in Schaumburg-Lippe. The former was *Infanterie-Regiment Graf Bülow von Dennewitz (6. Westfälisches) Nr.55.* whose staff and 3rd Battalion were located in Detmold with the 1st Battalion quartered in Hörter and the 2nd in Bielefeld. The 3rd Battalion's *Chef* was *Generalmajor Fürst* Leopold of Lippe-Detmold. Attached *à la suite* to the same battalion were three princes of Lippe, two with the rank of *Hauptmann*, Bernhard and Julius Ernst, and *Leutnant* Ernst, the Crown Prince of Lippe. The rifle battalion was *Westfälisches Jäger-Bataillon Nr.7*. It had no royal as its *Chef* but could boast a whole slew of princes of Schaumburg-Lippe including *General der Kavallerie* Adolf, the *Kaiser*'s brother-in-law mentioned earlier, *Oberst* Hermann, *Hauptmann* Moritz, *Oberleutnant* Ernst Wolrad and the *Leutnante* Stephan and Heinrich as *à la suite*.

The 55th Infantry Regiment could trace its origins to a Lippe infantry battalion created in 1807 during Napoleon's regime. In 1808, two companies fought with the French in Spain and only a handful of survivors returned. The following year, six companies were engaged in the campaigns in Austria and in the Tyrol. The entire battalion was moved to Spain in 1810/1811 and of its total strength of about 1,000 men, only 60 ever made it back home. Reconstituted in 1812 from two old and four new companies, the battalion joined the Prussian army in the occupation of Danzig and Kovel, returning to Danzig in late 1813. About 800 officers and men served in the siege of Mainz in 1814 and then fought in the "Hundred-Day War" against Napoleon in 1815 as part of the Lippe Waldeck Regiment (the name came from the time the deposed French Emperor arrived in Paris on March 20 to June 28 when Louis XVIII was restored to the throne for the second time following Napoleon's defeat at the Battle of Waterloo). In 1849 in the war against Denmark, the battalion was entrenched for three months near Düppeln and in 1866 with a complement of some 1,000 men again, it became part of the Prussian Main Army. In that campaign against Austria and its allies, the battalion lost its commander and an additional 13 men killed and 32 wounded.

On October 1, 1867, three officers and 254 men transferred to the Prussian Army itself as the 3rd Battalion of the 6th Westphalian Infantry Regiment No. 55. The soldiers wore the cockades of Lippe-Detmold and Schaumburg-Lippe according to their place of recruitment. The battalion participated in the Franco-Prussian War of 1870 as part of the 13th Infantry Division of the 7th Corps of the 1st Army. In the battle at Colombey east of Metz on August 14, 1870, the regiment had 145 men killed, about 5% of its strength. The regiment moved to the south of Paris around Auxerre after the siege and capitulation of the fortress of Metz. There it became part of the *Sudarmee* in January 1871. It saw some lively action near Vorges south of Besançon on January 26 in the course of pursuing the retreating French and at the time of the armistice two days later, it had moved through Salins and was on the march to Pontarlier. Thereafter, with the 7th Corps, the regiment occupied pleasant billets around Dijon where it was said that the men enjoyed the "pleasures" of the northern Côte-d'Or in the heart of Burgundy. During the entire war, the regiment's dead in combat amounted to about 6% of its effectives but, actually, illness was the greater menace (mostly typhoid fever in all likelihood). No figure on non-combat fatalities is available but during the siege of Metz in late 1870 for example, every third man was down sick.

Upon mobilization in 1914, the 55th Infantry Regiment was paired with the 2nd Westphalian (*Infanterie-Regiment Prinz Friedrich der Niederlande Nr.15.*) to form the 26th Infantry Brigade of the 13th Infantry Division, VII Army Corps. The 55th was in the sweep into Belgium in early August as part of von Bülow's 2nd Army. The fortified city of Liege was taken on August 7 and with it, the first two *Pour le Mérites* of World War I were earned. The first, on August 7, went to the Corps commander, *General der Infanterie* Otto von Emmich. The other, on the next day, went to the then *Generalmajor* Erich Ludendorff who had actually bluffed the Belgian commander into surrendering the city. Thereafter, the regiment fought on, entering French soil on August 25. It then participated in the ill-fated Battle of the Marne after which it settled into positions north of Reims. At the beginning of October, the 55th was moved to Artois where it stayed until March 1916. But its time there was not without event. In 1915, there were two hard fought battles there, that of Neuve Chapelle which began on March 10 and Festubert in May. Casualties were heavy among all the regiments of the division with those of one of the 55th's sister regiments in the division's other brigade, the 25th, in the Battle of Neuve Chapelle probably being all too typical. It had 21 officers and 1,031 non commissioned officers and men killed, wounded and missing in that two day engagement. The 55th was finally sent to rest and refit in the Cambrai area at the end of March 1916 before being thrown into what was called the cauldron of Verdun in early June. There it held the line in the Hill 304 sector where violent German attacks had been going on since the previous month and which continued in June until they were finally repulsed by the French. The regiment was then shifted to the other slug match that was going on along the Somme, arriving there in September. After one week, its losses were so heavy that it had to be relieved on September 19. By October, it was returned to the Hill 304 sector, there to remain until mid-May 1917.

The year 1917 was another one of trial for the men of the 13th Division. It launched important attacks along the Chemin des Dames on July 31 and again on August 2-3 but each time it was unable to retain the ground that was won. Losses among the 55th are not known but two of the division's other regiments, the 13th and 15th, each lost some 600 men. Immediately after the failed second attack, the division again had to be relieved over the night of August 3-4. It was back along the Chemin des Dames by October 11 replenished now not with Westfalians but replacements from the recruit depots of neighboring divisions. They were just in time to bear the brunt of the artillery preparations preceding the big French attack in that area that kicked off on October 23 and from the assault itself. Just in prisoners, the division lost 47 officers and 1,548 men. Two regimental commanders were among those captured and a third was killed (unfortunately, it is not known if any of them were the 55th's Commanding Officer). And once again, the division had to be reorganized. It was described as "exhausted" and "used up." Along the Chemin des Dames, in fact, it had not displayed its old form at all. Despite under strict orders not to cede ground but to hold positions at all costs, it had put up little resistance and as the figures indicate, large groups surrendered *en masse* together with their officers. After the pounding it took that October in what came to be called the Battle of La Malmaison, the Lippe regiment was considered to be of only mediocre worth. The 55th as well as the other then remaining two regiments in the division, the 13th and 15th (the 158th had been transferred in March 1915 to the 50th Division, a new formation, and never replaced thus consolidating the division into just a single brigade), scraped the barrel of Germany's manpower bowl for the necessary replacements. It received 1,000 men who were of 35 years of age or older and who had been serving on the Eastern Front. Earlier, the few Westfalians who could be brought in were mostly older men too coming from *Landsturm* battalions in the home area.

In the "Great Battle of France" in March 1918, however, the division redeemed itself and its performance was rated excellent. One measure of that was the price paid. It lost about 40% of its troops from the time of the opening of the German offensive on March 21 until it was relieved for a second time on April 11. After only 10 days rest during which it received returned wounded and replacements from the Class of 1919 to fill the gaps in its ranks, the division was again thrust back into the lines. For the rest of the war, it was in and out of action as the scales of the war tipped against Germany. In August, in the British counterattack along the Somme, the division lost 2,769 men as prisoners in the fighting around Villers-Bretonneux. At the end of the same month, another 3,400 went into the bag during the attempt to stem the British tide east of Albert. The division was so chewed up that it had to be withdrawn still another time. After a rest in quiet Alsace, its final engagements were in the Argonne where they faced the fresh Americans. Towards the end, in addition to everything else, the deadly Spanish flu took its toll as well. At the end of October, for example, the 13th Regiment was down to a mere 200 effectives.

CHAPTER XIII

THE MILITARY AWARDS OF THE PRINCIPALITY OF LIPPE
THE PRINCELY LIPPE HONOR CROSS

On October 25, 1869, Prince Leopold of Lippe and Prince Adolf Georg of Schaumburg-Lippe signed the founding statutes of what they called the Honor Cross of the Princely Joint House. Its purpose was to "reward outstanding services rendered to Ourselves and Our House and to enable us to give proof of Our favor and affection to deserving individuals." In a further paragraph in the same document they went on to say, "The award of Our Honor Cross is made on the joint decision of both Sovereigns to give a visible token of Our recognition to those who have earned an acknowledgment of Our esteem and gratitude by their outstanding services and self-sacrificing devotion as well as loyalty and honesty in their professions; and to honor those foreigners who have acquired merit in respect to Ourselves and Our country."

At its foundation, the order came in three classes designated 1st, 2nd and 3rd Class with associated Merit Medals in gold and silver. The 1st Class was to be worn at the neck while the other grades and the Merit Medals were to be worn in the buttonhole or on the left breast. The 1st and 2nd Classes were enameled badges while the 3rd Class was a plain silver cross with the enameled center medallion of the two higher grades. Bestowal of the awards was made conditional on the agreement of both reigning princes but it was allowed that in "exceptional cases" that the bestowal could be made unilaterally. In those cases, however, the other sovereign was to be notified "without delay." Upon the death of a recipient, the insignia was to be returned. This also applied in the case of promotion to a higher grade when the lower grade insignia was also to be returned. The ribbon was of red watered silk edged in gold and this configuration continued throughout the life of the award.

From the beginning, both sovereigns reserved for themselves alone the right to wear what in effect was a Grand Cross Star on a sash (referred to as *Stern nebts Cordon*). The name "Grand Cross," however, was not so named until a statute amendment of May 30, 1911. This restricted right was confirmed in the statute amendments of 1877 and again in 1890 when by mutual consent, the order was separated into its Lippe and Schaumburg-Lippe branches. The first liberalization of this provision came on May 30, 1906 when the right to wear the Star and Sash was extended to the reigning Princess and the Dowager Princess with smaller insignia. Finally, on May 30, 1911, this privilege could be bestowed on foreign sovereigns holding the 1st Class Honor Cross and princes of the Lippe house. The 1st Class badge was worn from a broad sash from the right shoulder to the left hip with an eight-pointed breast star on the left breast. Princes of the house could also wear the 1st Class badge at the neck.

In 1871, following the Franco-Prussian War, swords were authorized on insignia to indicate an award made for "distinction on active military service." A statute amendment of September 10, 1877 added the Swords-on-Ring feature. In these cases, both the higher grade insignia with Swords-on-Ring and the lower with Swords in the conventional position between the arms of the cross were to be retained and worn together.

More revisions came as a result of amended statutes dated October 23, 1887 in Detmold and November 4, 1887 in Steyrling. The order was expanded into four classes, 1st, 2nd, 3rd and 4th. The 1st Class was redesignated 1st Class with Crown, and the old 1st Class badge without crown became the 2nd Class, the old 2nd Class breast badge became the 3rd Class and the old 3rd Class silver cross became the 4th Class. And as a mark of special distinction, the 2nd Class badge could also be awarded with Oakleaves.

The Honor Cross of the Joint Houses of Lippe and Schaumburg-Lippe was founded in 1869. In 1890, it was separated into an award from each individual state by mutual (and amicable) agreement. For service in World War I, only five men in the *Fliegertruppe* received the order from Lippe. A staff *Major* was awarded the 2nd Class with Swords a day after the armistice and then Oakleaves were added to the badge in 1919 (the 2nd Class badge above has neither swords nor oakleaves). The 4th Class 2nd Division with Swords, the lowest grade of the order (below), was earned by four junior officer fliers. In both cases, the obverse of the badge is shown at the left and the reverse is shown on the right.

As a young officer, probably for the War of 1870, *Generaloberst* Alexander von Kluck, German 1st Army commander in 1914, received the Lippe Honor Cross 3rd Class with Swords.

Only five Grand Crosses with Swords of the Lippe Honor Cross were awarded for World War I including two to young princes of the house. King Ludwig of Bavaria was the third.

Generaloberst Kronprinz Rupprecht of Bavaria received his Grand Cross with Swords a day after Ludwig's, on December 13, 1917.

The last Grand Cross with Swords went to *Kaiser* Karl I of the Austro-Hungarian Empire dated between July 4 and July 6, 1918.

As mentioned, in 1890, the then ruling princes of Lippe and Schaumburg-Lippe decided to set aside the idea of a house order in common and go their separate ways each with his own award. This was, at the time, an amicable agreement and with only minor changes (those of Schaumburg-Lippe will be discussed in the chapter on that house order), the insignia and its nomenclature remained pretty much the same. Either sovereign now held the authority to bestow his house order without consultation with the other. Otherwise, all was the same in Detmold although a few more changes in the structure of its Honor Cross were still to come.

Although the Merit Crosses affiliated with the house order had no application to the fliers of World War I and are therefore not discussed here, to be complete, it should be mentioned that after a meeting with war veterans in 1905, Leopold decided the next year that holders of the Gold and Silver medals who had received them for bravery in the War of 1870 or who had distinguished themselves in that conflict could henceforth wear a pair of crossed swords on their ribbon. Then in the following year, on May 30, 1907, several other changes were made in the structure of the Honor Cross, namely:

- the 3rd Class could now be awarded with oakleaves as well as the 2nd Class.
- the 4th Class was divided in two termed 4a. and 4b.
    - 4a. was the same as the former 4th Class.
    - 4b. was also a silver cross of the same size but without a star design feature around the center medallion that was common to the other classes (to be described shortly). This grade was designated the Civil Honor Cross.

Two more changes occurred in the order's structure before the war began. On May 30, 1913 it was decreed that henceforth the 3rd Class with Oakleaves would no longer be conferred. In its place an Officer's Cross grade was established, a pin-back award worn on the left breast without ribbon (and without a Swords-on-Ring provision) that ranked between the Honor Cross 2nd Class and Honor Cross 3rd Class. Then on June 22, 1913, the Civil Honor Cross designation was dropped and it became the 4th Class 2nd Division. The old 4th Class was renamed the 4th Class 1st Division (the German word is "*Abteilung*" which has several meanings and is often translated as "section" in this case; either would be correct and this writer's choice of "division" is purely arbitrary).

Before going on with the customary description of the insignia themselves, something should be said about several unique awards for which no specific statutory authority seems to exist. Before the two principalities went their separate ways with their respective house orders, a 2nd Class Honor Cross with a 50 Jubilee Numeral was awarded in 1886 and then just once again in 1887. The exact configuration of this appurtenance is unknown but it could have been something similar to the year buttons seen on the Prussian Red Eagle and Crown Orders. These awards were made by Schaumburg-Lippe. Then after the split, Lippe came up with two variations of their own to its Honor Cross 1st Class. In 1898, one was awarded with Oak Wreath and in 1905, another was awarded with the combination of a Laurel and an Oak Wreath. Again, where these elements were placed is not known but Mr. Ludvigsen makes the reasonable suggestion that they were wreaths mounted between the arms of the cross (which is exactly what Oldenburg did when it added a Laurel Wreath as a mark of further distinction to its House and Merit Order of Peter Friedrich Ludwig in the last month of World War I).

The badge of the Lippe Honor Cross Grand Cross and 1st Class were similar and were approximately the same size being a white enameled, gold-edged Maltese cross with gold ball finials on the points of each arm. Both badges were surmounted by a gold princely crown. The center medallion of each had the rose of Lippe in red enamel set on a background of white enamel. Surrounding this was a blue enameled gold ring carrying the order's motto *FÜR TREUE UND VERDIENST* ("For Fidelity (or Loyalty) and Merit") in gold capital letters. The medallion and ring were applied over the eight-pointed star of Schwalenberg and Sternberg in gold. The reverse of the badges displayed a medallion of red enamel carrying the crowned monogram *L* (for the original founder, Leopold) surrounded by a gold ring (during the time the two principalities shared the house order in common, that is up until 1890, the monogram carried the initial *LA* (for the co-founders, Leopold and Adolf). The gold star of Schwalenberg and Sternberg was repeated on the reverse side. Swords, if present, were in gold. The breast star of the Grand Cross was a silver eight-rayed star of the usual design with a center medallion and ring like those on the badge. Missing, here, however, was the Schwalenberg and Sternberg star element.

The Honor Cross 2nd Class badge was the same size as the 1st Class but it lacked the crown and the ball finials on the points of its arms. The Oakleaves, if present, were in gold and mounted above the top arm of the cross in the usual manner. The 3rd Class badge was identical to the 2nd only smaller. The Officer's Cross was the same size as the 3rd Class but had the gold ball finials of the Grand Cross and 1st Class. Being a pin-back piece, the back was left in plain gilt. The 4th Class 1st Division badge had silver instead of enameled arms but retained the enameled medallion and ring as well as the Schwalenberg and Sternberg star in gold (gilt). The 4th Class 2nd Division badge lacked this star element and its reverse medallion was not enameled. The swords in these two cases were in silver.

To repeat some of the things already said, the ribbon for all grades of the Lippe Honor Cross was red watered silk with gold edges. The Grand Cross badge was worn from a broad sash over the right shoulder with the badge itself positioned on the left hip. Princes of the house could also wear the Grand Cross at the neck. Both the 1st and 2nd Class badges were worn at the neck with the 3rd and 4th Classes worn through the buttonhole or on the left breast. The Officer's Cross was worn on the lower left breast without a ribbon.

Even together, Lippe and Schaumburg-Lippe were small properties within the 2nd *Reich* with a combined land area of only 600 square miles, or less than 3% of the empire, and a 1900 population of about 182,000 (increased to nearly 200,000 by 1910). But during the period when the two principalities were administrating the award of the Honor Cross jointly, there was a rather large distribution of their house order. And considering the limited opportunities, the number of swords awards during this time, 1869 to 1890, was also a bit surprising. Appendix XXV shows the entire picture. By May 1914, the number of serving officers in the Royal Prussian Army and the 13th Royal Württemberg Army Corps who held just the Princely Lippe Honor Cross with Swords had dwindled to a handful however (Appendix XXVII). In the Imperial German Navy as of February 1918, the Rank List shows not a single serving officer then holding any class of the Lippe Honor Cross with Swords (Appendix XXVIII) and, of course, such was also the case when the November 1926 Navy Rank List was published. In the reconstituted *Reichsheer* of 1924, there were only 10 officers with a Lippe Honor Cross with Swords (Appendix XXIX).

Appendix XXVI shows the distribution of the Lippe only Honor Cross from 1890 on to the armistice in 1918 both with and without Swords broken down into two periods, 1890 to 1913 and 1914 to 1918. As we will shortly see, however, there is evidence of at least one immediate post-armistice award which was not entered on the roll (and thus not counted in the tabulations). This same recipient was then advanced to the next highest grade of the house order in 1919. There could well have been, therefore, other post-armistice awards that have not been accounted for here. Table 13-1 breaks out just the recorded swords awards during the period of the war and again shows a relatively liberal pattern (especially when compared to wartime swords awards of such house orders as those of Brunswick and Hesse).

Table 13-1
Awards of the Princely Lippe Honor Cross with Swords, 1914-1918

Award	Number
Grand Cross with Swords	5
1st Class with Swords	15
1st Class with Swords-on-Ring	1
2nd Class with Oakleaves and Swords	7
2nd Class with Swords	24
2nd Class with Swords-on-Ring	2
Officer's Cross with Swords	37
3rd Class with Swords	25
3rd Class with Swords-on-Ring	1
4th Class 1st Division with Swords	75
4th Class 2nd Division with Swords	47[1]
Total	**239**

Note 1: One of these was awarded to a Court Equerry and a second to a private tutor Doctor of Philosophy and may have been entered as swords awards on the roll by mistake.

As the table indicates, there were only five awards of the Grand Cross with Swords of the Princely Lippe Honor Cross during the war and since none of the often customary Prussian royalty nor any of its top military leaders were included, it might be of interest to some readers to name them. They were:

- *Rittmeister Prinz* Bernhard of Lippe on October 3, 1914.
- *Leutnant Prinz* Friedrich Wilhelm of Lippe on October 3, 1914.
- *König* Ludwig III of Bavaria on December 12, 1917.
- *Generaloberst Kronprinz* Rupprecht of Bavaria on December 13, 1917.
- *Kaiser* Karl I of the Austro-Hungarian Empire over July 4-6, 1918.

Both the young Lippe princes had held the Princely Lippe Honor Cross Grand Cross without Swords before the war as members of the princely house. The swords awards to the two Bavarian royals have no ready explanation. Leopold IV was neither *Chef*, *Inhaber* nor even *à la suite* to any of the Bavarian line regiments of infantry, cavalry or artillery. Nor is there any apparent connection between Leopold's house and that of the Austro-Hungarian Empire.

Five awards of the Honor Cross with Swords have been traced to airmen, not a bad number at all considering how relatively few swords awards were made overall. One was the Honor Cross 2nd Class which came on the day after the armistice to an aviation staff officer (it was the one just mentioned that does not appear on the roll; it was found on the man's service record). This recipient, whose short biography is the only one in this chapter, then was accorded the Oakleaves to his Honor Cross 2nd Class with Swords in 1919. The other four awards went to younger fliers, all in the 4th Class 2nd Division with Swords. No biographies on any of them appear here for the simple reason that try as this writer might over the many years that their awards have been known, nothing on their wartime careers has surfaced until just recently when Dr. H.M. Dieter Gröschel of Charlottesville, Virginia was able to piece together a few facts about two of them together. The four men were:

Leutnant Hannes Credé whose award was made on September 6, 1917 for service in *Flieger-Abteilung (A)274.*

Oberleutnant Karl Piderit whose award was made on December 19, 1917 for service in *Flieger-Abteilung 302.*

Leutnant Ernst Niedt whose award was made on February 25, 1918 for service at *Flieger-Ersatz-Abteilung 11.*

Leutnant Hans Thümmel whose awards was made on November 11, 1918 but there was no unit listed on the roll as to where it was earned.

Dr. Gröschel has found that as a *Leutnant*, Karl Wilhelm Dietrich Georg Piderit was lightly injured in a crash but could not find further information on Piderit's unit at the time or whether he was a pilot or an observer. Prewar, Piderit had been a member of *Mindensches Feldartillerie-Regiment Nr.58.* based in Minden, not far from Detmold. Piderit was also a recipient of the Princely Lippe War Honor Cross for Heroic Deed and its War Merit Cross, two decorations discussed in the next two chapters. There were two brothers, Hans and Helmut Thümmel, in the Lippe regiment, the 6th Westphalians No.55, at the start of the war. There was also a *Leutnant* Credé with them there and those affiliations, with Leopold IV being the *Chef* of its 3rd Battalion in Detmold, undoubtedly accounted for the awards to Hans Piderit and whom we assume to have been Hannes Credé. And now to the one recipient of the Princely Honor Cross with Swords about whom we can say a few more words.

MAJOR WILHELM HAEHNELT

The staff officer in the *Fliegertruppe* who was awarded the Princely Lippe Honor Cross 2nd Class with Swords on November 12, 1918 and who added the Oakleaves the following year was Wilhelm Haehnelt, born in the East Prussian city of Posen (now Poznan in Poland) to a retired *Oberstleutnant*. The father's influence was readily apparent when the son began cadet training when only 13 years old. Just before his 20th birthday, he completed his secondary education and was immediately appointed *Fähnrich* in *4. Niederschlesisches Infanterie-Regiment Nr.51.*, based in Breslau where the father died just four months into Wilhelm's military career. His progress was good considering promotion in the peacetime German Army came slowly. Just under a year later, the new *Fähnrich* was appointed *Leutnant* and shortly before his 30th birthday in 1904, he added the "pip" of an *Oberleutnant*. Already he wore one medal for his service, the *Kaiser Wilhelm-Errinerungsmedaille* (the Emperor Wilhelm Commemorative Medal or, as it was commonly known, the Centenary Medal). It was founded on March 22, 1897 by *Kaiser* Wilhelm II in remembrance of the 100th birthday of his grandfather, Wilhelm I, and was given to all ranks in the military as well as to veterans of wars going back as far as 1848.

Haehnelt's next honor was not a wearable award but an important one. On May 15, 1905, he was given a Sword of Honor in recognition of his turning in the best shooting record

Right: *Major* Wilhelm Haehnelt was the only flier to receive the Lippe Honor Cross 2nd Class with Swords which was awarded the day after the armistice and then Oakleaves were added in 1919. After being briefly in charge of a *Feldflieger-Abteilung* at the start of the war, the rest of his World War I service was as a highly regarded staff aviation officer with ever-increasing responsibilities.

Below: Haehnelt attends the farewell party for *Jasta 32*'s *Staffelführer*, *Oberleutnant* Otto Schmidt (seated center), who was on his way to take over *Jasta 29* on August 19, 1917 being eased out to allow a Bavarian to command the flight. Haehnelt wears the ribbon with crossed swords indicating the Knight's Hohenzollern he had received on February 26, 1917. Schmidt, with a final score of 20 victories, was recommended for a *Pour le Mérite* but it failed to be approved in time. On his left is the later 22-victory *Pour le Mérite* ace, *Leutnant* Rudolf Windisch, holder of the Waldeck Honor Cross with Swords among other high awards and who died in mysterious circumstances as a French prisoner-of-war after first having been reported as captured alive (see the Waldeck chapter for his biography).

Haehnelt was in charge of all aviation units of the German 2nd Army from February 1918 to the end of August and thus during the titanic battles in France. Here he converses with the then *Leutnant* Lothar *Freiherr* von Richthofen (wearing his *Pour le Mérite*), the Red Baron's younger brother.

in a competition within the 6th Army Corps (which was comprised of five infantry brigades, three cavalry brigades and two brigades of field artillery and thus no mean feat). Possibly this drew the attention of the higher-ups for Haehnelt was appointed to the War Academy four months later for a three year stint. In between, he had brief postings to an artillery regiment and one to a cavalry regiment. It appears he was being given broad experience in grooming him for bigger things to come. It was also during this time, in 1907, that he was given the *Südwestafrika-Denkmünze* (Southwest Africa Commemorative Medal). It is not recorded whether he received it in bronze for combatants or in steel for non-combatants. Almost certainly, however, it was the latter. He would not have had time to serve on active duty in that colony. He must have had something to do with getting troops ready to be shipped there or helped in the preparations for the campaign in other ways. Haehnelt next spent a couple of months aboard His Majesty's Ship Mecklenburg with a naval artillery section after passing out of the War Academy. His next assignment was a real shift. On October 1, 1908, he reported to *Luftschiffer-Bataillon Nr.1.* in Berlin and there earned the certificate of a *Freiballonführer* (free balloon pilot) in January of the following year. This much traveled man's next post was quite a plum. He was transferred to the Great General Staff for a period of two years. It was a sure sign that he was being looked at as an officer of great promise. As that experience was coming to an end, Haehnelt was promoted *Hauptmann* on September 13, 1911. He then reverted back to his original infantry regiment where he became one of its company commanders for an additional two years. Finally, on June 1, 1913, the call to aviation came.

On that date, Haehnelt reported to the Johannisthal field outside of Berlin to begin pilot training and continued his training after he was assigned to *Flieger-Bataillon Nr.4.* on September 10 under the command of the then *Major* Wilhelm Siegert. He must have switched his specialty because it was an *Observer's* Badge, not a Pilot's Badge, for which he qualified on May 1, 1914. When war came and the officers of the four *Flieger-Bataillonen* were parceled out to the *Feldflieger-Abteilungen*, Haehnelt took over the leadership of *Feldflieger-Abteilung 4* on the Western Front. He was now age 39 and with the diversified experience of his prewar assignments and an

Funeral ceremonies in the field for *Oberleutnant* Erich Löwenhardt with Haehnelt in his familiar greatcoat at far right. Löwenhardt, with 54 victories and the *Pour le Mérite*, was killed on August 10, 1918 after a mid-air collision. Hermann Göring is on Haehnelt's right in the first rank.

expanding air service, it was perhaps not surprising that he was relieved of that command on September 25 and moved up to staff work that would occupy him for the rest of the war. Just before the move and in recognition of his work after less than two months in the field, Haehnelt was awarded his first war decoration, the Iron Cross 2nd Class. As readers hardly need reminding, at this early stage of the war it was a highly regarded honor and would have been among the first to be awarded to an airman (the earliest aviation Iron Cross 2nd Class found by this writer was the one to the then *Leutnant* Ernst Eberstein of *Feldflieger-Abteilung* 14 on September 9, 1914.

Throughout the rest of 1914 and in 1915, 1916 and until April 1917, Haehnelt served as a *Stofl* (Staff Officer for Aviation) for the German 5th Army, exercising these responsibilities within a series of Army High Commands. This found him in Champagne in 1915 and at Verdun and on the Somme in 1916 and until early 1917. It was during this period that he received the majority of his wartime awards. These were:

- the Iron Cross 1st Class, August 16, 1915
- the Württemberg Friedrich Order Knight 1st Class with Swords, June 28, 1916
- the Bavarian Military Merit Order 4th Class with Swords, February 12, 1917
- the Knight's Cross with Swords of the Royal House Order of Hohenzollern, February 26, 1917
- the Austro-Hungarian Field Pilot's Badge, February 26, 1917

On April 12, 1917, Haehnelt was named the *Kofl* (Commander of Aviation) of the German 1st Army and remained in charge there until January 28, 1918 except for a couple of short interruptions for duties at *Idflieg*. He then took over as *Kofl* of the 2nd Army which saw him through the see-saw battles in France in the spring and summer. Just the day before he left to take up the *Kofl 2* post, he was promoted *Major*. In September, he moved up to Siegert's staff at *Idflieg* and was there when the war ended and when the day after the armistice he received the Lippe Honor Cross 2nd Class with Swords. Concurrent with that award came Lippe's War Merit Cross, a decoration founded in December 1914 that is discussed in the chapter after next. Haehnelt was still in uniform, now as the *Inspekteur der Flieger* (Inspector of Aviation) itself, when he added the Oakleaves to his 2nd Class cross on May 30, 1919. Try as one might, no reason has been found as to why this officer, born in East Prussia and never having served in the Lippe regiment, was accorded such high honors from the principality and why, also, they came as late as they did.

No photographs of any of the four fliers who received the Lippe Honor Cross 4th Class 2nd Division with Swords have been found but these views of aircraft may be typical of the types two of them flew. Above: *Fl.Abt. (A)274* with a typical mix of two-seaters in 1917. Front to rear, Rumpler C.IV 8267/16, Rumpler C.IV 6695/16, a Hannover Cl.II and a DFW C.V. *Lt.* Hannes Credé received his award in *(A)274* on September 6, 1917. Below: Hannover Cl.II (Rol) 513/18 with unknown crew at *FEA 11* in Brieg. *Lt.* Ernst Niedt received his award there on February 25, 1918. Even the unit's telephone number has been lettered on!

CHAPTER XIV

THE MILITARY AWARDS OF THE PRINCIPALITY OF LIPPE

THE WAR HONOR CROSS FOR HEROIC DEED

Prince Leopold IV of Lippe introduced two new military decorations on December 8, 1914. They were the War Honor Cross for Heroic Deed and the War Merit Cross (the latter to be discussed in the next chapter). Both were awarded for bravery in the face of the enemy but the lesser War Merit Cross was also given for contributions to the war effort on the home front. The requirements to earn the War Honor Cross for Heroic Deed were quite specific. In the language of the foundation statement, it was meant to "honor in a prominent manner the most outstanding heroism or a single death-defying wartime act. The bestowal is the result of an independent Highest decision of the Sovereign. The heroic deed has to be substantiated in the proposal register with the most accurate details. Bestowal is not dependent upon the award of the War Merit Cross or the Iron Cross."

Despite those fine words, the War Honor Cross for Heroic Deed was bestowed on a number of royals who were far removed from the dangers of the battlefield and on the two senior Army field commanders in 1916 (see Appendix XXX). In fact, the first award went to Prince Leopold himself on January 17, 1915. Thereafter, it was awarded a total of 740 times with the last coming on February 4, 1921. The year-by-year breakdown was:

1915	47
1916	115
1917	197
1918	354
1920/1921	27

The War Honor Cross for Heroic Deed (in German, *Kriegsehrenkreuz für heldenmütige Tat*) was a one-class, pin-back decoration shaped like the Iron Cross but struck in bronze-gilt. On the obverse, the rose of Lippe appeared in the center encircled by a wreath of laurels. On an upper line on the left arm of the cross the word *FÜR* appeared and opposite it on the

The Lippe War Honor Cross for Heroic Deed was founded on December 8, 1914 and was the principality's highest award strictly for heroism or, in the words of the foundation language, "a single death-defying" act. Despite that language, the decoration went to a number of royals and to Germany's two senior field commanders (see opposite page). In total, 740 crosses were awarded with 24 of them going to men at the time they were serving in the *Fliegertruppe*. In German, "for Heroic Deed" reads "*für heldenmütige Tat*" and these words appear on two lines on the horizontal arms of the cross. On the upper arm the crowned initial "*L*" appears standing for the founder Prince Leopold IV of Lippe. The lower arm has the foundation year date of "*1914*."

SOME IMPORTANT RECIPIENTS OF THE PRINCELY LIPPE WAR HONOR CROSS FOR HEROIC DEED

Rupprecht of Bavaria
June 7, 1915

Wilhelm II of Prussia
October 11, 1916

Paul von Hindenburg
October 13, 1916

Erich Ludendorff
October 13, 1916

Leopold of Bavaria
October 15, 1916

Oskar of Prussia
October 19, 1916

Crown Prince Wilhelm of Prussia
February 18, 1917

Ludwig III of Bavaria
December 12, 1917

right arm was the word *HELDEN*. On a line below *FÜR* was the word *MÜTIGE* and opposite was the word *TAT*. These were in raised block letters. The upper arm of the cross had the letter *L* topped by a small crown while the lower arm carried the year date *1914*. The reverse of the badge was plain.

Slightly over 3% of the awards of the decoration went to airmen (24 out of the total of 740). The most famous aviation recipient was (who else?) Manfred *Freiherr* von Richthofen. He received it on October 13, 1917 when his score stood at 61 and he was leading *Jagdgeschwader Nr.1*. It came during a period when the *Rittmeister* garnered several other awards from the smaller entities in the Empire which included the Hanseatic Cross from the city of Lübeck (September 22), the War Merit Cross from Brunswick (September 24) and the Cross for Faithful Service from Schaumburg-Lippe (October 10). The other aviation recipients of the War Honor Cross for Heroic Deed were far lesser lights (see Appendix XXXI). Enough has been written about von Richthofen to pass over him here without further comment on his career but the four biographies that follow make the point that his was the only "big" name on the list.

LEUTNANT FRANZ VON KERSSENBROCK

Franz von Kerssenbrock was another youth who was on track for the fashionable life of a cavalry officer in an elite unit of the peacetime German army when the war changed everything. In April 1914, not yet age 19, he had been appointed a *Fahnenjunker* in *Kürassier-Regiment von Driesen* (*Westfälisches*) *Nr.4.* based in Munster. With them he participated in the early battles in France until November when he was transferred to the Eastern Front. That service lasted until May 1915 when his application for a transfer to aviation was approved and he joined the *Fliegertruppe* the following month. Meantime, his commission had come through and that qualified him for observer training which was begun at *Flieger-Ersatz-Abteilung 5* in Hanover and completed at *FEA 2* at Döberitz and Schniedemuhl. His first posting was to *Feldflieger-Abteilung 1* in Serbia that September, participating in the Salonica campaign. May 1916 saw him back in the west again and then it was off to Russia late in the year for our much traveled young man. By this time, von Kerssenbrock had already been decorated with both the Iron Cross 1st and 2nd Class and the Lippe War Merit Cross. On January 10, during his change of venue, his already distinguished career to date was further recognized with Lippe's War Honor Cross for Heroic Deed. Concurrently, his further application to qualify as a pilot received the blessing of *Kogenluft* and beginning in February, he went through his courses at the Graudenz and Allstein military flying schools.

Von Kerssenbrock took up his new duties on the Western Front in June 1917 with *Flieger-Abteilung 1* (not his old *Feldflieger-Abteilung 1* but the former *FFl.Abt.45*, one of the numerous two-seater formations whose numbers were changed over the late 1916/early 1917 period). Almost immediately, his name appeared in the *Nachrichtenblatt* list for July 1917. He was credited with a first victory, a Spad on July 2, and a second, a Voisin, on the 6th. The fact that he received sole credit for them and did not share either success with an observer raises an interesting question, or, really, several questions. Was the name of the observer in his unit inadvertently omitted on both occasions? Possible, but not likely. Or was there a single-seater fighter assigned to *Fl.Abt.1* which von Kerssenbrock was flying when he scored these victories? Again, not likely since these were the days of the permanent *Jagdstaffel* formations and the time when fighters were parceled out in twos and threes to the *Flieger-Abteilungen* primarily to fly protection for their two-seaters was long gone. This leaves the possibility that an aggressive-minded man like von Kerssenbrock took the opportunity to moonlight a bit as a fighter pilot and was flying as a spare man with an adjacent or nearby *Jasta*.

The week previous to von Kerssenbrock's first two victories, a new fighter flight, *Jasta 39*, was formed at Hanover. The date of his posting to the unit is uncertain but it is quite likely that he was an original member or at least went out to Italy with it in mid-September after only three weeks of frontline operations on the Western Front. *Jasta 39*'s first Commanding Officer, *Leutnant* August Raben, was also the first to score and in quite spectacular fashion at that. On September 26, he downed two Caproni bombers. One of his men, the then

Opposite

Top: *Lt.* Franz von Kerssenbrock (far left) received the Lippe War Honor Cross for Heroic Deed on January 10, 1917 probably for his service in Serbia in late 1915 and early 1916 with *FFl.Abt. 1*. The original caption on this photograph reads "The Balkan Eagles of *Feldflieger-Abteilung 1*." The others are, left to right, *Lt.* Spurleder, *Lt.* Metzel, a "Death's Head" hussar, and *Vzfw*. Schluckebier. Von Kerssenbrock wears a cuirassier tunic with its distinctive rounded collar and the white cap with red band of his former cavalry regiment *von Driesen Nr.4*. The ribbon of his Lippe War Merit Cross appears under that of his Iron Cross 2nd Class.

Bottom: *FFl.Abt. 1* in Salonica with one of its Albatros C.Is probably shortly after its arrival in the Balkans. The men are, left to right, Schluckebier, Holler, Schindler, von Kerssenbrock, Stenzel, Schmidt, Jacobsen and Wendelmuth. Von Kerssenbrock, Karl Holler, Fritz Jacobson and Rudolf Wendelmuth all became successful fighter pilots later in their careers.

Top: *FFl.Abt. 1* newly arrived in Russia at their base in Burzency on November 11, 1916. The officer 3rd from the left is *Hptm.* Robert Holtzmann (Württemberg Friedrich Order and Saxe-Ernstine House Order) and the man on von Kerssonbrock's right, 5th from the left, is *Hptm.* Erich Preu (Württemberg Military Merit Order and its Gold Military Merit Medal). Spurleder and Metzel are 9th and 10th from the left.

Bottom: Von Kerssonbrock ended his career as a fighter pilot with *Jasta 39* in Italy. Its Albatros D.Va on the right carries the lozenge pattern camouflage on its rudder whereas the two D.IIIs have the more conventional overpainted white. The aircraft at the left with the stylized letter "K" is believed to be von Kerssonbrock's machine. After scoring four confirmed victories, two in the west and two in Italy, he fell in flames over the town of Conegliano on December 3, 1917.

Vizefeldwebel Wilhelm Hippert, an experienced pilot who had been credited with a victory in two-seaters was credited with the unit's next success on October 2. *Jasta 39* was in the thick of things when the great Austro-German attack known as the Battle of Caporetto was launched on a 20-mile front along the Izonzo on October 24. It turned into a disaster for Italian arms as its 3rd and 4th Armies collapsed under the assault. Of a total of some 305,000 casualties, all but 30,000 were troops which had surrendered. Drumhead Italian military courts shot deserters and supposed deserters by the hundreds. The battle very nearly knocked Italy out of the war and the British and French had to rush divisions to shore up their ally (and it was during this drive that a young Württemberg Mountain Battalion *Oberleutnant* named Erwin Rommel, the "Desert Fox" of World War II renown, led his troops in taking two vital mountain peaks and capturing 150 officers 9,000 men and 81 artillery pieces; the feat earned him the *Orden Pour le Mérite* on December 10).[1]

The Italian *Aeronautica Militare* was out in force on the first days of the offensive doing what they could to support their fast evaporating ground forces and paid dearly for it. On October 25, *Jasta 39* alone put in for nine claims, eight of which were confirmed. Single victories went to the *Vizefeldwebels* Ludwig Gaim and Bernhard Ultsch for Capronis and one Voisin each was chalked up to *Leutnante* Busch, Rudolf Bertelsmeier and Karl Überschaer (Überschaer had the one unconfirm, another Voisin). Hippert got a single-seater, possibly a Camel, possibly a Hanriot (the *Nachrichtenblatt* again is of no help; all of the day's victories on this front were marked down as "(victor) not decided" and the two fighters listed were identified as a Nieuport and a Spad). The star of the day was von Kerssonbrock himself. He shot down a Farman and a Voisin for his 3rd and 4th confirmed victories. The next day, October 26, was a virtual repeat of the previous day's harvest for the men of *Jasta 39*. Seven of the enemy were claimed and credited, six Capronis and one Voisin, although von Kerssonbrock was not successful this time. In fact, his "double" on the 25th were his last confirmed victories (he claimed a Caproni on November 7 but it was disallowed). Raben was wounded in combat 10 days later and von Kerssonbrock was appointed Acting Leader. It is unclear if he were ever formally appointed *Jasta 39*'s commander on the ground as well as in the air. On December 3, the dashing cuirassier was shot down in flames over Conegliano, thus ending the matter along with his life.

LEUTNANT LUDWIG FRITZ DORNHEIM

Six new *Jagdstaffeln* came on stream in December 1916 to join the 25 which had already been mobilized since the preceding August. One of the six was given the designation *Jasta 29*. Initially, at the end of January 1917, administration of the new formation was turned over to an old hand, the portly but capable *Hauptmann* Hermann Palmer. He was nominally its first leader but in reality he was more a housekeeper as equipment and personnel arrived and until a Commanding Officer who would lead *Jasta 29* in the air could be appointed.[2] That post was filled almost immediately. On February 5, a 24-year-old Regular Army man, *Leutnant* Ludwig Fritz Dornheim, got the job.

Dornheim had gone to war with the unit in which he had been commissioned in June 1912, *10. Rheinisches Infanterie-Regiment Nr.161*. Before 1914 ended, 14 of his brother officers had fallen in action, principally around Sedan in August and on the Marne in September, but Dornheim survived those first bloody months. The new year of 1915 saw him transferring to the *Fliegertruppe* and he started the course for observers at *Flieger-Ersatz-Abteilung 6* located in Grossenhain on March 9. He took the work in stride and less than two months later, on May 1, he joined *Feldflieger-Abteilung 60* for what turned out to be an eight month stint before he made another successful application, this time to qualify as a pilot. The first half of 1916 was spent at Adlershof near Berlin and the Leina field outside of Altenburg in Thuringia. With that behind him, he was returned to *60* briefly and after just several weeks, was assigned to the single-seater fighter detachment at Cologne. From there, he reported to *Jasta 7* on August 22. Just the day before, it had taken that new designation from a *Fokkerstaffel* that was operating with Army Group *Kronprinz* of the German 5th Army in the Verdun sector. Less than a month later, on September 20, Dornheim made a lateral move to *Jasta 5* which was in the

[1] One of the features Rommel captured was the 5,420 foot Monte Matajur. Whoever did that had been promised the *Pour le Mérite*. But the award went to a Company Commander in the 63rd Infantry Regiment, *Leutnant* Walther Schnieber, and not to Rommel. Schnieber and his men had actually taken an adjacent peak. Nonetheless, Schnieber received the award on October 27. But by November 10, Rommel had led the advance another 40 miles and crossed the Piave in pursuit of the fleeing Italians. In recognition of these further successes (and perhaps to rectify the mistake in not crediting him with the capture of Monte Matajur), his own *Pour le Mérite* came through on December 10. Also receiving the order that day was Rommel's Commanding Officer, *Major* Theodor Sproesser, for his role in the operations between October 24 and November 10.

[2] Palmer had commanded *Feldflieger-Abteilung 23* and under his tutelage there and its fighter detachment, *Kampfeinsitzer-Kommando Vaux*, the *Pour le Mérite* aces of 1916 Ernst *Freiherr* von Althaus, Rudolf Berthold, Hans-Joachim Buddecke, Wilhelm Frankl, Walter Höhndorf and Kurt Wintgens had made their names.

Right: Look closely and one can see the War Honor Cross for Heroic Deed just below the Iron Cross 1st Class on the tunic of *Lt*. Ludwig Fritz Dornheim. The photograph was taken during his all-too brief time as the leader of *Jasta 29*. He still wears the patch of his former *FFl.Abt. 60*.

Below: Before taking over *Jasta 29*, Dornheim served with *Jasta 5* where he scored his only two victories of the war. He stands 2nd from the right looking down on a distinguished visitor, the *Pour le Mérite* ace Ernst *Freiherr* von Althaus. The group may be celebrating the award of the order to *Jasta 5*'s commander, *Oblt*. Hans Berr (on von Althaus' right). Others who went on to ace status here are Edmund Nathanael (standing 2nd from the left), Hans Müller (seated on Berr's right) and Kurt Schneider (standing at the far right).

process of getting ready to move to the Somme front and taking on the new Halberstadt D-Type fighter. Dornheim was also given the responsibilities of Adjutant of the *Staffel* in addition to his flying duties.

Jasta 5 had come into being on August 21, the same day *Jasta 7* had taken on that designation. The unit was formed from *Kampfeinsitzer-Kommando* "*Ost*" (also called "*Avillers*") in the same German 5th Army area around Verdun and continued under *KEK* "*Ost*'s" Commanding Officer, *Oberleutnant* Hans Berr, who had scored two victories in March 1916 with the Fokker *Eindecker*. *Jasta 5*'s first recorded victories went to the then *Vizefeldwebel* Hans Müller whom those interwar German researchers frequently referred to in this treatise credit with three previous victories. Müller shot down a Voisin on August 26 and burned a balloon on the 31st. Berr himself was the next to score after *Jasta 5* had made its move to a field near Cambrai. On October 7, he brought down a French Caudron G.4 and a British B.E.12 (identified by the Germans, mistakenly, as a B.E.2). Dornheim's turn came on October 16. He got another Caudron for his own first victory and *Jasta 5*'s fifth. Recognition and recompense for the event were quick in coming. On October 25, Dornheim received both the Iron Cross 1st Class and his *Ehrenbecher*. It is possible that coincident with these awards he also received the Lippe War Merit Cross (confirmation of which was found in the archive in Detmold but without a recorded date). As already noted in the chapter on the awards of Hesse, that grand duchy also presented Dornheim with its General Honor Decoration "for Bravery" on December 16. The year 1916 was closed out in a most satisfactory fashion. On the day after Christmas, he sent a B.E.2c down for his second victory.

Dornheim's success on December 26 was tempered by the loss that day of *Jasta 5*'s star pilot and leading scorer, Hans Müller. In the early afternoon, Müller had claimed a B.E.2d and an F.E.2b within 40 minutes of each other. The German researchers marked them down as his 11th and 12th victories but it is likely that only one was confirmed and two of his earlier ones were similarly denied because his official score is usually listed as only nine. Shortly after dispatching his last quarry of the afternoon, Müller himself was seriously wounded and had to be rushed to hospital. Whether he had "only" nine victories or as many as 12, Müller, who was out of action for the rest of the war as a result of his wounding (he ended the war as a test pilot), never received his due when it came to decorations. He had held the Iron Cross 1st Class for some

Below: Dornheim's overpainted (color?) Albatros D.III with its light (white?) spinner in *Jasta 29*. A mechanic tinkers with the pipe leading to the wing radiator, here centrally located. Fittingly, the *Staffelführer*'s machine is lettered number "1."

Another party, this time in *Jasta 29*. Dornheim is the short officer standing 3rd from the left. Seated in the place of honor is *Lt*. Wilhelm Allmenröder here being playfully throttled by *Lt*. Hans Hermann von Budde. No doubt the occasion is the celebration of *Jasta 29*'s first confirmed victory, an observation balloon destroyed by Allmenröder on March 16, 1917.

months before his last flight. Had he been an officer with his length of service in the air, he could well have been up for a *Pour le Mérite* according to the standards of the day. His Commanding Officer, Berr, had just been awarded his "Blue Max" on December 4 with his score standing at 10. As a non-commissioned officer, any order was out of the question for Müller however. Still, Prussia had its honor decoration associated with the Royal House Order of Hohenzollern, the Member's Cross, or its Golden Military Merit Cross. But Müller was passed over for either of them. He otherwise could have been the first aviation recipient of one or the other (the first air award of the Member's Cross with Swords came on January 9, 1917 and the first air award of the Golden Military Merit Cross was not made until October 11 that year). Many another good man would be passed over for the honors that were his due but it would be hard to find a more deserving one than Hans Müller of *Jasta 5*.

January of 1917 and the first days of February were a slow time for the men of *Jasta 5* and for Dornheim as well. Towards the end of January, on the 26th, *Vizeflugmeister* Max Winkelmann, a naval rating, was shot down by ground fire and taken prisoner. The only victory scored since December 26 came on February 2 when *Leutnant* Hans Gutermuth got a D.H.2 for his first confirmed victory. And then on the 5th, the call came for Dornheim to take over *Jasta 29* from Palmer. This expression of confidence in his leadership potential was not lost on the authorities in Detmold. Acting with commendable speed, he was awarded the War Honor Cross for Heroic Deed on the 13th of the month. He was only the sixth airman so honored thus far in the war. Meantime, events in his new command continued apace. New pilots came in and were busy familiarizing themselves with their Albatros D.IIIs. In a test flight with one of these on February 15, *Leutnant* Hermann Klein, just arrived two days before, was severely injured in a crash to become the flight's first casualty.

More new pilots were absorbed and by March, Dornheim and his men were ready for action against the French. He very nearly became the first to score a victory against the enemy but lost that chance when his claim failed to be upheld. On March 11, he put in for a "*Gitterrumpf*" (lattice-tail), the generic name the German airmen gave to French and British "pushers" with their outsize tailbooms connecting the fuselage and wings to the tailplane and rudder. But even the entry in the *Jasta 29* War Diary noted that confirmation was "*fraglich*" (doubtful). And so it was. First scoring honors fell to one of the newcomers, *Leutnant* Wilhelm Allmenröder. He had come in on February

The solemn ceremonies for *Jasta 29*'s first fatality, *Vzfw*. Karl Möwe. Möwe lost his life in aerial combat on April 11, 1917. A chaplain delivers the eulogy as the men bid Möwe farewell. *Hptm*. Hermann Palmer, *Jasta 29*'s first CO, and Dornheim, his successor, are the two officers at the extreme left of those facing the open grave. Allmenröder is 4th from the left. A close inspection of the photograph shows Dornheim wearing his War Honor Cross for Heroic Deed and Allmenröder his Oldenburg Friedrich August Cross 1st Class pinned next to their Iron Crosses 1st Class and flight badges. The French credited *Capitaine* Armand Pinsard (below, marked by the arrow) with downing Möwe, Pinsard's sixth confirmed victory out of a total of 27. Dornheim himself had less than three weeks to live, falling in action on Sunday, April 29, 1917.

16 from the flying school at Paderborn and on March 16, he destroyed an observation balloon over Moiremont.[3] Five days later, he was awarded the often customary first victory Iron Cross 1st Class.[4]

Another victory followed on March 17. *Vizefeldwebel* Karl Möwe, who had joined *Jasta 29* on the same day as Allmenröder, was given credit for a Caudron near Mourmelon, his first and last victory. No further successes were achieved for the rest of the month and April, as it turned out, was equally without a single confirmed victory. But on the debit side of the ledger, there were the unit's first two fatalities during this period. Möwe paid with his life when mortally wounded in an air combat between St. Souplet and Auberive in Champagne on April 11. The second loss occurred on April 29 and was even more devastating to the men of *Jasta 29*. Around three that afternoon, the leader himself, Dornheim, was shot down and killed over Beine. He had worn Lippe's highest bravery honor for all of 76 days.

Purported to be the photograph of Dornheim's death crash on April 29, 1917. If so, he was flying an Albatros D.II in his final combat (the port side radiator can clearly be seen here). Why would a *Staffelführer* be using an obsolescent D.II at such a late date when *Jasta 29* was equipped with the improved D.III at this time? In any event, this aircraft was certainly not the overpainted D.III Dornheim is known to have used (see previous page). His victor is often claimed to have been *Sous Lt.* René Dorme, affectionately known as *Le Père Dorme* (below) despite being only 23-years old. Dorme, too, was shortly to die, being shot down in flames on May 25, 1917 after 23 confirmed victories by the later *Pour le Mérite* ace, *Lt.* Heinrich Kroll.

VIZEFELDWEBEL AUGUST BEGEMANN

Of the 24 aviation recipients of Lippe's War Honor Cross for Heroic Deed, only five were non-commissioned officers. The most highly decorated of the five was *Vizefeldwebel* August Begemann who was a long serving pilot in *Flieger-Abteilung 6*, earning Prussia's Golden Military Merit Cross there on April 11, 1918, one of the 69 airmen in the war to do so.

Like so many of the pilots in the two-seater formations, little was ever recorded of his wartime service. We know he joined *Flieger-Abteilung 6* on January 23, 1917 and by the time of his award of the Golden Military Merit Cross, he had flown over 180 successful flights over enemy lines, a large portion of which were in Flanders where his coolness under heavy ground fire drew praise. He was also cited for heroic achievements in general and for his "excellent abilities, enthusiasm, perseverance and nerve." Already, these characteristics had gained him both Iron Crosses, the Lippe War Merit Cross and

[3] In air historian's Peter Kilduff's article on the combat log of *Jasta 29* in the Summer 1979 issue of *Cross & Cockade Journal* (U.S.), he identifies the balloon as coming from the 36th Company with its observer, Adjutant (Warrant Officer) A. Bry, surviving.

[4] Wilhelm was to be transferred to *Jasta 11* on April 30, 1917 there to join his younger and soon-to-be-famous brother, Karl Allmenröder. Karl would earn the *Orden Pour le Mérite* on June 14 and end with a score of 30 before being shot down by ground fire on the morning of June 27, 1917 and killed. Wilhelm, despite a severe wounding on May 24, 1917 in aerial combat, survived the war. Both were recipients of the Oldenburg Friedrich August Cross 1st and 2nd Class and as such, their biographies appeared in Volume VI in this series.

The only aviation holder of both the Princely Lippe War Honor Cross for Heroic Deed and the Prussian Golden Military Merit Cross, *Vzfw.* August Begemann, shows off his decorations to good advantage on his immaculately tailored (for a non-commissioned officer) tunic in this pleasant pose. The second ribbon on his bar is his Lippe War Merit Cross. In the photograph at the right, he enjoys a smoke with fellow Golden Military Cross winner in *Fl.Abt. 6*, *Vzfw.* Ernst Nitschmann, who was the pilot for the *Pour le Mérite* observer in the unit, *Oblt.* Albert Müller-Kahle. Below: Begemann's regular observer was a *Leutnant* Doetsch who earned the Knight's Hohenzollern with Swords. He stands in front of their DFW C.V while Begemann perches on the fuselage.

on December 19, 1917, the War Honor Cross for Heroic Deed. Begemann's regular observer was a *Leutnant* Doetsch who didn't do badly himself in the orders and decorations department. In *Flieger-Abteilung 6*, he had been given the Knight 2nd Class with Swords of the Saxon Albert Order on July 24, 1917 and already possessing both Iron Crosses like Begemann, his award of the Knight's Cross with Swords of the Royal House Order of Hohenzollern appeared in the May 7, 1918 issue of the *Militär-Wochenblatt*. Since those listings lagged behind the actual bestowal date of an award by anywhere from three to six weeks or so, it seems most likely that the pair received their Prussian awards together.

There was another famous Emil and Franz team in *Flieger-Abteilung 6* at this time. The pilot was *Vizefeldwebel* Ernst Nitschmann (Golden Military Merit Cross on July 16, 1918) and his observer, *Oberleutnant* Albert Müller-Kahle (Hohenzollern House Order on October 11, 1917 and the *Orden Pour le Mérite* on October 13, 1918). Considering what all four went through, it was most fortunate, even remarkable, that they all survived the war.

LEUTNANT ARNO BENZLER

Once again, a pre-air service regimental connection accounted for the awards from Lippe that Arno (sometimes seen spelled as Arnd) Benzler received. Although born in the small town of Sterkrade near Düsseldorf in the Rhineland on October 14, 1985, Benzler was living in Detmold where his mother was a medical doctor. It was there he joined *Infanterie-Regiment Graf Bülow von Dennewitz (6. Westfälisches) Nr.55.*, the Lippe regiment, whose staff and 3rd Battalion were quartered there. He transferred to the army aviation arm in January 1916.

Benzler's initial training took place at *Flieger-Ersatz-Abteilung 6*, that large facility at Grossenhain in Saxony which was responsible for producing a number of Germany's most successful fliers, men such as the later *Pour le Mérite* aces Hans Berr, Walter Blume, Julius Buckler, Carl Degelow, Manfred von Richthofen (as an observer), Rudolf Windisch and Kurt Wüsthoff. Benzler moved to the military flying school at Mockau near Leipzig in mid-June 1916 and finished his training and staging at *Armee-Flug-Park 5* beginning in August and ending, finally, at the end of October. On November 6, he reached his first frontline unit, *Artillerie-Flieger-Abteilung 207*. Just over a month later, on December 14, 1916, Benzler and his observer were credited with a first victory, a Caudron they shot down above the ruins of Fort Douaumont, one of the fortresses that ringed the citadel of Verdun. Just two days before, Benzler's Pilot's Badge was authorized, evidence once again that in the Imperial German Army Air Service, that recognition had to be earned the hard way (not that most readers by now need to be reminded of that fact). Benzler's by-now customary *Ehrenbecher* was presented to him the day after New Year's 1917. A two-seater victory made him a logical candidate for a transfer to fighters and just a week later, Benzler, after passing through another *FEA*, was sent to the single-seater school at Paderborn a few miles south of Detmold to begin a new career. A month later, he drew *Jagdstaffel 32* as his home-to-be. *Jasta 32* had just been mobilized under the command of a Bavarian, *Oberleutnant* Heinrich Schwandner, who had been leading *Schutzstaffel 27* and who had also commanded its predecessor unit, *Kampfstaffel 36* of *Kampfgeschwader 6*. Schwandner was a highly regarded man and had been awarded the Bavarian Military Merit Order 4th Class with Crown and Swords on the previous December 28.

Jasta 32 began its first patrols in the Lorraine sector in March 1917 and immediately had a run of bad luck. On the 16th, Schwandner was shot down in flames and killed eight miles north of Luneville in a combat with two enemy planes. And that was not all. On the same day, *Leutnant* Lotar (also spelled Lothar) von Hausen had the misfortune to tangle with France's great Georges Guynemer. Guynemer wounded him and von Hausen was forced to come down in French lines. He lingered on until May 15 when he died in a military hospital in Toul.[5] Von Hausen had come into *Jasta 32* along with Benzler. Also joining the unit then were two other men who would go on to successful careers as fighter pilots. One was a man who is featured in the chapter in this book on the awards of the Principality of Waldeck, a Saxon named Rudolf Windisch. He would have an eventual score of 22 when shot down on May 27, 1918 and was reported to be alive although a prisoner-of-war. On that basis, the *Pour le Mérite* for which he had been proposed was approved on June 6. But he never surfaced after the armistice and his fate is clouded in mystery (see the Waldeck chapter for the full story). The other newcomer along with Benzler, von Hausen and Windisch was Hans Joachim Rolfes. He would score only one victory in *Jasta 32* but then as the leader of *Jasta 45* in 1918, he would run his string up to 17 confirmed, earning in the process the Knight's Cross with Swords of the Royal House Order of Hohenzollern.

[5] Von Hausen, also a Saxon whose regimental *Chef* was *Fürst* Heinrich XXVII of Reuss, was also highly decorated, holding the Saxon Knight's Crosses 2nd Class with Swords of its Merit and Albert Orders and from Reuss, its Honor Cross 3rd Class with Swords and posthumously, its War Merit Cross. A full biography on him appeared in Volume V.

Two nattily dressed pilots in *FFl.Abt. 207, Lt.* Arno Benzler in puttees and seated behind him, *Lt.* Werner Ulmer favoring what were called "walking out" trousers with straps under each boot to keep them neat. Benzler scored his first victory in *207* on December 14, 1916 but it did not bring an immediate Iron Cross 1st Class as it did to some airmen that early in the war. He would have to wait for it until the summer of 1917 by which time he was with *Jasta 32*. Benzler went on from there to a successful career as a fighter pilot ending with nine victories and the command of *Jasta 60* and two awards from Lippe and the Knight's Hohenzollern to show for it. Below: *Jasta 32*'s first aircraft were Roland D.IIs and the light blue paint applied to the underside of the fuselage of his checker-board marked Roland shows up well here. It looks like the dachshund wears a neck decoration!

Jasta 32 had yet to post a single confirmed victory when *Oberleutnant* Otto Schmidt was appointed its Commanding Officer on June 30, 1917. On the Friday following, July 6, its fortunes changed. Three victories were confirmed although in the process one of its men was lost. Schmidt himself, who had had a claim for a Farman forced down on the other side of the lines two days before disallowed, scored his own personal fifth by downing a Spad. Rolfes' one and only victory in *Jasta 32* came on this day, a Farman, and *Vizefeldwebel* Kurt Starck also got a Farman for his first victory. The man lost was *Vizefeldwebel* Manfred Stimmel who was shot down and taken prisoner by the French. Benzler was still scoreless as a fighter pilot when, at last, he was awarded the Iron Cross 1st Class on July 23. He was, in fact, still without another victory when he was transferred to *Jasta 45* on December 22. Rolfes had been given the command of the newly formed flight on December 17 and it would appear that Rolfes requested that Benzler join him there.

The change of venue was of no help to Benzler. He remained without another score all through January and February and then on March 7, he was nonetheless given a *Staffel* of his own and took over *Jasta 65*. Its first leader, *Leutnant* Hellmuth Contag, also an ex-*Jasta 29* man, had been killed in action the day before. This change acted like a tonic on Benzler. On both March 13 and again on the 16th, he downed Spads for victories number two and three after 15 months of air fighting. Then on the 18th, in a strange turn of events, Benzler was back in *45* to make room for *Leutnant* Otto Fitzner, himself only a three victory pilot from *Jasta 17*. Under Rolfes again, Benzler added a balloon to his bag on April 12.

The loss of still another *Jastaführer* gave Benzler the chance to have a command of his own again. On May 26, 1918, *Oberleutnant* Kurt von Rudno-Rudzinski, the scoreless leader of *Jasta 60*, was forced down in enemy lines and taken prisoner. The next day, Benzler got his job, this time for good. He would remain in charge of *60* until the end of the war except for a three week leave in September. The month of June turned out to be Benzler's best month with victories on the 2nd, 4th and 23rd. July was scoreless but it must nonetheless have been satisfying. Benzler's War Honor Cross for Heroic Deed was approved on the 15th, his second recognition for his former service to Lippe, having already received its War Merit Cross. His final victories of the war came on August 4 and 7 giving him a total of a most respectable nine in all. When he returned from his leave to take command again on October 1, things were in critical shape for the German *Luftstreitkräfte* with shortages of everything affecting its performance. As one of the "lesser" *Jastas*, Benzler's flight no doubt had its flying hours restricted, perhaps even spending days when it was entirely grounded, thus cutting into his and his men's chances for much further scoring. Even so, it was not only Lippe that paid him tribute in these closing months of the war. The September 3, 1918 issue of the *Militär-Wochenblatt* carried the news that Arno Benzler had been awarded the Knight's Cross with Swords of the Royal House Order of Hohenzollern by his All-Highest, the Emperor of Germany and the King of Prussia, in recognition of his long service, leadership and successful air combats.

Opposite
Jasta 60 was fully equipped with the superb Fokker D.VII by the second half of 1918. Top: It would appear Benzler has just returned from a sortie and has shed his helmet, goggles and flight togs and draped them over the lower right wing on the aircraft at the right to pose for the camera. Plainly visible is his War Honor Cross for Heroic Deed pinned next to his Iron Cross 1st Class. The small crossed swords on the "war ribbon" in the buttonhole signify the Hohenzollern Knight's Cross which he earned in August 1918, a month after his Lippe award. Below: Benzler and the men of his command in October 1918. Left to right: *Unteroffz./Vzfw.* Wunnenberg, *Vzfw.* Zimmermann, *Lt.* Dobberke, *Lt.* Schwager, Benzler, *Lt.* Wolf, *Lt.* Ritscherle, *Unteroffz./Vzfw.* Mack, *Vzfw.* Bollmann and an unknown *Vzfw.* Ritscherle was an eight-victory ace scoring in *Schusta 8* (3) and in *Jasta 60* (5). He earned Baden's Order of the Zähringen Lion and its Silver Merit Medal.

LIPPE WAR HONOR CROSS FOR HEROIC DEED RECIPIENTS WITHOUT BIOGRAPHIES

There were no precise regulations as to just how a pin-back badge like the War Honor Cross for Heroic Deed should be positioned on the tunic in relation to other badges like the Iron Cross 1st Class and a flight badge. Obviously, *Oblt.* Roland Müller, right, preferred this vertical arrangement. Müller earned his Lippe cross in *FFl.Abt. 27* on May 23, 1916. His ribbon bar shows the Iron Cross 2nd Class, the Lippe War Merit Cross and the Hessian General Honor Decoration "for Bravery." He served in Hesse's 117th Infantry Regiment at the start of the war. Müller and his pilot, *Lt.* Karl Germer, far right, were killed over Liaucourt on November 17, 1916 right after *FFl. 27* had been redesignated *Fl.Abt. (A)266*. At their elaborate funeral ceremonies, below, the *Ordenskissens* of both men were displayed but the second award on Germer's bar defies definite identification.

Above: The first of only two naval aviation recipients of the War Honor Cross for Heroic Deed, *Oberflgmst*. Ernst Boedecker, seated at the far right, with fellow enlisted pilots of *I. Mar.Feldjasta* on the field at Jabbecke in Flanders in the summer of 1917, about the time (June 15) of his award. Seated from left to right: Ottomar Hagenmüller († December 5, 1917), Karl Meyer (Golden Military Merit Cross – † December 31, 1917), Bertram Heinrich († August 31, 1918) and Boedecker. Standing, left to right: Hans Groth († March 26, 1918), Luitjen Luitjens († August 22, 1917) and Künstler.

Below: Detmold-born *Lt*. Ernst Hilker, in the center of the men of *Fl.Abt. (A)256* in the back row, was allowed little time to relish his award of the War Honor Cross for Heroic Deed. It was approved on December 4, 1917 and Hilker fell six weeks later, on January 14. Seated from left to right: *Vzfw*. Brocke, *Lt*. Wilke, *Oblt*. Weingarth, *Lt*. Hill, *Lt*. Weger and *Lt*. Fleischer. Standing left to right: *Hptm*. Beyersdorff, *Lt*. von Woisky, *Lt*. Hening, Hilker, *Lt*. von Esmarch and two men one of whom is *Rittm*. Hermann. The photograph was taken before September 24, 1917 when von Esmarch was killed in action.

Above: The brass listen in as War Honor Cross for Heroic Deed recipient, Manfred von Richthofen, and Tony Fokker, the helmeted figure with flight jacket over one of his trademark suits, converse. The subject, no doubt, is Fokker's new triplane which he demonstrated at Marckbeke on this day, Friday, August 31, 1917. Between the two men are the then Chancellor Georg Michaelis (July-October 1917) and with back also to camera, *General der Infanterie* von Arnim. Over Fokker's left shoulder *JG I*'s Adjutant, *Oblt.* Karl Bodenschatz, stands at a discreet distance. Between Fokker and Michaelis, *Hptm.* Viktor Carganico tries to eavesdrop. But why the presence of so many coal scuttle steel helmeted ground troops on an occasion like this?

Right: Each man awarded the War Honor Cross apparently had to sign a receipt for the badge and return the form to the orders chancery in Detmold. Here is von Richthofen's with his familiar signature dated 23 October 1917. The decoration was approved on the 13th. In effect, the form was something like a mini-service record with date and place of birth, religion, rank, job description, address in the field and entered by hand in the right column, a man's orders, decorations and, in this case, flight badges as well.

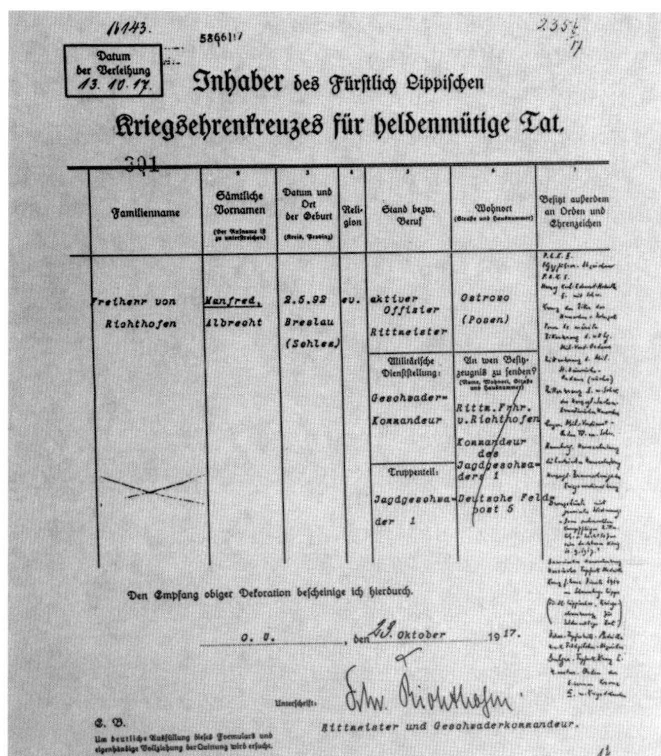

1143. 5866117 235 1/17

Datum der Verleihung 13. 10. 17.

Inhaber des Fürstlich Lippischen Kriegsehrenkreuzes für heldenmütige Tat.

301

1 Familienname	2 Sämtliche Vornamen (Der Rufname ist zu unterstreichen)	3 Datum und Ort der Geburt (Kreis, Provinz)	4 Religion	5 Stand bezw. Beruf	6 Wohnort (Straße und Hausnummer)	7 Besitzt außerdem an Orden und Ehrenzeichen
Freiherr von Richthofen	Manfred, Albrecht	2.5.92 Breslau (Schles.)	ev.	aktiver Offizier Rittmeister	Ostrowo (Posen)	
				Militärische Dienststellung: Geschwader-Kommandeur	An wen Besitzzeugnis zu senden? (Name, Wohnort, Straße und Hausnummer) Rittm. Frhr. v. Richthofen Kommandeur des Jagdgeschwaders 1	
				Truppenteil: Jagdgeschwader 1	Deutsche Feldpost 5	

Den Empfang obiger Dekoration bescheinige ich hierdurch.

O. U., den 23. Oktober 1917.

Unterschrift: Frhr. Richthofen.

Rittmeister und Geschwaderkommandeur.

E. B.

Um deutliche Ausfüllung dieses Formulars und eigenhändige Vollziehung der Quittung wird ersucht.

Jasta 22 in early 1917. *Lt.* Karl Stock, at far left and born near Detmold, received the War Honor Cross for Heroic Deed on January 7, 1918 for his service in *Jasta 6* where he scored his two victories of the war. Left to right: Stock, *Vzfw.* Wunsch, *Vzfw.* Hoppe, *Lt.* Rath, *Lt.* Josef Jacobs (later *Pour le Mérite*), *Oblt.* Hönemanns (CO), *Lt.* Collin, *Lt.* Herwath, *Lt.* George Meyer (proposed for the *Pour le Mérite*), *Lt.* Röhr, *Vzfw.* Grafbeissel, *Lt.* Fichtner and *Lt.* Karge. In *Jasta 48*, Stock and a fledgling pilot, *Lt.* Max Kerstling, were shot down and killed on February 3, 1918, both probably by Capt. H.H. Maddocks of No.54 Squadron, RFC, his 6th, 7th and final victories of the war. Below: The funeral ceremonies for Stock and Kerstling. Each man's *Ordenskissen* can be seen atop their coffins in a church possibly at Guise north of Laon. An entourage of high ranking officers follows the two coffins now mounted on wagons and heaped high with foliage. Where possible, the Germans spared no effort to bury their dead with the most impressive formalities.

CHAPTER XV

THE MILITARY AWARDS OF THE PRINCIPALITY OF LIPPE
THE WAR MERIT CROSS

On the same date that Prince Leopold IV of Lippe founded the War Honor Cross for Heroic Deed, December 8, 1914, he also established a second decoration for "special achievements" in the war called the War Merit Cross. It could be awarded to combatants for bravery and military merit and to non-combatants as well for contributions to the cause. For those at the front, it therefore became Lippe's lesser award for valor. Possession of an Iron Cross was not a prerequisite although in the case of all native recipients encountered so far, the War Merit Cross had to be in a man's possession before he could go on to the higher War Honor Cross for Heroic Deed. For those who were not citizens of Lippe or serving in a Lippe contingent, possession of the War Merit Cross was not a requirement in receiving the War Honor Cross in the first instance.

In appearance, the War Merit Cross closely resembled the War Honor Cross except that it was a conventional breast badge and worn from a ribbon. It was also slightly smaller than the War Honor Cross (41 mm x 41 mm vs. 45 mm x 45 mm). Unlike the War Honor Cross however, there was no inscription on the obverse of the War Merit Cross, just the rose of Lippe in the center surrounded by a laurel wreath and on the upper arm the crowned monogram *L* with the year date *1914* on the lower arm. There was an inscription on the reverse in block letters reading *FÜR* ("for") on the upper arm, *AUSZEICHNUNG IM* ("Distinction In") running across both horizontal arms and *KRIEGE* ("War") on the lower arm.

Combatants and non-combatants received the same badge, only the ribbon made the differentiation between the two. For combatants, the ribbon was yellow with narrow red side stripes and white end stripes. For non-combatants, the colors were reversed. The center stripe was white with the side and end stripes being red and yellow respectively. The non-combatant award was commonly referred to as coming "on the white ribbon." Awards continued to be made retrospectively as late as 1922. Combatant awards amounted to 18,374. Non-combatant awards totaled 1,116. Again, the large number of combatant awards precluded a detailed examination of the roll to extract the aviation recipients during this writer's one and only visit to the archive in Detmold.

Examples of a War Merit Cross in pin-back form are known to exist which suggest that a higher grade may have been under consideration. If so, it is almost certain it was never officially authorized. The authoritative work on the wearable decorations of Germany by *Dr*. Waldemar Hesse Edler von Hessenthal and Georg Schreiber makes no mention whatsoever of this version of the War Merit Cross. It is easy to see, however, why the idea may have been on the drawing board. Lippe's sister principality, Schaumburg-Lippe, had a pin-back version of its Cross for Faithful Service which was founded on November 18, 1914 (the decoration is discussed in the chapter on that award).

No full biographies of aviation recipients of the War Merit Cross are included here. The four biographies of holders of the War Honor Cross for Heroic Deed in the previous chapter were for men who also held the War Merit Cross. To conserve space, photographs and captions of other men in the *Fliegertruppe* who were awarded the War Merit Cross will have to suffice.

The Lippe War Merit Cross was founded in December 1914 at the same time as the War Honor Cross for Heroic Deed and was meant to recognize special achievements in war. It could be earned for bravery and military merit on the part of combatants and for merit on the home front by non-combatants. Below: The handsome bestowal certificate accompanying the decoration in this case is to *Lt.* Jean Laband who actually was assigned to *Idflieg* in Berlin at the time of his award despite the fact the document lists his pre-air service grenadier infantry regiment. Earlier, Leband had served with *Kagohl 2* in the west as an observer and was wounded in action at least once.

Leopold IV
Fürst zur Lippe
1914

Seine Hochfürstliche Durchlaucht der Fürst

haben Sich gnädigst bewogen gefunden, dem Leutnant d. R. im Garde Grenadier Regiment 5 Jean Laband

für besondere Auszeichnung im Kriege das

Kriegsverdienstkreuz

zu verleihen.

Zur Bestätigung wird dieses Besitzzeugnis ausgefertigt.

Detmold, den 13. Juni 1918.

Der Staatsminister.

Verleihungs-Urkunde.

Durch Verfügung des Chefs des Feldflugwesens
(Kommandierender General der Luftstreitkräfte)
vom 23.Februar 1917 Nr. 101803 Fl. ist dem

Leutnant d.R. Laband

das Beobachterabzeichen

verliehen worden.

Flughafen Metz, den 28. Februar 1917.

Kampfgeschwader 2, O.H.L.

Dewall

Hauptmann u. Kommandeur.

Lt. Jean Laband's cased Observer's Badge made by the Berlin firm of C.E. Juncker and its bestowal document signed by the Commanding Officer of *Kagohl 2* at the time, *Hptm.* Job-Heinrich von Dewall. In April 1917, von Dewall was given the Knight 1st Class with Swords of the Saxe-Ernestine House Order even though he had been taken prisoner the previous month. Below: This photograph of a DFW C.V that has piled up on a snowy field was among Laband's effects that survived the war but there was no indication that it necessarily had any connection with him. On the other hand, it could have been the occasion of an injury or wounding that resulted in his Wound Badge in Black.

Generalleutnant Walter von Eberhardt, first Inspector of the German Army Air Service. The last three awards on his bar are the Lippe War Merit Cross, the Hamburg Hanseatic Cross and the Bremen Hanseatic Cross. Prewar, he also held the Lippe Honor Cross 2nd Class.

Leutnant Konstantin von Kleist-Retzow at the time of his being the Commanding Officer of *Reihenbildzug 3* (Serial Camera Detachment 3). In addition to the Lippe War Merit Cross, he held both Iron Crosses, the Royal House Order of Hohenzollern and the Bavarian Military Merit Order.

Below: Non-fatal crash of Albatros C.V 1212/16 of *Feldflieger-Abteilung 25* on the Verdun Front. The crew of von Kleist-Retzow and his pilot, a *Lt.* Krautmacher, seem none the worse for wear. A member of the ground crew holds a portion of the splintered prop while the unit's *Werkmeister* (literally, foreman) appears none too happy about the damage to nose and undercarriage.

Von Kleist-Retzow and his pilot, *Gefr*. Friedrich Weisert, were both killed in an accidental crash of their aircraft on October 7, 1917 at Azannes near Verdun. Right: Von Kleist-Retzow's *Ordenskissen* on top his coffin displays the awards mentioned on the previous page. Those of Weisert's are hidden by the floral tributes. Below: The funeral procession carrying the two coffins begins. The first coffin is von Kleist-Retzow's preceded by an officer carrying his *Ordenskissen*. At the lower left, the officer with *Pickelhaube* in charge of the honor guard awaits while one of his steel-helmeted men can just be seen as he presents arms.

CHAPTER XVI

THE MILITARY AWARDS OF THE PRINCIPALITY OF LIPPE
THE MILITARY MERIT MEDAL

Prince Paul Alexander Leopold of Lippe who ruled as Leopold II (1802-1851) established the Military Merit Medal on May 16, 1832 as a reward for those in the military "who, on account of a long and blameless period of service, distinction in campaigns in which they have participated or in any other way have made or will make themselves deserving." The campaigns referred to in this founding statement were those between 1805 and 1815.

The medal was struck in dark bronze and was throughout its lifetime worn from a bright red ribbon with narrow yellow edge stripes. In the center on the obverse the entwined crowned initials of the founder *P A L* appeared. Under this in a semi-circle was the inscription *DEM MILITAIR VERDIENSTE* ("The Military Meritorious") in block letters. These elements were surrounded by a bound wreath of oak. On the reverse the five-petalled rose of Lippe appeared in the center surrounded, again, by the bound wreath of oak.

The medal, according to *Herr* Jörg Nimmergut's *Deutsche Orden Und Ehrenzeichen Bis 1945*, was awarded a total of 144 times of which there were 55 given in the period 1839-1887, 26 between 1887-1908 and 63 between 1908-1915. The last award of the medal in this striking was on November 20, 1915. In 1908, the statutes were renewed with slightly different but essentially the same qualifying language. It was now meant to "reward honorably those persons who by their long, unblemished period of service, distinction in campaigns in which they participated or in other ways have especially distinguished themselves militarily." For military merit in the field the medal's ribbon now came with a pair of crossed swords in silver. During the reign of Leopold IV (1905-1918), there were only four such awards, three to members of the *Schutztruppe* in German Southwest Africa and one to a *Feldwebel* in *1. Hannoverisches Infanterie-Regiment Nr.74.* whose Commanding Officer was *Oberst* Friedrich Wilhelm, *Prinz zur Lippe-Detmold.*

There was a second striking of the medal in 1915 for awards recognizing military merit in the field. Instead of crossed swords as a device fixed to the ribbon, the medal itself now featured crossed swords in its design. These appeared in bronze under the inscription on the obverse of the medal. According to Nimmergut again, there were a total of 1,945 such awards for service in World War I.

Some confusion exists as to the retention and proper wear for recipients of the Military Merit Medal who also held Lippe's War Merit Cross which was instituted on December 8, 1914 (and which has already been discussed). One directive states that the Military Merit Medal with Swords was to be returned upon the award of the War Merit Cross. Yet another states that "to honor a recipient's war service," the Military Merit Medal with Swords was to be worn immediately after the War Merit Cross and "ahead of all other Lippe orders and decorations." The latter practice certainly prevailed in the case of the only known aviation recipient of the Military Merit Medal with Swords whose short biography follows. This man, Gottlieb Vothknecht, is known to have received not only the War Merit Cross but also Lippe's highest bravery decoration a non-commissioned officer could receive in the war, the War Honor Cross for Heroic Deed. In the photograph on his military pass that is reproduced here, we can clearly see that the third award on his *Feldschnalle* is the ribbon for the Military Merit Medal. Preceding that, although tightly folded, is undoubtedly the ribbon for the War Merit Cross. And in first position on the bar, of course, is the ribbon for his Iron Cross 2nd Class. He also wears the Iron Cross 1st Class next to his War Honor Cross

The obverse (left) and reverse (right) of the Lippe Military Merit Medal in its second striking. Originally founded in 1832, the first striking did not have crossed swords on the obverse of the medal itself. Then in 1908, while the medal remained unchanged, a pair of silver crossed swords were affixed to the ribbon to indicate military merit in the field. The second striking came in 1915 and now the swords appeared on the medal rather than on the ribbon. A total of 1,945 awards of the medal was made for World War I service.

for Heroic Deed and his Pilot's badge. Yet this seems to contradict another provision that applied to the Military Merit Medal with Swords when it was instituted. This stated that the medal was to be given to non-commissioned officers and men of the 2nd Battalion of the 55th Westphalian Infantry Regiment (*Infanterie-Regiment Graf Bülow von Dennewitz*) "who as Lippe citizens became unfit for service due to wounding or illness acquired in the field and who were not awarded, or proposed for, the Iron Cross 2nd Class." Our man Vothknecht obviously held *both* Iron Crosses. It would appear, therefore, that the provisions just mentioned were waived in Vothknecht's case, a condition encountered before when restrictions laid down in the beginning for a certain award were not always followed in every case subsequently.

OFFIZIER-STELLVERTRETER GOTTLIEB VOTHKNECHT

Gottlieb Vothknecht was born in the town of Schlangen which lies just south of Detmold. His initial military service and what he might have done in the *Fliegertruppe* prior to his becoming a pilot in one of the first *Jagdstaffeln* to be formed is not known. His story, what little there is of it, begins with his transfer from *Jasta 14* to *Jasta 24* on December 4, 1916. Initially equipped with Albatros D.IIs, six new Albatros D.IIIs were delivered to its airfield at Mörchingen in Alsace on January 13, 1917 (for those who are interested in such details, the numbers of three of these aircraft were recorded in the *Jasta 24* War Diary, these being 1922/16, 1950/16 and 1963/16). The next day, *Jasta 24*'s first war patrols were flown. They were without event other than the then *Vizefeldwebel* Karl Lorenz was forced to land in Albatros D.II 1735/16 with a shot-up propeller. *Jasta 24*'s first success in the air did not come until February 25 and the honor of posting that fell to none other than Vothknecht. Near Saargemünd, he intercepted Sopwith 1 1/2 Strutter 9739, part of a bombing flight from No.3 Wing, RNAS. The pilot was Flight Sub/Lt. L.E. Smith and his observer was Air Mechanic 1st Class R.S. Portsmouth. Portsmouth was killed outright and Smith was taken prisoner but died of his wounds.

For the next week, there was little flying but on March 3, the then *Vizefeldwebel* Friedrich Altemeier was credited with his first and the unit's second victory when he downed a French Nieuport 17.[1] Vothknecht figured in the *Staffel*'s next successes which came on March 9. At just after noon (German Time) on that day, *Offizier-Stellvertreter* Anton Dierle scored first when he downed another French Nieuport north of Parroy Wood east of Nancy.[2] Then a little over an hour later, still over Parroy Wood, Dierle and Vothknecht teamed up to bring down a Salmson-Moineau SM. 1, a two-seater from *Escadrille F.45*. The *Nachrichtenblatt* confirmed the victory, identifying the enemy plane as a Martinsyde and giving the credit to Vothknecht (whether it was clear Vothknecht played the major role in bringing the plane down or whether the two airmen tossed a coin to determine who would get the credit or whether Dierle merely stepped aside in view of his earlier victory that day is

[1] As a recipient of the Saxon Friedrich August Medal, a biography on Altemeier appeared in Volume III in this series.

[2] As a recipient of the Baden Silver Karl Friedrich Merit Medal, a biography on Anton Dierle appeared in Volume VI in this series. His story was told in conjunction with his twin brother, Johann, also a recipient of this award, Baden's highest bravery recognition to non-commissioned officers.

The only known aviation recipient of the Military Merit Medal with Swords was *Offizier-Stellvertreter* Gottlieb Vothknecht who scored two confirmed victories in *Jasta 24* in the early months of 1917. This is his military pass stamped with the seal of the *Kommandeur der Flieger im Heimatgebiet* (Commander of Aviation in the Home Establishment). We see here that he was entitled to draw pay of 205 *Reichmarks* per month which included 150 marks flight pay which all ranks in the *Fliegertruppe* received. Next to his Iron Cross 1st Class and Pilot's Badge, Vothknecht is wearing his Lippe War Honor Cross for Heroic Deed, the Principality's highest bravery award a non-commissioned officer could earn. On his small bar the Iron Cross 2nd Class, the Lippe War Merit Cross and its Military Merit Medal are represented by ribbons. With these three awards, he may well have been Lippe's most highly decorated non-commissioned officer who served in an aviation contingent in the war.

unknown). The *Nachrichtenblatt*'s mistake is not an uncommon one but as air historian Richard Duiven has found in his researches, the SM.1 was the only large Allied aircraft lost in that area on March 9.

Recognition for Vothkenecht's accomplishments in his first two months of flying with *Jasta 24* was immediately forthcoming. The very next day after this second success, the award of his War Honor Cross for Heroic Deed was approved. Since this was the senior bravery award that a non-commissioned officer could earn from Lippe, he already held its Military Merit Medal with Swords and its War Merit Cross but, unfortunately, neither the circumstances of these awards nor their dates have been discovered. Another award caught up with Vothknecht on March 14. On that day, both he and Altemeier received their *Ehrenbechers*. Although the air action picked up in the ensuing weeks, Vothknecht was unable to score again when on April 10, he was abruptly assigned to the *Stabsoffizier Heimatgebiet* (Staff Officer in charge of aviation in the Home Establishment) for disposal to other duties. And there we lose track of him for the rest of the war.

CHAPTER XVII

THE PRINCELY HOUSE OF SCHAUMBURG-LIPPE

The means by which Philipp, the youngest son of Simon VI, Count of Lippe, inherited the lands of Alverdissen, Lipperode and Uhlenburg in the early 17th century and from which the Princely House of Lippe emerged were recounted in that earlier chapter. Here, briefly, is how its smaller appendage, Schaumburg-Lippe, came about.[1] In 1646, Philipp acquired more territory from his sister Elizabeth who was the mother of Otto V, last Count of Schaumburg and Holstein-Pinneberg, who had died in 1640. With this, he gained sovereignty over parts of the county of Schaumburg on the Weser River and adopted the title Count of Schaumburg, Lippe and Sternberg. It was from that that the name Schaumburg-Lippe was derived.

Philipp's great-great-grandson, Count Georg, was granted Sovereign Status by joining Napoleon I's Confederation of the Rhine when it was formed in 1806 and took the title of Prince the following year. He ruled as Georg I until his death in 1860. From then until the dynasty ceased to reign, the line of succession was quite straightforward passing from father to eldest son. After Georg I, Adolf Georg sat on the throne as Adolf I until his own death in 1893. His successor was Stephan Albrecht, a General of Cavalry in the Prussian Army, who assumed the title Georg II. It was Georg II's youngest brother, readers may recall, who briefly held the regency in Lippe while the matter of succession there was being thrashed out in the courts. Georg II died in 1911 and his first-born son, Adolf Bernhard Moritz Ernst Waldemar, became the last reigning prince of Schaumburg-Lippe, with the title Adolf II. He was forced to abdicate on November 16, 1918.

Readers may also recall that in World War I, the two principalities fielded two units, the 55th Infantry Regiment in Lippe and the 7th Westphalian *Jäger* Battalion in Schaumburg-Lippe, both elements of the 26th Infantry Brigade, 13th Infantry Division, VII Army Corps. The origins of the 7th *Jägers* went back to 1815 when the 2nd (Rhenish) *Schützen* Battalion was formed.[2] In 1821, it became the 3rd (Westphalian) Rifle Detachment based in Cleve. Expanded as the 7th *Jäger* Battalion in 1848, the unit was transferred to Düsseldorf. In 1860, it was renamed the Westphalian Rifle Battalion No. 7 and moved to its final base in Bückeburg, the capital city of Schaumburg-Lippe, in 1867. The ruling princes of Schaumburg-Lippe became the unit's chiefs in 1869.

In its former incarnation as the 3rd (Westphalian) Rifle Detachment, the unit was deployed in the revolutionary disturbances in the Rhineland in 1832 and again in similar uprisings in 1848 as the 7th *Jäger* Battalion. It fought in Schleswig in 1849 when the German Confederation came to the aid of German nationalist rebels who opposed the complete incorporation of the duchy into Denmark and in that campaign lost its commanding officer in combat. The battalion served again in the 1864 war against Denmark as part of the Army of the Elbe. Its only losses there were due to cholera. In the Franco-Prussian War of 1870/71, the battalion was part of the 1st Army and the *Südarmee* along with the Lippe Regiment von Dennewitz and fought in the same areas (see the discussion of its campaigning in the chapter on the Princely House of Lippe). The 7th *Jäger's* combat casualties were small (3% killed) but

[1] The 1910 Census gave Schaumburg-Lippe a population of 46,652 and a land territory of 131,400 square miles. Similar figures for Lippe were 150,937 and 469,400 respectively.

[2] A *Schütze* is a rifleman or sharpshooter; a *Jäger* is a trained huntsman or game-keeper serving as a rifleman or sharpshooter; they were also called *Gelernter Jäger* (huntsman by trade).

on October 1, 1870, during the siege of Metz, 60% of its officers and men were incapacitated due to illness, probably typhoid fever.

So far as the role of the 7th *Jägers* in World War I was concerned, please refer back to the actions of its sister regiment, the Lippe 55th, which were discussed in the chapter on that princely house.

Right: Georg II (ruled 1893-1911) wearing the pre-1890 Grand Cross Breast Star for Princes with Swords-on-Ring (right) of the two joint Houses' Honor Cross.

Far right: Adolf II (ruled 1911-1918) in the uniform of *Husaren-Regiment König Wilhelm I. (1. Rheinisches) Nr.7.* wearing his 1st Class Honor Cross at the neck.

Three princes of the Schaumburg-Lippe House, Moritz (left), Wolrad (center) and Heinrich (right). Wolrad and Heinrich also wear Grand Cross insignia of the Saxe-Ernestine House Order. Their mother was the eldest daughter of Prince Moritz of Saxe-Altenburg, Duke of Saxony.

CHAPTER XVIII

THE MILITARY AWARDS OF THE PRINCIPALITY OF SCHAUMBURG-LIPPE

THE PRINCELY SCHAUMBURG-LIPPE HONOR CROSS

When in 1890, by mutual consent, the Honor Cross which had previously been jointly administered by Schaumburg-Lippe and Lippe as a house order in common was separated, only small changes in the Schaumburg Lippe insignia were made to differentiate between the two. On the obverse of the Schaumburg-Lippe badges, silver nettle leaves were added around the enameled red rose in the center medallion. On the reverse, the enamel on the medallion was changed from red to blue and the crowned monogram was changed from *L A* (for the co-founders of the order from both principalities, Leopold and Adolf) to *A G* (for the founder-prince of Schaumburg-Lippe, Adolf Georg). Another change came about after Prince Adolf came to the throne in April 1911. He directed that the white enameled obverse center medallions on the insignia upon which the red rose of Lippe now surrounded by silver nettles rested be switched to translucent red. No doubt this was to emphasize his independence from and disdain for his cousin in Lippe, Prince Leopold IV. The exact date when this was to become effective has not been found but the medals scholar and historian Eric C. Ludvigsen suspects it took place sometime in September 1911. He bases this on the fact that there was a 39-day gap between awards, extending from September 2 to October 11 that year. At no other time during the year did such a gap exceed 23 days.

There were some other small differences between the insignia of the two principalities and the structure of their respective house orders after 1890 which need to be mentioned but to avoid needless and tedious repetition, a complete description of the badges of each grade of the Schaumburg-Lippe Honor Cross will be omitted since in so many respects they were otherwise identical to those of Lippe. The other differences in the Schaumburg-Lippe insignia and the structure of its house order from those of Lippe were:

- There was no Grand Cross grade. The Honor Cross 1st Class was the highest grade.

- The Officer's Cross which was founded in the revised statutes of October 23, 1899 was surmounted by a gold princely crown without the ball finials that appeared on the Lippe Officer's Cross. And instead of having a plain gilt reverse, the Schaumburg-Lippe Officer's Cross carried the crowned monogram *A G* on a cross-hatched background without any enameling.

- In the same October 23, 1899 revised set of statutes, a crown as a mark of special distinction was added to the 3rd and 4th Class crosses.

- The 4th Class grade did not have a 1st and 2nd Class Division as did the Lippe 4th Class grade. The Schaumburg-Lippe 4th Class badge was the same as the Lippe 4th Class 1st Division badge except for the center and reverse medallion changes that have already been noted.

While swords awards for the Lippe house order were rare, if we can believe the 1890-1918 Schaumburg-Lippe Honor Cross roll, they were virtually non-existent during that period. It shows only the following number of first instance swords awards as well as those with Swords-on-Ring indicative of an earlier swords award:

Honor Cross 1st Class with Swords 1
Honor Cross 1st Class with Swords-on-Ring 1
Honor Cross 2nd Class with Swords 0
Honor Cross 2nd Class with Swords-on-Ring 3

When Schaumburg-Lippe and Lippe decided in 1890 to each have their own house order and not administer the Honor Cross jointly, small changes in the Schaumburg-Lippe insignia were made to differentiate between the two. On the obverse of the badges (left), small silver nettles were added to the red rose of Lippe in the center medallion. On the reverse, the enamel on the medallion was changed from red to blue and the monogram was changed to *A G* to represent the initials of Prince Adolf Georg who was the Schaumburg-Lippe cofounder of the Honor Cross in 1869 along with Prince Leopold of Lippe. Everything remained the same until 1911 when young Prince Adolf assumed the throne in Bückeburg. He had no love for his cousin in Detmold and directed that the enamel on which the rose and nettles rested be changed from white to translucent red, perhaps to emphasize his independence or to spite his relative or possibly both.

The Schaumburg-Lippe Honor Cross 4th Class with Swords of the 2nd Type with the red center. The roll of the house order shows that during World War I, only one award of this grade was made with Swords and not only that but that it was the only swords award of the order in the war in any grade. Several researchers believe, however, there were other swords awards which were simply not recorded as such on the roll. In any event, swords awards of the order were rare throughout its history.

Officer's Cross with Swords 0
Officer's Cross with Swords-on-Ring 1
Honor Cross 3rd Class with Swords 1
Honor Cross 3rd Class with Swords-on-Ring 1
Honor Cross 4th Class with Swords 1

The one swords award of the Honor Cross 1st Class was made in 1912, the 3rd Class award in 1905 and the 4th Class in 1916, the latter thus being the only swords award, according to the roll, that was made during the war.[1] Others more authoritative in these matters than this writer who have also examined the roll strongly suspect that some of the entries during this period were, in fact, swords awards and were merely not noted as such since there were recipients, although in the minority, who did hold military ranks (unfortunately, the roll gives only last names with no indication, in respect to officers, of the unit in which the man was serving). The total number of awards made in the war years themselves, although relatively few as opposed to those made between 1890 and the start of the war, would support that view. Also, a number of insignia of the post-1911 type with swords have been seen, many more than can be supported by just the three noted above (but collectors beware: there are a number of both Schaumburg-Lippe and Lippe Honor Cross insignia on the market today that are recently made pieces, particularly in the higher grades with such appurtenances as swords and oakleaves). Taking only the awards of the Schaumburg-Lippe Honor Cross made from August 2, 1914 through November 11, 1918, here is the total picture year-by-year by grade (the one 4th Class Honor Cross with Swords has been included):

[1] The recipient was a *Leutnant* von Blumenthal who received the Schaumburg-Lippe Honor Cross 4th Class with Swords on October 10, 1916. He was possibly the von Blumenthal who in 1914 was a member of *Husaren-Regiment König Wilhelm I. (I. Rheinisches) Nr.7.* to which, as a *Major*, ruling Prince Adolf of Schaumburg-Lippe was attached *à la suite*.

Table 18-1

	1914	1915	1916	1917	1918	Total
1st Class	1	8	4	6	3	22
2nd Class	1	4	3	4	6	18
Officer's Cross	0	8	17	9	12	46
3rd Class	0	5	13	10	25	53
4th Class	0	4	19	6	13	42
Total	**2**	**29**	**56**	**35**	**59**	**181**

Note: The total picture for awards from 1890 to 1918 is shown in the Appendix.

With this rather bleak picture in respect to swords awards of the Schaumburg-Lippe Honor Cross, the reader may be disappointed (as this writer was) but not surprised that it cannot be established whether even the two "flying princes" of Prussia received the order with Swords much less an airman of less exalted station. Princes Friedrich Sigismund and Friedrich Karl were awarded the Honor Cross 1st Class on November 20, 1915 and April 27, 1916 respectively. But there is no indication that their insignia came with Swords. Had either held the order in that grade prewar, then we could be certain that a second presentation would have added the swords.[2] Neither did however and yet both were on active service so why not swords? Only one early birdman has been found who held the Honor Cross prewar, without Swords of course. He was the then *Oberleutnant* Albert Mühlig-Hofmann with *Flieger-Bataillon Nr.2.* at the start of the war. One thing is certain. Schaumburg-Lippe, not unlike some of the smaller German states, chose to rely primarily on a bravery decoration to recognize gallantry in action rather than its house order. And it is to that award we now turn.

[2] Both princes, by right of birth, held the Grand Commander of the Royal House Order of Hohenzollern before the war. During the war, swords were added to their insignia.

Kogenluft, Generalleutnant Ernst von Hoeppner, Commanding General of the *Luftstreitkräfte*, (Army) Air Force, "touches fingers" with *Leutnant* Karl-Emil Schäfer as he is introduced to him by the Commanding Officer of *Jasta 11*, Manfred von Richthofen. The others in line, left to right, are: *Lt.* von Hartmann, *Lt.* Krefft, Schäfer, *Lt.* Lothar von Richthofen, *Lt.* Brauneck and *Lt.* Hintsch. At far left, *Hptm.* Sorg, *Kofl* of the 6th German Army. The General's visit was sometime in the March/April 1917 period when the older von Richthofen was on his 31-victory roll during those two months. Prewar, as an *Oberst*, von Hoeppner received the Schaumburg-Lippe Honor Cross 2nd Class in May 1909. It would have had the white enameled center like the badge below.

Prince Friedrich Sigismund of Prussia, far left suiting up in *Feldflieger-Abteilung 22* with "Death's Head" Hussar cap, received the Schaumburg-Lippe Honor Cross 1st Class on November 20, 1915 but it is not known whether it came "with Swords" or not.

Prince Friedrich Karl of Prussia, in flight clothes conversing with other officers with his skull-marked Albatros D.I 410/16 being moved in, was awarded his Schaumburg-Lippe Honor Cross 1st Class on April 27, 1916 (again, it is not clear if it came "with Swords"). Friedrich Karl was the Deputy Leader of *Flieger-Abteiling (A)258* but took every opportunity to fly with *Jasta Boelcke* as a fighter pilot. On March 31, 1917, he was forced down between the lines and in attempting to escape, he was wounded in the back and taken prisoner by Australians. By his own statement, he was well cared for but died of his injuries nonetheless in a British hospital just one week later.

Above: A headgear collector's dream! Officers of the *Fliegertruppe* in parade uniforms immediately following the concluding critique of the *Kaiser* Maneuvers of 1912. The then *Leutnant* Alfred Mühlig-Hofmann, 4th from the right in shako (and also at left in more suitable flight attire), was awarded the Schaumburg-Lippe Honor Cross 4th Class (without Swords) on June 23, 1913. Here he is wearing his two earlier honors, the Prussian Crown Order 4th Class (without Swords) and the Mecklenburg Griffin Order Knight's Cross. Promoted *Oberleutnant*, Mühlig-Hofmann was serving with *2. Kompanie Flieger-Bataillon Nr.2.* in Graudenz when war was declared. The other officers lined up are, left to right, *Oblt.* Hofer, unknown, *Lt.* Fink, *Lt.* Baron von Ascheberg, *Hptm.* von Dewall, *Lt.* Junghans, *Lt.* Lau, *Lt.* Reinhardt, *Oblt.* Keller, *Lt.* Funck, *Lt.* Coerper, *Lt.* Engwer, *Lt.* Mahncke, 3 unknowns, *Lt.* Fisch, *Lt. Freiherr* von Freyburg, *Lt.* Blüthgen, *Lt.* Kastner, *Lt.* Schmickaly, *Lt.* Berger, *Oblt.* Albrecht, *Rittm.* von Hantelmann, *Lt.* Förster, 2 unknowns, *Lt.* Joly, unknown, *Lt.* von Scheele, 4 unknowns, Mühlig-Hofmann, *Oblt.* von Falkenstein, *Lt.* Reiche and unknown.

Right: Albert Mühlig-Hofmann qualified as a military pilot before the war and at its outbreak, went into the field, spending 11 months with *Feldflieger-Abteilung 17*. There on the Eastern Front in January 1915, he poses with Fokker M.8 whose military designation was A.1, this being serial number A.195/14. He was promoted *Hauptmann* that month and took the command of *FFl.Abt. 38* on May 13, 1915. Beginning in mid-July 1916 and for almost two years, he was involved in staff and development work, first with *Idflieg*, then as the head of the ordnance depot *Abteilung A*. On June 21, 1918, he again went to the front as the Commanding Officer of *Fl.Abt. (A)219* where he finished out the war.

Below: On the field at the Fokker factory in Schwerin, Mühlig-Hofmann converses with the designer-pilot Tony Fokker. Behind them is one of Fokker's new D-Type biplane fighters. With leather jacket and helmet in its pocket, Fokker probably either has or is about to demonstrate his new plane (for which so much was hoped but which turned out to be totally outclassed by the Albatros and Halberstadt counterparts). Looking on is the *Pour le Mérite* ace, *Oblt.* Hans Joachim Buddecke, just returned from Turkey and in the process of taking over the new *Jasta 4* in August 1916.

CHAPTER XIX

THE MILITARY AWARDS OF THE PRINCIPALITY OF SCHAUMBURG-LIPPE

THE PRINCELY SCHAUMBURG-LIPPE CROSS FOR FAITHFUL SERVICE

For the War of 1870, Prince Adolf Georg of Schaumburg-Lippe created a decoration named the Cross for Faithful (or Loyal) Service which he presented to personal associates during his service on the staff of the VII Army Corps and as *Chef* of the *Bückeburg Jägers*. For World War I, Prince Adolf II renewed the award on November 18, 1914 but extended its distribution well beyond just his own circle. Now it was open to all in the military as well as to non-combatants although its primary candidates were officers and men serving in the *Westfälisches Jäger-Bataillon Nr.7., Husaren-Regiment König Wilhelm I. (I. Rheinisches) Nr.7.*, and those in the 2nd Cavalry Division to which the regiment belonged and *Husaren-Regiment Landgraf Friedrich II. von Hessen-Homburg (2. Kurhessisches) Nr.14*. In addition to a breast badge version of the 1870 cross, Adolf established a pin-back badge. It assumed something of the function of the 1870 cross in that it went to members of reigning houses only, both his own and others, although it was never officially designated a higher grade of-the-decoration.

Except for a change in monogram and the year date, the badges of 1870 and 1914 were the same. The badge for both the breast and pin-back versions was a Geneva cross, a form of Greek cross with arms of the same length and width although, here, the arms curved slightly outward at each end. Both were struck in bronze-gilt. On the obverse, there was a crowned monogram *A* in the center. The words *FÜR*, *TREUE* and *DIENSTE* appeared on the top, left and right arms of the cross respectively. On the bottom arm, there was the year date *1914*. The reverse of both badges was plain. The breast badge's combatant ribbon was bright blue with a narrow white center stripe, two slightly broader white side stripes and very narrow blue end stripes. For non-combatants, the ribbon was white with narrow red side stripes and blue end stripes, these being of equal width. The cross did not have to be returned upon the death of the recipient.

The roll of the 1914 Cross for Faithful Service is separated into three categories, "Members of Reigning Houses," "Officers and Equivalent Persons" and "Non-Commissioned Officers and Men." On the former, there are 36 names, half of which carry the notation "with and without ribbon" and half of which do not. It is clear that "without ribbon" refers to the pin-back badge and "with ribbon" means the breast badge. The first 10 awards went to eight princes of the Schaumburg-Lippe house (including Adolf II), the Duke of Saxe-Altenburg and the Prince of Waldeck-Pyrmont, all dated September 25, 1914 (obviously, in view of the November 1914 renewal date of the decoration, this was a retroactive one). These were all for both badges. From there it is hit and miss. Some royals, minor ones at that, are shown as receiving both badges; others, far more exalted, have no indication after their names that they received anything more than just the breast badge. For example, the award to *Kaiser* Wilhelm II on January 6, 1915 does not carry the "with and without ribbon" notation. It hardly seems possible that Duke Ernst II of Saxe-Altenburg and Prince Friedrich of Waldeck-Pyrmont would receive the pin-back badge while the King of Prussia and Emperor of all Germany would be given only a mere breast badge. This had led some to suspect that all 36 royals on this roll got both badges despite the notations which seem to indicate the contrary. The names of these recipients and the dates of their awards are shown in Appendix XXXVI.

The number of "ordinary" awards of the Cross for Faithful Service dating from 1914 to as late as 1923 were:

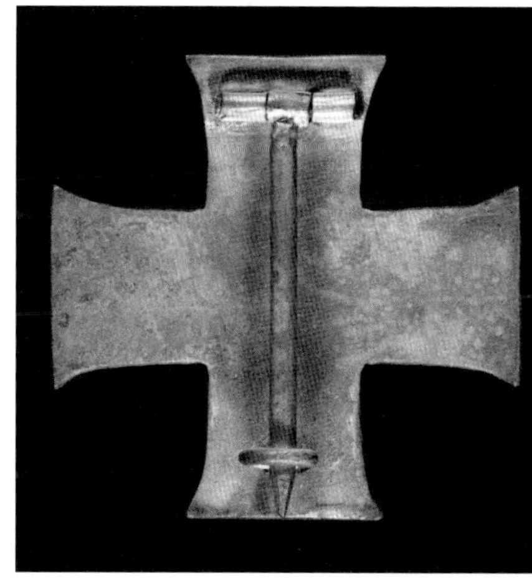

Prince Adolf II of Schaumburg-Lippe renewed the Cross for Faithful Service on November 18, 1914. Established for the War of 1870, it had been given then to personal associates of Prince Adolf Georg. For World War I, its distribution was broadened to include all the military and non-combatants as well. A special *Stekkreuz* (pin-back cross) was also created for princes of reigning houses. The most famous aviation recipient of the regular cross was the leading ace of the war, *Rittmeister* Manfred *Freiherr* von Richthofen. Below: The bestowal certificate for the Cross for Faithful Service to a rifleman dated a week after the armistice.

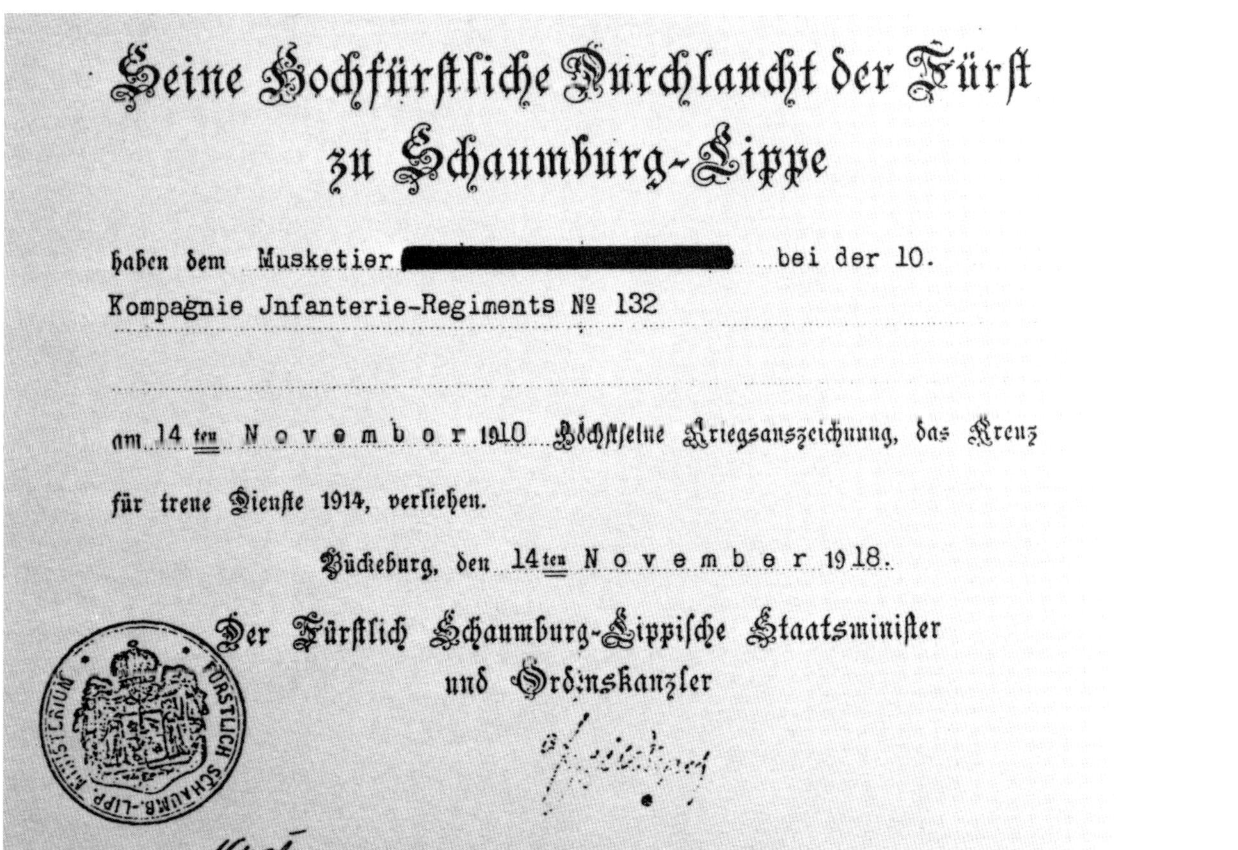

Seine Hochfürstliche Durchlaucht der Fürst
zu Schaumburg-Lippe

haben dem Musketier [redacted] bei der 10.
Kompagnie Jnfanterie-Regiments № 132

am 14 ten N o v e m b e r 1910 Höchstseine Kriegsauszeichnung, das Kreuz
für treue Dienste 1914, verliehen.

Bückeburg, den 14ten N o v e m b e r 1918.

Der Fürstlich Schaumburg-Lippische Staatsminister
und Ordenskanzler

FÜRSTLICH SCHAUMB.-LIPP. MINISTERIUM

Nr. 1649 der Ordensliste.

SOME MILITARY LEADERS WITH THE SCHAUMBURG-LIPPE CROSS FOR FAITHFUL SERVICE

Generaloberst von Bissing, on December 2, 1914

General der Kavallerie von Einem on December 2, 1914

Generalfeldmarschall von Hindenburg on February 17, 1916

Above: *General der Infanterie* Ludendorff on February 17, 1916. Right: *Kaiser* Karl of the Austro-Hungarian Empire on November 7, 1917 and *Kaiser* Wilhelm II of the German Empire on January 6, 1915.

Members of Reigning Houses and Officers: 2,174
Non-Commissioned Officers and Men: 7,942
Non-Combatants: 281
Total: 10,397

The study of the rolls to determine aviation recipients of the Cross for Faithful Service was made difficult by several factors. First, the original entries were made by hand and the writing appears to have deteriorated when the original lists were transferred to microfiche. Many of the characters in the men's names and the other entered information are badly broken up. Deciphering that is difficult, even for others familiar with the old *Schrift*. In addition, most entries lack first names altogether and in all too many cases, unit designations in which the award was earned are lacking as well. Under those conditions, identifying aviation recipients is no easy matter unless encountering a famous name. Then, too, it seems evident in a number of instances where a unit is listed, that the unit was an airman's pre-air service unit even though he earned the award in an aviation contingent. With all these limitations, it is perhaps not surprising, but nonetheless disappointing, to have to report that despite the large number of total awards, less than 50 air recipients 22 officers and 24 non-commissioned officers, could be found (these men are shown in Appendices XXXVII and XXXVIII). Among the officers, only a few names will be familiar to most students of German World War I aviation history. Among the ranks, it is doubtful even one name will strike a chord. The most recognized name on the rolls is that of *Rittmeister* Manfred *Freiherr* von Richthofen. Also there is the next most famous recipient of the decoration, von Richthofen's fellow *Pour le Mérite* ace, the 30-victory *Leutnant* Karl-Emil Schäfer. But, still, the rolls leave us in some confusion as to whether Schäfer's award was earned in the ground troops or later in the air. What evidence exists points to a ground award prior to his transfer to the *Fliegertruppe*, as will be explained on the following pages.

LEUTNANT KARL-EMIL SCHÄFER

Much has been written about the short but spectacular fighter pilot career of Karl-Emil Schäfer, undoubtedly because he proved to be one of Manfred von Richthofen's most successful pupils and those around *der Zirkusdirektor* ("the Ringmaster"), including others like Werner Voss, Kurt Wolff, Karl Allmenröder and the Baron's younger brother, Lothar, have always seemed to have attracted more than a fair share of attention from World War I aviation biographers. Like those others, too, Schäfer's victories have been well documented particulary in the recent work by British historian Trevor Henshaw in his highly praised *The Sky Their Battlefield*. There is, therefore, little new that can be said about the man that most readers do not already know. But, for the record, he can hardly be overlooked in a book like this and some words about him would not be out of place.

In the summer of 1914, Schäfer had traveled to London and was in France when the war clouds loomed ominously. He arrived back in Germany in just the nick of time to answer the call to the colors. Schäfer had already discharged his compulsory military service with the 10th *Jäger* Battalion but as a reservist and at age 22, he was, of course, subject to recall. But instead of reporting to his old unit, he was assigned to *Reserve Jäger-Bataillon Nr.7.* in Bückeburg (which affiliation would result in his award from Schaumburg-Lippe). After being promoted *Vizefeldwebel* in just the first weeks of the war and receiving the Iron Cross 2nd Class (on September 19), he was seriously wounded in the left thigh at the end of the month. Judging from a description of the wound, which opened a hole four to five centimeters wide, he was probably hit by an explosive, or dumdum, bullet. He downplayed his injury as just a flesh wound when informing his parents but it sidelined him for a good six months. Promotion to *Leutnant* and a transfer to the air service followed. How many times have we seen this pattern? A crippling wound gave a German soldier the chance to get out of the trenches and into the seemingly less demanding job of riding in an airplane.

Schäfer arrived at *Flieger-Ersatz-Abteilung 8* at Graudenz on January 16, 1916 and from there proceeded to the flying school at Köslin at the end of the month. Early in May, his courses successfully completed, it was back to *FEA 8* ready for a frontline assignment. This came on June 22 and he joined *Kampfstaffel 8* of *Kampfgeschwader 2* on the Western Front. The cauldron of Verdun was still at full boil and the long expected Anglo-British offensive along the Somme was in days of kicking off (the bombardment preliminary to the attack on July 1 would begin on June 24). But things were stirring in the east too. The one and only at-first successful Russian drive of the war, dubbed the Brusilov Offensive after the commander of the Russian Southwest Army Group, had smashed through the lines of the Austrian Fourth and Seventh armies in June and not for the last time, the Germans were called upon to reinforce their ally. *Kagohl 2* was one of the air units rushed there in July, making its base at Kowel in the Ukraine. The crisis had passed but the Russians were stirring again in August and *Kagohl 2* was busily employed in bombing troop concentrations, rail junctions and supply dumps. So little aerial

Above: Karl-Emil Schäfer as a young *Leutnant* in his pre-air service days became the subject of one of the popular Sanke post cards of the day. The ribbon under that of the Iron Cross 2nd Class is undoubtedly that of the Schaumburg-Lippe Cross for Faithful Service. After his death, an unknown artist drew in all his orders and decorations using the same photograph. Left and opposite: Two views of Schäfer with Albatros D.II 1724/16 when he was in the fighter detachment of *Kasta 11* of *Kagohl 2* based at Metz over the winter of 1916/1917. It was here on January 22 that Schäfer was credited with his first confirmed victory, a Caudron. The "bulls-eye" marking on the fuselage of 1724/16 was repeated on the top side of both the left and right elevators.

opposition was present that the German two-seater formations had virtually no fighter support. We have only sketchy details of Schäfer's time on the Eastern Front. His *Kasta* leader was a *Rittmeister* Ziegler and Schäfer often flew with a *Leutnant Freiherr* von Grote as his observer. *Kasta 8*'s complement were mostly Albatros C.IIIs (Schäfer says he and Grote flew C.674 with a 150 hp Benz engine and he also mentions a Rumpler C. machine (probably a C.I) with a 160 hp engine). It was also at Kowel that Schäfer would have made the acquaintance of another then unknown pilot, one *Leutnant* Manfred *Freiherr* von Richthofen. They must have formed a good bond even then for in mid-February 1917 when Schäfer was again back in the west and now with *Kasta 11* of *Kagohl 2* and von Richthofen's star had already begun its ascent, Schafer could telegram the new *Pour le Mérite Träger* (wearer) and *Staffelführer* asking whether von Richthofen could use him. The answer was immediately in the affirmative.

Schäfer's appeal to his former fellow two-seater pilot was not without some substance. Upon his return to the west, he and four other young pilots formed a fighter detachment within *Kagohl 2* at Metz. They were all *Leutnante* and except for the last named about whom nothing more is known, they were all fated to die within the year as members of *Jagdstaffels* to which they were soon posted. In addition to Schäfer, there was Werner Albert (killed on May 10, 1917 in *Jasta 31*), Lotar (or Lothar) *Freiherr* von Hausen (shot down and captured on March 16, 1917 and died of injuries on May 15, 1917 as a member of *Jasta 32*), Paul Hermann (killed on April 19, 1917 in *Jasta 31*), Franz von Scheele (February 4, 1917 in *Jasta Boelcke*) and a man named Stern. It was in his new role with *Kasta 11* that Schäfer scored his first victory when he brought down a Caudron east of the St. Mihiel salient near Pont-a-Mousson. He seemed to be just the kind of man von Richthofen was looking for and after moving through *Armee-Flug-Park 6* on February 21, he joined *Jasta 11* at its Brayelle field on the western outskirts of Douai the same day.

Schäfer began his remarkable string of victories in *Jasta 11* on March 4 and by the end of the month he had added six more giving him a total number of eight confirmed. Of all of Manfred von Richthofen's charges in *Jasta 11*, Schäfer was now in the lead in the scoring column. His closest competitors were Karl Allmenröder and Kurt Wolff who both ended the month with five confirmed victories each. March 6 and March 9 were the big days for Schäfer during the month when he scored "doubles" on both occasions. They were big days for the *Staffel* as well with four scored overall on the 6th and five on the 9th. These victories plus the five shot down on the 4th earned *Jasta 11* a mention in the March 11 Order of the Day of the German 6th Army with the leader, von Richthofen, Schäfer, Allmenröder and Wolff being cited by name for their accomplishments. The latter three were praised for shooting down three enemy planes from a group of seven "Vickers" single-seaters inside German lines and forcing two others to go down on the other side of the lines. The victims were F.E.8s of No.40 Squadron, RFC and, actually, four were lost with three of their pilots captured while the fourth, wounded, escaped by

Above: In attempting to bring down his second victim on March 3, 1917, Schäfer's synchronization gear malfunctioned and he shot up his own propeller. Upon his safe return, the damage was photographed. The experience hardly affected his performance. Victory number two was scored the next day. Before the month was out, he would raise his confirmed victories to a total of eight.

Below: Victory number 11, the second of the day, came on April 6, Sopwith Triplane N.5457 of No.1 Squadron, RNAS. Despite what appears to be a total wreck, possibly burned out as well, the pilot, Flight Sub-Lt. N.D.M. Hewitt, survived to be taken prisoner.

jumping from his burning aircraft in British lines. Schäfer himself had to make a forced landing after the combat with his aircraft shot up but himself unharmed.

"Bloody April" and especially *Jasta 11*'s contribution to the carnage suffered that month by the RFC and the RNAS has also been so well documented that it is unnecessary to go into much detail but some of the highlights of Schäfer's role in it should be mentioned. In fact, in terms victories and honors, it was the greatest month of his short life. When it ended, he had raised his score to 23, had received Prussia's two highest gallantry awards for officers and had been given a command of his own. He would be leaving *Jasta 11* with runner-up standing among von Richthofen's successful pilots having been eclipsed only by the astonishing 22 victories posted by Kurt Wolff that month which brought his total up to 27. Schäfer had passed the 10-victory mark on April 6 by downing two B.E.2s that day. Von Richthofen could now submit Schäfer's name for the Hohenzollern House Order. Similarly, when Schäfer was credited with his 20th victim on April 21, he was equally eligible for the even more coveted *Orden Pour le Mérite*. News of his Hohenzollern reached him on April 26 and at the same time he was ordered to assume the command of *Jasta 28* whose commander, *Oberleutnant* Rudolf Lang, was being kicked upstairs (ironically, it had been Manfred von Richthofen who had relieved Lang of the command of *Jasta 11* in January 1917). Unbeknown to Schäfer was that his *Pour le Mérite* had also been approved that day but that news did not reach him until a few days later and he was only able to telegraph his parents about the great event on April 30 after he was already over at *Jasta 28*. He was lucky to have been alive to receive both honors. On April 4, he had made a forced landing at Roucoucourt and was slightly injured. Then on the 22nd, his aircraft was hit by ground fire and he was downed again, but this time between the lines as darkness was falling that evening. It was touch and go but he was able to work himself back to the safety of the German trenches.

Schäfer's parents may have been pleading with him to take some leave after all that he had been through in the past two months and now that he was laden with honors. If so, he dispelled any chance of that when he wrote them on May 10 that leave at the moment was out of the question. As he put it, "one cannot just assume a new position and at the same time ask his employer for a holiday." The *Staffel* first had to hit its stride. And under Schäfer's leadership, hit it it did with the *Staffelführer* showing the way. Already, as of May 10, he had added three new kills to his score. By the end of the month, he had added three more. There was another star in Schäfer's new command. *Offizier-Stellvertreter* Max Müller, a diminutive but feisty Bavarian who had scored his initial five victories in *Jasta 2*, ended the month with a total score of 13. Others who were inspired by Schäfer's example were *Leutnant* August Hanko who scored his third on May 25 while on the same day, *Vizefeldwebe* Karolus Bärenfänger got his first.

On the early afternoon of June 4, Schäfer was leading nine of his men when they intercepted a flight of D.H.4s from No.55 Squadron, RFC on their way to bomb the rail lines near Ingelmunster. There was a running fight to their objective and it continued as the bombers made the run back to their own lines. In the melee, Schäfer knocked down A.7420 over Moorslede, killing its crew. Victory number 30 was to be his last, or at least officially. The official Royal Air Force historian provides this report of Schäfer's final combat:

> In the afternoon of the 5th a formation of seven F.E.2d's of No.20 Squadron had a running fight with about fifteen Albatros Scouts over the Ypres-Menin road. The German leader, in a red Albatros, early attacked one of the F.E.'s and mortally wounded its pilot, Lieutenant W.W. Sawden, who dived for home closely pursued by the Albatros. Another of the F.E.2d's (pilot, Lieutenant L. Satchell, observer, Second Lieutenant T.A.M.S. Lewis) went to the assistance of Lieutenant Sawden and engaged the red Albatros in a combat lasting fifteen minutes. The German pilot showed exceptional skill and tenacity, but, eventually, a burst of bullets from the F.E.2d at very close range shattered a part of the Albatros, which broke up in the air and crashed near Zandvoorde. The pilot proved to be Lieutenant Karl Schaefer, one of the foremost German fighting pilots who had, at the time of his death, thirty Allied aeroplanes to his credit.

Sawden was able to make it back with his uninjured observer, Lt. R. Mck. Madill, before he died of his wounds but the F.E. was a complete write-off and therefore, technically, Schäfer's 31st victory.

Just the day before his death, another award for Schäfer was approved and one wonders if he ever knew of it. It was the Bavarian Military Merit Order 4th Class with Swords which had gone to his former leader in *Jasta 11*, Manfred von Richthofen, on April 29.[1] Also approved that June 4 was the same order for Kurt Wolff, now leading *Jasta 29*, and on June

[1] For many years, based on statements by the late eminent German medals authority, *Dr.* Kurt-Gerhard Klietmann, and the presence of such a badge on his *Ordenskissen*, it was believed (and repeated by this writer) that von Richthofen held the Bavarian Military Merit Order in the 3rd Class and with both Crown and Swords. Research by Dr. Dieter H.M. Gröschel and the Director of the War Archive in Munich, *Dr.* Achim Fuchs, have proved it was just the 4th Class of the order without Crown. For the full story, see the Errata and Addenda chapter in Volume VI in this series.

Schäfer was awarded the *Orden Pour le Mérite* on April 26, 1917, three days after his 23rd victory. He lived to wear it for less than six weeks and consequently, photographs of him wearing the badge are rare. These are of rather poor quality, probably taken with a small personal camera. Above: Schäfer and the leader of *Jasta 18*, *Oblt.* Karl von Grieffenhagen, put on their best smiles. Right: Schäfer converses with a *Lt.* Wünnenberg at left, the later *Pour le Mérite* observer, *Oblt.* Hermann Fricke (with cane) and a fourth unknown officer. Below right: His badge here almost looks like it was touched in but the photograph was taken when he was in *Jasta 28*, a command he assumed on April 27.

Opposite
Top: "Under New Management." D.H.4 A.2140 ('2') of No.55 Squadron, RFC gets a face lift. Schäfer brought it down in German lines on the afternoon of April 8 for his 13th victory of the war.

Bottom: A familiar yet classic image of *Jasta 11* at the peak of its fame in "Bloody April" 1917. These men accounted for 89 enemy planes that month (individual victories shown in brackets). In the cockpit of the Albatros D.III, the leader, *Rittm.* Manfred von Richthofen (21). Standing, left to right, *Lt.* Carl Allmenröder (4), *Lt.* Hans Hintsch (0), *Vzfw.* Sebastian Festner (10), *Lt.* Karl-Emil Schäfer (15), *Lt.* Kurt Wolff (22), *Lt.* Georg Simon (1) and *Lt.* Otto Brauneck (0). Seated, *Lt.* Karl Esser (0) and *Lt.* Konstantin Krefft (1). On the ground, *Lt.* Lothar von Richthofen (15). Festner would not survive the month, crashing to his death on April 25.

Above: Schäfer, now clearly wearing his *Pour le Mérite*, puts on his best "walking out" dress blues as he hosts the ladies from the Lille theater troop at Wasquehl, home of *Jasta 28*. In the background we can pick out, left to right, *Lt*. Wenig, *Lt*. Ray, *Vzfw*. Bärenfänger, *Vzfw*. Wagner, *Lt*. Welss and *Lt*. Hanko. Next to Schäfer on the floor, an impish grin on his face, is *Lt*. Karl Bolle, a future *Pour le Mérite* ace himself. In providing this photograph and the one below, aviation historian, Alex Imrie, added the note, "Sorry. 'Don't know the girls' names!"

Below: Still another party for the ladies from Lille. The same *Jasta 28* men are in attendance plus *Lt*. Friedrich Graepel (with the kitten). Schäfer, monocle in right eye, has loosened his tunic displaying his *Pour le Mérite* slightly askew on its ribbon. Someone has playfully draped a pair of fox furs on Schäfer's shoulders. Bolle once again appears to be having a grand old time.

23, Karl Allmenröder who was to die in combat four days later and Lothar von Richthofen then in hospital from his wounding on May 13 were similarly honored. But what about Schäfer's Cross for Faithful Service? The confusion about when he received it stems from entries on the roll to two Schäfers (first names omitted), both in the 7th Reserve *Jägers*. One award is dated June 19, 1916, the other on September 19, 1917. The first if it were to be "our" Schäfer would have been prior to his air service days and the second, of course, would have meant a posthumous award, possible but not likely. That it might have been awarded after his death cannot be ruled out completely and, as we know, many entries on rolls for an award to an airman show his pre-air service unit (as was the case, incidentally, with Schäfer's award of the Bavarian Military Merit Order; there his unit is listed as the 10th *Jägers* even though he never served with it during the war years). The best evidence, however, that the June 1916 date is probably the correct one comes from his portrait photograph on Sanke postcard number 507, reproduced on page 294. Under the ribbon of his Iron Cross 2nd Class, the young *Leutnant* is wearing a second ribbon with the color spacing similar to the Schaumburg-Lippe cross. Nor is there any evidence of a flight badge in this photograph (or an Iron Cross 1st Class for that matter) and there is no air service insignia (the winged propeller device) on either epaulet.

Had Schäfer been granted a bit more time in his new command, almost surely he would have been in store for another award. *Jasta 28* was a Württemberg contingent and many of its members came to wear its orders and decorations (see Volume IV in this series). Later in the month Schäfer was killed, on June 28, Max Müller, then with 18 confirmed victories, and August Hanko still with just his three, were awarded the Württemberg Gold Military Merit Medal (a decoration that could go equally to non-commissioned officers and junior commissioned officers). Schäfer's successor as *Staffelführer, Hauptmann* Otto Hartmann, already had earned Württemberg's Gold Military Merit Medal and the Knight's Cross of its highest bravery award, the Military Merit Order, so there was not much more Württemberg could do for him before he was killed in action on September 3, 1917. The man who took over from him, *Oberleutnant* Werner Jahns, like Schäfer, had little time to make his mark with the authorities in Stuttgart. He fell on September 24 after less than three weeks on the job. The next, and as it turned out, the last, leader of *Jasta 28*, *Leutnant* Emil Thuy with a *Pour le Mérite* and a final score of 32 confirmed victories (some lists credit him with as many as 35), survived the war and earned two Württemberg orders while in command, the Knight 2nd Class with Swords of its Friedrich Order on June 6, 1918 and the Knight's Cross of its Military Merit Order

A macabre scene. Said to be the remains of Schäfer and his Albatros on the afternoon of June 5, 1917, here being surveyed by a glum looking crowd of German soldiery. In attacking an F.E.2d of No.20 Squadron, RFC whose pilot he mortally wounded, Schäfer came under the fire of a second "Fee" and after a combat lasting 15 minutes, his aircraft broke up in the air and he crashed to his death. Below: An unknown officer carries Schäfer's *Ordenskissen* in his funeral procession while in the second photograph, Bolle can be identified by his light cuirassier's service cap.

Thought to be the funeral ceremonies in church for Karl-Emil Schäfer. The number of awards on the *Ordenskissen* correspond to those he earned but the photograph is not sharp enough to identify all of them. Certainly, there is a *Pour le Mérite* on its broad ribbon at the top of the cushion and the placement and number of awards do not correspond with the known *Ordenskissens* for fliers like Carl Allmenröder, Kurt Wintgens or Kurt Wolff for whom similar ceremonies were conducted.

Oberst Hermann von der Lieth-Thomson, Chief of Staff to the Commanding General of the (Army) Air Force, received the Schaumburg-Lippe Cross for Faithful Service on April 17, 1916 in his earlier role as *Chef des Feldflugwesens* (Chief of Field Aviation). In the same month a year later, he was awarded the *Orden Pour le Mérite* for his role in carrying out the re-organization and expansion of the air services. But typical of many high ranking officers with a long string of other awards, he affects here a more modest "black and white front" (i.e., just Prussian awards), his *Pour le Mérite* and Iron Cross 1st Class.

the following month, on July 25. But whether Schäfer might have been similarly honored became academic with his untimely death. What does matter is that he did indeed render "faithful service" as his star briefly but brilliantly shone in the skies over Flanders.

OBERST HERMANN VON DER LIETH-THOMSEN

The fourth aviation recipient on the roll of the Schaumburg-Lippe Cross for Faithful Service (so far as can be determined anyway) was the then Chief of Field Aviation, *Major* Hermann von der Lieth-Thomson. It came on April 17, 1916, a year before he would be decorated with the *Orden Pour le Mérite* for his part in reorganizing the German Army Air Service along with his nominal superior, *Generalleutnant* Ernst von Hoeppner. The word "nominal" is used here since Thomsen along with the equally capable and even more energetic *Major* Wilhelm Siegert are credited by most with being the real brains behind the development of German aviation in the war. But the post of Commanding General required a man of just that rank and von Hoeppner was tapped for it even though he had had no technical experience, being mainly a line cavalry and staff officer. He was fortunate in having Thomsen as his number one man and Chief-of-Staff.

On October 6, 1916, von Hoeppner was named to the new post of *Kommandierenden General der Luftstreitkräfte* (*Kogen-*

luft) and the new organization absorbed Thomsen's office of *Feldflugchef*. He had been promoted *Oberstleutnant* on March 22, 1916 and now he and von Hoeppner were responsible for all formations of the Army Air Service at the front and for the Home Establishment including training, development and supply. Only the German Naval Air Service and the Bavarian Inspectorate of Aviation did not fall under *Kogenluft*'s purview. Thomsen had come to his job as Chief of Field Aviation with a solid background in engineering and transportation being at various times involved with the fortifications surrounding the cities of Metz and Strasbourg before the war as well as serving with an engineer battalion and a railway regiment plus important staff jobs with units in the field. Evidence of his value in these wide ranging assignments can be seen from the impressive list of awards that he accumulated along the way. They were:

- Prussian Crown Order 4th Class on January 7, 1897
- Prussian Red Eagle Order on September 10, 1910
- Austrian Military Merit Cross 3rd Class on July 9, 1911
- Mecklenburg Griffin Order Honor Cross on August 7, 1912
- Saxe-Weimar Order of the White Falcon Knight 1st Class on October 4, 1912
- Prussian Officer's Long Service Cross for 25 Years on June 11, 1913
- Saxon Albert Order Knight 1st Class on January 5, 1914
- Württemberg Crown Order Knight 1st Class on April 22, 1914

Thomsen's World War I service gained him another long array of awards:

- Iron Cross 2nd Class on August 29, 1914
- Iron Cross 1st Class on September 29, 1914
- Bavarian Military Merit Order 4th Class with Crown and Swords on January 13, 1915
- Austrian Military Merit Cross 3rd Class with War Decoration on March 19, 1915
- Saxon Albert Order Knight 1st Class with Swords on July 9, 1915
- Saxon Albert Order Knight 1st Class with Crown and Swords on December 15, 1915
- Royal House Order of Hohenzollern Knight's Cross with Swords on January 17, 1916
- Austrian Order of the Iron Crown 3rd Class with War Decoration on February 1, 1916
- Schaumburg-Lippe Cross for Faithful Service on April 17, 1916
- Brunswick War Merit Cross on May 3, 1916
- Bulgarian St. Alexander Order (grade unknown) - September 15, 1916
- *Orden Pour le Mérite* on April 8, 1917

As the photograph of Thomsen reproduced here shows, he was a well proportioned man. Or, better, one might say he was a big man for a big job.

Above: *Hptm.* Hilmar *Frhr.* von Bülow (with goggles) and his pilot, *Offz.-Stv.* Wilhelm Grübbel, in *FF1.Abt. 1*. Von Bülow earned his Cross for Faithful Service there on December 23, 1914, the second known aviation recipient of the decoration. A native of Schaumburg-Lippe, he became a highly decorated CO of two-seater formations, receiving awards from six other German states (see his biography in Volume IV in this series). A squadron puppy perches on the wing just above the wheel painted with the national marking. Right: Von Bülow and the *Pour le Mérite* observer, *Oblt.* Hermann Fricke, at Avricourt on June 23, 1918. Von Bülow had been Fricke's commander in *FFl.Abt. 11* in 1915 and 1916 and at this time, von Bülow was in charge of *Fl.Abt. (A)223*.

Left: The then *Oblt.* Paul Backhaus, standing 3rd from the right, received his Cross for Faithful Service in *Kagohl 2* on July 14, 1916. This photograph is believed to have been taken around December 1915 when the unit was in the process of changing its designation from the cover name of *Brieftauben-Abteilung-Metz* to *Kampfgeschwader 2*. In the pilot's seat of the Rumpler G.II is *Hptm.* Fritz Prestien and manning what appears to be an early model 2 cm Becker cannon is a man named Hacheburg. Standing at the extreme right is *Lt.* Franz Ray, the later 17-victory ace. Backhaus served in *Kagohl 2*'s *Kasta 7* until June 13, 1916 when he was appointed the leader of sister *Staffel*, *Kasta 12*. Then on November 17 that year, he was named the commander of *Jasta 23* and coincident with that, was promoted *Hptm.* There he scored his one and only victory of the war on May 21, 1917, credited with a Spad. He was returned to two-seaters three months later and saw out the war as the CO of *Fl.Abt. (A)259* there earning the Württemberg Friedrich Order Knight 1st Class with Swords on February 20, 1918.

Of the 22 officers in the *Fliegertruppe* known to have received the Cross for Faithful Service, an uncommonly high number, six in all, earned it for their service in the same unit, *Fl.Abt. 22*. Above: Two of these recipients are shown here, *Oblt*. Julius Liebrecht, 3rd from the left, on May 22, 1917 and *Lt*. Ernst Hein on February 27, 1918, at far left. Flanking Liebrecht are a *Lt*. Baumann on his right and a *Lt*. Richter on his left.

Below: Another group of *Fl.Abt. 22* personnel in comfortable quarters complete with a phonograph. Liebrecht is standing 2nd from the right and Baumann, a Bavarian later with *Fl.Abt. (A)287b* and here with monocle, stands 4th from the left. The two seated officers at the left are a *Hptm*. Pretzell and on his left an *Oblt*. von Damnitz. Others are unidentified but could include one or more of the other *Fl.Abt. 22* recipients of the decoration.

Above: Hardly dressed in their Sunday best, the two von Richthofen brothers greet their father on the steps of the chateau *Jasta 11* occupied at Roucourt southeast of Douai. No wonder the boys are in working clothes. It is the second half of "Bloody April," a month in which Manfred scored 21 victories and Lothar 15. Six months later, on October 10, Manfred would receive Schaumburg-Lippe's Cross for Faithful Service. Three days after that, the Principality of Lippe, not to be outdone by its smaller neighbor, presented him with its War Honor Cross for Heroic Deed.

Below: *Rittm.* Egon Hugo *Graf* von Beroldingen, with a belt of comic opera proportions, points out some aerial action to King Wilhelm II of Württemberg and his entourage at his command, *FEA 10* at Böblingen just outside of Stuttgart, in September 1917. The badge at his neck is not the *Pour le Mérite* but the *Ehrenritter* (Knight of Honor) of the *Johanniterorden* (Order of St. John). Von Beroldingen was awarded the Cross for Faithful Service on July 22, 1918 to add to his two Iron Crosses, the Hohenzollern, the Württemberg Knight's Military Merit Order and Friedrich Order Knight 1st Class with Swords and Saxony's Albert Order Knight 1st Class with Swords.

CHAPTER XX

THE MILITARY AWARDS OF THE PRINCIPALITY OF SCHAUMBURG-LIPPE

THE MILITARY MERIT MEDAL

A Military Merit Medal in Schaumburg-Lippe was founded on May 30, 1850 by Prince Georg Wilhelm who ruled as Georg I (1806-1860). It could be awarded without respect to rank. The medal was in silver and smaller than its counterpart in Lippe (30 mm vs. 35 mm for the second striking of the latter medal). On the obverse, emulating the medal in Lippe, the crowned entwined initials of the founder *G W*, appeared in the center surrounded by a bound wreath of laurels. On the reverse, again much like its sister principality's award, there was an inscription, this one reading *FÜR MILITAIR VERDIENST* ("For Military Merit"). From the beginning, however, the reverse also carried a pair of swords below the inscription, in this case crossed cavalry sabers. Around these elements was a similar bound wreath of laurels. The ribbon was red with rather wide light blue edge stripes.

According to *Herr* Jörg Nimmergut's *Deutsche Orden Und Ehrenzeichen Bis 1945*, there were 58 awards of this medal of which 14 were presented initially on June 15, 1850. The medal was also awarded with the inscription *Düppeler Höhen den 17. April 1849* ("Denmark Heights the 17th April 1849") engraved around the rim. There were only two recipients of the medal in this form. For the War of 1870, during the reign of Adolf I (1860-1893), 583 medals were awarded and these carried an additional pair of crossed silver cavalry sabers affixed to the ribbon. For World War I with Adolf II now on the throne (1911-1918), the same medal sufficed but now military awards carried a pair of crossed silver swords in the Roman, or straight, style on the ribbon. There were also awards of the medal with a *Genfer Kreuz auf dem Band* (Geneva, or Red, Cross on the ribbon) for charitable work connected with the war effort. Women receiving this medal wore it from a bow. Nimmergut provides no figures for the number of awards of these medals for World War I. This writer was unable to find a roll for the Military Merit Medal with Swords for the war but one was discovered for the medal mit "*Rotem Kreuz*" ("with 'Red Cross'") which contained a total of 522 names. Lacking a roll for the military version of the medal therefore, nothing can be said about possible aviation recipients of the decoration. With the renewal of the Cross for Faithful Service so early in the war however, it is unlikely that there were many, if any, airmen who came to receive the award for service in World War I.

Following the pattern established in its sister principality of Lippe, a Military Merit Medal was instituted in Schaumburg-Lippe on May 30, 1850. The medal itself remained the same up to and throughout World War I but there were several minor variations, principally in the style of swords affixed to the ribbon for the War of 1870 and the 1914-1918 war (see text for full details). The photograph above left displays the reverse of the medal with the obverse shown in the photograph at the right. Whoever the recipient was, he obviously chose to display the reverse facing forward with the Roman, or straight, style of swords used for World War I awards on its ribbon. This was common practice with many medals whose obverse displayed initials while the reverse side was considered more attractive and more descriptive by certain recipients and who thus chose to "flop" the medal when worn.

CHAPTER XXI

THE GRAND DUCAL HOUSES OF MECKLENBURG-SCHWERIN AND MECKLENBURG-STRELITZ

Mecklenburg-Schwerin

Mecklenburg-Strelitz

When its recorded history began in the 10th century, the area in north central Germany that extended along the Baltic Sea called Pomerania and a part of which became the Grand Duchies of Mecklenburg-Schwerin and Mecklenburg-Strelitz was inhabited by heathen Slavic tribes whom the Germans called "Wends." In still another attempt to subdue them, a crusade led by Henry the Lion of Saxony and Albert the Bear of Brandenburg was mounted in 1147. It was largely unsuccessful at the time but in subsequent years, the Wends were at last subjugated and forced to accept Christianity. One of the Slav princes was a man named Niklot, head of the Obotrite tribe. His grandson, Heinrich Borwin I, was created a prince of the Holy Roman Empire in 1170 and became Prince of Mecklenburg in 1179. It was from this line that the houses of both Mecklenburgs descended and the fact of their Slavic origins makes them unique among the reigning families of Germany.

In 1227, the eastern section of the area became an independent principality known as Pomerelia and was annexed to Poland in 1294. Through the three turbulent centuries that followed, it remained a part of Poland but in 1772, in the first Polish partition, it was ceded to Prussia and incorporated as the province of West Prussia. Meantime, the other principality, Pomerania, remained a duchy of the Holy Roman Empire and its princes were raised to ducal rank in 1348. The duchy was divided into Mecklenburg-Schwerin and Mecklenburg-Güstrow in 1621. During the Thirty Years War, both dukes were deposed by the imperial general Albrecht von Wallenstein in 1628 and forced to flee their lands. Von Wallenstein was awarded the territory as an hereditary fief by the Holy Roman Emperor but Gustavus II of Sweden retook it in 1631 and restored the dukes to their thrones. Mecklenburg was again a duchy of the Holy Roman Empire and in 1637, it was turned over to the elector of Brandenburg. In the Peace of Westphalia the following year, *Vorpommern* (Hither Pomerania, the western part) was given to Sweden while *Hinterpommern* (Farther Pomerania, the eastern part) went to Brandenburg. The line of Mecklenburg-Güstrow died out in 1701 and that of Mecklenburg-Strelitz took its place, the same year that the rule of primogeniture was introduced in both duchies.

As a result of the Northern War (an effort to break Swedish supremacy in the Baltic), Sweden lost about half of its Pomeranian holdings in 1720 to what was now the kingdom of Prussia (as from 1701 when the Brandenburg elector Friedrich III had himself crowned as "king in Prussia" and took the title King Friedrich I). Sweden retained the rest of its Pomeranian holdings until 1806 when the Holy Roman Empire was dissolved in the face of Napoleon I's Confederation of the Rhine. Napoleon occupied the Swedish part of Pomerania but upon making peace with the Swedes in 1809, he restored it to them. Then in the Treaty of Kiel in 1814, Sweden handed over its remaining holdings there to Denmark in exchange for Norway. After Napoleon's final defeat, the Congress of Vienna (1814-1815) in redrawing the map of Europe saw Denmark ceding its share of Pomerania to Prussia, receiving the province of Lauenburg in return. In the process, both duchies were elevated to the status of grand duchies with Duke Friedrich Franz I assuming the title of Grand Duke of Mecklenburg-Schwerin on June 14, 1815 and Duke Karl that of Grand Duke of Mecklenburg-Strelitz two weeks later. All Mecklenburg was now firmly in Prussian hands. Both grand duchies joined the German Confederation of 1815 that replaced the old Holy

Roman Empire and in the 1866 war with Austria, sided with Prussia. And both became members of the German Empire upon its founding in 1871 after the conclusion of the successful war with France. In World War I, with a combined population (as of 1910) of approximately three-quarter million subjects (but only a little over 100,000 of them in Strelitz), the two grand duchies fielded two infantry regiments, one rifle battalion, two regiments of cavalry and two of artillery. Their origins go back to the 18th century.

In 1782, Mecklenburg-Schwerin added a new grenadier regiment (*Prinz Friedrich*) to the existing ducal horse body guard and the two infantry regiments, *Regiment von Both* and *Regiment von Gluer. Regiment Prinz Friedrich* became a *Leib* regiment and *Regiment von Both* a grenadier regiment in 1785. One thousand Mecklenburg infantrists were sold as mercenaries to Holland in 1788 and fought there against the French revolutionary army, suffering considerable losses before they returned home in 1796. By 1805, there were two *Leib* grenadier and one infantry regiments in the Mecklenburg army. When the French illegally occupied Mecklenburg in 1806, the army was dissolved. The duchy was then forced to throw in its lot with the French and joined Napoleon's Confederation of the Rhine, the last German state to do so. It had to provide the French army with four battalions of infantry which became the Mecklenburg Brigade. Two of its companies engaged the Prussian *Freikorps Schill* in 1809, half-heartedly it seems since one of the companies lost almost all of their men due to desertion. The entire brigade went to Russia in 1812 as part of Napoleon's *Grande Armeé* of 500,000 strong and of the 1,700 Mecklenburgers who set out with it, only 34 returned. With "the Little Corporal" having deserted the remnants of his army and taking refuge in Paris, Prussia was the first of Napoleon's allies to desert and Mecklenburg went over with it.

Mecklenburg recruited three new infantry battalions and also established an artillery battery with two cannons and two howitzers for the so-called "War of Liberation." Its grenadier guard battalion fought the French in Northern Germany and a volunteer *Jäger* battalion took on the Danes. During Napoleon's ephemeral rule of one hundred days following his return from exile on Elba, one of the Mecklenburg guard battalions and one of its musketeer battalions were engaged against his reconstituted forces. With the Corsican finally crushed at Waterloo in June, 1815 and his threat to Europe over for good, a period of reconstruction of the Mecklenburg army set in. In 1819, the first squadron of *Cheveaulegers* was established. It was expanded to a regiment in 1831 and its horsemen were renamed "dragoons" in 1837. Meantime, the army by 1821 had grown to three infantry battalions plus an artillery detachment of eight guns and formed part of the German Confederation's 10th Corps. In 1845, two *Jäger* companies were added to the 1st Infantry Battalion and in 1857, the entire unit was designated a *Jäger* battalion. Together with the dragoons, they participated in the 1848 Schleswig campaign when forces of the German Confederation came to the aid of the rebels protesting Denmark's attempt to incorporate Schleswig into Denmark completely. In the revolutionary year of 1848, the Mecklenburgers were again mustered against the uprisings spreading across Europe and were part of the Prussian units that put down the revolutionaries in Baden the next year while the dragoons were used to keep order at home. The two infantry battalions were enlarged to regiments in 1863 and in the 1864 war with Denmark, were employed in both frontline actions and in guard duties along the coast. In the short but decisive war of 1866 whereby a triumphant Prussia removed Austria from German affairs forever, one of the Mecklenburg regiments remained at home while the other and the dragoons served under Grand Duke Friedrich Franz II, a Colonel General in the Prussian army and commander of the Prussian Reserve Corps and saw action in one of the minor engagements around Würzburg (the battle that decided the war took place at Sadowa (Königgrätz to the Prussians) on July 3, 1866 in East Bohemia).

A major reform in the state's military took place in 1867. It was incorporated into the Prussian army as the Grand Ducal-Mecklenburg force. It consisted of *Grossherzoglich Mecklenburgisches Grenadier-Regiment Nr.89., Grossherzoglich Mecklenburgisches Füsilier-Regiment Nr.90., Grossherzoglich Mecklenburgisches Jäger-Bataillon Nr.14., 1. Grossherzoglich Mecklenburgisches Dragoner-Regiment Nr.17*, and the newly erected *2. Grossherzoglich Mecklenburgisches Dragoner-Regiment Nr.18*. The 89th Grenadier's 2nd Battalion was Strelitz infantry (it had begun as a body guard company in 1701) and based in Neustrelitz, the capital city of the Grand Duchy (it was founded in 1733 after the earlier ducal residence in Strelitz burned down in 1712). The 89th's staff and other two battalions were based in Schwerin, that Grand Duchy's capital city (becoming such in the early 17th century).

Grand Duke Friedrich Franz II was still on the Schwerin throne when the Franco-Prussian War broke out in 1870 and he took command of the newly formed 13th Army Corps. As the Germans crossed the border into Alsace on August 4, the corps was at first assigned coastal guard duties against possible French naval landings. When it was clear that no such threat was imminent, the Mecklenburg 17th Division which included the two dragoon regiments and the artillery detachment was moved to France in September and took part in the siege of Toul. From there, the division joined the investment line around

The co-founders of the Grand Ducal Mecklenburg Order of the Wendish Crown, Friedrich Franz II of Schwerin (left) and Friedrich Wilhelm of Strelitz. Friedrich Franz also established the Military Merit Cross in Schwerin in 1848 while Friedrich Wilhelm followed suit on March 10, 1871 with his Cross for Distinction in War. The Wendish Crown was only awarded rarely for military achievement.

Right: Friedrich Franz IV ruled in Schwerin during World War I. Here he wears the Collar and Grand Cross of the Wendish Crown with Breast Star and the Grand Cross of the Mecklenburg Griffin Order at the hip from its sash.

Far right: Adolf Friedrich VI was on the throne in Strelitz when he committed suicide on February 24, 1918. In this pose, he wears a Knight's badge of the Griffin Order on his bar to represent its Grand Cross and the Grand Cross breast stars of the Wendish Crown and Anhalt Order of Albert the Bear.

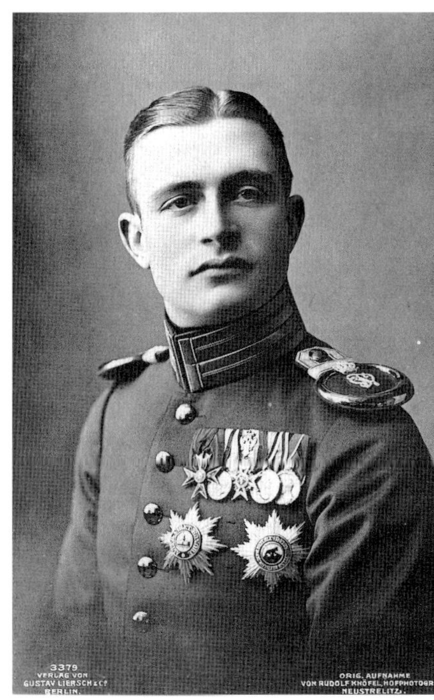

Paris, at Rambouillet southwest of Versailles in early November. It was during this time that illness felled a number of the Mecklenburgers – typhoid fever according to contemporary sources – with as many as 20-25% of its men reporting sick each day. The formation of strong French armies to relieve Paris caused the Detachment Grand Duke Mecklenburg (DGDM) to be attached to the German 3rd Army at Dreux, due west of Versailles. While the detachment was on the march to Le Mans en route to Tours, the seat of the French Government of National Defense, the German 2nd Army of some 45,000 men at Orleans were suddenly threatened by a strong enemy force of 200,000. DGDM was ordered to the 2nd Army's assistance and reached its right wing after forced marches. There they met the attacking XVI and XVII Corps of the French Army of Orleans under General Antoine Chanzy which were trying to breach the investment ring around Paris from the south. The Grand Duke used all his forces (the 17th and 18th Divisions, the 1st Bavarian Corps and the 4th and 6th Cavalry Divisions) in the Battle of Loigny-Poupry. The French charged the Bavarians but the 17th Mecklenburgers struck at the French right flank and with excellent support from cavalry and artillery, the Bavarians and the Mecklenburgers pushed the French back, not without casualties (the *Jägers* lost about a quarter of their strength). Another French attack from the east was checked by the 22nd Division. The German 2nd Army was then ordered to take Orleans. While it was engaged with the French XV Corps on December 3, XVI Corps tried to reinforce them but ran into the detachment forces which stopped the relief. On the next morning, the battle resumed and the 17th Division moved energetically along the western side of the Orleans to Paris highway. After some skirmishes with French defensive positions, the division reached the western gates of Orleans around six in the evening. The commanding officer, General Hermann von Tresckow, negotiated the city's surrender.

With just one day of rest, the detachment moved against the French army that General Chanzy had regrouped along the Loire southwest of Orléans. 17th Division marched on the left wing and met the French advance guard near Meung on December 7. In heavy fighting, especially by one battalion of the 2nd Mecklenburg infantry near Langlochere, the French were pushed back in a northwesterly direction. The right wing of the DGDM reached Ouzuerle-Marché and on the next day, both wings moved toward Beaugency when they were attacked by a strong French force, well supported by artillery, near Cravant. The French were repulsed and the 17th Division followed them along the Loire and took Beaugency. The division supported the Bavarians against another heavy French attack on December 9, finally forcing the enemy to retreat. The French stood their ground the next day but as the Grand Duke was in the process of organizing a major assault the next morning, December 11, General Chanzy ordered a retreat.

The weather had turned miserable and both the retreating French and their pursuers had to march through muddy country. The 17th Division followed the French to the Loire and then on to Vendôme where a strong French force awaited. After a brush with the enemy at Pezon on December 15, the 2nd German Army moved to attack Vendôme on the 17th. Again, Chanzy pulled out his troops and headed for Le Mans. Six weeks of marching through mud, ice and snow had done in the German soldiers, however, and they were unable to carry the pursuit beyond the Loire. They were on the march again after a few days of rest and occupied Chartes and remained there until December 24. Chanzy, who had been resting his own troops at Le Mans and receiving reinforcements and replacements for his losses, now decided to try on his own to break the ring around Paris. He attacked Vendôme with two strong columns as well as Briare on the Loire southeast of Orleans. The Detachment that was now reconstituted as the 13th Corps under the Grand Duke along with 2nd Army moved against Chanzy in the direction of Le Mans and ran into Chanzy's troops at Vendôme on January 6. Six terrible days of winter fighting ensued after which Chanzy's new army was forced to retire back towards Le Mans. Outside the city, in excellent positions in the Huisne Valley, the French made a stand. Purely by luck, the German 19th Corps under General Voigts-Rhetz attacked the weakest point of the French defenses which were manned by untrained and poorly armed conscripts. The Germans broke through and the entire French line collapsed. The French withdrew but the Germans were too exhausted to pursue. 13th Corps was transferred to Rouen a few days later after the German 1st Army had had its last battle in the west against the French Army of the North under Faidherbe. The armistice was signed, finally, on January 28, 1871.

After the Franco-Prussian War, the army of the new German *Reich* was reorganized by the Military Convention of 1872. The Mecklenburg Contingent became part of the Prussian 9th Army Corps. The artillery detachment of Field Artillery Regiment No.9 joined the newly formed Holstein Field Artillery Regiment No.24 in Güstrow in 1872 as its 1st Detachment with four batteries. The third battery was the Strelitz unit garrisoned in Neustrelitz. The Grand Ducal Mecklenburg Field Artillery Regiment No.60 was formed from this regiment in 1899 and was stationed in Schwerin. The dragoon regiments were renamed the 1st and 2nd Grand Ducal Mecklenburg Dragoon Regiments No.17 and No.18. The grenadier and fusilier regiments were enlarged by one battalion each in 1893 and the

Jäger Battalion No.14 was transferred from Schwerin to Colmar in Alsace in 1890 as part of the XV Army Corps.

The losses of the Mecklenburg contingents in the War of 1870 are shown in Table 21-1:

Table 21-1
Losses of the Mecklenburg Contingents in the War of 1870

Unit	Strength at Mobilization	Total Losses	%	Killed	Wounded	Prisoners	Died of Illness (mostly typhoid)
Grenadier Regiment 89	3,100	445	(14%)	107	250	12	76
Fusilier Regiment 90	3,144	722	(23%)	214	429	7	72
Jäger Battalion 14	795	243	(31%)	67	127	23	26
Dragoon Regiment 17	660	55+	(8%+)	22	25	8	?
Dragoon Regiment 18	626	53	(8%)	12	20	6	15
Total	**8,325**	**1,518+**	**(18%+)**	**422**	**851**	**56**	**189**

In World War I, the Mecklenburg contingents except for the 14th *Jägers* formed the 17th Division of the 9th Army Corps along with the 75th Bremen and the 76th Hamburg Infantry Regiments (the 162nd Infantry from Lübeck was assigned to the 17th Reserve Division). The 17th was to give a good account of itself despite a high casualty rate. It was only in the final months of the war that discipline broke down in some units. From first to last, except for brief periods of rest and reorganization due to attrition, the division was in action along the Western Front.

The division was part of von Kluck's 1st Army that invaded neutral Belgium on August 4. The Mecklenburg Grenadier and Fusilier regiments were present at Liége when the fortress was stormed on the 6th and taken on the 7th. The division then pushed on to the French border and the goal of Paris. By the 20th, it had reached Louvain (the destruction of the city by the Germans in retaliation for what was claimed to be civilian sniping and the infamous burning of its ancient library did not begin until August 26). The 17th was one of six of von Kluck's divisions that engaged the regulars of the British 3rd and 5th Divisions at Mons on the 23rd, forcing the "Old Contemptibles" of the BEF to withdraw towards Maubeuge-Jenlain the next day. The 17th then skirted Maubeuge and moved on through Nesle and Roye, reaching the north bank of the Aisne on September 1. On September 4, von Kluck's army began its fatal swing southeast across the Marne instead of driving on behind Paris as had been called for by the Von Schlieffen Plan and thereby moved across the front of von Bülow's 2nd Army. In the First Battle of the Marne that ensued, the Mecklenburgers were heavily engaged, especially between the 6th and the 8th during which the withdrawal of the 9th and 3rd German Army Corps opened a gap along the German front which eventually widened to 30 miles and into which Allied troops poured. The battle ended on September 10 and in the retreat from the Marne, the 17th recrossed the Aisne the next day. It halted on the 13th and fought in actions that lasted from September 16 to 21. Position warfare had set in on the 1st German Army front however. In the first six weeks of the conflict, 1st Army had marched some 375 miles from the German border to east of Paris and then back to the Aisne.

In October 1914, the 17th Division took over trenches on the left bank of the Oise and remained in that sector until mid-October 1915. During that period, in March, one of the Hanse regiments, the 76th from Hamburg, was transferred to the 111th Division which was being newly formed near Brussels. The 17th's next move was to Champagne where it occupied positions in Sabot Wood (Souain) and along the St. Hilaire-St. Souplet road for the rest of that year and until June 1916. There a French assault had begun on September 27 in conjunction with the British drive known as the Battle of Loos farther to the north. The French continued to attack, the Germans counterattacked and so it went with little accomplished except more names on the casualty lists of both sides. In June, the 17th was finally pulled out of the line and sent to the rear for rest and reinforcements. But it was clear it was merely being refitted for the coming action on the Somme where the long expected Anglo-French offensive north and south of the river opened on July 1. It was another blood bath. The British losses, particularly on the opening day, were horrendous (nearly 60,000 in killed, wounded and missing) but so were those of the

German defenders including the 17th. Its casualties between July 10 and 25 were so severe that even at the battle's height it had to be withdrawn. By mid-August, reconstituted once again, it was thrown back into the fray just in time to face a French attack south of the Somme on a 12-mile front on September 4 in the Barleux-Belloy sector.

At the beginning of October 1916, the badly mauled division was transferred to Artois where there had been see-saw actions between the opposing armies throughout 1915 and early 1916 but which was now relatively quiet. It held the line there between Roelincourt and Bailly opposite Arras until December 24. Early in the new year, around January 9, the division was back in the line in the Py sector south of the Ancre. There the British were pushing ahead and on February 7 around Grandcourt and on February 17 at Miraumont, the Mecklenburgers again incurred serious losses. During the time of the voluntary German withdrawal to prepared positions on the so-called Hindenburg Line between February 25 and April 5 (the only major change in the trench line in early 1917), the division was relieved along the Somme and was rested southwest of Douai from the end of March until the beginning of April. On the 10th of that month, it found itself back in Artois where the Battle of Arras and Vimy had been launched by the British the day before. It occupied the Oppy-Gavrelle sector and took such heavy losses in front of Gavrelle on April 23 and 24 that it was again relieved the following day. Just one company of the 90th Fuseliers had lost 115 men for example. After regrouping, the division went back into the lines in a quiet sector west of Cambrai until the end of May and then rested once again in the Cambrai area to prepare for its next ordeal, It was during this time that the desperate need for replacements resulted in the 89th Grenadiers receiving all native Mecklenburgers who were members of the four regiments of the 12th Infantry Division.

The 17th Division's next ordeal turned out to be Flanders. For the moment, however, it had a bit of a respite. The second stage of the battle known as Third Ypres was due to kick off on July 31. Three days before that, the division was pulled out but not before having taken heavy losses as a result of the two weeks of intense bombardment (more than three million shells) that preceded the attack. For the next five weeks, it sat in the relative safety of a quiet part of the lines south of the Cambrai-Bapaume road. That short holiday was over when it entrained for Flanders on September 23 and was assigned to the Polygon Wood sector northeast of Ypres. On September 26, the British took the rest of Polygon Wood despite a counterattack by the 17th which failed and in which its losses were so great that it had to be withdrawn after only two days in the lines. The Bremen 75th Division, the 1st Hanseatic, lost 30 officers and 1,000 men in these engagements. The British intelligence report summed up the situation when it wrote, "After the last combats of Flanders (July and September 1917), the 17th Division was considered having its combative force perceptibly diminished on account of its losses." The Mecklenburgers and their Hanse comrades were sent from the wasteland that was Flanders to another rest area and from there to positions south of Lens on October 17, now quiet after British attacks in that sector during the summer and early fall. They would remain there until February 1918.

In the opening four days of the first of the German 1918 offensives, the 17th Division advanced southeast of Arras towards Amiens but had to be relieved on March 25 having lost 50% of its effectives. It was back in the lines on April 1 until the 10th when it had to be withdrawn, resting first near Cambrai and then at Valenciennes. The division had suffered particularly around Bucquoy on April 5 and while off the lines, received a draft of some 1,300 replacements. It was back in the Bucquoy sector for a month beginning on May 24 when it was again rested until July 17. Then it moved to Laon a week later and from there marched in stages to the Vesle front near Reims where the Second Battle of the Marne had been opened by the Germans on July 15 only to be challenged by the Franco-American counter-stroke three days later. The division went into action on August 1 and was in stubborn retreat thereafter. The 89th Grenadiers received a special mention in the Orders of the Day praising its conduct on August 28 against the Americans at Bazoches. Relief was again necessary by mid-September but after only three days, it was thrust back into the fight. There followed off and on engagements through October in Champagne with a final move to the Ardennes at the end of the month where on the 29th, the division lost 558 prisoners. Nonetheless, the 90th Fusiliers drew praise in the German communiqué the following day for the resistance they had put up. But at the end on November 11, the division had been so reduced in numbers that it could muster, according to the British assessment, "but one or two battalions."

To go back to just before the turn of the century, in Mecklenburg-Schwerin, Grand Duke Friedrich Franz IV, the only son of Friedrich Franz III, succeeded to the throne upon his father's death on April 10, 1897. The new ruler was only a youth, having just turned 15 the day before. Until his 19th birthday in 1901, he reigned under the Regency of his uncle, Duke Johann Albrecht of Prussia. Friedrich Franz was to hold the throne throughout World War I. In Mecklenburg-Strelitz, Grand Duke Adolf Friedrich V had died on the eve of the war, on June 11, 1914. His elder son took the title Grand Duke Adolf

Friedrich VI. Never married, he committed suicide by shooting himself on February 24, 1918. The next surviving male in line for succession was his 1st cousin once removed, Karl Michael. But Karl Michael had already renounced any right to the throne by letter dated June 24, 1914 and on August 7 of that same year, had become a naturalized Russian citizen even as the German and Russian armies were having their first clashes. There had always been close dynastic connections between the Mecklenburg families and the Romanovs. Karl Michael held the rank of Lieutenant General in the Russian army and was a knight of Russia's highest order of knighthood and chivalry, the Order of St. Andrew. With Adolf Friedrich's death, the throne in Strelitz was left vacant and when Friedrich Franz was forced to abdicate on November 14, 1918, he acted on behalf of Strelitz as well as on behalf of Schwerin.

By the time of World War I, the Mecklenburgs had two house orders which were administered jointly. The senior one was the House Order of the Wendish Crown. Its exclusivity was protected by the second, the Griffin Order. The Order of the Wendish Crown was given out only sparingly and was rarely awarded for military achievement. The Griffin Order, on the other hand, served the military establishment as well as the civil sector, particularly prewar. Eric C. Ludvigsen, the medals expert, in undertaking an extensive study of the Griffin Order, also had some interesting comments on the Order of the Wendish Crown in a monograph published in *The Journal of the Orders and Medals Society of America, Volume 41, Number 12, December 1990* (Mr. Ludvigsen modestly entitled the work "An Outline" in acknowledging that there were many gaps in the available information but in truth, his paper on the Griffin Order is probably as close to being the definitive history of the order and a detailed description of its insignia that we are ever to have in the English language). Mr. Ludvigsen estimates that from its founding in 1864 until it became obsolete in 1918, there were as few as 2,154 awards of the Wendish Crown in all grades and that further, fully 40%-45% of these were not the order itself but, rather, its two affiliated decorations, the Gold and Silver Merit Crosses. He found that, as of 1906, only a handful of the highest ranking military had any grade of the order and then only because they held government or court positions. The number of domestic recipients of the order was limited by the statutes in each grade at any one time. During the 1914-1918 period, these were 10 for the Grand Cross, 25 for the Grand Commander, 55 for the Commander and 90 for the Knight. Only the Grand Cross grade was awarded "with Swords" and these went to princes of the reigning houses. But there was at least one exception to this, the Grand Cross with Gold Crown and Swords to *Generalfeldmarschall* von Hindenburg on November 24, 1915.

Because of its limited application to the military, no detailed description of the handsome insignia of the Order of the Wendish Crown need concern us here. Perhaps it is sufficient to note only that essentially the same crosses and breast stars served both houses with only two minor variations to distinguish between the two. The most visible difference was the motto carried around the center medallion on the crosses and breast stars. For Schwerin it was *Per Aspera Ad Astra* ("Through Struggle to the Stars" – the motto, incidentally, for the British Royal Air Force as well). For Strelitz it was *Avito Viret Honore* ("He Flourishes in Hereditary Honor"). The other distinguishing mark was the entwined initials of the original founders of the order which appeared on the reverse of the medallions on the crosses (the reverse of the breast stars was plain). For Schwerin it was *F F* (for Grand Duke Friedrich Franz II). For Strelitz it was *F W* (for Grand Duke Friedrich Wilhelm). The ratio of awards between the two houses was on the order of three for Schwerin to one for Strelitz.

It is appropriate to discuss the Griffin Order in greater depth because of its application to the military even though, as we shall see, it never became an award for bravery in the face of the enemy in World War I. The idea for creating a second order in Mecklenburg originated in Schwerin during the time Grand Duke Friedrich Franz II was on the throne there. But nothing had been done about it when he died in 1883. It fell to his successor, Friedrich Franz III, to implement the concept which he did on September 15, 1884. At its institution, there were five grades, Grand Cross, Grand Commander, Commander, Honor Cross and Knight. There were no affiliated decorations comparable to the Merit Crosses of the Order of the Wendish Crown. The Honor Cross was a pin-back badge, the equivalent of the Officer's Cross grade that subsequently was established in the structure of many other Imperial German orders. At the time, however, this grade was a new innovation. Then in 1904, a Knight's Cross with Crown was added ranking just ahead of the plain Knight's Cross. It was to be awarded as a mark of "higher distinction, in isolated cases." In practice, it came to be not uncommon at all. The Grand Cross, Grand Commander and Commander could also be awarded *mit Diamanten* ("with Diamonds") as a mark of special favor. Only the Grand Cross was awarded *mit Schwertern* ("with Swords") and this embellishment was meant for princes of the grand ducal families.[1] The Grand Cross went to these princes around the time of their 15th birthdays and with it came a Knight's Cross

---

[1] Other grades of the Griffin Order with swords have been seen. Some feel they could well have been badges made up with the possible intent of actually awarding them. Others believe they are merely artful works by fakers. The collecting fraternity has been plagued in recent years by copies of the Griffin Order Grand Cross badges and stars, both with and without swords.

which was worn on mounted groups of medals to represent the Grand Cross when full insignia was not worn.

A Grand Cross badge with Swords and Oakleaves exists which in his study Mr. Ludvigsen believes was a circa 1917 unique award presented by Grand Duke Friedrich Franz IV in Schwerin to his cousin in Strelitz, Grand Duke Adolf Friedrich VI, quite possibly upon the occasion of the latter's promotion to *Generalmajor* on November 6, 1917. Adolf Friedrich had seen active service in the field as a colonel of cavalry and one must wonder what role, if any, his wartime experiences played in his suicide just three months later.

Prior to 1904, the order in any grade was rarely awarded within Mecklenburg-Strelitz. Then in August of that year, the two rulers concluded an agreement whereby the Grand Ducal Mecklenburg Griffin Order, as it was termed, was to be administered in common with each Grand Duke a Grand Master. The then-existing statutes served for both houses augmented by a number of new provisions governing the administration of the order. It is believed the same ratio of awards between the two grand duchies that applied to the Order of the Wendish Crown was continued for the Griffin Order, or perhaps increased a bit in favor of Schwerin in a proportion of four to one instead of three to one.

The griffin was a mythical beast with the body and legs of a lion and the beak and wings of an eagle. It was the oldest element of Mecklenburg heraldry, first appearing on the seals of the princes of Mecklenburg and Rostock in the early 13th century. The same insignia served for awards from both houses. The crosses of the Griffin Order were plain in the extreme yet handsomely wrought. They were a Maltese cross with the only embellishment being a small center medallion on the obverse. In this, the cross reflected the Prussian influence that was described in the case of the Order of Henry the Lion in Brunswick when new grades of similarly simple design were added to that otherwise highly ornate order. The badges of the Griffin Order also used the same so-called "pie slice" suspension seen in such Prussian orders as that of the Black Eagle, the military division of the *Orden Pour le Mérite* and the *Johanniter Orden*. The badges were enameled red and edged in gold (silver-gilt actually in the case of all issue badges). Merely saying "enameled red" does not adequately describe the beauty of the jeweler's art in this case. Mr. Ludvigsen says it much better when he writes that the arms of the crosses were "enameled in transparent red with convex surfaces tapering down to the edges. The underlying metal is cut to take the enamel, in a champleve-style pattern of dashed lines parallel to the arm edges and joining along a line bisecting the arms lengthwise." The effect was particularly striking. The badges

A second order, the Griffin Order, was founded in the Mecklenburgs by Friedrich Franz III of Schwerin in 1884. From 1904, it was administered jointly by both grand duchies. Prewar, it was widely awarded within the military establishment but less so in World War I and never, as far as can be determined, for outright bravery. It was beautifully enameled in translucent red and swords were used only on Grand Crosses going to princes of the two houses. Above: The Honor Cross, a pin-back badge. Below: The Knight's Cross which also came with Crown.

of the three higher grades were fully enameled on both sides whereas the reverse of the Honor Cross and both Knight's Crosses were left in plain matte gilt. The center medallion displayed (in Mr. Ludvigsen's words again) a "highly modeled" griffin in silver-gilt facing heraldic right. There was no reverse medallion on the issue badges.

The breast stars of the Grand Cross and Grand Commander were of a more conventional design reflecting, perhaps, the Russian influence. Both had blunted silver rays of eight points but the four diagonal rays on the Grand Commander breast star were shortened and since the same center medallion was used on both stars, this provided instant eye differentiation. In the center of the medallion, the "highly modeled" griffin again appeared in silver-gilt. Surrounding this was a transparent red-enameled ring upon which the order's motto, *Altior Adversis*, was applied in silver-gilt block letters (one scholar translates the Latin to mean "Enobled in Adversity" while another Drefers "Exalted in Adversity"). The Grand Cross breast star was at first worn on the right side. In 1902, this was switched to the more conventional position of the left side. From the beginning, the Grand Commander star was worn on the left breast. The ribbon for the sash, neck cravats and breast ribbons was the same except for width, bright yellow with narrow red edge stripes, an eye-pleasing complement to the red and gold enameled badges.

In prewar rank lists, the Griffin Order shows up with considerable regularity among the military. Records in the archive in Schwerin do not disclose to what extent it was employed for military merit in World War I. As already mentioned, there is no recorded instance of it being used to reward bravery in the face of the enemy. Instead, both grand duchies relied on their respective war crosses to recognize the combatant (these awards are discussed in the two chapters that immediately follow). So little did the late medals authority, *Dr.* K.-G. Klietmann, regard the Griffin Order as a military award that he did not even include it in his treatise *Pour le Mérite und Tapferkeitsmedaille* (although, rather curiously, he did include the Order of the Wendish Crown). The only instance where the Griffin Order came into play in World War I in respect to aviation that has been discovered by this writer was a brief account found in the Schwerin archive. It occurred on the occasion of a visit by Grand Duke Friedrich Franz IV of Mecklenburg-Schwerin on August 29, 1918 to the airfield at Müritzsee where he observed a program of flight and mock combat demonstration. In attendance also were representatives of the Inspectorate of the Air Service (*Inspektion der Fliegertruppe - Idflieg*) and the Inspectorate of Aircraft Aviation (*Inspektion der Flugzeugwesens*). The Grand Duke obviously felt it desirable that he express his appreciation to the heads of these two services, to members of their staffs and to the Commanding Officer of the airfield and his Adjutant. He chose the Griffin Order as the means to do so and the following awards were forthcoming:

Honor Cross	*Oberstleutnant* Wilhelm Siegert, head of *Inspektion der Fliegertruppe* *Major* Felix Wagenführ, head of *Inspecktion der Flugzeugwesens*
Knight's Cross with Crown	*Hauptmann* Siegfried Reinhardt, on staff of *Inspektion der Fliegertruppe*
Knight's Cross	*Oberleutnant* Hans Karl Bauer, Adjutant to Commanding Officer, Müritzsee Airfield *Oberleutnant* Emil Flörke, Adjutant, *Inspektion der Fliegertruppe* *Oberleutnant* Conrad von Raczelk, on staff of *Inspektion der Fliegertruppe* *Oberleutnant* Fritz Sprungmann, Adjutant, *Inspektion der Flugzeugwesens*

In addition, a *Hauptmann* Cörper who was on hand from the aviation section of the War Ministry received the Mecklenburg-Schwerin Military Merit Cross 2nd Class. The Grand Duke's choice of the Griffin Order for the other gentlemen can only be speculative but perhaps it was because they already possessed his Military Merit Cross (the roll of that award could not be located in the archive in Schwerin so, as we shall see, the known recipients in aviation contingents are far below the actual number). We do know from the roll of the Strelitz counterpart award, the Cross for Distinction in War, that Siegert as a *Major* with *Idflieg* received that award in the 2nd Class so its is reasonable to assume he may well have already had the Schwerin cross. There was one final award noted in connection with the Grand Duke's visit to Müritzsee and this the most curious of all. The Commanding Officer of the airfield, *Hauptmann* August Joly, was decorated with the Strelitz cross in the 2nd Class. With his rank and station, one would think that he, too, would have been a recipient of the

Prewar, the later heads of the German Army Air Service, Ernst von Hoeppner and Hermann von der Lieth-Thomsen, shown together at the right, both held the Griffin Order Honor Cross. The Inspector of Air Service during the war, *Oberstlt.* Wilhelm Siegert (below in the back seat of a staff car with Thomsen) and the Inspector of Aircraft Aviation, *Major* Felix Wagenführ (below right) both were awarded the Honor Cross on August 29, 1918 having been present at an air show attended by the Grand Duke of Mecklenburg-Schwerin. Bottom: The record in the Schwerin archive of Siegert's Honor Cross. While the line under the right-hand column would seem to indicate he held no other Mecklenburg awards, we know that he received the Strelitz Cross for Distinction in War 2nd Class.

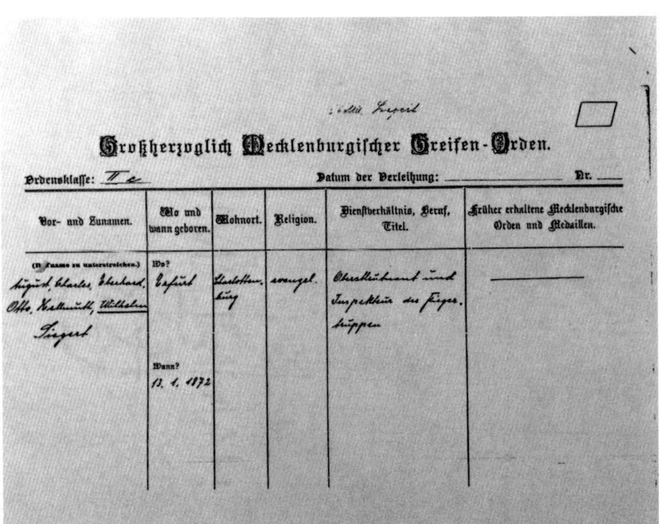

Großherzoglich Mecklenburgischer Greifen-Orden.

Ordensklasse: II a Datum der Verleihung: ______ Nr. ___

Vor- und Zunamen.	Wo und wann geboren.	Wohnort.	Religion.	Dienstverhältnis, Beruf, Titel.	Früher erhaltene Mecklenburgische Orden und Medaillen.
(Rufname zu unterstreichen.) August, Charles, Eberhard, Otto, Hellmuth, Wilhelm Siegert	Wo? Erfurt Wann? 13. 1. 1872	Charlottenburg	evangel.	Oberstleutnant und Inspekteur der Fliegertruppen	______

Griffin Order, particularly since his Adjutant got a Knight's Cross. Did he already have it? It does not show as one of his immediate prewar awards. And why Strelitz? Again, it is guesswork but he, too, could have had the Schwerin cross and with the Grand Duke of the Strelitz branch now dead and the throne vacant, Friedrich Franz undoubtedly had the right to approve Strelitz awards as well.

Just a few other officers who served in the *Fliegertruppe* are known to have possessed the Griffin Order prewar. As a *Generalmajor* and commanding the 17th Infantry Brigade, Ernst von Hoeppner, the later head of the *Luftstreitkräfte*, had the Honor Cross as did the man who would become his Chief-of-Staff, the then *Major* Hermann von der Lieth-Thomson who on the eve of the war was in *Eisenbahn-Regiment Nr.2*. Knight's Crosses were held by *Oberleutnant* (later *Hauptmann*) Albert Mühlig-Hofmann in *Flieger-Bataillon Nr.2.* and *Hauptmann* Franz Geerdtz in *Flieger-Bataillon Nr.3.*, his being with Crown.

CHAPTER XXII

THE MILITARY AWARDS OF THE GRAND DUCHY OF MECKLENBURG-SCHWERIN

THE MILITARY MERIT CROSS

The Military Merit Cross was founded on August 5, 1848 by Grand Duke Friedrich Franz II initially to recognize bravery in the campaign against Denmark that year over the Schleswig-Holstein question. Subsequently, it was extended to men and women who made contributions on the home front to war efforts. From its institution all the way up to and through World War I, the same basic insignia served for these purposes. What did change in a series of different coinages was a year date on the cross to reflect a particular conflict.

The badge was a *cross pattée* in bronze-gilt (sometimes referred to as "cannon bronze") that was clearly based an the Prussian Iron Cross including the beading around its edges. From the beginning, it came in two classes, 1st and 2nd. The 1st, like the Iron Cross 1st Class, was a pin-back piece worn without a ribbon on the lower left breast. The 2nd Class was worn from a ribbon usually in conjunction with other awarded breast badges on a bar but sometimes merely looped through a buttonhole on the front of the tunic. The ribbon remained unchanged during the decoration's lifetime. For combatants, it was the same ribbon as that employed by the Duchy's House Order of the Wendish Crown, pale blue with narrow yellow (inner) and red (outer) edge stripes. Non-combatant awards came with a ribbon with the colors reversed, red with narrow blue (inner) and yellow (outer) edge stripes. These became known as awards on the "red ribbon." On the obverse of the cross, the initials of the founder, *F F*, appeared in raised letters. On the upper arm, there was a small molded crown and on the lower arm, the appropriate year date. The reverse of the 1st Class badge was plain but on the back of the 2nd Class badge the inscription *Für Auszeichnung im Kriege* ("For Distinction in War") appeared on three lines.

The first crosses carried the year date *1848* but when that dispute continued into the following year, new crosses were struck with the date *1849*. Mecklenburg-Schwerin was not directly involved in the Italian War of 1859 in which Austria lost Lombardy but some of its military observers and Austrian officers received crosses bearing that date.

War again erupted with Denmark over the status of Schleswig-Holstein in 1864 and this time, Denmark lost the provinces for good. This campaign occasioned crosses marked *1864*. Next were crosses dated *1866* and *1870* for the war with Austria that drove it out of German affairs forever and the war against France that united the whole of Germany. In the 1877 war between Russia and Turkey, Mecklenburg-Schwerin's sympathies were clearly on the side of Russia and although it took no direct part, it awarded crosses marked that year to some Russian and Romanian royals and some of its own officers who, again, were on hand as military observers. There were Mecklenburgers in the East Asian Expeditionary Corps during the Boxer Rebellion in 1900-1901 and 2nd Class crosses were struck with the date *1900* for those who had displayed "distinguished behavior." In suppressing the native uprisings in Germany's African colonies in 1905 and 1906, especially in German Southwest Africa, 2nd Class crosses were awarded without any year date at all. Finally, we come to 1914 when, as to be expected, crosses bearing that year date once again were awarded. Grand Duke Friedrich Franz IV actually did not renew the decoration until February 28, 1915 but awards were made retroactive to the start of the war. The 1st Class crosses were struck in both a flat style and a slightly concave style. The last awards for the war were not processed until the end of May 1924.

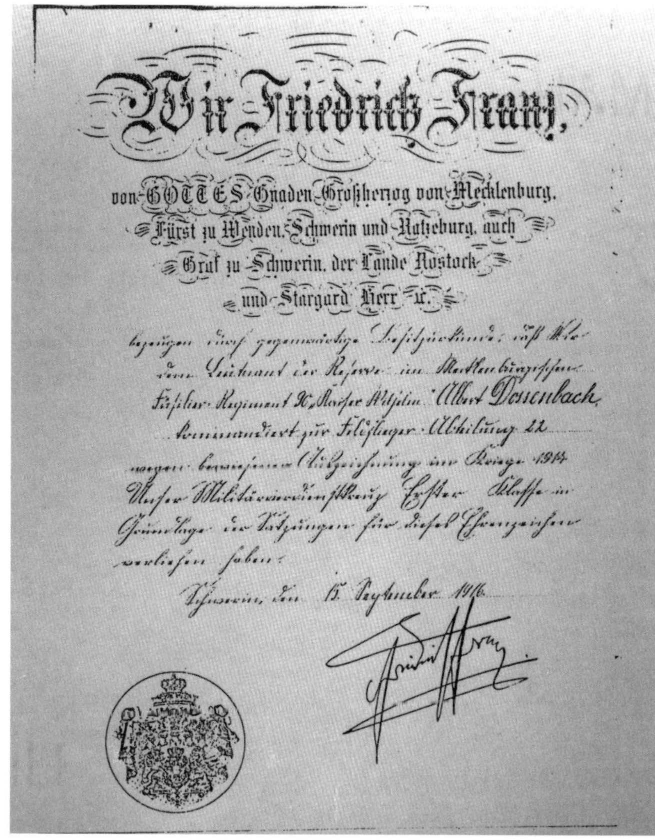

Wir Friedrich Franz,
von GOTTES Gnaden Großherzog von Mecklenburg,
Fürst zu Wenden, Schwerin und Ratzeburg, auch
Graf zu Schwerin, der Lande Rostock
und Stargard Herr &c.

bezeugen durch gegenwärtige Besitzurkunde, daß Wir dem Leutnant der Reserve im Mecklenburgischen Füsilier-Regiment 90, Kaiser Wilhelm, Albert Dossenbach, kommandiert zur Fliegerabteilung 22 wegen bewiesener Auszeichnung im Kriege 1914 Unser Militärverdienstkreuz Erster Klasse in Gemäßheit der Satzungen für dieses Ehrenzeichen verliehen haben.

Schwerin, den 15. September 1916.

Grand Duke Friedrich Franz IV of Mecklenburg-Schwerin renewed its Military Merit Cross on February 28, 1915. It had served in various wars and campaigns since its founding in 1848 with only the year date changing. Closely resembling the Iron Cross, it was, however, struck in bronze-gilt. The 1st Class (above) was a pin-back badge. Below. The obverse and reverse of the 2nd Class breast badge. Right: The bestowal document for the 1st Class award to the later *Pour le Mérite* two-seater and fighter pilot, Albert Dossenbach, September 15, 1916.

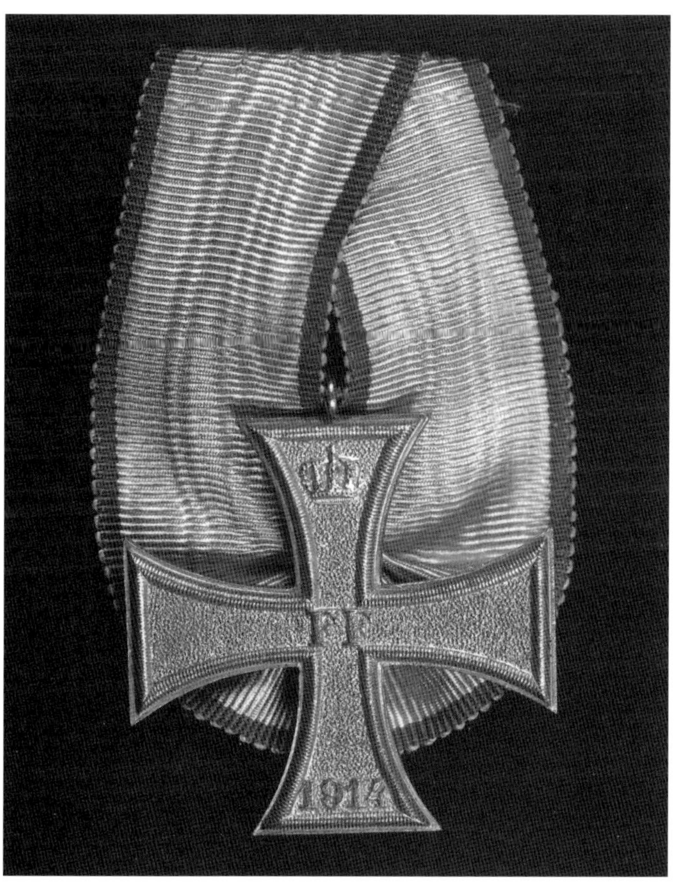

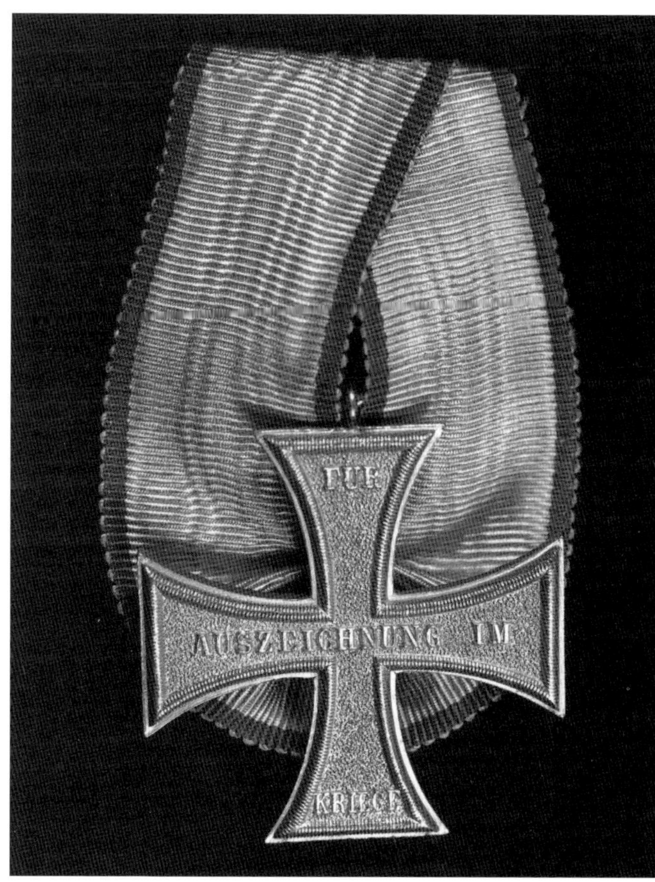

Two visits by this writer to the archive in Schwerin in 1996 failed to uncover anything close to a roll of World War I recipients of the Military Merit Cross, merely snippets of information whereas, as we shall see in the next chapter, far more, but nonetheless not complete, information was obtained on Mecklenburg-Strelitz's counterpart decoration, the Cross for Distinction in War. Of necessity, therefore, the relatively few fliers known to have received the cross in one or both classes have had to come from a number of other sources. Certainly, the 56 men who have been found represent only a fraction of the actual total which could number several times that figure (see Appendix XXXIII). Seven of the more prominent aviation recipients have already been given biographical treatment in earlier volumes in this series because of the other awards they earned. Very little on them will appear here as a result. For reference purposes, the men and the volume or volumes in which they were given the fullest treatment were:

Karl Bolle	Volume IV
Albert Dossenbach	Volume VI
Hermann Fricke	Volumes II and V
Walter Hahn	Volume V
Erich Killinger	Volume VI
Günther Plüschow	Volume VI
Karl Schweikhardt	Volume VI

There were two other well known airmen, both successful fighter pilot leaders, who received the Schwerin cross in both classes, the *Pour le Mérite* 30-victory ace, Ulrich Neckel, and Kurt-Bertram von Döring whose air service spanned the entire war and who was credited with 11 victories. Both men have come up in previous volumes although neither was accorded a full biography. Most readers are familiar with the high points of their careers thanks, for example, to books like the Norman Franks et al Grub Street productions. Thus they will be given their due here only by a few photographs which will be equally familiar to many readers.

Strangely missing from the known aviation recipients of the Schwerin Military Merit Cross is the name of Prussia's most highly decorated flier, Manfred *Freiherr* von Richthofen. Even though the decoration was given out widely to men who were neither native Mecklenburgers nor who had ever served in a Mecklenburg contingent and despite his growing fame beginning in late 1916, he never received it. In fact, of the five grand duchies in the empire, only Hesse saw fit to recognize him. He was passed over by Baden, Oldenburg and the two Mecklenburgs (but see the next chapter on his failed nomination for the Strelitz cross).

For the reasons already stated, this chapter will be slim on biographies of those who did receive the Schwerin cross, just two plus a third who may have been a possible recipient. The first man, a fighter pilot, will be much more familiar to readers than the other two, observers both and typically, all but forgotten today.

OBERLEUTNANT HANS-HELMUT VON BODDIEN

The scion of an old Mecklenburg family, Hans-Helmut von Boddien was appointed a *Fahnenjunker* in *Kürassier-Regiment-Königin (Pommersches) Nr.2.* just a few weeks shy of his 19th birthday, the son of a retired army *Major* who had died when Helmut was only seven years old. The youth made good progress in his peacetime regiment, advancing to *Fähnrich* on May 23, 1911 and receiving his commission as *Leutnant* a year later, on May 22, 1912 (with his Patent reverting back to May 1910). The cavalryman honed his skills at the Officer's Riding School in Paderborn for nine months, ending his courses there on July 30, 1913. Upon the outbreak of war, he was seconded to *Reserve-Ulanen-Regiment Nr.2.* and in close combat with an enemy horseman in a patrol clash, received a wound in his upper right arm from the thrust of the trooper's lance. It took him nearly a year before he was fit enough for duty and after a short stint as a battalion adjutant with the 55th Reserve Infantry Regiment, he rejoined the 2nd Uhlans. In December 1915, his transfer to aviation came through, another member of the cavalry who saw scouting in the air a logical extension of his training. He reported to *Flieger-Ersatz-Abteilung 5*'s observer school at Hanover on the 7th.

By mid-June 1916, von Boddien was ready for the front and joined *Feldflieger-Abteilung 18*. There, he and his pilot, *Leutnant* Friedrich-Wilhelm Lübbert, rated a mention in the *Kofl* report of the 6th German Army for their "gallant behavior" in January 1917. Having put in nearly a year of arduous two-seater work and with a commendation to his credit, his application for pilot training could hardly be turned down. Accordingly, he left what was now designated *Flieger-Abteilung 18* and arrived at *FEA 11* in Brieg on May 24, 1917. It took him only one month to get the knack of flying and either on the 24th itself or the 25th, he joined the prestigious *Jasta 11*. These were momentous days at its base at Harlebeke in Flanders. On the 24th, *Jasta 11*, along with *Jastas 4, 6* and *10*, had been ordered to form the first *Jagdgeschwader* "for the purpose of winning and securing air superiority in crucial combat sectors." All four flights were to assemble on one field

After the customary service as a two-seater pilot, *Oblt*. Hans-Helmut von Boddien joined *Jasta 11* in late June 1917. From an old Mecklenburg family, he was a recipient of the Schwerin Military Merit Cross in both classes. At the left in the photograph above, he stands with the *Pour le Mérite* flier, Karl Allmenröder and Allmenröder's rather beat-up, overpainted red Albatros D.III. Allmenröder had but a day or two to live, being shot down by ground fire on June 27, 1917. At right, von Boddien with one of *Jasta 11*'s Fokker Dr.1 triplanes.

Von Boddien commanded *Jasta 59* from January 1918 until his serious wounding on September 27. There he scored his five victories of the war. In 1919, he fought the Russian Red Army in Lithuania with *Flieger-Abteilung 424* with whom he is shown here, the tall figure 4th from the right with his distinctive cuirassier's cap. He never returned from a mission on November 29 and his exact fate was never determined.

"if possible" (this occurred on July 2 when all moved to the aerodrome at Marckebeke). On June 25, the formal appointment of *Rittmeister* Manfred *Freiherr* von Richthofen as squadron leader was made by *Kogenluft*. Within the week, *Jagdgeschwader Nr.1*'s staff was in place. *Oberleutnant* Karl Bodenschatz came over from *Jasta "Boelcke"* as adjutant, a job he had performed there. *Leutnant* Konstantin Krefft, one of *Jasta 11*'s early pilots who had scored his first and second victories in March and April 1917, became the technical officer "for the time being" and von Boddien, it is believed, was assigned as the administrative officer although only Bodenschatz was not expected to fly as well (Bodenschatz, an ex-infantry officer, never qualified as either a pilot or an observer).[1] Krefft, however, crashed on August 11 when he suffered engine failure over the Marckebeke field but was not seriously injured. It is nonetheless doubtful that he did much flying after that and he ended the war with just those two 1917 victories. Von Boddien, too, was unsuccessful in the air during his time with *Jasta 11*. In fact, his only mention in the War Diary of *JG 1* came on an entry for December 10, 1917. There it was noted that *Leutnant* Eberhardt Mohnicke "flew into" the aircraft of von Boddien, now an *Oberleutnant*, from behind during a combat. Mohnicke's machine crashed but he, too, escaped unscathed. Von Boddien, with elevators gone as a result of the collision, somehow managed to get back to his own field and executed a smooth landing, no mean feat.

At the end of January 1918, despite his having no luck in scoring a confirmed victory, von Boddien was transferred to the newly formed *Jasta 59* as its second commander (the first, *Leutnant* Walter Höhne, one of the original pilot's in Boelcke's *Jasta 2* and one of the few survivors of that early group, was being sent back to the now *Jasta "Boelcke"* in an attempt to restore it to is former prominence, a job the worn-out man was not up to and he handed the command over to the same Karl Bolle just mentioned as one of more illustrious holders of the Mecklenburg-Schwerin Military Merit Cross only a month later). *Jasta 59* turned out to be one of the lesser scoring fighter units as many of the higher-numbered *Jastas* formed in December 1917 and early 1918 were unless they were blessed

[1] As a recipient of Baden's Zähringen Lion Order, a biography of Bodenschatz appeared in Volume VI in this series.

with a superstar.[2] From its first confirmed success on March 10, 1918 until the end, *Jasta 59* pilots were credited with only 20 victories in all. Yet von Boddien did more than his share, with a total of five for himself and ending up as the leading scorer in the unit. And had his career not been cut short by a wound in combat, he might have done much better. He had scored himself for the first time on March 23 but it was not until August and September that he really started going, getting confirmed victories twice in each month including a "double" on September 24. Then in a fight with D.H.9s that were being escorted by S.E.5as on a bombing mission on September 27, von Boddien was hit my a machine gun bullet in the right shin-bone and forced to break off and return home. His wound was serious enough to require three months' hospitalization and thus he was put out of action for the rest of the war. But like many of his peers at this time, his service to his country was not over. Both within Germany and on its borders, left-wing revolutionaries were threatening the postwar German government with a takeover. Von Boddien was one who volunteered to join the paramilitary formations created by those on the right to crush these forces. In his case, it was a journey to Lithuania which the Russian Red Army was attempting to seize. He flew in a unit designated *Flieger-Abteilung 424* and while on a flight on November 29, 1919, he did not return. No trace of him was ever found. Whether he died that day as a result of hostile action, or whether he suffered a fatal crash, or whether, perhaps, he even survived a forced landing in enemy lines only to be executed (a not uncommon fate meted out to prisoners taken by both sides), remains unknown. What is known is that his long service during World War I was well regarded and well rewarded. In addition to the Mecklenburg-Schwerin Military Merit Cross in both 1st and 2nd Class, his other awards, all undated unfortunately, were both Iron Crosses, the Knight's Cross with Swords of the Royal House Order of Hohenzollern and the Lippe War Merit Cross.

Author's Note: Appreciation is expressed to Mr. Albert Rebours of Chatou, France for the information on von Boddien's prewar service and for his awards list.

[2] Notable exceptions were 21 pilots in such units who scored in double-digits. They and their units were (total victories in brackets): In *Jasta 45*: *Lt.* Gustav Dörr 35, *Vzfw.* Karl Schlegel 22, *Lt.* Hans Rolfes 16 (17). In *Jasta 46*: *Lt.* Oskar Hennrich 20, *Lt.* Robert Heibert 12 (13). In *Jasta 50*: *Lt.* Hans von Freden 16 (20). In *Jasta 52*: *Lt.* Paul Billik 23 (31). In *Jasta 56*: *Lt.* Franz Piechulek 12 (14). In *Jasta 58*: *Lt.* Martin Demisch 10. In *Jasta 61*: *Lt.* Siegfried Büttner 10 (13). In *Jasta 62*: *Lt.* Max Näther 26. In *Jasta 66*: *Lt.* Arthur Laumann 23 (28), *Lt.* Werner Preuss 22, *Lt.* Rudolf Windisch 14 (22). In *Jasta 68*: *Lt.* Fritz Pütter 16 (26). In *Jasta 72*: *Lt.* Karl Menckhoff 19 (39). In *Jasta 74*, *Oblt.* Theodor Camman 10 (12). In *Jasta 76b*: *Lt.* Walter Böning 11 (17). In *Jasta 79b*: *Lt.* Hans Böhning 12 (17). In *Jasta 81*: *Vzfw.* Dietrich Averes 10, *Vzfw.* Alfons Nagler 10.

HAUPTMANN ERNST EBERSTEIN

Ernst Eberstein was one of the few early airmen who went off to war in 1914 and who, except for time off both attending and commanding observer schools during the course of the war, was returned to an active command rather than remaining in staff positions. His awards testify to the fact that his work was highly regarded both at the front and behind the lines.

Eberstein gained his commission as *Leutnant* in *3. Niederschlesisches Infanterie-Regiment Nr.50.* on July 22, 1906. Just when he made the switch to aviation before the war is not known but he was posted to *Feldflieger-Abteilung 14* on the Eastern Front on August 2, 1914, quickly proving himself as evidenced by his award of the Iron Cross 2nd Class when the war was just over a month old. The date was September 9, 1914 and as readers are well aware, an Iron Cross in any grade so early on was an exceptional event. Eberstein's cross even predates the one given to the later *Pour le Mérite* ace, Rudolf Berthold. His award was made the following week, on the 13th, and at the time, was only the second such award within the entire German 2nd Army. Berthold's came for his valuable reconnaissance's in the west, on the Marne (Berthold was still an observer at the time). Eberstein's was for the reports he turned in on Russian troop movements leading up to the decisive German victory at Tannenberg (August 27-30, 1914) and which resulted in untold Russian fatalities, 92,000 prisoners taken and the suicide of the commander of the trapped Russian 2nd Army, General Aleksandr Samsonov. Only remnants of his force escaped. The fliers of *FFl.Abt. 14* proved the value of aerial reconnaissance although many of the more hidebound German brass were still loathe to accept, or act upon, the findings of these pioneer aviators. And before 1914 ended, Eberstein's efforts were rewarded with promotion to *Oberleutnant* (November 8) and the authorization of his Observer's Badge (November 19).

1915 was another busy year for Eberstein, the first seven months of which saw him still in Russia with *14*. On February 15, he received the Iron Cross 1st Class and while enemy aerial opposition was virtually nil, the war on the ground continued with German and Austrian advances into Russian-held territory continuing in February and May. We have an interesting account of an event on May 26 related by Eberstein himself. At 3:30 a.m. on that Wednesday morning, word was received at *41*'s airfield at Ortelsburg that a lone Russian aircraft was approaching the area. A frequent pilot of Eberstein's was *Leutnant* Ernst Canter who won fame along with his observer, *Leutnant* Mertens, when they delivered the report on the eve of the Battle of Tannenberg that Samsonov's and Rennen-

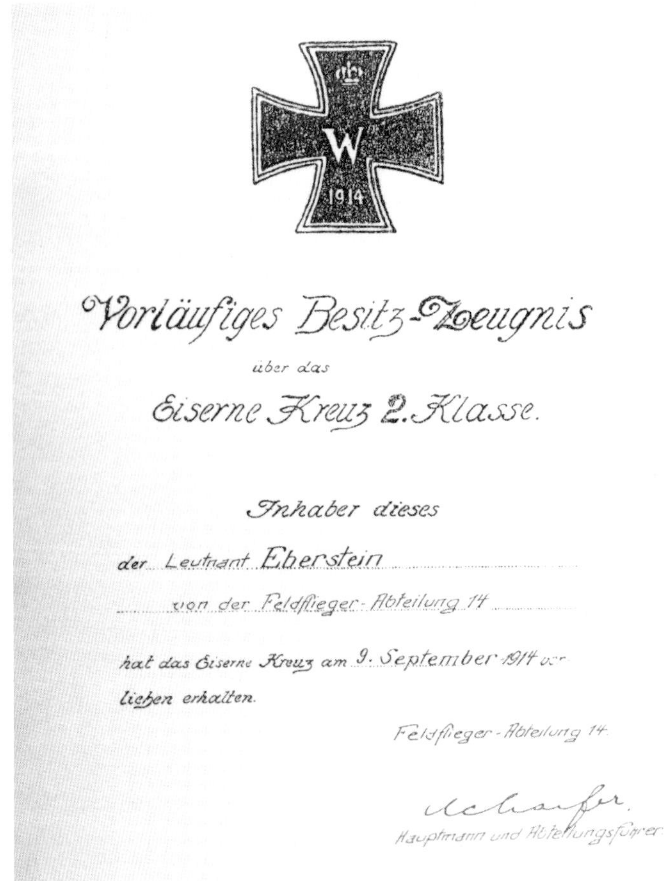

W
1914

Vorläufiges Besitz-Zeugnis
über das
Eiserne Kreuz 2. Klasse.

Inhaber dieses
der Leutnant Eberstein
von der Feldflieger-Abteilung 14
hat das Eiserne Kreuz am 9. September 1914 verliehen erhalten.

Feldflieger-Abteilung 14.

Schafer.
Hauptmann und Abteilungsführer

Opposite
Top: The then *Leutnant* Ernst Eberstein, left with an Aviatik B-Type sometime in 1915, won an exceptionally early Iron Cross 2nd Class when he received it on September 9, 1914 for his reconnaissances on the Russian Front that contributed to the decisive German victory at Tannenberg. Their work was all the more remarkable since he and the men of his unit, *FFl.Abt. 14*, were flying the slow and unwieldy *Taube* (dove) monoplane already obsolete.

Bottom: "The Fliers of Tannenberg." Men of *FFl.Abt. 14* with Eberstein 3rd from the left. Two of his comrades there, *Lt.* Canter, 2nd from the left, and *Lt.* Mertens, 3rd from the right, were credited with delivering a crucial report which materially affected the course of the battle.

Right above: The up-turned Albatros B.II of Eberstein on *FFl.Abt. 14*'s airfield at Ortelsburg in Russia on May 26, 1915, the result of his pilot's attempt to turn back when it had engine trouble at low level after take-off. Thereafter, Eberstein lectured young pilots never to turn in such circumstances but always land by going straight ahead.

Right and below: After a year of frontline service, Eberstein imparted some of his hard-earned experience to newcomers at *FEA 7*'s observer school. In both photos, he is marked by the arrow. His pilot, left, was a *Lt.* Kelch. The school's CO was a *Hptm.* Aumann, probably center with the Iron Cross 1st Class.

Eberstein commanded the Observer's School at Schwerin from October 12, 1916 until December 18, 1917 whose souvenir booklet he autographed. He then took over *Flieger-Abteilung 26* and remained in charge there until the outfit was disbanded a month after the armistice.

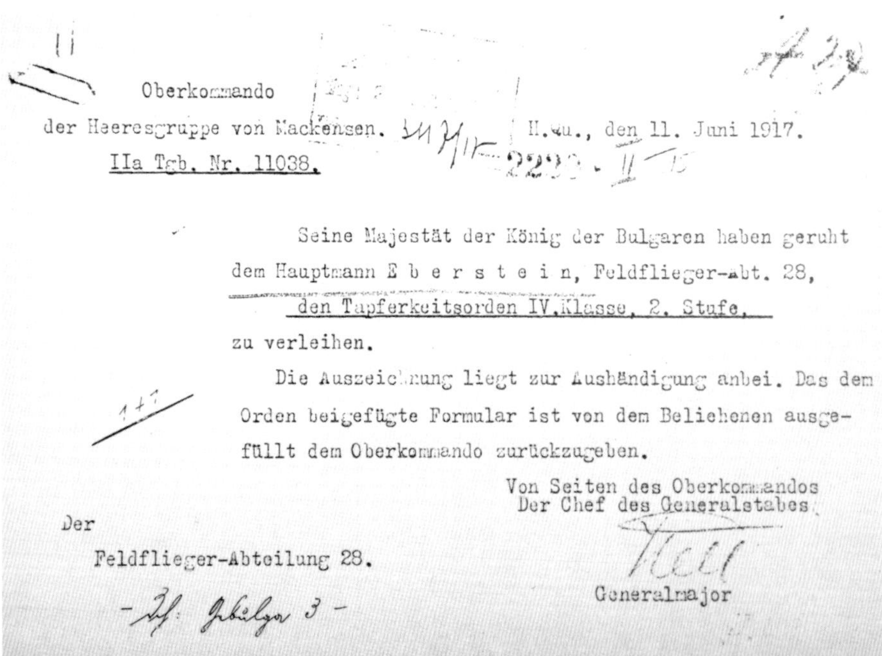

Oberkommando
der Heeresgruppe von Mackensen. H.Qu., den 11. Juni 1917.
IIa Tgb. Nr. 11038.

Seine Majestät der König der Bulgaren haben geruht dem Hauptmann E b e r s t e i n, Feldflieger-Abt. 28, den Tapferkeitsorden IV.Klasse, 2. Stufe, zu verleihen.

Die Auszeichnung liegt zur Aushändigung anbei. Das dem Orden beigefügte Formular ist von dem Beliehenen ausgefüllt dem Oberkommando zurückzugeben.

Von Seiten des Oberkommandos
Der Chef des Generalstabes

Generalmajor

Der
Feldflieger-Abteilung 28.

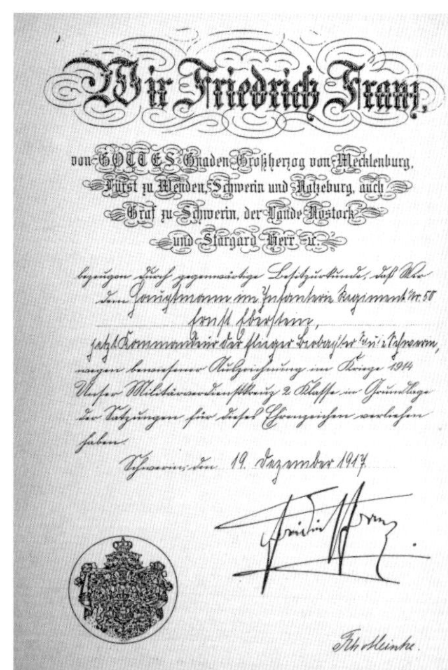

Wir Friedrich Franz,
von Gottes Gnaden Großherzog von Mecklenburg,
Fürst zu Wenden, Schwerin und Ratzeburg, auch
Graf zu Schwerin, der Lande Rostock
und Stargard Herr. etc.

Schwerin, den 19. Dezember 1917

Above: The notice dated 11 June 1917 attesting to Eberstein's award of the Bulgarian Bravery Order 4th Class 2nd Degree for his service in his old *FFl.Abt. 28* in the fall of 1916. Right: A parting present from Schwerin dated 19 December 1917 awarding Eberstein his Mecklenburg-Schwerin Military Merit Cross 2nd Class.

kampf's armies were operating independently which helped in the decision to attack Samsonov's forces without fear of Rennenkampf coming to their aid.[3] But on this particular day, Eberstein's assigned pilot was a man named Krahnen. Together, the pair drove to their field only to find their Albatros B.II's engine malfunctioning. So Eberstein commandeered a second B.II and the pair took off (he does not tell us just what they expected to do in their unarmed aircraft against the Russian marauder however). Just as they lifted off, the engine of this plane began knocking and they began to lose altitude. Eberstein shouted back to Krahnen ordering him to keep straight ahead and pour on more gas. The Albatros failed to respond so Eberstein told his pilot to keep on but get the tail down for a landing. They were now only 10 meters above ground and instead of heeding Eberstein's advice, Krahnen banked in a potentially fatal attempt to return to their field. Luckily, they made it but upon landing, Krahnen ran into the hangar tent which housed Eberstein's regular aircraft damaging its tail and giving a mechanic there a slight knock. The Albatros they were

[3] Canter and Mertens delivered their report to *General der Infanterie* Hermann von François, commander of the German 1st Corps. Some historians have called von François the true victor at Tannenberg for ignoring second-in-command Ludendorff's caution and for pushing on to deliver the decisive blow on the last day. Others believe von François has been overpraised and the Russians at that stage, as von Hindenburg, the Supreme Commander, would later say were no longer seeking victory but their own destruction. Berlin gave the credit for the victory to von Hindenburg, awarding him his *Pour le Mérite* on September 2 (Ludendorff had already been decorated with what was only the second *Pour le Mérite* of the war on August 8 for his role in the capture of the fortress of Liége). Von François would not receive his own *Pour le Mérite* until May 14, 1915 for the success and breakthrough at Gorlice-Tornow in Galicia on May 2.

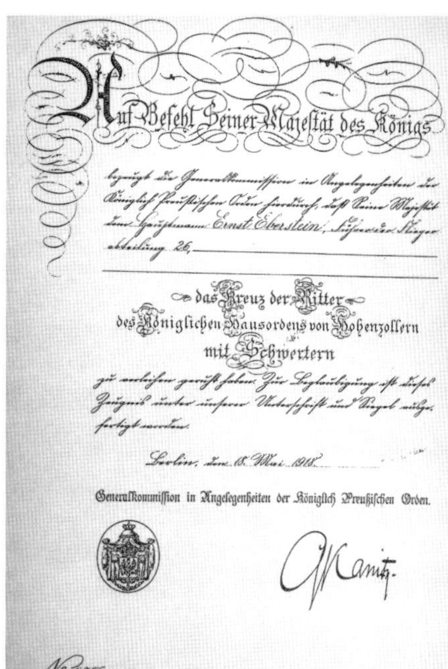

Auf Befehl Seiner Majestät des Königs

bezeugt die Generalkommission in Angelegenheiten der Königlich Preußischen Orden hierdurch, daß Seine Majestät dem Hauptmann Ernst Eberstein, Führer der Flieger-abteilung 26,

das Kreuz der Ritter des Königlichen Hausordens von Hohenzollern mit Schwertern

zu verleihen geruht haben. Zur Beglaubigung ist dieses Zeugnis unter unserer Unterschrift und Siegel ausgefertigt worden.

Berlin, den 18. Mai 1918.

Generalkommission in Angelegenheiten der Königlich Preußischen Orden.

Kanitz

№ 6856.

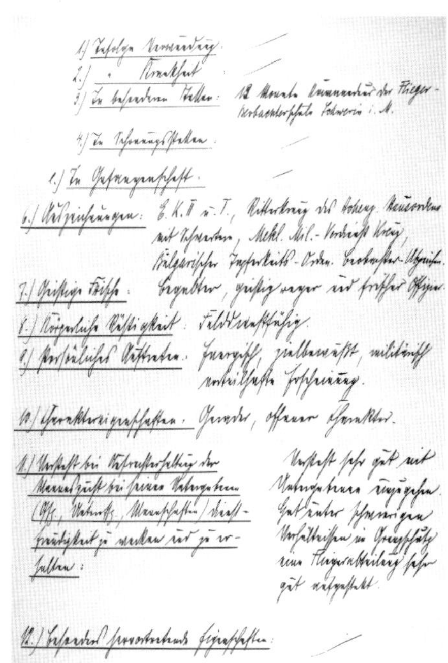

Above: Like many of his peers, Eberstein joined the paramilitary right wing forces fighting the Communists in the revolutions which engulfed Germany after the war. Taken at that time, this pose shows off all his wartime awards. The eagle-like devices on the collar of his tunic are unlike any *Freikorps* insignia known to this writer. Could they be of Eberstein's own creation, perhaps alluding to the mythical griffin of Mecklenburg? Right: The bestowal document to his Hohenzollern House Order dated 18 May 1918 and a page from a postwar fitness report in which his orders and decorations are listed (item No. 6).

flying up-ended and in Eberstein's own words was "*kaputt*." Neither Eberstein nor Krahnen were injured but thereafter, Eberstein always lectured young pilots that if they experienced engine trouble, always go straight on, never attempt to turn.

Eberstein got his first respite from the front on August 13, 1915 when he was ordered to report to *Flieger-Ersatz-Abteilung 7* for a month's tour of duty at the observer's school in Cologne-Bützweilerhof where the first courses there were being conducted. The head instructor was a *Hauptmann* Aumann but, what with a year's experience under his belt, it is safe to assume that Eberstein was there as one of his chief assistants and not as a pupil. In mid-October, Eberstein was back in action again, this time with *FFl.Abt. 66* and on December 18, was promoted *Hauptmann*. Nearly nine months went by after that until he took charge of *FFl.Abt. 28* on September 4, 1916. Then it was back to school again but this time as the Commanding Officer of the observer's school at Schwerin with effect from October 12 the same year. A delayed award from the Bulgarians reached Eberstein on June 11, 1917. It was in the form of its Bravery Order 4th Class, 2nd Degree (a breast badge; the 4th Class, 1st Degree was a pin-back decoration), recognizing his service to them as the leader of *FFl.Abt. 28* in Army Group von Mackensen on the Eastern Front.

On December 18, 1917, Eberstein assumed his last command, *Flieger-Abteilung 26*, and remained in that post until a month after the armistice when the unit was dissolved. It was during this time that Eberstein received the award that brings him into this treatise as well as his most important Prussian recognition. A day after taking over *26*, Prince Franz IV signed the diploma awarding Eberstein the Schwerin Military Merit Cross 2nd Class. Then on May 18, 1918, the head of the General Commission on Royal Prussian Orders in Berlin, a man named Kanitz, signed a similarly impressive document giving Eberstein title to the Knight's Cross with Swords of the Royal House Order of Hohenzollern. But like the man in the previous biography, still more was asked of Eberstein despite the war being over. He, too, participated in the *Freikorps*' actions against the revolutionaries and in 1919 served in an outfit called *Freikorps Schlesien*. Fortunately, and unlike that previous subject, Eberstein survived albeit to an uncertain future in a defeated Germany.

LEUTNANT OTTO-MARTIN *GRAF* VON SCHWERIN

The late World War I German researcher and author, A. Edward Ferko, obtained an interesting account of the capture by the British of an observer in *Feldflieger-Abteilung 66* in Salonika on January 17, 1917. The man was *Leutnant* Otto-Martin *Graf* von Schwerin with whom Mr. Ferko corresponded in 1984. Unfortunately, for our purposes, Mr. Ferko never determined von Schwerin's full awards list so it cannot be stated with any certainty that he was, in fact, a recipient of the war cross from the grand duchy from which his family drew their name. But may we not speculate that in all likelihood the nobleman would have possessed the decoration? In any event, having an account of an action in one of the participant's own words makes it worthy of inclusion, Schwerin cross or not.

Lt. Otto-Martin *Graf* von Schwerin with one of his pilots, *Unteroffz.* A. Ostenkötter, in *FFl.Abt. 66* on the Salonika Front in 1916. It is not known with certainty whether his noble name put him in line for the grand duchy's Military Merit Cross but it seems a reasonable possibility. With another pilot, *Unteroffz.* Christian Bohnensiek, on a reconnaissance on January 17, 1917 just a day before he was to go on leave, the pair had the misfortune to be attacked by two B.E.12s near the British aerodrome at Lahana. Trapped and with von Schwerin's machine gun jammed, they had no choice but to land where in a vain attempt, they tried to burn their Albatros C.VII. The action in which they were taken prisoner is described in von Schwerin's own words in the text.

On Sunday, January 14, 1917, von Schwerin already had leave papers in his pocket and was preparing to return home to Germany the next day. He decided that he should take one last series of photographs of the front against which he could check any changes in enemy dispositions upon his return. He and his pilot, *Unteroffizier* Christian Bohnensiek, took off in their Albatros C.VII 1302/16. Across the way, at their airfield in Lahana, two pilots, one from No. 17 Squadron, RFC and the other from its sister unit, No. 47 Squadron, RFC, rose for what would turn out to be an eventful patrol for them both. The 17 pilot was the later Major Gilbert Ware Murlis-Green who already had been credited with two confirmed victories in the previous four weeks. The other man was the later Captain Franklin Geoffrey Saunders who was as yet unblooded. Both were in single-seater B.E.12s, 6601 and 6603 respectively. As the pair came across von Schwerin's aircraft, let us now pick up his own words using the exact language in his letter to Mr. Ferko:

Sharing in the victory over von Schwerin and his pilot was the later Major Gilbert Ware Murlis-Green, here straddling the fuselage of his second victory, an Albatros D.V on January 4, 1917. He already wears the ribbon of the British Military Cross which was gazetted three days earlier. He would go on to add two Bars to the M.C. and earn the Distinguished Service Order with one Bar. Below: This is his spectacular original five-gallantry British awards medal bar with service and foreign decorations spanning the years 1914-1945. Once in the collection of the Foundation for Aviation World War I, it was subsequently donated to the RAF Museum, Hendon.

"When intercepted by a British machine, I signaled it to my pilot. He looked around, spotted another machine and steered down to it for a fight. We were now positioned between two enemies, one level, the other above, Captain Green apparently. In the following fight, my machine gun very quickly got stuck as it frequently did (Bergmann) and we became as good as defenseless. The only chance was to try and get across to our lines. But it was far and Captain Green could easily prevent it. So we had to land and destroy the plane, I tried to kick a hole into the tank, but with the padded felt overshoes we wore on flight, it was impossible and the last measure to fire a starshell under the tank raised only lots of smoke and ... nothing. In the meantime, people came running and we had to watch them taking possession of a brand new Albatros complete with pilot and observer as an involuntary contribution to the war museum."

Both Murlis-Green and Saunders were credited with a shared victory. Murlis-Green had already been decorated with the British Military Cross which was gazetted on January 1, 1917 in a general citation. For his first two victories in Salonika, he was put in for a Bar which was gazetted on February 13, 1917. He went on to a distinguished career, achieving eight victories in all, including the first German Gotha brought down at night when he forced it to ditch in the Channel on December 18-19, 1917. The Distinguished Service Order was given to him on June 18, 1917 after his fourth, fifth and sixth victories in March 1917 and a Bar was added to it on December 18, 1917 for his work against the German raiders over England. The Gotha victory brought him a 2nd Bar to his M.C. on January 7, 1918. His gallantry group puts Murlis-Green in the front ranks of Britain's most highly decorated airmen of World War I. This writer recalls Mr. Ferko telling him that in his contacts with von Schwerin, the Count had only the highest praise for both the British airmen who brought him down.

AVIATION RECIPIENTS OF THE MECKLENBURG-SCHWERIN MILITARY MERIT CROSS WITHOUT BIOGRAPHIES

(See Appendix XXXIII for Grade Awarded and Date of Award Where Known)

New observers-to-be at the school at Jüterborg during the course given there from March 30 to May 12, 1917. The officer at the extreme left may be the school's commander and the *Hptm.* Friedrich Behrens who served in *FFl.Abt. 47* and *Fl. Abt. 37*. None of the others named in the photograph are known to have held the award.

One of the "Hornets of Zeebrügge," the observer, *Lt.z.See* Erich Boenisch, strikes a jaunty pose, cigar and all. One victory over a Nieuport 12 two-seater on May 5, 1916.

Jasta 4 pilots in 1917 with their leader, the then *Oblt.* Kurt-Bertram von Döring (left and standing 4th from left above). Others who can be identified are *Vzfw.* Ernst Clausnitzer (standing 2nd from left), *Vzfw.* Linus Patermann (5th from left), *Lt.* Busso von Alvensleben (6th from left) and *Lt.* Wilhelm Schultze (8th from left). Seated center is the later *Pour le Mérite* 22-victory ace, *Lt.* Hans Klein.

Above: The officers of the *Sud-Armee's Fl.Abt. (A)220* in August 1917 at their casino in Nowosioscka in southeast Galicia. A *Hptm.* Fleischfresser, 6th from left wearing his 1st Class cross, was the *Abteilungsführer*. Others are, left to right, *Lt.* Warmbier, *Lt. Frhr.* von Levetzow, *Lt.* Hesse, *Lt.* Schulze, *Oblt.* von Münster, Fleischfresser, *Lt.* Perisberg, *Lt.* Poethmann, *Lt.* Elsner and *Lt.* Wiegand. What, no squadron mascot?

Right and below: The *Fokker-Werke-Schwerin GmbH* was located in the Grand Duchy's capital city and here in his trademark plaid suit, Tony Fokker receives his 2nd Class cross from the Grand Duke himself on February 12, 1916. A Fokker M.17 is in the background. The post card below "with his new monoplane" is a much prized one by today's collectors.

Despite his lengthy air service which began in *FFl.Abt. 31* and progressed through *Jasta 15* to the commands of *Jasta 37* and *Jasta 38* until he was killed over Predejci in Macedonia on June 12, 1918, *Oblt.* Kurt Grasshoff was never able to score a confirmed victory. We will let others speculate on the color scheme of his Albatros D.III 2135/16 here in *Jasta 37* but none can deny that the sunburst on the fuselage made for a striking effect. His pre-air service unit was *Grossherzoglich Mecklenburgisches Jäger-Bataillon Nr.14.* whose *Chef* was Duke Johann Albrecht.

The Grand Duke of Mecklenburg-Schwerin visits *FFl.Abt. 11* on June 25, 1916. Two Schwerin 2nd Class recipients are in this group, *Oblt.* Hermann Fricke and *Lt.* Walter Hahn. Left to right, *Lt.* von Manteufel, *Offz.-Stv.* Lehmann, *Oblt.* Fromm, *Lt.* von Schütz, *Lt.* van Wersch, Fricke, *Oblt.* Lackner, (Rank?) *Graf* von Bernstorff, the Grand Duke, *Lt.* de Bea, *Hptm.* von Bülow (CO), *Offz.-Stv.* Grübbel, (Rank?) Grevin, Duke Paul of Mecklenburg, *Oberst* Reitze, Hahn, *Lt.* Schwabedissen, *Vzfw.* Peterson and *Gefr.* Ruckser. In all, 14 men who served in *FFl.Abt. 11* at one time or another earned the Schwerin cross in the 2nd Class, a high number for one unit.

Prewar test flight of an August Euler pusher with Prince Heinrich of Prussia, himself a licensed pilot (November 1910), in attendance. *Oblt.* Ferdinand Hiddessen whose story appears in the chapter on Hesse is on the Prince's left. He was one of the earliest recipients of the Schwerin cross in *FFl.Abt. 11*. 2nd from the right is August Euler himself.

Lt. Hans Körner, at far right in the group photograph above with his 1st Class cross present, joins others in *Jasta 19* celebrating the award of the Hohenzollern House Order to their leader, *Lt.* Hans Pippart, seated 2nd from right, news of which reached the unit on May 14, 1918 which was also Pippart's 30th birthday. Left: A mottled photo of Körner's zig-zagged marked Fokker Dr.1 in *Jasta 19*. He scored four victories there and three in earlier units.

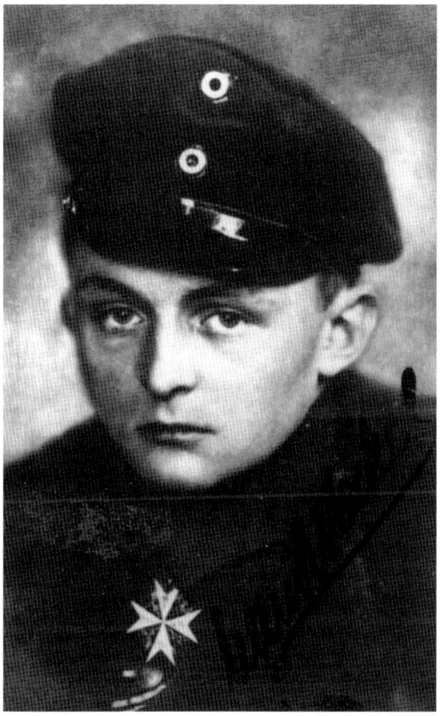

Four of the known recipients of the *Orden Pour le Mérite* also were awarded the Schwerin Military Merit Cross. They were Karl Bolle, Albert Dossenbach, Hermann Fricke and this man, *Lt.* Ulrich Neckel. Biographies on the first three have appeared in earlier volumes in this series. Neckel scored 30 confirmed victories in *Jasta 12* and *Jasta 6* and his *Pour le Mérite* on November 8, 1918 was the second last award given to an airman (the one on the next day to Carl Degelow of *Jasta 40* was the last award ever in its military form). By Allied standards, Neckel became an "ace" when he shot down his 5th confirmed victory on February 26, 1918. At right is that aircraft in German hands. S.E.5a B.548 was piloted by 2/Lt. C.H. Crosbee of No.24 Squadron, RFC who survived to be taken prisoner. There is no evidence that Neckel and Crosbee ever met but there are accounts on other occasions where Neckel went out of his way to meet the enemy fliers he engaged and even brought them presents of much welcome chocolates and cigarettes.

The ribbons on the bar of *Oblt*. Wolfgang Plüschow attest to his Iron Cross 2nd Class and his 2nd Class Schwerin cross but he wears his Austro-Hungarian Field Pilot's Badge in a most unusual position on his left breast above his Observer's Badge. Converting to fighters, he joined *Jasta 11* in October 1916 and was killed in *Jasta 39* on July 5, 1918. His Fokker D.II was one of 25 ordered in the D.2380-D.2404/16 series. A failure, it was soon relegated to training and backwater areas of the war, but still in its pristine factory finish here.

Lt. Friedrich Schumacher, 5 victories in *Jasta 10*, wounded in combat July 24, 1918.

Lt. Karl Stutzer, an observer in *Fl.Abt. (A)283* who fell in action on July 5, 1917.

The framed photograph of the deceased Bavarian *Pour le Mérite*/Military Max-Joseph fighter pilot recipient *Lt.* Max *Ritter* von Mulzer, looks down on the party of *Fl.Abt. (A)208* officers celebrating the birthday of *Oblt.* Krieg in late April 1918. Seated left to right, *Lt.* Schmidt, unknown, *Hptm.* Ihn, *Major* Hohl, Krieg and *Hptm.* Usbek. Hohl and Usbek sport homemade "*Pour le Mérites*" (*mit Eichenlaub* no less) in honor of the occasion. Usbek's Schwerin 1st Class cross can just be seen over a glass on the well-laden table.

Hptm. Bruno Wentscher was one of the 2nd Class Schwerin cross recipients in *FFl.Abt. 11*, his award being made retroactive to December 18, 1914. Wentscher was a prewar pilot with license 406 issued on May 20, 1913.

Fl.Abt. 33 with two of its men before they went on to earn their *Pour le Mérites*. *Lt.* Wilhelm Griebsch, 5th from left, received his on September 30, 1918 in *Fl.Abt. (A)213* and *Oblt.* Paul *Freiherr* von Pechmann, 7th from the left, was just about to get his in *33* on July 31, 1917. The tall man 11th from the left is a *Hptm.* Zorn wearing his 1st Class Schwerin cross. From left to right, *Vzfw.* Homann, *Unteroffz.* Gesper, *Lt.* Bechtle, *Lt.* Eichler, Griebsch, *Lt.* Semmler von Pechmann, *Hptm.* Plaeschke, *Vzfw.* Bahr, Zorn, *Vzfw.* Droth, *Lt.* Bertsch, *Unteroffz.* Ingenhofen, unknown, *Lt.* Müller, *Lt.* Mangold and *Lt.* Filbry. Mascot's name unknown.

Hptm. Hellmuth Wilberg was another *FFl.Abt. 11* recipient of both the Schwerin and Strelitz crosses in the 2nd Class as the first CO of the unit, August 2, 1914 to July 27, 1915. He is seen at the left with Hermann Göring in his observer days and the later *Pour le Mérite Jasta 5* leader, Hans Berr (wearing his *FFl.Abt. 60* arm patch). The locale is Metz-Freskaty. Göring's Iron Cross 1st Class dates this photograph after March 22, 1915.

Wilberg then became *Kofl* of the 4th German Army and remained in that job until the armistice. In late August or September 1917, he escorted Prince Otto von Hapsburg of Austria-Hungary to *Jasta 10*'s airfield at Marckebeke to inspect the brand new Fokker F.I 103/17 assigned to its leader, Werner Voss (in the cockpit). Wilberg, wearing the Austrian Military Merit Cross 3rd Class with War Decoration, is behind the Prince with von Döring immediately behind Wilberg.

Wilberg, with *Grossordenschnalle*, in the funeral parade in Courtrai on September 18, 1917 for the fallen (September 15) *Pour le Mérite* leader of *Jasta 11*, *Oblt*. Kurt Wolff. who was killed in the second prototype triplane, F.1 102/17. Far left is von Döring with *Gen.d.Inf*. Friedrich Sixt von Arnim between him and Wilberg. Behind them, left to right, *Oblt*. Kurt Scheffer, *Lt*. Gisbert-Wilhelm Groos, *Lt*. Alfred Gerstenberg and *Lt*. Karl Meyer.

Above: Four ladies (plus one chaperon) are outnumbered 20 to 1 by men of *Fl.Abt. (A)205* and other visitors (two of whom are in "civvies"). All (except perhaps the chaperon) seem to be having a fine old time but identities are lacking. Thus we don't know who the fellow seated on the floor at far right wearing the 1st Class Schwerin cross may be.

Right: Another unknown Schwerin cross recipient, possibly from *Fl.Abt. A284*, wearing an interesting cluster in his buttonhole comprising the Iron Cross 2nd Class and a Knight 2nd Class with Swords of the Baden Zähringen Lion Order in addition to his Schwerin decoration. There was a *Lt.* Hans Schroeder who received the Baden order in *FFl.Abt. 58/ Fl. Abt. (A)284*'s predecessor designation, on September 29, 1916. Could this be he?

CHAPTER XXIII

THE MILITARY AWARDS OF THE GRAND DUCHY OF MECKLENBURG-SCHWERIN

THE CROSS FOR DISTINCTION IN WAR

The Mecklenburg-Strelitz Cross for Distinction in War was instituted on March 3, 1871 by Grand Duke Friedrich Wilhelm to recognize military merit in the just-concluded Franco-Prussian war and like its already-existing counterpart decoration in Schwerin, was open to all ranks. In selecting the name he did for the award, the Grand Duke chose the same phrase, *Für Auszeichnung im Kriege*, that appeared on the reverse of the 2nd Class Schwerin cross. The Strelitz cross was a breast badge that was struck in two versions, the only difference between the two being the inscription that appeared on the obverse.[1] At the time of its foundation, there was no 1st Class pin-back badge as there was in Schwerin.

The Cross for Distinction in War was a *cross pattée* struck in silver with a beaded-edge and a prominent center medallion which on both sides was surrounded by a wreath of laurels. The inscription on the obverse of one version was *Tapfer und Treu* ("Brave and Faithful") set on three lines and on the other *Für Tapferkeit* ("For Bravery") on two lines, both in block letters. The reverse was the same in each case, the crowned entwined initials of the founder, *F W*, in the center of the medallion. Like the 2nd Class Schwerin cross, both versions used the same ribbon as that of the Mecklenburg House Order of the Wendish Crown, pale blue with narrow yellow (inner) and red (outer) edge stripes. And like its sister decoration in the other grand duchy, the Strelitz cross could be given to non-combatants for contributions to the war effort. In these cases, the colors of the ribbon were reversed just as they were in Schwerin, red with narrow pale blue and yellow edge stripes, the so-called "red ribbon."

The version with the *Tapfer und Treu* inscription constituted the bulk of the awards of the 1871 cross. According to Peter Ohm-Hieronymussen's study *Die Mecklenburg-Strelitzer Orden und Ehrenzeichen*, 269 of these were awarded, 180 in 1871 and another 89 in 1872. Only 14 awards of the *Für Tapferkeit* version were made, all in 1871. While the founding statement said these were meant for "princely persons," in fact, the only royal recipient among the 14 was Grand Duke Friedrich Wilhelm himself according to Ohm-Hieronymussen's findings (could other such awards within the Grand Ducal House merely have gone unrecorded?). The other recipients ranged from the Chief of the General Staff, *Generalfeldmarschall* Helmuth *Graf* von Moltke whose brilliant tactics were given the main credit for France's defeat in the recent war, down to six other General officers, three Colonels and three Majors.

On August 11, 1914, the then ruling Grand Duke Adolf Friedrich VI who had just assumed the throne exactly two months earlier upon the death of his father renewed the decoration for World War I. In so doing, he moved more quickly that did his cousin in Schwerin who did not renew his Military Merit Cross until February of the following year. Again, there were the two versions of the breast badge with the inscriptions previously used and both badges were in silver (the crosses began to be struck in silvered bronze in 1916 due to the precious metals shortages). Two small changes were made however. On the reverse, the crowned entwined initials were changed to *A F* and the year date *1914* appeared on the lower arm of the cross. On New Year's Day 1915, a 1st Class pin-back cross in silver (silvered metal from 1917) was authorized for repeated acts of outstanding bravery to be worn on the left breast without a

[1] The founding document stated that the inscriptions were on the obverse of both crosses. Yet the authoritative work *Die Ehrenzeichen des Deutschen Reiches* by von Hessenthal and Schreiber places them on the reverse. In practice, the badges were usually worn with the inscriptions facing front in any event.

Grand Duke Adolf Friedrich IV of Mecklenburg-Strelitz renewed the Cross for Distinction in War, first instituted for the War of 1870, on August 11, 1914. It came in two versions, one with the inscription *Für Tapferkeit* ("For Bravery") and another with the inscription *Tapfer und Treu* ("Brave and Faithful"). Both were breast badges worn from the ribbon of the House Order of the Wendish Crown.

The cross with the *Für Tapferkeit* legend was awarded only 25 times with all recipients being royals or high ranking General officers with field commands. The cross with the other legend was much more widely awarded with one authority stating 8,131 awards of this version being made between 1914 and 1923 after which retroactive awards for World War I ceased.

On January 1, 1915, a 1st Class pin-back cross with only the *Für Tapferkeit* inscription was created whereupon the breast badges became known as the 2nd Class. Rolls for these awards in the archive in Schwerin do not appear to be complete but it would appear that there were at least 414 awards of the 1st Class Cross for Distinction in war for service in World War I.

ribbon. There was only one version carrying the inscription *Für Tapferkeit*. The year date *1914* also appeared on the lower arm of the cross. The reverse was plain but except for the fact that this badge's arms were slightly curved and not flat, the cross was identical to the 1914 striking which now became known as the 2nd Class.

Appendices XXXIV through XXXVII show the frequency of awards found in the Army rank lists of 1914 and 1924 and in the Navy lists of 1918 and 1926. These would suggest that the decoration, especially in the 1st Class (after 1915), was not that widely awarded. In fact, the 2nd Class in the *Tapfer und Treu* version was given out quite widely although the number of known *Fliegertruppe* recipients was relatively small in proportion to the total (see Appendices XL and XLI). The Ohm-Hieronymussen study found a total 8,131 2nd Class awards with the *Tapfer und Treu* inscription from 1914 to 1923 but this writer's inspection of the rolls came up with only 52 sure approvals to men in the air service. This could well be understated because no full, complete roll of the award could be located in the searches by this writer in the archive in Schwerin which were also considerably augmented by help from *Professor Dr. Dr.* Holger Steinle of the *Deutsches Technikmuseum Berlin*. There were some seven separate listings, several without any dates of bestowal. There were only 25 awards of the 2nd Class cross with the *Für Tapferkeit* inscription. In addition to the royals of a number of German states and the ruler of at least one of Germany's allies in the war, its recipients included high ranking General officers and one civilian, the Prussian War Minister (see Appendix XXXIX). Ohm-Hieronymussen lists only 21 recipients of the 1st Class *Für Tapferkeit* cross between 1915 and 1918. They also were royals, at least one Allied ruler and high ranking officers. Their names checked with the research done by this writer. But in addition, other 1st Class recipients' names were found on a list in the archive including six men in the *Fliegertruppe*. Those 21 recipients plus the six airmen are shown in Appendix XXXVIII. This list totaled 419 names with five crossed out, presumably deletions for one reason or the other. A total of 419 (or 414) awards of the 1st Class cross for World War I seems much more likely than a mere 21. Finally, and only for the medals specialists, two lists totaling 470 names were found for awards of the 2nd Class *Tapfer und Treu* cross on the "red ribbon" and another list contained the names of awards of that decoration to 127 women (with one name deleted). The first recipient among the women was the Grand Duchess Elizabeth of Mecklenburg-Strelitz.

Two recipients of the Cross for Distinction in War were key figures in the organization and deployment of the Imperial German Army Air Service. One was its top man, *Generalleutnant* Ernst von Hoeppner who was awarded both the 1st Class cross and the 2nd Class *Tapfer und Treu* cross. The other was *Major* Wilhelm Siegert who so ably headed up the Inspectorate of Aviation (*Idflieg*) in Berlin. He was awarded the same 2nd Class cross as von Hoeppner. The lists upon which their names appear are undated but their positions at the time of award are given and, clearly, both were in the *Fliegertruppe* when their crosses were approved. One name that might be expected to appear in view of these two awards would be that of von Hoeppner's Chief-of-Staff and right hand man, *Oberst* Hermann von der Lieth-Thomsen. But not only does his name not appear on these lists but a personnel record found in the archive in Freiburg im Breisgau in which all his prewar and wartime awards are given fails to show anything from Mecklenburg-Strelitz (but he did receive the Mecklenburg Griffin Order Honor Cross (without Swords) on August 7, 1912 as a *Major* on the Great General Staff; strange, then, that one of the Mecklenburgs didn't see fit to do something for him in the course of the war).

Two other names are of even greater interest. They are those of the two most famous airmen that Germany produced during the war (Max Immelmann notwithstanding), Oswald Boelcke and Manfred von Richthofen about whom so much has been written in earlier volumes in this series and in untold numbers of books and articles elsewhere. In Volume V, the fact that a 2nd Class *Tapfer und Treu* cross was Boelcke's original awards which are in the possession of a family member was first discussed. Search as this writer did for corroboration of the award in the archive in Schwerin, there was nothing of the sort there.

Still, that proves nothing conclusively. We cannot be sure that the lists which were found contain the names of all recipients. The case of Manfred von Richthofen is without doubt the most interesting of all. The roll where he appears, the fifth of the seven with dates between 1916 and 1918 for awards of the 2nd Class *Tapfer und Treu* cross, gives the disposition of the proposals for the award, whether they were approved or turned down. In the latter case, and there are many, the term used is "*Ad Acta*," or "To File," i.e., not approved. And opposite von Richthofen's name is that very notation.

He was proposed for the award on September 16, 1917 at the height of his career (61 victories) and the decision shelving the proposal is dated September 24. How could the grand duchy turn its back on Germany's premier fighter pilot? Did they come up with the excuse, like the Bavarians did in denying him the Military Max-Joseph Order, that he was not a native? But if Boelcke, certainly no Mecklenburger either, got the award, why not von Richthofen? More needs to be discovered to get the answers to these intriguing questions.

There are no other "big" names on these lists of other aviation recipients of the Cross for Distinction in War. Thus this chapter ends with no new biographics and just a few photographs – a disappointing note.

Above: *Generalleutnant* Ernst von Hoeppner, above left, as the Commanding General of the Air Force (*Kogenluft*) was one of only 18 known General officers to receive the Cross for Distinction in War 1st Class. He was also a recipient of the 2nd Class of the decoration with the inscription *Tapfer und Treu*. The available rolls, however, show no comparable recognition for his able Chief-of-Staff, *Oberst* Hermann von der Lieth-Thomsen, standing to von Hoeppner's left.

Right: The number two key man on the staff of the Army Air Service was *Oberstlt.* Wilhelm Siegert who headed up the Inspectorate of Aviation (*Idflieg*) in Berlin. He, too, was recognized by Mecklenburg-Strelitz with its 2nd Class *Tapfer und Treu* Cross for Distinction in War.

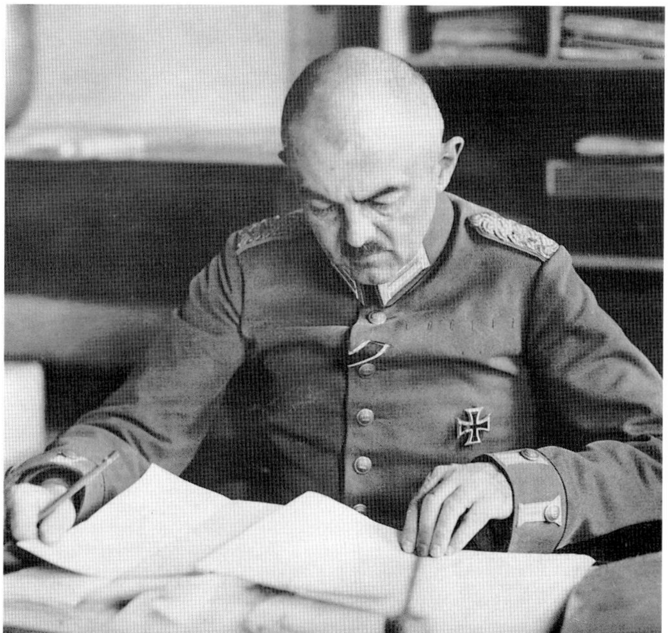

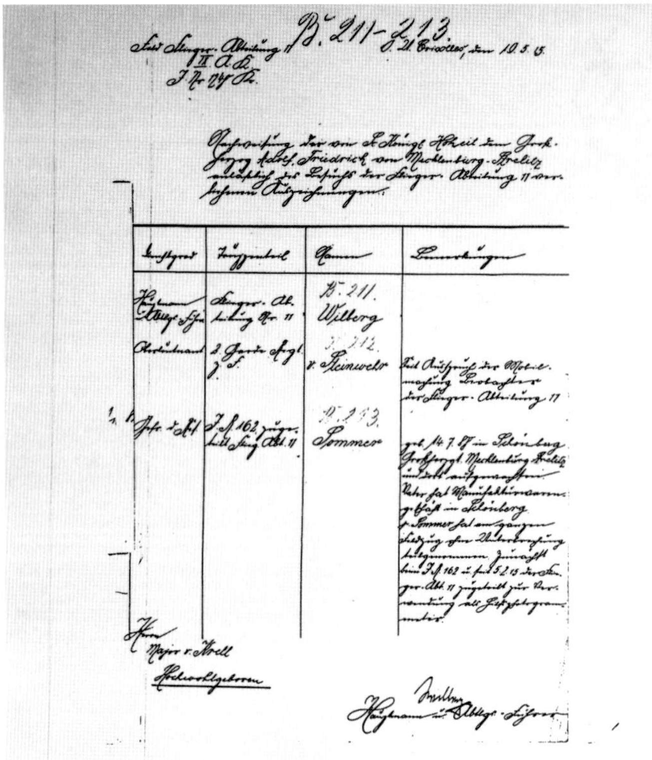

B. 211-213.

B. 211. Wilberg

B. 212. v. Steinwehr

B. 213. Sommer

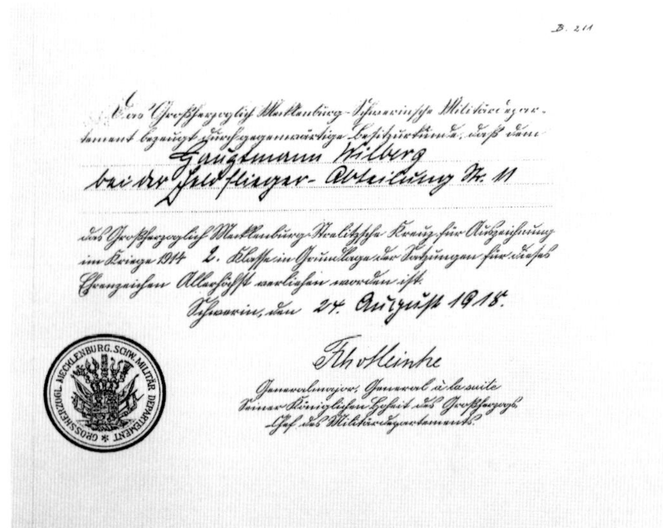

Hauptmann Wilberg

Schwerin, den 24. August 1918.

The register dated 10 May 1915 listing the award of the Cross for Distinction in War 2nd Class to three *FFl.Abt. 11* men, *Hptm.* Hellmuth Wilberg, *Oblt.* Wulff von Steinwehr and a *Gefr.* Sommer. Above: Certificate dated 24 August 1918 confirming Wilberg's decoration with the Schwerin Military Department stamp.

Wilberg, as *Kofl 4* in early September 1917, greets the men of *Jasta 11*. In the line-up left to right, *Hptm.* Reinhard, *Oblt.* Scheffer, *Oblt.* Lothar von Richthofen, *Lt.* Groos, *Lt.* Mohnicke, *Oblt.* Löwenhardt (hidden by Wilberg), *Lt.* Meyer, *Lt.* Müller, unknown, *Lt.* von der Osten and *Oblt.* Gerstenberg. Behind Wilberg, the *JG 1* CO, *Rittm.* Manfred von Richthofen, an unknown on Wilberg's staff and *Oblt.* Bodenschatz, the *JG 1* Adjutant. The lines on this print point to numbers not seen here which identified the personnel in this photograph.

Hptm. Kurt *Freiherr* von der Goltz was one of only four junior officer airmen known to have received the 1st Class Cross for Distinction in War. At the time, he was in *AFA 230* and had earned the 2nd Class earlier on August 16, 1915 as an *Oblt.* in *FFl.Abt. 28.*

Lt. Joachim *Freiherr* von Maltzahn won his 2nd Class cross in *3. Garde-Rgt. zu Fuss* and as an observer with *FFl.Abt. 48*, he was wounded in an air battle over Ammerzweiler in Alsace and died in hospital at Mulhouse (Mühlhausen) on June 11, 1915.

The officers (grouped together standing in the back row, most wearing goggles on their service caps) and men of *FFl.Abt. 38* at Brussels. The handwritten inscription was dated 7 November 1914. *Lt.* Heinz Junge received the Cross for Distinction in War 1st Class on December 15, 1915 for service in this unit. Mecklenburg-Schwerin Military Merit Crosses recipient, the later *Rittm.* Kurt-Bertram von Döring, started his frontline service with *38* but the date is unknown. It is therefore not possible to say if he is in this group but it is likely that Junge is somewhere here. One must wonder if *38* was still flying the obsolete Taube which forms the backdrop.

53A

Opposite
The display of the original awards of *Hptm.* Oswald Boelcke in the possession of a family member displayed on an *Ordenskissen*. On the left running down diagonally to the Iron Cross 1st Class are three breast badges not mounted on his order bar, the Bulgarian Bravery Order 4th Class 2nd Degree, the Mecklenburg-Strelitz 2nd Class *Tapfer und Treu* Cross for Distinction in War and the Württemberg Military Merit Order Knight. None of the rolls of the Strelitz cross which were found contain his name however. At right, one of Boelcke's *Feldgrau* uniforms appears along with a *Feldschnalle* of his below. Missing on that are ribbons for both the Strelitz cross and the Württemberg order (records confirm the award of the latter piece). The ribbons represent the Iron Cross 2nd Class, the Knight's Hohenzollern (curiously, on the statute ribbon), the Prussian Life Saving Medal, the Anhalt Bear Order 1st and 2nd Class (with swords missing on the 2nd Class), the Anhalt Friedrich Cross, the Bavarian Military Merit Order, the Saxe-Ernestine House Order, the Turkish Imtiaz Medal in Silver, the Turkish War Medal and the Bulgarian order.

Opposite below: Fall of 1916: Tony Fokker points out features of his new but soon-to-be-maligned Fokker D.I to *Hptm.* Waldemar von Buttlar (I) and others while Boelcke (II) and fellow *Pour le Mérite* recipient Wilhelm Frankl confer in the background.

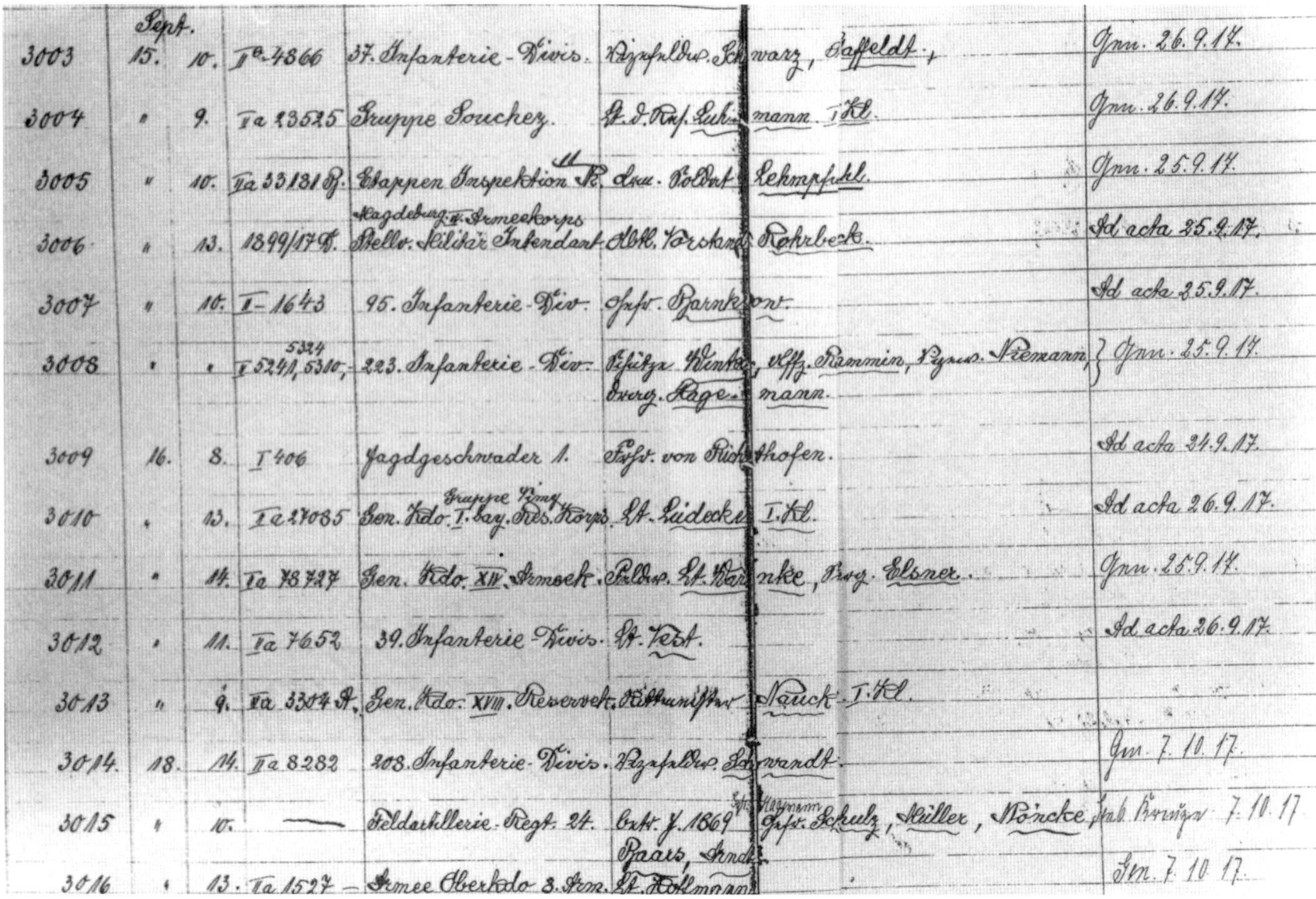

	Sept.					
3003	15.	10.	Ic 4866	37. Infanterie-Divis.	Vizefeldw. Schwarz, Saffeldt.	Gen. 26.9.17.
3004	"	9.	Ia 13525	Gruppe Souchez.	Lt. d. Res. Luhmann. I Kl.	Gen. 26.9.17.
3005	"	10.	IIa 33131	Etappen Inspektion II.	Lehmpfuhl.	Gen. 25.9.17.
3006	"	13.	1899/17	Stellv. Militär Intendant Magdeburg IV. Armeekorps	Rohrbeck.	Ad acta 25.9.17.
3007	"	10.	I-1643	95. Infanterie-Div.	Gefr. Barnkow.	Ad acta 25.9.17.
3008	"	"	I 5241, 5310, 5324	223. Infanterie-Div.	Winkler, Uffz. Rammin, Niemann, Hagemann.	Gen. 25.9.17.
3009	16.	8.	I 406	Jagdgeschwader 1.	Frhr. von Richthofen.	Ad acta 24.9.17.
3010	"	13.	Ic 27085	Gen. Kdo. I. bay. Res. Korps Gruppe Prinz	Lt. Lüdecke I. Kl.	Ad acta 26.9.17.
3011	"	14.	Ic 78727	Gen. Kdo. XIV Armeek.	Lt. Warnke, Elsner.	Gen. 25.9.17.
3012	"	11.	Ia 7652	39. Infanterie Divis.	Lt. Test.	Ad acta 26.9.17.
3013	"	9.	Ia 3304	Gen. Kdo. XVIII. Reservek.	Rittmeister Nauck I. Kl.	
3014	18.	14.	IIa 8282	208. Infanterie-Divis.	Vizefeldw. Schwandt.	Gen. 7.10.17.
3015	"	10.	—	Feldartillerie-Regt. 24.	Gefr. Schulz, Müller, Röncke, Paats, Arndt	7.10.17
3016	"	13.	Ia 1527	Armee Oberkdo 3. Arm.	Lt. Kollmann	Gen. 7.10.17.

Above: The page from the roll for the award of the Cross for Distinction in War 2nd Class which gives the dates of a man's proposal and in the column at the right, the disposition of the matter in each case. Here, on entry number 3009, we can see that on September 16, 1917, "*Frhr.* von Richthofen" of *Jagdgeschwader 1* was proposed for the decoration and on September 24, 1917, the recommendation was filed away ("*Ad Acta*") and not acted upon. Had it been approved, the notation would have been "*Gen.*" (*Genehmigen*, or "approved") as can be seen in the case of the majority of the entries on this portion of the roll. It would not be the only time that the great von Richthofen was proposed for an award which failed to materialize (see text for another example of this happening to him). Below: The next month, on October 18, von Richthofen, 5th from the left in his *Uhlan* tunic and *Tschapka* (lancer's helmet), attended the wedding of his old *Kagohl 1* comrade, *Hptm.* Fritz Prestien, to the left of the bride, at Reinhardsbrunn Castle in Gotha. Von Richthofen's *Grossordenschnalle* spans most of his chest so one might say that his Cross for Distinction in War wasn't really missed.

CHAPTER XXIV

THE PRINCELY HOUSE OF WALDECK AND PYRMONT

The Principality of Waldeck might be called the poor cousin of the other German States. Small, only 433 square miles, hilly and forested, agriculture was its principal industry. The 1910 census put the population at just over 61,000 making it one of the most sparsely settled regions of the 2nd Reich (only the Grand Duchies of Mecklenburg-Schwerin and Mecklenburg-Strelitz had fewer people per square mile). From 1900 to 1910, the principality's population increased by less than 3,800 people. It had been so deeply in debt that upon entering the North German Confederation fashioned by Bismarck in 1867, it was unable to meet the financial obligations of membership and Prince Georg Viktor was forced to turn over most of his royal prerogatives to Prussia effective with the 1st of January 1868. He kept his title and a few other rights including the granting of orders and decorations.

The House of Waldeck went back to the Count of Schwalenberg, Widukind III, in the 12th century. His descendants were elevated to Counts of the Holy Roman Empire in 1349 and by inheritance, acquired the County of Pyrmont in 1631. The dignity of *Hoch-und Wohlgeboren* (High and Well-Born) was granted in 1627. Count Christian Ludwig who died in 1706 added some minor properties and in the process fathered 25 children between his two wives. Two of his sons were the ancestors of the two branches of the family that then formed. One line, the Princes of Waldeck and Pyrmont, was founded by Friedrich Anton Ulrich and in January 1712, he was raised to the rank of Prince and given the dignity of *Hochgeboren* (Highborn). In June 1815, the reigning prince adopted the title Serene Highness. The other son of Christian Ludwig, Josias, founded the line Counts of Waldeck and Pyrmont and his descendants were as of August 1844, addressed as Your Illustrious Highness. On the Princes of Waldeck and Pyrmont side of the family, Georg II ruled from 1813 to 1845. He was succeeded after his death by his second son, Georg Viktor, his first born son having died as an infant. George Viktor held the throne until his death in 1893. It was under his reign that the awards we will be discussing were instituted. His first marriage produced six children, five girls and a boy. The boy, first-born and christened Friedrich, took over upon his father's death and was the last ruler of the principality. A General of Cavalry in the Prussian Army, Friedrich was forced to abdicate on November 13, 1918 following the armistice whereupon Waldeck became another of the Free States in postwar Germany.

In 1815, the Principality of Waldeck (as we will henceforth shorten its full name) contributed three companies of infantry and one of *Jäger* (fusilier) to the Army of Confederation. The traditions of this small contingent went back to 1681. Since that time, the principality's troops had seen service in most of the wars on the European continent and had served overseas as mercenaries in the pay of the Dutch and Venetians as well as the British in the American Revolution. Prussia assumed the financial support of what had now become a Fusilier Battalion in a convention that was signed in 1862. Under the terms of that agreement, officers of the Waldeck battalion had to take commissions in the Prussian service and swear allegiance to the King of Prussia or lose their pensions and chances for promotion (only one officer failed to accept these terms). A second convention with Prussia was concluded on August 6, 1867. And with that, the battalion was disbanded. Its officers were spread around other Prussian contingents with 16 officers and 182 men joining the 83rd Prussian Infantry Regiment that had been formed in 1866. These troops formed the 3rd Battalion of the regiment garrisoned at Waldeck's capital city, Arolsen and the regiment shortly was given a new name, *Infanterie-Regiment von Wittich (3. Kurhessisches) Nr.83*. (*3. Kurhessisches* meaning "3rd Electoral Hessian"). In 1875, Georg Viktor became the regiment's *Chef* and in 1897, Prince Friedrich was named the chief of the 3rd Battalion and then of the entire regiment in 1913. Four princes of the house were attached to the regiment *à la suite*, three of Friedrich's sons, Crown Prince Josias and the Princes Max and Georg Wilhelm, and the only child of George Viktor's second marriage, Wolrad, who was killed in action on October 17, 1914 near Morslede as a *Leutnant* in the 23rd Hessian Dragoon Guards.

During the Franco-Prussian War, the von Wittich regiment was in the 22nd Prussian Division, a part of the 11th Corps. It suffered serious losses at the Battle of Wörth on August 6, 1870 (12% killed or wounded) and at Sedan on September 1 (9% casualties including the regimental commander). During the fighting for Orléans, the 22nd Division was assigned to the 1st Bavarian Corps and attacked the city on October 10 and 11, occupying it. This action was even more bloody. By its end, the 83rd had lost all its staff officers, the regiment was in the hands of a 1st Lieutenant and the battalions were being commanded by 2nd Lieutenants. Reinforced, the 22nd Division then stormed Châteaudun and moved on to Chartres where it was assigned to a newly formed detachment, *Grossherzog von Mecklenburg*. Its mission was to assist the 2nd Army in blocking any French forces from getting through them from the south and west to relieve Paris. The regiment next took part in the reoccupation of Orléans on December 3-4 and in the engagement at Beaugency-Cravant on December 8-12. The 13th Corps, as the Mecklenburg detachment was now called, advanced on Le Mans where French General Chanzy had assembled a large force. But his forces collapsed when attacked over January 10-12, 1871. The Prussians followed the retreating French to Alençon and had its last battle of the war at l'Aigle on January 21. One week later, Bismarck inked his name on the armistice papers, Paris was occupied for one day and the war was over for all practical purposes (the fortress of Belfort held out until February 16). The German Empire under Wilhelm I had already been proclaimed at Versailles on January 18 and in the Treaty of Frankfurt which was ratified on May 21, France was forced to cede all of Alsace except the Territory of Belfort and a large part of Lorraine to Germany and pay an indemnity of $1 billion over a three year period. The seeds of World War I had been sewn.

The Waldeck regiment's losses during the war were heavy. Based on its strength at the start of the campaign, 40% of its troops were casualties (13% killed and 27% wounded). Twenty of its officers were killed and 40, including that regimental commander, had been wounded. The regiment started with 59 officers so, on paper, the officer corps had been wiped out (but, of course, there were replacements for these casualties along the way). It was because of the 83rds' tenacity in battle in the War of 1870 that it was given the honor of being named "The Iron Regiment."

In the 1914-1918 war, the 83rd Regiment, still a part of the 22nd Infantry Division, began its baptism of fire on the Western Front and ended there as well. But in between, it spent most of its campaigning on the Eastern Front. The 43rd Brigade of the division of which the 83rd was one of its two regiments was present at the capture of the fortress city of Liége on August 7, 1914 and would have pressed on with the rest of the German Army thrusting at Paris had it not been for Russia having mobilized much faster than the German General Staff had anticipated and was actually invading East Prussia. The 22nd Division was one of those pulled off the Western Front and shipped east to counter that threat. By October, they were in Poland and would remain there until May 1915 taking part in the counter offensives against the Russians. In the latter half of that year, it saw combat in the Mackensen offensive in Galicia and spent 1916 first in Lithuania, then back again in Galicia to help stem the Brusilov Offensive that summer and fall and finished out the year in Romania (which had declared war on Austria on August 27 when the Russians appeared as though they might carry the day). But it was back to Galicia again in January of 1917 and more hard fighting until the end of October when the 83rd was again part of a strategic shift of forces, this time with Russia virtually out of the war to put the full weight of the German Army on winning the war in the west. It got a bit of a rest in the now largely quiet Verdun area before the spring storms broke. It fought in that general sector and was heavily engaged in the Second Battle of the Marne in July until relieved on August 7, the division having lost some 400 taken prisoner. It was thrown back into the thick of it along the Somme in September and was still engaged in the stubborn fighting retreat of the German Army west of the old Mons battlefield when the 11th hour of the 11th day of the 11th month came. An appraisal by American intelligence rated the 22nd Division as only third class in its 1918 performance but, almost grudgingly it would seem, had to admit that although it had made little headway on the Marne, on defense it performed better than many other German divisions which received a higher rating overall. Thirty eight of the 83rds' Regular Army officers who numbered 113 when they marched off to war were killed during the course of it (supposed non-combatants like the regiment's doctors not included), or one in three.

Among these were five young *Leutnante* who later transferred to the *Fliegertruppe* and there met their deaths (see Appendix II). Three of them held the Waldeck house order and it is their stories, or at least as much as is known about them, and those of the men who received the award but survived as fliers that we now tell. We start with the most famous recipient of them all after the customary background on the order itself.

CHAPTER XXV

THE MILITARY AWARDS OF THE PRINCIPALITY OF WALDECK
THE MERIT CROSS

As the noted medals authority, Eric C. Ludvigsen, said in an excellent monograph on the old Waldeck Military Merit Cross that appeared in the April 1975 issue of the *Journal of the Orders and Medals Society of America*, the practice of awarding orders and decoration came late to the Principality of Waldeck. Up to 1854, the extent of Waldeck's awards were a long service clasp in three grades established in 1848 and a series of commemorative medals first struck in 1850 going back to the Wars of the Liberation in Napoleonic times.

Then on May 3, 1861, a Military Merit Cross in two classes was founded by Prince Georg Viktor. After a Regency under his mother, Princess Emma, he had just come into his own right on August 17, 1852, seven months after his 21st birthday. Georg Viktor went one step further on January 14, 1871 when he established the Merit Order, again in two classes. In September 1878, a Silver Merit Medal was added. Georg Viktor died on May 12, 1893 and was succeeded by his elder son, Friedrich. Now a complete realignment of Waldeck awards took place. The Military Merit Cross and the Merit Order disappeared and in their place a single award, named the Merit Cross, came into being. As Mr. Ludvigsen also says, one can only speculate as to why the two earlier honors were abolished. But Mr. Ludvigsen's conclusion that Friedrich probably felt that service to the state and his house could be adequately rewarded by a single, fully-developed decoration, one without recourse to separate civil and military distinctions, appears perceptive, This all happened in 1896 in an unpublished decree dated March 28.

The new Merit Cross was virtually identical in appearance to the now defunct Merit Order (the use of the term "Cross" rather than "Order" followed the terminology used by the house orders of the principalities of Reuss, Schwarzburg-Rudolstadt and Schwarzburg-Sondershausen but not by the principalities of Hohenzollern, Lippe and Schaumburg-Lippe where the term "Order" was retained). The Merit Cross was initially founded in four grades, 1st through 4th Class. Each badge was a Maltese cross. For the three higher grades, the arms of the cross were in white enamel with gold edges. The 4th Class badge was plain silver. The 1st Class badge was surmounted by a gold crown. The 2nd Class badge was suspended from an inverted gold oak leaf, a feature of the old 1st Class Military Merit Cross. The order was expanded in 1899 by the addition of a Gold Merit Medal to accompany the 1878 Silver Merit Medal. In addition, an entirely new decoration was instituted. This was the Honor Cross (to be discussed in the next chapter). It ranked between the 4th Class Merit Cross and the Gold Merit Medal. Finally, coming into the new century, an Officer's Cross was created in 1912. As customary, it was a pin-back piece and ranked between the 2nd and 3rd Class grades. There was no breast star for the Merit Cross 1st Class, consistent with the house orders of most of the other principalities (Lippe-Detmold being the exception). With the Officer's Cross, Waldeck's house order had now been fully fleshed out and there were no more additions or amendments up to and during World War I.

The badge of the Merit Cross was classic in design and had an especially attractive center feature around the medallion. The medallion itself displayed a red enameled *cross moline* on a white enameled ground surrounded by a gold ring. Emanating from the medallion there was a black and gold enameled star of eight rays. On the 1st Class badge only, the star feature was further surrounded by a gold-ringed, blue-enameled larger medallion which carried the separated inscription *Dem Ver dien ste* ("to the Meritorious"). This additional medallion and the

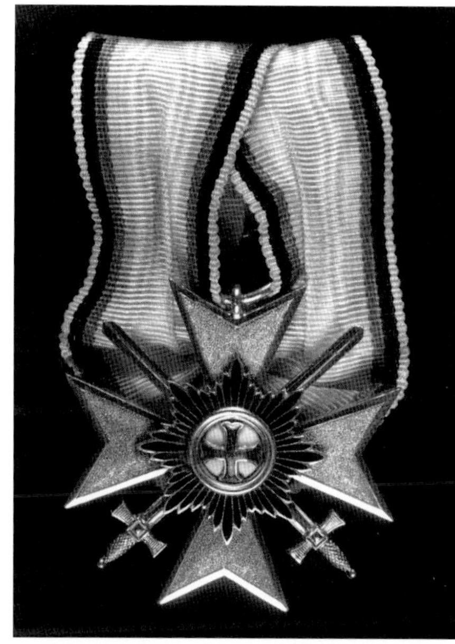

Above: The Princely Waldeck Merit Cross was instituted on January 14, 1871 at a time when the principality had another award in being which had the rather confusing name Military Merit Cross. Actually, it was a decoration (although in appearance and wear, it took the form of an order) and ceased to exist in 1896. The plain Merit Cross then became Waldeck's only military award for officers and its only house order. Above left, the obverse of the 3rd Class cross with Swords (swords to the insignia came about mainly in World War I) and at the right, the 4th Class badge with Swords. They were the same except for enameled arms on the 3rd Class and for the finish, gold edges on the 3rd Class and matte silver on the 4th Class. In the center, the reverse of the 3rd Class cross.

Right: Prince Friedrich succeeded to the throne in 1893. The lead-off medal on his order bar is the *Kaiser* Wilhelm Commemorative Medal (commonly called the Centenary Medal) founded by *Kaiser* Wilhelm II in 1897 to mark the 100th birth date of his grandfather. Thus that also dates this photograph and yet the Prince still chooses to wear the now defunct Waldeck Military Merit Cross 1st Class at the neck with its inverted oak leaf. Below that, he wears the Grand Cross badge of the Prussian Red Eagle Order and the 1st Class Honor Cross of Lippe. The breast stars appear to be those of the Grand Cross of the High Order of the Prussian Black Eagle and the Baden Zähringen Lion Order. The other medals on his bar cannot all be identified with certainty but are undoubtedly commemorative and jubilee awards similar to the Centenary Medal.

SOME HOLDERS OF THE WALDECK MERIT CROSS 1st CLASS WITH SWORDS

(Rank at Time of Award)

Oberleutnant Prinz Heinrich XXXIII of Reuss, November 15, 1914

Generaloberst August von Mackensen, March 30, 1915

Generalfeldmarschall Paul von Hindenburg, May 9, 1916

Generalleutnant Erich Ludendorff, May 9, 1916

General der Infanterie Hermann von François, January 16, 1918

General der Artillerie Max von Gallwitz, May 9, 1918

inscription were omitted on the four lower grades of the order which created, in the opinion of some, an even cleaner appearance. The reverse medallion on the 1st Class badge was in plain gold and displayed the crowned initials of the order's founder, *G V*, (Georg Viktor). For the other grades with the exception of the Officer's Cross the reverse medallions were likewise plain, gold for all but the 4th Class, but carried an inscription, *FÜR VERDIENST* ("For Merit"), rather than the crowned initials. The back side of the Officer's Cross was plain.

The 1st and 2nd Class badges were worn at the neck from a cravat. The 3rd and 4th Class badges were worn on the breast or looped through a buttonhole on the tunic from narrower ribbons. The Officer's Cross was pinned to the lower left breast of the tunic and as such, needed no ribbon. At first, the ribbon was a rather darkish yellow with narrow red and black side stripes and a thinner yellow edge stripe, similar to the ribbon employed on the Principality of Reuss' Honor Cross (its house order). But when the order came to be given "with Swords," the ribbon of the old Military Merit Cross was substituted. This was an equally pleasing combination of colors with white being the predominant one and therefore, again in the opinion of some, making this one of the more distinctive ribbons in the galaxy of those used on Imperial German awards.

The broad white center stripe was flanked by narrow yellow, red and black side stripes followed by an even more narrow white edge stripe. Some sources have stated that the practice of adding swords to the insignia began with the advent of World War I and that this was confirmed by a cabinet order dated March 27, 1915. But an examination of the last Army Rank List just before the outbreak of the conflict shows that already there had been a few awards of the Merit Cross with Swords (see Appendix LII). Using the nomenclature employed in Prussia for bravery awards, this "war ribbon" reflected the heraldic colors of the principality. That same rank list, incidentally, also showed a few serving officers with the old Merit Order, five in all, and a few more, 14 if the count is correct, with the old Military Merit Cross earned for earlier service.

In 1985, a fine booklet entitled *Geschichte der Orden und Ehrenzeichen des Fürstentums Waldeck und Pyrmont* ("History of the Orders and Decorations of the Principality of Waldeck and Pyrmont") written by Gert Efler of Alsfeld, Germany was published. Among much else, it gave the numbers for wartime awards of the order and its affiliated decorations. Apart from a few photographs of men wearing their awards, there was no name-by-name list of recipients. So in order to discover the aviation holders of these awards, this writer went to Marburg in 1995 where in the Hessian State Archive there the rolls can be found. And there the laborious job of copying out the names and numbers of those men was undertaken. This information was put on hold while earlier volumes in this series covering states other than Waldeck were being completed. Happily, this was trumped in 1998 when Erhard Roth of Leipzig had his own findings published in a work entitled *Verleihungen von militarischen Orden und Ehrenzeichen des Fürstentums Waldeck im Ersten Weltkrieg 1914-1918* ("Bestowal of the Military Orders and Decorations of the Principality of Waldeck in the First World War 1914 1918"). This was much more complete than either of the other two studies because *Herr* Roth listed the recipients of these awards by not only grade and date but also by name. His findings are shown in Appendix LVI. In Appendix LVIII, these are compared with those of *Herr* Efler and this writer.

There are some minor discrepancies in numbers between what three different people found, but nothing of great significance. In the case of this writer's numbers, one reason for some of the differences could simply have been errors in tabulating the data. More than that however, missing from the rolls that he was provided were several periods where there were gaps in the data. For these reasons and because *Herr* Roth provides names even down to the frequently awarded Silver Merit Medal with Swords which *Herr* Efler and this writer only estimated (due to time constraints on the part of this writer), his study is not only more useful but also probably the more definitive of the other two. Using his data, therefore, the following picture for wartime awards of the Merit Cross with Swords emerges:

Table 25-1

Award	Number
Merit Cross 1st Class with Swords	27
Merit Cross 2nd Class with Swords	20
Officer's Cross with Swords	23
Merit Cross 3rd Class with Swords	72
Merit Cross 4th Class with Swords	580
Total	**722**

For such a tiny state as Waldeck, this was a fairly generous distribution of its house order. The number of 1st Class awards may be understated however. While the list of those recipients contains expected names like senior Prussian Army field leaders such as *Generalfeldmarschall* Paul von Hindenburg, the then (1916) *Generalleutnant* Erich Ludendorff and *Generaloberst* August von Mackensen and only two royals from other minor German states, missing are the names of the often customary "courtesy" awards to the *Kaiser*, the Prussian Crown Prince and the heads of state of Germany's Austrian and Turkish allies. Perhaps these were simply never recorded. Appendix LVIX shows the names of the four known aviation recipients of the Merit Cross (plus the airmen who earned the affiliated decorations) and Appendix LX shows the names of six men known to have received their cross in the ground troops before transferring to the air service (plus the two who, like them, earlier won Waldeck decorations). Then, just to round things out, we have a tabulation showing swords awards of the order held by men who appear in the available rank lists, before, during and after the war. Like the earlier ones presented for swords awards of the other states covered in this book, we can see how few serving officers there were who held swords insignia of the order during these periods. And finally, and this primarily for the medals specialists, Appendix LVII shows the number of non-swords awards to military personnel by grade and year for the order and the three decorations. With that, we now proceed with a discussion of the recipients of Princely Waldeck awards who are of interest to us. We begin with the man who, unquestionably, was the order's most distinguished aviation recipient.

OBERLEUTNANT MAXIMILIAN VON COSSEL

The date was May 7, 1916. The locale was the *Kasino* of *Feldflieger-Abteilung 62* near its airfield at La Brayelle just outside of Douai on the Western Front. The unit's Commanding Officer, *Hauptmann* Hermann Kastner, had gathered his men together to make a few remarks on the occasion of *62's* first full year of operational flights against the enemy. With justifiable pride, he cited some of its accomplishments. His two-seaters, augmented in the summer of 1915 by the new Fokker *Eindecker*, had logged some 1,000 sorties. They had covered more than 55,000 miles of ground. Twenty-five enemy planes had been claimed with 20 of them having been brought down in German lines. And all this was accomplished with the loss of only two of their own aircraft. Finally, two of its men had been recognized with Prussia's supreme military tribute to officers, the *Orden Pour le Mérite*.

At Kastner's side that evening sat one of the recipients of that order. He was the newly promoted *Oberleutnant* Max Immelmann. Both he and a former *62* man, Oswald Boelcke who was now based down at Verdun, had become the first airmen to receive the award when each had scored his eighth confirmed victory on January 16, 1916. On the date of Kastner's little speech, Immelmann had since added six more while his arch rival for top scoring honors in the German Army Air Service, Boelcke, had done him one better with his tally now totaling 15. Both men were national heroes, acclaimed throughout Germany for their accomplishments and respected by their opponents in the air. Kastner's small audience on that Sunday in May included two men who, in contrast, were unknown to the public at large. One was a seasoned observer who had been with the *Abteilung* for nine months, the then 23-year-old *Leutnant* Maximilian von Cossel. The other was a freshly arrived pilot only 19 years of age on his first frontline posting, *Unteroffizier* Rudolf Windisch. Neither could know that a short five months later they, too, would become household names for a feat that saw them decorated by no less a personage than their All-Highest War Lord, the *Kaiser* himself.

Maximilian von Cossel was a Prussian, born in the Brandenburg town of Jüterbog, 35 miles south of its capital city Potsdam. Looking to the army as a career, he joined *Feldartillerie-Regiment General-Feldzeugmeister (2. Brandenburgisches) Nr.18.* at age 18 at its base in *Frankfurt-an-der-Oder*, 62 miles east of Berlin. He was slated to be officer material but first he had to move through the ranks which he did quite smartly, being promoted *Gefreiter* (January 27, 1912, the *Kaiser*'s birthday), then to *Unteroffizier* (March 13, the same year) from which he was jumped to *Fähnrich* 10 weeks later (May 22). Von Cossel's *Patent* as *Leutnant* came less than a year later, on February 18, 1913. The war was only two months old when he was detached from his artillery regiment and sent directly to *Feldflieger-Abteilung 7* on September 29, 1914 for observer training wearing the ribbon of an Iron Cross 2nd Class he had been awarded just the week before. At this early stage of the war, such training was really "hands-on" as evidenced by the fact that he was wounded on January 11, 1915. Recuperation took all of February and March but he was able to report back to *7* on April 1 wearing another just recently awarded recognition for his work, this being his Observer's Badge authorized on March 23. Then his move to *62* came on August 4 where during the month before, great things had happened.

The first *Eindecker* had arrived at *62* in late June and after a demonstration by the designer, Anthony Fokker, himself a brilliant pilot, Boelcke took it up for the first time on the 24th. But he was still making regular patrols in one of the unit's new armed two-seaters, LVG C.I 32/15. And it was in this ship that Boelcke and his observer, *Leutnant* Heinz Helmut von Wühlisch, scored their first victory on July 4 when von Wühlisch poured 83 rounds into a French Morane Parasol two-seater which crashed ironically enough on the family estate of

Compared to the fighter pilots, few two-seater men were that well known that they became the subjects of the popular patriotic post cards of the day. *Oberleutnant* Maximilian von Cossel was the exception appearing on two by himself and several others in conjunction with other men. He was the only airman of the war to earn the Princely Waldeck Merit Cross in the 3rd Class with Swords for an exploit pulled off in October 1916 on the Russian Front. But even before that, as the card at the left attests, he was considered one of "our successful airmen." Von Cossel mailed a copy of this card home from the Douai airfield in late 1915 showing him before he had received his Iron Cross 1st Class. In the other card, we see him not long after the October event, now with the Iron Cross 1st Class and a ribbon bar denoting his Iron Cross 2nd Class, the Knight's Cross with Swords of the Royal House Order of Hohenzollern (which also came for his October 1916 heroics), the Waldeck Merit Cross 3rd Class with Swords and the Hanseatic Cross from Lübeck. Both the Waldeck Merit Cross and the Lübeck Hanseatic Cross were a direct result of his flying in support of ground troops from regiments from that principality and free city.

one of the young French victims, a Count de Rochefocault. Thereafter, Boelcke took to the *Eindecker* exclusively but in another bit of irony, it was Immelmann who first scored in the machine. On August 1, following Boelcke in a second Fokker that had arrived, Immelmann managed to force a B.E.2 down that had had no chance to defend itself. It was out on a bombing job and in order to carry a heavier load, the observer had been left behind. The hapless pilot was lucky to have escaped with just a slight wound in his left arm. The next day, Immelmann was awarded the Iron Cross 1st Class, an initial victory often bringing a man this decoration (von Wühlisch had received one for his July 4 success; Boelcke, already possessing the award had to settle for a written commendation). From that point on, Boelcke and Immelmann began their steady march up the scoring ladder. Early November brought each what were almost certainly the first air awards of a Knight's Cross with Swords of the Royal House Order of Hohenzollern – a prelude to their *Pour le Mérites* – after both had reached a score of six.

But the main job of *62* was not air fighting, however rewarding that was for the few who flew against generally inferior foes with a synchronized gun firing forward. Especially vulnerable were the Moranes, Farmans, Voisins and B.E.-Types with which many German fighter pilots fattened their scores in those early days of the air war. The important work of reconnaissance, photography and bombardment was still carried on by *62's* two-seaters and at this von Cossel excelled – so

Dem Leutnant v. Cossel im Fuß-artillerie-Regiment Nr. 18

ist das von Seiner Majestät dem Kaiser und König unter dem 27. Januar 1914 genehmigte Abzeichen für Beobachtungsoffiziere aus Flugzeugen verliehen worden, worüber dieses Besitzzeugnis ausgestellt wird.

Berlin, den 23. März 1915.

Der stellv. General-Inspekteur des Militärverkehrswesens

Nr. 114.

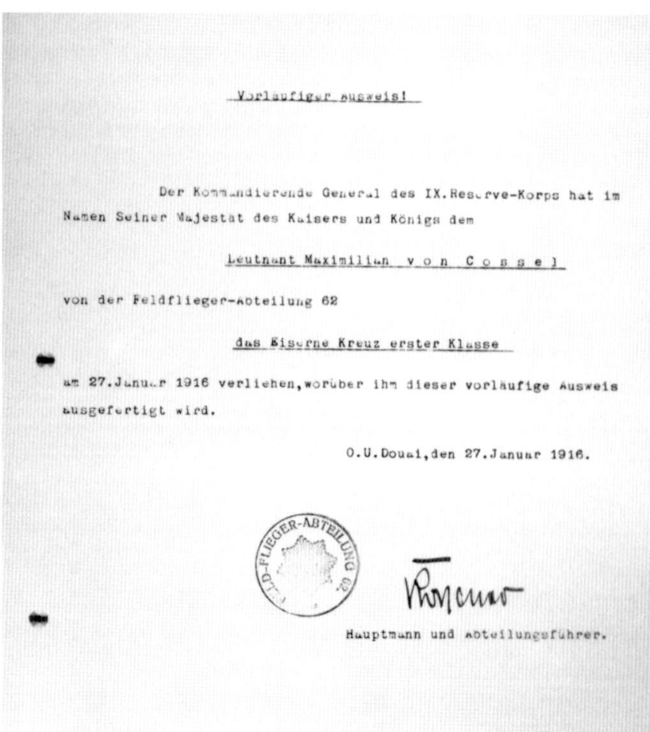

Vorläufiger Ausweis!

Der Kommandierende General des IX. Reserve-Korps hat im Namen Seiner Majestät des Kaisers und Königs dem

Leutnant Maximilian von Cossel

von der Feldflieger-Abteilung 62

das Eiserne Kreuz erster Klasse

am 27. Januar 1916 verliehen, worüber ihm dieser vorläufige Ausweis ausgefertigt wird.

O.U. Douai, den 27. Januar 1916.

Hauptmann und Abteilungsführer.

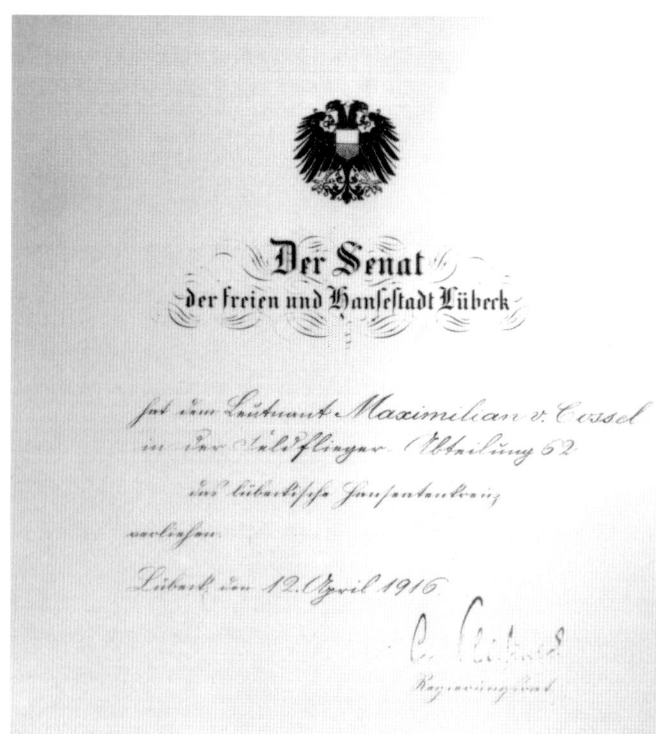

Der Senat der freien und Hansestadt Lübeck

hat dem Leutnant Maximilian v. Cossel in der Feldflieger-Abteilung 62 das lübeckische Hanseatenkreuz verliehen.

Lübeck, den 12. April 1916.

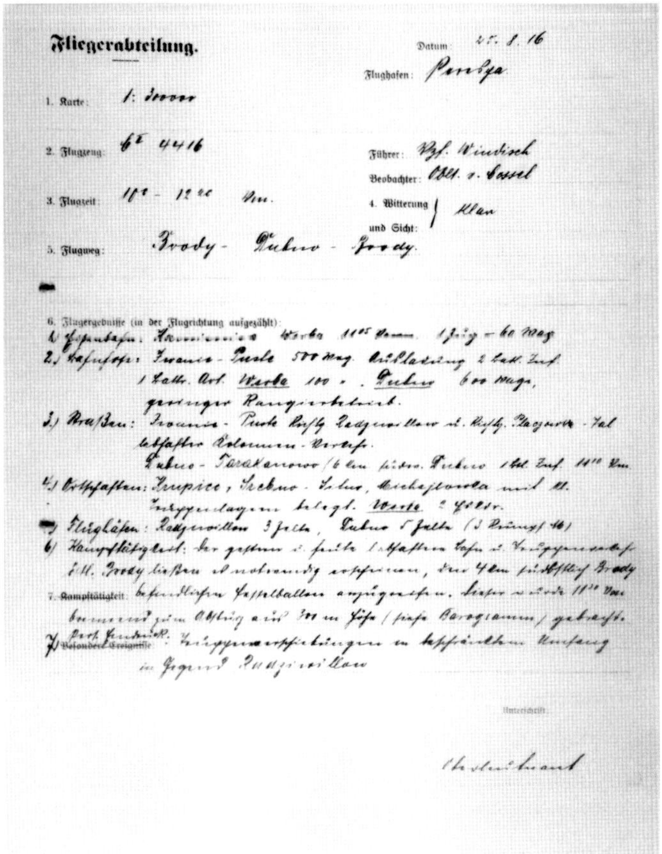

Fliegerabteilung.

Datum: 25. 8. 16

Flughafen: Perespa

1. Karte:

2. Flugzeug: 4416

Führer: Vzfw. Windisch

Beobachter: Oblt. v. Cossel

3. Flugzeit:

4. Witterung und Sicht: klar

5. Flugweg: Brody - Dubno - Brody

6. Flugergebnisse (in der Flugrichtung aufgezählt):

7. Kampftätigkeit:

Besondere Ereignisse:

Unterschrift:

Von Cossel's flight report for August 25, 1916 from the Perespa airfield in the Ukraine with *Vzfw.* Rudolf Windisch as his pilot. Handwritten point #6 details the observation balloon they downed in flames. See text for the full translation.

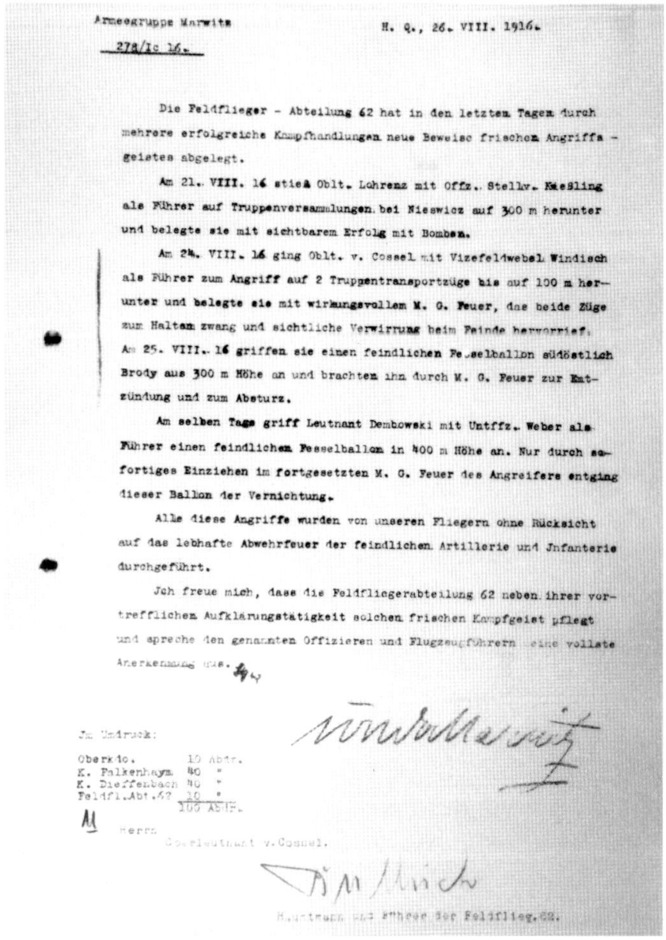

Armeegruppe Marwitz H. Q., 26. VIII. 1916.

278/Ic 16.

Die Feldflieger - Abteilung 62 hat in den letzten Tagen durch mehrere erfolgreiche Kampfhandlungen neue Beweise frischen Angriffs - geistes abgelegt.

Am 21. VIII. 16 stieß Oblt. Lohrenz mit Offz. Stellv. Kießling als Führer auf Truppenversammlungen bei Nieswicz auf 300 m herunter und belegte sie mit sichtbarem Erfolg mit Bomben.

Am 24. VIII. 16 ging Oblt. v. Cossel mit Vizefeldwebel Windisch als Führer zum Angriff auf 2 Truppentransportzüge bis auf 100 m herunter und belegte sie mit wirkungsvollem M. G. Feuer, das beide Züge zum Halten zwang und sichtliche Verwirrung beim Feinde hervorrief.

Am 25. VIII. 16 griffen sie einen feindlichen Fesselballon südöstlich Brody aus 300 m Höhe an und brachten ihn durch M. G. Feuer zur Entzündung und zum Absturz.

Am selben Tage griff Leutnant Dembowski mit Untffz. Weber als Führer einen feindlichen Fesselballon in 400 m Höhe an. Nur durch sofortiges Einziehen im fortgesetzten M. G. Feuer des Angreifers entging dieser Ballon der Vernichtung.

Alle diese Angriffe wurden von unseren Fliegern ohne Rücksicht auf das lebhafte Abwehrfeuer der feindlichen Artillerie und Infanterie durchgeführt.

Ich freue mich, dass die Feldfliegerabteilung 62 neben ihrer vortrefflichen Aufklärungstätigkeit solchen frischen Kampfgeist pflegt und spreche den genannten Offizieren und Flugzeugführern meine vollste Anerkennung aus.

v. d. Marwitz

Im Umdruck:
Oberkdo. 10 Abdr.
K. Falkenhayn 40 "
K. Dieffenbach 40 "
Feldfl.Abt.62 10 "
100 Abdr.

Herrn Oberleutnant v. Cossel.

Bullrich
Hauptmann und Führer der Feldflieg. 62.

Commendation for *FFl.Abt. 62* from *General der Kavallerie* Georg von der Marwitz which singles out von Cossel's and Windisch's balloon attack. The *Abteilungsführer, Hptm.* Artur Bullrich who took over in September 1916, testifies to the communication's "correctness."

Opposite

Top: The handsome diploma for von Cossel's Observer's Badge which was authorized on March 23, 1915 not untypically identifies him by his pre-air service ground contingent whose full title was *Feldartillerie-Regiment General-Feldzeugmeister (2. Brandenburgisches) Nr.18.* and not the flying unit in which he earned it, *Feldflieger-Abteilung 7*. The foundation date for the badge was the *Kaiser*'s birthday. The Pilot's Badge was created exactly one year earlier, on January 27, 1913. Along with the Observer's Badge, a Commemorative Aviator's Badge came into being, originally for men who could no longer function on active duty as pilots or observers and later for three years service in the *Fliegertruppe*. Finally, for the Army Air Service, a Gunner's Badge, another birthday present from the *Kaiser*, was added on January 27, 1918.

Bottom left: January 27 was also a big day for von Cossel but not his birthday (which was on January 7 in 1893). On that date in 1916, he was awarded the Iron Cross 1st Class.

Bottom right: Von Cossel's valuable reconnaissance work where the 162nd Infantry Regiment from Lübeck faced the enemy earned him the Lübeck Hanseatic Cross from the city's Senate on April 12, 1916.

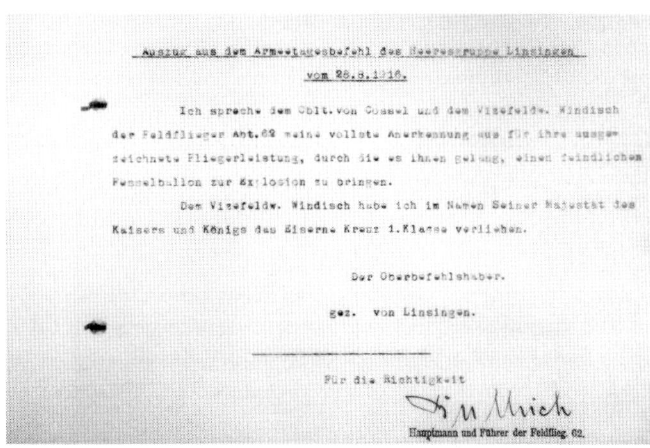

Auszug aus dem Armeetagesbefehl der Heeresgruppe Linsingen vom 28.8.1916.

Ich spreche dem Oblt. von Cossel und dem Vizefeldw. Windisch der Feldflieger Abt.62 meine vollste Anerkennung aus für ihre ausgezeichnete Fliegerleistung, durch die es ihnen gelang, einen feindlichen Fesselballon zur Explosion zu bringen.

Dem Vizefeldw. Windisch habe ich im Namen Seiner Majestät des Kaisers und Königs das Eiserne Kreuz 1.Klasse verliehen.

Der Oberbefehlshaber.

gez. von Linsingen.

Für die Richtigkeit

Bullrich
Hauptmann und Führer der Feldflieg. 62.

Now *General der Infanterie* Alexander von Linsingen adds his congratulations to von Cossel and Windisch for destroying the Russian balloon and in the name of His Majesty, the Emperor and King, awards Windisch his Iron Cross 1st Class on August 28, 1916.

much so, in fact, that his own Iron Cross 1st Class came on January 27, 1916 (the *Kaiser*'s birthday again and this time the celebration the military was obliged to hold on that day each year must have been especially sweet for von Cossel).

Von Cossel's "wholly outstanding service," as it was termed, earned him and the pilot with whom he was flying at the time, a *Vizefeldwebel* Müller, a special commendation in an Order of the Day signed by the Commanding General of the German IX Reserve Corps, *General der Infanterie* Max von Boehn. Dated 20 March 1916, it praised the crew's work, especially singling out a valuable three-quarters of an hour reconnaissance on the previous day that had brought back valuable information on British troop dispositions in the Artois sector in which von Boehn's troops were deployed. Von Cossel's performance on this occasion and undoubtedly similar work during this period that resulted in his next wearable award. Part of von Boehn's command was the 17th Reserve Division. And two of the 17th's elements were *Infanterie-Regiment Lübeck (3. Hanseatisches) Nr.162.* and its sister unit, *Schleswig-Holsteinisches Infanterie-Regiment Nr.163.* (von Boehn was *Chef* of the latter regiment). These units had been in Artois near Lens since October 1915 (Lens was only 12 miles from Douai). In recognition of von Cossel's help to the men of the 162nd Regiment, the Senate of Lübeck voted him its Hanseatic Cross on April 12. It would not be the last time that von Cossel would be decorated for his work on behalf of the ground forces of another German state.

Von Cossel and Müller received more praise in another IX Reserve Corps Order of the Day on May 9. Both were cited for "nearly 80 successful frontline flights" and again, the March 19 sortie was singled out as being especially noteworthy. The communiqué also announced that in the name of His Majesty, the *Kaiser*, Müller had been awarded the Iron Cross 1st Class. As in Boelcke's case when von Wühlisch received his 1st Class cross, von Cossel had to settle only for the satisfaction of knowing that his efforts were recognized and appreciated by higher headquarters. It would have been too early and too much to expect that the next step up from his own Iron Cross 1st Class, the prestigious Knight's Cross with Swords of the Royal House Order of Hohenzollern, could have been his at this time. Up to now, there had been only three awards of a Hohenzollern to officers in the German Army Air Service, the fighter pilots Boelcke, Immelmann and a man who had just been decorated with the *Pour le Mérite* the month before, Hans-Joachim Buddecke, and none as yet had gone to an observer (the first of them to win the Hohenzollern was Paul *Freiherr* von Pechmann who received the order on September 13, 1916; he would also be the first observer (of eight in all) to earn the *Pour le Mérite*). How different things would be for von Cossel in this respect, however, in just five short months.

Events far to the east now had a marked effect on the majority of the men of *Feldflieger-Abteilung 62*. On June 4, 1916, the one and only successful Russian drive of the war kicked off on a 200-mile front (it was also the last large-scale Russian attack of the war). It was called the Brusilov Offensive after the commander of the Russian Southwest Army Group, Aleksei Brusilov. In short order, his four armies smashed the Austrian lines and the Austrian Fourth and Seventh Armies were swallowed up. Ultimately, the Brusilov Offensive ran out of steam after only three months and although the Central Powers lost more than 600,000 men, including 400,000 that were marched into captivity, the key objectives of Lembeg and Lublin were never taken and the Russians suffered even greater casualties, something like one million of them, and their best troops too. After that, things were ripe for revolution. But in the beginning, the offensive posed a grave threat. Despite the continuing blood bath at Verdun and unmistakable signs that Haig's long promised offensive of his own was going to take place either in Flanders (Haig's choice) or closer to Verdun somewhere along the Somme (which is what Joffre successfully lobbied for), Germany had no choice but to come to the aid of its tottering ally and divert precious resources from the west to the east. One of the air units transferred was *Feldflieger-Abteilung 62* (another was *Feldflieger-Abteilung 4b*). But only its two-seaters were to pack up and train it across Germany and into Russian Poland. Aerial opposition on the Russian Front was virtually non-existent and *62's* fighter aircraft could be better employed right where they were. So men like von Cossel and Windisch said their goodbyes to their fighter escort comrades who, on June 12, became an independent force known as *Kampfeinsitzer-Kommando III* or *Kampfeinsitzer-Kommando Douai*. Left behind were such stalwarts as Immelmann and a handsome young Bavarian who was beginning to make a name for himself, *Leutnant* Max Mulzer. The two-seater men entrained on June 15 and would never see either Immelmann or Mulzer again. Immelmann would be killed in air combat three days later. Mulzer would die testing a new Albatros D.I (424/16) three months later, on September 26 (but not before earning both the *Pour le Mérite* and his home state's premier bravery award, the Military Max-Joseph Order, which conferred personal nobility thus making him Max *Ritter* von Mulzer).[1]

[1] As prominent airmen, the names of several of the other fliers that have been mentioned in the preceding paragraphs appear in earlier volumes in this series with considerable frequency. For the fullest treatment of their wartime careers, see Volumes III and V for Boelcke and Immelmann, Volume I for von Mulzer and Volume II for von Pechmann.

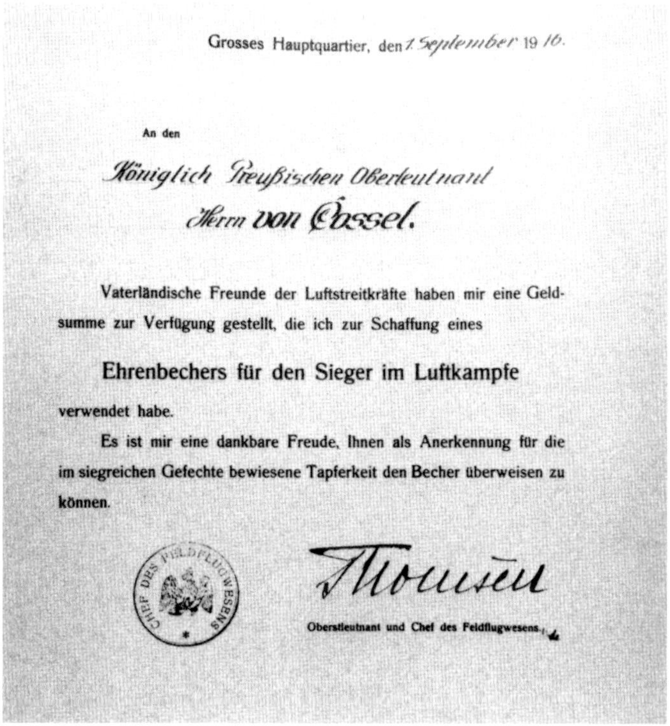

Grosses Hauptquartier, den 1. September 1916.

An den

Königlich Preußischen Oberleutnant

Herrn von Cossel.

Vaterländische Freunde der Luftstreitkräfte haben mir eine Geldsumme zur Verfügung gestellt, die ich zur Schaffung eines

Ehrenbechers für den Sieger im Luftkampfe

verwendet habe.

Es ist mir eine dankbare Freude, Ihnen als Anerkennung für die im siegreichen Gefechte bewiesene Tapferkeit den Becher überweisen zu können.

Chef des Feldflugwesens

Thomsen

Oberstleutnant und Chef des Feldflugwesens.

Von Cossel's balloon victory was his first (but not his last). It brought the customary *Ehrenbecher* on September 1 with his document signed by the then *Feldflugchef*, Hermann von der Lieth-Thomsen. The wording reads, "Fatherland friends of the Air Force have given me a sum of money with which I ordered a Goblet of Honor for the Victor in Air Battle. It is my grateful pleasure to present it for bravery and success in victory." This is not von Cossel's actual cup but is identical to the silver one he received.

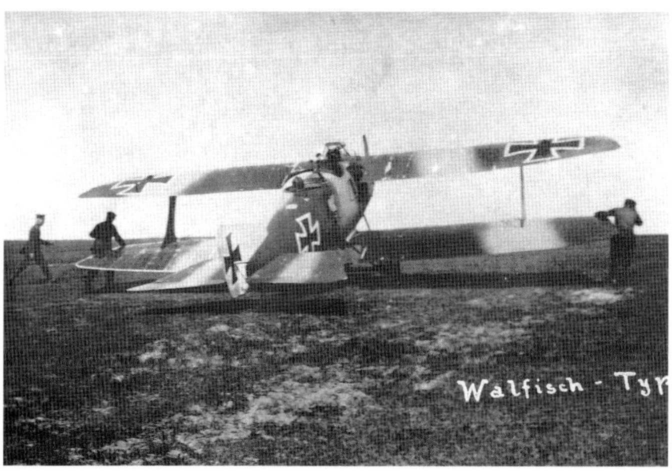

The LFG Roland C.II, popularly and appropriately known as the *Walfisch* ("whale"), also made it on post cards of the day. Von Cossel and Windisch were flying in 4416 when they burned the Russian balloon. Windisch's *Ehrenbecher* came three weeks after von Cossel's, on September 22. Why the slight delay one must wonder?

It took four days for the men and their equipment to train across Germany and Poland and just about the time they arrived at what was to be their airfield at Perespa near Sokal in the Ukraine, the Brusilov Offensive had been temporarily contained due to the exhaustion of the Russian troops and the problems of supply to their extended lines. Von Cossel now began regular flights with Windisch who began to catch up with his observer in terms of recognition and rewards. Von Cossel himself had been promoted *Oberleutnant* just before the orders came that split up *62's* two-seaters and fighters (the date was June 6). Now, during the second full week of July 1916, in rapid succession Windisch's Pilot's Badge was authorized (July 10 and one might observe, about time too), he was awarded the Iron Cross 2nd Class (on the 12th) and promoted *Vizefeldwebel* (on the 13th). Their biggest day since arriving in Russia came on August 25. On an observation flight that lasted two hours and 20 minutes, in addition to noting a number of enemy troop and train movements and dispositions, they pulled off the unusual feat of downing a tethered Russian balloon, unusual enough for a two-seater on any front but especially so in Russia. Upon landing back at Perespa, von Cossel, as the airplane commander, filed the following report which well described what otherwise would have been just another routine patrol:

> Date: 25.8.16.
> Airport: Perespa
>
> 1. Map: 1:300,000
> 2. Aircraft: C.II 4416
> Pilot: *Vzf.* Windisch
> 3. Flying Time: 1000 - 1220 a.m.
> Observer: *Oblt.* v. Cossel
> 4. Weather and View: Clear
> 5. Flight Route: Brody - Dubno - Brody
> 6. Results of Flight (listed in the direction of flight):
>
> 1) Railroad: Kaminienica-Wreba 11:05 a.m. 1 train - 60 wagons
> 2) Railway Stations: Iwanic-Puste 500 wag. disembarking 2 btns. infantry, I btry. art. Werba 100 wag. Dubno 600 wag. some train shunting activity.
> 3) Roads: Iwanic-Puste in direction of Radziwillow & direction of Placzowika Valley lively traffic of columns. Dubno-Tarakanowo / 6 km southwest of Dubno I btn. infantry 11:10 a.m.
> 4) Places: Krupice, Srebno-Sitno, Michajlowka occupied with small troop camps. Werba 2 squadr.
> 5) Airports: Radzewillow 3 tents, Dubno 5 tents (3 fuselage a/c)
> 6) Combat Activity: The lively rail and troop traffic yesterday and today east of Brody made it seem necessary to attack the captive balloon stationed 4 km southeast of Brody. It was downed in flames at 11:30 a.m. from 300 m (see barogram).
> 7) Pers. Impression: Troop movements on a limited scale in area of Radziwillow.
>
> Signature
> *Oberleutnant*

The destruction of the Russian balloon rated mentions in Orders of the Day of both Army Group Marwitz under whose command *62* was operating and the overall command on the front, Army Group Linsingen (named, respectively, for *General der Kavallerie* Georg von der Marwitz and *General der Infanterie* Alexander von Linsingen, both holders of the *Orden Pour le Mérite mit Eichenlaub* since 1915). But more than that, the Linsingen congratulatory message to the two men also contained the news that Windisch was being awarded an immediate Iron Cross 1st Class. But still, nothing but the paperwork for von Cossel until with remarkable dispatch in his case, his *Ehrenbecher für dem Sieger im Luftkämpfe* was approved on the first of September. Windisch, on the other hand, had to wait until the 22nd of the month before his victory cup became official, a three or four week delay in the approval process after the event itself being more the norm. Was this quicker recognition for von Cossel an effort to give him something as soon as possible since a decoration was still not in the offing?

The Russian offensive was on its last legs but the High Command was still concerned. Down came the order, "the fliers must disrupt the Rowno-Brody rail line by all possible means." The line was just a single track that carried vital supplies and troops from the main Russian base at Rowno to the front at Brody 60 miles to the southwest. This was familiar ground to von Cossel and Windisch who had made repeated flights over the area and who had photographed the territory so that maps could be pieced together giving them the lay of the land. Already they were discussing the idea of sabotaging the line by flying von Cossel in with explosive charges that he would plant at a critical point, conventional bombing from the air being ruled out as not likely to have any chance of success at all. Both well knew the risks of putting a plane down on a field where, as von Cossel wrote, a depression in the ground, a tree stump or even a mole's tunnel could cause their aircraft to nose over and a propeller to break. Then they would be in a real fix, at the mercies of either an illiterate populace or enemy soldiery who would have no love for German airmen whose depredations

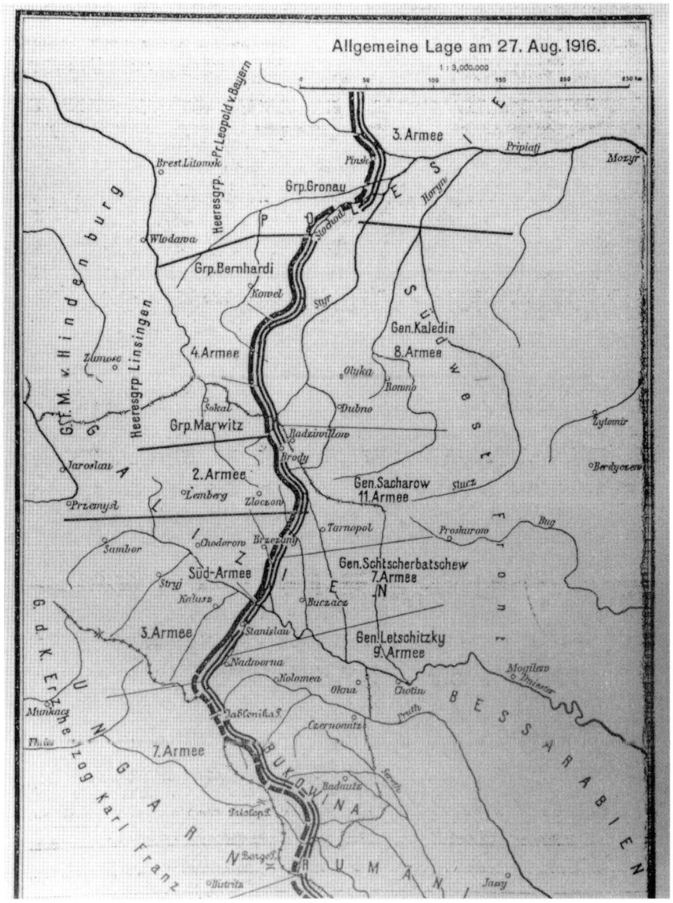

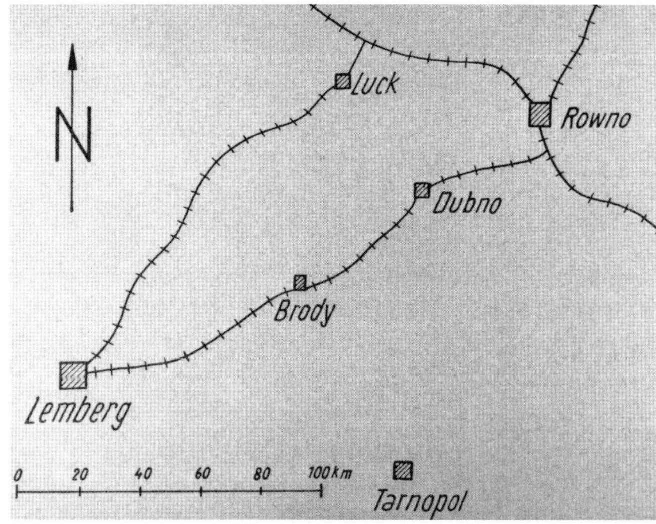

The front line in the Ukraine as of August 27, 1916 shown at the left. Above: The Russian rail line running between Rowno and Brody. It was this vital supply link that the German High Command wanted disrupted "by all possible means" and which provided the motivation for the spectacular sabotage job that von Cossel and Windisch pulled off on October 2-3, 1916.

Below: It is believed that this stunning photograph of the two men and their proud crew was taken soon after their return on October 3, possibly even that very day (but, obviously, not before they had changed into their best uniforms not only for the camera but also for their date with the *Kaiser* and the Prince of Waldeck-Pyrmont and the awards they would soon receive from them). The light "stripe" on the fuselage is not a marking but a shadow cast by the top wing.

POST CARDS! POST CARDS!

The original uncropped photograph of von Cossel and Windisch proudly wearing their just-bestowed Prussian and Waldeck awards dressed in their Sunday best.

The same photograph was then lifted by the Berlin photographer Sanke and became one of the most popular and widely distributed of these patriotic post cards of the day.

were only too well known to them. But both von Cossel and Windisch agreed; with careful preparations and with "some luck," they could pull it off.

First, they had to pick a likely spot for their landing, one that was open enough to permit a landing and a take-off not just once but twice for it had been decided that Windisch could not stay. He would have to drop von Cossel off and then return the following day to bring him out. Also, the place had to be close enough to the rail line for von Cossel to make it there on foot and yet far enough away so that the guards stationed along the tracks would not have observed the German plane landing. The place they chose was about six miles from the rail line. Then there was the matter of supplies. Without divulging the true purposes of the explosive charges they needed for fear of spies learning of their intentions, they conned these out of a German engineering company near their airfield. But then there was a hang-up about the electric detonator that was also necessary. There were only two of these to be had in the entire area but they were able to get their hands on one of these too. The extra cans of petrol needed for refueling were no problem since their mission had the blessing of their *Abteilungsführer*.

Everything was ready to go by the end of September and in complete darkness at 4:45 on the morning of October 2, they took off in their LFG Roland C.II *Walfisch* (quite possibly 4416, the aircraft used in their balloon victory in August). Stashed inside the plane were their supplies including a knapsack weighing over 100 pounds containing the explosives, detonator, wire and entrenching tools that von Cossel would

Not frequently seen but more decorative, this card showing the two heroes also adds an account of their daring exploit. So great was the pair's reputation that on the card at the right, they took center stage surrounded by the first 10 aviation recipients of the *Orden Pour le Mérite*, fighter pilots all.

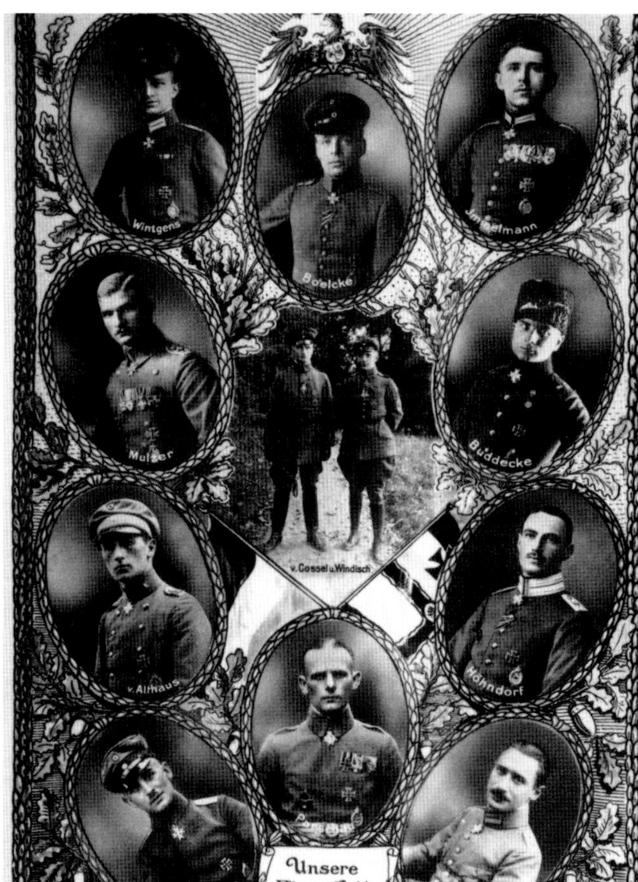

need to do his work. The Roland "Whales" were prone to be nose heavy anyway so the extra load had to be placed judiciously to compensate for that. The front on a direct line from their field was only 30 miles away and the railroad another 15 miles beyond that. But in order to avoid detection, Windisch flew a more southeasterly route of some 60 miles in order to cross the lines at a heavily wooded and thus less populated point. As they approached their pre-selected landing spot, "a fiery red sun" (as von Cossel wrote) broke through the morning mist as if on cue and Windisch set the plane down "like a feather." Von Cossel went on:

> Then it was out of the old barge! Sacks into the woods! The heavy stuff firmly strapped to my back so it wouldn't shift; every minute lost was a chance for the Cossacks to swoop down upon us. Now with only myself to hold onto one wing, the engine was revved up so the aircraft could turn around. A handshake. Good hunting! And away! Windisch flew home.

In the take-off however, the mission almost ended then and there. A peasant in a horse-drawn cart who had not been seen before was plodding across the millet-stubbled field. Windisch was forced to veer around the obstacle. The horse bolted, the peasant fell backwards into the cart but von Cossel was sure that in the man's fright, he had not realized that he had almost been run over by an enemy airplane. With Windisch now safely on his way, von Cossel made his final preparations. First there was the matter of altering his appearance, just enough so as not to draw attention to himself should he encounter any suspicious people along the way but not enough to be accused of being out of uniform and, if caught, executed as a spy. He stashed his flight clothing on the site and donned a half-length fur-collared jacket that he had had the foresight to pack. This covered his tunic and could pass for civilian garb if he was spotted from afar. He smeared mud on his *Oberleutnant*'s "pip" and gilt winged propeller device on each epaulet to obscure them. He muddied his boots and removed the cockades from his service cap. To complete his appearance as just a wandering peddler with pack, he cut a sapling and fashioned it into a walking stick. Armed with a pistol and knife, von Cossel was ready to go.

Following his map pieced together from aerial photographs, von Cossel made for his objective, pausing about two and one-half miles away from the rail line just before the forest ended. It was still too early so he consumed some of the food he carried. Within his view was the town of Zdolbunowo whose rail yards at that very moment were under bombardment by two German planes. Both were coming under intense Russian antiaircraft fire. Downplaying his own precarious position, von Cossel later wrote that he was glad not to be in their place. At 4:00 p.m., he felt it was time to move on without waiting for dusk. He passed children tending livestock and farmers in their fields but no one paid him any notice. He reached the rail line before it was dark only to find a signal block station around a curve in the tracks. There were some railway personnel and soldiers on guard in and around the building. Now he had to wait for complete darkness before his next moves.

After dark, von Cossel slithered up to the tracks "like a Sioux Indian" to begin placing his charges under the rails and attaching the blasting caps. He was interrupted frequently by the continuous passage of trains which forced him to withdraw and hide in the tall grass to avoid being picked up in the glare of the locomotives' headlights. It was exhausting and nerve-wracking work but it was finally done. Two cables were run back some 150 yards to a shallow trench he had hollowed out with his shovel. There he attached the detonator and waited. It was still too early to act because he wanted to give the enemy as little time as possible to find him after the charges were blown. He ate a bit more and warmed himself from a flask of rum that was part of his kit (it seems every contingency had been anticipated!). Meantime, there was nothing to do but watch more trains go by unmolested. When midnight finally came, however, he felt he should wait no longer. The moment of truth had arrived.

Soon another train's headlight pierced the otherwise all-black night (the moon had set). It appeared to be a long consist, just the target that was wanted. Von Cossel had marked the spot where his charges had been planted by one of the telephone poles that ran alongside the track. When the engine approached that point, he turned the arm on the detonator to complete the circuit. There was a blinding flash and the rumble of a powerful explosion. The engine jumped the splayed tracks, derailed and pulled about 10 of its goods wagons after it before it plowed to a halt. Von Cossel could see that the cars were loaded with automobiles, railway equipment and "other nice things." There were also shouts from the signal block station and a siren went off. It was high time for him to make his getaway. But before he left, he had the presence of mind to reel in the cables so his position could not be traced and to further confuse just who had perpetrated the wicked deed, a recent copy of *The Times* of London was left behind.

The weather had now changed and von Cossel made his way back to the landing site in a heavy rain. This time, he took as direct a route as possible, fearing that a search party could be on his trail. He even walked directly through the village of Spasow where the few people that were up at that hour seemed to be surprised to see an obvious stranger passing by. He tightened his grip on the gun he carried but no one tried to approach him. When he reached his objective, he checked that the surrounding woods were clear and then had to wait, hoping, even while he laid out the agreed-to ground recognition signals, that the weather at Perespa had not been so bad that Windisch had had to abort his flight. It was about 5:00 that morning when von Cossel thought he had picked up a sound. But then it died away only to come back again into what became a steadily increasing drone of an engine -probably the most welcome sound he would ever hear. Von Cossel had also packed a "good Zeiss telescope" and through this glass he picked up a *Walfisch* just under the cloud layer being buffeted by strong winds. Windisch had not let him down. The ground markers guided him to another perfect landing and there were warm handshakes all-around. Windisch reported that on his way he had flown over the scene of von Cossel's night's work and there were three trains backed up behind the wreck. The line was indeed

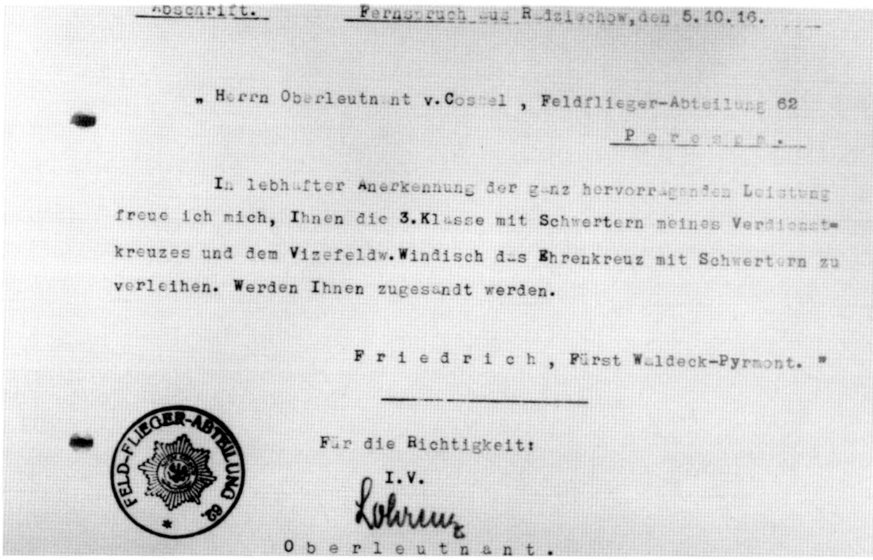
Abschrift. Fernspruch aus R[illegible]schow, den 5.10.16.

„ Herrn Oberleutnant v. Cossel , Feldflieger-Abteilung 62

P e r e s p a .

In lebhafter Anerkennung der ganz hervorragenden Leistung freue ich mich, Ihnen die 3.Klasse mit Schwertern meines Verdienstkreuzes und dem Vizefeldw.Windisch das Ehrenkreuz mit Schwertern zu verleihen. Werden Ihnen zugesandt werden.

F r i e d r i c h , Fürst Waldeck-Pyrmont. "

Für die Richtigkeit:

I.V.

Lohrenz

O b e r l e u t n a n t .

The transcript of a telephoned message from His Serene Highness Prince Friedrich of Waldeck-Pyrmont to von Cossel at the Perespa field expressing his pleasure in making his awards to him and to Windisch.

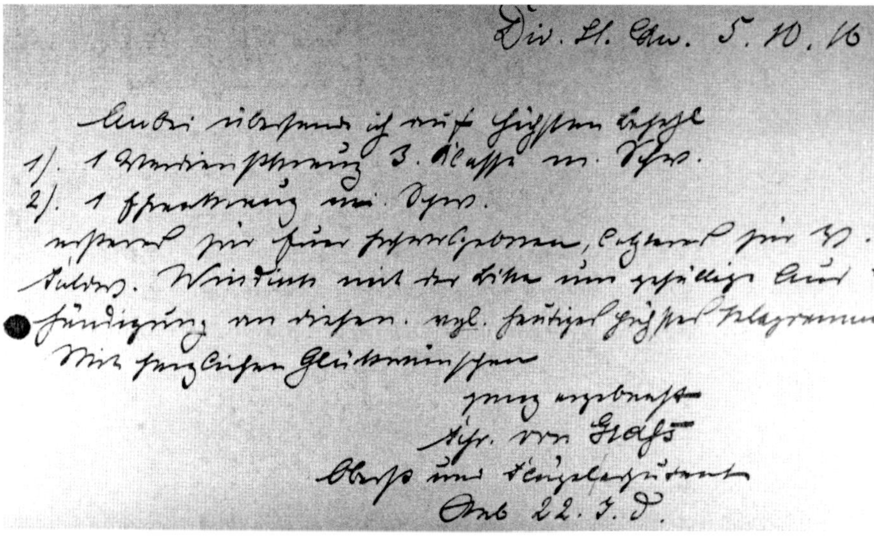
Div. St. Qu. 5.10.16.

[illegible]

1/ 1 Verdienstkreuz 3. Klasse m. Schw.

2/ 1 Ehrenkreuz m. Schw.

[illegible]

Mit herzlichen Glückwünschen

ganz ergebenst

Frhr. von Grass

Oberst und Flügeladjutant

Stab 22. I. D.

On the same date, the *Flügeladjutant* of the 22nd Infantry Division of which the 83rd Waldeck Regiment was a part, an *Oberst Freiherr* von Grass, sends along the insignia and offers his best wishes "most humbly." And this from a full Colonel to a mere *Oberleutnant* and *Vizefeldwebel*!

Württemberger Zeitung

Stuttgart. | Neueste Meldungen. | Sonntag, 8. Okt.

Ein Handschreiben des Kaisers an General v. Linsingen.

Berlin, 7. Okt. (WTB.)

Wie die Kriegsberichterstatter melden, hat der Kaiser bei seiner Anwesenheit in Kowel folgende Ordensauszeichnungen verliehen: Dem Generalstabschef des Oberbefehlshabers-Ost, Obersten Hoffmann, den Orden Pour le mérite, dem im Heeresbericht genannten Flieger, Oberleutnant v. Cassel, das Ritterkreuz des Hohenzollerischen Hausordens mit Schwertern und dem Vizefeldwebel Windisch den Kronenorden mit Schwertern.

Außerdem wird noch folgendes Handschreiben des Kaisers an den General der Infanterie v. Linsingen bekannt:

Mein lieber General v. Linsingen!

Die Ihnen unterstellte Heeresgruppe, in der deutsche und österreichische Truppen in treuer Kameradschaft vereint sind, hat sich in langen, schweren Kampfeswochen in der Verteidigung der Ostfront, in der sie an besonders gefährdeter Stelle unerschütterlich ausharrt, unvergänglichen Ruhm erworben. Der Mut und die Ausdauer, mit der Ihre braven Truppen immer wieder den Anstürmen des an Zahl weit überlegenen Gegners die Stirn bieten und sie blutig zum Scheitern bringen, sind jeden Lobes wert. Ihnen aber, mein lieber General, gebührt hierbei das Verdienst der nie ermüdenden, tatkräftigen und planvollen Führung und der vorausschauenden fürsorgenden Umsicht. Meiner Zufriedenheit und dankbaren Anerkennung wünsche ich deshalb heute dadurch Ausdruck zu geben, daß ich Sie unter Belassung in dem Verhälinis à la suite des Grenadierregiments König Friedrich Wilhelm IV. (erstes pommersches) Nr. 2 zum Chef des 1. hannoverschen Infanterieregiments Nr. 74 ernenne, indem ich weiß, daß es gewiß Ihren Wünschen entspricht, mit dem tapferen, unter Ihren Augen schlachterprobten Regiment Ihres hannoverschen Heimatlandes für immer in Beziehung zu treten.

Großes Hauptquartier, 5. Oktober 1916. (Gez.) Wilhelm I. R.

A page from a Stuttgart newspaper featuring the text of a congratulatory handwritten letter from the *Kaiser* to General von Lingsingen but which is preceded by news of a *Pour le Mérite* to *Oberst* Max Hoffmann and the special Prussian orders to von Cossel and Windisch.

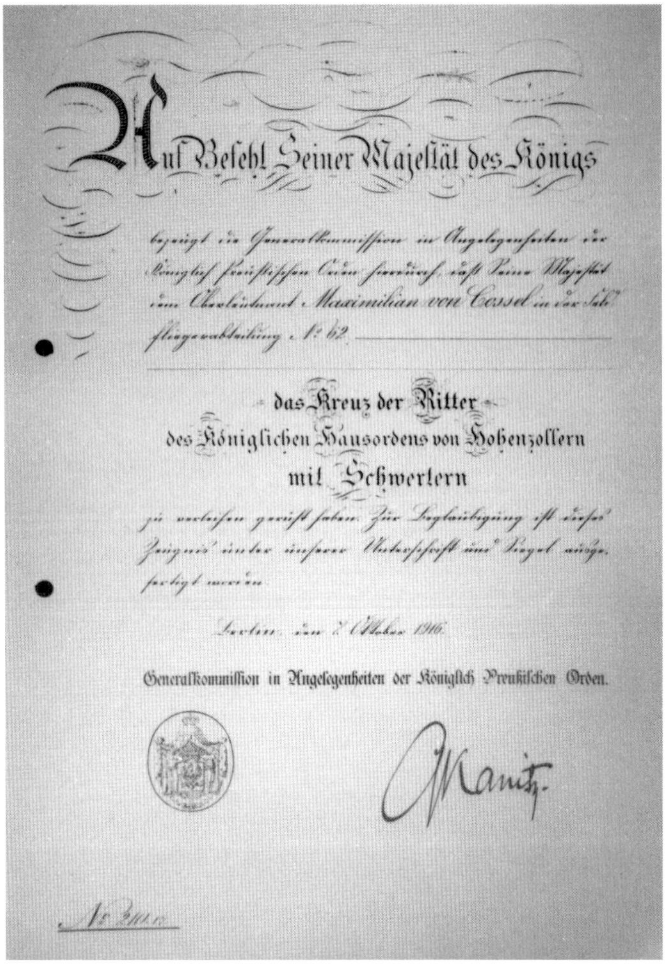

Auf Befehl Seiner Majestät des Königs

bezeugt die Generalkommission in Angelegenheiten der Königlich preußischen Orden hierdurch, daß Seine Majestät dem Oberleutnant Maximilian von Cossel in der Feldfliegerabteilung Nº 62

das Kreuz der Ritter
des Königlichen Hausordens von Hohenzollern
mit Schwertern

zu verleihen geruht haben. Zur Beglaubigung ist dieses Zeugnis unter unserer Unterschrift und Siegel ausgefertigt worden.

Berlin, den 7. Oktober 1916.

Generalkommission in Angelegenheiten der Königlich Preußischen Orden.

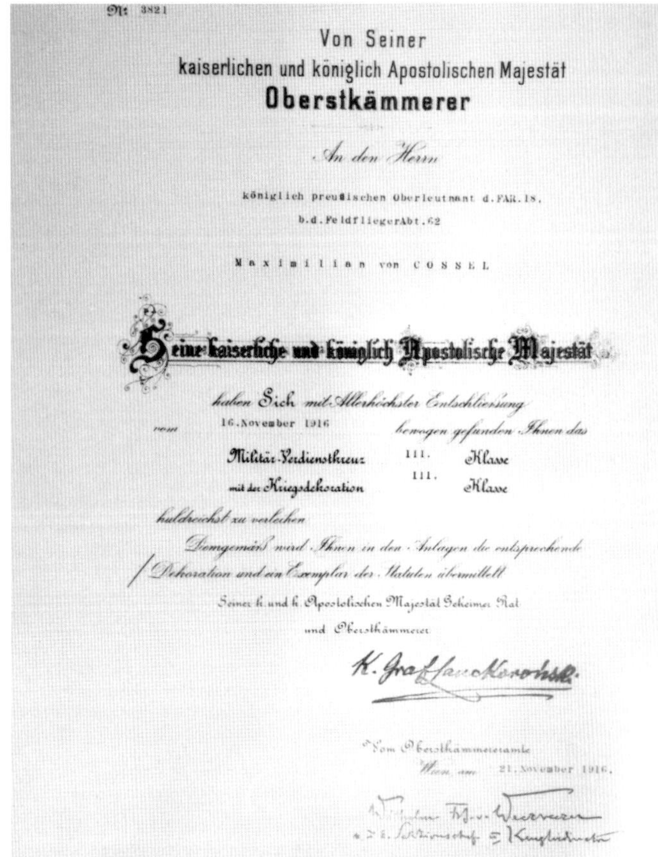

Nr 3821

Von Seiner
kaiserlichen und königlich Apostolischen Majestät
Oberstkämmerer

An den Herrn

königlich preußischen Oberleutnant d.FAR.18,
b.d.Feldfliegerabt.62

Maximilian von COSSEL

Seine kaiserliche und königlich Apostolische Majestät

haben Sich mit Allerhöchster Entschließung vom 16.November 1916 bewogen gefunden Ihnen das

Militär-Verdienstkreuz III. Klasse
mit der Kriegsdekoration III. Klasse

huldreichst zu verleihen.

Demgemäß wird Ihnen in den Anlagen die entsprechende Dekoration und ein Exemplar der Statuten übermittelt.

Seiner k. und k. Apostolischen Majestät Geheimer Rat
und Oberstkämmerer

K. Graf Lanckoroński

Vom Oberstkämmereramte
Wien, am 21.November 1916.

Ich habe dem Oberleutnant
Maximilian von Cossel
das Abzeichen für Verwundete in schwarz verliehen.

Der Inspekteur.

Berlin, den 31. März 1920.

More documents and the actual orders and decorations of Maximilian von Cossel. Upper left, the *Urkunde* to his Knight's Hohenzollern with Swords with his name gracefully lettered in. Penmanship was an art in those days. Upper right, that to his Austrian Military Merit Cross 3rd Class with War Decoration. Right, his Black Wound Badge certificate. For the Army, these were created on March 3, 1918 but not generally handed out until that summer. Von Cossel had to wait until his return from captivity for his. Opposite, von Cossel's impressive array of wartime and postwar awards. See the text opposite the color 2nd Cover for a full identification.

blocked (how Windisch was able to observe this in the early morning darkness was not explained; perhaps Russian working parties were using some kind of illumination in their efforts to clear the tracks). With celebratory cigars lit, von Cossel's gear was stored in the plane and they took off for home.

Acclamation for their exploit was instantaneous. What they had done was called a brave deed that had raised the air service to a new and previously unattained level. Within days, they became national heroes when the press back in Germany got hold of the story, much to the misgivings of the local command and von Cossel himself who would have preferred the enemy not find out just how the feat had been accomplished. But before that there were tangible rewards that only added to the public's fascination with the event. The Waldeck regiment, *Infanterie-Regiment von Wittich (3. Kurhessisches) Nr.83.*, was one of the units of the German 22nd Division manning this part of the front. The 83rd's *Chef* was the reigning Prince of Waldeck-Pyrmont, *General der Kavallerie* Friedrich, and prewar, two of the Principality's young princes and then later two more were *à la suite Leutnante* to the regiment. What von Cossel and Windisch had done was considered by Friedrich to be a direct assist to his cause which deserved to be recognized with decorations under his control. Just two days after the event, on October 5, a telegram addressed to von Cossel arrived at the *Abteilung* signed by Friedrich saying that it gave him great pleasure to award von Cossel with his Merit Cross 3rd Class with Swords for his "outstanding achievement." It also stated that Windisch was being given his Honor Cross with Swords (a decoration affiliated with the order meant for non-commissioned personnel which will be discussed in the next chapter). This was followed up by a letter of the same date from a Colonel and Aide-de-Camp on the staff of the 22nd Division again addressed to von Cossel that included the two insignia themselves. Von Cossel was "kindly" requested to pass the second badge on to Windisch.

The fact that von Cossel's cross came in the 3rd Class was a mark of special appreciation on Friedrich's part. The majority of the only 72 awards of this grade of the house order during the war went to men with the rank of Major (there were 19 awards to men of lower ranks, eight to *Hauptleute*, four to

Oberleutnante including von Cossel's and seven to *Leutnante*). And, as it turned out, it was the only award of the war of a 3rd Class cross with Swords to a member of the *Fliegertruppe*. The exclusivity of Windisch's Honor Cross with Swords will be discussed further in the next chapter as well but suffice it to say here, it, too, represented a high regard for what he had done. Up to the time of his award, it was only the 55th of the war (out of an eventual total of a mere 154) and Windisch's was the first of just two that went to airmen. There were two lesser merit medals that he could have received so it appears there was a conscious effort to put Windisch's award on a par with the one going to von Cossel. On top of all this, most of Waldeck's awards went to its own people and von Cossel, as we have seen, was a Prussian and Windisch a native of the Kingdom of Saxony. But Waldeck was not to be alone in honoring the two young warriors. By a happy set of circumstances, the *Kaiser* happened to be on an inspection trip in the vicinity and he was not about to be upstaged in the matter of orders and decorations.

Both von Cossel and Windisch were ordered to report to His Majesty whereupon he personally decorated each man. Von Cossel received his long awaited and well deserved Hohenzollern Knight's Cross with Swords. The badge, still in the possession of his widow happily along with his other awards, was in genuine gold, a rarity then because by now such insignia were being made in silver-gilt and other substitute materials due to a precious metals shortage in Germany. This could suggest that it came from a private stock of awards that the *Kaiser* carried with him (for him, nothing but gold would do is a logical conclusion). What is more certain is that there hadn't been time to work the award through the regular approval process. The date of von Cossel's Hohenzollern appears variously as October 5 (on his service record) and October 7 (on his bestowal document), thus almost immediately after the event. It is doubtful the Prussian General Orders Commission in Berlin was even consulted in the matter, something which had happened before. In 1915, when there were just a handful of swords awards of the Knight's Hohenzollern, the *Kaiser* had infuriated the bureaucrats at the Orders Commission by willy-nilly handing out the prestigious honor to staff officers in his retinue who were far removed from the dangers of the battlefield. Obviously, Wilhelm felt he could do what he wanted; after all, it was *his* house order. And he more than demonstrated his royal right in respect to Prussian orders when it came to Windisch's award. If the boys in Berlin raised an eyebrow when not being asked to put their stamp of approval on von Cossel's Hohenzollern in advance, they must have had a conniption when they learned what the *Kaiser* had given the young enlisted pilot.

Windisch was presented with the Prussian Crown Order 4th Class with Swords which directly contravened the statutes of this and other orders. Within the military, orders were the exclusive provence of the officer class. They were not meant for non-commissioned personnel. In Prussia, only the Iron Cross was shared by officers and men alike. For the troops, Prussia had two higher decorations that the *Kaiser* could have (one should say, should have) drawn upon. One was an honor decoration affiliated with the Hohenzollern House Order called the Member's Cross. The other was the Golden Military Merit Cross. The first turned out to be Prussia's most exclusive honor of the war for, with Swords, there were only 17 awards with 11 of these ultimately going to airmen. The second became generally recognized as Prussia's highest bravery honor for men in the ranks with the vast majority of the total of 1,770 awarded for World War I coming in 1918. In all, 69 crosses went to men in the *Fliegertruppe*. But perhaps the *Kaiser* can be forgiven for what would otherwise seem as largess in bestowing an order on Windisch. As of the date of his investiture (October 5 seems to have been the actual date), there had been no awards of a Member's Cross with Swords thus far in the war (the first, and it was to an airman, came on January 9, 1917) and the first award of a Golden Military Merit Cross would occur only 10 days *after* Windisch received his Crown Order (this to an infantryman). There was also another factor that may have influenced the *Kaiser*'s decision. Von Cossel's widow has said that what Wilhelm really wanted to do was promote Windisch to *Leutnant* but he was thwarted in this because that prerogative rested with Windisch's Saxon superiors. Either there wasn't time to clear that matter with Dresden or they weren't ready to act that quickly. Thus an order to a man who, so far as the *Kaiser* was concerned, should have been made an officer was not so out of line after all. And yet, this case remains the only one ever discovered in the annals of the German Army where an enlisted man received an order. It is strange that more was not said about this unique event at the time.

The two men posed for the photographer, gloved, belted and dressed in their best uniforms, wearing their respective awards looped through a buttonhole on their tunics. It quickly became the subject of a patriotic post card widely circulated throughout Germany. Von Cossel explained how the word of their daring deed was released despite his misgivings in a letter to a *Fraulein* Henner von der Malsburg in the village of Rittergut Eichenberg near Ihringshausen in the District of Kassel. After a few personal family notes, he also tells of his hobnobbing with royalty:

Fliers of *FFl.Abt. 25* and officers and men temporarily assigned to it from other units at Vouziers in November 1915. The unit's CO at the time was the later *Pour le Mérite* holder, *Hptm.* Leo Leonhardy. He is in the center, wearing glasses with his head tilted back and holding what appears to be a formidable thorned walking stick (a Teutonic shillelagh perhaps?). Towering directly behind him is the youthful figure of *Lt.* Emil Flörke who was to earn the Waldeck Merit Cross 4th Class with Swords on January 20, 1916. Besides Leonhardy and Flörke, a number of these men became highly decorated in the course of the war. The *Pour le Mérite*, Military Karl Friedrich and Zähringen Lion Order holders, Hermann Göring and Bruno Loerzer, are standing 2nd and 4th from the left. Peering through the bannister to Flörke's left is *Lt.* Karl Vogel, a recipient of the Württemberg Military Merit Order and Gold Military Merit Medal. On the stairs in the light *Litewka* is *Oblt.* Ernst Veiel, another Württemberger with its Military Merit and Friedrich Orders. The cherubic face over Veiel's left shoulder belongs to the then *Offz.-Stv.* Willy Rosenstein. His awards included both the Gold and Silver Württemberg Military Merit Medals and Baden's Zähringen Lion Order. (Below) One of *25*'s AEG "large battle planes" which, with as many as three machine guns and a crew of four, flew protection for the unit's two-seaters (von Richthofen derisively dubbed them "apple barges").

What could have been the occasion for *Fl.Abt. 19*'s CO, *Lt.* (first name?) van der Emde, seated in the center, and the debonair officer on his left to have garlands of greenery and flowers festooned on their heads? Van der Emde was an observer and from other photographs, including the one below, we know the other man was a pilot. So perhaps the group was celebrating an especially successful mission by the pair. At any rate, van der Emde and the officer on his right were being playful with their Knight's Crosses by wearing them at the neck à la a *Pour le Mérite*. Van der Emde's 4th Class Waldeck Merit Cross with Swords, earned on January 16, 1918, can barely be seen. The Ducal Saxe-Ernestine House Order on his unknown comrade is in full view. None of the other men in either photograph besides van der Emde and the squadron mascot can be identified either. The Teddy is an original Steiff, worth a small fortune to collectors today.

10 October 1916

Dear Henner,
Cordial thanks for your dear letter. Mother was more pleased than frightened. She is particularly happy that she may be able to come to Mons to receive my first nephew or niece. So, you were in Klingemuhl; I remember it well from a patrol on horseback. Had a few very nice months there and later on, the regimental aide-de-camp told me that a mounted patrol from Kottbus to Frankfurt did not mean that I can visit relatives on the way to feeding my horse and myself.

Close by here are troops from Kassel. On the day before yesterday, Windisch and I dined with His Highness, Prince Friedrich of Waldeck-Pyrmont, and the commander of the 22nd Division, Excellence Dieffenbach. The former had already given us his orders by telegram with very kind words. The fact that we had been ordered to report to His Majesty and were decorated by His Majesty personally will be reported by the newspaper journalists. Yes, yes, the publicity. The relatives are naturally glad when the name appears in the paper, therefore the many congratulations. But a repetition of the film will be made more difficult because the Russians will now alert the entire population. Ludendorff was so delighted by the affair that he disregarded my and the High Command's wishes regarding an announcement.[2]

To you, your Mother and Elizabeth cordial greetings
In a hurry!

Your Troddelmax J.[3]

For von Cossel now, his war in the east was coming to an end. Even bigger things were in the offing. On November 17, he was named to command a unit of his own, *Kampfstaffel 12* of *Kampfgeschwader 2*. He was headed back to his old stamping grounds on the Western Front. And coincident with that move came some rather belated recognition from the Austrians in appreciation of his labors on behalf of their armies. Just the day before he got his new command, he was awarded the Austrian War Merit Cross 3rd Class with War Decoration and then on Christmas Eve 1916, the Austrian Field Pilot's Badge caught up with him. By that time, *Kasta 12* was operating in Lorraine. And it was near the city of Nancy, Lorraine's economic center, that on successive days in January of the new year, on the 23rd, 24th and 29th, von Cossel was reported to have made balloon attacks. None of these, apparently, were successful or at least none resulted in an official confirmation that any had been destroyed. In a moment, we will comment more on his penchant for going after these dangerous targets.

By March 1917, *Kasta 12* with von Cossel still in command had been moved over to the Aisne sector in Champagne. The cocky French General Robert Nivelle, now Commander-in-Chief of the French armies, was about to unleash an offensive that he confidently boasted would win the war. The Germans pulled the plug on him when they learned of his plans and had begun to move back to the heavily fortified Hindenburg Line (the Germans called it the Siegfried Line) in early February. It resulted in their front being shortened by 27 miles which translated into an increased defensive strength, the equivalent of which was like having eight new divisions on hand. What had once been a vulnerable salient was now a solid line running from Arras in the north down to the ridge known as the Chemins des Dames in the south. Still, Nivelle was not deterred. He even arrogantly proclaimed, "The greater their numbers, the greater my victory." The French *poilu* ("hairy one") went over the top on April 16. The weather turned horrible and the French losses were even worse. In 10 days they got nowhere. The offensive was called off, Nivelle was sacked and the first of the great French mutinies of 1917 began on April 29 with troops bleating like sheep being led to the slaughter which, in fact, they were. We can assume that von Cossel and his men were in the thick of all this.

On June 5, von Cossel was switched over to the command of *Kasta 8*, another component of *Kagohl 2*. And there, on the 25th, he had another big day. Flying with a *Vizefeldwebel* Grabow, the crew were credited with not one but two balloons brought down. Von Cossel, now with three of the huge gas bags to his credit, had pulled off what appears to have been an unprecedented feat for a two-seater man. From available records, mainly the *Nachrichtenblatt* covering the period from January 1917 through August 1918, single balloon victories were recorded during that time by only seven two-seater crews. None of them repeated for a second balloon victory. So von

[2] The word "film" is a German word coined by German airmen in World War I to denote a special deed. An example of a sentence in German using the word might be, "*Wir haben einen Film gedreht*," or "We did a special job."

[3] "*Troddel*" in German means a tassel or swordknot. "Max," of course, was a contraction of von Cossel's first name. He could be joking about the knot on an officer's dress dirk but an informed German speaker has said that "*Troddel*" might also be local slang for "*Trotten*" which means to jog or trudge along, possibly a reference to von Cossel's recent sojourn behind enemy lines. Also, "*Trottel*" is the German word for an idiot or a blockhead. "*Troddel*" could also be slang for that word and if he used it here with that meaning, it would be typical of von Cossel's self-deprecating ways which were so much a part of this man's admirable character.

Cossel in all liklihood can claim the title of the two-seater balloon "ace" of the German Army Air Service in World War I. But disaster, always the specter in an airman's life, was but days away. On June 28, von Cossel was shot down in unknown circumstances and made a prisoner of war.[4]

The Treaty of Versailles was signed by the allies and Germany on June 28, 1919 but the former, especially the French, were slow to release their captives. Von Cossel returned home via Bremen on February 8, 1920 and was formally released from service on the 12th. Two final honors were still to come but there was another that was not to be his.

On March 31, 1920, his Wound Badge in Black was approved in recognition of the one he had suffered more than five years earlier and then on September 12, 1921, von Cossel was given the *Charakter* (the dignity or title but meaning here the rank) of *Hauptmann*. For the honor that never came, we rely on an interview with von Cossel's widow that took place first in the 1970s and which has been followed up since on several occasions. She has said that his name was in channels for a *Pour le Mérite* at the time of his capture but nothing had come of it by the time of the armistice. Thus von Cossel joined a number of other men who had been proposed for the award but who for various reasons (death, the Kaiser's abdication before approval or in at least one other case, capture by the enemy) would never receive it.[5] After the war, many of these men made vigorous attempts to get the postwar government to sanction their *Pour le Mérites* (and the Hohenzollern House order too). In all such cases, these applications were turned down with equal tenacity (one applicant, Hermann Frommherz, was finally told on May 23, 1919 by an exasperated *Major* Wilhelm Haehnelt, the former *Kofl* of the German 2nd Army in 1918, that "additional petitions for the bestowal of the *Orden Pour le Mérite* and the Hohenzollern House Order with Swords are a waste of time" (Frommherz, however, had received his Hohenzollern on September 30, 1918). And so on that disappointing note, we close out the career of one of the most outstanding German observers of the war.[6]

OTHER AVIATION RECIPIENTS OF THE WALDECK MERIT CROSS WITH SWORDS

Only three other men besides von Cossel are known to have been awarded the Waldeck Merit Cross with Swords when members of the *Fliegertruppe*. There may well have been a few others who were not picked up as fliers in the roll of the order. The reasons are familiar. In many cases only last names are given without the man's unit being recorded. The three whom we know were airmen each received the order in the 4th Class with Swords as was appropriate to their rank of *Leutnant* at the time. Not much has been found on the wartime careers of the trio (in fact, not even their first names in two cases). What little is known on each follows.

LEUTNANT EMIL FLÖRKE

Emil Flörke received his cross on January 20, 1916. His unit is recorded as *Feldflieger-Abteilung 5*. This may be in error. A week and one day later, on January 28, 1916, he was awarded the Hanseatic Cross from Bremen. It was for his service in *Feldflieger-Abteilung 25*, not *5*. And the only photograph of him that we have, reproduced here, was definitely taken in *25*. Flörke's pre-air service contingent was the Waldeck Regiment, the 83rd Infantry, in which he was commissioned June 16, 1911. It was that affiliation which accounted for his Waldeck award when it came time to recognize him. As already mentioned in the chapter on the Grand Ducal Houses of Mecklenburg-

---

[4] Von Cossel was interned in a French camp so if he were downed by an allied airman (he could have come down due to engine trouble or ground fire too of course), the liklihood would have been the flier was French. The chances of his victor being an ace to boot is slight but in that category, there were three French aces who had confirmed victories that day. One was *Sous/Lieutnant* Maurice Arnoux: of *N.49*, an "enemy aircraft," his first of five. Another was *Capitaine* Alfred Auger of *N.3*, an "enemy aircraft," his seventh and last. The third was *Lieutenant Alexandre* Marty of *N.77*, a two-seater, his second of seven. Arnoux's victory was shared with *Marechal-des-Logis* de Belleville, not an ace himself. The man who scored a probable on June 28 was *Adjutant* Rene Montron of *N.48*, an "enemy aircraft." He had 11 confirms.

[5] The other case where a man proposed for a *Pour le Mérite* was captured before the award was approved and never received it involved *Leutnant* Paul Billik. As the leader of *Jasta 52*, he was long overdue for a Hohenzollern House Order when he finally received it on July 25, 1918, the day of his 27th or 28th victory (sources differ on this point). With that in hand, he was then able to be proposed for the higher honor. On August 10, however, the day after his 30th and 31st victories, he was forced to land in allied lines with a shot-up engine. Despite all his credentials for the award, he, too, was passed over leading one to believe that despite the honorable circumstances of his capture, the authorities took a dim view of a nominee now in enemy hands. For biographies on these failed recipients, see Volume II in this series. Since that was published, other failed nominees have been found (see Volume III, page 236 and Volume V, page 311).

[6] Had von Cossel's nomination for the *Pour le Mérite* been acted upon with reasonable dispatch, he could well have been the first German observer of the war to receive it. In the event, the first award to an observer went to the then *Oberleutnant* Paul *Freiherr* von Pechmann, then in *Flieger-Abteilung 33*, on July 31, 1917. As an illustration of the inequity that existed then (and would continue throughout the war) between awards of the order to fighter pilots as opposed to men serving in other flight capacities, at the time of von Pechmann's *Pour le Mérite*, 22 awards of the order had been made. All but two of them had gone to fighter pilots, one being to a two-seater pilot just before he converted to fighters (Albert Dossenbach) and the other to a bomber squadron commander (Ernst Brandenburg).

Schwerin and Mecklenburg-Strelitz, Flörke, now an *Oberleutnant* and Adjutant to Wilhelm Siegert, the head of *Idflieg*, was given the Knight's Cross of their Griffin Order at the same time his boss was decorated with the Griffin Honor Cross on August 29, 1918. The circumstances of those awards are described in that chapter.

Flörke continued to serve in the postwar *Reichsheer* where he was promoted *Hauptmann* on October 1, 1923 and was still in that grade as late as 1932. From the rank lists in those years, we can fill out his other wartime decorations which were comprised of both Iron Crosses, as would be expected, the Oldenburg Friedrich August Cross in both 1st and 2nd Class and the Wound Badge in Black.

LEUTNANT MÜLLER

Which of the many Müllers who served in the German military in World War I was the aviation recipient of the Waldeck Merit Cross will probably never be discovered (fully 132 Müllers who were airmen died during or immediately after the war; undoubtedly, many more with the same surname survived). Our only clue is that he received his award on September 13, 1916 for service in *Kampfgeschwader 2*. Thus he probably was a comrade of both Erwin Böhme and Manfred von Richthofen who served with the unit in the Ukraine that summer and who in August were chosen by the famous Oswald Boelcke to join his newly forming *Jagdstaffel 2* in the west. "Our" Müller may even be in the only known photograph of von Richthofen taken on the Eastern Front while he was in *Kagohl 2* which was reproduced on page 322 of Volume V in this series.

LEUTNANT VAN DER EMDE

Van der Emde was the Commanding Officer of *Flieger-Abteilung 19* when he received his Merit Cross with Swords on January 16, 1918. That, and the fact that he survived the war, is all that is known except, perhaps, for one thing. He must have had a slightly irreverent streak in him judging by the way he is wearing his order in one of the photographs seen here.

RECIPIENTS OF THE WALDECK MERIT CROSS WITH SWORDS PRIOR TO TRANSFERRING TO THE *FLIEGERTRUPPE*

LEUTNANT FRIEDRICH-WILHELM WICHARD

Service records, when they can be found, are invaluable in our search for information on the wartime careers of the men in whom we are interested. Thus it was fortunate that one on Friedrich-Wilhelm Wichard was located in the military archive in Freiburg im Breisgau. It allows a much fuller discussion of his service than many of these other recipients of the Waldeck Merit Cross.

The 20-year-old Wichard volunteered at the start of the war, becoming a section leader in the Waldeck 83rd Reserve Infantry Regiment before being tapped for a month's officer candidate course in early 1915. He was commissioned *Leutnant* in his regiment on March 20 that year but was wounded in action in Galicia just three months later, on June 13. Two awards in recognition of his leadership followed. The Iron Cross came on June 23 and his Waldeck Merit Cross 4th Class with Swords was approved not long afterwards (August 22 was entered on his service record, the date on the roll of the order is September 9, 1915). That October, he was successful in transferring to aviation and initially took his pilot training at Köslin and then finished up in early May 1916 at *Flieger-Ersatz-Abteilung 8* in Graudenz. On the 13th of the month, he was posted to *Feldflieger-Abteilung 58* followed by assignments with *Feldflieger-Abteilung 18* and *Artillerie-Flieger-Abteilung 217*. During this period, on December 5, 1916, he qualified for his Pilot's Badge. His final two-seater duties were with *(A)257* lasting from September 28, 1916 to January 27, 1917.

With no break for familiarization with single-seater aircraft or fighter tactics, Wichard was transferred to *Jagdstaffel 24* directly from *(A)257*, arriving there on the very next day, January 28. One report has it that his assignment was that of the unit's *O.z.v.B.*, or Adjutant, which would explain his spending no time at a *Jastaschule*. If so, Wichard was not the man to just push pencils behind a desk. April 21, less than three months after reporting in, found him up in the air that day in Albatros D.III 2096/16 that carried the prominent marking "Vera" on its fuselage. He was bent on a balloon attack which, if successful, would have been a first victory for him. His eagerness was his undoing. He was shot down and taken prisoner by the French. They kept him until June 18, 1918 when

No photograph of *Lt*. Friedrich-Wilhelm Wichard, the first of six men known to have been awarded the Waldeck Merit Cross 4th Class with Swords before transferring to aviation, has been found so this one of an unknown crew in *FFl.Abt. 58*, one of Wichard's early units, will have to do. What is the crew pointing to? Something that the mechanics have not attended to? Oh dear!

The aircraft in the photograph above is Otto C.I 544/15, later assigned to *FFl.Abt. 58* but here it is on the field at Schleissheim outside of Munich and home to the Royal Bavarian Army Air Service and its training and replacement center, *Flieger-Ersatz-Abteilung 1*.

Wichard was shot down and taken prisoner by the French on April 21, 1917 when attacking a balloon as a member of *Jasta 24*. His "Vera," still in its overpainted French markings, was turned over to the Americans and graces this display in an exhibition of captured materiel.

he was handed over to the Swiss. It is likely that Wichard was in such poor health, whether from injuries received in being shot down or illness of some sort, that he was no longer considered a threat as a released POW and the Swiss were willing to take care of him. The *Jasta 24* War Diary says that he was seriously wounded in the April 21 incident so it may well have been that he had still not healed (but, curiously, the War Diary places the date of the attack as April 19, not the 21st) and the French were not particularly well known for the tender care of their prisoners. Another indication that Wichard was not a well man is the fact that he was not released by the otherwise correct Swiss until June 17, 1919, fully seven months after the armistice. But finally back home, he became one of those given a retrospective award of the Iron Cross. He had received it in the 2nd Class back in his infantry days on June 23, 1915. Now it was the 1st Class, dated September 9, 1919. It had been a long wait in between.

LEUTNANT RICHARD EISENBERG

Just a one-line entry in the German loss list is about all that is known of *Leutnant* Richard Eisenberg's service in the *Fliegertruppe*. As an observer in *Flieger-Abteilung (A)206*, he was shot down on February 10, 1918 and succumbed to his injuries the next month, on March 21. He was another 83rd Infantry officer who won his cross in Galicia, his coming a month after Wichard's, on October 12, 1915.

LEUTNANT WILHELM SCHULTZE

One week after Eisenberg's award, on October 19, 1915, *Leutnant* Wilhelm Schultze got his 4th Class Cross with Swords in the Galician campaign with the Waldeck regiment (there were fully 17 awards of the 4th Class Cross with Swords to young officers in the 83rd Infantry in September and October 1915 in addition to Schultze's and those to Wichard and Eisenberg). His transfer to aviation came right after the first of the following year with his pilot training beginning at *Flieger-Ersatz-Abteilung 6* in Grossenhain, Saxony on February 3. This was followed by a six-week course on single-seater fighters that began on September 16 at *FEA 7* then at Cologne (it moved to Brunswick on March 1, 1917) and finally, with eight months of preparation under his belt, he landed at *Armee-Flug-Park 10* on October 31 to find out whether he might be posted to one of the new *Jagdstaffeln* which had been coming on line since August. But he was to be disappointed in that, at least for the present time. Like most pilots out of the schools at that time, some two-seater experience was in store for him.

Schultze drew *Feldflieger-Abteilung 55* as his first frontline posting and served with them until late the following March when a spot opened up for him in *Jasta 4*. He reported to his new Commanding Officer, the ex-Mecklenburg dragoon, the then *Oberleutnant* Kurt-Bertram von Döring, on March 29 (it has often been stated that the *Staffelführer* at this time was not von Döring but *Leutnant* Wilhelm Frankl who had received the *Pour le Mérite* back on August 12, 1916 following his eighth confirmed victory. Notes taken from the *Jasta 4* War Diary by one of those interwar German researchers, however, make it von Döring who took over on January 12, 1917 when its first leader, *Oberleutnant* Hans-Joachim Buddecke went off for his second tour of duty in Turkey). Frankl, who became popularly known as "the Jew with the Blue Max," an original member of Buddecke's command, apparently continued on as just a regular pilot in the unit despite his outstanding record (he had 15 confirms when the change of command occurred and when he was killed on April 8, 1917, his score had gone up to 20, including four two days before he fell; despite his having converted to Christianity to marry, his Jewish origins could well have worked against him as they did, for example, when all record of him as a *Pour le Mérite* flier was expunged during the Hitler regime). But whoever was leading *Jasta 4*, the outfit had not been having the kind of good fortune it had had in the beginning. It had gone into action on the aerodrome at Chateau Vaux with its new Halberstadt fighters on August 25, 1916. With stalwarts like Rudolf Berthold and Otto Bernert as well as Buddecke and Frankl, it had gotten off to a fast start, being credited with 13 enemy planes in September and another four the next month. But then there were only three in November, all scored by just one pilot, Bernert. Then nothing at all until a single victory in March 1917. And there matters stood when Schultze showed up. Although he could claim no part in it, things turned completely around in April – "Bloody April" of 1917.

Jasta 4 claimed 15 British planes and one balloon in the Royal Flying Corps blood bath that occurred in April 1917. May, June and July went by with another 30 claims. Particularly

Jasta 4 and friends near its Marckebeke field in Flanders in October 1917. *Lt.* Wilhelm Schultze, at the extreme left, won his Waldeck Merit Cross 4th Class with Swords in the infantry in 1915. There is no evidence of his being wounded shortly before to account for the bandage around his chin. It almost appears as though he had one big toothache. Schultze scored one victory but was killed on November 30, 1917 in a mid-air collision with the German ace, Rudolf Wendelmuth, the leader of *Jasta 20*. The men are, left to right: Schultze, *Lt.* Busso von Alvensleben, unknown, unknown, *Oblt.* Oskar *Frhr.* von Boenigk (*Pour le Mérite* October 25, 1918), unknown, the then *Oblt.* Kurt-Bertram von Döring (CO), *Lt.* Hilde, *Lt.* Egon Koepsch, unknown, *Lt.* Karl Hertz, unknown, possibly a *Lt.* Kraul and another unknown. It appears the men are in working dress. No flying badges and only one Iron Cross 1st Class are in evidence on their tunics.

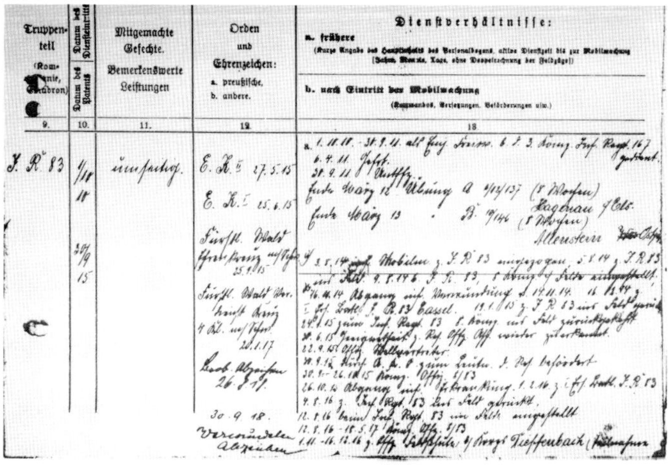

A portion of the service record of observer *Lt.* Friedrich Niedernhöfer attesting to his awards including both the Waldeck Honor Cross and its Merit Cross 4th Class with Swords. To the right, the tranquil countenance of *Lt.* Viktor von Pressentin, another Merit Cross recipient, belies his proficiency as a deadly fighter pilot, 15 victories in two months before being killed himself.

effective was a future *Pour le Mérite* man, *Leutnant* Hans Klein, who alone had 16 confirms by the end of July. Another youngster who would go on to earn the same award and was briefly a commander of *Jasta 4*, *Leutnant* Kurt Wüsthoff, had burst on the scene and had scored his sixth on the last day of the month. The leader, von Döring, had raised his bag to five. August was therefore something of a let-down with only five more victories credited to the unit but one of them was Schultze's, or it was so as far as the Germans were concerned. On the 18th, he put in for his first victory, an R.E.8 downed over Boesinghe. The British admitted to battle damage to three of their R.E.8s that day with two of their crews wounded but all three aircraft got back safely. And even though the action for *Jasta 4* continued hot and heavy in the next months to come (19 enemy planes in September and four more in October), Schultze was unable to score again. Wüsthoff was the lone victor in the unit in November, three early in the month giving him 26 in all and the *Pour le Mérite* to drape around his neck on the 22nd of the month. The last day of November was also the last day for Wilhelm Schultze. In a combat over Fontaine-Notre Dame west of Cambrai, at 11:35 a.m. German Time, his Pfalz D.III collided in the air with the Albatros flown by *Leutnant* Rudolf Wendelmuth, the 14-victory leader of *Jasta 20*, and both men were killed.[6]

[6] For a biography of Wendelmuth, who has always interested air historians as possibly being the pilot of the "red-nosed Albatros" that briefly cooperated with the legendary Werner Voss in Voss' fatal combat on September 23, 1917, see Volume V in this series.

LEUTNANT FRIEDRICH NIEDERNHÖFER

Of the nine recipients of the Waldeck Merit Cross with Swords that we are discussing here, *Leutnant* Friedrich Niedernhöfer is the only one of them who won two of the principality's bravery awards. His pre-air service was also in the 83rd Infantry Regiment and it was with them that he earned both. As a *Vizefeldwebel* he received the Waldeck Honor Cross with Swords (the decoration is discussed in the next chapter) on October 12, 1915 according to the roll (entered as September 25, 1915 on his service record), in another of the Galician campaign at that time. Then after having won his commission, he added the 4th Class Merit Cross with Swords on January 20. 1917 (this time the service record agrees), the regiment having just returned to Galicia from service in Moldavia (Romania). Earlier in 1915, on successive months, he had had the distinction for a non-commissioned officer to earn the Iron Cross 2nd Class on May 27, 1915 and then the 1st Class on June 25, quite a tribute coming as they did so close together. Were it not for the one page of his service record that is pictured here (unfortunately, the other pages are not in hand; if they were, we would have more details), we would not even have known that Niedernhöfer later became an airman. But there we can clearly see the entry for his Observer's Badge dated August 26, 1918. Nothing more other than he survived the war, not even the unit or units in which he flew, has been discovered.

LEUTNANT VIKTOR VON PRESSENTIN (KNOWN AS VON RAUTTER)

This is another, to us, rather strange case of a man forsaking his original German surname, preferring to be called by another one altogether. And of the six known awards of the Waldeck Merit Cross with Swords that went to men in ground units before their transfer to the air service, von Pressentin's (as we shall continue to call him) was the only one not earned by an infantry officer. Rather, von Pressentin wore the more dashing tunic of a *Leutnant* from the *3. Garde-Ulanen-Regiment* in Potsdam (the Guard regiments were stationed either in Berlin itself or nearby, in Potsdam and Spandau). And like all the socially prestigious guard regiments, the 3rd Guard Uhlans were full of "vons" along with a generous smattering of *Grafs* and *Freiherrn* and even a *Prinz* here and there from a minor German house. So, one might ask, why would our cavalryman-later-turned-airman come in for an award from the tiny Principality of Waldeck? In fact, how come, in addition to von Pressentin's 4th Class cross there were at least 30 such awards for officers in the unit during the war? The answer, as is so often the case in these otherwise seemingly unconnected awards, lies in a royal personage attached to the regiment *à la suite*. Here he was *General der Kavallerie* Friedrich, Prince of Waldeck and Pyrmont. Von Pressentin's Merit Cross was approved on January 20, 1917.

For an airman who would post such a fine record as a fighter pilot, von Pressentin got a rather late start in the air service. He began training on the 1st of August 1917 at *Armee-Flug-Park 14* and then took pilot courses at *Flieger-Ersatz-Abteilung 5*, Hanover, from late September until the middle of January 1918 when he attended the observer's school at Königsberg (one wonders what they had in mind for him for what turned out to be more than a month of this kind of instruction). At any rate, by February 28, it was off to the *Jastaschule* at Valenciennes for two weeks of fine tuning as a fighter pilot. His first orders, cut on March 11, had him slated for *Jagdstaffel 59*, not too exciting a prospect because it was a new, start-up formation which had just scored its first victory the day before. But those orders were reversed within a few days and he headed for *Jasta 4*, a much more seasoned outfit as we have seen.

Almost immediately, von Pressentin became *Jasta 4*'s star performer. The unpopular 26/27 victory *Pour le Mérite* ace, Kurt Wüsthoff, had been moved up to the staff of *Jagdgeschwader 1* and in the absence of the appointment of a new *Staffelführer*, von Pressentin had taken over as Acting Leader. He began his own victory skein on March 28 when he downed a Camel (called an S.E.5 in German records). Two more victories were scored in April and then he really got going in May with 12 credited to him in that month alone. With his star rising so fast, von Pressentin might well have been looked upon as a logical choice for taking over Wüsthoff's job permanently. But, no, towards the end of von Pressentin's string, on May 22, an outsider was named. He was the then 23-victory ace, Ernst Udet. Von Pressentin's days under Udet were fated to be few. His last victory, the 15th overall, came on the last day of May when he bagged a familiar target, a Breguet 14 (he had already gotten three of these tough two-seater opponents before). But in the action that day, he failed to return. All the *Jasta 4* War Diary could record on May 31, 1918 was that he had fallen in an air battle. More details have surfaced in the book *Above the Lines* produced by the Norman Franks team. There it is stated that immediately after von Pressentin downed his Breguet on the 31st, he was in turn shot down in flames southwest of Soissons by another Breguet. Since much of the victory data in that book is believed to come from records assembled by the late *Dr*. Gustav Bock, an impeccable researcher if there ever was one, those were undoubtedly the true circumstances of von Pressentin's demise.

A postscript on von Pressentin's awards needs to be mentioned. His rapid scoring in May 1918 put him in position to be considered for the Hohenzollern House Order, anytime from the middle of the month on when he reached the 10-victory level. Long gone were the days of 1916 when such approvals linked to scores were almost automatic. Things like a Hohenzollern went through channels now and these things took time. And time was running out for von Pressentin. Unless the proposal had gone in promptly on, say, May 15, and Berlin had acted with immediate dispatch, he would have been dead before the award was approved. And Prussia did not make posthumous awards generally. But generalities are always dangerous. In von Pressentin's case, he was one of the few exceptions. His Hohenzollern was announced in the August 17, 1918 *Militär-Wochenblatt*. The other late careful historian, A. Edward Ferko, had evidence that the actual approval date for the award was July 13, 1918 and that sounds about right, the *Wochenblatt* announcement often coming four to six weeks after the actual event. One thing does need to be straightened out however. Von Pressentin did not receive the Prussian Golden Military

Merit Cross, a non-commissioned officer's decoration in any event, as has been reported in a recent publication on the records of World War I German aces.

LEUTNANT HANS-ERNST LAURISCH

The vast majority of fighter pilots who spent any time at all in a *Kampfeinsitzerstaffel* (single-seater fighter home defense section or flight) had had previous experience in a *Jagdstaffel*. Many were transferred to the *Kests* having not made it in the more demanding, pressure cooker climate of daily frontline flights against the best the enemy had to offer. Others were deemed to need a break and later went back to a *Jasta*. *Leutnant* Hans-Ernest Laurisch, according to most records, went directly from his two-seater unit where he had posted an outstanding record to a *Kest* where he was to lose his life. But once again, the late A.E. Ferko had scraps of information that suggest Laurisch, too, had been given his chance in a *Jasta*, in his case the famous *Jasta Boelcke*.

Laurisch, the last of the 83rd Infantry Regiment men discussed here, won his Merit Cross 4th Class with Swords on August 13, 1917. His new trade as a pilot in *Flieger Abteilung (A)254* was already well under way when news of the award's approval reached him but it was in recognition of his earlier infantry leadership and not for a signal event that had occurred six weeks before. On June 27, he and his observer, a *Leutnant* Thiede, shot down a Spad over Berry-au-Bac. Then a week after his Merit Cross recognition, on August 20, the pair did it again. And again it was a Spad downed over Toter Mann. Few indeed were German two-seater crews who could claim two enemy fighters destroyed. Perhaps such an exceptional performance was the reason for Laurisch's next move (if the Ferko records are correct). He is said to have arrived at *Jasta Boelcke* on November 28, a fighter pilot aspirant fresh out of *Jastaschule II*. If so, he would have made the customary courtesy call on his Commanding Officer, *Leutnant* Erwin Böhme, who, as described in the chapter on Brunswick awards, was to be killed in action the very next day.

What is certain is that Laurisch scored no further victories in his new berth. In fact, he was allowed precious little time to prove himself. On December 13, the former 17th Brunswick hussar, *Leutnant* Walter von Bülow-Bothkamp, came in from *Jasta 36* to take command, only to fall on January 6. The short, stocky *Leutnant* Max Müller already loaded with honors which, in value, rivaled those of Manfred von Richthofen (see especially the biographies of him which have appeared in Volume I and Volume IV in this series) was named to lead *Jasta B* in von Bülow's place, probably just in the air initially; whether he would have ever been confirmed as its leader on the ground is questionable because at this stage of the war, it would have been unusual for a Bavarian to lead a Prussian formation. The very next day, January 7, Laurisch was unceremoniously "put at the disposal of *Idflieg*," in other words, transferred out and available for reassignment. Was it a matter of Laurisch not measuring up to Müller's standards? Who is to know now for Muller himself fell or jumped to his death on January 9 from his Albatros as it went down ablaze from the guns of an R.E.8 observer (in death, Müller would become Max *Ritter* von Müller when he was posthumously awarded the Knight's Cross of the Bavarian Military Max-Joseph Order in March 1919).

At the end of July 1918, we next find Laurisch in his final assignment, the home defense unit *Kest 4b* based in Freiburg im Breisgau in Baden. On either July 30 or 31, he lost his life. The German Honor Rank List for 1914-1918 published in 1926 shows the latter date but other sources say July 30. It is not clear, either, whether his death was due to enemy action or to an accident. The Honor Rank List merely contains the abbreviation "*abg*." That could stand for "*abgeschossen*" (shot down) or "*abgestürzt*" (crashed). Small comfort for him whatever the circumstances.

CHAPTER XXVI

THE MILITARY AWARDS OF THE PRINCIPALITY OF WALDECK THE HONOR CROSS

A new Waldeck decoration called the Honor Cross was introduced on July 4, 1899. Within the military, it went to men below the rank of *Leutnant* and was the senior award open to them. The Honor Cross closely resembled the Merit Cross 4th Class in that it was also in matte silver although slightly smaller and had the same enameled white center medallion with the red enamel *cross moline* surrounded by a gold ring. What immediately distinguished the Honor Cross from the Merit Cross 4th Class was the absence of the eight-rayed star feature of the house order badges. The reverse medallion of the Honor Cross carried the inscription *FÜR VERDIENST* ("For Merit") on two lines.

Swords on an Honor Cross indicated, as might be expected, an award made for brave deeds or distinguished service in the presence of the enemy. For service in World War I, a total of 154 awards of the Honor Cross with Swords were made (plus just five without Swords) to men in the military. It went generally to natives of the principality and to those serving in the Waldeck regiment (although we have already encountered a major exception to those provisions in the previous chapter and will hear more about him shortly). It was also necessary that a recipient possess the Iron Cross (the grade was not specified and the presumption, therefore, is that just the Iron Cross 2nd Class was sufficient). The small number of swords awards of the Honor Cross made it one of the least common of Imperial Germany's World War I bravery decorations and an example of one is highly prized by collectors today.

For heroic achievements in the air, only two fliers are known to have been awarded the Honor Cross with Swords. One was the previously mentioned *Vizefeldwebel* Rudolf Windisch. The other was *Offizier-Stellvertreter* Ludwig Friedewald, a two-seater pilot also. 'More on Windisch's career follows, particularly after he had converted to fighters. What is known of Friedewald's service is also included. Only one man who earned the Honor Cross with Swords in the ground troops and later transferred to the *Fliegertruppe* has been found, *Leutnant* Friedrich Niedernhöfer. As a later recipient of the Merit Cross 4th Class with Swords, he, too, appeared in the previous chapter. There could well have been others in Niedernhöfer's category, men who received the Honor Cross with Swords before switching over to the air arm. The absence of first names and unit designations in all too many cases on the roll have prevented identifying any other such recipients however.

LEUTNANT RUDOLF WINDISCH

Those reading this book sequentially will have already learned of the heroics of the then *Vizefeldwebel* Rudolf Windisch on the Eastern Front in the summer and fall of 1916 and the awards they merited. But let us go back now to the beginning of his military career before briefly reprising those events and then going on with the rest of his story. Just before the war broke out, Windisch at age 17 had started his compulsory training as a one-year volunteer with the Dresden quartered *12. Infanterie-Regiment Nr.177*. Dresden was also Windisch's birthplace where he came into the world on January 27, 1897 (also, coincidentally, the *Kaiser*'s 38th birthday that year). When the gray tide entered Luxembourg in the first days of the war and then stormed through Belgium and France, the 177th Infantry, as an element of the Saxon 1st Army Corps, was part of that force on its way to the crucial meeting on the Marne. In the withdrawal that followed, the 177th ended up north and west

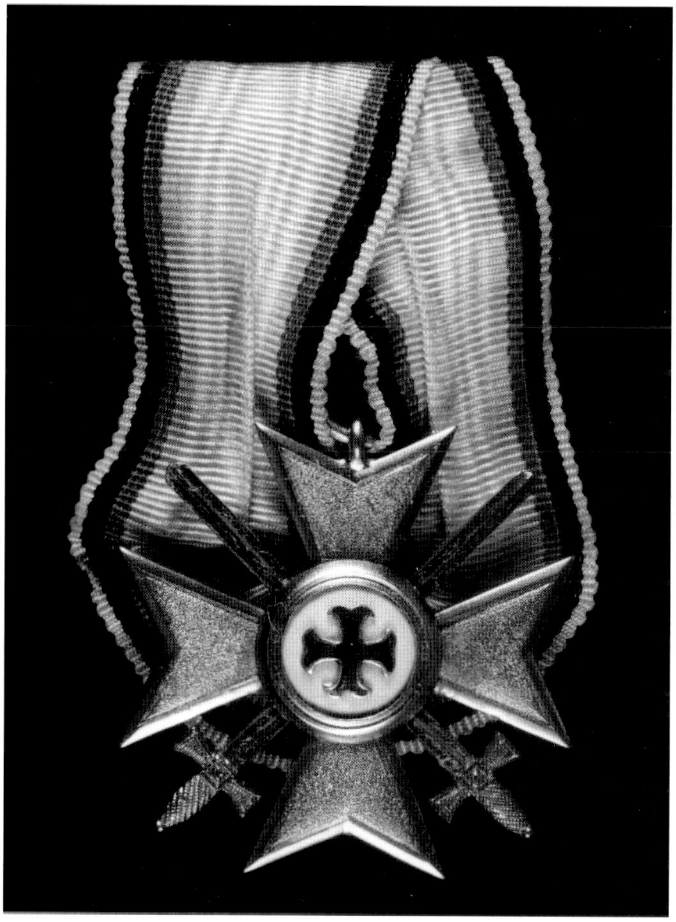

The Waldeck Honor Cross was founded on July 4, 1899 and was the principality's highest decoration within the military for men below the rank of *Leutnant*. During World War I, it was awarded only 159 times, 154 of which were with Swords, the insignia seen here (obverse on the left, reverse on the right). Swords awards indicated that the recipient had performed some especially brave deed or deeds in the face of the enemy. To earn it, a man also had to have the Iron Cross in his possession and the award was not generally conferred on those who were not Waldeck citizens or serving in the Waldeck regiment. Those factors account for its exclusivity and made it one of the least frequently bestowed bravery decorations of the war. And also why, so far as is known, only two fliers received the Honor Cross with Swords for exploits in the air. Swords awards of the Honor Cross used the same ribbon as the one employed on swords awards of the Waldeck Merit Cross, its house order, which was the old white ribbon with narrow yellow, red, black and white end stripes of the former and by the time of World War I, defunct Waldeck Military Merit Cross.

of Reims where the lines finally stabilized (and where they were to remain until 1918).

In the bitter trench warfare that ensued, Windisch was wounded by a grenade on November 21, not seriously but enough to require hospitalization. He was first attended to at the field hospital in Laon and then, no doubt to the joy of his family, he was shipped to *Ersatzlazarett I* (Reserve Hospital 1) in Dresden for further treatment. There he was attended to by a Dr. Lahmann who ran a sanitarium in the city whose emblem was said to be a running stag (more on that later). It was during his recuperation that Windisch put in for a transfer to the air service which was accepted (as were so many similar applications by wounded men who apparently had had enough of trench life and saw in aviation a more exciting way to make their contribution to the war effort). Windisch had long been captured by aviation and at age 14, his handmade glider had won a prize at an exhibition.

At the turn of the year, Windisch was released from hospital and reported to the large aviation training and supply facility at Grossenhain conveniently located some 20 miles from Dresden. His initial indoctrination concluded, he was sent off to the Leipzig-Lindenthal school on February 22, 1915 to get some hands-on flying. Coincident with a promotion to *Unteroffizier* on June 10, he was assigned back to Grossenhain and its *Flieger-Ersatz-Abteilung 6*. The war would have to wait a bit longer for him. So good a pupil had he been that he had been earmarked an instructor. This job lasted until the middle of April 1916. After the usual staging at an *Armee-Flug-Park*, he was assigned to *Feldflieger-Abteilung 62* on the 1st of May and that's where we found him in the previous chapter a week later listening to his Commanding Officer recite the accomplishments of the unit in its first full year of operation. Then came the previously described shift of *62* to the Ukraine in the middle of June. Things for Windisch began to move ahead rapidly. On July 10, with the required number of frontline flights now entered in his log, he was authorized to wear the Pilot's Badge (three to four months of combat flying being about par for the course in earning it oftentimes). Then two days later came the Iron Cross 2nd Class and the day after that, promotion to *Vizefeldwebel*.

The balloon victory on the 25th of the following month which brought Windisch the Iron Cross 1st Class and his *Ehrenbecher* have already been described as has the biggest event of his wartime career to that time, his ferrying his observer to a landing spot behind enemy lines and then returning the next day to bring him safely home and the acclaim that was waiting both of them. In addition to the immediate award of Windisch's Honor Cross with Swords from a grateful Prince Friedrich of Waldeck whose 83rd Regiment faced the Russians in this sector, the *Kaiser*'s who-cares-what-the-statutes-say presentation of the Prussian Crown Order 4th Class with Swords has likewise received considerable comment. This would be an appropriate place to explore that fact in more detail, despite the fact that much of what follows has already been previously discussed.

The granting of a Prussian order, or any order for that matter, to a non-commissioned officer was without precedent. So far as it is known, this is the only time it ever happened in the long history of Prussian awards and there is no record of it ever happening again. As already explained, the *Kaiser* had two much more logical and at the time, perhaps even more prestigious options. One was Prussia's Golden Military Merit Cross which became in World War I what was accepted as the highest bravery award that could be bestowed on non-commissioned officers. As such, it was referred to as the *Pour le Mérite für Unteroffiziere* (or more irreverently as the "*Pour le Mérite* for the Little Man"). But as of the date of Windisch's order from the Emperor, no Golden Military Merit Cross had as yet been awarded in World War I (the first, to an infantryman, would, however, come within the month, on October 15, so the idea of starting to bestow it was obviously in channels at the time of Windisch's Crown Order which was officially dated October 5). The Golden Military Merit Cross had first been awarded in the 1866 war with Austria and most recently, in the colonial campaigns, the last being in 1906 to a *Feldwebel* in the *Schutztruppe* in Cameroon, but only a total of 38 times in all those years (there were no further awards of the cross in 1915; the next was on June 14, 1917 followed by 53 more that

The then *Vzfw.* and later *Lt.* Rudolf Windisch as captured on contemporary post cards by the firm of W. Sanke in Berlin. In the boyish pose at the left, he wears the Iron Cross 1st Class given him for scoring his first victory, a Russian balloon brought down on August 25, 1916 while flying with his observer, *Oblt.* Maximilian von Cossel. The center card depicts him after he had returned to the Western Front but wearing decorations earned in the east. After the Iron Cross 2nd Class we see the Prussian Crown Order 4th Class with Swords, the Waldeck Honor Cross with Swords, the Silver Saxon St. Henry Medal and the Austrian Bravery Medal in Silver 2nd Class. In the card at the right, an artist has used the same photograph and has drawn in a representation of the *Orden Pour le Mérite*, an honor he never lived to wear.

Above: A Roland C.II and a brace of Fokker *Eindeckers* on the aerodrome of *Feldflieger-Abteilung 62* on the Western Front in 1916 before the two-seaters were transferred to the Ukraine in the middle of June. This C.II appears in the overall pale blue/gray doped finish that was typical of most of the initial production machines.

Below: In another photo of this scene, air historian Peter M. Grosz in his Windsock Datafile 49 called it a "gorgeous" line-up and pointed out that a variety of exhaust stacks could be seen and that some of the aircraft had bomb racks installed under the fuselage.

year; 1918 saw the vast majority of the total of 1,770 bestowed in World War I, 1,715 of them). The other option open to the *Kaiser* would have been the Cross of a Member of the Royal Hohenzollern House Order with Swords, an honor decoration affiliated with the order but meant for non-commissioned personnel too. As such, it would have made the perfect counterpart to the Knight's Cross with Swords of the Royal Hohenzollern House Order which the *Kaiser* presented to Windisch's observer, Maximilian von Cossel, on this occasion. But the Member's Cross, too, had yet to be awarded in the war. The first did not come until January 9, 1917 (in all, only 17 awards of the Member's Cross with Swords were made in the war with 11 of them going to airmen). So what made the *Kaiser*, who was well aware of the regulations concerning orders if anyone was, overreach himself and do something as extraordinary as what he did?

It has already been suggested in the previous chapter that since, according to von Cossel's widow, it was really his desire to reward Windisch with a commission but since he did not have that authority when it involved a man in the Royal Saxon Army and for whatever reason was not able or didn't try to get Dresden to agree with that proposition, that he reached into his

Above: Almost certainly it is Windisch who sits in the pilot's seat of this captured British F.E.2, already stripped of its Lewis guns. The circumstances of its downing are unknown but it certainly was not a victory pose for Windisch. His first confirmed victory would not come until August 25, 1916 when he and von Cossel burned a Russian balloon southeast of Brody. The man in the observer's cockpit is unknown. Below: An overpainted Roland C.II of *FFl.Abt. 62* with the distinctive shark's mouth that also marked the machine in which Windisch and von Cossel made their famous raid behind Russian lines over October 2/3, 1916. This C.II also had the whimsical "curtains" painted on the windows.

bag and came up with an order. Was it then pique on his part that his Royal Wish had not been agreed to by the Saxons and since in his mind Windisch was deserving to be an officer and therefore an order would do? Or was it actually merely a matter of convenience, taking out an award that happened to be on hand? After all, he couldn't very well decorate von Cossel and not do something for the other participant in the affair. Probably the matter is of little consequence to most, but it has always fascinated this writer.

While Saxony might not have been quite ready to elevate Windisch to officer rank, they couldn't very well overlook what he had done in view of all the fuss being made about him and von Cossel in the press. So on October 16, Windisch was given the Saxon Silver St. Henry Medal. This decoration was affiliated with Saxony's highest military tribute for officers, the Military St. Henry Order. There was a higher grade of the decoration, the Gold St. Henry Medal but Windisch was passed over for it and, contrary to what has been written elsewhere, was never to receive it. It was probably around this time (the date has not been found) that the Austrians, too, felt they should come through for Windisch just as they would for von Cossel on November 16 when he received their Military Merit Cross 3rd Class with War Decoration. For Windisch, it was their Silver Bravery Medal 2nd Class. So in some only four months of action, he had a chestful of one order, five decorations and his flight badge to display his prowess as a flier to the world.

As it was with von Cossel, Windisch's theater of war was about to change soon after their escapade together. Both men were transferred to *Kampfstaffel 12* of *Kampfgeschwader 2*, left the Ukraine and headed for the Western Front. And there, on December 5, Windisch got the good news that he had been given his commission. So it had only been two months for the Saxons to agree with the *Kaiser* that he was first class officer material. That also marked the end of his association with the dashing von Cossel however. The next day, Windisch moved over to *Kagohl 2*'s sister unit, *Kasta 11*. Even bigger change was on the docket for him in the new year of 1917. With the expansion of the *Jagdstaffeln* that had been going on, many an experienced two-seater pilot was being shifted over to the new air arm. Windisch joined one of the new units, *Jagdstaffel 32*, on February 20, two days ahead of its official mobilization date. *Jasta 32* went into action the following month but despite three months of flying in Lorraine and another three patrolling the skies on the Aisne and in Champagne, Windisch proved to be a slow starter in terms of victories. His first did not come until September 18 by which time *Jasta 32* was flying over the old Verdun battlefield. He scored once more that month and before the year was out, three more times in November. He was on his way and the next year would see him go on to become one of Germany's premier *Kanonen* of the war (Windisch's complete list of victories will be shown in a table at the end of his biography). And it was also in November, on the 4th, that Saxony again recognized what the new young officer was up to and awarded him the Knight 2nd Class with Swords of its Albert Order. And with that, now is the time and place to make a long overdue correction.

In the 1960s and early 1970s, the much respected medals authority in Berlin, *Dr.* Kurt-Gerhard Klietmann, was graciously assisting the early efforts of this writer to determine the awards of German airmen in World War I. Access to West German archives for that kind of information which would show up on service records (if they had survived that is) was in many cases restricted to direct family members only. But *Dr.* Klietmann had his methods and he also had voluminous records of his own. He was able to provide data that otherwise would not have been obtainable at that time (the situation has much eased since then and the laws concerning *Datenschutz*, the protection of personnel information, have been relaxed more and more). Of course, in those years, the archives behind the Curtain were completely closed to westerners. Nonetheless, one of the lists of awards provided by *Dr.* Klietmann were those of Rudolf Windisch. That included his unique Crown Order 4th Class with Swords and his other awards including what was said to have been the Albert Order Knight 1st Class with Swords. That statement was accepted by this writer and so in writing about recipients of that order, it was always the 1st Class and not the 2nd Class that Windisch was said to have received. That probably should have been questioned more than it was on those occasions. The Saxon *Grundsätze für Verleihhung Allerhöchster Ordensauszeichnungen* (Principles for Bestowal of All-Highest Orders Distinctions) clearly lay out the ground rules. Rank was the determinant, not the degree of an man's bravery. *Oberleutnante* and *Leutnante* would receive the Albert Order in the 2nd Class in the first instance. Only *Majore* and *Hauptleute* would get the 1st Class Knight's Cross. The only way the two junior officer ranks could earn an Albert Knight 1st Class were if he already possessed the Albert Knight 2nd Class and had also been awarded the Saxon Merit Order 2nd Class with Swords, an order a step above the Albert. And the Merit Order Windisch never received. With the fall of the Wall, archives such as the one in Dresden are now open and it was visited by this writer in 1992 in connection with his work on Volume III in this series dealing with the aviation awards of the Kingdom of Saxony. The roll of the Albert Order found there was far from complete with the last entry for an award of the order to an airman being dated March 16, 1917.

Above: Windisch, still a non-commissioned officer and still in the Ukraine with *FFl.Abt. 62*, must have gotten in some single-seater time there with this Pfalz E.II (the Pfalz company logo is just visible on top of the cowling which appears to be in need of a bit of a paint job at that). The Pfalz Es were even inferior to the Fokker *Eindeckers* which themselves were exceptional for the day only due to their synchronized machine gun.

Left: Windisch and friend in a seldom-seen picture. His ribbon bar now shows a slightly different arrangement with that of his St. Henry Medal in third place and his Waldeck Honor Cross in fourth place. Actually, as a Saxon, he could have placed that kingdom's award ahead of his Prussian Iron Cross and Crown Order.

Opposite, top: *Jasta 32* on a chilly day in the summer of 1917 form up for a group photograph on the steps of their requisitioned living quarters with two unidentified mess boys awaiting the mens' pleasure. Windisch joined *Jasta 32* when it was mobilized in February 1917. Standing with their feet on the ground, left to right (total victory scores in brackets) are: *Lt.* Wilhelm Eckenberg (0 - *O.z.b.V.*), *Lt.* Fritz Kieckhäfer (8) and *Lt.* Hans-Joachim Rolfes (17). On the first step: Windisch (22). On the second step: *Vzfw.* Walter Starke (?), *Oblt.* Otto Schmidt, *Staffelführer* (19 or 20), *Lt.* Lothar Zenkominierski (3) and *Vzfw.* Franz Tabaka (1). In the back row: a *Lt.* Richter (?). *Lt.* Werner Ulmer (0), *Vzfw.* Kurt Petzinna (2), *Vzfw.* Konrad Poralla (0) and *Lt.* Otto Hohmuth (4). But, again, where are the squadron puppies?

Bottom: A trio of *Jasta 32* pilots well bundled up for a high altitude flight. Left to right: Rolfes, Windisch and Zenkominierski. Rolfes scored only one victory with *Jasta 32* but then became a superstar with *Jasta 45* achieving 16 more victories there.

Two views of the famous dragon-marked French Spad in German markings that some say Windisch flew in combat during his time as the leader of *Jasta 66*. The snowy field in the photograph above suggests it could have been shortly after he took over on January 24, 1918 after leaving *Jasta 32* with a short two week stay in *Jasta 50* in between. Just before leaving *32*, he shot down a Spad on January 4. Could it be this machine? But a prominent British air historian says Windisch "collected" this Spad from *Jasta 50* on March 10. Windisch's next victory, another Spad, didn't come until March 15 but who can say whether there wasn't a late snow and that this was, in fact, an aircraft from one of his early *Jasta 66* victories? However it came into Windisch's possession, it would be natural that he would want to test its capabilities. Spads were his most favorite target. It seems to be a target, too, for his Great Dane (above) as Windisch wags a naughty-naughty finger at the beast. Below, we see him in the same aircraft when the temperature had turned more agreeable.

Thus Windisch's order didn't show up on that list. Subsequently, *Herr* Erhard Roth of Leipzig did much better work at the archive and in respect to the Albert Order, found aviation awards as late as March 23, 1918. There Windisch is listed as receiving the Knight 2nd Class with Swords on November 4, 1917 for his work in *Jasta 32*. So in this respect, small a matter though it is, the record now stands corrected and we can move on to the final months in the life of Rudolf Windisch.

In the first days of January 1918, on the 3rd and 4th, Windisch scored again bringing his total number of victories now to a highly respectable eight. Just two years earlier, Oswald Boelcke and Max Immelmann had become the first aviation recipients of the *Orden Pour le Mérite* immediately after each had scored his eighth victory. But the days of a Blue Max for eight victories had long passed and there was no special recognition for Windisch having reached that mark. Then, strangely it would seem on the surface, he was pulled out of *Jasta 32* on January 10 and sent to *Jasta 50*, a unit that had been formed the previous month and was just arriving at the front. Had Windisch been appointed to lead the formation, the transfer would have made sense. But he was sent there just as a regular pilot since the command had gone to an older hand, *Leutnant* Heinrich Arntzen, who came in from *Jasta 15* with six victories to his credit. Windisch's leaving *Jasta 32* was probably due to the fact that it had been named a unit belonging to the Royal Bavarian Army back in July 1917 and the process of bringing in its own people and transferring out "foreigners" had been going on since then. And they had finally gotten around to him. At any rate, *Jasta 50* was only a way stop, and a very short one at that.

On January 24, Windisch was appointed the first Commanding Officer of still another new fighter flight, *Jasta 66*. It went into action in February and, fittingly, he opened the game book when he was given confirmation of a Spad shot down on March 15. There then followed a string of five more victories before the end of the month. March 24 was the big day. He pulled off the "hat trick" on two afternoon patrols that day. Let Windisch describe the action himself:

> On 24 March 1918, I took off at 1:35 p.m. with *Vizefeldwebel* Schäfer and *Offizier-Stellvertreter* Beyer of my *Jagdstaffel 66* for a combat patrol. North of Chauny we were attacked by seven Spads and had a dogfight for about 10 minutes after which the enemy planes flew away. I dove after one Spad between Chauny and Ablecourt which I had had under observation for a long time. I caught up with him near Manicamp and fired at a distance of 200 to 300 meters and then my guns jammed. The enemy infantry flier – a Spad two-seater – went down slowly in the direction of Noyen towards the ground and then, near Bretigny, turned over on the ground and began to burn.
>
> At 4:10 p.m. in the afternoon I took off again with four planes of my flight. We flew over Chauny at 3000 meters when I saw a squadron of enemy Spads. We went to 3,300 meters to get above the squadron of 12 to 14 Spads. The enemy flew over Chauny-Terguiers to just before La Fere where the other four planes and myself attacked. I began shooting at the highest Spad from a short distance until he went down. The result, according to *Gefreiter* Sonneck, was that it burned on the ground. I myself could not see this as I was attacking another opponent who, after about 200 rounds, went down in flames. Its crash into a small stand of trees was observed by *Gefreiter* Sonneck. The other Spads had dispersed in the combat and so I went after another. I could not do anything more, though, because I had expended all my cartridges.
>
> On the day before I was able to shoot down a Sopwith biplane near Baristo so that inside of 10 days the number of my victories has reached 14.

This was enough to merit a commendation for the *Staffelführer* from the boss, *Generalleutnant* Ernst von Hoeppner, which showed that the name of von Cossel hadn't been forgotten either. It said:

> The victories of *Leutnant* Windisch and his *Jagdstaffel 66* show me that *Leutnant* Windisch, along with his fine former observer, *Oberleutnant* von Cossel, possesses not only attention to the task and has the spirit of attack but also has the ability to lead a fine *Jagdstaffel*. I give *Leutnant* Windisch and his *Jagdstaffel* 66 my full recognition and wish them further success.

Von Hoeppner had more than just a written tribute in mind for Windisch. It was at this time that a recommendation was forwarded to Berlin that Windisch receive the Knight's Cross with Swords of the Royal Hohenzollern House Order. His 14 victories and position as leader of his own *Jasta* clinched the matter. The announcement of the award appeared in the April 18, 1918 issue of the *Militär-Wochenblatt*. As the reader has heard before, these announcements typically followed the actual approval date of the award some four to six weeks later. The pace slowed a bit in April, just three victories but was capped by a "double" on the 21st, both Spads by now his favorite target. May saw the resumption of his rapid scoring and by the 16th of the month, his total had gone over the 20 mark to 21. His

Above: Men of *Jasta 66* at rest. Seated left to right: *Lt.* Paul Turck (10 victories), unknown, *Vzfw.* Heinrich Hünninghaus (4 victories), unknown and failed nominee for the *Orden Pour le Mérite Lt.* Werner Preuss (22 victories). Back row: Unknown and *Lt.* Rudolf Windisch.

Right: Having a little fun with *Jasta 66*'s duty board for the camera. At left, *Lt.* Wilhelm Schulz, Windisch's successor as *Staffelführer* but himself killed in action on June 25, 1918 after scoring six victories. On top, *Vzfw.* Erich Sonneck irreverently thumbs his nose. He survived with a score of six victories too. At right, Windisch. The date is March 22, 1918. He would score his 11th victory the next day and the "hat trick" on the 24th, his best day of the war. The board gives the details for take-off readiness, stand by (or stand to) and independent flights.

name was now in channels again, this time for the biggest prize of all – a *Pour le Mérite*. It had been said back in 1916 when accidents and combat had taken the lives of early *Pour le Mérite* airmen like Immelmann, Parschau, Wintgens and von Mulzer that getting the award was tantamount to a death sentence for a fighter pilot. Prophetic words for Windisch too.

On Monday, May 27 at 1:25 p.m., Windisch took off for the usual routine after-lunch patrol. He was in a new Fokker D.VII, believed to be 2035/18, with a prominent personal marking of a leaping stag on each side of its fuselage, his tribute to Dr. Lahmann's clinic in Dresden and the treatment at the good doctor's hands. Over Couvrelles, he dispatched victim number 22, a Spad two-seater, but then came under attack himself. A bullet punctured his fuel tank and he was forced to land in enemy lines although, fortunately, there was no fire. All subsequent indications were that he survived and had been taken prisoner probably unwounded as well. First, in a German advance in the area shortly thereafter, both the burned-out wreckage of his 22nd victory and his Fokker were found. The landing gear of Windisch's plane had been wiped out in the forced landing but otherwise the machine was pretty much intact and there was no blood stain in the cockpit. On the other hand, a photograph of what was purported to be Windisch's Fokker (unfortunately, not available for reproduction here) has appeared in an article about him in a German flying magazine. This shows a badly knocked about D.VII with most of its fabric gone, either burned off or stripped, possibly souvenired. Whatever the condition of his plane, more reassuring news came in in the next days. A note dropped over the German lines told of his being captured and that he was all right. Further, the Red Cross in Stuttgart told Windisch's parents that they had picked up an announcement that their son, according to a British headquarters, was in French hands and had not been injured. There were other indications that he was all right. A certain Englishman living in Montreaux, Switzerland, an H.H. Cohen, confirmed that Windisch was alive but where the source of that information came from was not stated. Finally, statements supposedly made by several captured French airmen said that Windisch had indeed been made a prisoner.

If Windisch were dead, that would undoubtedly have ended the possibility of his ever receiving the *Pour le Mérite*. As we have seen, a Prussian award made posthumously was very much the exception. Being alive but in captivity reduced one's chances for the award as we have also seen with von Cossel and the fighter pilot, Paul Billik. But with every indication that Windisch had survived and his prisoner of war status not held against him this time, his proposal for the high honor proceeded on its course. The *Kaiser* gave his blessing and above his

In the early afternoon of May 27, 1918, Windisch took off in what many believe to be this very machine, Fokker D.VII 2035/18 with a leaping white (?) stag, the marking of the clinic in Dresden whose doctor treated him for the wounds he suffered in the trenches in November 1914. Shortly after scoring his 22nd confirmed victory, Windisch was himself shot down, landing in French lines. The first reports categorically stated that though taken prisoner, he was safe. On that basis, the *Pour le Mérite* that had been working itself through the approval process went forward and he became an official recipient on June 6. But although there was one probably apocryphal story that he was shot trying to escape, his true fate has never surfaced. All that is known is that he never returned alive after the war. There are several theories which are explored in the text, the darkest of which is that he could have been murdered by frontline troops and the matter was hushed up.

signature on the bestowal document the name of Rudolf Windisch and the date 6 June 1918 were neatly written in. The badge itself was entrusted to *Kogenluft* to be held until the man could return from captivity to claim it himself (presumably, it was eventually returned to the orders commission since it could only go to the man, not to parents or other next-of-kin). We now enter the dark phase of the story.

Windisch never returned after the armistice. There seem to be no records that he ever even existed in captivity. One fanciful tale right out of Hollywood has surfaced which has no substantiation whatsoever. This has it that Windisch and another captured German flier were picked up and entertained overnight by a French squadron before they were to be packed off to a prison camp the next day. The pair attempted to steal a Spad two-seater and make their escape in it but both were shot and killed. It is almost useless to speculate what really happened but two possibilities are worth mentioning. One is that the photograph of the gutted D.VII referred to earlier was, in fact, his and that Windisch perished on the spot and found an anonymous grave. The other is that either on the scene of the crash or as he was being led to the rear Windisch was shot out of hand by frontline troops not known for kindness to prisoners in general but especially not so to airmen who were wont to strafe them and the matter passed away as just another act of violence in a violent war. In relating the stories of these young men one always tries to end things on a conclusive note. In the case of Rudolf Windisch, this will probably never be possible.

Table 26-1
The Victories of Leutnant Rudolf Windisch

No.	Date	Type	Location	Unit
1.	August 25, 1916	Observation Balloon	4 km. southeast of Brody	*FFl.Abt.62*
2.	September 18, 1917	Paul Schmitt	Fleury	*Jasta 32*
3.	September 27, 1917	Spad	Belleville	*Jasta 32*
4.	November 1, 1917	Spad	West of Bray	*Jasta 32*
5.	November 7, 1917	Spad	Leuilly-Brancourt	*Jasta 32*
6.	November 19, 1917	Spad	Laval	*Jasta 32*
7.	January 3, 1918	Observation Balloon	Villers	*Jasta 32*
8.	January 4, 1918	Spad	South of Staubecken	*Jasta 32*
9.	March 15, 1918	Spad	Vitry-Reims	*Jasta 66*
10.	March 17, 1918	Spad	Vitry-Reims	*Jasta 66*
11.	March 23, 1918	Sopwith Two-Seater	Le Buin Fe	*Jasta 66*
12.	March 24, 1918	Spad Two-Seater	Chemy	*Jasta 66*
13.	March 24, 1918	Spad	Tergnier	*Jasta 66*
14.	March 24, 1918	Spad	Tergnier	*Jasta 66*
15.	April 11, 1918	Breguet	South of Noyen[1]	*Jasta 66*
16.	April 21, 1918	Spad Single-Seater	Guy[1]	*Jasta 66*
17.	April 21, 1918	Spad Single-Seater	Guy[1]	*Jasta 66*
18.	May 3, 1918	Observation Balloon	Juvigny[1]	*Jasta 66*
19.	May 4, 1918	Spad	Carlepoint[1]	*Jasta 66*
20.	May 15, 1918	Spad Single-Seater	Trosly-Loire[1]	*Jasta 66*
21.	May 16, 1918	Spad Single-Seater	Thiescourt[1]	*Jasta 66*
22.	May 27, 1918	Spad Two-Seater	Couvrelles	*Jasta 66*

Note 1: These locations from *Above the Lines*. Others from notes made from war diaries by interwar German researchers.

Source: Notes made from war diaries by interwar German researchers.

OFFIZIER-STELLVERTRETER LUDWIG FRIEDEWALD

When Ludwig Friedewald, likely the only other aviation recipient of the Honor Cross with Swords, could pin on that decoration, it took its place ahead of the only other two Waldeck bravery awards that were open to men in the ranks, the Gold and the Silver Merit Medals with Swords, both of which Friedewald had earned. That distinction of winning all three was shared by probably no more than 10 other men, and maybe even a few less than that. It is difficult to determine the precise number of men who pulled off this triple play during the war due to the previously mentioned and all-too-frequent absence of first names and units on the rolls of these awards. But certainly for an airman, it was a unique feat.

Friedewald, then 31, won the Silver on June 4, 1917 for heroism in *Reserve-Infanterie-Regiment Nr.56.* as an overage-in-grade *Gefreiter*. Almost certainly, this was a late award, just catching up with him, because he had already transferred to the *Fliegertruppe* by that time. It would have to have been earned before November 10, 1916, his date of entry into the air service and his start of pilot training. *R.I.R. 56.* was heavily engaged right from the February 21, 1916 kick-off of the Battle of Verdun and it was no doubt here that it was won. Friedewald had been a truck driver and skilled mechanic before the war, talents that would have made him an attractive candidate for a pilot's berth. From 1917 on, he would serve in two-seaters on the Western Front and post an outstanding record with long range reconnaissance flights his particular forte. Although available data, which are by no means complete, do not show that Friedewald was ever credited with a confirmed victory it is known that an at least two occasions he returned with a seriously wounded observer, evidence enough that he was involved in a number of tough air battles.

By January 1918, Friedewald, now a *Vizefeldwebel* (another indication of the regard in which he was held by his superiors), was flying with *Flieger-Abteilung (A)261* and it was with them that he picked up his Gold Merit Medal on February 8. To that and his Silver he added the Honor Cross on May 7. It is a shame that a photograph of him wearing the three awards has not been found (in fact, no photograph of the man at all unfortunately). If we had one, we could see the unusual line-up of three identical ribbons on his chest since, as also mentioned, each decoration employed the white "war ribbon" of the old Military Merit Cross, Waldeck's first wearable award for individual achievement.[1]

And with those three honors, Waldeck had done all it could for their non-commissioned officer native son. A commission,

The 40-victory *Pour le Mérite* ace, *Lt.* Carl Degelow, flew a similarly marked Fokker D.VII as the CO of *Jasta 40*. A close inspection of both leaping stags shows small differences in execution, due no doubt to different touches by the squadron artists.

[1] Three other instances of three awards sharing identical ribbons going to a single individual, two fliers and one who was an infantryman, come to mind. The fliers were the *Pour le Mérite* fighter pilots, Otto Könnecke and Karl Thom. The infantryman was *Leutnant* Walter Kühn. Könnecke as a non-commissioned officer had been awarded the Iron Cross 2nd Class and the Golden Military Merit Cross. After being commissioned and with the *Pour le Mérite* still to come, he received the Knight's Cross with Swords of the Royal Hohenzollern House Order (the only one of the aviation Golden Military Merit Cross holders to get this intermediate award before the *Pour le Mérite*). As Prussian military awards, all three employed its black and white war ribbon. For Thom, it was the combination of the Iron Cross 2nd Class, the Golden Military Merit Cross and the Member's Cross with Swords of the Royal Hohenzollern House Order. Kühn had been awarded the Saxon Gold and Silver St. Henry Medals before being made *Leutnant*. Then he received the Knight's Cross of the Saxon Military St. Henry Order., The ribbon for each was likewise the same, pale blue with lemon-yellow edge stripes, the military colors of the kingdom. Könnecke and Thom survived the war but Kühn did not. His Knight's St. Henry was approved on November 24, 1916 and he had almost two more years of tough campaigning ahead of him. On October 15, 1918, he suffered his eighth wound of the war and was taken prisoner by the British. In their captivity he died three days later.

of course could have brought the Merit Cross with Swords but that was not to be (and, had that happened, wouldn't a row of *four* identical ribbons have been something!).

Waldeck may have been through with Friedewald but Prussia wasn't. His continued commendable work in *(A)261* merited his third Prussian award too (he had already received the Iron Cross 1st and 2nd Class). And it came just in time too. On October 28, 1918, he became the 64th airman of the war to earn the Golden Military Merit Cross (along with two other air awards of the decoration that day). As usual, the citation was mostly a general one, praising his many flights against the enemy, his all-around good work, consistent performance under fire and his coolness in dangerous situations. But it also singled out one flight on August 30, 1918 when he and his unnamed observer brought back extremely valuable photographs. There were only three additional air awards of the Golden Military Merit Cross before the end. Then it, too, along with the military form of its counterpart *Orden Pour le Mérite*, passed into history.

THE GOLD AND SILVER MILITARY MERIT MEDALS

As already mentioned, a Silver Merit Medal associated with the Merit Cross of Waldeck was instituted on September 26, 1878. Then on July 4, 1899, at the same time the Honor Cross was created, a Gold Military Merit Medal was added. During the war, 410 Gold Medals were awarded with Swords (perhaps as many as 412 or 413 – see Appendix LVI). Waldeck was, as would be expected, more liberal with the award of its Silver Medal. The best figure we have for swords awards of this decoration comes to 4,204 (see Appendix LVI also).

Any at-length discussion of aviation awards of these two decorations during the war is unnecessary for the simple reason only two such recipients have been identified. A Gold Medal with Swords went to *Vizefeldwebel* Ludwig Friedewald in *Flieger-Abteilung (A)261* on February 8, 1918. He had already earned the Silver Medal with Swords on June 4, 1917 for his prior service in the ground troops and would go on to win the Honor Cross with Swords in *(A)261* on May 7, 1918, this, too, mentioned in the previous chapter. The single known aviation recipient of the Silver Medal with Swords was a *Flieger* (Private) Wilhelm Reuter who received it for unknown reasons on November 13, 1918. Even his unit was not identified on the roll but the rank was unique to the *Fliegertruppe* and being as low as it was, the man quite likely was not on flying status but served in some other capacity, perhaps a member of the ground crew or even a clerk.

Opposite
The Waldeck Silver Military Merit Medal was instituted first, on September 26, 1878. Then on July 4, 1899, the Gold Military Merit Medal was added. The Silver (above) displayed the crowned initials of the then reigning prince, Georg Viktor. By the time the Gold came out, Friedrich was on the throne and the obverse of this grade showed the eight-ray star with the *cross moline* of Pyrmont that appeared on the badges of the house order. On the reverse, both grades carried the legend *FÜR VERDIENST* ("For Merit"). The swords were fully finished on both sides. Here the Gold Military Merit Medal is seen on an order bar fitted between a Prussian Enlisted Long Service Cross for 15 Years' service and a Franz Joseph I coinage Austrian Bronze Bravery Medal.

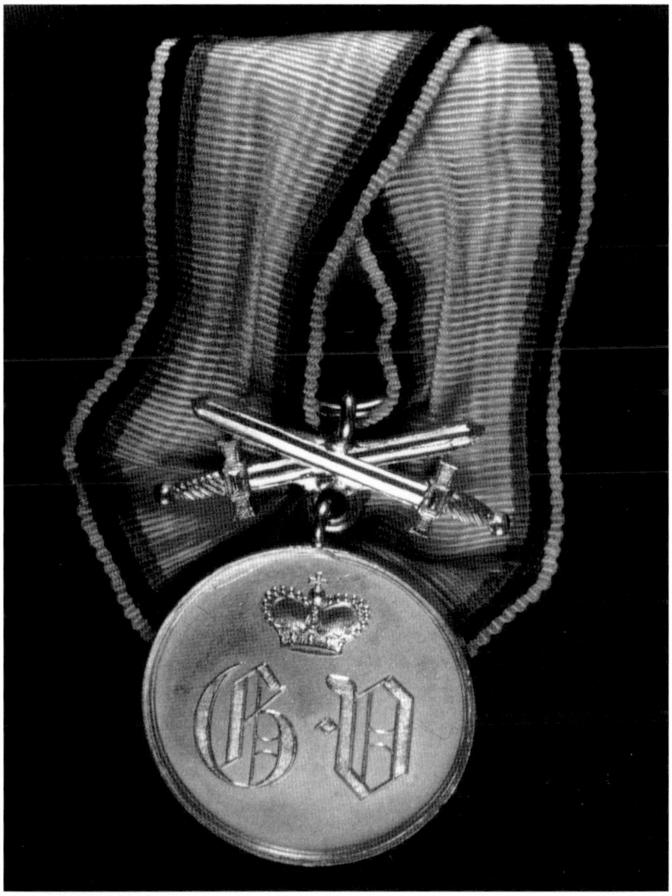

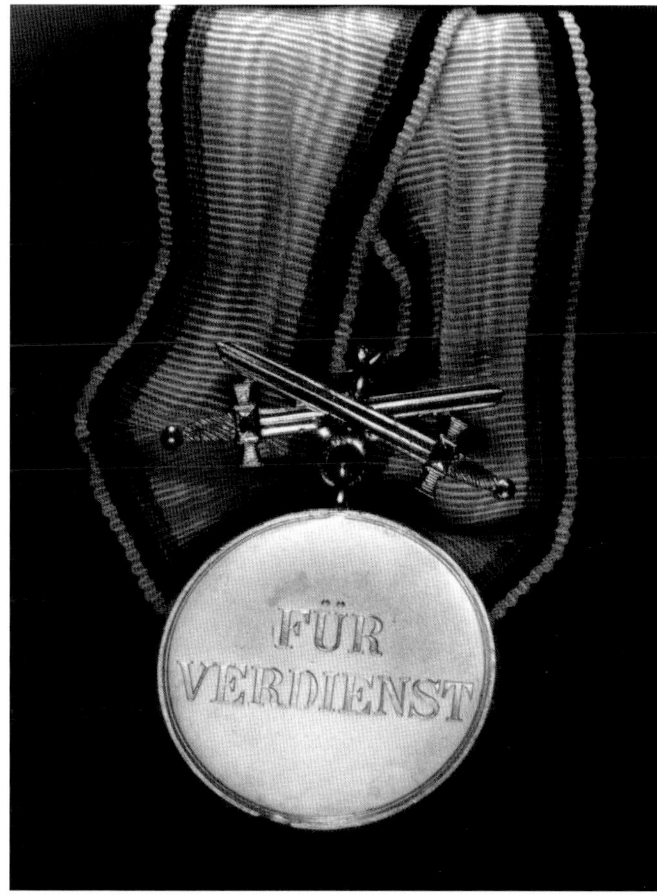
FÜR
VERDIENST

FÜR
VERDIENST

CHAPTER XXVII

THE FREE HANSE CITIES OF BREMEN, HAMBURG AND LÜBECK

Bremen, Hamburg and Lübeck are still known today as Free Hanse Cities. Once they were key members of an association known as the Hanseatic League. The League's origins are obscure but it emerged as early as the 11th century as a mercantile group of medieval German towns. Originally, a *Hansa* was a company of merchants trading with foreign lands which had banded together for reasons of mutual security and protection and which sought exclusive trading rights for themselves and wherever possible, a monopoly on trade. It was made necessary by the absence of a strong central German national government which might otherwise have provided support for their business.

By the time of the 13th century, the League had become a force to be reckoned with as it pushed its operations eastward in the wake of the German settlement of the Slavic lands along the Baltic. In 1241, Lübeck and Hamburg had already reached a treaty of mutual protection. Branches existed as far away as London and towns on the continent from Holland to Poland joined together to form a powerful organization backed up with troops in support. Throughout this time, however, the north German cities remained its most influential members. The League probably reached its zenith when it defeated the forces of Waldemar IV of Denmark and with the signing of the Treaty of Stralsund in 1370, gained a virtual monopoly on trade throughout Scandinavia. It suffered a major setback in 1441, though, when the Dutch attacked and successfully took over trade in the Baltic. Thereafter, the League's fortunes fluctuated and by the 1500s, it began to decline in importance. One reason, perhaps inevitable due to the large number of members (from somewhere less than 100 to as many as 160), was internal dissension. But there were other reasons, too, not the least of which was the growth of more centralized states and in particular, restrictions put on trade by the German princes as they grew in power as well as the vigorous expansion by the English and the Dutch with their own fleets of merchant ships. The last diet (assembly) of the League was held in 1669 and although it was never formally dissolved, it began to fall apart after that until the only remaining members were the cities of Bremen, Hamburg and Lübeck.

By the time of World War I, each of the three cities fielded an infantry regiment. All three were elements of the *IX. Armee-Korps* which was headquartered in the Hamburg suburb of Altona. Two of the regiments, *Infanterie-Regiment Bremen (1. Hanseatisches) Nr.75.* and *Infanterie-Regiment Hamburg (2. Hanseatisches) Nr.76*, were assigned to the 17th Mecklenburg Division's 33rd Infantry Brigade. The third, *Infanterie-Regiment Lübeck (3. Hanseatisches) Nr.162.*, was part of the 17th's 81st Infantry Brigade based in Lübeck itself. We begin their histories at the time when the man dubbed "The Monster," by his enemies and more charitably "the Little Corporal" by others, Emperor Napoleon I, was in the final stages of his nearly successful attempt at the domination of all Europe.

In the 1813 War of Liberation, Bremen, Hamburg and Lübeck had formed a Hanse Legion. After the war, these troops became part of the 2nd Division of the 10th Corps of the German Confederation Army. In 1834, the cities signed a military convention with Oldenburg that took the Hanse Brigade under unified command. This convention was canceled in 1851 and the cities attached their forces to Prussia. The Free City of Bremen had contributed 1,000 men to the Hanse Legion but reduced that number to some 500 foot and 90 horse soldiers which were organized as a battalion and a squadron respectively together with the Lübeck contingent in the Confederation Army. It formed its own infantry battalion in October 1866 but this was dissolved by the Prussian Military Convention on October 1, 1867. Then with companies from Pomeranian regiments and recruits from dissolved Hanoverian regiments, the battalion was reorganized as Infantry Regiment No.75 and renamed the 1st Hanse Regiment.

The Free City of Hamburg created a battalion of five musketier and one *Jäger* companies in 1814 and enlarged its forces to two battalions in 1815. It contributed 1,300 foot and horse soldiers to the Hanse Legion and after that was dissolved, it formed its own military unit with an infantry battalion of six companies, an artillery company and a squadron of dragoons, 1,050 men in total. Additionally, there were 400 night watchmen and a rather strong militia. The city was also partially fortified at this time. In 1834, Hamburg sent a *Jäger* detachment instead of one of artillery to the Confederation army. The troops were used in the city to suppress revolutionary demonstrations earlier in 1832 and again in 1848 and one battalion was sent to Schleswig for the campaign there in 1848. During the 1866 war with Austria and her allies, the Hamburg contingent was part of the Main Army but did not see action. Its only losses were 13 men to cholera. In 1867, the Hamburg infantry was dissolved. Suitable soldiers were taken into the newly formed 76th Infantry Regiment. The 1st and 2nd Battalions of the new regiment were garrisoned in Hamburg and the regiment was renamed the 2nd Hanse Regiment.

The Free City of Lübeck had formed a citizen's militia in 1815 which consisted of one active and one reserve battalion. In the Hanse Brigade, it shared a battalion and a squadron with Bremen. After the dissolution of the Oldenburg convention in 1851, Lübeck formed a battalion of four companies with 600 men. This force was abolished in 1867 and men considered suitable as well as a few officers were taken into the 3rd Fusilier Battalion of the newly formed Prussian Infantry Regiment No.76 stationed in Hameln. The fuseliers were moved to Lübeck in October 1867 where the non-commissioned officers and men were housed in private quarters until new barracks were constructed between 1869 and 1871. When the German army was enlarged in 1897 and the new Infantry Regiment Lübeck No.162 was formed from companies of Mecklenburg regiments and other units including the 75th and 76th regiments, Lübeck's request that their fuseliers stay in the town was accepted. They then became the 2nd Battalion of the new regiment which was designated the 3rd Hanse Regiment.

In the Franco-Prussian war, the two Hanse regiments were part of the Grand Duke of Mecklenburg's 13th Corps in the Mecklenburg 17th Division. They were initially assigned to guarding the North Sea coast but then on July 25, 1870, were transferred to the front in France. Their participation in the campaign was the same as the Mecklenburg infantry already described. They also suffered heavily from the typhoid epidemic with the 1st Regiment reporting a sick list of 440 men on October 1, about 13% of its force. Both Hanse regiments had severe losses, the 76th Infantry especially at the Battle of Loingy-Poupry on December 2 and the 75th at Beaugency-Cravant later that month. By December 16, the 76th was down to 59% of its mobilization strength. The regiment again fought valiantly at the Battle of Le Mans between January 10 and 12, 1871. Losses of the two regiments in the War of 1870 consisted of 17% of the strength of the 75th Regiment and 27% of that of the 76th (comparable data for the 162nd are lacking). The 75th had 131 men killed, 389 wounded and 56 dead from illness. The 76th had 248 killed, 554 wounded and 40 dead from illness.

The Bremen 75th and Hamburg 76th Infantry Regiments marched into Belgium in August 1914 as part of the 17th Infantry, the Mecklenburg division, along with its other two regiments, the 89th Grenadiers and the 90th Fuseliers. The two Hanse regiments' service was therefore described in the previous chapter on the Mecklenburg Grand Ducal Houses. That of the other Hanse regiment, the 162nd, which was part of the 17th Reserve Division, followed a similar track during the war but should be briefly discussed nonetheless. Unlike its sister regiments, however, it did not participate immediately in the invasion of Belgium but was used to guard the coast of Schleswig-Holstein in the event of an Allied landing there. When that threat failed to materialize and all the Allied forces in the west were engulfed in the conflict in Flanders and France, the division was entrained for Belgium on August 23.

Following behind the German advance, it was moved to the Valenciennes area on September 9 and from there to the Oise. The division saw its first taste of battle there around Chauny on the right bank of the river, south of Noyon from September 15 to 20. In the first week of October, it was moved to Roye and incurred heavy casualties in action there. From the middle of November through the end of the year, the 17th Reserve occupied static positions in the trench warfare that had set in.

While continuously on the Western Front during 1915, the division saw no significant action during the year. Its main involvement in 1916 was along the Somme beginning in late July and continuing on until the middle of August when it had to be pulled out for rest and reorganization due to losses after which it held the line north of Lens until it was returned to the Somme in September where that battle still raged. In the Le Transloy-Combles sector around September 21, the division was cut in half taking casualties amounting to 51% of its strength. After being relieved around October 10, it was in the line in Flanders from late October until the end of January 1917. The division was then rested for a month and returned to the same sector in Flanders after that. It was next moved to Artois at the end of March to help stem the British offensive on the Arras Front. On April 9 alone, it again took very heavy casualties including 2,100 of its men taken prisoner. By the 12th, the 17th Reserve had to be relieved, rested and reorganized once again. The remainder of 1917 was a repeat of the same terrible drill. It was back in line southwest of Cambrai at the end of April until the end of May, fought again in Artois in June and was in and out of the fighting there and finally, just before 1917 was over, back in Flanders by mid-November where the division suffered heavily again. For the 162nd Lübeckers, there were mixed reports during this time. The regiment was praised for great stubbornness in successful attacks near Becclacre in Flanders on December 14. But earlier, on June 18 in front of Arras, it was reported to have refused an order to advance.

The early 1918 winter months were a quiet time for the men of the 17th Reserve and its 162nd Infantry as it was generally along the Western Front as everyone braced for the big German offensive that was expected now that Russia was out of the war and the Americans were still not ready. The division's role was to be along the Lys where with other German divisions it launched an attack aimed at Messines on April 9. Considerable ground was gained but the cost was heavy. The 17th had to be relieved on April 22 and was out of action until early June. Two battalion commanders and many company commanders had fallen during the two weeks on the Lys. A whole new command structure had to be replaced and absorbed. After rigorous training, the division was again deemed fit and was thrown into the Noyon offensive on the Oise where it was very seriously mauled in a French counterattack on June 16. Now on the defensive, the 17th Reserve faced further French onslaughts and severe losses required it to be taken out of the line on September 9. After another month's rest, it was engaged at Le Cateau where it fell back against British drives from then until November 3 when its final relief came. Its resistance in that last month of the war against overwhelming odds was said to have been of a "high order."

THE HANSEATIC CROSSES

The governing bodies of the three Free Hanse Cities of Bremen, Hamburg and Lübeck each agreed on issuing a war cross in a common design with similar provisions for recognizing military merit at the front and helping the war effort at home. The Senates of each city formally ratified the idea in quick succession, in Lübeck on August 21, 1915 followed by Hamburg on September 10 and Bremen on September 14. At the front, it was meant for members of the 75th Bremen Infantry Regiment, the 76th from Hamburg and for those in the 2nd Battalion of the Lübeck 162nd Regiment. The crews of the His Majesty's Ships Bremen, Hamburg and Lübeck were also eligible as were citizens of each town who might be serving in other contingents. At home, it could be awarded to those engaged in voluntary nursing of the war wounded and sick. But just as we have seen with seemingly rather strict limitations on who was and who was not eligible for a certain award as specified in a foundation statement, the ground rules were relaxed in the case of the Hanseatic Crosses too. Many others, not serving in a Hanse unit nor a native himself, came to be awarded one (or more) of the city's crosses.

The decoration was in the form of a St. George cross, that is one with straight arms but in this case, with ends that curved slightly inwards. The issue badges were in silvered copper-bronze with dark red enameled arms which showed underlying radial lines bordered by a narrow silver edge on the obverse. There was a center medallion which displayed the arms of the awarding authority. For Bremen, it was a diagonal silver key pointing upwards. For Hamburg, it was a triple-towered castle also in silver. Both of these were on a red enameled background. For Lübeck, it was a black double-headed eagle with a small shield in the center which was horizontally divided, half white (top) and half red (bottom). This was set upon a gilt background. The reverse of all three crosses was the same, in plain silver with the gothic letters *Für Verdienst* ("For Merit") curved around the top of the medallion and in the center on three lines, *im Kriege 1914* ("in War 1914"). The traditional colors of the Hanseatic League, red and white, in various combinations were used for the ribbon of each. For Bremen, there were five white stripes and four red stripes, each of equal width. For Hamburg, the ribbon was white with narrow red side stripes. For Lübeck, the ribbon was half white and half red. The late *Dr.* K.-G. Klietmann in his *Pour le Mérite und Tapferkeitsmedaille* stated that in the course of the war and for retrospective awards immediately thereafter, a total of 20,018 awards of the Bremen cross were made. He made an estimate of some 50,000 for the Hamburg cross and had no figure for the Lübeck cross. In a visit to the archive in Lübeck, time prevented an accurate count of the roll found there but with a population (as of 1910) of less than half of Bremen (116,599 for Lübeck vs. 299,526 for Bremen), an estimate of 10,000 for the Lübeck cross might not be far off.

The three Free Hanse Cities of Bremen, Hamburg and Lübeck issued war crosses of a common design for their own citizens, troops serving in their infantry regiments and sailors on the three ships named after the cities. The only differences were the arms on the obverse center medallion of each, a key for Bremen (left), a castle for Hamburg (center) and an eagle for Lübeck (right) as well as a different arrangement of the red and white stripes on each ribbon. The Lübeck Senate authorized its award on August 21, 1915 followed by Hamburg on September 10 and Bremen on September 14. The reverse of each cross (below, center) was the same. Also below, one of the early designs submitted for the Hamburg cross which was rejected, obverse on the left and reverse on the right. The inscription, *Fuer Verdienst Im Kriege* ("For Merit in War"), survived however.

As just mentioned, a roll of recipients of the Lübeck cross was found. There was also a roll existing for the Bremen cross in that city. But nothing like that in the Hamburg archive could be found despite the full cooperation of the officials and staff there, only many housekeeping details such as the design, manufacture and costs of its cross. Yet even the Bremen and Lübeck rolls were not complete. Some names of aviation recipients of one or the other cross are missing, men who from other documentation are known to have held the award. To those official lists, then, these additional names have been added in the case of Bremen and Lübeck. For Hamburg, of necessity, the names of aviation recipients that have been assembled come from a variety of other sources. These are all shown in the final appendices at the back of this volume.

A number of German airmen including many of the more outstanding figures were recipients of a Hanseatic Cross as might be expected given the numbers awarded. The mighty Manfred von Richthofen got all three, the only known flier to have been so recognized. His runner-up for top scoring honors and the highest scoring German ace to survive the war, Ernst Udet, was given two as was the 29-victory *Jasta* leader, Harald Auffarth. The *Pour le Mérite* fliers Julius Buckler, Friedrich Christiansen, Wilhelm Frankl, Max Immelmann, Josef Jacobs, Otto Kissenberth, Albert Müller-Kahle, Max *Ritter* von Mulzer, Theo Osterkamp, Lothar von Richthofen, Gotthard Sachsenberg, Paul Schreiber and Josef Veltjens each received one of the crosses. No attempt will be made in this chapter to reprise anything of their careers which, in any event, have already been covered (for Buckler, in this volume; for the others in earlier volumes). The following photo gallery with only the briefest of captions will have to suffice. But, hopefully, most of the photographs will be new ones to a goodly portion of the readership.

And with this, the final chapter in the book, we come to the end of a long road. It all began with the publication of Volume I on Bavarian awards in 1988. In there, a commitment was made to cover the aviation awards of all the other entities in the 2nd German Empire. Now, three other kingdoms, five grand duchies, six duchies, seven principalities, three cities and a total of seven volumes later, we have been fortunate with the help of many others to have fulfilled that promise. As Paul wrote to Titus, "*Bonum certamen certavi, cursum consumavi, fidem servavi.*"[1]

[1] "I have fought the good fight, I have finished the race, I have kept my word."

An unknown but presumed recipient of the Bremen Hanseatic Cross with a representation of the city's coat-of-arms applied to his Brandenburg W.12 2002. As might be expected, naval airmen, both sea- and land-based, came in for a high proportion of the awards of the Hanseatic Crosses

Above: *Oblt*. Harald Auffarth, Bremen and Hamburg Crosses with Pfalz D.VIII in *Jasta 29*. 29 victories. Below: *Lt*. Hans von Buttlar, Lübeck Cross in *Jasta 15* on June 26, 1918.

Vzfw. Karl Angermeyer, Hamburg Gross. Killed in crash on May 3, 1918.

The then *Oblt*. Friedrich Christiansen, Hamburg Cross, chatting up a high ranking visitor at Zeebrügge in 1917. (Right) *Vzfw*. Ernst Clausnitzer, Hamburg Cross, *Jasta 4*, POW July 16, 1917.

Funeral of *Oblt*. Walter Evers, Lübeck cross, *Jasta 77b* leader, killed in action May 15, 1918 after scoring eight victories.

Left: 6th victory of *Lt*. Wilhelm Frankl, Hamburg cross, *FFl.Abt. 40/KEK Vaux*, May 21, 1916, crew POW. Right: Frankl astride wreckage of 7th victory, August 2, 1916, crew of Morane BB 5181 killed. 6th victory gained Frankl the Hohenzollern House Order.

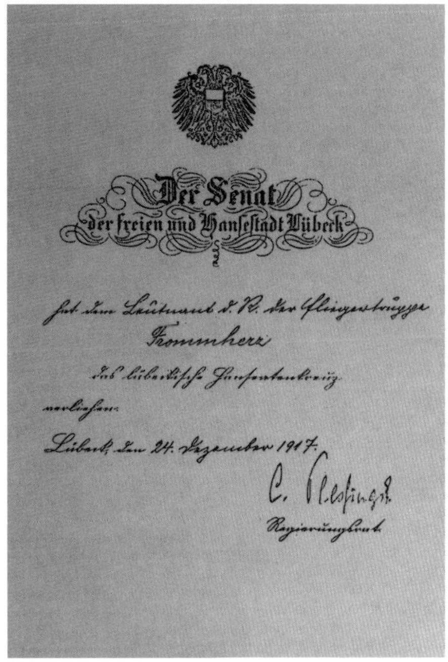

Der Senat
der freien und Hansestadt Lübeck

hat dem Leutnant d. R. der Fliegertruppe
Frommherz
das lübeckische Hanseatenkreuz
verliehen.
Lübeck, den 24. Dezember 1917.
C. [illegible]
Regierungsrat

Left: *Lt*. Hermann Frommherz, Lübeck cross, 32/33 victories, with Fokker Triplane in *Jasta* "*Boelcke*" and award document. Right: *Lt*. Walter Göttsch, Hamburg cross, 20 victories.

Left: Göttsch in cockpit of a Fokker D.II in *Jasta 8* where he scored 17 of his victories. Right: Göttsch was killed on April 10, 1918 in this Fokker Dr.1 419/17 as leader of *Jasta 19*.

Lt. Bertram Heinrich, Hamburg cross, *I. Marine Feldjasta*, 10/12 victories, with Fokker E.V 160/18. Heinrich was killed on August 31, 1918 and buried with fellow casualty, *Lt*. Werner Bastian.

Lt.z.See Wilhelm Herrenknecht, Lübeck cross, *See Flgst. Zeebrügge*.

Lt. Carl Heinrich Hertz, Hamburg cross, KIA May 9, 1918, *Jasta 59*.

Lt. Hans Joachim von Hippel, Bremen cross, two victories in *Jasta 5*.

Above: *Lt*. Otto Hunzinger, Hamburg cross, *Jasta* "*Boelcke*." Right: *Oblt*. Max Immelmann (center), Hamburg cross.

Men of *FFl.Abt. 11* with enemy souvenir. Josef Jacobs, 3rd from left, Walter Hahn, 4th from left, both with Hamburg cross.

Oblt. Erwin Jollassee (foreground), Hamburg cross, with his slightly pranged Albatros C.V in *FFl.Abt. 32*, Somme, Autumn 1916.

Pilots and observers of *Fl.Abt. (A)259* with CO *Hptm*. Klepke, Hamburg cross, in the center.

AFP 2 1916. *Hptm*. Martin Zander between two British POWs. With goggles, *Hptm*. Normand Knackfuss, both men awarded the Hamburg cross.

Lt.z.See Theodor Lodemann, Hamburg cross, in Albatros D.Va 7315/17, KIA July 4, 1918. *Ehrenpreis* for 1st victory on May 9, 1918.

Jasta 33 CO, *Oblt*. Heinrich Lorenz, Lübeck cross, 2nd from left. *Lt.* Friedrich Ehmann at far right.

Jasta 37 CO, *Lt*. Georg Meyer, Bremen cross, with his Fokker D.VII and ground crew. 24 victories.

Lt. Gustav Nolte, Hamburg cross, *Jasta 18*. Killed on July 28, 1917 after 3 victories.

Lt. Friedrich Noltenius, Bremen cross, *Jastas 27, 6* and *11*. Credited with 21 victories.

Lt. Kurt Polborn, Lübeck cross, naval aviation staff and *I. See Fliegerabteilung*.

Hptm. Hermann Palmer, Hamburg cross, in white tunic, CO of *FFl.Abt. 23*. Seated next to him, Otto Bernert still with his Observer's Badge.

Lt. Leopold von Raffay, Hamburg cross, *Jastas 34* and *6*, two victories, known as "Poldi." A *Jasta 6* triplane awaits him in the background.

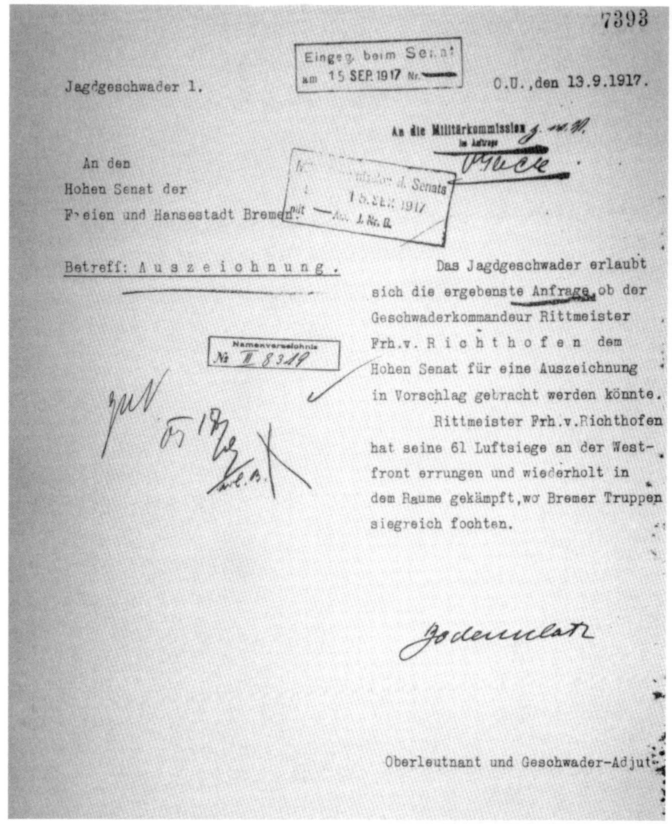

7393

Eingeg. beim Senat am 15 SEP. 1917

Jagdgeschwader 1. O.U., den 13.9.1917.

An die Militärkommission

An den
Hohen Senat der
Freien und Hansestadt Bremen.

Betreff: Auszeichnung.

Das Jagdgeschwader erlaubt sich die ergebenste Anfrage, ob der Geschwaderkommandeur Rittmeister Frh.v. Richthofen dem Hohen Senat für eine Auszeichnung in Vorschlag gebracht werden könnte.

Rittmeister Frh.v.Richthofen hat seine 61 Luftsiege an der West-front errungen und wiederholt in dem Raume gekämpft, wo Bremer Truppen siegreich fochten.

Bodenschatz

Oberleutnant und Geschwader-Adjut.

The von Richthofen brothers, Lothar (above left), each received the Hamburg cross with Manfred also getting those from Bremen and Lübeck. Above: The application to the Bremen Senate signed by Bodenschatz on September 13, 1917 for its cross mentioning his then 61 victories. The award was approved on September 25.

Left: *Lt.z.See* Hans Rolshoven, Lübeck cross, 3 victories, killed in accident May 6, 1918. Above: *Lt.* Richard Runge, Hamburg cross, in Albatros D.V, *Jasta 18*, eight victories.

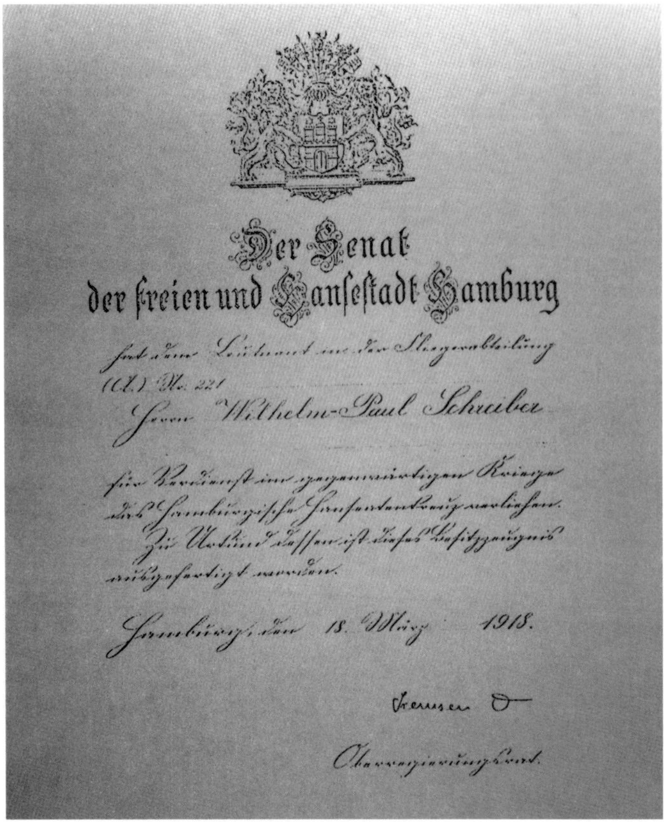

Der Senat
der freien und Hansestadt Hamburg
hat dem Leutnant in der Fliegerabteilung
(A) Nr. 221
Herrn Wilhelm-Paul Schreiber
für Verdienst im gegenwärtigen Kriege
das Hamburgische Hanseatenkreuz verliehen.
Zu Urkund dessen ist dieses Besitzzeugnis
ausgefertigt worden.
Hamburg, den 18. März 1918.

Above: Bestowal document for Hamburg Hanseatic Cross to later posthumous *Pour le Mérite* observer, *Lt.* Paul Schreiber, *Fl.Abt. (A)221*. Above: *Lt.* Julius Schulte-Frohlinde, Bremen cross, 4 victories in *Jasta 11*. Left: *Oblt.* Ernst Sieverts, Hamburg cross, *FFl.Abt. 62* Saxon St. Henry and Albert Order recipient. Below: Observer *Lt.* Walter Schwabedissen, 2nd left, Hamburg cross, with pilot, *Unteroffz.* Wilhelm Grübbel, 3rd left, in *FFl.Abt. 11* and Aviatik C.III, Chauny, 1916.

Famous crew of *Lt.* Alexander Stein (left) and *Oberflgmstr.* Paul Fabeck of "Wolfchen," the eyes of *SMS* Wolf, both with Lübeck cross.

Left: The then *Vzfw.* Ernst Udet, Hamburg and Lübeck crosses, with his Fokker D.III 368/16 in *KEK Habsheim* in 1916. A dummy "observer" was fixed to the fuselage to fool enemy attackers that it was a two seater with a rear gunner. Below: A choice view of Udet's Fokker D.VII "Lo!"

Lt. Josef Veltjens, Bremen cross, taking stock of a captured S.E.5a, possibly D.6094 of No.56 Squadron, RAF credited to him on August 10, 1918 in *Jasta 15* for his 24th victory (in sequence). Veltjens' winged arrow-marked Fokker D.VII with floral bouquet and placard lettered "24."

CHAPTER XXVIII

"FAMOUS CHESTS"

This chapter illustrating the replicated groups of the orders and decorations awarded to selected airmen has been a feature of these books since Volume IV. The awards themselves are genuine but are not those actually belonging to the recipient, hence the term "famous chests." These are groups that once were in the collection of the Foundation for Aviation World War I and are now in the German Technical Museum, Berlin. None here have appeared in earlier volumes. Many of the groups which contained awards covered in those earlier books also had awards which have been discussed here. For reference purposes, these were:

Volume IV:
- Otto Kissenberth (Hamburg Hanseatic Cross)
- Hermann Palmer (Hamburg Hanseatic Cross)
- Ernst Udet (Hamburg and Lübeck Hanseatic Crosses)
- Wolfgang Zorer (Hessian General Honor Decoration "for Bravery")

Volume V:
- Ernst von Althaus (Brunswick War Merit Cross and Hessian General Honor Decoration "for Bravery")
- Hans Berr (Brunswick War Merit Cross and Hamburg Hanseatic Cross)
- Max *Ritter* von Mulzer (Hamburg Hanseatic Cross)
- Theo Osterkamp (Hamburg Hanseatic Cross)

Volume VI:
- Friedrich Christiansen (Hamburg Hanseatic Cross)
- Hermann Frommherz (Bremen Hanseatic Cross)
- Theo Osterkamp (Hamburg Hanseatic Cross)
- Karl Schweikhardt (Mecklenburg-Schwerin Military Merit Cross)

Above: A replication of the *Grossordensschnalle* of *Vzfw*. Fritz Beckhardt: The Iron Cross 2nd Class, the Hessian General Honor Decoration "for Bravery" and the Princely Hohenzollern Silver Merit Medal with Swords.

Below: A replication of the *Grossordensschnalle* of *Lt*. Julius Buckler: The Iron Cross 2nd Class, the Golden Military Merit Cross, the Hessian General Honor Decoration "for Bravery," the Württemberg Silver Military Merit Medal and the Hamburg Hanseatic Cross. The Württemberg award is speculative (see text for explanation).

Above: A replication of the *Grossordenschnalle* and unmounted awards of *Oblt.* Hans-Joachim Buddecke: On the bar: The Iron Cross 2nd Class, the Knight's Hohenzollern with Swords, the Saxon Military St. Henry Order Knight, the Bavarian Military Merit Order 4th Class with Swords and the Brunswick War Merit Cross. Unmounted left: The Turkish Gold Imtiaz Medal with Sabers and the Gold Liakat Medal with Sabers. Unmounted right: The Silver Imtiaz Medal with Sabers and the Silver Liakat Medal with Sabers.

Below: A replication of the *Grossordensschnalle* of *Oblt.* Maximilian von Cossel: The Iron Cross 2nd Class, the Knight's Hohenzollern with Swords, the Waldeck Merit Cross 3rd Class with Swords, the Lübeck Hanseatic Cross and the Austrian Military Merit Cross 3rd Class with War Decoration.

Above: A replication of the *Grossordensschnalle* of *Rittm.* Kurt-Bertram von Döring: The Iron Cross 2nd Class, the Knight's Hohenzollern with Swords, the Mecklenburg-Schwerin Military Merit Cross 2nd Class, the Reuss Honor Cross 3rd Class (without Swords) and the Austrian Military Merit Cross 3rd Class with War Decoration. Left: The pin-back Mecklenburg-Schwerin Military Merit Cross 1st Class.

Below: A replication of the *Grossordenschnalle* of *Generalleutnant* Walter von Eberhardt: The Iron Cross 2nd Class, the Prussian Life Saving Medal, the Prussian 25-Year Officer's Long Service Cross, the Centenary Medal, the Oldenburg Friedrich August Cross 2nd Class, the Lippe War Merit Cross, the Hamburg Hanseatic Cross and the Bremen Hanseatic Cross.

Above: A replication of the *Grossordensschnalle* of *Oblt.* Herman Fricke: The Iron Cross 2nd Class, the Knight's Hohenzollern with Swords, the Brunswick War Merit Cross with "Proved" Clasp to the 1918 2nd Class award, the Mecklenburg-Schwerin Military Merit Cross 2nd Class and the Ducal Saxe-Ernestine House Order Knight 2nd Class with Swords. Right: The pin-back 1918 Brunswick War Merit Cross 1st Class.

Below: A replication of the *Grossordensschnalle* of *Lt.* Konstantin von Kleist-Retzow: The Iron Cross 2nd Class, the Knight's Hohenzollern with Swords, the Bavarian Military Merit Order 4th Class with Swords and the Lippe War Merit Cross.

Above: A replication of the *Grossordensschnalle* of *Lt*. Otto Parschau: The Iron Cross 2nd Class, the Knight's Hohenzollern with Swords, the Brunswick War Merit Cross and the Austrian Military Merit Cross 3rd Class with War Decoration.

Below: A replication of the *Grossordensschnalle* of *Oblt*. Albert Müller-Kahle: The Iron Cross 2nd Class, the Knight's Hohenzollern with Swords, the Bremen Hanseatic Cross, the Bavarian Military Merit Order 4th Class with Swords, the Oldenburg Friedrich August Cross 2nd Class and the Saxon Albert Order Knight 2nd Class with Swords. This unconventional alignment of awards with the Bremen and Oldenburg decorations ahead of the Bavarian and Saxon orders was the manner in which Müller-Kahle wore his awards postwar.

Above: A replication of the *Grossordensschnalle* of *Hptm.* Albert Mühlig-Hofmann: The Iron Cross 2nd Class, the Knight's Hohenzollern with Swords, the Prussian Crown Order 4th Class (without Swords), the Bavarian Military Merit Order 4th Class with Swords, the Mecklenburg Griffin Order Knight and the Schaumburg-Lippe Honor Cross 4th Class (without Swords).

Below: A replication of the *Grossordensschnalle* of *Lt.* Karl-Emil Schäfer: The Iron Cross 2nd Class, the Knight's Hohenzollern with Swords, the Schaumburg-Lippe Cross for Faithful Service and the Bavarian Military Merit Order 4th Class with Swords. This sequence of awards on the bar follows that which an artist painted on a photograph of Schäfer. No photograph of him wearing an order bar is known to exist.

Above: A replication of the *Grossordensschnalle* of *Lt.* Carl-August von Schoenebeck: The Iron Cross 2nd Class, the Knight's Hohenzollern with Swords, the Baden Zähringen Lion Order Knight 2nd Class with Swords, the Princely Hohenzollern Honor Cross 3rd Class with Swords and the Hamburg Hanseatic Cross.

Below: A replication of the *Grossordensschnalle* of *Lt.* Rudolf Windisch: The Saxon Albert Order Knight 1st Class with Swords, the Saxon Silver St. Henry Medal, the Iron Cross 2nd Class, the Knight's Hohenzollern with Swords, the Prussian Crown Order 4th Class with Swords, the Waldeck Honor Cross with Swords and the Austrian Silver Bravery Medal 2nd Class. As a Saxon, it would be correct to wear his bravery awards from that kingdom ahead of those from Prussia. Later research, however, indicates that Windisch received the Albert Order Knight in the 2nd Class and not the 1st.

ERRATA AND ADDENDA

This chapter, too, has been a regular feature in the series since Volume III. It permits the record to be set straight where earlier errors were made and the inclusion of new information and photographs which were not to hand at the time the volume in question was published. Much of what follows comes from readers whose comments and permission to reproduce the photographs have the author's grateful appreciation.

VOLUME I

Page 21: It was said here that Walter *Ritter* von Lichtenberger was born in the Rhineland. Von Lichtenberger was born in Speyer which is in today's Rhineland-Pfalz but at the time of World War I, Speyer was considered a part of the Kingdom of Bavaria.

Page 39: It was said here that Eduard *Ritter* von Dostler's first wartime award was the Bavarian Life Saving Medal. The date given was August 21, 1914. That was, in fact, the bestowal date of the award but it came for saving two men in his engineer battalion from drowning on June 15, 1914. Hence, it was not technically a wartime award.

Page 39: It was further stated on this page that von Dostler scored no victories while a member of *Jasta 13*. Wrong! Von Dostler was credited with a Caudron west of Verdun while flying with *Jasta 13*. It was his second confirmed victory.

Page 124: In the lower photograph on this page, it was speculated that the Gold Bavarian Bravery Medal recipient, Fritz Danker, may have been one of the men pictured in *Jasta 32b* in 1918. A specialist in that unit's history in Germany has the names of all the men in this particular photograph and Danker is not one of them.

VOLUME II

Page 50: It was stated that Maximilian von Cossel was a native of the Principality of Waldeck. Not so. Von Cossel was born on January 7, 1893 in Jüterbog in Prussia (Brandenburg).

Page 129: A German historian has discovered another flier who was unsuccessfully proposed for the *Orden Pour le Mérite*. He was *Leutnant* Hans Ziegler of *Flieger-Abteilungen (A)273* and *(A)270* whose recommendation was made in September 1918 for outstanding long range reconnaissance flights. His name should also be added to the list of recipients of the Knight's Cross with Swords of the Royal House Order of Hohenzollern which appeared as Appendix XIV in this volume. Ziegler's award was approved on April 9, 1918.

Page 147: In Footnote 2 on this page it was speculated that the 14-victory ace, Edmund Nathanael, would have seemed worthy of something more from Prussia than just the Iron Cross 1st and 2nd Class which he received. It has now been determined that despite the fact his name did not appear on a postwar list of recipients of the Member's Cross with Swords of the Royal House Order of Hohenzollern, he did, in fact, receive that honor decoration affiliated with the order. The reason his name was omitted was because he was a Jew.

Page 198: In respect to Ludwig Friedewald's award, it was stated that there were 153 bestowals of the Waldeck Honor Cross with Swords for service in World War I. The correct figure is 154.

Appendix XIV: A number of additional aviation recipients of the Knight's Cross with Swords of the Royal house Order of Hohenzollern, not listed in this appendix nor mentioned in the Errata and Addenda chapters of subsequent volumes in this series, have been found. The men, the known aviation units in which they served and the dates of their awards are:

Rank and Name of Recipient	Unit(s) in Which Recipient is Known to Have Served	Date of Award
Hptm. Erwin Barends	*FFl.Abt. 20*	March 2, 1918[1]
Oblt. Josef Bauch	*FFl.Abt. 3b, Schusta 23b, Fl.Abt. (A)291b*	July 16, 1918
Hptm. Fritz Berthold	*FFl.Abt. 56, Fl.Abt. 300, Schusta 25,*	July 1, 1918
Hptm. Ernst Eberstein	*FFl.Abt. 14, Fl.Abt. 66, FFl.Abt. 28, Fl.Abt. 26*	May 18, 1918
Oblt. Walter Ewers	*Fl.Abt. 26, Jasta 8, Jasta 12, Jasta 77b*	April 21, 1918
Oblt. Hermann Fricke	*FFl.Abt. 11, Fl.Abt. 3, Rhb. 2*	March 14, 1917
Hptm. Waldemar Klepke	*FFl.Abt. 45, Fl.Abt. (A)259, Grufl 16*	April 17, 1918
Hptm. Günther Lohmann	*Fl.Abt. 31*	October 31, 1918
Oblt. Jürgen Lüdecke	*Fl.Abt. (A)254, Jasta 36, Schlasta 6*	July 5, 1918
Lt. Karl Plauth	*Fl.Abt. (A)204, Jasta 20, Jasta 51*	November 8, 1918
Lt. August-Albert Ploch	*Fl.Abt. (A)202*	June 8, 1918
Hptm. Ernst Stagl	*FFl.Abt. 1b, FFl.Abt. 9b, Schusta 14*	January 31, 1918
Oblt. Theodor Triendl	*FFl.Abt. 6b, Kasta 31, Schusta 26b, Fl.Abt. (A)287b*	May 2, 1918
Lt. Hans Ziegler	*Fl.Abt. (A)273, Fl.Abt. (A)270*	April 9, 1918

Note 1. Barends' award was announced in this issue of the *Militär-Wochenblatt*. The actual approval date has not been found.

Three more recipients of the Knight's Hohenzollern with Swords have been found who earned their awards in 1918 but the exact dates in that year are not as yet known. They are:

Oblt. Hans-Helmut von Boddien, *FFl.Abt. 18, Jasta 11, Jasta 59.*
Lt. Otto Creutzmann, *Kagohl 4, Jasta 20, Kest 4, Jasta 43, Jasta 46.*
Hptm. Artur König, *FFl.Abt. 3b, AFA 103b, Fl.Abt.(A)288b.*

The following men have been previously listed as recipients of the order but without dates of their awards. The announcements of them in the *Militär-Wochenblatt* have been traced however. These give an approximate idea of when the awards were actually approved (the announcements came anywhere from several weeks to several months after the event itself). Their known aviation units have been given before and will not be repeated here. The men are:

Rank and Name of Recipient	Issue of *Militär-Wochenblatt*
Lt. Raven von Barnekow	November 14, 1918
Oblt. Hans Bethge	August 20, 1918
Hptm. Ernst Böhmer	August 9, 1917
Rittm. Anton von Brederlow	April 30, 1918
Lt. Joachim von Busse	November 9, 1918
Hptm. Friedrich Cranz	November 3, 1918
Lt. Karl Drum	April 18, 1918
Hptm. Fenske	August 17, 1918
Lt. Reinhold Otto Foell	October 19, 1918
Hptm. Egloff *Freiherr* von Freyburg-Eisenberg-Allmendincen	December 28, 1917
Hptm. Ulrich Grauert	August 14, 1917
Lt. Walter Gronau	May 7, 1918
Oblt. Jürgen von Grone	March 12, 1918
Oblt. Johannes Ludwig *Graf* von Hachenburg	July 23, 1918

Hptm. Oskar von dem Hagen	November 14, 1918
Lt. Eberhard von Harbou	June 28, 1917
Hptm. Mohr	August 18, 1917
Lt. Friedrich Nielebock	December 28, 1917
Hptm. Adolf Sorche	March 12, 1918
Hptm. Walter Surén	May 19, 1918
Hptm. Werner Taeufert	June 12, 1917
Lt. Emil Thuy	November 20, 1917
Oblt. Rüdiger von Wedel	October 29, 1918
Hptm. Hellmuth Wilberg	November 10, 1917

Appendix XVI: As noted, it can now be stated that *Offizier-Stellvertreter* Edmund Nathanael was a recipient of the Member's Cross with Swords of the Royal House Order of Hohenzollern. His award was announced in the June 5, 1917 issue of the *Militär-Wochenblatt* but his name was omitted from a postwar list of recipients because he was a Jew. Nathanael's biography appeared in Volume V in this series.

VOLUME IV

Page 14: The correct number of air awards of the Member's Cross with Swords should be 11, not 10, thus raising the total for World War I to 17. This correction should also be made in the same chapter on frequently mentioned Prussian awards in Volumes V and VI.

Page 97: Fokker D.VII 5056/18 was not an OAW-built machine according to two experts who should know. It was built at the Fokker factory and accepted as flight-worthy on September 18, 1918. Thus it could not have been at the front on September 14, 1918 and was not the D.VII flown in a balloon attack by Friedrich Noltenius that day. The number of Noltenius' aircraft is yet to be determined.

Page 238: Johannes Leistner was awarded the Knight's Cross of the Saxon Military St. Henry Order on January 12, 1916 for service in *Feldflieger-Abteilung 59*, not 5 as stated here.

Appendix XIV: To the list of aviation recipients of the Württemberg Friedrich Order, the name of *Hauptmann* Bruno Wentscher should be added. He served in *Feldflieger-Abteilung 53, Artillerie-Flieger-Abteilung 243* and *Flieger-Abteilung (A)202* and was awarded the Knight's Cross 1st Class with Swords of the order on June 9, 1917.

VOLUME V

Page 16: An interesting sidelight to the young nobleman, Georg *Freiherr* von Saalfeld who was killed in action on April 29, 1916, is the fact that in a fall when age 15, he had lost a leg. Despite that, he completed his courses as a fully qualified military pilot.

Page 88: The comments here about the possibility of Edmund Nathanael receiving either the Prussian Golden Military Merit Cross or the Member's Cross with Swords of the Royal Hohenzollern House Order are no longer relevant. As already mentioned twice, he did receive the latter award but was not put on the official list of recipients because of his Jewish ancestry.

Page 94: The speculation here that Nathanael was not awarded the Member's Cross because he was killed before it could be approved and in keeping with the Prussian practice of not making posthumous awards, the idea was shelved is likewise now irrelevant.

Page 144: The identities of the two officers in the photograph at the top of this page were reversed. *Hptm.* Funck is on the right and *Oblt.* Wittkowski is on the left holding the riding crop. The reader who pointed out this correction also noted that in the album of *Offz.-Stv.* Franz Hilger, who was Wittkowski's pilot on 71 missions in *Fl.Abt. (A)209*, he spelled the *Abteilung Führer*'s name "Funk," not "Funck." It is therefore also quite possible that the *Hptm.* Werner Funck whose biography appears on pages 116 and 117 in this volume and the *Hptm.* Funck or Funk who is pictured with Wittkowski here are one and the same person.

Page 157: The same correspondent who provided the above information also points out a mistaken identification on this page. In the photograph of the four men straddling the Pfalz D.IIIa fuselage, the first man on the left was identified by Hilger as Neunhofen in his album. The man in question is undoubtedly the *Vzfw.* Fenke who appears in the other four photographs on this page.

Appendix VI: *Leutnant* Hans Webers' unit in which he earned the Saxe-Weimar Wilhelm Ernst War Cross was *Flieger-Abteilung 41*, not *47* as stated. The date of the award in 1918 has since been discovered. It was May 6.

Appendix XIII: To the list of known aviation recipients of the Silver Merit Medal with Swords of the Ducal Saxe-Ernestine

House Order, the name of the then *Unteroffizier* Reinhold Jörke should be added. He received it on May 15, 1917 when he was serving in *Jasta 12*. The issuing duchy was Altenburg.

Appendix XV: To the list of known aviation recipients of the Saxe-Meiningen Cross for Merit in War, the name of *Leutnant* Werner Johannes should be added. He received it on May 26, 1915 when he was serving in *Feldflieger-Abteilung 26*. On the roll, only his pre-air service unit was listed but he was very much in the *Fliegertruppe* at the time, being killed in action on July 19, 1915. The recipient of the Saxe-Meiningen Cross in *Flieger-Abteilung 41* on January 19, 1918, *Leutnant* Weber, had the first name Hans, not Paul as stated.

VOLUME VI

Page 11: The seventh award on the order bar of Grand Duke Friedrich I of Baden was misidentified. It was not the Knight's Cross of the Order of Berthold I but, rather, that of the Netherlands Military Order of William.

Page 14: In the English translation of the German leaflet illustrated here, the name of the French president was misspelled. It should be "Poincaré," not "Poincarré."

Page 21: Von Hindenburg's full name is written "Paul Beneckendorff und von Hindenburg," and not "Paul von Beneckendorff und Hindenburg" as it was here.

Page 37: *Grufl 11* was assigned to the 1st, 4th and 18th German Armies according to one correspondent and not the 11th German Army.

Page 38: The same mistake concerning *Grufl 11* was repeated in the caption on the lower photograph on this page. Also, a reliable historian reports that at no time did *Flieger-Abteilung (A)261* serve on the Eastern Front as stated.

Page 65: The crew of the Aviatik pictured here was, in fact, Hermann Göring and Bruno Loerzer but Göring was not in the rear pilot's seat of this B-Type but up front in the observer's position on these unarmed machines. The impeccable source for these identifications also dates the photograph as being taken on November 26, 1914 in *Feldflieger-Abteilung 25*.

Page 81: Most historians now agree that Rudolf von Eschwege was flying an Albatros D.III an not a Halberstadt D.II when he met his death on November 21, 1917.

Page 84: It is also mentioned here that von Eschwege was flying a Halberstadt D.II.

Page 139: In the caption under the top photograph on this page, it was speculated that *Leutnant* Paul Döge may have been present with these men of *Kampfstaffel 15* of *Kampfgeschwader 3*. A recently obtained photograph of Döge (reproduced on page 436) would seem to confirm that he is the man kneeling, 4th from the left in the front row.

Page 168: At the time the interview with the late-Air Vice Marshal John O. Andrews in which he discussed his shooting down the German ace, Stephan Kirmaier, was published in Volume VI, the source of the interview was not known to this writer who had been given the transcript by a now deceased air historian. Subsequently, the interviewer has been found to be Barrington Gray, Esq. of Hertford, England. Apologies are due Mr. Gray for not having given him proper attribution and appreciation for preserving this bit of history.

Page 203: An historian in Germany has information that in addition to the awards given to *Vizefeldwebel* Eduard Böhme mentioned here, he also received the Württemberg Gold Military Merit Medal.

Page 208: It was stated here that *Vizefeldwebel* Willy Glinkermann was a fighter pilot in *Feldflieger-Abteilung 68* and then was attached to *KEK Habsheim*. An historian in Germany points out that Glinkermann was with *KEK Habsheim* from its inception while always still carried as an official member of *FFl.Abt. 68*.

Page 213: *Leutnant* Aloys Brandenstein who appears in the lower photograph on this page was neither a *Freiherr* nor a von according to a reliable source.

Page 221: It was stated here that the famous No.56 Squadron, RFC ace, Captain R.A. Maybery, was thought to have been brought down by *Vizefeldwebel* Artur Weber of *Jasta 5*. The definitive biographer of the history of No.56 Squadron, Alex Revell, Esq. of Penzance, Cornwall, England, reminds us that in his book, *High in the Empty Blue*, Mayberry's death is fully documented. Mayberry was shot down on December 19, 1917 by *K-Flakbatterie 108* and buried close by the crash site by the Germans.

Page 221: Another historian has provided a few more details on the career of Silver Karl Friedrich Military Merit Medal recipient, *Vizefeldwebel* Gustav Kautzmann. After service in

Feldflieger-Abteilung 51/Flieger-Abteilung 20 where he earned that decoration, he was transferred to *Flieger-Abteilung 300 "Pascha"* in Palestine upon leaving *Fl.Abt. 20* on March 17, 1917. In the article entitled *Wings over Sinai and Palestine* by Dieter H.M. Gröschel, M.D. and Jürgen Ladek (*Over the Front*, Volume 13, Number 1, Spring 1998) which discusses the operations of *Fl.Abt. 300 "Pascha"* from April 1916 until November 1917, Kautzmann is mentioned twice. Of particular interest is the fact that on June 18, 1917, the Rumpler C.1 piloted by Kautzmann was attacked by two British D.H.1a aircraft and claimed shot down "out of control." Kautzmann was apparently unscathed but his observer, a *Leutnant* von Oettinger, was severely wounded.

Page 224: The Commanding Officer of *Offizier-Stellvertreter* Emil Meinecke at *Flieger-Abteilung 6* in Chanak-Kale, Turkey was not *Oberleutnant* Theo Croneiss as stated but, rather, *Hauptmann* Carl Croneiss, Theo's brother.

Page 243: It was stated here that *Jasta Ober-Ost* was an independent fighter formation of the German *Süd-Armee* in Russia. An ever-vigilant historian in Germany writes to say that *Jasta Ober-Ost* was not a part of the *Süd-Armee* but was part of the *Oberste Heeresleitung* (Supreme Command) operating only on the central and northern sectors of the Eastern Front. The *Süd-Armee* had its own fighter detachments, *Flieger-Abteilung 24* and *Flieger-Abteilungen (A)220* and *(A)242*.

Page 244: One of the interwar German researcher's notes, not the one referred to here, does state that *Vizefeldwebel* Wilhelm Anton Seitz served with *Jasta 68* in the last weeks of the war.

Page 249: In the photograph on this page of men of *Jasta 29*, it was speculated that the person at the extreme right might have been *Vizefeldwebel* Eugen Weiss. Through the courtesy of still another German historian and researcher, we now have a photograph of Weiss (reproduced on page 436). From that, it is clear Weiss is not in the photograph on this page.

Page 292: The description here of an accident involving *Leutnant* Franz Brandt of *Jasta 19* and the death of *Unteroffizier* Josef Schreiner of *Flieger-Abteilung (A)257* on April 8, 1917 was totally wrong. In fact, Brandt was not being ferried by Schreiner. Hardly! Brandt shot down the LVG being piloted by Schreiner by mistake, killing him and wounding his observer, probably a *Leutnant* Plange of *(A)257* who was a casualty that day.

Page 295: The man identified in these photographs as *Leutnant* Wallerth was actually *Leutnant* Clemens Vollert. Because he was wearing an Observer's Badge, it was suggested here that he might have been a visitor to *Jasta 76b*. Not the case. Vollert joined *Jasta 76b* as its Adjutant on November 18, 1917. He had earned the Bavarian Observer's Badge on August 2, 1916 while serving with *Feldflieger-Abteilung 6b*.

Page 313: One of the German contributors to whom we are indebted for setting matters right makes two comments on Table 10-10 shown on this page. First, *Oblt.* Karl von Grieffenhagen should read *Oblt.* Heino Grieffenhagon (no von). Second, this correspondent is convinced that Kurt Wintgens was never assigned to *KEK Vaux*. Wintgens came from *KEK Falkenhausen* when joining *KEK Bertincourt* of the recreated German 1st Army at the beginning of the Somme battles in July 1916. *KEK Bertincourt* became the nucleus of *Jasta 1* and *Jasta 2* when they were formed that August.

Page 339: It was stated that Wilhelm Allmenröder scored the second victory of *Jasta 29*, and his first, on March 16, 1917 and first scoring honors had gone to another pilot of the unit on March 11. That other man was *Leutnant* Ludwig Dornheim, *Jasta 29*'s leader. His claim on March 11 was not upheld, however. So Wilhelm Allmenröder was the first to score in the new unit after all.

Page 345: *Leutnant* Heckner's first name was Max.

Page 356: *Leutnant* Roland Hauck should read *Leutnant* Roland Nauck.

Page 357: Two name corrections need to be made in the photograph of men of *Jasta 20* at the bottom of this page. *Leutnant* Heiss should read *Leutnant* Meiss and his first name was Werner. *Leutnant* Landgraf's first name was Erich.

Page 360: The full name of *Oberleutnant* von Dazur was Waldemar Baron von Dazur.

Page 364: The first name of the *Leutnant* Schleth pictured with Ernst Udet in *Jasta 37* was probably Heinrich who may have been the unit's Adjutant at this time and not just visiting.

Appendix XI: *Lt.* Effrem Rosetti-Sozescu should read *Lt.* Effrem Rosett-Solescu.

Appendix XXV: *Oblt.* Waldemar von Dazur should read *Oblt.* Waldemar Baron von Dazur.

New photographs of *Lt.* Arthur Laumann (left, with Tony Fokker in 1918 and right, earlier in that year in *Fl.Abt. (A)265).* His companion is not identified nor is the little pooch. When historian Peter Grosz saw this photo of the men with the LVG C.V, he remarked, "What a gorgeous propeller!" Below: Original bestowal documents to *Pour le Mérite* airmen are rare (Laumann's is below left) but even more rare is the example of the Imperial Decree certificate from the Prussian General Orders Commission "in reference to the bestowal of the *Ordens Pour le Mérite*" (below right) dated, ironically, on Armistice Day 1918.

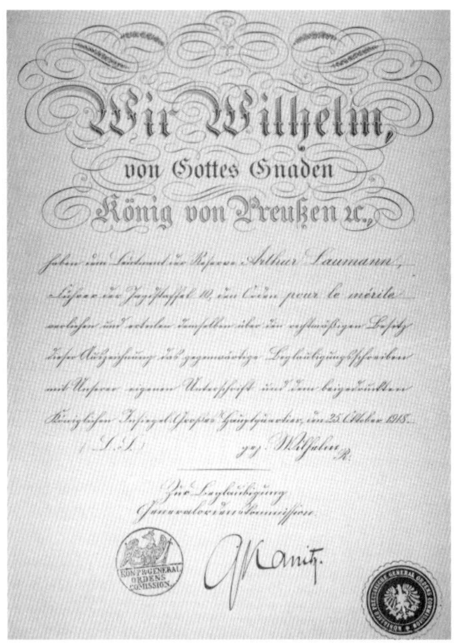

Wir Wilhelm,
von Gottes Gnaden
König von Preußen rc.

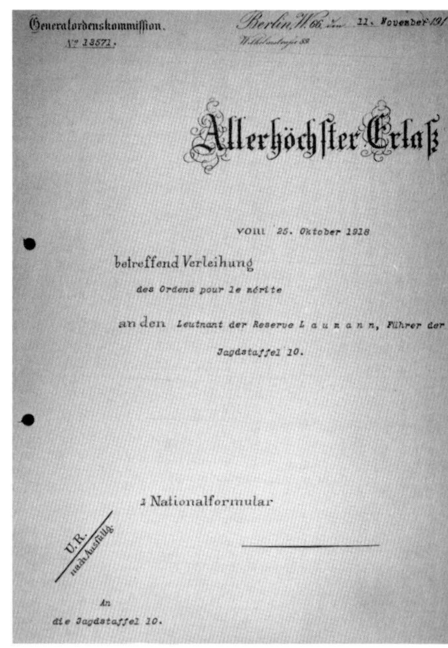

Generalordenskommission.
Nr 33571.

Berlin, W 66, den 11. November 1918.

Allerhöchster Erlaß

vom 25. Oktober 1918

betreffend Verleihung
des Ordens pour le mérite
an den Leutnant der Reserve L a u m a n n, Führer der Jagdstaffel 10.

1 Nationalformular

An
die Jagdstaffel 10.

Below: The full complement of *Bosta 19* of *Bogohl 4* under the command of the *Pour le Mérite Hptm.* Hermann Köhl during its December 1917 - February 1918 sojourn in Italy. Some 77 men can be counted here. Köhl is marked with the "X" 2nd from the far left. The eight aircraft in the background, one AEG N.1, four DFW C.Vs and three AEG G.IVs have been identified by Mr. Grosz. In doing so, he commented that the AEG N.1 was "super rare."

Right: An interesting directive relating Saxon bravery awards to a man's rank. The symbols indicate its Merit Order (*VR*), Albert Order (*AR*), Albert Cross (*AK*), Honor Cross (*EK*) and Friedrich August Medals (*FAM*). The symbol, *AO*, means the Albert Order Officer's Cross.

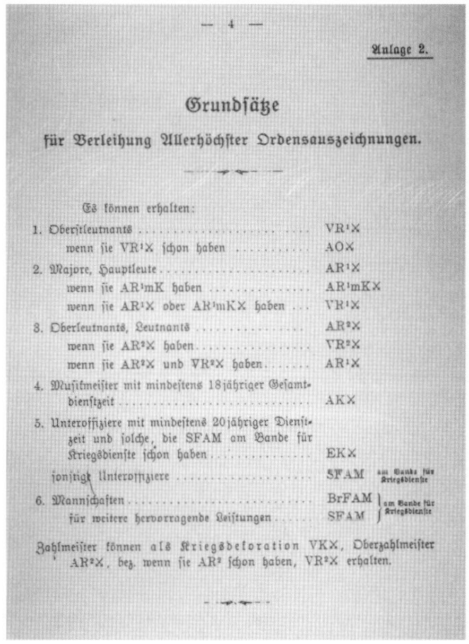

— 4 —

Anlage 2.

Grundsätze

für Verleihung Allerhöchster Ordensauszeichnungen.

Es können erhalten:

1. Oberstleutnants .... VR^{1}X
   wenn sie VR^{1}X schon haben .... AOX
2. Majore, Hauptleute .... AR^{1}X
   wenn sie AR^{1}mK haben .... AR^{1}mKX
   wenn sie AR^{1}X oder AR^{1}mKX haben ... VR^{1}X
3. Oberleutnants, Leutnants .... AR^{2}X
   wenn sie AR^{2}X haben .... VR^{2}X
   wenn sie AR^{2}X und VR^{2}X haben ...... AR^{1}X
4. Musikmeister mit mindestens 18jähriger Gesamtdienstzeit .... AKX
5. Unteroffiziere mit mindestens 20jähriger Dienstzeit und solche, die SFAM am Bande für Kriegsdienste schon haben .... EKX
   sonstige Unteroffiziere .... SFAM am Bande für Kriegsdienste
6. Mannschaften .... BrFAM } am Bande für Kriegsdienste
   für weitere hervorragende Leistungen ..... SFAM }

Zahlmeister können als Kriegsdekoration VKX, Oberzahlmeister AR^{2}X, bez. wenn sie AR^2 schon haben, VR^{2}X erhalten.

Far right: The first aviation recipient of the Saxon Military St. Henry Order was the then *Lt.* Egbert Kühn, left with unknown pilot. Kühn's biography appeared in Volume III. Both are wearing prewar Prussian Crown Orders 4th Class (without Swords) probably in *FFl.Abt. 3*.

Right: This might be just another burned-out machine were it not for the sharp eyes of Mr. Grosz. It is Max Immelmann's death crash which could be identified by the twisted wheel. This view is one not seen before by either Mr. Grosz or this writer.

Below: The caption on this photograph says that a *Lt.* Folksdorf is being decorated with a Saxon order by a *Hptm.* Köbrich in front of his Rumpler G.III. No record of a Saxon award to a Folksdorf has been found but field investiture photos are rare nonetheless.

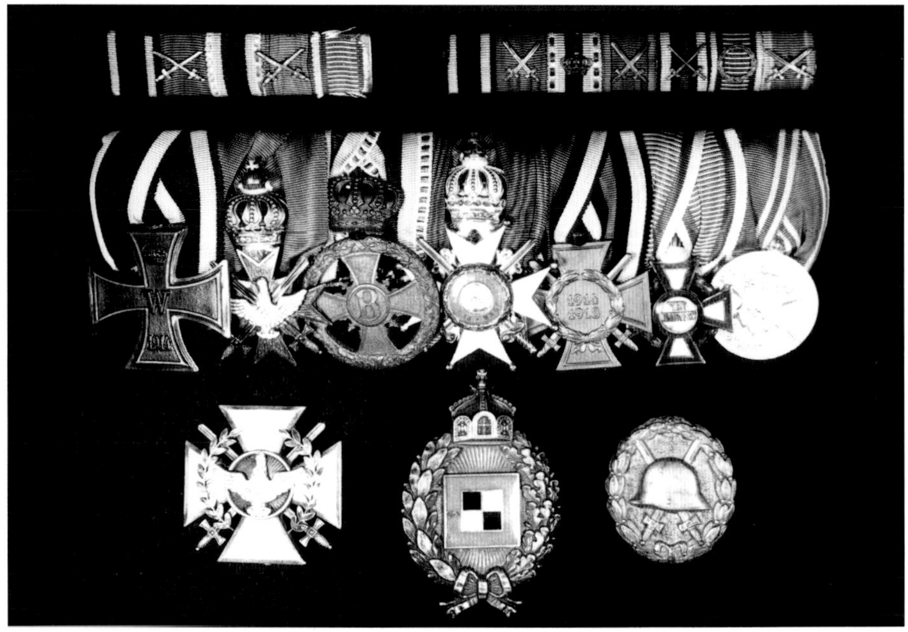

The original awards of *Lt.* Hans Weber, an observer with *Fl.Abt. 41*, with an impressive array of four Thuringian State awards made all the more so due to the man's rank and youth. On the bar following the Iron Cross 2nd Class, the Knight 2nd Class with Swords of the Saxe-Weimer Order of the White Falcon, the Saxe-Meiningen Cross For Merit in War and the Knight 2nd Class with Swords of the Ducal Saxe-Ernestine House Order. On the left of his Observer's Badge, the Saxe-Weimar Wilhelm Ernst War Cross. Two small ribbon bars complete this splendid group.

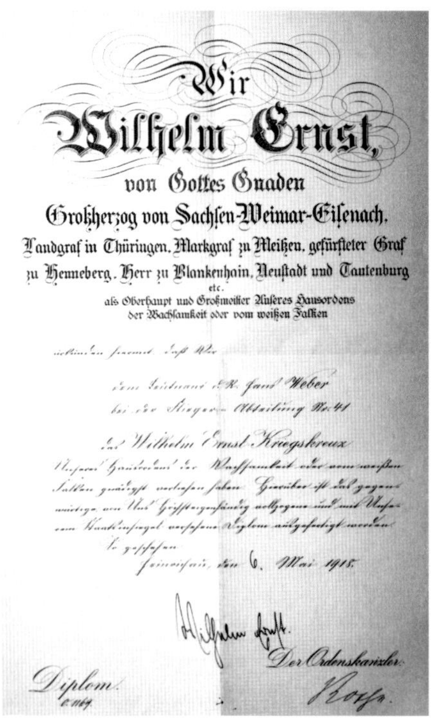

Wir
Wilhelm Ernst,
von Gottes Gnaden
Großherzog von Sachsen-Weimar-Eisenach,
Landgraf in Thüringen, Markgraf zu Meißen, gefürsteter Graf zu Henneberg, Herr zu Blankenhain, Neustadt und Tautenburg
etc.
als Oberhaupt und Großmeister Unseres Hausordens der Wachsamkeit oder vom weißen Falken

dem Leutnant d. R. Hans Weber
bei der Flieger-Abteilung Nr. 41
das Wilhelm Ernst-Kriegskreuz

den 6. Mai 1918

Diplom

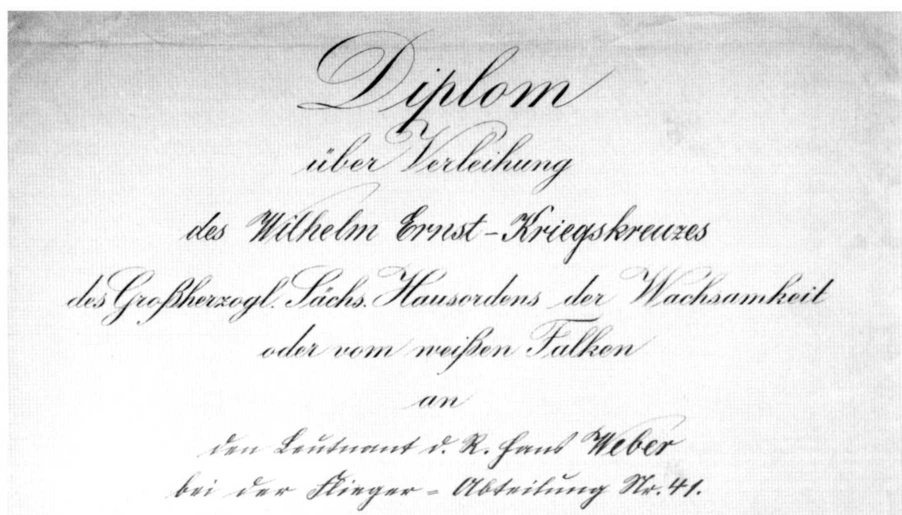

Diplom
über Verleihung
des Wilhelm Ernst-Kriegskreuzes
des Großherzogl. Sächs. Hausordens der Wachsamkeit
oder vom weißen Falken
an
den Leutnant d. R. Hans Weber
bei der Flieger-Abteilung Nr. 41.

Left: Weber's bestowal document to the Order of the White Falcon. Above: The certificate to his Wilhelm Ernst War Cross. Medal specialists will be interested in its language tying the decoration to the White Falcon (also called the House Order of Vigilance). It is believed that the original intent may have been to have the pin-back badge an Officer's grade of the order rather than a decoration standing on its own. Little has been learned on the exploits that earned Weber such high recognition. Any further information on the man's career would be gratefully received.

Left: A previously unpublished (by this writer) photograph of *Offz.Stv.* Edmund Nathanael, holder of two Saxe-Weimar decorations. It has now been determined that he was awarded the Hohenzollern Member's Cross with Swords shortly before his death in action. His name was never carried on the official list of recipients in the 1930s because Nathanael was a Jew. Right: A new (to this writer) photograph of Saxe-Ernestine House Order holder, *Lt.* Rudolf Wendelmuth, here with his Albatros D.V 1111/17 with a broken lower right wing. The number "1" on its fuselage suggests this was taken in *Jasta 20* which he commanded for just over a month in 1917 before he was killed on November 30 in a mid-air collision with a wingmate.

Left: The first ribbon on *Offz.-Stv.* Reinhold Jörke's bar has at last been established. It is that of the Saxe-Ernestine Silver Merit Medal with Swords, awarded May 15, 1917 in *Jasta 12*. The third ribbon may be the Bremen Hanseatic Cross but if so, his name was not picked up on the roll. Above: The burial of Saxe-Meiningen Cross for Merit in War recipient, *Lt.* Werner Johannes and his pilot, *Unteroffz.* August Ströbel. Johannes was killed on July 19, 1915 and Ströbel died of injuries on July 27. They became the first victory of the later great French ace, Georges Guynemer, and his *mechanicien* (Mechanic) Charles Guerder. Johannes and Ströbel, members of *FFl.Abt. 26*, came down in flames southeast of Soissons.

A new aviation recipient of the Anhalt Ducal House Order of Albert the Bear with Swords has been found since the publication of Volume V. But that's only part of the story of *Hptm.* Hans Hesse (right). Mobilized at the start of the war with *FFl.Abt. 12*, his Albatros Taube was forced down in neutral Holland on August 19, 1914 (shown above under guard). He gave his parole but then escaped to Germany. Upon learning that Hesse had violated his officer's oath, the *Kaiser* ordered him sent back. Eventually, Hesse was repatriated but was reduced in rank to *Flieger* (aviation Private). Records are skimpy but it appears that he went out to Serbia in 1916 and served in *FFl.Abt. 57* and possibly put in some time as a fighter pilot with *Jasta 25* in Macedonia. There he must have redeemed himself, was reinstated as an officer and by the fall of 1917, was back in the *Kogenluft*'s good graces and ready to make an historic flight (see next page).

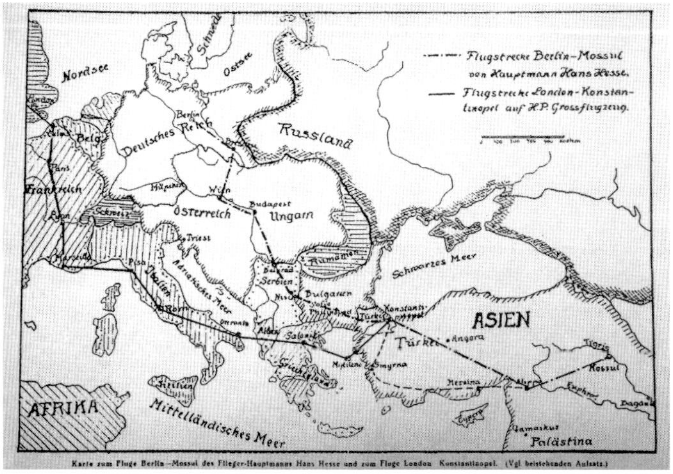

Towards the end of 1917, Hesse made a long-range solo flight from Berlin to Mossul, then a city in the Ottoman Empire near the present day city of Baghdad, the capital of Iraq. He did it in series of hops landing in 13 spots in between. He flew this by-then overage-in-grade Albatros B.II on the entire journey, appropriately lettered with his itinerary. The front cockpit was closed over and the space was filled with added fuel tanks to see him through. His route is traced in the sketch above, He became known as "*Der Bagdad Flieger*."

Prewar, Hesse was a member of *Anhaltisches Inf.-Rgt. Nr.93.* and in recognition of his feat, he was awarded the Knight 1st Class with Swords of the Ducal House Order of Albert the Bear on December 31, 1917 in view of that earlier affiliation. He is also known to have received the Turkish War Medal (the Germans called it the *Eiserne Halbmond*, or "Iron Crescent") and the Turkish "*Sichel*." That seems to imply a second Turkish award (the logical one would be the Silver Liakat Medal with Sabers) but *Sichel* in German means "crescent" too. We hope to find out more about this interesting man who went from *Leutnant* to *Flieger* and back to *Hauptmann*.

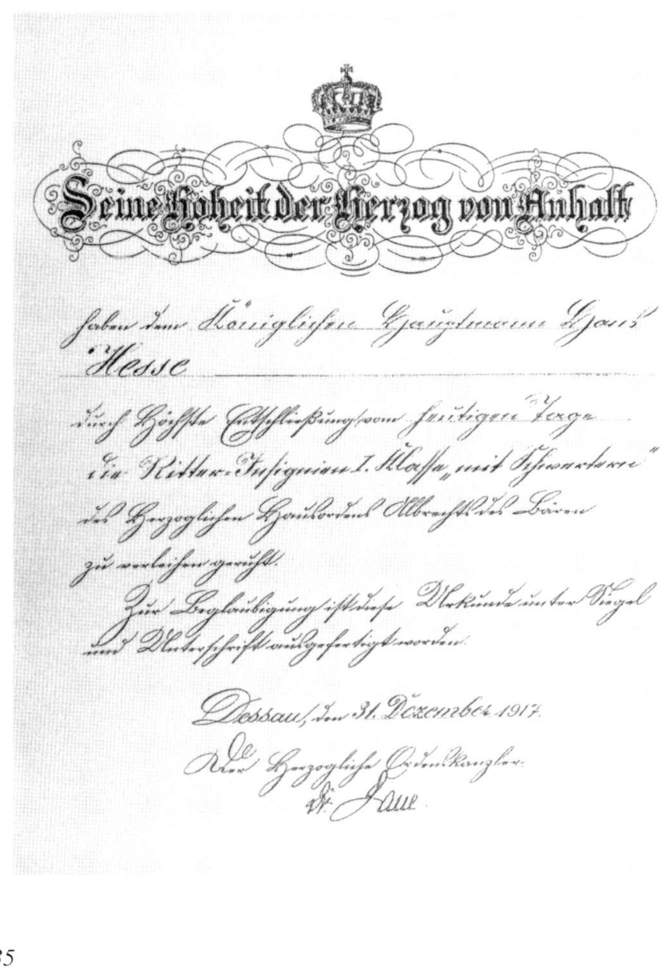
Seine Hoheit der Herzog von Anhalt

Hesse

Dessau, den 31. Dezember 1917.

Above: Anhalt Bear Order and *Pour le Mérite* recipient, *Lt.z.See* Gotthard Sachsenberg, leader of the naval land-based *Jagdgeschwader* in Flanders, poses with his spectacularly marked Fokker D.VII.

Right: At the time Volume VI was published, no photograph of Baden's Zähringen Lion Order holder, *Lt.* Paul Döge, was to hand. But now we see him here. With *Bogohl 3*, the so-called *England Geschwader*, Döge survived one crash of his Gotha but not the second. He was killed in the early morning of January 29, 1918 in a failed landing attempt near Ghent when returning from the first 1918 night raid on London.

Above right: Similarly, a likeness of Baden Silver Karl Friedrich Military Merit Medal winner, *Vzfw.* Eugen Weiss, was unavailable for Volume VI. But here he is, too, contributed by a reader and resplendent with his Karl Friedrich and plain Silver Merit Medal flanking his 2nd Class Iron Cross. Weiss also was awarded the Merit Cross of the Zähringen Lion Order but that award for some reason is not present here.

ANOTHER NEW DISCOVERY!

In Volume V, a photograph of Manfred von Richthofen during his brief time with *Kagohl 2* on the Eastern Front in the summer of 1916 was published on page 322, perhaps the first time any record of his being there had been seen by most readers. Now, through the courtesy of another German historian, we have an equally rare view of him at the time of his earlier service with *BAO* at Ghistelles on the Western Front shortly after, as his first biographer, Floyd Gibbons, so luridly put it, he had shed "his first tiny drop of blood for the Fatherland for which he was later to give his life."

Here we see von Richthofen at the left (sans his Observer's Badge) with a *Freiherr* von Könitz next to him followed by *Lt.* Hans *Freiherr* Haller von Hallerstein. The man on the extreme right's identity is not known. What makes this photograph so interesting is the small bandage on von Richthofen's little finger on his right hand. On September 4, 1915, he was on a bombing run with his pilot, *Lt.* Georg Zeumer. In attempting to point out where their bombs were hitting, one of the propeller blades grazed the finger. Upon landing and after an initial examination, he was transferred to a nearby naval hospital where the diagnosis was "a complicated fracture of the right little finger tip." He was given a tetanus shot and the finger was splinted. The healing process was "unremarkable" and he was released from hospital on September 10 and declared fit for flight duty. Afterwards, von Richthofen wrote, "this did not increase my fondness for bombing planes." Appreciation is again expressed to the person who so generously provided this, the last photograph in the last book in this series, and who permitted its publication here.

• • •

Readers interested in the history of World War I aviation, its operations, aircraft and personnel, as well as those who have a similar interest in orders, decorations and medals, are urged to consider subscriptions to the journals of three non-profit aviation societies and two similar organizations devoted to the study of the military and civil awards of all nations. In addition, there are two worthwhile publications, one covering the aircraft of the period, primarily British and German, which are technical masterpieces and photographic treats, and the other dealing with the latest in the field of World War I aircraft modeling, including colors and markings (and much else).

The three aviation societies are Cross & Cockade International, The League of World War I Aviation Historians and World War I Aero. The first publishes a quarterly journal under the title *Cross & Cockade International Journal*, the second another quarterly journal with the title *Over the Front* and the third a journal called *World War I Aero - The Journal of the Early Aeroplane* (as the title of the latter implies, it also covers aviation prewar while the other two are almost entirely restricted to the 1914-1918 period). All three are highly professional publications, well illustrated and well worth the modest subscription rates.

The two medal societies are the Orders and Medals Research Society in England and the Orders and Medals Society of America in the United States. Both publish informative journals on a regular basis, OMRS quarterly and OMSA six times a year.

The other two publications are magazines entitled *Windsock Datafiles* and *Windsock International*. While the first is technically oriented and the second directed primarily at the modeling crowd, others not necessarily specializing in those fields will find much of interest in both.

For further details, please contact:

Membership Secretary, Cross & Cockade International, 5 Cave Drive, Bristol, BS16 2TL, England.

Membership Secretary, The League of World War I Aviation Historians, 3127 Penrose Place, Cincinnati, OH 45211, U.S.A.

Membership Secretary, World War I Aero, 15 Crescent Road, Poughkeepsie, NY 12601, U.S.A.

Membership Secretary, The Orders and Medals Research Society, P.O. Box 133, Chertsey, Surrey, KT16 8YY, England.

Membership Secretary, The Orders and Medals Society of America, P.O. Box 198, San Ramon, CA 94583, U.S.A.

Windsock Datafiles and/or Windsock International, Albatros Productions Limited, 10 Long View, Berkhamstead, Herts. HP4 1BY, England.

As always, the courtesy of a stamped, self-addressed envelope with 1st Class postage in the U.S. or sufficient International Reply Coupons for air mail postage elsewhere would be appreciated by these organizations, all but two of which are non-profit.

APPENDICES

Appendix I
Abbreviations Used in Tables in the Appendices

Ranks

Flg.: Flug
Frhr.: Freiherr
Fw: Feldwebel
Gefr.: Gefreiter
Gen.: General
Hptm.: Hauptmann
Korv.Kpt.: Korvettenkapitän
Kpt.: Kapitän
Kptlt.: Kapitänleutnant
Lt.: Leutnant
Mech.: Mechaniker
Mstr.: Meister
Oberstlt.: Oberstleutnant
Oblt.: Oberleutnant
Offz.: Offizier
Rittm.: Rittmeister
Sgt.: Sergeant
Stv.: Stellvertreter
Vz.: Vize
Vzfw.: Vizefeldwebel
Z.: zur

Other Terms

(A): Artillerie
Abt: Abteilung
AFA: Artillerie-Flieger-Abteilung
AFP: Armee-Flug-Park
AKN: Armee-Kommando-Nord
Art.: Artillerie
"B": "Boelcke"
b: Bayerische
BAO: Brieftauben-Abteilung-Ostende
Bat.: Bataillon
Beob.: Beobachter
BG: Bombengeschwader
Bogohl: Bombengeschwader der Oberste Heeresleitung
Bosta: Bombenstaffel
d.: der
Erz.: Ersatz
FAR: Feldartillerie-Regiment
FEA:: Flieger-Ersatz-Abteilung
Feldart.: Feldartillerie
FFL.: Feldflieger-Abteilung
Fl.: Flieger
Flg.: Flug
Flgst.: Fliegerstation
FS: Fokkerstaffel
Füsil.: Fusilier
Fussart.: Fussartillerie
Geschw.: Geschwader
Gr.: Gruppe
Grufl: Gruppenführer der Flieger
Hus.: Hussar
Idflieg: Inspektion der Fliegertruppen
Inf.: Infanterie
Jasta: Jagdstaffel
JG: Jagdgeschwader
JGr.: Jagdgruppe
Kagohl: Kampfgeschwader der Oberste Heeresleitung
Kasta: Kampfstaffel
KEA: Kampfeinsitzer-Abteilung
KEK: Kampfeinsitzer-Kommando
Kest: Kampfeinsitzerstaffel
Kofl: Kommandeur der Flieger
Kooenluft: Kommandierenden General der Luftstreitkräfte
KS: Kampfstaffel
Küst.: Küste
Mar.: Marine
Nr.: Nummer
O.H.L.: Oberste Beeresleitung
Pion.: Pionierkorps
Res.: Reserve
Rfa.: Riesenflugzeug-Abteilung
Rgt.: Regiment
Rhbldz./Rbz.: Reihenbildzug
Schlasta: Schlachtstaffel
Schusta: Schutzstaffel
Stofl: Stabsoffizier der Flieger

Appendix II
Officer Fatalities in the *Fliegertruppe* Who Had Been Seconded from Ground Contingents of States and Cities Covered in this Book, 1914-1918
(Listed Alphabetically by Unit)

State/City	Regimental/Battalion Affiliation	Rank and Name of Fatality	Unit at Death and Date of Death
Brunswick	*Braunschweigisches-Inf.-Rgt. Nr.92.*	*Oblt.* Friedrich von Campe	*Bogohl 4* - August 8, 1918
		Oblt. Friedrich *Freiherr* von Dalwig	*FFl.Abt. 21* - September 3, 1914
		Lt. Ernst von der Lippe	*Fl.Abt. 26* - June 18, 1917
	Braunschweigisches-Hus.-Rgt. Nr.17.	*Lt.* Konrad von Bülow	*Finnische Fliegertruppe* - August 11, 1918
		Lt. Walter von Bülow	*Jasta Boelcke* - January 6, 1918
		Lt. Harald Heidemann	*FEA 8* - July 23, 1916
		Lt. Georg Heine	*Kagohl 1* - February 26, 1916
		Lt. Johannes Klamroth	*FEA 9* - October 11, 1917
		Lt. Fritz Kutsche	*FFl.Abt. 26* - October 18, 1916
		Lt. Eduard von Marcard	*Fl.Abt. 12* - March 17, 1917
		Lt. Walter von Rieck-Eggebert	*FEA 3*
		Lt. Alexander Schlieper	*Fl.Abt.(A)204* - April 30, 1917
	Niedersächsisches Feldart.-Rgt. Nr.46.	*Lt.* Ernst Barthauer	*Jastaschule 1* - February 27, 1918
		Lt. Rudolf Matthaei	*Jasta 46* - April 17, 1918
		Lt. Heinrich Kunckell	*Fl.Abt. (A)279* - November 12, 1917
		Lt. Friedrich von Thomsen	*Bogohl 3* - January 28/29, 1917
Hesse	*Leibgarde-Inf.-Rgt. (1. Grossherzoglich Hessisches) Nr. 115.*		
		Oblt. Hans Joachim Buddecke	*Jasta 18* March 10, 1918
		Lt. Ernst Ewald	*FEA 10* - February 18, 1917
		Lt. Georg Hofsess	*Fl.Beob.Schule Schwerin* - June 26, 1917
		Lt. Wilhelm Preissmann	*FEA 14* - October 14, 1918
		Hptm. Heinrich Scanzoni von Lichtenfels	*Flugzeug Zentral Abnahme-Kommando* (Berlin) - October 29, 1916
		Lt. Hans Schmidt	*Fl.Abt. 9* - May 1, 1917
		Lt. Otto *Freiherr* von Wangenheim	*FFl.Abt. 72* June 21, 1916
		Lt. Bodo von der Wense	*Jasta 6* - August 11, 1918
	Inf.-Rgt. Kaiser Wilhelm (2. Grossherzoglich Hessisches) Nr. 116.		
		Lt. Kurt Bornemann	*AFP 2* - January 5, 1916
		Lt. Paul Dotzenroth	*Fl.Abt. 17* - October 25, 1917
		Lt. Friedrich Hofmann	*Jasta 11* - June 30, 1918
	Inf.-Leibrgt. Grossherzogin (3. Grossherzoglich Hessisches) Nr. 117.		
		Oblt. Roland Müller	*Fl.Abt. (A)266* - November 17, 191
		Hptm. Fritz Wieter	*Rfa 501* - May 10, 1918
		Lt. Hans Henning von Winterfeld	*FFl.Abt. 18* - July 25, 1915
		Oblt. Fritz von Zangen	*FFl.Abt. 18* - October 5, 1914
	Inf.-Rgt. Prinz Carl (4. Grossherzoglich Hessisches) Nr. 118.		
		Lt. Otto Fresenius	*Kagohl 7* - September 4, 1916
		Lt. Walter Holtz	*Fl.Abt. (A)231* - May 20, 1917

State/City	Regimental/Battalion Affiliation	Rank and Name of Fatality	Unit at Death and Date of Death
		Hptm. Franz Külp	*Fl.Abt. 35* - August 9, 1917
		Lt. Hans Varges	*Fl.Abt. (A)202* - October 19, 1917
		Lt. Johann Wennesheimer	*Fl.Abt.9* - May 29, 1918
	5. Grossherzoglich Hessisches Inf.-Rgt. Nr. 168.		
		No Wartime Fliegertruppe Casualties[1]	
	Garde-Dragoner-Rgt. (1. Grossherzoglich Hessisches) Nr. 23.		
		Lt. Oskar Degener	*Geschw.Schule Paderborn* - October 11, 1918
		Lt. Karl *Freiherr* von Nordeck zur Rabenau	*FEA 3* - July 5, 1915
		Lt. Erich Peucer	*Fl.Abt. 14* - November 15, 1917
		Lt. Otto Reichardt	*Flugzeugmeisterei* - September 3, 1918
	Leib-Dragoner-Rgt. (2. Grossherzoglich Hessisches) Nr. 24.		
		Lt. Alex Jagenburg	*Fl.Abt. 23* - August 16, 1918
	1. Grossherzoglich Hessisches Feldart.-Rgt. Nr. 25.		
		No Wartime Fliegertruppe Casualties	
	2. Grossherzoglich Hessisches Feldart.-Rgt. Nr. 61.		
		Lt. Werner Steinhäuser	*Jasta 11* - June 26, 1918
	Grossherzoglich Hessische Train-Abteilung Nr. 18.		
		Lt. Phillipp Gross	*Fl.Abt. (A)214* - April 27, 1917
		Lt. Theodor Corty	*Rfa 501* - August 11, 1918
Hohenzollern	*Füsilier-Rgt. Fürst Karl Anton von Hohenzollern (Hohenzollernsches) Nr. 40.*		
		No Wartime *Fliegertruppe* Casualties	
	Hohenzollernsches Fussart.-Rgt. Nr. 13.	No Wartime *Fliegertruppe* Casualties	
Lippe/Schaumburg-Lippe			
	Inf.-Rgt. Graf Balow von Dennewitz (6. Westfälisches) Nr. 55.		
		Lt. Friedrich Bracksieck	*Fl.Abt. (A)202* - January 20, 1918
	Westfälisches Jäger-Bat. Nr. 7.[2]	*Lt.* Fritz Müller	*BAO* - February 10, 1915
Mecklenburg	*Grossherzoglich Mecklenburgisches Grenadier-Rgt. Nr. 89.*		
		Lt. Richard Grüter	*Jasta 17* - April 1, 1918
		Lt. Otto Lange	*Fl.Abt. (A)262* - April 23, 1918
	Grossherzoglich Mecklenburgisches Füsilier-Rgt. Nr. 90. Kaiser Wilhelm		
		Lt. Karl-August Bockhahn	*AFP 10* - March 16, 1916
		Lt. Albert Dossenbach	*Jasta 10* - July 3, 1917
		Oblt. Otto *Freiherr* Marschalck von Bachtenbrock	*AFP 2* - January 5, 1916
		Lt. Willi Plath	*FEA 6* - January 23, 1917
		Lt. Max Traun	*FFl.Abt. 59* - November 10, 1916
		Oblt. Helmuth von Zanthier	*Kagohl 3* - September 5, 1917
		Lt. Gerhard Zantz	*Fl.Abt. (A)277* - September 17, 1917

State/City	Regimental/Battalion Affiliation	Rank and Name of Fatality	Unit at Death and Date of Death
	Grossherzoglich Mecklenburgishes Jäger-Bat. Nr. 14.		
		Oblt. Kurt Grasshoff	*Jasta 38* - June 12, 1918
	1. Grossherzoglich Mecklenburgisches Dragoner-Rgt. Nr. 17.		
		Lt. Friedrich Niemann	*FEA 7* - July 27, 1917
		Lt. Eberhard Wenck	*Fl.Abt. 2* - August 19, 1917
	2. Grossherzoglich Mecklenburgisches Dragoner-Rgt. Nr. 18.		
		Lt. Tilo von Döring	*Bogohl 2* - June 1, 1918
		Lt. Karl-Hubertus von Plessen	*Jasta 59* - May 16, 1918
	Holsteinisches Feldart.-Rgt. Nr. 24. Grossherzoglich Mecklenburgisches		
		No Wartime Fliegertruppe Casualties	
	Feldart.-Rgt. Nr. 60.	*Lt.* Friedrich Kurz	*Fl.Abt.(A)275* - September 22, 1917
Waldeck	*Inf.-Rgt. von Wittich (3. Kurhessisches) Nr. 83.*		
		Lt. Richard Eisenberg	*Fl.Abt. (A)206* - March 21, 1918
		Lt. Hans-Ernst Laurisch	*Kest 4b* - July 30, 1918
		Lt. Walter Schulte	*Fl.Abt. (A)213* - December 27, 1917
		Lt. Wilhelm Schultze	*Jasta 4* - November 30, 1917
		Lt. Helmut Staats	*Fl.Beob.Schule Königsberg* - September 26, 1917
Bremen	*Inf.Rgt. Bremen (1. Hanseatisches) Nr. 75.*		
		Oblt. Friedrich Giesekr	*FFl.Abt. 67* - September 24, 1916
		Lt. Walter Groll	*FFl.Abt. 59* - November 10, 1916
		Lt. Hans Alfred Stentzler	*Fl.Abt.18* - September 27, 1917
Hamburg	*Inf.Rgt. Hamburg (2. Hanseatiches) Nr. 76.*		
		Oblt. Dietrich von dem Borne	*Fl.Abt. 6* - July 29, 1918
		Oblt. Robert von Renesse	*Fl.Abt. 30* - January 29, 1918
Lübeck	*Inf.-Rgt. Lübeck (2.- Hanseatisches) Nr. 162.*		
		Lt. Hans-Werner Müller	*Fl.Abt.(A)243* - April 6, 1917

Notes:

1. *Lt.* Wilhelm Schmidt served in *5. Grossherzoglich Hessisches Inf.-Rgt. Nr.168.* before transferring to the *Fliegertruppe*. He was killed in an air crash on April 29, 1919 assigned to *Flieger 21 Ost Nord.*

2. *Lt.* Karl-Emil Schäfer served in *Westfälisches Jäger-Bat. Nr.7.* before transferring to the *Fliegertruppe*. In the Honor Rank List of the Former German Army, his pre-air service unit is given as *6. Badisches Inf.-Rgt. Kaiser Friedrich III. Nr.114.* There his death in action on June 5, 1917 is correctly recorded but there is no evidence that he ever served with this infantry regiment.

Source:
Ehren-Rangliste des ehemaligen Deutschen Heeres

Appendix III
Serving Officers in the Royal Prussian Army and the 13th (Royal Württemberg) Army Corps as of May 6, 1914 Holding the Ducal Brunswick Order of Henry the Lion with Swords

Grade of the Order	Generals	Field Grade Officers[1]	Captains	1st and 2nd Lieutenants
Grand Cross with Swords	3	0	0	0
1st Class with Swords	0	0	0	0
Commander 1st Class with Swords	1	0	0	0
Commander 2nd Class with Swords	3	0	0	0
Officer's Cross with Swords	0	0	0	0
Knight Ist Class with Swords	0	0	0	0
Knight 2nd Class with Swords	1	3	10[2]	2[3]
4th Class with Swords	0	0	0	0

Notes:
Included are officers in related branches such as the Medical and Veterinarian services, the Marine infantry (*Seebataillonen*) and those in the colonies (*Ostasiatisches Marine-Detachment* and *Schutztruppen*) as well as officers in the reserves and militia (*Landwehr*).

1. Colonels, Lt. Colonels and Majors
2. Including three in the *Schutztruppe*.
3. Including one in the *Schutztruppe*.

Source:
Rangliste der Königlich Preussischen Armee und des XIII. (Königlich Württembergischen) Armeekorps für 1914.

Appendix IV
Serving Officers in the Imperial German Navy as of February 14, 1918 Holding the Order of Henry the Lion

Award	Flag Admirals	Full Officers[1]	Junior Lieutenants[2]	Officers[3]
Grand Cross with Swords	2	0	0	0
Grand Cross	1	0	0	0
1st Class with Swords	0	0	0	0
1st Class	2	0	0	0
Commander 1st Class with Swords	0	0	0	0
Commander 1st Class	2	0	0	0
Commander 2nd Class with Swords	0	0	0	0
Commander 2nd Class	2	1	0	0
Officer's Cross with Swords	0	0	0	0
Officer's Cross	1	2	0	0
Knight 1st Class with Swords	0	0	0	0
Knight 1st Class	0	2	0	0
Knight 2nd Class with Swords	0	1	0	0
Knight 2nd Class	0	1	0	1
4th Class with Swords	0	0	0	0
4th Class	0	0	1	0

Notes:
Included are officers in related branches such as Marine infantry, Engineering and Medical Services as well as officers in the reserve.

1. Captains, Commanders and Lieutenant Commanders
2. Lieutenants
3. Lieutenants Junior Grade, Ensigns and Cadets

Source:
Rangliste (Dienstaltersliste) der Kaiserlich Deutschen Marine für das Jahre 1918. Nach dem Stande vom 14. Februar 1918.

Appendix V
Serving Officers in the German Army as of April 1, 1924 Holding the Order of Henry the Lion

Award	Generals	Field Grade Officers[1]	Captains	1st and 2nd Lieutenants
Any Grade of the Order Higher than Knight 1st Class with or without Swords	0	0	0	0
Knight 1st Class with Swords	0	0	0	0
Knight 1st Class	3	1	0	0
Knight 2nd Class with Swords	0	0	0	0
Knight 2nd Class	2	4	0	0
4th Class with Swords	0	0	0	0
4th Class	1	6	6	0

Note:
1. Colonels, Lieutenant Colonels and Majors

Source:
Rangliste des Deutschen Reichsheeres nach dem Stande vom 1. April 1924.

Appendix VI
Awards of the Ducal Brunswick Order of Henry the Lion, 1908-1918
O'Connor Research

Grade of the Order	1908	1909	1910	1911	1912	1913	1914	1915	1916	1917	1918	Total
Grand Cross with Swords	0	0	0	0	0	0	0	0	1	0	0	1
Grand Cross without Swords	1	21	15	2	4	9	26	2	2	2	0	84
1st Class with Swords	0	0	0	0	0	0	0	0	0	1	0	1
1st Class without Swords	4	29	15	5	8	25	20	2	6	4	1	119
Commander 1st Class with Swords	*	3	0	0	0	1	0	0	0	0	0	4
Commander 1st Class without Swords	*	21	23	12	11	17	26	2	7	4	0	123
Commander 2nd Class with Swords	*	2	1	0	0	2	1	0	0	0	0	6
Commander 2nd Class without Swords	*	25	21	22	14	24	35	6	7	16	3	173
Officer's Cross with Swords	2	1	0	1	0	0	0	0	0	0	0	4
Officer's Cross without Swords	18	48	31	19	18	26	32	18	3	7	4	224
Knight 1st Class with Swords	*	3	0	1	0	0	0	0	0	0	0	4
Knight 1st Class with Swords-on-Ring	*	0	0	0	0	0	0	1	0	0	0	1
Knight 1st Class without Swords	*	56	41	39	21	49	48	49	29	49	7	383
Knight 2nd Class with Swords	*	1	0	0	0	1	0	0	0	0	0	2
Knight 2nd Class without Swords	*	49	85	41	58	88	53	74	36	25	9	518
4th Class with Swords	1	0	0	0	0	0	0	0	0	0	0	1
4th Class without Swords	26	97	76	42	38	72	99	42	16	31	5	544
Merit Cross 1st Class with Swords	*	0	0	0	0	2	1	0	0	0	0	3
Merit Cross 1st Class with Swords	*	70	66	70	36	64	65	98	67	64	7	607
Merit Cross 2nd Class Swords	*	6	0	2	0	2	1	0	0	0	0	11
Merit Cross 2nd Class without Swords	*	137	105	89	59	86	127	101	91	46	13	854
Honor Decoration 1st Class	*	223	108	185	107	178	169	99	76	72	13	1,230
Honor Decoration 2nd Class	*	114	133	66	76	68	30	100	62	67	6	722

* = 1908 entries are omitted on the roll

Source:
O'Connor, research in *Niedersächsisches Staatsarchiv in Wolfenbüttel, 1995.*

Appendix VII
Comparison of Findings of Awards of the Ducal Brunswick Order of Henry the Lion, 1908-1918[1] with and without Swords
Reckewell/Fischer Study vs. O'Connor Research

Grade of the Order	Reckewell/Fischer Study		O'Connor Research	
Grand Cross	86	(incl. 2 with Swords)[2]	85	(incl. 1 with Swords)
1st Class	120	(incl. 2 with Swords)	120	(incl. 1 with Swords)
Commander 1st Class	129	(incl. 4 with Swords)	127	Uncl. 4 with Swords)[3]
Commander 2nd Class	179	(incl. 6 with Swords)	179	(incl. 6 with Swords)[3]
Officer's Cross	228	(incl. 3 with Swords)	228	(incl. 4 with Swords)
Knight 1st Class	380	(incl. 5 with Swords)	393	(incl. 4 with Swords)[3]
Knight 2nd Class	529	(incl. 2 with Swords)	520	(incl. 2 with Swords)[3]
4th Class	532	(incl. 1 with Swords)	545	(incl. 1 with Swords)
Merit Cross 1st Class	604	(none with Swords)	610	(incl. 3 with Swords)[3]
Merit Cross 2nd Class	865	(none with Swords)	865	(incl. 11 with Swords)[3]
Honor Decoration Ist Class	1,223		1,230[3]	
Honor Decoration 2nd Class	720		722[3]	
Totals:	**5,595**	**(incl. 25 with Swords)**	**5,624**	**(incl. 37 with Swords)**

Notes:
The Reckewell/Fischer Study also shows swords awards on unspecified dates made retroactivelyfor the War of 1870. Presumably, these were awards with swords in the "on-Ring" position. The numbers were:

Grand Cross 1
Commander 1st Class 2
Commander 2nd Class 6
Knight 1st Class 20

Reckewell/Fischer also lists 50 Merit Cross 1st Class with Swords and 150 Merit Cross 2nd Class with Swords given retroactively for the War of 1870. The Merit Crosses never employed the Swords-on-Ring configuration so these awards would have had the swords in the conventional position, between the arms of the cross.

The O'Connor research discovered only one Swords-on-Ring award during the 1908-1918 period, this being a Knight 1st Class in 1915.

1. The Reckewell/Fischer Study covers awards from May 8, 1908 through 1918. The O'Connor research covers awards from the beginning of 1908 through 1918.

2. Presumably, this includes the known Grand Cross with Swords award to *Generalfeldmarschall* Paul von Hindenburg. This award was not on the roll of the order at the Wolfenbüttel archive.

3. 1908 entries are omitted on the roll.

Sources:
Reckewell/Fischer, *Orden, Ehren- und Abzeichen des Herzogtums Braunschweig-Lüneburg von 1809 bis 1908*, 1987
O'Connor, research at *Niedersächisches Staatsarchiv in Wolfenbüttel*, 1995

Appendix VIII
Comparison of Findings of Awards of the Ducal Brunswick Order of Henry the Lion, 1913-1918, with and without Swords
Dr. K.-G. Klietmann Study vs. O'Connor Research

Grade of the Order	Klietmann Study	O'Connor Research
Grand Cross	13	42
1st Class	23	59
Commander 1st Class	32	57
Commander 2nd Class	64	94
Officer's Cross	60	90
Knight 1st Class	156	232
Knight 2nd Class	184	286
4th Class	169	265
Totals:	**701**	**1,125**

Sources:
Klietmann, *Pour le Mérite und Tapferkeitsmedaille*, 1966
O'Connor, research at *Niedersächisches Staatsarchiv in Wolfenbüttel*, 1995

Appendix IX
Serving Officers in the Imperial German Navy as of February 14, 1918 Holding the Brunswick War Merit Cross

Admirals	Flag Officers[1]	Lieutenants[2]	Junior Officers[3]
4	22	34	53

Notes:
Included are officers in related branches such as Marine infantry, Engineering and Medical Services as well as officers in the reserve.

1. Captains, Commanders and Lieutenant Commanders
2. Lieutenants
3. Lieutentants Junior Grade, Ensigns and cadets

Source:
Rangliste (Dienstaltersliste) der Kaiserlich Deutschen Marine für das Jahre 1918. Nach dem Stande vom 14. Februar 1918.

Appendix X
Serving Officers in the German Army as of April 1, 1924 Holding the Brunswick War Merit Crosses

Award	Generals	Field Grade Officers[1]	Captains	1st and 2nd Lieutenants
War Merit Cross 1st Class and 2nd Class with "Proved" Clasp	0	9	11	8
War Merit Cross 1st Class and 2nd Class	4	18	18	13
War Merit Cross 2nd Class with "Proved" Clasp	0	1	2	2
War Merit Cross 2nd Class	6	57	38	20

Note:
1. Colonels, Lieutenant Colonels and Majors

Source:
Rangliste des Deutschen Reichsheeres nach dem. Stande vom 1. April 1924.

Appendix XI
Serving Officers in the German Navy as of November 20, 1926 Holding the Brunswick War Merit Crosses

Award	Admirals	Flag Officers[1]	Full Lieutenants[2]	Junior Officers[3]
War Merit Cross 1st Class and 2nd Class with "Proved" Clasp	0	0	0	0
War Merit Cross 1st Class and 2nd Class	0	0	1	0
War Merit Cross 2nd Class with "Proved" Clasp	0	0	0	0
War Merit Cross 2nd Class	0	6	5	1

Notes:
Included are officers in related branches such as the Engineering and Medical services.

1. Captains, Commanders and Lieutenant Commanders
2. Lieutenants
3. Lieutenants Junior Grade and Ensigns

Source:
Rangliste der Deutschen Reichsmarine. Nach dem Stande vom 20. November 1926.

Appendix XII
Recipients of the Brunswick War Merit Crosses Who Served in Aviation Contingents, 1914-1918
(Listed Alphabetically)
X = Received the Award but Date Not Known

Rank and Name of Recipient	Unit(s) in Which Recipient is Known to Have Served	1st Class Cross	2nd Class Cross
Lt. Paul Achilles	*II. Seefl.Abt., 5. Marine Jasta*		X
Lt. Hanns Eugen von Albert	*FEA 1*		January 27, 1918
Oblt. Ernst *Freiherr* von Althaus	*FFl.Abt. 23, KEK Sivry, KEK Vaux, Jasta 4, Jasta 14, Jasta 10*		October 23, 1915
Oblt. Walter Aschoff	*Kagohl 3, Bogohl 3*	X	X
Oblt. Hans Berr	*FFl.Abt. 60, Fokkerstaffel Avillers, KEK Ost (Avillers), Jasta 5*		X
Lt. Joachim von Bertrab	*FFl.Abt. 71, Fl.Abt. (A)276, Jasta 30*		X
Lt. Eugen Beusch	*FEA 7*	July 1918	May 1916
Lt. Erwin Böhme	*Kagohl 2, Jasta 2, Jasta 29, Jasta "B"*		X
Lt. Martin Böhme	*Rfa 501*		X
Lt. z. See Hans Otto Bork	*Seeflgst. Flandern II.*		X
Oblt. Hans-Joachim Buddecke	*FFl.Abt. 27, FFl.Abt. 23, Turkei, Jasta 4, Jasta 30, Jasta 18*		October 23, 1915
Lt. Otto Brandes	*Jasta 15, Jasta 24*	May 30, 1918	X
Lt. Conrad von Bülow	*Jasta 18, Jasta 14, Jasta 19, Finnisches Fliegertruppe*		X
Lt. Harry von Bülow	*FFl.Abt. 53, Fl.Abt. (A)272*, Jasta 36, Jasta "B"		X
Oblt. Karl Döring	*Kasta 31b, Fl.Abt. 287b*		March 22, 1917
Oblt. Richard Flashar	*FFl.Abt. 33, Kagohl 2, Jasta 5, JGr. 2*		X
Oblt. Hermann Fricke	*FFl.Abt. 11, Fl.Abt. 3, Rhbldz. 2*	June 24, 1918	February 28, 1915
Rittm. Hans-Achim von Grone	*FFl.Abt. 21, FFl.Abt. 54, Fl.Abt. II. (Turkei)*		April 25, 1917
Lt. Ernst Hamster (Hamscher)	*Jasta 37, Jasta 65*	X	X
Lt. Georg von Hantelmann	*Jasta 18, Jasta 15*	October 1918	September 1917
Lt. Georg Hauptvogel	*Seeflgst. Flandern I.*		X
Lt. Georg Heine	*BAO, Kagohl 1*		January 27, 1915
Oblt. Hermann Heise	*Kasta Köln, Kasta Trier, Kasta 31, Sonderstaffel S.1, Schusta 20*	X	X[1]
Lt. z. See Gerhard Holland	*I. See Fl.Abt., II. See Fl.Abt., Seeflgst. Helgoland, Seeflgst. Borkum, Seeflgst. List*		X
Oblt. Werner Jahns	*Jasta 18, Jasta 28*		X
Lt. Johannes Klamroth	*FEA 9*		X
Hptm. Martin Körner	*Turkei, Fl.Abt. (A)269*		X
Oberst Hermann von der Lieth-Thomsen	*Feldflugchef, Kogenluft*		May 3, 1916
Lt. Ernst von der Lippe	*Fl.Abt. 26*		X
Oblt. Günther Lüdeke	*Jasta 36, Schlasta 6*		July 15, 1915
Oblt. Argen Lüdeke	*Fl.Abt. (A)254, Schlasta 6*	September 1917 ?	November 3, 1915
Lt. Eduard von Marcard	*Kagohl 4, FFl.Abt. 12, Fl.Abt. 12*		X
Lt. Rudolf Matthaei	*Kagohl 2, Jasta 21, Jasta 5, Jasta 46*		Spring 1915
Lt. Willy Meyer	*FFl.Abt. 31*		X
Rittm. Deodat *Graf* von Oriola	*FFl.Abt. 21, Fl.Abt. 21*		X
Lt. Otto Parschau	*FFl.Abt. 22, BAO, Kagohl 1, AKN, FFl.Abt. 32*		X

Rank and Name of Recipient	Unit(s) in Which Recipient is Known to Have Served	1st Class Cross	2nd Class Cross
Oblt. Curt Rabe	*FFl.Abt. 5, Fl.Abt. (A)223, Jasta 27*	X	June 21, 1915
Lt. Walter von Rieck-Eggebert[2]	*FEA 3*		X
Rittm. Manfred *Freiherr* von Richthofen	*FFl.Abt. 69, BAO, Kagohl 2, Jasta 2, Jasta 11, JG 1*	? (see text)	September 24, 1917
Lt. Alex Schlieper	*Fl.Abt. (A)204*		X
Lt. Achatz *Graf* von der Schulenburg	*FFl.Abt. 40*		X
Hptm. Karl Seber	*FFl.Abt. 23, Fl.Abt. 23*		? (see text)
Hptm. Friedrich Starke	*FFl.Abt. 21, Fl.Abt. (A)275, Bogohl 4*		January 11, 1915
Lt. Burkart Strauch	*Fl.Abt. (A)234, Jasta 4, Jasta 41*	November 1918	January 1917[1]
Hptm. Theodor Triendl	*FFl.Abt. 6b, Kasta 31b, Schusta 26b, Fl.Abt. (A)287b*		March 22, 1917
Rittm. Luitpold *Graf* von Wolfskeel	*FFl.Abt. 2b, Fl.Abt. 45b*	March 25, 1915	X
Lt. Erich Wurm	*Fl.Abt. (A)237*		
Lt. Walter Zwilgmeyer	*Fl.Abt. 13*		X

Notes:
1. Received the "Proved" clasp to the War Merit Cross 2nd Class in 1918.

2. Prewar, Rieck-Eggebert received the Brunswick Merit Decoration for Arts and Science 2nd Class.

Sources:
Bundesarchiv-Kriegsarchiv, Freiburg i. Br.
Die Braunschweiger Husaren als Flieger im Weltkrieg 14/18, Oberleutnant a. D. Curt Rabe
Die Braunschweiger Husaren im Weltkriege 1914/1918, Erster Teil, Berlin, 1922
Die Braunschweiger Husaren im Weltkriege 1914/1918, Zweiter Teil, Berlin, 1923
Die Braunschweiger im Weltkriege 1914-1918, Brunswick, 1920
Ferko, A.E. Archive
Obituaries
Photographs

Appendix XIII
Serving Officers in the Royal Prussian Army and the 13th (Royal Württemberg) Army Corps as of May 6, 1914 Holding the Grand Ducal Order of Philipp the Magnanimous

Grade of the Order	Generals	Field Grade Offices[1]	Captains	1st and 2nd Lieutenants
Grand Cross with Crown and Swords	1	0	0	0
Grand Cross with Swords	2	0	0	0
Grand Cross with Crown	7	0	0	0
Grand Cross	14	10	9	2
Commander 1st Class with Swords	2	0	0	0
Commander 1st Class with Crown	1	0	0	0
Commander 1st Class	18	2	3	0
Commander 2nd Class with Swords	5	0	0	0
Commander 2nd Class with Crown	4	0	0	0
Commander 2nd Class	28	5	2	3
Honor Cross	14	28	3	0
Knight 1st Class with Crown and Swords	1	0	0	0
Knight 1st Class with Swords	3	2	0	0
Knight 1st Class with Crown	1	11	1	0
Knight 1st Class	8	116	61	6
Knight 2nd Class with Swords	0	2	20[2]	2
Knight 2nd Class with Crown	0	0	2	1
Knight 2nd Class	4	37	69	28

Notes:
Included are officers in related branches such as the Medical and Veterinarian services, the Marine infantry (*Seebataillionen*) and those in the colonies (*Ostasiatisches Marine-Detachment* and *Schutztruppen*) as well as officers in the reserves and militia (*Landwehr*).

1. Colonels, Lieutenant Colonels and Majors
2. Including one in the *Seebatallion* and one in the *Schutztruppe*

Source:
Rangliste der Königlich Preussischen Armee und des XIII. (Königlich Württembergischen) Armeekorps für 1914.

Appendix XIV
Serving Officers in the Imperial German Navy as of February 14, 1918 Holding the Grand Ducal Order of Philipp the Magninanimous and the General Honor Decoration "for Bravery"

Grade of the Order/Decoration	Admirals	Flag Officers[1]	Full Lieutenants[2]	Junior Officers[3]
Grand Cross with Crown	1	0	0	0
Grand Cross	2	0	0	0
Commander 2nd Class with Swords	1	0	0	0
Commander 2nd Class	6	1	0	0
Knight 1st Class with Swords	1	0	0	
Knight 1st Class	1	3	1	0
Knight 2nd Class with Crown	0	0	1	0
Knight 2nd Class	0	7	1	0
General Honor Decoration "for Bravery"	3	9	20	58

Notes:
This rank list does not contain awards of the Warrior's Honor Decoration in Iron. Included are officers in related branches such as the Marine Infantry, Engineering and Medical services as well as officers in the Reserve.

1. Captains, Commanders and Lieutenant Commanders
2. Lieutenants Senior Grade
3. Lieutenants Junior Grade, Ensigns and Cadets
4. An *Oberleutnant* in the *Marineinfanterie*

Source:
Rangliste (Dienstaltersliste) der Kaiserlich Deutschen Marine für das Jahre 1918. Nach dem Stande vom 14. Februar 1918.

Appendix XV
Serving Officers in the German Army as of April 1, 1924 Holding the Grand Ducal Order of Philipp the Magnanimous with Swords, the Warrior's Honor Decoration in Iron and the General Honor Decoration "for Bravery"

Grade of the order/Decoration	Generals	Field Grade Officers[1]	Captains	1st and 2nd Lieutenants
Knight 2nd Class with Swords	0	2	0	0
Warrior's Honor Decoration in Iron	0	8	3	7
General Honor Decoration "for Bravery"	8	89	65	59

Note:
1. Colonels, Lieutenant Colonels and Majors

Source:
Rangliste des Deutschen Reichsheeres nach dem Stande vom 1. April 1924.

Appendix XVI
Serving Officers in the German Navy as of November 20, 1926 Holding the Grand Ducal Order of Philipp the Magnanimous with Swords, the Warrior's Honor Decoration in Iron and the General Honor Decoration "for Bravery"

Grade of the Order/Decoration	Admirals	Flag Officers[1]	Full Lieutenants[2]	Junior Officers[3]
Any Grade of the Order of Philipp the Magnanimous with Swords	0	0	0	0
Warrior's Honor Decoration in Iron	0	0	0	0
General Honor Decoration "for Bravery"	1	2	0	4

Notes:
Included are officers in related branches such as Engineering and Medical services.

1. Captains, Commanders and Lieutenant Commanders
2. Lieutenants Senior Grade
3. Lieutenants Junior Grades and Ensigns.

Source:
Rangliste der Deutschen Reichsmarine. Nach dem Stande vom 20. November 1926.

Appendix XVII
Recipients of the Hessian Warriors' Honor Decoration in Iron Who Served in Aviation Contingents, 1917-1918
(Listed Alphabetically)

Highest Wartime Rank and Name of Recipient	Unit(s) in Which Recipient is Known to Have Served	Date of Award (if known)
Vzfw. Fritz Beckhardt	*Schusta 11, Jasta 26, Kest 2*	?
Lt. Julius Buckler	*Art.Fl.Abt. 209, Jasta 17*	November 5, 1917
Hptm. Hans Busch	*FFl.Abt. 11, Fl.Abt. (A)202*	May 15, 1917
Vzfw. Karl Czapeh	*Fl.Abt. (A)284*	October 2, 1918
Hptm. — Hüttig	*Fl.Abt. (A)283*	?
Lt. Walter Graf	*I. Mar.FFl.Abt.*	September 4, 1917
Oblt. Friedrich-Carl Hanesse	*Fl.Abt. (A)225, Schusta 9, Schlasta 2*	?
Vzflugmstr. — Mayer	*Mar. Feldjasta I, II, III*	?
Lt. Oscar Rousselle	*FFl.Abt. 32, FFl.Abt. 23, Jasta 4*	?

Sources:
Bundesarchiv-Kriegsarchiv, Freiburg i. B.
Ferko, A.E. Archive
Photographs
Rangliste des Deutschen Reichsheeres 1924-1932

Appendix XVIII
Recipients of the Hessian General Honor Decoration "for Bravery" Who Served in Aviation Contingents, 1914 -1918
(Listed Alphabetically)

Highest Wartime Rank and Name of Recipient	Unit(s) in Which Recipient is Known to Have Served	Date of Award (if known)
Unteroffz. Carl Abelmann	*in der Fliegertruppe*	May 30, 1915[1]
Oblt. Karl Abert	*FFl.Abt. 2b, Fl.Abt. 45b*	November 17, 1915
Lt. Ernst Adler	*Fl.Abt. (A)218*	?
Oblt. Ernst *Frhr.* von Althaus	*FFl.Abt. 23, KEK Sivry, KEK Vaux, Jasta 4, Jasta 14, Jasta 10*	?
Lt. Adolf Auer	*Jasta 40*	November 17, 1915
Hptm. Wilhelm Baur de Bataz	*FFl.Abt. 27, Fl.Abt. (A)242, Fl.Abt. (A)275*	January 30, 1915
Vzfw. Fritz Beckhardt	*Schusta 11, Jasta 26, Kest 2*	?
Rittm. Anton von Brederlow	*FFl.Abt. 27, FFl.Abt. 69, Kasta 21, Jasta 17, Fl.Abt. 38, Fl.Abt. 17, JGr. 11*	September 20, 1914
Lt. Ulrich Buchholz	*FFl.Abt. 60, Kagohl 2, Jasta 20*	?
Lt. Julius Buckler	*Art.Fl.Abt. 209, Jasta 17*	?
Hptm. Hans Busch	*FFl.Abt. 11, Fl.Abt. (A)202*	December 18, 1914
Lt. Karl Christ	*Kagohl 6, Kagohl 5, Jasta 28w*	?
Hptm. Job-Heinrich von Dewall	*FFl.Abt. 6, BAO, Kagohl 3, Kagohl 2*	April 1, 1915
Lt. Albert Dietlen	*FFl.Abt. 60, Jasta 23, Jasta 41, Jasta 58*	November 25, 1916
Lt. Ludwig Dornheim	*FFl.Abt. 60, Fl.Abt. (A)275, Jasta 7, Jasta 5, Jasta 29*	December 16, 1916
Lt. — Friedrichs	*in der Fliegertruppe*	August 8, 1917[1]
Lt. Kuno Heribert Fütterer	*FFl.Abt. 45, Fl.Abt. 1, Bogohl 6*	?
Lt. — Gröger	*in der Fliegertruppe*	August 22, 1917[1]
Lt. Walter Graf	*I. Mar.FFl.Abt.*	August 31, 1916
Lt. Hans Gutermuth	*Jasta 6, Jasta 5*	?
Lt. Ernst Hamster (Hamscher)	*Jasta 37, Jasta 65*	May 7, 1917
Oblt. Friedrich-Carl Hanesse	*Fl.Abt. (A)255, Schusta 9, Schlasta 2*	?
Rittm. Sittig Heinrich Ferdinand von Hellsdorf	*FFl.Abt. 19, FFl.Abt. 44*	?
Lt. Franz Hemer	*Fl.Abt. (A)283, Jasta 6*	?
Oblt. Josef Hilgers	*Fl.Abt. (A)292*	?
Lt. Friedrich Hofmann	*Jasta 11*	?
Vzfw. Richard Hort	*Schusta 21*	August 14, 1917
Oblt. Ludwig Keiper	*FFl.Abt. 24, Fl.Abt. 1, Fl.Abt. 15*	?
Hptm. Alfred Keller	*FFl.Abt. 27, FFl.Abt. 40, Kagohl 1, Bogohl 1*	?
Lt. Rolf *Frhr.* von Lersner	*Kagohl 1, Jasta "B," Kagohl 3*	?
Vzfw. — Marcard	*in der Fliegertruppe*	August 8, 1917 1.
Lt. — Mayer	*in der Fliegertruppe*	August 8, 1917 1.
Vzflgmstr. — Meyer	*Mar.Feldjasta I, Mar.Feldjasta II, Mar.Feldjasta III*	?
Oblt. Roland Müller	*FFl.Abt. 27, Fl.Abt. (A)266*	?
Lt. Walter Niesen	*Art.Fl.Abt. 203*	?
Oblt. Karl Obert	*FFl.Abt. 26*	May 4, 1916
Lt. Herbert Pfeifer	*Fl.Abt. (A)226*	?
Hptm. Erich Quade	*FFl.Abt. 66, FFl.Abt. Heyder, FFl.Abt. 54, Fl.Abt. (A)260*	?

Highest Wartime Rank and Name of Recipient	Unit(s) in Which Recipient is Known to Have Served	Date of Award (if known)
Rittm. Manfred *Frhr.* von Richthofen	*FFl.Abt. 69, Kagohl 2, Jasta 2, Jasta 11, JG 1*	?
Lt. Gustav Ritzert	*in einer Kampfstaffel*	October 25, 1916 1.
Hptm. Heinrich Scanzoni von Lichtenfels	*FFl.Abt. 41*	?
Hilfzahlmstr. Heinrich Schneider	*Fl.Abt. (A)266*	December 25, 1917
Oblt. Hans Schüz	*FFl.Abt. 34, FFl.Abt. 2*	January 18, 1915
Hptm. Julius Schulz	*FFl.Abt. 5*	?
Oblt. Heinrich Schwandner	*FFl.Abt. 2b, Kasta 36, Schusta 27b, Jasta 32*	April 28, 1915
Hptm. Julius Staab	*FFl.Abt. 2b, FFl.Abt. 4b, FFl.Abt. 7b, Fl.Abt. (A)293*	February 20, 1917
Lt. Werner Steinhäuser	*Fl.Abt. (A)261, Jasta 11*	July 15, 1915
Oblt. — Vogeley	*FFl.Abt. 26*	in 1916
Oblt. Erich Rudiger von Wedel	*Jasta 11*	September 28, 1915
Lt. Norbert Welkoborsky	*FFl.Abt. 32, Fl.Abt. (A)263*	July 9, 1918
Hptm. Erich Wilok	*FFl.Abt. 18, Fl.Abt. (A)265*	?
Hptm. Werner Zahn	*FFl.Abt. 6, FFl.Abt. 41*	?
Hptm. Eduard Zimmermann	*FFl.Abt. 38, FFl.Abt. 34, Fl.Abt. (A)274*	December 7, 1915
Hptm. Eduard Wolgang Zorer	*FFl.Abt. 54, Schusta 7, Kagohl 1*	?

Note

1. These dates are from the German aviation magazine *Flugsport*'s issue that mentioned the award without listing the recipient's aviation unit. They are not the dates on which the award was approved.

Sources:

Badische Generallandesarchiv, Karlsruhe
Bayerische Hauptstaatsarchiv, Abteilung IV, Kriegsarchiv, Munich
Bundesarchiv-Kriegsarchiv, Freiburg i. B.
Die Generale der deutschen Luftwaffe 1935-1945, Teil II., Band 1, 2, 3
Feldflieger-Abteilung 11 Personnel Roster, August 2, 1914 to November 10, 1916
Ferko, A.E. Archive
Flugsport, Various issues, 1914-1918
Photographs
Rangliste des deutschen Reichsheeres 1924-1932
Rangliste der Deutschen Reichsmarine 1926

Appendix XIX
Serving Officers in the Royal Prussian Army and the 13th (Royal Württemberg) Army Corps as of May 6, 1914 Holding the Princely Hohenzollern Honor Cross with Swords

Grade of the Order	Generals	Field Grade Officers[1]	Captains	1st and 2nd Lieutenants
Honor Cross 1st Class with Swords	2	0	0	0
Honor Commander Cross with Swords	0	0	0	0
Honor Cross 2nd Class with Swords	0	0	0	0
Honor Cross 3rd Class with Crown and Swords	0	0	0	0
Honor Cross 3rd Class with Swords	1	0	0	0

Notes:
Included are officers in related branches such as the Medical and Veterinarian services, the Marine infantry (*Seebatallionen*) and those in the colonies (*Ostasiatisches Marine-Detachment* and *Schutztruppen*) as well as officers in the reserves and militia (Landwehr).

1. Colonels, Lieutenant Colonels and Majors.

Source:
Rangliste der Königlich Preussischen Armee und des XIII. (Königlich Württembergischen) Armeekorps für 1914.

Appendix XX
Serving Officers in the Imperial German Navy as of February 14, 1918 Holding the Princely Hohenzollern Honor Cross with Swords

Grade of the Order	Admirals	Flag Officers[1]	Full Lieutenants[2]	Junior Officers[3]
Honor Cross 1st Class with Swords	1	0	0	0
Honor Commander Cross with Swords	0	0	0	0
Honor Cross 2nd Class with Swords	0	1	0	0
Honor Cross 3rd Class with Crown and Swords	0	0	0	0
Honor Cross 3rd Class with Swords	0	0	2	1

Notes:
Included are officers in related branches such as Marine infantry, Engineering and Medical Services as well as officers in the reserve.

1. Captains, Commanders and Lieutenant Commanders
2. Lieutenants
3. Lieutenants Junior Grade, Ensigns and Cadets

Source:
Rangliste (Dienstaltersliste) der Kaiserlich Deutschen Marine für das Jahre 1918. Nach dem Stande vom 14. Februar 1918.

Appendix XXI
Serving Officers in the German Army as of April 1, 1924 Holding the Princely Hohenzollern Honor Cross with Swords

Grade of the Order	Generals	Field Grade Officers[1]	Captains	1st and 2nd Lieutenants
Honor Cross 1st Class with Swords	1	0	0	0
Honor Commander Cross with Swords	1	0	0	0
Honor Cross 2nd Class with Swords	4	1	0	0
Honor Cross 3rd Class with Crown and Swords	1	13	0	0
Honor Cross 3rd Class with Swords	0	17	10	14
Gold Merit Cross with Swords	0	0	0	1
Silver Merit Cross with Swords	0	0	1	1

Note:
1. Colonels, Lieutenant Colonels and Majors

Source:
Rangliste des Deutschen Reichsheeres nach dem Stande vom 1. April 1924.

Appendix XXII
Recipients of the Princely Hohenzollern Honor Cross 3rd Class with Swords Who Served in the *Fliegertruppe*, 1914-1920
(Listed in Order of Receipt as Shown on the Roll)

No. on Roll	Rank at Time of Award and Name of Recipient	Unit in Which Recipient Earned the Award	Date of Award
69	*Lt.* Franz Biwer	*Füsil.-Rgt. 40.*[1]	January 31, 1915
91	*Hptm.* Erwin Barends	*FFl.Abt. 20*	April 16, 1915
133	*Oblt.* Heinz von Pflugk-Harttung	*FFl.Abt. 12*	June 30, 1915
180	*Hptm.* Ernst Dreebsel	*FFl.Abt. d. Armme Einem*[2]	November 30, 1915
256	*Oblt.* Lothar Baas	*FEA 2*	July 1, 1916
334	*Lt.* Günther Schroth	*FFl.Abt. 42*[3]	December 1, 1916
349	*Lt.* Oskar Wilhelm Türk	*Res.-Feldart.-Rgt. 239*[4]	December 12, 1916
481	*Lt.* Josef Deigendesch	*Res.-Inf.-Rgt. 74.*[5]	August 7, 1917
520	*Lt.* Gustav Salffner	*Fl.Abt. (A)214*	August 25, 1917
528	*Hptm.* Carl Schwab	*Fl.Abt. (A)223*	September 18, 1917
544	*Lt.* Carl-August von Schoenebeck	*Jasta 11*[6]	October 12, 1917
560	*Oblt.* Georg Weber	*Fl.Abt. (A)298*	August 29, 1917
746	*Oblt.* Heinz-Hellmuth von Ahlisch	*Generalkommando XIV.*[7]	April 16, 1918
755	*Lt.* Erich Lindemann	*Res.-Inf.-Rgt. 249.*[8]	April 25, 1918
765	*Lt.* Otto Keller	*Bosta 9, Bogohl 8*	May 22, 1918
833	*Lt.* Xaver Luib	*Bosta 8, Bogohl 6*	June 19, 1918
873	*Lt.* — Vater	*Fl.Abt. (A)209*	August 13, 1918
877	*Oblt.* — von Prittwitz und Gaffron	*Fl.Herresgr. Eichhorn-Kiew*	August 21, 1918
885	*Lt.* Friedrich Neu	*Fl.Abt. 48*	August 30, 1918
938	*Lt.* Joachim Albrecht *Graf* von Rothenburg	*Sächsischen Garde-Reiter-Regiment*	August 27, 1919[9]

Notes:
1. Biwer later served in *Art.Fl.Abt. 206* and *Fl.Abt. (A)224*.
2. Drechsel was *Kofl 3* on the date of his award.
3. Schroth had joined *Jasta 19* one week before the date of his award.
4. Türk later served in *Fl.Abt. (A)280*.
5. Deigendesch later served in *Fl.Abt. 1*.
6. An incident in von Schoenebeck's flight training days formed the basis for his award (see text for details).
7. Von Wuhlisch had earlier served in *FFl.Abt. 62, Fl.Abt. 32* and *Schusta 10*. on the date of his award, he was on the staff of the XIV Army Corps.
8. Lindemann later served in an unknown unit of the *Fliegertruppe*. In view of the fact that his was an 1918 award, this may be a case of listing his pre-air service regiment instead of the air service contingent in which it was actuall earned.
9. *Graf* von Rothenburg was a qualified observer (unit unknown). This may also be a situation like Lindemann's. The award itself was made retroactive to October 29, 1918.

Source:
Staatsarchiv, Sigmaringen

Appendix XXIII
Recipients of the Princely Hohenzollern Gold Honor Medal with Swords Who Served in the Fliegertruppe, 1914-1918
(Listed in Order of Receipt)

No. on Roll	Rank at Time of Award and Name of Recipient	Unit in Which Recipient Earned His Award	Date of Award
162	*Zahlmstr.-Stv.* Anton Kaus	*Art.Fl.Abt. 214*	May 18, 1916
276	*Vzfw.* Andreas Oswald	*Res.-Jäger-Bat. 16*[1]	April 18, 1917
335	*Vzfw.* Karl Käppeler	*Fl.Abt. (A)252w*	August 8, 1917
336	*Vzfw.* Martin Gelle	*AFP 3*	August 8, 1917
375	*Schirrmstr.* Adolf Lörch	*AFP 1*	October 20, 1917
587	*Vzfw.* Karl Siebenrock	*Fl.Abt. (A)236*	August 23, 1918
619	*Schirrmstr.* Paul Küpper	*Fl.-Depot Nord*	October 14, 1918

Notes:
1. Oswald later served in *Fl.Abt. (A)250*.

An *Offz.-Stv.* Willy Westphal received the Gold Honor Medal with Swords on December 4, 1916 for service in *Jäger-Bat. Nr. 5*. An *Offz.-Stv.* Willy Westphal joined the *Fliegertruppe* in August 1916 after service in the infantry and ended commanding a flight in *Schlasta 20* where he earned the Prussian Golden Military Merit Cross on August 7, 1918. It is possible that these are one and the same.

Sources:
Flieger des Weltkrieges, Inhaber des Goldenen Militär-Verdienst-Kreuzes, Heft 9, Berlin, 1942
Staatsarchiv, Sigmaringen

Appendix XXIV
Known Aviation Recipients of the Princely Hohenzollern Silver Merit Medal with Swords, 1914-1918
(Listed Alphabetically)

Rank at Time of Award and Name of Recipient	**Unit(s) in Which Recipient is Known to Have Served**
Vzfw. Fritz Beckhardt	*Schusta 11, Jasta 26, Kest 2*
Vzfw. Andreas Emele	*Jasta 80*
Flieger Josef Fischer	*Fl.Abt. 7*
Gefr. Eduard Gebhard	*FFl.Abt. 50*
Kraftfahrer — Herre	*Fl.Abt. (A)241*
Gefr. Johann Kohle	*in der Fliegertruppe*
Unteroffz. Bruno Lehle	*Fl.Abt. (A)271*
Flieger Alfred Lendle	*Fl.Abt. 10*
Funker Ernst Menzel	*Fl.Abt. (A)248*
Flugmech. Obermaat Erich Mielke	*II. Mar. FFl.Abt.*
Flieger Albert Moll	*in der Fliegertruppe*
Flugzeugmonteur Wilhelm Otto	*Fl.Abt. 12*
Flieger Hunibald Saupp	*Schusta 16*
Fliegerfunker Karl Soherer	*Idflieg*
Unteroffz. Heinrich Schröck	*Fl.Abt. (A)248*
Flieger Josef Weiss	*Jasta 1*

Sources:
Hohenzollerisches Gedenkbuch, 1914-1918, Hechingen, 1927
Staatsarchiv, Sigmaringen

Appendix XXV
Awards of the Honor Cross of the Princely Joint House, 1869-1890

	Lippe	Schaumburg-Lippe	Joint	Total
1st Class with Swords	14	21	1	36
1st Class without Swords	94	177	11	282
2nd Class with Swords	0	0	0	0
2nd Class with Swords-on-Ring	1	4	0	5
2nd Class with Oakleaves	5	1	0	6
2nd Class with 50 Jubilee Numeral	0	2	0	2
2nd Class without Swords	39	80	1	120
3rd Class with Swords	5	16	0	21
3rd Class with Swords-on-Ring	8	2	0	10
3rd Class without Swords	115	166	6	287
4th Class with Swords	73	13	0	86
4th Class without Swords	175	265	5	445
Total	**529**	**747**	**24**	**1,300**

Sources:

Liste der vom Sr. Durchlaucht dem Fürsten Adolph Georg zu Schaumburg-Lippe mit dem Fürstlich Lippischen Ehren-Kreuze begnadigten Personen, Volume I, Bückeburg Branch, *Schaumburg/des. L4*, No. 21, pp 26-73

Liste der vom Sr. Durchlaucht dem.Fürsten Leopold zur Lippe mit des Fürstlich Lippischen Ehrenkreuze begnadigten Personen, Volume I, Bückeburg Branch, *Schaumburg/des. L4*, No. 21, pp 99-126

Nordhein-Westfälisches Staatsarchiv, Detmold, Reconstructed Lippe House Order Roll of the Lower Saxon State Archives, Research by Eric C. Ludvigsen

Appendix XXVI
Awards of the Princely Lippe Honor Cross, 1890-1913 and 1914-1918

	1890-1913	**1914-1918**	**Total**
Grand Cross with Swords	0	5	5
Grand Cross without Swords	5	5	10
1st Class with Swords	0	15	15
1st Class with Swords-on-Ring	2	1	3
1st Class with Laurel and Oak Wreath	1	0	1
1st Class with Oak Wreath	1	0	1
1st Class without Swords	124	5	129
2nd Class with Oakleaves and Swords	0	7	7
2nd Class with Swords	0	24	24
2nd Class with Swords-on-Ring	6	2	8
2nd Class with Oakleaves	59	7	66
2nd Class without Swords	157	17	174
Officer's Cross with Swords	0	37	37
Officer's Cross without Swords	15	33	48
3rd Class with Swords	0	25	25
3rd Class with Swords-on-Ring	2	1	3
3rd Class with Oakleaves	21	0	21
3rd Class without Swords	236	40	276
4th Class 1st Division with Swords	5	75	80
4th Class 1st Division without Swords	469	92	561
4th Class 2nd Division with Swords	0	47	47
4th Class 2nd Division without Swords	76	75	151
Total	**1,179**	**513**	**1,692**

Source:
Nordhein-Westfälisches Staatsarchiv, Detmold - Reconstructed Lippe House Order Roll of the Lower Saxon State Archives, Research by Eric C. Ludvigsen

Appendix XXVII
Serving Officers in the Royal Prussian Army and the 13th (Royal Württemberg) Army Corps as of May 6, 1914 Holding the Princely Lippe Honor Cross with Swords

Grade of the Order	Generals	Field Grade Officers[1]	Captains	1st and 2nd Lieutenants
Honor Cross 1st Class with Swords[2]	1	1	0	0
Honor Cross 3rd Class with Swords[2]	3	1	0	0
Honor Cross 4th Class with Swords[3]	0	1	5[4]	0

Notes:
Included are officers in related branches such as the Medical and Veterinarian services, the Marine infantry (*Seebatallionen*) and those in the colonies (*Ostasiatisches Marine-Detachment* and *Schutztruppen*) as well as officers in the reserves and militia (*Landwehr*).

1. Colonels, Lt. Colonels and Majors
2. Joint awards from Lippe and Schaumbuge-Lippe up to 1890
3. Lippe only awards from 1890 to 1914; no indication of which division
4. Including two in the Schutztruppen

Source:
Rangliste der Königlich Preussischen Armee und des XIII. (Königlich Württembergischen) Armeekorps fur 1914.

Appendix XXVIII
Serving Officers in the Imperial German Navy as of February 14, 1918 Holding the Princely Lippe War Honor Cross for Heroic Deed and the War Merit Cross

Award	Admirals	Flag Officers[1]	Full Lieutenants[2]	Junior Officers[3]
Any Grade of the Honor Cross with Swords	0	0	0	0
War Honor Cross for Heroic Deed	0	1	0	1
War Merit Cross	0	1[4]	12	12

Notes:
Included are officers in related branches such as the Marine infantry, Engineering and Medical Services as well as officers in the reserve.

1. Captains, Commanders and Lieutenant Commanders
2. Lieutenants
3. Lieutenants Junior Grade, Ensigns and Cadets
4. Award made on the ribbon for non-combatants

Source:
Rangliste (Dienstaltersliste) der Kaiserlich Deutschen Marine für das Jahre 1918. Nach dem. Stande vom 14. Februar 1918.

Appendix XXIX
Serving Officers in the German Army as of April 1, 1924 Holding the Princely Lippe Honor Cross with Swords, the War Honor Cross for Heroic Deed and the War Merit Cross

Award	Generals	Field Grade Officers[1]	Captains	1st and 2nd Lieutenants
Honor Cross 2nd Class with Swords	1	0	0	0
Honor Cross 3rd Class with Swords	0	1	0	0
Honor Cross 4th Class with Swords[2]	0	3	4	1
War Honor Cross for Heroic Deed	1	2	3	5
War Merit Cross	3	48	44	27

Notes:
1. Colonels, Lieutenant Colonels and Majors
2. The Rank List does not distinguish between the 4th Class Honor Cross 1st Division and the 4th Class Honor Cross 2nd Division

Source:
Rangliste des Deutschen Reichsheeres nach dem Stande vom 1. April 1924.

Appendix XXX
Some Important Recipients of the Princely Lippe War Honor Cross for Heroic Deed
(Listed in Order of Receipt)
(- Known to Have Also Received the Lippe War Merit Cross)*

No. on Roll	Title or Rank and Name of Recipient	Date of Award
1	*Prinz* Leopold IV of Lippe	January 17, 1915
6	*Generaloberst Kronprinz* Rupprecht of Bavaria	June 7, 1915
149	*Kaiser* Wilhelm II of Prussia*	October 11, 1916
150	*Generalfeldmarschall* Paul von Hindenburg	October13, 1916
151	*General der Infanterie* Erich Ludendorff	October 13, 1916
154	*Prinz* Leopold of Bavaria	October 15, 1916
155	*Prinz* Oskar of Prussia	October 19, 1916
260	*Kronprinz* Wilhelm of Prussia	February 18, 1917
404	*König* Ludwig III of Bavaria	December 12, 1917
405	*Prinz* Wilhelm of Hohenzollern	December 14, 1917

Source:
Nordrhein-Westfälisches Staatsarchiv, Detmold

Appendix XXXI
Aviation Recipients of the Princely Lippe War Honor Cross for Heroic Deed, 1914-1918

(Listed in Order of Receipt)

(- Known to Have Also Received the Lippe War Merit Cross)*

No. on Roll	Rank and Name of Recipient	Unit in Which Recipient Earned the Award	Date of Award
24	*Rittm.* Iwan von Stietencron	*Heeresgr. v. Mackensen*	October 10, 1915
82	*Oblt.* Roland Müller*	*FFl.Abt. 27*	May 23, 1916
164	*Lt.* Franz von Kerssenbrock*	*in der Fliegertruppe*[1]	January 10, 1917
173	*Lt.* Karl Piderit*	*FEA 6*	February 13, 1917
179	*Offz.Stv.* Gottlieb Vothknecht	*Jasta 24*	March 10, 1917
186	*Lt.* Ludwig Dornheim*	*Jasta 29*	February 13, 1917
213	*Lt.* Hermann Büscher*	*Fl.Abt. (A)258*	April 26, 1917
233	*Oberflgmstr.* Ernst Boedecker	*Mar.Landflieger-Abt.*	June 15, 1917
301	*Rittm.* Manfred *Freiherr* von Richthofen	*JG 1*	October 13, 1917
344	*Lt.* Karl Fricke*	*FEA 11*	November 20, 1917
354	*Vzfw.* August Begemann	*Fl.Abt. 6*	December 19, 1917
362	*Oblt.* Leopold Kuhlmann	*Fl.Abt. (A)256*	December 4, 1917
363	*Lt.* Ernst Hilker	*Fl.Abt. (A)256*	December 4, 1917
378	*Lt.* Karl Stock*	*Jasta 6*	January 7, 1918
382	*Lt.* Hans Lindemann	*Fl.Abt. (A)217*	January 7, 1918
400	*Flgmstr.* Fritz Schilling	*II. Mar.FFl.Abt.*	January 7, 1918
429	*Lt.* Theo Prüssner	*Bogohl 7*	April 18, 1918
431	*Lt.* Hermann Günter	*Fl.Abt. (A)213*	April 18, 1918
533	*Lt.* Wilhelm Schröder	*Fl.Abt. (A)213*	April 18, 1918
576	*Lt.* Arno Benzler*	*Jasta 60*	July 15, 1918
589	*Vzfw.* Hermann Vehmeier	*Schlasta 18*	July 8, 1918
601	*Lt.* Fritz Fromme*	*Fl.Abt. (A)265*	August 20, 1918
651	*Lt.* Hans Rohdewald	*Fl.Abt. (A)232*	October 18, 1918
703	*Lt.* Walter Wiegrebe	*Fl.Abt. (A)224*	November 1, 1918

Note:

1. The unit in which von Kerssonbrock earned his War Honor Cross for Heroic Deed is not listed on the roll. He served in Salonika in 1916 with *Feldflieger-Abteilung 1* and with *Jasta 39* in 1917. It was probably in the former unit that his award came.

Source:

Nordrhein-Westfälisches Staatsarchiv, Detmold

Appendix XXXII
Awards of the Princely Schaumburg-Lippe Honor Cross, 1890-1913 and 1914-1918

	1890-1913	**1914-1918**	**Total**
1st Class with Swords	1	0	1
1st Class with Swords-on-Ring	1	0	1
1st Class without Swords	227	31	258
2nd Class with Swords	0	0	0
2nd Class with Swords-on-Ring	2	1	3
2nd Class with Oakleaves	20	6	26
2nd Class without Swords	341	21	362
Officer's Cross with Swords	0	0	0
Officer's Cross with Swords-on-Ring	1	0	1
Officer's Cross with 50 Jubilee Numeral	2	0	2
Officer's Cross without Swords	186	62	248
3rd Class with Swords	1	0	1
3rd Class with Swords-on-Ring	1	0	1
3rd Class with Crown	4	1	5
3rd Class without Swords	443	83	526
4th Class with Swords	1	1	2
4th Class with Crown	7	1	8
4th Class without Swords	542	75	617
Total	**1,780**	**282**	**2,062**

Source:
Niedersächsisches Staatsarchiv in Bückeburg, Research by Eric C. Ludvigsen

Appendix XXXIII
Serving Officers in the Royal Prussian Army and the 13th (Royal Württemberg) Army Corps as of May 6, 1914 Holding the Princely Schaumburg-Lippe Honor Cross with Swords

Grade of the Order	Generals	Field Grade Officers[1]	Captains	1st and 2nd Lieutenants
Honor Cross 1st Class with Swords[2]	1	0	0	0
Honor Cross 1st Class with Swords-on-Ring[2]	1	0	0	0
Honor Cross 4th Class with Swords[3]	0	0	1[4]	0

Notes:
Included are officers in related branches such as the Medical and Veterinarian services, the Marine infantry (*Seebatallionen*) and those in the colonies (*Ostasiatisches Marine-Detachment* and *Schutztruppen*) as well as officers in the reserves and militia (*Landwehr*).

1. Colonels, Lt. Colonels and Majors
2. Joint awards from Schaumburg-Lippe and Lippe up to 1890
3. Schaumburg-Lippe only awards from 1890 to 1914
4. The recipient was in the Schutztruppe

Source:
Rangliste der Königlich Preussischen Armee und des XIII. (Königlich Württembergischen) Armeekorps für 1914.

Appendix XXXIV
Serving Officers in the Imperial German Navy as of February 14, 1918 Holding the Princely Schaumburg-Lippe Cross for Faithful Service

	Admirals	Flag Officers[1]	Full Lieutenants[2]	Junior Officers[3]
Cross for Faithful Service	4	2	2	2

Notes:
Included are officers in related branches such as the Marine infantry, Engineering and Medical Services as well as officers in the reserve.

1. Captains, Commanders and Lieutenant Commanders
2. Lieutenants, Lieutenants Junior Grade and Ensigns

Source:
Rangliste (Dienstaltersliste) der Kaiserlich Deutschen Marine für das Jabre 1918. Nach dem Stande vom 14. Februar 1918.

Appendix XXXV
Serving Officers in the German Army as of April 1, 1924 Holding the Princely Schaumburg-Lippe Honor Cross with Swords and the Cross for Faithful Service

Award	Generals	Field Grade Officers[1]	Captains	1st and 2nd Lieutenants
Honor Cross 3rd Class with Swords	0	0	1	0
Cross for Faithful Service	2	32	31	27

Notes:
1. Colonels, Lieutenant Colonels and Majors

Source:
Rangliste des Deutschen Reichsheeres nach dem Stande Vom 1. April 1924.

Appendix XXXVI
Members of Reigning Houses Who Received the Princely Schaumburg-Lippe Cross for Faithful Service, Pin-Back and Breast Badges, 1914-1918
(Listed in Order on the Roll)

No. on Roll	Name of Recipient	Pin-Back Badge	Breast Badge	Date of Award
1	Prince Adolf of Schaumburg Lippe[1]	yes	yes	September 25, 1914[2]
2	Prince Adolf of Schaumburg-Lippe[3]	yes	yes	September 25, 1914[2]
3	Prince Otto of Schaumburg-Lippe	yes	yes	September 25, 1914[2]
4	Prince Friedrich of Schaumburg-Lippe	yes	yes	September 25, 1914[2]
5	Prince Albrecht of Schaumburg-Lippe	yes	yes	September 25, 1914[2]
6	Prince Moritz of Schaumburg-Lippe	yes	yes	September 25, 1914[2]
7	Prince Wolrad of Schaumburg-Lippe	yes	yes	September 25, 1914[2]
8	Prince Stephan of Schaumburg-Lippe	yes	yes	September 25, 1914[2]
9	The Duke of Saxe-Altenburg	yes	yes	September 25, 1914[2]
10	The Prince of Waldeck-Pyrmont	yes	yes	September 25, 1914[2]
11	The German Emperor and King of Prussia	no[4]	yes	January 6, 1915
12	Prince Leopold of Prussia	no	yes	March 20, 1915
13	Prince Heinrich of Schaumburg-Lippe	yes	yes	March 23, 1915
14	The Duke of Anhalt	yes	yes	April 17, 1915
15	Prince Max of Schaumburg-Lippe	yes	yes	April 20, 1915
16	The Duke of Saxe-Meiningen	yes	yes	May 25, 1915
17	Duke Ulrich of Württemberg	no	yes	June 14, 1915
18	The Grand Duke of Hesse	no	yes	July 2, 1915[5]
19	Prince Philipp of Hesse	no	yes	June 15, 1915[5]
20	Prince Christian of Schaumburg-Lippe	yes	yes	August 31, 1915
21	Archduke Josef Ferdinand	no	yes	December 9, 1915
22	Archduke Heinrich Ferdinand	no	yes	December 9, 1915
23	Prince Waldemar of Prussia	no	yes	December 27, 1915
24	The Sultan of the Ottoman Empire	yes	yes	April 15, 1916
25	Czar Ferdinand of Bulgaria	yes	yes	April 28, 1916

No. on Roll	Name of Recipient	Pin-Back Badge	Breast Badge	Date of Award
26	Crown Prince Boris of Bulgaria	no	yes	April 28, 1916
27	Prince Cyrill of Bulgaria	no	yes	April 28, 1916
28	The Grand Duke of Mecklenburg-Strelitz	no	yes	August 25, 1916
29	The Grand Duke of Oldenburg	no	yes	March 2, 1917
30	Heir Grand Duke Nikolaus of Oldenburg	no	yes	March 2, 1917
31	Prince Eugen of Schaumburg-Lippe	no[6]	yes	July 15, 1917
32	Prince Friedrich Sigismund of Prussia	no	yes	August 14, 1917
33	Emperor Karl of the Austro-Hungarian Empire	yes	yes	November 7, 1917
34	Prince Felix of Parma	no	yes	December 4, 1917
35	Prince Renee of Parma	no	yes	December 4, 1917
36	Archduke Max	no	yes	January 10, 1918

Notes:

1. This Prince Adolf was the reigning Prince of Schaumburg-Lippe, Adolf II.
2. Since the Cross for Faithful Service was renewed on November 18, 1914, these dates must have been retroactive.
3. This Prince Adolf was a *General der Kavallerie*, fourth son of Adolf I.
4. The roll shows no indication that *Kaiser* Wilhelm II received the pin-back version of the Cross for Faithful Service. In view of the fact that the monarchs of the Austro-Hungarian Empire, Bulgaria and the Ottoman Empire each received a pin-back cross in addition to the breast badge, this omission may be in error.
5. The roll dates Prince Philipp of Hesse's award ahead of that to the Grand Duke of Hesse which would have been unlikely. Since that would be unlikely, one or the other of these dates may be wrong.
6. The roll shows no indication that Prince Eugen of Schaumburg-Lippe received the pin-back version of the Cross for Faithful Service. Since all the other princes on the roll did get both the pin-back and the breast badges, this omission may be in error.

Source:
Niedersächsisches Staatsarchiv in Bückeburg

Appendix XXXVII
Aviation Recipients of the Princely Schaumburg-Lippe Cross for Faithful Service, 1914-1919 Officers and Equivalent Persons

(Listed in Order of Receipt)

No. on Roll	Rank and Name of Recipient	Unit in Which Recipient Earned the Award	Date of Award
4	*Oblt.* Karl von Apell	*FFl.Abt. 28*	October 31, 1914
133	*Hptm.* Hilmar *Frhr.* von Bülow	*FFl.Abt. 1*	December 23, 1914
152	*Hptm.* — Gissot	*FFl.Abt. 21*	January 4, 1915
598	*Lt.* Hans-Otto *Graf* von Nostitz	*FFl.Abt. 59*	November 13, 1915
831	*Major* Hermann von der Lieth-Thomsen	*Chef des Feldflugwesens*	April 17, 1916
919	*Oblt.* Paul Backhaus	*Kagohl 2*	July 14, 1916
1457	*Oblt.* Julius Liebrecht	*Fl.Abt. 22*	May 22, 1917
1459	*Lt.* Walter Scharpf	*Fl.Abt. 22*	May 23, 1917
1624	*Rittm.* Manfred *Frhr.* von Richthofen	*JG 1*	October 10, 1917
1635	*Lt.* Hans Arimond	*Fl.Abt. 22*	October 19, 1917
1636	*Lt.* Hermann Gütmeister	*Fl.Abt. 22*	October 19, 1917
1637	*Lt.* Kurt Richter	*Fl.Abt. 22*	October 19, 1917
1879	*Lt.* Ernst Hein	*Fl.Abt. 22*	February 27, 1918
1947	*Lt.* Maximilian *Frhr.* von Gregory	*Fl.Abt. (A)277*	April 24, 1918
1965	*Lt.* Klaus Seemann	*Fl.Abt. 303*	May 24, 1918
1986	*Lt.* August Kinter	*Fl.Abt. (A)231*	June 13, 1918
2039	*Rittm.* Egon Hugo *Graf* von Beroldingen	*FEA 10*	July 22, 1918
2084	*Lt.* Nikolaus *Graf* von Luckner	*FEA 5*	August 15, 1918
2085	*Lt.* Ernst Paland	*FEA 5*	August 15, 1918
2086	*Lt.* Karl Ruthe	*FEA 5*	August 15, 1918
2087	*Lt.* Ernst Peck	*FEA 5*	August 15, 1918
2117	*Lt.* (?) Kuno *Frhr.* von Hoverbeck (known as von Schoenaich)	*FEA 6*	September 5, 1918

Source:
Niedersächsisches Staatsarchiv in Bückeburg

Appendix XXXVIII
Aviation Recipients of the Princely Schaumburg-Lippe Cross for Faithful Service, 1914-1918 Non-Commissioned Officers and Men
(Listed in Order of Receipt)

No. on Roll	Rank and Name of Recipient	Unit in Which Recipient Earned the Award	Date of Award
1339	*Flieger* Heinrich Löfker	*FFl.Abt. 46*	September 9, 1915
1405	*Vzfw.* Friedrich (?) Ebeling	*FEA 8*	October 2, 1915
1948	*Gefr.* Ernst Bruns	*FFl.Abt. 46*	February 10, 1916
2225	*Unteroffz.* Emil Thielker	*FFl.Abt. 61*	April 15, 1916
2700	*Flgmaat* Wilhelm Geils	*I. Seeflieger-Abt.*	August 14, 1916
2936	*Landsturmann* Wilhelm Wessel	*Flgst. Elbing*	September 23, 1916
4234	*Flieger* Karl Söchtig	*Fl.Abt. (A)273*	March 17, 1917
4807	*Gefr.* — Stock	*Fl.Abt. 16*	July 31, 1917
5058	*Unteroffz.* Heinrich Büse	*Fl.Abt. 28*	September 24, 1917
5512	*Unteroffz.* Wilhelm Heinemeyer	*Fl.Abt. (A)240*	January 16, 1918

(this was followed by a second roll beginning with number 1)

No. on Roll	Rank and Name of Recipient	Unit in Which Recipient Earned the Award	Date of Award
59	*Unteroffz.* Anthony Reiter	*Fl.Abt. 30*	March 6, 1918
64	*Flieger* Friedrich Lungershausen	*Fl.Abt. 28*	March 13, 1918
430	*Unteroffz.* Ernst Pfänder	*Fl.Abt. (A)273*	May 10, 1918
778	*Gefr.* August Haase	*Fl.Beob.Schule Thorn*	May 15, 1918
884	*Sgt.* Maximilian Flaig	*AFP 18*	July 22, 1918
1059	*Flieger* Friedrich Schmid (or Schnier)	*Fl.Abt. (A)268*	August 21, 1918
1133	*Vzfw.* Wilhelm Hillner	*FEA 5*	August 15, 1918
1134	*Sgt.* Willi Hellming	*FEA 5*	August 15, 1918
1223	*Flieger* Erhard Hünlich	*Stab d. Kofl 3*	September 18, 1918
400	*Waffenmstr.-Stv.* Adolf Diederichs	*Bogohl 3*	November 5, 1918
452	*Funker* Wilhelm Dreyer	*Fl.Abt. (A)209*	November 12, 1918
541	*Flgzeugmatrose* Friedrich Holle	*Kofl d. Land-Flieger*	November 14, 1918
548	*Offz.-Stv.* Viktor Fabrice	*Jastaschule II*	November 14, 1918
609	*Funker* Wilhelm Weimann	*Fl.Abt. (A)213*	November 14, 1918

Source:
Niedersächsisches Staatsarchiv in-Bückeburg

Appendix XXXIX
Serving Officers in the Royal Prussian Army and the 13th (Royal Württemberg) Army Corps as of May 6, 1914 Holding the Mecklenburg-Schwerin Military Merit Cross

Grade of the Cross	Generals	Field Grade Officers[1]	Captains	1st and 2nd Lieutenants
1st Class	2	0	0	0
2nd Class	18	4[2]	22[3]	4

Notes:
Included are officers in related branches such as the Medical and Veterinarian services, the Marine infantry (*Seebatallionen*) and those in the colonies (*Ostasiatisches Marine-Detachment* and *Schutztruppen*) as well as officers in the reserves and militia (*Landwehr*).

1. Colonels, Lt. Colonels and Majors
2. Including one in the *Schutztruppe*
3. Including four in the *Schutztruppe*

Source:
Rangliste der Königlich Preussischen Armee und des XIII. (Königlich Württembergischen) Armeekorps für 1914.

Appendix XL
Serving Officers in the Imperial German Navy as of February 14, 1918 Holding the Mecklenburg-Schwerin Military Merit Cross

Grade of the Cross	Admirals	Flag Officers[1]	Full Lieutenants[2]	Junior Officers[3]
1st Class	3	7	8	3
2nd Class	9	47	80	95

Notes:
Included are officers in related branches such as the Marine infantry, Engineering and Medical Services as well as officers in the reserve. Awards on the Red Ribbon not included.

1. Captains, Commanders and Lieutenant Commanders
2. Lieutenants
3. Lieutenants Junior Grade and Ensigns

Source:
Rangliste (Dienstaltersliste) der Kaiserlich Deutschen Marine für das Jahre 1918. Nach dem Stande vom 14. Februar 1918.

Appendix XLI
Serving Officers in the German Army as of April 1, 1924 Holding the Mecklenburg-Schwerin Military Merit Cross

Grade of the Gross	Generals	Field Grade Officers[1]	Captains	1st and 2nd Lieutenants
1st Class	4	22	18	27
2nd Class	10	88	73	55

Notes:
1. Colonels, Lieutenant Colonels and Majors. Awards on the Red Ribbon not included.

Source:
Rangliste des Deutschen Reichsheeres nach dem. Stande vom 1. April 1924.

Appendix XLII
Serving Officers in the German Navy as of November 20, 1926 Holding the Mecklenburg-Schwerin Military Merit Cross

Grade of the Cross	Admirals	Flag Officers[1]	Full Lieutenants[2]	Junior Officers[3]
1st Class	0	3	0	0
2nd Class	4	14	3	4

Notes:
Included are officers in related branches such as the Engineering and Medical Services. Awards on the Red Ribbon not included.

1. Captains, Commanders and Lieutenant Commanders
2. Lieutenants
3. Lieutenants Junior Grade and Ensigns

Source:
Rangliste der Deutschen Reichsmarine. Nach dem Stande vom 20. November 1926.

Appendix XLIII
Known Recipients of the Mecklenburg-Schwerin Military Merit Crosses Who Were Members of Aviation Contingents

(Listed Alphabetically)
(P = Date of Proposal, not Date of Award)

Rank and Name of Recipient	Aviation Units in Which Recipient Served	1st Class and Date (if known)	2nd Class and Date (if known)
Hptm. Friedrich Baerens	*FFl.Abt. 47, Fl.Abt. 37*		X
Lt. Gustav Banse	*FFl.Abt. 6, Grufl 9*		X
Oblt. z. See Günther Barg	*Mar. Flgst. Nest, Mar. Flgst. Apenrade*		X
Lt. Raven *Frhr.* von Barnekow	*Jasta 4, Jasta 20, Jasta 1*		June 10, 1915 (P)
Kptlt. Hermanri Berthold	*II. See-Fl.Abt., Mar. Luftfahrwesen*		X
Oblt. Heinrich von Blanc	*FFl.Abt. 11*		X
Hptm. Ernst Mhmer	*FFl.Abt. 11*		X
Lt. Walter Boenicke	*Fl.Abt. (A)202, Fl.Abt. (A)213, Fl.Abt. 39*		March 5, 1916
Lt. z. See Erich Boenisch	*Mar. Luft Fl.Abt. Johannisthal, See Flgst. Warnemünde, See Flgst. Zeebrügge*		X
Oblt. Hans-Helmut von Boddien	*FFl.Abt. 18, Jasta 11, Jasta 59*	X	X
Oblt. Karl Bolle	*KG 4, Jasta 28w, Jasta "Boelcke"*		X
Lt. Erwin Burk	*FFl.Abt. 11*		X
Hptm. Hans Busch	*FFl.Abt. 11, Fl.Abt. (A)202, Idflieg*		July 19, 1915
Lt. Ernst Datan	*Fl.Abt. (A)264*	X	X
Hptm. Eberhardt von der Decken	*FFl.Abt. 11*		
Rittm. Kurt-Bertram von Döring	*FFl.Abt. 38, Fl.Abt. (A)227, Jasta 4, Jagdgr. 4, JG 1, Jasta 66, Jasta 1*	X	X
Lt. Albert Dossenbach	*FFl.Abt. 22, Jasta 2, Jasta 36, Jasta 10*	September 29, 1916	September 15, 1914
Hptm. Ernst Eberstein	*FFl.Abt. 14, FFl.Abt. 66, Fl.Abt. 26*		December 19, 1917
Hptm. Egloff *Frhr.* von Freyburg Eisenberg-Allmendingen	*FFl.Abt. 11, BAO, FFl.Abt. 5, Fl.Abt. (A)239, Grufl 5*		X
Hptm. — Fleischfresser	*Fl.Abt. (A)202*	X	X
Herr Anthony Fokker	*Fokker-Werke-Schwerin GmbH*		February 12, 1916
Oblt. Hermann Fricke	*FFl.Abt. 11, Fl.Abt. 3, Rbz. 2*		X
Oblt. Heinz Funke	*Fl.Abt. (A)256, Schlasta 3*		X
Lt. Hugo Glüer	*Mar.Land Fl.Abt., I. Mar. FFl.Abt., See Flug Versuchs Kommando Warnemünde*		X
Oblt. Kurt Grasshoff	*FFl.Abt. 31, Jasta 15, Jasta 37, Jasta 38*	X	X
Lt. Walter Hahn	*FFl.Abt. 11*		X
Hptm. Hans Eduard von Heemskerck	*FFl.Abt. 11, FFl.Abt. 42, FFl.Abt. 5, Fl.Abt. 300 "Pascha," Heeresgr. F (Palestina)*		X
Korv.Kpt. Max Hering	*See Flug Versuchs Kommando Warnemünde*		X
Oblt. Ferdinand von Hiddessen	*FFl.Abt. 11, BAO*		X
Lt. Max Kessler	*Mar.Land Fl.Abt.*		September 28, 1917
Lt. z. See Erich Killinger	*Mar.Luft Fl.Abt. Johannisthal, See Flgst. Putzig, See Flgst. Libau, See Flgst. Zeebragge, See Flgst. Ostende*	Proposed (?)	Proposed
Lt. Hans Orner	*Jasta 8, Jasta 27, Fl.Abt. (A)246, Jasta 19*	X	X
Lt. Hans Knoll	*II. Mar. FFl.Abt., Mar. Land Fl.Abt.*		September 28, 1917
Lt. Wilhelm Kreitz	*Luftfahrwesen d. Mar. Korps, I. Mar. FFl.Abt.*	June 29, 1918	X
Lt. Ernst Krüger	*Jasta 4*	X	X

Rank and Name of Recipient	Aviation Units in Which Recipient Served	1st Class and Date (if known)	2nd Class and Date (if known)
Lt. Wulf Krueger	*Mar. Fl.Abt. Johannisthal, See Flgst. Putzig, See Flgst. Libau, See Flgst. Warnemünde, Torp. Staffel Flensburg, Sonder Kommando II., Torp. Staffel Zeebrügge*		May 25, 1917 (P)
Kptlt. Walter Langfeld	*I. See.Fl.Abt., See Flgst. Helgoland, Sonder Kommando I., See Fl.Abt. Oberkommando Meerengen, Stab b. Mar. Flugchef*	X	X
Lt. Ulrich Neckel	*Fl.Abt. 25, Jasta 12, Jasta 19, Jasta 6*	X	X
Oblt. Hans-Henning von Oertzen	*FFl.Abt. 31, Fl.Abt. 33*	X	X
Kptlt. Rudolf Pechel	*I. See Fl.Abt.*		X
Kptlt. Günther Plüschow	*Mar. Flgst. Tsingtau, See Flgst. Libau, See Flgst. Holtenau, Mar. Flgst. Zeebrflgge, Mar. Flgst. Seddin*	X	X
Oblt. Wolfgang Plüschow	*FFl.Abt. 8, Jasta 11, Jasta 39*		X
Obermaat — Prüss	*II Mar. FFl.Abt.*		June 3, 1918
Lt. Christian Franz von Scheele	*FFl.Abt. 32, BAM, KG 2, Jasta "Boelcke"*		April 27, 1915
Lt. Hans-Argen von Schlichting	*Osmanisches Fliegertruppe, FEA 11*		X
Oblt. Carl Alexander von Schmidt	*Stofl Niemen-Armee*		July 21, 1915 (P)
Vzfw. Fritz Schumacher	*Jasta 10*	X	X
Hptm. Karl Schwab	*FFl.Abt. 11, Fl.Abt. (A)210*		X
Hptm. Karl Schweikhardt	*FFl.Abt. 20, FFl.Abt. 11,*		X
Lt. Karl Stutzer	*Fl.Abt. (A)283*	X	X
Hptm. Usbek	*Fl.Abt. (A)208*	X	X
Hptm. Bruno Wentscher	*FFl.Abt. 11, FFl.Abt. 53, AFA 243, Fl.Abt. (A)202*		December 18, 1914[1]
Hptm. Helmuth Wilberg	*FFl.Abt. 11, Kofl 4*		X
Kptlt. Georg von Winterfeld	*See Flug Versuchs Kommando, See Flgst. Helgoland*		X
Lt. Joseph Wolferseder	*Fl.Abt. 45b*		April 11, 1916
Hptm. Zorn	*Fl.Abt. 33*	X	X

Notes:
1. These are retroactive award dates. The Schwerin Military Merit Cross was not reinstituted for World War I until February 28, 1915.

(P) Date of proposal, not date of award. Actual approvals are not known in these cases.

Sources:
Bundesarchiv-Militärarchiv, Freiburg im Breisgau
Deutsches Technikmuseum, Berlin
Die Generale der deutschen Luftwaffe 1935-1945, Teil II, Band 1, 2, 3
Ehrenrangliste der Kaiserlich Deutschen Marine 1914-1918
Feldflieger-Abteilung 11 vom 2. August 1914 bis 10. November 1916
Ferko Archive
Mecklenburgisches Landeshauptarchiv, Schwerin
Rangliste des Deutschen Reichsheeres, 1924-1932
Rangliste (Dienstaltersliste) der Kaiserlich Deutschen Marine, 1916 and 1918
Rangliste der Deutschen. Reichsmarine, 1926
Photographs

Appendix XLIV
Serving Officers in the Royal Prussian Army and the 13th (Royal Württemberg) Army Corps as of May 6, 1914 Holding the Mecklenburg-Strelitz Cross for Distinction in War

	Generals	Field Grade Officers[1]	Captains	1st and 2nd Lieutenants
Cross for Distinction in War	5	4[2]	0	0

Notes:
Included are officers in related branches such as the Medical and Veterinarian services, the Marine infantry (*Seebatallionen*) and those in the colonies (*Ostasiatisches Marine-Detachment* and *Schutztruppen*) as well as officers in the reserves and militia (*Landwehr*).

1. Colonels, Lieutenant Colonels and Majors
2. Including three in the *Schutztruppe*

Source:
Rangliste der Königlich Preussischen Armee und des XIII. (Königlich Württembergischen) Armeekorps für 1914.

Appendix XLV
Serving Officers in the Imperial German Navy as of February 14, 1918 Holding the Mecklenburg-Strelitz Cross for Distinction in War

Grade of the Cross	Admirals	Flag Officers[1]	Full Lieutenants[2]	Junior Officers[3]
1st Class	0	1	2	0
2nd Class	1	3	4	5

Notes:
Included are officers in related branches such as the Marine infantry, Engineering and Medical Services as well as officers in the reserve.

1. Captains, Commanders and Lieutenant Commanders
2. Lieutenants
3. Lieutenants Junior Grade and Ensigns

Source:
Rangliste (Dienstaltersliste) der Kaiserlich Deutschen Marine für das Jahre 1918. Nach dem Stande vom 14. Februar 1918.

Appendix XLVI
Serving Officers in the German Army as of April 1, 1924 Holding the Mecklenburg-Strelitz Cross for Distinction in War

Grade of the Cross	Generals	Field Grade Officers[1]	Captains	1st and 2nd Lieutenants
1st Class	0	5	1	2
2nd Class	1	16	12	5

Notes:
1. Colonels, Lieutenant Colonels and Majors.

Source:
Rangliste des Deutschen Reichsheeres nach dem Stande vom 1. April 1924.

Appendix XLVII
Serving Officers in the German Navy as of November 20, 1926 Holding the Mecklenburg-Strelitz Cross for Distinction in War

Grade of the Cross	Admirals	Flag Officers[1]	Full Lieutenants[2]	Junior Officers[3]
1st Class	0	0	0	0
2nd Class	0	0	1	0

Notes:
Included are officers in related branches such as the Engineering and Medical Services.

1. Captains, Commanders and Lieutenant Commanders
2. Lieutenants, Lieutenants Junior Grade and Ensigns

Source:
Rangliste der Deutschen Reichsmarine. Nach dem Stande vom 20. November 1926.

Appendix XLVIII
Members of Reigning Houses, High Ranking Officers and Men in the *Fliegertruppe* Known to Have Received the Mecklenburg-Strelitz Cross for Distinction in War 1st Class, 1915-1918
(Listed in Order of Appearance on the Roll)

No. on Roll	Title or Rank and Name of Recipient	Title or Command Responsibility or Unit in Which Recipient Earned the Award	Date of Award (if shown)
1a.	*Grossherzog* Adolf Friedrich IV	Grand Duke Mecklenburg Strelitz	
1b.	*Gen. d. Inf.* Ferdinand von Quast	Commander IX Army Corps	
5.	*Generaloberst* Alexander von Kluck	Commander German Ist Army	
13.	*Lt.* Heinz Junge	*FFl.Abt. 38*	December 15, 1915
18.	*Generalleutnant* Stengel	Commander 17th Infantry Division	
19.	*Generaloberst* Karl von Einem	Commander German 3rd Army	
20.	"*Seine Majestät d. Kaiser u. König*"	See Note 1.	
21.	*Generaloberst* Hans von Plessen	Commander Supreme Headquarters	
25.	*Sultan* Muhamed Reschad Chan V	Ruler of the Ottoman Empire	
32.	*Gen. d. Inf.* Hans von Beseler	General Government Warsaw	
35.	*Generalfeldmarschall* Paul von Beneckendorff und Hindenburg	Supreme Commander East	
51.	*Hptm.* Kurt *Freiherr* von der Goltz	*AFA 230*	
66.	*Gen. d. Art.* Max von Gallwitz	Commander German 2nd Army	
70.	*Generalleutnant* Nieber	Commander Tnspectorate of Bases	
71.	*Gen. d. Inf.* Max von Böhn	Commander IX Army Corps	
72.	*Generalfeldmarschall* Luitpold	Crown Prince Bavaria	
73.	*Generalleutnant* Hermann von Kuhl	Chief of General Staff, Army Group Crown Prince	
94.	*Generaloberst* Ludwig *Freiherr* von Falkenhausen	Commander German 6tb Army	
106.	*Generaloberst* von Heeringen	Commander Coastal Defences	
130.	*Generalleutnant* Ernst von Hoeppner	Commander Air Force	
178.	*Vzfw.* Friedrich Mathies	*Jasta 20*	
193.	*Gen. d. Inf.* Erich Ludendorff	Supreme Headquarters	
194.	*Gen. d. Inf.* Moritz *Freiherr* von Lyncker	Chief of Military Cabinet	
223.	*Generalfeldmarschall* Hermann von Eichhorn	(no command responsibility listed)	
317.	*Lt.* Werner Janell	*Flieger Bomben Lehr Abt. Frankfurt o.d. Oder*	
394.	*Oblt.* Erich Stoecker	*Fl.Abt. (A)260*	
406.	*Lt.* Kurt Maller	*Kagohl 1*	

Notes:

1. From the entry which reads in its entirety "His Majesty the Emperor and King," it is not clear whether this refers to *Kaiser* Wilhelm II of Prussia or Kaiser Franz Joseph of Austria-Hungary. In his book *Die MecklenburgStrelitzer Orden und Ehrenzeichen*, the author, Peter Ohm-Hieronymussen, lists Franz Joseph as the recipient, perhaps based on information found elsewhere. In view of the award to the Sultan of Turkey which follows on the roll, this conclusion seems reasonable.

2. Von Eichborn was a *Generaloberst* and in command of the German 10th Army when be received the *Orden Pour le Mérite* on August 18, 1915 and the *Orden Pour le Mérite mit Eichenlaub* on September 28, 1915.

Source:
Mecklenburgisches Landeshauptarchiv, Schwerin

Appendix XLIX
Recipients of the Mecklenburg-Strelitz Cross for Distinction in War 2nd Class with Inscription "*für Tapferkeit*" (roll undated)
(Listed in Order of Appearance on the Roll)

No. on Roll	Title or Rank and Name of Recipient	Title or Command Responsibility
1.	*Grossherzog* Friedrich Franz IV	Grand Duke of Mecklenburg-Schwerin
2.	*Herzog* Paul	Duke of Mecklenburg-Schwerin
3.	*Fürst* Wilhelm	Prince of Hohenzollern
4.	*Generaloberst* Alexander von Kluck	Commander of the German 1st Army
5.	*Herzog* Leopold Friedrich II	Duke of Anhalt
6.	*Prinz* Eitel Friedrich	Prince of Prussia and Commander of the 1st Guard Infantry Division
7.	*Generaloberst* Karl von Einem	Commander of the German 3rd Army
8.	*Kronprinz* Friedrich August Georg	Crown Prince of Saxony
9.	*Herzog* Ernst August	Duke of Brunswick
10.	"*Seine Majestät der Kaiser und König*"	See Note 1.
11.	*General der Infanterie* Moritz *Freiherr* von Lyncker	Chief of the Military Cabinet
12.	*Excellenz* Wild von Hohenborn	Prussian War Minister
13.	*General der Infanterie* Erich von Falkenhayn	Chief of the General Staff
14.	*Sultan* Muhamed Reschad Chan V	Ruler of the Ottoman Empire
15.	*Generalfeldmarschall* Paul von Beneckendorff und Hindenburg	Supreme Commander East
16.	*General der Infanterie* Hans von Beseler	General Government Warsaw
17.	*Generalleutnant* Erich Ludendorff	Chief of the General Staff, Supreme Command East
18.	*General der Infanterie* Max von Fabeck	(no command responsibility listed)[2]
19.	*Fürst* Adolf	Prince of Schaumburg-Lippe
20.	*Kronprinz* Luitpold	Crown Prince of Bavaria
21.	*Herzog* Georg II	Duke of Saxe-Meiningen
22.	*General der Artillerie* Max von Gallwitz	Commander of the German 2nd Army
23.	*König* Friedrich August III	King of Saxony
24.	*Generaloberst* Ludwig *Freiherr* von Falkenhausen	Commander of the German 6th Army
25.	*Generalfeldmarschall* Hermann von Eichhorn	(no command responsibility listed)[3]

Notes:

1. From the entry which reads in its entirety "His Majesty the Emperor and King," it is not clear whether this refers to *Kaiser* Wilhelm II of Prussia or *Kaiser* Franz Joseph of Austria-Hungary. In his book *Die Mecklenburg-Strelitzer Orden und Ehrenzeichen*, the author, Peter Ohm-Hieronymussen, lists Franz Joseph as the recipient, perhaps based on information found elsewhere. While in view of the award to the Sultan of Turkey which follows on the roll this conclusion seems reasonable, it should be noted that on the order bar of Wilhelm II, there is a 2nd Class Cross for Distinction in War present. It is not possible to determine which inscription this cross carried but the presumption would have to be that it was the one reading *für Tapferkeit*.

2. Von Fabeck was a *General der Infanterie* and in command of the German 1st Army when he received the *Orden Pour le Mérite* on August 23, 1915.

3. Von Eichhorn was a *Generaloberst* and in command of the German 10th Army when he received the *Orden Pour le Mérite* on August 18, 1915 and the *Orden Pour le Mérite mit Eichenlaub* on September 28, 1915.

Source:
Mecklenburgisches Landeshauptarchiv, Schwerin

Appendix L
Members of the *Fliegertruppe* Known to Have Received the Mecklenburg-Strelitz Cross for Distinction in War 2nd Class with Inscription "*Tapfer und Treu*"
(Listed in Order of Appearance on Each Roll)

No. on Roll	Rank and Name of Recipient	Unit in Which Recipient Earned the Award	Date of Award (if shown)
Roll No. 1			
113.	*Lt.* Joachim *Freiherr* von Maltzahn	*3. Garde-Rgt. zu Fuss*	
Roll No. 2			
205.	*Oblt.* Walter Wehrig	*FFl.Abt. 11*	May 10, 1915
211.	*Hptm.* Hellmuth Wilberg	*FFl.Abt. 11*	May 10, 1915
212.	*Oblt.* Wulff von Steinwehr	*FFl.Abt. 11*	May 10, 1915
213.	*Gefr.* — Sommer	*FFl.Abt. 11*	May 10, 1915
Roll No. 3			
471.	*Oblt.* Karl Schwab	*AFA 223*	
758.	*Generalleutnant* Ernst von Hoeppner	*Kogenluft*	
759.	*Oblt.* Eltze	*Kogenluft*	
760.	*Major* Wilhelm Siegert	*Idflieg*	
762.	*Lt.* Otto Reinhardt	*in der Fliegertruppe*	
763.	(no rank) Hellmut Michael	*Riesen Flugzeug Ers-Abt.*	
Roll No. 4			
777.	*Oblt.* Kurt *Freiherr* von der Goltz	*FFl.Abt. 28*	August 16, 1915
1671.	*Lt.* Fritz Witte	*FFl.Abt. 44*	June 16, 1916
1898.	*Vzfw.* Ernst Schildein	*FFl.Abt. 34*	
1968.	*Gefr.* Carl Otto	*FFl.Abt. 30*	
2014.	*Offz.-Stv.* Friedrich Matthies	*Kasta 28, Kagohl 5*	
2204.	*Lt.* Rudolf Hagemeister	*AFA 206*	
2436.	*Wachtmstr.* Wilhelm Gebert	*AFA 229*	
2844.	*Rittm.* Egon Weinschenk	*Fl.Abt. 26*	April 24, 1917
2845.	*Lt.* Joachim Kortüm	*in der Fliegertruppe*	April 24, 1917
3309.	*Flieger* Ernst Schflssler	*Fl.Abt. 38*	July 12, 1917
3811.	*Werkmstr.* Hermann Schiebe	*II. See Fl.Abt.*	September 20, 1917
4927.	*Unteroffz.* Adolf Rolff	*Fl.Abt. (A)223*	
4928.	*Flieger* Paul Winter	*Fl.Abt. (A)223*	
5488.	*Unteroffz.* Otto Förber	*Fl.Abt. (A)275*	
5634.	*Gefr.* Wilhelm Geyer	*Fl.Abt. 30*	
5952.	*Feldwebel* Friedrich Köhn	*II. See Fl.Abt.*	
6312.	*Gefr.* Karl Utech	*Grufl 13*	

Sources:
Ferko Archive (*Feldflieger-Abteilung 11 vom 2. August 1914 bis 10. November 1916*)
Mecklenburgisches Landeshauptarchiv, Schwerin
Photographs

Appendix LI

Members of the *Fliegertruppe* Proposed for the Mecklenburg-Strelitz Cross for Distinction in War 2nd Class with Inscription "*Tapfer und Treu*" 1916-1918 and Disposition of the Proposal

(Listed in Order of Appearance on Roll No.5)

No. on Roll	Rank and Name of Person Proposed	Proposing Authority	Disposition of Proposal
131.	*Vzfw.* — Schildein	*Chef des Feldflugwesen*	Approved August 1, 1916[1]
205.	*Offz.-Stv.* — Matthies	*Chef des Feldflugwesen*	Approved August 26, 1916[2]
722.	*Oblt.* — Ahrens	*Fl.Abt. (A)258*	To File March 8, 1917
1068.	*Rittm.* — Weinschenk	*Kogenluft*	Approved April 16, 1917[3]
1068.	*Lt.* — Kortüm	*Kogenluft*	Approved April 16, 1917[4]
1521.	*Flieger* — Maas	*Armee Oberkommando 11.*	To File August 22, 1917
1521.	*Flieger* — Schtissler	*Armee Oberkommando 11.*	Approved June 14, 1917[5]
1716.	*Gefr.* — Müller	*Fl.Abt. (A)205*	Bestowal Document sent to (A)205 (undated)
3009.	(no rank) *Frhr.* von Richthofen	*Jagdgeschwader 1.*	To File September 24, 1917
3032.	*Lt.* — Arppe	*Fl.Abt. (A)284*	Bestowal Document sent to Military Department Schwerin on September 20, 1917
3170.	*Unteroffz.* — Michael	*Riesen Flugzeug Ers. Abt.*	Document not bestowed dated September 20, 1917[6]
3192.	*Kanonier* — Becker	*Kogenluft*	Approved October 19, 1917
3192.	*Lt.* — Ruthenberg	*Kogenluft*	Approved October 19, 1917
3192.	*Lt.* — Pfeiffer	*Kogenluft*	Not approved October 19, 1917
3255.	*Oblt. z. See* — Krämer	*Chef d. Marine-Kabinett*	Approved November 17, 1917
3255.	*Flgzeugmech.* Viktor Piper	*Chef d. Marine-Kabinett*	Approved November 17, 1917
3698.	*Flieger* Paul Winter	*Generalkommando d. X. Armeekorps*	Approved February 1, 1918[7]
3859.	*Vzfw.* — Matthies	*Kogenluft*	Approved February 4, 1918[8]
3886.	*Oblt.* — Ahrens	*Fl.Abt. (A)258*	To File February 4, 1918
3956.	*Kraftfahrer* — Maibauer	*Kogenluft*	Approved February 4, 1918
4029.	*Flieger* — Cyril Lundbeck	*Fliegerhallen und Zelte Abt.*	Approved June 17, 1918
4230.	(no rank) — Geyer	*Kogenluft*	Approved May 5, 1918
4230.	(no rank) — Witte	*Kogenluft*	Witte proposed for the 1st Class; Approved May 5, 1918; Bestowal Document sent to Witte.
4337.	(no rank) — Schröder	*Kogenluft*	Approved April 24, 1918
4360.	(no rank) — Förber	*Kofl 3*	Approved April 19, 1918[9]
4457.	(no rank) — Scheel	*Kogenluft*	Approved May 15, 1918
4457.	(no rank) — Schmidt	*Kogenluft*	Approved May 15, 1918
4740.	*Lt.* — Pollwitz	*Kogenluft*	Pollwitz proposed for the 1st Class; Approved August 15, 1918.
4740.	*Gefr.* — Utech	*Kogenluft*	Approved August 15, 1918[10]
6258.	*Hptm.* — Fisch	*Idflieg*	Bestowal Document sent (recipient not indicated; undated)[11]
6292.	*Lt.* Joachim Brauer	*Fl.Abt. (A)224w*	Proposal questioned on December 13, 1918[12]
6350.	*Flieger* — Hintze	*Armee Oberkommando 2.*	Disposition unclear[13]

Notes:
1. *Vzfw*. Ernst Schildein's award for service in *FFl.Abt. 34* without date appears on Roll No. 4, Appendix XL

2. *Offz.-Stv*. Friedrich Matthies' award for service in *Kagohl 5* without date appears on Roll No. 4, Appendix XL.

3. *Rittm*. Egon Weinschenk's award for service in *Fl.Abt. 26* dated April 24, 1917 appears on Roll No. 4 in Appendix XL.

4. *Lt*. Joachom Kortüm's award for service in an unnamed unit dated April 24, 1917 appears on Roll No. 4 in Appendix XL. Kortöm served as a pilot in *Fl.Abt. (A)216* from November 7, 1916 to March 21, 1917 and was assigned as a test pilot at Adlershof from March 22, 1917 to March 9, 1918.

5. *Flieger* Ernst Schuussler's award for service in *Fl.Abt. 38* dated July 12, 1917 appears on Roll No. 4 in Appendix XL.

6. Hellmut Michael's award for service in Riesen *Flugzeug Ers. Abt*. appears on Roll No. 3 in Appendix XL. No rank or date is indicated there.

7. *Flieger* Paul Winter's award for service in *Fl.Abt. (A)223* appears without date on Roll No. 4 in Appendix XL.

8. *Offz.-Stv*. Friedrich Matthies' award for service in *Kagohl 5* appears without date on Roll No. 4 in Appendix XL.

9. *Unteroffz*. Otto Förber's award for service in *Fl.Abt. (A)275* appears without date on Roll No. 4 in Appendix XL.

10. *Gefr*. Karl Utech's award for service on the staff of *Grufl 13* appears without date on Roll No. 4 in Appendix XL.

11. *Hptm*. Willy Fisch served as *1. Adjutant* at *Idflieg* from October 1, 1916 to September 24, 1917.

12. After *Lt*. Joachim Brauer's name on this roll, there is an entry reading "*Staatsangeh. - 6 Wochen 13.12.18.*" This is apparently an inquiry concerning Brauer's citizenship with six weeks after December 13, 1918 allowed for an answer. There is no indication on the roll as to the final disposition of the award.

13. There is no indication on the roll as to the final disposition of the award proposal for *Flieger* Hintze.

Sources:
Die Generale der deutschen Luftwaffe 1935-1945, Teil II, Band I und 2 Mecklenburgisches Landeshauptarchiv, Schwerin
Photographs

Appendix LII
Serving Officers in the Royal Prussian Army and the 13th (Royal Württemberg) Army Corps as of May 6, 1914 Holding the Princely Waldeck Merit Cross with Swords

Grade of the Order	Generals	Field Grade Officers[1]	Captains	1st and 2nd Lieutenants
Merit Cross 1st Class with Swords	0	0	0	0
Merit Cross 2nd Class with Swords	1	0	0	0
Officer's Cross with Swords	0	0	0	0
Merit Cross 3rd Class with Swords	0	0	0	0
Merit Cross 4th Class with Swords	0	0	3[2]	0

Notes:
Included are officers in related branches such as the Medical and Veterinarian services, the Marine infantry (*Seebatallionen*) and those in the colonies (*Ostasiatisches Marine-Detachment and Schutztruppen*) as well as officers in the reserves and militia (*Landwehr*).

1. Colonels, Lieutenant Colonels and Majors.
2. Including one in the *Schutztruppe*
3. Two field grade officers and four Captains held the old Military Merit Cross 3rd Class.

Source:
Rangliste der Königlich Preussischen Armee und des XIII. (Königlich Württembergischen) Armeekorps fur 1914.

Appendix LIII
Serving Officers in the Imperial German Navy as of February 14, 1918 Holding the Princely Waldeck Merit Cross with Swords

Grade of the Order	Admirals	Flag Officers[1]	Full Lieutenants[2]	Junior Officers[3]
Merit Cross 1st Class with Swords	1	0	0	0
Merit Cross 2nd Class with Swords	0	0	0	0
Officer's Cross with Swords	0	0	0	0
Merit Cross 3rd Class with Swords	0	0	0	0
Merit Cross 4th Class with Swords	0	0	2	1

Notes:
Included are officers in related branches such as Marine infantry, Engineering and Medical Services as well as officers in the reserve.

1. Captains, Commanders and Lieutenant Commanders
2. Lieutenants
3. Lieutenants Junior Grade, Ensigns and Cadets

Source:
Rangliste (Dienstaltersliste) der Kaiserlich Deutschen Marine für das Jahre 1918. Nach dem Stande vom 14. Februar 1918.

Appendix LIV
Serving Officers in the German Army as of April 1, 1924 Holding the Princely Waldeck Merit Cross with Swords

Grade of the Order	Generals	Field Grade Officers[1]	Captains	1st and 2nd Lieutenants
Merit Cross 1st Class with Swords	0	0	0	0
Merit Cross 2nd Class with Swords	0	0	0	0
Officer's Cross with Swords	0	0	0	0
Merit Cross 3rd Class with Swords	0	1	10	1
Merit Cross 4th Class with Swords	0	6	6	6

Note:
1. Colonels, Lieutenant Colonels and Majors

Source:
Rangliste des Deutschen Reichsheeres nach dem Stande vom 1. April 1924.

Appendix LV
Serving Officers in the German Navy as of November 20, 1926 Holding the Princely Waldeck Honor Cross with Swords

Grade of the Order	Admirals	Flag Officers[1]	Full Lieutenants[2]	Junior Officers[3]
Honor Cross 1st Class with Swords	0	0	0	0
Honor Commander Cross with Swords	0	0	0	0
Honor Cross 2nd Class with Swords	0	0	0	0
Honor Cross 3rd Class with Crown and Swords	0	0	0	0
Honor Cross 4th Class with Swords	0	4	0	0

Notes:
Included are officers in related branches such as Engineering and Medical services.

1. Captains, Commanders and Lieutenant Commanders
2. Lieutenants
3. Lieutenants Junior Grade and Ensigns

Source:
Rangliste der Deutchen Reichsmarine. Nach dem Stande vom 20. November 1926.

Appendix LVI
Awards of the Princely Waldeck Merit Cross, Honor Cross and Merit Medals with Swords, 1914-1918

	1914	1915	1916	1917	1918	Total
Merit Cross 1st Class with Swords	6	7	3	5	6	27
Merit Cross 2nd Class with Swords	1	6	3	2	8	20
Officer's Cross with Swords	2	11	2	6	2	23
Merit Cross 3rd Class with Swords	7	27	12	12	14	72
Merit Cross 4th Class with Swords	48	189	86	106	151	580
Total	**64**	**240**	**106**	**131**	**181**	**722**
Honor Cross with Swords	2	41	12	27	72	154
Gold Merit Medal with Swords	29	120	59	72	130	410
Silver Merit Medal with Swords	—	—	—	—	—	4,204

Note:
Yearly awards of the Silver Merit Medal with Swords not tabulated.

Source:
Verleihungen von militärischen Orden und Ehrenzeichen des Fürstentums Waldeck im Ersten Weltkrieg 1914-1918, Erhard Roth, Offenbach am Main, 1998

Appendix LVII
Awards of the Princely Waldeck Merit Cross, Honor Cross and Merit Medals without Swords to Military Personnel, 1914-1918

	1914	1915	1916	1917	1918	Total
Merit Cross 1st Class	0	0	1	0	1	2
Merit Cross 2nd Class	0	1	2	0	0	3
Officer's Cross	0	1	1	1	4	7
Merit Cross 3rd Class	0	1	0	2	2	5
Merit Cross 4th Class	0	1	0	6	15	22
Total	**0**	**4**	**4**	**9**	**22**	**39**
Honor Cross	0	0	3	1	1	5
Gold Merit Medal	0	0	2	2	3	7
Silver Merit Medal	0	2	8	0	4	14

Source:
Verleihungen von militärischen Orden und Ehrenzeichen des Furstentums Waldeck im Ersten Weltkrieg 1914-1918, Erhard Roth, Offenbach am Main, 1998

Appendix LVIII
Comparison of Findings of Princely Waldeck Awards with Swords, 1914-1918 Erhard Roth Study vs. Gert Efler Study vs. O'Connor Research

Award and Year		Roth Study	Efler Study	O'Connor Research
Merit Cross 1st Class with Swords				
	1914	6	6	6
	1915	7	7	7
	1916	3	4	4
	1917	5	6	6
	1918	6	4	4
	Total	**27**	**27**	**27**
Merit Cross 2nd Class with Swords				
	1914	1	3	3
	1915	6	3	3
	1916	3	3	3
	1917	2	1	1
	1918	8	9	9
	Total	**20**	**19**	**19**
Officer's Cross with Swords				
	1914	2	2	2
	1915	11	10	10
	1916	2	2	2
	1917	6	6	6
	1918	2	2	2
	Total	**23**	**22**	**22**
Merit Cross 3rd Class with Swords				
	1914	7	8	8
	1915	27	26	26
	1916	12	12	12
	1917	12	16	16
	1918	14	6	4*
	Total	**72**	**68**	**66**

* Last entry on roll is 12 March 1918

Award and Year		Roth Study	Efler Study	O'Connor Research
Merit Cross 4th Class with Swords				
	1914	48	51	49
	1915	189	186	187
	1916	86	87	88
	1917	106	132	123
	1918	151	148	116*
	Total	**580**	**604**	**563**

* Last entry on roll is 16 September 1918

Award and Year		Roth Study	Efler Study	O'Connor Research
Honor Cross with Swords				
	1914	2	2	2
	1915	41	40	40
	1916	12	12	12
	1917	27	32	21*
	1918	72	72	68
	Total	**154**	**158**	**143**

* Pages from late July and late October 1917 are missing from the roll

Award and Year		Roth Study	Efler Study	O'Connor Research
Gold Merit Medal with Swords				
	1914	29	30	30
	1915	120	121	121
	1916	59	62	62
	1917	72	82	82
	1918	130	117	118
	Total	**410**	**412**	**413**
Silver Merit Medal with Swords*				
	Total	**4,204**	**ca. 3,500**	**ca.3,520**

* Yearly awards not tabulated in Efler Study and O'Connor Research

Sources:
Roth, *Verleihungen von militärischen Orden und Ehrenzeichen des Fürstentums Waldeck im Ersten Weltkrieg, 1914-1918*, 1998
Efler, *Geschichte der Orden und Ehrenzeichen des Fürtstentums Waldeck und Pyrmont*, 1985
O'Connor, research at *Hessisches Staatsarchiv Marburg*, 1995

Appendix LIX
Known Recipients of Waldeck Awards Who Earned Them as Members of the *Fliegertruppe*, 1914-1918
(Listed in Order of Receipt)

Rank and Name of Recipient	Unit in Which Recipient Earned His Award	Date of Award
Merit Cross 3rd Class with Swords		
Oblt. Maximilian von Cossel	*FFl.Abt. 62*	October 11, 1916
Merit Cross 4th Class with Swords		
Lt. Emil Flörke	*FFl.Abt. 5*	January 20, 1916
Lt. — Müller	*Kagohl 2*	September 13, 1916
Lt. — van der Emde	*Fl.Abt. 19*	January 16, 1918
Honor Cross with Swords		
Vzfw. Rudolf Windisch	*FFl.Abt. 62*	October 11, 1916
Vzfw. Ludwig Friedewald	*Fl.Abt. (A)261*	May 7, 1918
Gold Merit Medal with Swords		
Vzfw. Ludwig Friedewald	*Fl.Abt. (A)261*	February 8, 1918
Silver Merit Medal with Swords		
Flieger Wilhelm Reuter	*in der Fliegertruppe*	November 13, 1918

Source:
Verleihungen von militärischen Orden und Ehrenzeichen des Fürstentums Waldeck im Ersten Weltkrieg 1914-1918, Erhard Roth, Offenbach am Main, 1998

Appendix LX
Known Recipients of Waldeck Awards Earned for Service Prior to Joining the *Fliegertruppe*, 1914-1918
(Listed in Order of Receipt)

Rank and Name of Recipient	Date of Award	Later Known Aviation Unit(s)	Comments
Merit Cross 4th Class with Swords			
Lt. Friedrich-Wilhelm Wichard	September 9, 1915	*FFl.Abt. 58, FFl.Abt. 16, Fl.Abt. (A)217, Fl.Abt. (A)257, Jasta 24*	Shot down and wounded in balloon attack with *Jasta 24* April 21, 1917. P.O.W.
Lt. Richard Eisenberg	October 12, 1915	*Fl.Abt. (A)206*	Shot down with *(A)206* February 10, 1918. Died of injuries March 21, 1918.
Lt. Wilhelm Schultze	October 19, 1915	*FFl.Abt. 55, Jasta 4*	Killed with *Jasta 4* on November 30, 1917
Lt. Friedrich Niedernhöfer	January 20, 1917	*in einer Flieger-Abteilung*	Survived the war.
Lt. Viktor von Pressentin (known as von Rautter)	January 20, 1917	*Jasta 59, Jasta 4*	Killed with *Jasta 4* on May 31, 1918.
Lt. Hans-Ernst Laurisch	August 13, 1917	*Fl.Abt. W254, Jasta Boelcke, Kest 4b*	Died July 31, 1918 of injuries on July 30, 1918 with *Kest 4b.*
Honor Cross with Swords			
Vzfw. Friedrich Niedernhöfer	October 12, 1915	*in einer Flieger-Abteilung*	Survived the war.
Silver Merit Medal with Swords			
Gefr. Ludwig Friedewald	June 4, 1917	*Fl.Abt. (A)261*	Survived the war.

Sources:

Ehren-Rangliste des ehemaligen Deutschen Heeres, Berlin, 1926

Unsere Luftstreitkräfte 1914-1918, Berlin, 1930

Verleihungen von militärischen Orden und Ehrenzeichen des Fürstentums Waldeck im Ersten Weltkrieg 1914-1918, Erhard Roth, Offenbach am Main, 1998

Appendix LXI
Aviation Recipients of the Bremen Hanseatic Cross as Shown on the Roll at the Staatsarchiv Bremen, 1915-1921
(Listed in Order of Receipt)

No. on Roll	Rank and Name of Recipient	Unit in Which Recinient Earned the Award	Date of Award
160	*Lt.* Werner Wieting	*FFl.Abt. 33*	December 17, 1915
283	*Hptm.* Rudolf Müller	*FEA 2*	December 28, 1915
409	*Lt.* Emil Flörke	*FFl.Abt. 25*	January 28, 1916
659	*Lt.* Eberhard Grauert	*FFl.Abt. 56*	February 8, 1916
822	*Oblt.* Wilhelm Linck	*FFl.Abt. 18*	February 15, 1916
1443	*Hilfsmann* Johannes Jacobi	*SeeFlgst. Zeebrügge*	March 17, 1916
1649	*Lt.* Albert Müller	*AFA 202*	April 4, 1916
1732	*Flieger* Julius Koch	*Versuchs u. Übungsflugpark Kraft*	April 14, 1916
1786	*Unteroffz.* Karl Denicke	*FEA 9*	April 18, 1916
2107	*Lt.* Heinrich Klatte	*FFl.Abt. 70*	May 2, 1916
2488	*Flieger* Karl Feiss	*FEA 9*	June 9, 1916
2604	*Gefr.* Georg Hunzelmann	*FFl.Abt. 42*	June 16, 1916
2643	*Vzfw.* Wilhelm Hübner	*FFl.Abt. 25*	June 20, 1916
2917	*Lt.* Andraeas Thielebeule	*FEA 5*	July 11, 1916
3345	*Flieger* Heinrich Vahlenkamp	*AFP 13*	August 11, 1916
3435	*Unteroffz.* Georg Wulf	*FFl.Abt. 40*	August 18, 1916
3510	*Lt.* Karl Pokrantz	*FFl.Abt. 54*	August 29, 1916
3884	*Lt.* Hans-Alfred Stentzler	*Mil.Fl.Schule Hamburg-Fühlsbuttel*	October 17, 1916
4628	*Lt.* Henry Becker	*II. See Fl.Abt.*	December 12, 1916
4639	*Lt.* Karl Meierdirks	*Kasta 16, Kagohl 3*	December 12, 1916
4706	*Lt.* Wilhelm Scholvin	*AFP von Strantz*	December 22, 1916
4832	*Lt. z. See* Arthur Neesen	*Seeflugzeug Kommando Warnemünde*	January 9, 1917
4967	*Lt.* Werner Güldenpfennig	*FEA 4*	January 19, 1917
5009	*Flugmaat* Wilhelm Berger	*II. See Fl.Abt.*	January 19, 1917
5180	*Vzfw.* Helmuth Struckmann	*FFl.Abt. 3*	February 13, 1917
5389	*Flieger* Wilhelm Walter	*Kasta 16, Kagohl 3*	March 2, 1917
5596	*Vzfw.* Gottlieb Sander	*Fl.Abt. (A)286b*	March 20, 1917
5712	*Obermaat* Hermann Hoffmann	*I. Mar.FFl.Abt.*	March 20, 1917
5730	*Gefr.* Reinhold Winkler	*FFl.Abt. 70*	March 20, 1917
5962	*Lt.* Christian Lahnsen	*Jasta 25*	April 3, 1917
5964	*Flieger* Heinrich Behrens	*Kofl 1*	ADril 3, 1917
5965	*Lt.* Konrad Edzard	*FFl.Abt. 68*	April 3, 1917
6410	*Gefr.* Wilhelm Flieger	*Versuchs u. Übungsflugpark West*	May 11, 1917
6411	*Lt.* Wilhelm Jaeger	*Fl.Abt. (A)249*	May 11, 1917
6533	*Vzfw.* Gustav Konitzky	*Fl.Abt. 42*	May 11, 1917
6732	*Unteroffz.* August Flohr	*Fl.Abt. (A)261*	April 3, 1917
6733	*Rittm.* Egon *Graf* von Beroldingen	*Fl.Abt. (A)261*	April 3, 1917
7112	*Flugzedgobermaat* Heinrich Evers	*II. See Fl.Abt.*	June 26, 1917
7113	*Obermatrosen* Johann Huckemeyer	*See Flgst. Flandern I*	June 26, 1917
7340	*Vzfw.* Karl Caletschky	*Fl.Abt. (A)279*	July 6, 1917
7941	*Lt.* August Stoltze	*FEA Braunschweig*	August 31, 1917
7956	*Flugobermaat* Heinrich Schmidt	*SeeFlgst. Konstanza*	August 31, 1917
7966	*Unteroffz.* August Emme	*Jasta 18*	August 31, 1917
8154	*Unteroffz.* Johann Antholn	*Fl.Abt. 30*	September 14, 1917
8164	*Flieger* Adolf Carstens	*Kagohl 1*	September 14, 1917

No. on Roll	Rank and Name of Recipient	Unit in Which Recinient Earned the Award	Date of Award
8238	*Unteroffz.* Otto Markmann	*Kofl 1*	September 14, 1917
8239	*Flieger* Wilhelm Runger	*Kofl 6*	September 14, 1917
8319	*Rittm.* Manfred *Frhr.* von Richthofen	*JG 1*	September 25, 1917
8544	*Vzfw.* Walther Goot	*Jastaschule II*	October 12, 1917
8869	*Lt.* Hans Böhning	*Jasta 36*	November 2, 1917
8870	*Vzfw.* Heinrich Knigge	*Fl.Abt. (A)253*	November 2, 1917
8871	*Flieger* Karl Wrede	*Fl.Abt. (A)223*	November 2, 1917
9045	*Unteroffz.* Ernst Röschmann	*Fl.Abt. (A)255*	November 27, 1917
9193	*Oblt. z. See* Ferdinand Rasch	*Mar. Land-Fl.Abt.*	December 6, 1917
9224	*Vzfw.* Rudolf Presuhn	*FEA 3*	December 14, 1917
9225	*Lt.* Alfons Meyer	*Fl.Abt. (A)293*	December 14, 1917
9534	*Lt.* Robert Schlömer	*Fl.Abt. (A)243*	January 11, 1918
9607	*Lt.* Gustus Röschmann	*Fl.Abt. (A)241*	January 11, 1918
9608	*Unteroffz.* Fritz Albrecht	*Fl.Abt. (A)280*	January 11, 1918
9893	*Gefr.* Hermann Lübeck	*Fl.Abt. (A)231*	February 19, 1918
9957	*Flieger* Robert Meier	*Fl.Abt. (A)244*	February 19, 1918
10065	*Unteroffz.* Harald Schwarmann	*Kofl 10*	February 19, 1918
10081	*Vzfw.* Karl Heinz	*Flieger Staffel 31*	February 19, 1918
10129	*Unteroffz.* Wilhelm Lüning	*Schusta 8*	March 1, 1918
10303	*Gefr.* Alfred Stimmper	*Fl.Abt. (A)209*	March 30. 1918
10323	*Hptm.* Ernst Nordmann	*Fl.Abt. (A)234*	March 30, 1918
10798	*Lt.* Erich Ewald	*Kofl d. Marinekorps*	April 2, 1918
10799	*Flugobermaat* Walter Schindler	*Kofl d. Seeflieger*	April 2, 1918
10800	*Flugmaat* Heinrich Blume	*Kofl d. Seeflieger*	April 2, 1918
10801	*Kapitän z. See* Linus Roehr	*Kofl d. Marinekorps*	April 2,1918
10933	*Unteroffz.* Wilhelm Düe	*Fl.Abt. 21*	April 16, 1918
10943	*Flieger* Wilhelm Harnssen	*Jagdstaffeln O.H.L. I*	April 16, 1918
10946	*Gefr.* Hermann Nullmeyer	*Fl.Abt. 27*	April 16, 1918
10947	*Flieger* Engelbart Forst	*Fl.Abt. (A)255*	April 16, 1918
11081	*Unteroffz.* Dietrich Dunker	*Jasta 27*	April 26, 1918
11088	*Flieger* Hermann Wichmann	*Fl.Abt. (A)251*	April 26, 1918
11089	*Flieger* Ernst Müller	*Fl.Abt. (A)251*	April 26, 1918
11355	*Gefr.* Gustav Tölken	*Jasta 56*	May 14, 1918
11382	*Unteroffz.* Friedrich Klemm	*Fl.Abt. (A)240*	May 14, 1918
11487	*Flieger* Robert Jahns	*Fl.Abt. 13*	May 24, 1918
11569	*Oblt.* Wilhelm Brimmer	*Idflieg*	June 4, 1918
11625	*Flieger* Paul Schilling	*Fl.Abt. 300 "Pascha"*	June 4, 1918
11632	*Flieger* Heinrich Wehselau	*Kofl 3*	June 4, 1918
11707	*Oblt.* Julius *Graf* von Schaesberg-Thannheim	*Fl.Abt. (A)274*	June 11, 1918
11731	*Gefr.* Georg Andreae	*Schusta 7*	June 11, 1918
11759	*Unteroffz.* Robert Güldner	*Jasta 38*	June 11, 1918
11957	*Lt.* Ernst Hartert	(Unit Illegible)	July 5, 1918
11986	*Vzfw.* Hermann Ewig	*Kofl "A"*	July 5, 1918
12040	*Oblt.* Hans Eggers	*Fl.Abt. (A)236*	July 5, 1918
12068	*Hptm.* Johannes Deves	*Fl.Abt. (A)243*	July 5, 1918
12105	*Lt.* Curt Vocke	*FEA 3*	July 16, 1918
12264	*Unteroffz.* Otto Diederichs	*Schlasta 37*	July 30, 1918
12268	*Oblt.* Harald Auffarth	*Jasta 29*	July 30, 1918
12709	*Flugmstr.* Georg Thünemann	*I. Mar. FFl.Abt.*	September 3, 1918
12728	*Flugmech.maat* Heinrich Ebeling	*II. See Fl.Abt.*	September 3, 1918

No. on Roll	Rank and Name of Recipient	Unit in Which Recipient Earned the Award	Date of Award
12807	*Lt.* Hermann Donandt	*SeeFlgst. Windau*	September 3, 1918
12921	*Flieger* Paul Holtmann	*Fl.Abt. (A)267*	September 27, 1918
12980	*Lt.* Friedrich Russell	*FEA 11*	September 27, 1918
13129	*Unteroffz.* Wilhelm Ahlers	*Fl.Abt. 38*	October 18, 1918
13159	*Unteroffz.* Hubert Decker	*Bosta 17, Bogohl 3*	October 18, 1918
13160	*Flieger* Fritz Voll	*Kofl 1*	October 18, 1918
13311	*Sergeant* Otto Nachtigall	*Riesen-Flugzeug-Ersatz-Abt. Cöln*	October 29, 1918
13416	*Unteroffz.* Georg Boerjes	*Jasta 39*	November 5, 1918
13417	*Flieger* Heinrich Wiedemann	*Jasta 5*	November 5, 1918
13418	*Unteroffz.* Louis Ebeling	*FEA 7*	November 5, 1918
13610	*Lt.* Erich Karwath	*Fl.Abt. (A)222*	January 3, 1919
13861	*Gefr.* Wilhelm Hasenbein	*Jasta 52*	January 10, 1919
13880	*Gefr.* Heinrich Bädecker	*Jasta 11*	January 10, 1919
14044	*Flieger* Georg Helmken	*Kofl 3*	April 15, 1919
14229	*Vzfw.* Heinrich Bätjer	*Fl.Abt. 404*	July 9, 1919
14385	*Lt.* Carl Mohrs	*FEA 255*	October 15, 1919
14490	*Vzfw.* Johann Lorenz	*Fl.Abt. (A)230*	July 15, 1920
14536	*Lt.* Otto Schultz	*I. Mar. FFl.Abt.*	July 15, 1920
14575	*Unteroffz.* Erich Thornählen	*Fl.Abt. (A)284*	July 15, 1920
14682	*Gefr.* Heinrich Lüders	*Schusta 5*	November 20, 1920
14844	*Flieger* Ferdinand Girod	*Flgst. St. Stefano (Turkei)*	July 20, 1921

Source:
Staatsarchiv Bremen

Appendix LXII
Other Known Recipients of the Bremen Hanseatic Cross Who Were Members of Aviation Contingents
(Listed Alphabetically)

Rank and Name of Recipient	Unit in Which Recipient Earned the Award (if known)	Aviation Units in Which Recipient Served	Date of Award (if known)
Generalleutnant Walter von Eberhard	*Idflieg*		
Lt. Hans Joachim von Hippel	*Fl.Abt. 37, Jasta 5,*	*Jasta 71*	
Generalleutnant Ernst von Hoepper	*Chef d. Generalstabs d. 3. Armee*		November 3, 1915
Lt. Georg Meyer	*Inf.-Rgt. Nr. 75.*	*FFl.Abt. 69, Fl.Abt. (A)253, Jasta 22, Jasta 7, Jasta 37*	
Oblt. Albert Müller-Kahle	*AFA 202*	*AFA 202, FFl.Abt. 47, Fl.Abt. (A)215, Fl.Abt. 6*	March 10, 1916
Lt. Friedrich Noltenius	*FAR 13.*	*Fl.Abt. W234, Jasta 27, Jasta 6, Jasta 11*	March 24, 1916
Lt. Julius Schulte-Frohlinde	*Ers. Pion.-Rgt. Nr. 9.*	*Jasta 41, Jasta 11*	March 14, 1916
Oberstlt. Wilhelm Siegert	*Idflieg*	*BAO, Stofl 1, Idflieg*	January 25, 1918
Lt. Josef Veltjens		*FFl.Abt. 23, Jasta 14, Jasta 18, Jasta 15*	

Sources:
Bundesarchiv-Militärarchiv, Freiburg im Breisgau
Ferko Archive
Siegert Letter
Senat der Freien und Hansestadt Hamburg Staatsarchiv
Staatsarchiv Bremen
Photographs

Appendix LXIII
Known Recipients of the Hamburg Hanseatic Cross Who Were Members of Aviation Contingents
(Listed Alphabetically)
(P = Date of Proposal, not Date of Award)

Rarik and Name of Recipient	Aviation Contingents in Which Recipient Served	Date of Award (if known)
Hptm. Karl Albrecht	*Fl.Abt. (A)205*	September 13, 1917
Offz.-Stv. Karl Angermeyer	*I. Mar. Feldjasta, II. Mar. Feldjasta*	
Vzflgmstr. Hans Antonius	*II. See Fl.Abt., I. See Fl.Abt.*	July 20, 1918
Oblt. Harald Auffarth	*FFl.Abt. 27, Fl.Abt. (A)266, Jasta 18, Jasta 29*	October 14, 1918
Hptm. Erwin Barends	*FFl.Abt. 20*	
Oblt. Hans Berr	*FFl.Abt. 60, FS Avillers, KEK Ost (Avillers), Jasta 5*	
Flgmaat — Blume	*See Flgst. Flandern I*	July 21, 1918 (P)
Hptm. Eberhard Bohnstedt	*FFl.Abt. 23*	
Lt. Julius Buckler	*AFA 209, Jasta 17*	
Lt. Wolfgang von Chamier-Glisczinski	*Fl.Abt. 12, Fl.Abt. 13*	
Kptlt. Friedrich Christiansen	*See Fl.Abt. Holtenau, See Flgst. Zeebrügge, II. See Fl.Abt.*	May 3, 1916 (P)
Vzfw. Ernst Clausnitzer	*Jasta 4*	
Oblt. Waldemar von Dazur	*Jasta 20*	
Lt. Paul Degetau	*FFl.Abt. 11*	
Lt. Paul Deichmann	*Fl.Abt. 8*	
Lt. z. See Heinrich Droege	*1. See Fl.Abt., See Flgst. Libau, See Fgst. Windau, See Flg. Versuchs Komm.*	
Lt. Wilhelm Drückhammer	*Mar. Küst. Fl.Abt. Flandern*	February 17, 1918[1]
Generalleutnant Walter von Eberhardt	*Idflieg*	
Lt. Otto Eckstein	*FFl.Abt. 24, FFl.Abt. 62, Fl.Abt. (A)264, Idflieg*	
Lt. Hans Engel	*FFl.Abt. 11*	
Oblt. Martin Fiebig	*KG 3/BG 3*	
Hptm. Max Fischinger	*FEA 5*	January 10, 1916
Lt. Wilhelm Frankl	*FFl.Abt. 40, KEK Vaux, FFl.Abt. 23, Jasta 4*	May 10, 1915
Vzf lgmstr. Hartmut Frosch	*See Flgst. Zeebrügge*	September 16, 1917
Lt. Heinrich Geigl	*KS 36/KG 6, Jasta 34b, Jasta 16b*	June 4, 1917
Lt. Otto Gienapp	*Mar. Land FliAbt. Johannisthal*	
Lt. Walter Göttsch	*FFl.Abt. 33, Jasta 8, Jasta 19*	
Oblt. z. See Eduard Hahn-Echenagucia	*I. Mar. FFl.Abt., II. Mar. FFl.Abt., See Flgst. Zeebragge, II. See Fl.Abt., Mar. Feldjasta*	
Lt. Walter Hahn	*FFl.Abt. 11*	
Oblt. Friedrich-Carl Hanesse	*Fl.Abt. (A)225, Schusta 9, Schlasta 2, Schlachtgr. 3*	
Lt. Bertram Heinrich	*I. Mar. Land Fl.Abt., I. Mar. Feldjasta*	February 19, 1918
Kpt. z. See Hans Herr	*Mar. Luftfahrwesen d. Mar.Korps*	May 7, 1917 (P)
Lt. Carl Heinrich Hertz	*Jasta 28, Jasta 4, Jasta 59*	
Lt. Rüdiger von Heyking	*KG 2*	
Generalleutnant Ernst von Hoeppner	*Kogenluft*	November 5, 1915
Lt. Otto Hunzinger	*Jasta "Boelcke"*	
Oblt. Max Immelmann	*FFl.Abt. 10, FFl.Abt. 62, KEK III*	
Lt. Josef Jacobs	*FFl.Abt. 11, KEK West, Jasta 22, Jasta 7*	
Flgmaat — Jany	*See Flgst. Flandern I*	July 21, 1918 (P)
Oblt. Erwin Jollasse	*FFl.Abt. 32, Fl.Abt. (A)263, Kofl 7*	
Lt. Friedrich Jordan	*II. Mar. Fl.Abt., II. See Fl.Abt.*	November 18, 1916 (P)
Lt. Arthur Jost	*I. Mar. Land Fl.Abt., Mar. Land Fl.Abt. Johannisthal*	

Rarik and Name of Recipient	Aviation Contingents in Which Recipient Served	Date of Award (if known)
Lt. z. See Erich Killinger	*Mar. Land Fl.Abt. Johannisthal, See Flgst. Putzig, See Flgst. Libau, See Flgst. Zeebragge, See Flgst. Ostende*	
Oblt. Otto Kissenberth	*FFl.Abt. 9b, Jasta 16b, Jasta 23b*	
Hptm. Werner Klepke	*FFl.Abt. 5, FFl.Abt. 18, FFl.Abt. 45, Fl.Abt. (A)259, Grufl 6*	
Kptlt. Hubert-Waldemar Klein	*See Flgst. Helgoland, See Flgst. Borkum, I. See Fl.Abt., See Flgst. Libau*	
Hptm. Normand Knackfuss	*FEA 1, Fl.Abt. (A)252*	December 10, 1917
Oblt. z. See Erwin Koch	*See Flgst. Helgoland, See Flgst. Wilhelmshavn, Land Flgst Zeebrügge*	July 21, 1918 (P)
Lt. Friedrich Leesemann	*Fl.Abt. (A)230, Fl.Abt. 11, Jagdgr. 3*	
Lt. Adalbert Lehner	*Mar. Land Fl.Abt., Land Fl.Abt. Nordholz*	
Unteroffz. Emil Liebert	*Jasta 30*	
Lt. Ludwig Liebig	*See Flgst. Borkum, See Flgst. Norderney, See Flgst. List*	
Lt. z. See Theodor Lodemann	*1. Mar. Fl.Abt., Seeflgst. Angernsee, See Flgst. Zeebrügge*	July 4, 1918[2]
Lt. Bruno Majewski	*I. Mar. FFl.Abt., Mar. Luftfahrwesen, Grufl Küste, Mar. Sonderstaffel, Mar. Schlasta II.*	May 8. 1916
Lt. Hans Mantel	*II. Mar. FFl.Abt., Fl. Verband Ostende*	
Lt. Kurt Monnington	*Jasta 12, FFl.Abt. 67, Jasta 22, Jasta 15, Jasta 18*	June 27, 1916
Lt. Max *Ritter* von Mulzer	*FFl.Abt. 4b, FFl.Abt. 5b, FFl.Abt. 62, FFl.Abt. 32, KEK Nord, KEK 3*	
Lt. Gustav Nolte	*Jasta 18, Jasta 36*	
Flgmstr. — Ochs	*Schusta 1*	
Lt. Theo Osterkamp	*Land Flgst. Wilhemshavn, II. Mar. Land Fl.Abt., I. Mar. Land Fl.Abt., I. Mar. Feldjasta*	
Hptm. Hermann Palmer	*FFl.Abt. 3, FFl.Abt. 23, Jasta 29, Grufl 2*	
Oblt. Heinrich Plambeck	*Mar. FFl.Abt., Mar. Land Fl.Abt., 1. See Fl.Abt., Stab Mar. Flugchef*	
Kptlt. Ganther Plüschow	*Mar. Flgst. Tsingtau, See Flgst. Libau, See Flgst. Holtenau, Mar. Flgst. Zeebrügge, Mar. Flgst. Seddin*	
Lt. Otto Praesent	*I. Mar. FFl.Abt., Mar. Land Fl.Abt., See Flgst. Xanthi*	May 14, 1917 (P)
Lt. Hans Prüter	*See Flgst. Zeebrügge, See Flgst. Ostende, Mar. Land Fl.Abt. Johannisthal*	February 17, 1918
Lt. August Raben	*Schusta 7, Jasta 36, Jasta 39, Jasta 15, Jasta 18*	
Lt. Leopold von Raffay	*Jasta 34, Jasta 6*	
Lt. Hans von Raussendorf	*II. Mar. FFl.Abt., Mar. Land Fl.Abt.*	May 8. 1918
Oblt. Lothar *Freiherr* von Richthofen	*KG 4, Jasta 11*	
Rittm. Manfred *Freiherr* von Richthofen	*FFl.Abt. 69, BAO, KG 2, Jasta 2, Jasta 11, JG 1*	
Lt. Theodor Rumpel	*Fl.Abt. (A)280, Jasta 26, Jasta 16b, Jasta 23b*	
Lt. Richard Runge	*Jasta 18*	
Lt. z. See Gotthard Sachsenberg	*II. Mar. FFl.Abt., See Flgst. Zeebrügge, Mar. JG*	
Lt. Max Schick	*Jasta 76b*	
Lt. Carl-August von Schoenebeck	*Fl.Abt. (A)203, Jasta 11, Jasta 59, Jasta 33*	
Lt. Wilhelm Paul Schreiber	*Fl.Abt. (A)221*	March 18, 1918
Lt. Walter Schwabedissen	*FFl.Abt. 11*	
Vzflgmstr. Ernst Schwarz	*Seeflgst. Flandern I*	October 6, 1917
Lt. Hans Schwarz	*Jasta 75*	
Oblt. Ernst Sieverts	*FFl.Abt. 62*	
Obermaat Georg Spengler	*I. Mar. FFl.Abt.*	February 19, 1918
Lt. Ernst Steinadler	*Mar. Luftfahrwesen, I. Mar. FFl.Abt., Mar. Kaste Fl.Abt.*	
Lt. Georg Stolzenbach	*I. See Fl.Abt., Seeflgst. Libau, See Flgst. Windau*	
Major Hans Streccius	*FFl.Abt. 13, KG 2, Kofl 5 Flgmech. Truelsen Mar. Küste Fl.Abt. III*	February 17, 1918
Kptlt. Bernhard von Tschirschky und Boegendorff	*Mar. Fl.Abt., II. See Fl. Abt., Kofl d. See Fl. b. Mar.Korps*	September 16, 1917
Lt. Otto Tuercke	*Mar. Land Fl.Abt.*	March 27, 1918

Rarik and Name of Recipient	Aviation Contingents in Which Recipient Served	Date of Award (if known)
Lt. Ernst Udet	*AFA 206, FFl.Abt. 68, KEK Habsheim, Jasta 15, Jasta 37, Jasta 11, Jasta 4*	
Hptm. Richard Walter	*KS 13/KG 3, BS 13/BG 3*	
Lt. Karl Wendt	*II. Mar. FFl.Abt., Mar. Land Fl.Abt., I. See Fl.Abt.*	
Lt. Bernhard Wladicka	*II. See Fl.Abt.*	September 16, 1917
Lt. Jakob Wolff	*KEA 1, FFl.Abt. 34, FFl.Abt. 71, FS Metz, KS West, Jasta 17*	
Flgmech. Obergast	*Zander Seefrosta*	May 8, 1916
Hptm. Martin Zander	*FFl.Abt. 9, KG 1, Jasta 1*	

Notes:
1. Drückhammer died in Blankenberg on January 29, 1918. His cross was mailed to his father with a letter of condolence on April 15, 1918.
2. Lodemann was killed near Ypres on July 4, 1918, the same day his award was approved.

Sources:
Bundesarchiv-Kriegsarchiv, Frieburg im Breisgau
Ehrenrangliste der Kaiserlich Deutschen Marine 1914-1918
Ferko Archive
Rangliste (Dienstaltersliste) der Kaiserlich Deutschen Marine für das Jahr 1916. und 1918.
Senat der Freien und Hansestadt Hamburg Staatsarchiv
Photographs

Appendix LXIV
Aviation Recipients of the Lübeck Hanseatic Cross as Shown on the Roll at the *Hansestadt Lübeck Archiv*, 1915-1918
(Listed in Order of Receipt)

No. on Roll	Rank and Name of Recipient	Unit in Which Recipient Earned the Award	Date of Award
207.	*Lt.* Joachim von Borcke	*FEA 5*	November 10, 1915
55.	*Flieger* — Busche	*FFl.Abt. 46*	November 20, 1915
—	*Flieger* H.K. Chiffard	*AFP 13*	December 22, 1915
292.	*Unteroffz.* Willi Rohweder	*FFl.Abt. 66*	December 22, 1915
357.	*Flieger* Wilhelm Peter	*AFP 13*	December 22, 1915
536.	*Lt.* Antonius Müller	*FFl.Abt. 21*	January 12, 1916
564.	*Flieger* Max Drether	*FFl.Abt. 61*	February 19, 1916
564.	*Flieger* Adolf Jessen	*FFl.Abt. 61*	February 19, 1916
564.	*Unteroffz.* Erich Sadowski	*FFl.Abt. 61*	February 19, 1916
705.	*Unteroffz.* Siegmund Gerdes	*FFl.Abt. 50*	March 8, 1916
728.	*Lt.* Olaf Bergengrün	*FFl.Abt. 24*	March 8, 1916
800.	*Korv. Kpt.* Friedrich Brehmer	*II. See Fl.Abt.*	March 22, 1916
943.	*Lt.* Maximilan von Cossel	*FFl.Abt. 62*	April 12, 1916
943.	*Oblt.* Ernst von Gosner	*FFl.Abt. 62*	April 12, 1916
943.	*Vzfw.* Alois Müller	*FFl.Abt. 62*	April 12, 1916
—	*Oblt.* — Behrenz	*Armee Oberkommando 3*	May 24, 1916
—	*Hptm.* — Fach	*FFl.Abt. 9*	November 25, 1916
354.	*Unteroffz.* Hans Möller	*FEA 2*	January 10, 1917
2260.	*Obermatrosen* Carl Paetan	*I. See Fl.Abt.*	January 10, 1917
2595.	*Oblt.* Fritz Bollbrugge	*FFl.Abt. 13*	March 3, 1917
2972.	*Unteroffz.* G.H. Brattström	*AFP 2*	May 9, 1917
2920.	*Unteroffz.* Wilhelm Kähler	*Fl.Abt. (A)217*	May 16, 1917
—	*Fluganwärter* Josef Gulembiewsky	*See FlgSt. Zeebrügge*	June 6, 1917
—	*Lt.* Wilhelm Herrenknecht	*See FlgSt. Zeebrügge*	June 6, 1917
—	*Flugmaat* Karl Huthmacher	*See FlgSt. Zeebrügge*	June 6, 1917
—	*Lt. z. See* Erich Killinger	*See FlgSt. Zeebrügge*	June 6, 1917
—	*Flugmstr.* Wilhelm Klissendorf	*See FlgSt. Zeebrügge*	June 6, 1917
—	*Lt. z. See* Hans Rolshoven	*See FlgSt. Zeebrügge*	June 6, 1917
—	*Kptlt.*, Bernhard von Tschirschky und Boegendorff	*See FlgSt. Zeebrügge*	June 6, 1917
3683	*Flieger* Fritz Löper	*Schusta 21*	August 29, 1917
3802	*Lt.* Reinhard Grosse	*Fl.Abt. (A)264*	September 15, 1917
3929	*Rittm.* Manfred *Frhr.* von Richthofen	*JG 1*	September 22, 1917
4150	*Flieger* Hans Lembecke	*Fl.Abt. (A)203*	November 17, 1917
—	*Oblt.* — *Graf* von Bernstorff	*in einer Riesenflgzg. Abt.*	December 15, 1917
4545.	*Unteroffz.* Friedrich Lübcke	*Fl.Abt. (A)243*	January 2, 1918
4442.	*Gefr.* Alfons Hildebrandt	*Fl.Abt. 5*	February 2, 1918
4846.	*Offz.Stv.* Carl Schmidt	*I. See Fl.Abt.*	February 2, 1918
4442.	*Flieger* — Müller	*Kofl 5*	March 6, 1918
4442.	*Lt.* — Schwarzkopf	*Fl.Abt. 5*	March 6, 1918
5219.	*Lt.* Alexander Stein	*SMS Wolf*	March 19, 1918
—	*Flgmstr.* Paul Fabeck	*SMS Wolf*	March 20, 1918
5505.	*Lt.* Felix	*See FlgSt. Ostende*	June 5, 1918
5505.	*Lt. z. See* Max Reinhard	*I. See Fl.Abt.*	June 5, 1918
—	*Lt.* Hans von Buttlar	*Jasta 15*	June 26, 1918

No. on Roll	Rank and Name of Recipient	Unit in Which Recipient Earned the Award	Date of Award
5639.	*Gefr.* Fritz Härtig	*Fl.Abt. (A)267*	July 17, 1918
—	*Lt.* Ernst Henchel	*Fl.Schule Hannover*	August 24, 1918
—	*Lt.* Ernst Udet	*Führer einer Jasta*[1]	August 24, 1918
705.	*Lt. z. See* Karl Geissler	*I. See Fl.Abt.*	August 28, 1918
5505.	*Flgmaat* Hans Bachner	*I. See Fl.Abt.*	August 28, 1918
5505.	*Flganwärter* Aufwarth Frank	*I. See Fl.Abt.*	August 28, 1918
5505.	*Flgobermaat* Alfred Gruber	*I. See Fl.Abt.*	August 28, 1918
5505.	*Lt.* Karl Schönhagen	*I. See Fl.Abt.*	August 28, 1918
5505.	*Lt.* Hugo Stangen	*I. See Fl.Abt.*	August 28, 1918
5970.	*Freg.Kpt.* Hermann Buchholz	*I. See Fl.Abt.*	August 28, 1918
5970.	*Oblt. z. See* Karl Holzapfel	*I. See Fl.Abt.*	August 28, 1918
5970.	*Flgmstr.* Wolf Prigge	*I. See Fl.Abt.*	August 28, 1918
5970.	*Lt. z. See* Otto Regendanz	*I. See Fl.Abt.*	August 28, 1918
5970.	*Lt. z. See* — Schmidt	*I. See Fl.Abt.*	August 28, 1918
—	*Hptm.* — Beckers	*FEA 7*	Septemner 10, 1918
6047.	*Gefr.* Wilhelm Hamman	*Fl.Abt. 303*	September 21, 1918
5275.	*Flieger* August Benn	*Fl.Abt. 42*	September 25, 1918
6354.	*Lt.* Julius Greifenhagen	*Fl.Abt. (A)275*	October 2, 1918
6354.	*Lt.* Lorenz Lünz	*Fl.Abt. (A)273*	October 2, 1918
6400.	*Lt.* — Danker	*FEA 5*	October 9, 1918
6400.	*Rittm.* — von Keller	*FEA 5*	October 9, 1918
6630.	*Werkmstr.* Silvester Adamczak	*Fl.Abt. 22*	November 20, 1918
6630.	*Vzfw.* Wolf Elsner	*Fl.Abt. 22*	November 20, 1918
6582.	*Flieger* Hans Langhoff	*Grufl 2*	November 20, 1918

Note:
1. Udet was assigned to *Jasta 4* as its leader on May 22, 1918 and confirmed in the position on June 3, 1918. He would be promoted *Oberleutnant* on September 11, 1918.

Source:
Hansestadt Lübeck Archiv

Appendix LXV
Other Known Recipients of the Lübeck Hanseatic Cross Who Were Members of Aviation Contingents
(Listed Alphabetically)

Rank and Name of Recipient	Unit in Which Recipient Earned the Award (if known)	Aviation Units in Which Recipient Served	Date of Award (if known)
Oblt. Walter Ewers		*Fl.Abt. 26, Jasta 8, Jasta 12, Jasta 77b*	February 26, 1916
Lt. Hermann Frommherz	*FEA 5 (Fl.Schule Lübeck)*	*KS 20/KG 4, KS 20/KG 1, Jasta "Boelcke," Jasta 27*	December 24, 1917
Oblt. Heinrich Lorenz		*KG 1, Jasta 19, Jasta 1, Jasta 33*	
Lt. Kurt Polborn		*Luftfahrwesen d. Mar.Korps, I. See Fl.Abt.*	
Lt. Georg Rieke		*KG 4*	

Sources:
Bundesarchiv-Kriegsarchiv, Freiburg im Breisgau
Ehrenrangliste der Kaiserlich Deutschen Marine 1914-1918
Generallandesarchiv, Karlsruhe
Rangliste (Dienstaltersliste) der Kaiserlich Deutschen Marine für das Jahr 1916.

SELECTED BIBLIOGRAPHY

Official Documents:

Flieger-Formationen, Teil 10, Luftstreitkräfte, Abschnitt B., Berlin, 1918

Militär-Wochenblatt, veröffenliche preussische Ordens-Verleihung 1914-1918

Nachrichtenblatt der Luftstreitkräfte, February 18, 1917 - October 22, 1918

Books and Periodicals:

Albedyll, Krister Reinhold George Ernst von, *Gedenkblätter der Königen-Kürassiers*, Pasewalk, 1919

Bodenschatz, Karl, *Hunting with Richthofen* (translation of *Jagd in Flanderns Himmel* and annotations by Jan Hayzlett), London, 1996

—. *Jagd in Flanderns Himmel*, Munich, 1935

Bowen, E.V., *The Prussian and German Iron Cross*, Colchester, 1986

Bowyer, Chaz, *Royal Flying Corps Communiques 1917-1918*, London, 1998

Bruce, J.M., *The Aeroplanes of the Royal Flying Corps (Military Wing)*, London 1982

Carr, William, *A History of Germany 1815-1985*, 3rd Edition, New York, 1987

Cole, Christopher, *Royal Air Force Communiques 1918*, London 1990

—. *Royal Flying Corps Communiques 1915-1916*, London 1990

Deiss, F.W., *Die Hessen im Weltkrieg 1914-1918*, Charlottenburg, 1928

Eberhardt, Walter von, *Unsere Luftstreitkräfte 1914-1918*, Berlin, 1940

Efler, Gert, *Geschichte der Orden und Ehrenzeichen des Fürstentums Waldeck und Pyrmont*, Alsfeld, 1984

Ferko, A.E., *Fliegertruppe 1914-1918*, Salem, 1980

—. *Fliegertruppe 1914-1918 Nr. 2*, Salem, 1987

Fischer, Bruno, *Ehrenbuch des ordens vom Militar-Verdienst-Kreuz e.V.*, Berlin, 1960

Franks, Norman, *Who Downed the Aces in WW I*, London, 1996

Franks, Norman L.R., Bailey, Frank W. and Duiven, Rick, *Casualties of the German Air Service*, London, 1999

—. *The Jasta War Chronology*, London, 1998

Franks, Norman L.R., Bailey, Frank W. and Guest, Russell, *Above the Lines*, London, 1993

—. *Bloody April ... Black September*, London, 1995

Franks, Norman, Guest, Russell and Alegi, Gregory, *Above the War Fronts*, London, 1997

Geile, Willi, *Im Marineverordnungsblatt*, Hagen, 1989

—. *Im Militär-Wochenblatt April 1914 bis November 1918*, Hagen, 1985

Gilbert, Martin, *First World War Atlas*, London, 1970

Gray, Peter and Thetford, Owen, *German Aircraft of the First World War*, London, 1978

Gritzner, Maximilian, *Handbuch der Ritter-und Verdienstorden*, Graz, 1962

Grosz, Peter M. and Haddow, G.W., *The German Giants*, London, 1962, 1969 and 1988 Editions

Grosz, Peter M., *Fokker Fighters D.I-IV*, Berkhamsted, 1999

—. Windsock Datafile, Berkhamsted, 1986-2000 (Odd Numbers 1 - 84)

Hamelman, William E., *The History of the Prussian Pour le Mérite Order, 1888-1918*, Dallas, 1985

Hayward, J.B., *The Times Diary and Index of the War, 1914-1918*, London, 1985

Henshaw, Trevor, *The Sky Their Battlefield*, London, 1995

Hessenthal, Dr. Waldemar Hesse Edlen von and Schreiber, Georg, *Die Ehrenzeichen des Deutsches Rei*ches, Berlin, 1940

Hildebrand, Karl Friedrich, *Die Generale der deutschen Luftwaffe 1935-1945, Band I, II, III*, Osnabrück, 1990

Imrie, Alex, *Fokker Fighters of World War One*, London, 1986

—. *German Air Aces of World War One*, Poole, 1987

—. *German Bombers of World War One*, London, 1990

—. *German Fighter Units 1914-May 1917* and *German Fighter Units June 1917-1918*, London, 1978

—. *German Naval Air Service*, London, 1989

—. *Pictorial History of the German Army Air Service*, Chicago, 1973

—. *The Fokker Triplane*, London, 1992

Jackson, Robert, *Air War Flanders 1918*, Shrewsbury, 1998

Kastner, Reinhard, *Bayerische Flieger im Hochgebirge*, Gröbenzell, 1998

Kilduff, Peter, *Germany's First Air Force 1914-1918*, London 1991

—. *Over the Battlefronts*, London, 1996

—. *Richthofen - Beyond the Legend of the Red Baron*, London, 1993

— *The Illustrated Red Baron*, London, 1999

—. *The Red Baron Combat Wing*, London, 1997

Klietmann, Dr. K.-G., *Pour le Mérite und Tapferkeitsmedaille*, Berlin, 1966

Link, Eva and Gauggel, Heinz, *Fürstlich flohenzollernsche Orden und Ehrenzeichen*, Fridingen, 1985

Ludvigsen, Eric C., *The Military Merit Cross of the Principality of Waldeck, The Medal Collector*, Volume 26, Number 4, April 1975

Mittler, E.S., *Ehren Rangliste des ehemaligan Deutsches Heeres*, Berlin, 1926

—. *Rangliste des activen Dienstandes der königlich Preussischen Armee und des XIII. (königlich Württembergischen) Armeekorps*, Berlin, 1914

—. *Rangliste des Deutschen Reichheeres 1924-1932*, Berlin 1924-1932

—. *Rangliste (Dienstaltersliste) der Kaiserlich Deutschen Marine für das Jahr 1916 und für das Jahr 1918*, Berlin, 1916 and 1918

Moller, Hanns, *Geschichte Der Ritter Des Ordens Pour le Mérite Im Weltkrieg, Band I. und II*, Berlin, 1935

Neumann, Georg P., *In der Luft unbesiegt*, Munich, 1923

Nimmergut, Jörg, *Bänderkatalog Orden & Ehrenzeichen Deutschland 1800-1945*, Munich, 1991

—. *Deutsche Orden und Ehrenzeichen bis 1945, Anhalt-Hohenzollern and Limburg-Reuss*, Munich, 1997 and Sachsen-Württemberg, Munich, 1999

—. *Deutschland-Katalog 1991/92 Orden und Ehrenzeichen 1800-1945*, Munich, 1991

O'Connor, Neal W., *Aviation Awards of Imperial Germany in World War I and the Men Who Earned Them, Volume I, II, III, IV, V and VI*, Princeton, 1988-1999

Ohm-Hieronymussen, Peter, *Die Mecklenburg-Strelitzer Orden und Ehrenzeichen*, Copenhagen, 2000

Gphaus, Franz-Josef, *Das Preussische Goldene Militär-Verdienst-Kreuz*, Berlin, 1936

Patzwall, Klaus D., *Das Preussische Goldene Militär-Verdienst-Kreuz*, Band 2, 1986

Pieters, Walter, M., *Above Flanders Fields*, London, 1998

Pivka, Otto von, *Brunswick Troops 1809-15*, London, 1985

—. *The Black Brunswickers*, Reading, 1973

Pivka, Otto von and Fosten, Bryan, *Napoleon's German Allies: Hesse*, London, 1982

Porret, D., *Les AS francaise de la Grande Guerre*, Tome I, Tome II, Bevaix, 1978

Purves, Alec A., *The Medals, Decorations & Orders of the Great War 1914-1918*, London, 1975

Reckewell, Roger and Fischer, Jens, *Orden, Ehrenzeichen- und Abzeichen des Herzogtums Braunschweig-Lüneburg von 1809 bis 1908*, Brunswick, 1987

Rimell, Raymond L., *The German Army Air Service in World War One*, London, 1985

Roth, Erhard, *Verleihungen von militärischen Orden und Ehrenzeichen des Fürstentums Waldeck im Ersten Weltkrieg 1914-1918*, Offenbach, 1998

Sauer, Werner, *Der Königlich Hausorden von Hohenzollern*, Steinau an der Strasse, 1979

Shores, Christopher, Franks, Norman and Guest, Russell, *Above the Trenches*, London, 1990

—. *Above the Trenches Supplement*, London, 1996

Sobbe, Freiherr von, *Geschichte des Braunschweigisches Infanterie-Regiment Nr. 92. im Weltkriege 1914-1918*, Berlin, 1929

Stoelzel, Alfred, *Ehrenrangliste der Kaiserlich Deutschen Marine 1914-18*, Berlin, 1930

Supf, Peter, *Das Buch der deutschen Fluggeschichte*, Stuttgart, 1958

Treadwell, Terry C. and Wood, Alan C., *German Knights of the Air*, London, 1997

Ursinus, Oskar, *Flugsport*, Frankfurt am Main, January 4, 1914-December 1919

Van Wyngarden, Greg, *Von Richthofen's Flying Circus*, Berkhamsted, 1994

Various Authors

Cross & Cockade International (formerly *Cross & Cockade of Great Britain*), Volumes 1 through 32

Cross & Cockade Journal (U.S.), Volumes 1 through 26

Deutsches Soldatenjahrbuch, for the years 1957 through 1999

Hohenzollernisches Gedenkbuch 1914-1918, Hechingen, 1927

History of the Two Hundred and-Fifty-One Divisions of the German Army Which Participated in the War (1914-1918), London, 1989

Voigt, Günther, *Deutschlands Heere bis 1918*, Osnabrück, 1982

Westermann, Georg, *Die Braunschweiger Husaren im Weltkriege 1914/1918*, Oldenburg, 1922

Werner, Johannes, *Briefe Eines Deutschen Kampffliegers An Ein Junges Mädschen*, Leipzig, 1930

Williamson, H.J., *The Roll of Honour Royal Flying Corps and Royal Air Force for the Great War 1914-18*, Dallington, 1992

Zuerl, Walter, *Pour le Mérite-Flieger im Weltkrieg*, Munich, 1938

GLOSSARY OF TERMS

Formations and Organizations

Abteilung: Detachment or unit (but in English often translated as "squadron")

Armee-Flug-Park (AFP): Army aviation supply depot

Armeestaffel der Oberkommando (AOK): Army section or flight of the High Command

Artillerie-Flieger-Abteiling (AFA): Artillery cooperation aviation detachment or unit

Artillerie-Regiment: Artillery regiment

Bataillon: Battalion

Bombengeschwader (Bogohl) (BG): Bombardment squadron

Bombenstaffel (Bosta) (BS): Bombardment section or flight

Brieftauben-Abteilung-Metz/Ostende (BAM) (BAO): Carrier Pidgeon Detachment or Unit Metz/Ostend (cover names for the first two bombardment squadrons)

Brigade: Brigade

Chef des Feldflugwesens (Feldflugchef): Chief of Field Aviation

Englandgeschwader: England Squadron (a reference to *Kampfgeschwader/Bombengeschwader 3*)

Ettapen-Flugzeug-Park (ETP): Army aviation supply depot in the Zone of Communications

Feldartillerie: Field artillery

Feldflieger-Abteilung (FFl.Abt.): Field aviation detachment or unit

Feldlazarett: Field hospital

Festungsflieger-Abteilung: Fortress aviation detachment or unit

Flieger-Abteilung (Fl.Abt.): Aviation detachment or unit

Flieger-Abteilung (A) (Fl.Abt. (A)): Artillery cooperation aviation detachment or unit

Flieger-Bataillon: Aviation battalion

Flieger-Ersatz-Abteilung (FEA): Aviation replacement detachment or unit

Fliegerschule: Aviation training school

Fliegerstation (Flgst.): (Naval) air station

Fliegerhallen und Zelte Abteilung: Hangar and Tent Department

Fliegertruppe: (Army) Aviation Troop or Air Service

Fokkerstaffel (FS): Section or flight equipped with E-Type aircraft

Freikorps: Paramilitary forces formed to fight the Communists in the postwar revolutions

Füsilier-Regiment: Rifle regiment

Garde: Guard

Geschwader: Squadron

Grenadier-Regiment: Grenadier Regiment

Gruppenführer der Flieger (Grufl): Officer or staff attached to Corps headquarters rrsponsible for the deployment of aviation units assigned to a Corps

Halbgeschwader: Aviation squadron half the usual strength

Heeresgruppe: Army Group

Husaren-Regiment: Hussar regiment

Infanterieflieger (Ifl): Infantry cooperation aircraft, flight or flier

Infanterie-Regiment: Infantry regiment

Inspektion der Fliegertruppe (Idflieg): Inspectorate of (Army) Aviation or Air Service

Jäger-Regiment: Rifle regiment
Jagdgeschwader (JG): Permanent grouping of four *Jagdstaffeln*
Jagdgruppe (JGr.): Temporary tactical grouping of several *Jagdstaffeln*
Jagdstaffel (Jasta) (J.): Fighter section or flight
Jastaschule: Fighter pilot training school

Kampfeinsitzer-Abteilung (KEA): Single-seater detachment or unit
Kampfeinsitzer-Kommando (KEK). Single-seater fighter command or establishment
Kampfeinsitzerstaffel (Kest): Single-seater home defense section or flight
Kampfgeschwader (Kagohl) (KG): Fighting squadron
Kampfstaffel (Kasta) (KS): Fighting section or flight
Kette: Several aircraft of the same section or flight
Kommandeur der Flieger (Kofl): Officer or staff attached to Army headquarters responsible for the deployment of aviation units assigned to an Army
Kommandierenden General der Luftstreitkräfte (Kogenluft): Commanding General of the (Army) Air Service or his staff
Kommando: Command or establishment
Kompanie: Company
Kürassier-Regiment: Cuirassier regiment
Küsten: Coastal

Landflieger-Abteilung (Land Fl.Abt.): Land-based (Navy) aviation detachment or unit
Landflugstation (Land Flgst.): Land-based (Navy) air station
Landwehr: Territorial Force or Militia
Leib: Body or Life Guard
Luftschiff: Airship
Luftstreitkräfte: (Army) Air Force or Air Service
Luftwaffe: German Air Force 1935-1945 and present day

Marine: Navy or naval ground forces
Matrosenartillerie: Naval artillery

Oberste Heeresleitung: (Army) High Command

Pionier-Bataillon: Engineer battalion
Proviant-Kolonne: Supply column

Reich: Empire
Reichsheer: Postwar German army to 1933
Reihenbildzug-Abteilung (Rbz.): Detachment or unit equipped with serial film strip cameras
Riesenflugzeug-Abteilung (Rfa.): Detachment or unit equipped with "Giant" aircraft

Schlachtgeschwader: Permanent grouping of four to six Schlachtstaffeln
Schlachtgruppe: Temporary tactical grouping of several *Schlachtstaffeln*
Schlachtstaffel (Schlasta): Attack section or flight
Schutzstaffel (Schusta): Protection section or flight
Seeflieger-Abteilung (See Fl.Abt.): Naval aviation detachment or unit
Seeflugstation (See Flgst.): Naval air station
Seefrontstaffel (Seefrosta): Naval front section or flight
Stabsoffizier der Flieger (Stofl): Officer or staff for aviation within an Army

Ulanen-Regiment: Cavalry lancer regiment

Versuchs und Ubungspark: Testing and training park

Aircraft Types
A. -: Single engine monoplane without armament
B. -: Single engine biplane without armament
C. -: Single engine biplane with armament
D. -: Single engine, single-seater biplane with armament
E. -: Single engine, single-seater monoplane with armament
F. -: Single engine, single-seater triplane with armament (prototype models)
G. -: Multi-engine biplane with armament
J. -: Single engine, two-seater armored biplane for infantry cooperation work
L. -: Multi-engine biplane with armament
R. -: Biplane with three to six enRines with armament ("Giant" aircraft)
S. -: Single engine, two-seater armored biplane with armament
CL. -: Light C-Type two-seater biplane with armament
DJ. -: Single engine, single-seater armored aircraft with armament
Dr. -: Single engine, single-seater triplane with armament (production models)
GL. -: Light G-Type biplane with armament

Ranks: German, Other than Medical Officers
Admiral: Admiral (equivalent to U.S. Navy full Admiral)

Fähnrich: Ensign, Cadet or Officer Candidate
Fahnenjünker: Officer Cadet or Ensign
Feldmarschalleutnant: Lieutenant Field Marshal (no equivalent U.S. rank)
Feldwebel (Fldw.): Sergeant
Feldwebelleutnant (Fldwlt.): Sergeant Lieutenant (equivalent to U.S. Warrant Officer)

Flieger: Private in the Army Air Service
Flügeladjutant: Wing Adjustant or Aide-de-Camp
Flugmaat (Flgmaat.): Petty Officer in the Naval Air Service
Flugmeister (Flgmstr.): Petty Officer in the Naval Air Service
Flugobermaat (Flgobermaat.): Chief Petty Officer in the Naval Air Service
Flugzeug-Mechaniker (Flgzeug-Mech.): Aircraft mechanic, rigger or fitter
Fregattenkapitän (Fregkpt.): Frigate Captain (equivalent to U.S. Navy full Commander)
Funker: Radio or wireless operator or telegraphist

Gefreiter (Gefr.): Private 1st Class
General der Artillerie (der Flieger, der Kavallerie, der Infanterie): General of Artillery (of Aviation, of Cavalry, of Infantry) (equivalent of U.S. Lieutenant General)
Generalfeldmarschall: General Field Marshal (equivalent of U.S. General of the Army)
Generalleutnant: Lieutenant General (equivalent of U.S. Major General)
Generalmajor: Major General (equivalent of U.S. Brigadier Ceneral)
Generaloberst: Colonel General (equivalent of U.S. four-star General)
Grossadmiral: Grand Admiral (equivalent of U.S. Admiral of the Fleet)

Hauptleute/Hauptmann (Hptm.): Captains/Captain
Hilfzahlmeister: Assistant Paymaster

Kapitän zur See (Kapt. z. See): Naval Captain (equivalent of U.S. Navy Captain)
Kapitänleutnant (Kptlt.): Captain Lieutenant (equivalent of U.S. Navy full Lieutenant)
Korvettenkapitän (Korvkpt.): Corvette Captain (equivalent of U.S. Navy Lieutenant Commander)

Landsturmann: Local Militiaman
Leutnant (Lt.): Lieutenant (equivalent of U.S. 2nd Lieutenant)
Leutnant zur See (Lt. z. See): Naval Lieutenant (equivalent of U.S. Navy Ensign)

Major: Major
Mechaniker: Mechanic

Oberflugmeister (Oberflgmstr.): Chief Petty Officer in the Naval Air Service
Oberleutnant (Oblt.): Senior Lieutanant (equivalent of U.S. 1st Lieutenant)
Oberleutnant zur See (Oblt. z. See): Naval Senior Lieutenant (equivalent of U.S. Navy Lieutenant Junior Grade)
Oberst: Colonel
Oberstleutnant (Oberstlt.): Lieutenant Colonel
Offizier-Stellvertreter (Offz.-Stv.): Acting Officer

Portepee-Fähnrich: Officer Candidate wearing the officer's sword knot
Portepeeträger: Senior non-commissioned officer wearing the officer's sword knot

Reichsmarschall: Marshal of the German Nation (World War II)
Rittmeister (Rittm.): Captain of Cavalry

Seekadet: Naval Cadet
Sergeant: Sergeant

Unteroffizier (Unteroffz.): Corporal (also a generic term for all non-commissioned officers

Vizeadmiral: Vice Admiral (equivalent to U.S. Navy Vice Admiral)
Vizefeldwebel (Vzfw.): Vice Sergeant or Vice Sergeant Major
Vizeflugmeister (Vzflgmstr.): Vice Petty Officer in the Naval Air Service
Vizewachtmeister (Vzwachtmstr.): Vice Sergeant or Vice Sergeant Major of Artillery or Cavalry

Wachtmeister (Wachmstr.): Sergeant Major of Artillery or Cavalry
Werkmeister (Werkmstr.): Foreman (senior non-commissioned ground officer in an aviation unit)

Zahlmeister: Paymaster
Zugführer: Platoon Leader

Ranks: German, Medical Officers
Assistenzarzt: Assistant Physician or Surgeon (equivalent of a Leutnant)

Generalarzt: Physician or Surgeon General (equivalent of an Oberstleutnant)
Generaloberarzt: Senior Physician or Surgeon General (equivalent of an Oberst)
Generalstabarzt: Staff Physician or Surgeon General (equivalent of a Generalmajor)

Oberarzt: Senior Physician or Surgeon (equivalent of an Oberleutnant)
Oberstabsarzt: Senior Staff Physician or Surgeon (equivalent of a Major)

Stabsarzt: Staff Physician or Surgeon (equivalent of a Hauptmann)

Unterarzt: Junior Physician or Surgeon (equivalent to a *Fähnrich*), also a One-Year Volunteer in the Medical Service

Rank data furnished by Dieter H.M. Gröschel, M.D.

Ranks: French
Adjutant: Warrant Officer
Adjutant-Chef: Chief Warrant Officer
Aspirant: Officer Candidate

Brigadier: Corporal of Artillery or Cavalry

Capitaine: Captain
Caporal: Corporal
Caporal Fourrier: Quartermaster Corporal
Chef de Bataillon: Major of Infantry
Chef d'Escadron: Major of Artillery
Chef d'Escadrons: Major of Cavalry
Colonel: Colonel
Commandant: Major

Général d'Armée: General of the Army (equivalent to U.S. four-star General)
Général de Brigade: Major General or Brigadier General
Général de Division: Lieutenant General

Lieutenant: Lieutenant
Lieutenant Colonel: Lieutenant Colonel

Maréchal de France: Field Marshal
Maréchal-des-Logis: Sergeant of Artillery or Cavalry
Maréchal-des-Logis-Chef: Sergeant Major of Artillery or Cavalry
Mecanicien: Mechanic

Sergeant: Sergeant
Sergeant-Fourrier: Quartermaster Sergeant
Sergeant-Major: Sergeant Major or 1st Sergeant
Soldat: Private
Sous-Lieutenant: 2nd Lieutenant

Rank data furnished by Frank W. Bailey

Other Terms: German
Abzeichen: Badge
Allgemeine Gesellschaft (AG): General company
Amerika Programm: America Program, the expansion of the German Army Air Serice which was undertaken beginning in June 1917
Ausländer: Foreigner
ausser Dienst (a.D.): Released from service, i.e., retired

Bandschnalle: Ribbon clasp
Beobachter: Observer
Bewährungs: Proved or certified
blauer Max: Blue Max (nickname for the *Orden Pour le Mérite*)

Chef: Chief

Doppeldecker: Biplane
Drillich: Fatigue dress

Ehenbecher dem Sieger im Lufkampfe: Honor Goblet to the Victor in Air Battles
Ehrenpreis: Prize of Honor (German Naval Air Service equivalent to the Army Air Service *Ehrenbecher* but a trophy rather than a goblet)
Eichenlaub: Oak leaf
Eindecker: Monoplane
Einsitzer: Single-seater aircraft
Erzherzog: Archduke
Excellenz: Excellency

Fackeltanz: Torch Dance
Feldgrau: Field gray (as in a uniform)
Feldschnalle: Bar with small ribbons denoting awards
Flieger-Formationen: Aviation Units (title of a table of German Army Air Service)
Flugsport: Sport Flying (title of a German aviation magazine)
Freifrau: Baroness
Freiherr: Baron
Fürst: Prince or sovereign
Führer: Leader, but in aviation also the Commanding Officer as in *Abteilungsführer* or *Staffelführer* or a pilot as in *Flugzeugführer*

Gitterrumpf: Aircraft fuselage with lattice-tail construction
G.m.b.H.: Limited company
Graf: Count

Grossherzog: Grand Duke
Grosskomtur: Grand Commander (as in the grade of an order)
Grosskreuz: Grand Cross
Grossordensschnalle: Bar with ribbons from which full size awards are suspended)
Gymnasium: Grammar school, secondary school

Hauptstaatsarchiv: Main state archive
Heeresbericht: Army Report
Heft: Paper-covered book
Herzog: Duke
Herr: Mister or sir

Ingenieur: Engineer
Inhaber: Member or owner

Kaiser: Emperor
Kanone(n): Cannon or gun but in aviation also ace (or aces)
Kasino: Officer's mess
Klasse: Class (as in the grade of an order)
König: King
Kommandant: Commanding Officer
Kommandeur: Commander
Komtur: Commander (a grade of an order)
Kreuz: Cross
Kriegsarchiv: Military archive
Kriegstagebucb (KTB): War Diary
Kronprinz: Crown Prince
Kurfürst: Elector

Lichtbild: Photograph
Litze: Braid (as a designation of rank on a uniform)

Medaille: Medal
Militär-Wochenblatt: Weekly Military Journal
mit Brillanten: With Brilliants (genuine or paste stones embellishing orders insignia)
mit Eichenlaub: With Oak Leaf (an added distinction on an order)
mit der Krone: With Crown (an added distinction on an order or decoration)
mit Schwertern: With Swords (an added element on an order or decoration indicating an award made for military merit or bravery)
mit Schwertern am Ringe: With Swords-on-Ring (an added element indicating an earlier award of the same order mit Schwertern)

Nachrichtenblatt: Intelligence Journal
Nazi: Acronym for the National Socialist German Workers Party

Oesterreich: Austria
Offizier zur besonderen Verwendung (O.z.b.V.): Officer Assigned for Special Duties or Adjutant
ohne Schwertern: Without Swords (indicative of an award made in peacetime or of a noncombat nature in wartime for an order or decoration that could be awarded *mit Schwertern*)
Orden Pour le Mérite: Order for Merit
Ordenskissen: Orders cushion (for displaying awards at a military funeral)
Ost: East

Patent: Commission
Pelzmütze: Fur cap
Pickelhaube: Spiked helmet
Portepeeoffiziere: Officers wearing the sword knot
Prinz: Prince

Rangliste: Rank List
Reichsmark: Unit of German currency in circulation at the time of World War I
Reichsminister: Federal Minister
Reserve: Reserve
Rex: King (Latin)
Ritter: Knight
Ritterkreuz: Knight's Cross
Ritterschaft: Knighthood or body of knights
Ruhmesblätter: Pages of Honor (as in annals)
Rumpf: Fuselage

Schlachtfliegerei: Attack aviation
Schloss: Castle
Schnaps: Alcoholic beverage
Schrift: Handwriting
Spartakist: Left-wing revolutionary postwar movement named after the gladiator, Spartacus, who led a slave rebellion against the Roman Empire and who was killed in 71 B.C.
Staatsarchiv: State archive
Stern: Star (as in the grade of an order)
Stufe: Step but here meaning a grade of an award
Sud: South

Tapferkeitsmedaille: Bravery medal
Turkei: Turkey

Ungarn: Hungary

Vogts: Imperial stewards

Walfisch: Whale
West: West

zur Disposition (z.D.): At the disposal of, i.e., in the Reserves and subject to recall
zur Landung gezwungen Flugzeug (z.L.g.F.): Aircraft forced to land

Other Terms: Belgian and French
Armée de l'Air: French Air Service
As: Ace
Aviation Militaire: Belgian Air Service

BM.: Breguet Michelin

Chevalier: Knight
Couronne: Crown
Croix de Guerre: War Cross

Escadrille: Squadron

Group de Bombardment: Bombardment Group

Lafayette Escadrille: Lafayette Squadron
Légion d'Honneur: Legion of Honor
Les Cigognes Groupe de Combat: The Stork Fighter Group

Medaille Militaire: Military Medal
MF.: Maurice Farman
MS.: Morane-Saulnier

N.: Nieuport

Officier: Officer

Rosette: Rosette

Sop.: Sopwith
Spa.: Spad

INDEX OF NAMES IN MAIN TEXT

NOTES

NOTES

NOTES

NOTES

NOTES

NOTES

NOTES

NOTES

NOTES

NOTES

NOTES

NOTES

Also from the Publisher

British Aeroplanes Before the Great War. *Mike Goodall*. For the very first time, the history of British pre-World War I aircraft has been gathered together in one volume, with more than 900 of them well illustrated. This new book constitutes a most valuable contribution about a remarkable period in aviation history and is a memorial to the bravery and inventiveness of the intrepid pioneers of that far off era. Among the many famous manufacturer's covered are Avro, Sopwith, Shorts, and Bristol. Many lesser known designers and builders such as Martin-Handasyde and Howard Wright are also given ample coverage.
Size: 8 1/2"x11" • over 930 b/w photographs • 300 pp.
ISBN: 0-7643-1207-3 • hard cover • $59.95

French Aeroplanes Before the Great War. *Leonard E. Opdycke*. This is a catalog of the aeroplanes of the nearly 700 French builders who worked before the onset of World War I. Most of these aeroplanes flew – some did not – but all of them reflect the extraordinary vitality and sense of optimism that powered the aeronautical world before the future of the aeroplane began to become clearer in wartime. Some of the machines appear in these pages probably for the first time in print; others are rarely seen. Readers are invited to enter the Grand Palais, as they might have in 1908 or 1909, to enjoy these marvelous aircraft.
Size: 8 1/2" x 11" n 840 b/w photos, line drawings • 288 pp.
ISBN: 0-7643-0752-5 • hard cover • $59.95

British Aviation Squadron Markings of World War I: RFC • RAF • RNAS. *Les Rogers*. Years in the making, this book covers the wide variety of markings used by British aviation units in World War I. Organized numerically by squadron number the book includes both textual and photographic examples for nearly all RFC, RAF, and RNAS squadrons. Many of the photographs are published here for the first time, and the color profiles offer a representative selection of units, aircraft, and color schemes. A classic book.
Size: 9"x12" • over 800 b/w photographs, 150 color aircraft profiles • 296 pp.
ISBN: 0-7643-1284-7 • hard cover • $69.95

Flying Officers of the United States Navy 1917-1919. This book, originally published just after World War I, is the definitive reference to United States Naval aviators in World War I. Also included: a history of naval aviation operations in World War I.
Size: 8 1/2" x 11" • over 2000 b/w photographs • 304pp.
ISBN: 0-7643-0219-1 • hardcover • $49.95

The Camel Drivers: The 17th Aero Squadron in World War I. *Otis Lowell Reed & George Roland*. The 17th Aero Squadron flew Sopwith Camels under British command along the Western Front during the summer of 1918. This definitive work on the 17th Aero Squadron in World War I is drawn from a wide range of official and personal sources, including original squadron records (found in an attic!), numerous interviews, letters written home, and half a dozen diaries—including one kept by a German pilot flying in opposition.
Size: 8 1/2" x 11" • over 200 b/w photographs • 160 pp.
ISBN: 0-7643-0071-7 • hardcover • $45.00

First to the Front: The Aerial Adventures of 1st Lt. Waldo Heinrichs and the 95th Aero Squadron 1917-1918. *Charles Woolley*. The 95th Aero Squadron was the first American pursuit squadron to fly over the front in March 1918 and 1st Lt. Waldo Heinrichs was one of its original members. Told through the words of those who served, Heinrichs' richly written diary forms the nucleus of the story supported by contemporary letters, anecdotes, and combat reports from many of the other flyers. Photos, most unpublished from the personal albums of the participants, show planes, places and personnel.
Size: 8 1/2" x 11" • over 280 b/w photos, color aircraft profiles • 240 pp.
ISBN: 0-7643-0749-5 • hard cover • $49.95

New England Aviators 1914-1918 Vol.1: Their Portraits and Their Records. This two volume set originally appeared in 1919 in limited quantities—original copies are now highly sought collectibles. Both volumes of New England Aviators are now available in new quality editions. 542 New England pilots—who flew with the USAAC, USN, USMC and British and French air forces—are given short biographical entries and most appear in World War I era photographs. New England Aviators is a superb, detailed reference for World War I and aviation historians, as well as uniform and insignia collectors.
Size: 6" x 9" • over 200 b/w photographs • 472 pp.
ISBN: 0-7643-0345-7 • hardcover • $49.95

New England Aviators 1914-1918 Vol.2: Their Portraits and Their Records. This is the second volume of the set. New England Aviators is a superb, detailed reference for World War I and aviation historians, as well as uniform and insignia collectors.
Size: 6" x 9" • over 250 b/w photographs • 480 pp.
ISBN: 0-7643-0346-5 • hardcover • $49.95

The Lafayette Flying Corps: The American Volunteers in the French Air Service in World War I. *Dennis Gordon*. Includes detailed biographies of the 269 volunteer American airmen and gunners of France's Service Aeronautique who flew in sixty-six pursuit and twenty-seven bomber/observation squadrons over the Western Front – also included are the thirty-eight pilots of the Escadrille Lafayette. It is an accurate and absorbing account of the lives and combat experiences of the men who later formed the nucleus of the American Expeditionary Force squadrons. Contains comprehensive research, including details of war casualties and survivors, and many unpublished photographs.
Size: 8 1/2" x 11" • over 320 and b/w photographs • 504 pp.
ISBN: 0-7643-1108-5 • hard cover • $59.95

Wings of Honor: American Airmen in WWI. *James J. Sloan*. *Wings of Honor* is a compilation of all United States pilots, observers, gunners and mechanics who flew against the enemy in World War I. Covered are Americans who flew with the French and British air services, U.S. Navy aviators, the 103rd Pursuit Squadron, the 1st Balloon Group, the 1st Pursuit Group, the 1st Corps Observation Group, American bomber units, the 2nd Pursuit Squadron, the 3rd Pursuit Group, and all other units in which Americans flew.
Size: 8 1/2 x 11" • over 350 b/w photos • 460 pp.
ISBN: 0-88740-577-0 • hardcover • $45.00

United States Naval Aviation 1910-1918. *Noel Shirley*. The author of this book, based upon over thirty years of research into the subject of World War I aviation, and based upon both primary and secondary reference sources, has compiled into one source a complete history of the early development of naval aviation in the United States. He then discusses the manner and role that the naval aviation service applied to the war effort during 1917-1918. Detailed discussion is also provided regarding the role of Marine Corps aviation during this time period.
Size: 8 1/2" x 11" • over 320 and b/w photographs • 336 pp.
ISBN: 0-7643-1179-4 • hard cover • $59.95

U.S. Navy/U.S. Marine Corps Aircraft: Two Classics in One Volume. *William T. Larkins*. William T. Larkins's illustrated surveys of Navy and Marine Corps aircraft remain two of the most valuable books about these airplanes ever written. These two volumes have become classics eagerly sought by aviation buffs worldwide. The criteria against which serious aviation research is measured, they remain the definitive record of the formative years for Navy and Marine Corps aviation. Larkins's emphasis is on squadron use, experimental and one-of-a-kind types, insignia, colors and marking schemes, technical innovations, and the service duty and tactical deployment of the various aircraft.
Size: 6" x 9" • over 1,000 photos • 608 pp.
ISBN: 0-88740-742-0 • hardcover • $39.95